The OS/2 Warp Survival Guide

Doug Azzarito
&
David W. Green

WILEY

John Wiley & Sons, Inc.
New York • Chichester • Brisbane • Toronto • Singapore

Doug Azzarito:
*To my wife, Sandy, and my daughters, Teresa, and Gina,
who supported me through the long days and sleepless nights
during the development of OS/2, only to be rewarded with long days and sleepless nights
while writing this book.*

*To the dedicated team of programmers
who put their lives on hold and gave everything to make OS/2 Warp a reality.*

David W. Green:
To my son, Robert. May he live long and prosper.

Designations used by companies to distinguish their products are often claimed as trademarks. In all instances where John Wiley & Sons, Inc., is aware of a claim, the product names appear in initial capital or all capital letters. Readers, however, should contact the appropriate companies for more complete information regarding trademarks and registration.

This text is printed on acid-free paper.

Copyright © 1995 by John Wiley & Sons, Inc.

All rights reserved. Published simultaneously in Canada.

This publication is designed to provide accurate and authoritative information in regard to the subject matter covered. It is sold with the understanding that the publisher is not engaged in rendering legal, accounting, or other professional services. If legal advice or other expert assistance is required, the services of a competent professional person should be sought.

Reproduction or translation of any part of this work beyond that permitted by Section 107 or 108 of the 1976 United States Copyright Act without the permission of the copyright owner is unlawful. Requests for permission or further information should be addressed to the Permissions Department, John Wiley & Sons, Inc.

Library of Congress Cataloging-in-Publication Data:

International Standard Book Number (ISBN): 0 471-06083-6

Printed in the United States of America
10 9 8 7 6 5 4 3 2 1

Table of Contents

Foreword .... *xvii*
    About the Authors xviii
    Acknowledgments xviii
    Trademark Acknowledgments xix
    Warning and Disclaimer xx

Preface .... *xxi*
    Who Should Read This Book xxii
        New OS/2 Users xxii
        Current OS/2 Users xxii
        Advanced OS/2 Users xxiii
        DOS and Windows Users Migrating to OS/2 Warp xxiii
    How This Book Is Organized xxiv
    Conventions Used in This Book xxv
        Special Information Icons xxvi
        Typographical Conventions xxvii

Introduction .... *xxix*

Chapter 1: Prepare to Warp *1*
    Hardware Requirements 2
        Microprocessors 2
        System Architecture 4
        System Memory 5
        Hard Disk Drives 6
        Video Displays 7
        Pointing Devices 8
        CD-ROM Drives 8
        Multimedia Hardware 10
        Miscellaneous Hardware 10

Software Requirements 11
   Existing DOS Software 11
   Existing Windows Software 12
   Existing OS/2 Software 12
Getting Ready for the Installation 13
Considering Multiple Operating Systems 14
   Considering Your Boot Options 14
Hard Disk Partitions 15
   Primary and Extended/Logical Partitions 15
Choosing the Proper File System 18
   The File Allocation Table (FAT) 19
   The High Performance File System 19
Disk Partitioning Examples 21
   Real DOS Users 21
Deciding Which OS/2 Warp Features to Install 25
   Quick Installation 25
   Advanced Installation 26
Considering Your OS/2 Warp Configuration 26
   Country 27
   Keyboard 27
   Mouse 27
   Serial Device Support 28
   Primary and Secondary Displays 28
   Advanced Power Management 28
   PCMCIA Support 28
   CD-ROM Device Support 29
   Printer 29
   Multimedia Device Support 29
   SCSI Adapter Support 30
Summary 30

Chapter 2: Installing OS/2 Warp *31*
Start 31
   FDISK Screen 36
OS/2 Warp System Configuration 48
   Country 50
   Keyboard 51
   Mouse (Pointing Device) 52

Table of Contents

  Serial Device Support 53
  Primary Display... 54
  Secondary Display 56
  Advanced Power Management (APM) Support...................... 56
  PCMCIA Support 57
  CD-ROM Device Support 58
  Printer Support 59
  Multimedia Device Support 60
  SCSI Adapter Support 61
 Selective Installation 63
  Options Menu 65
  Software Configuration Menu 66
 First Boot 74
  If OS/2 Warp Doesn't Seem to Start 74
  The OS/2 Tutorial 75

Chapter 3: Warping in the Workplace Shell 77

 What's New with the Warp Workplace?... 78
  LaunchPad.. 78
  BonusPak 79
  Pickup Feature 80
  Default Folder Views 80
  Other Desktop Enhancements.. 80
  Changes to the Context Menus 80
 Warp Basics... 81
  Workplace Shell Objects.. 82
  Getting Object-Oriented with the Mouse................................. 84
   Selecting an Object 85
   Starting a Program Object 86
   Opening a Folder Object... 86
   Moving an Object 86
   Copying an Object... 87
   Creating a "Shadow" of an Object 87
   Picking Up an Object.. 87
   Deleting an Object 88
   Drag-and-Drop 88
   Exiting OS/2 Warp (Shutdown)... 89

- Basic Window Controls 90
  - Object Icon 93
  - Title Bar 93
  - Hide/Minimize Button 94
  - Maximize/Restore Button 94
  - Menu Bar 94
  - Frame 94
  - Information Area 95
  - Scroll Bars 95
- Using Menus and Option Controls 96
  - Pull-Down Menus 96
  - Cascade and Conditional Menus 96
  - Dialog Boxes 97
  - Radio Buttons 98
  - Drop-Down Lists 98
  - Check Box 98
  - Push Buttons 98
  - Spin Buttons 98
- Using the Pop-Up Controls 99
  - Context Menus 99
  - The Window List 101
- Visual Clues in the Warp Workplace 102
  - Colors and Shading 102
  - Hatch Lines and Borders 102
  - Cursor Shapes 103
- A Look Inside the OS/2 Warp Folders 103
  - The OS/2 System Folder 104
    - Command Prompts Folder 105
    - Drives Folder 106
    - Games Folder 109
    - Minimized Window Viewer 110
    - Productivity Folder 111
      - Clipboard Viewer 112
      - Enhanced Editor 114
      - Icon Editor 115
      - OS/2 System Editor 116
      - Picture Viewer 117
      - Pulse 118

Table of Contents

    Seek and Scan Files 118
    Shredder Object 120
    Startup Folder 120
    System Setup Folder 121
  The Templates Folder 122
    Bitmap.BMP 123
    Mixed (and Solid) Color Palettes 123
    Data File 123
    Digital Audio.WAV 123
    Folder 123
    Font Palette 124
    Icon.ICO 124
    Metafile.MET 124
    PIF File.PIF 124
    Pointer.PTR 124
    Printer 125
    Program 125
    Scheme Palette 125
  The Information Folder 126
    Application Considerations 127
    Command Reference 128
    Glossary 129
    Master Help Index 130
    Multimedia 131
    Performance Considerations 132
    Printing in OS/2 133
    READ.ME 133
    REXX Information 134
    Tutorial 135
Virtual Desktop Devices 136
  The LaunchPad 136
  The Printer Object 137
  The Shredder Object 139

Chapter 4: The OS/2 Warp BonusPak 141

  Installing from the BonusPak Diskettes 142
  Installing from the BonusPak CD-ROM 142
  IBM Information Superhighway: The Internet Access Kit (IAK) ... 143

CompuServe 144
    CIM for OS/2 145
    Member Signup 146
HyperACCESS Lite 146
IBM Internet Connection for OS/2 147
    Introduction to the IBM Internet Connection 148
    IBM Internet Dialer 148
    Retrieve Software Updates 150
    Gopher 151
    WebExplorer 152
    NewsReader/2 153
    Ultimedia Mail/2 "Lite" 154
    Internet Utilities 156
        3270 Telnet 157
        Dial Other Internet Providers 157
        FTP-PM 158
        Telnet 159
    IBM Internet Customer Service 160
        Customer Assistance 160
        Registration 161
    Application Templates 162
IBM Works and the Personal Information Manager 163
    Appointments 164
        Alarm 167
        Launch 168
        Recurring... 169
            Event Monitor 170
    Planner 171
    Year Calendar 172
    To-Do List 173
    Address/Phone Book 176
        Outgoing Calls 179
        Incoming Calls 181
        Phone Dialer 181
        Phone Log 182
    Contact List 183
    Notepad 184
    Word Processor 188

Table of Contents

Spreadsheet	189
Chart	191
Data Filer (Database)	193
Creating a New Database	194
Designing the Form	195
Entering Data	196
Viewing Your Database	196
Printing Your Database	197
Report Writer	197
Editing a Report	198
Viewing and Printing a Report	199
FaxWorks for OS/2	199
Person to Person/2	201
The Address Book	202
The Call Manager	204
The Chalkboard Application	205
The Clipboard Manager	206
The Talk Application	207
The Video Application	208
Stills Capture	209
Multimedia Extensions	209
Ultimedia Video IN for OS/2	210
Ultimedia Viewer (The Light Table)	211
Summary	213

Chapter 5: Customizing OS/2 Warp 215

What Can I Customize?	215
Using the Settings Notebooks	217
Folder Object Settings	221
View Tab	221
Icon View	223
Tree View	225
Details View	227
Include Tab	229
Sort Tab	232
Background Tab	233
Background Images	234
Color Backgrounds	235

Menu Tab	236
File Tab	238
Window Tab	243
General Tab	246
Lockup Tab	249
Archive Tab	252
Desktop Tab	253
Folder Settings Summary	254
Program Object Settings	254
Program Tab	256
Session Tab	259
Association Tab	261
Type Tab	263
Program Settings Summary	264
System Setup Objects	264
Add Programs	265
Country	267
Time Tab	268
Date Tab	269
Numbers Tab	270
Create Utility Diskettes	271
Device Driver Install	271
Font Palette	271
Changing Fonts	272
Adding and Editing Fonts	273
Keyboard	274
Timing Tab	274
Mappings Tab	275
Special Needs Tab	276
General Tab	277
Mixed Color Palette	277
Changing Colors	279
Editing a Color	280
Mouse	281
Timing Tab	281
Setup Tab	282
Mappings Tab	283
Pointers Tab	285

Comet Cursor Tab	286
General Tab	287
Scheme Palette	287
Changing Schemes	288
Editing a Scheme	289
Selective Install	289
Selective Uninstall	291
Solid Color Palette	292
Sound	293
Sound Tab	293
Warning Beep Tab	295
Spooler	295
Spool Path Tab	295
Print Priority Tab	296
System	297
Screen Tab	298
Confirmations Tab	300
Title Tab	301
Window Tab	302
Input Tab	304
Print Screen Tab	305
Logo Tab	306
General Tab	307
System Clock	307
Date/Time Tab	308
View Tab	308
Alarm Tab	310
System Information Tool	311
WIN-OS/2 Setup	313
3.1 Session Tab	313
Data Exchange Tab	314

Chapter 6: Getting Warped: Exercises in Virtual Reality 317

Virtual Reality in the Workplace Shell	318
File System Objects	319
Folder Objects	320
File Objects	320
Program File Objects versus Program (Reference) Objects	321

Reference Objects for Data File Objects 322
Device Objects 324
Shadow Objects 325
Keep "Real" Objects off Your Desktop 326
Exercises in Virtual Reality 327
Exercise 1: Copying a Program File Object 328
    The Wrong Way 328
    The Right Way 329
Exercise 2: Creating a Program Object 330
Exercise 3: Creating a Work Area 332
Exercise 4: Using the Virtual Clipboard 338
Exercise 5: Creating a Desktop Window 342
Exercise 6: Building a File Manager (Warp Drive) 343
Exercise 7: Controlling the Virtual with the Real 345
Exercise 8: Using the Find Utility 346
    Using Find Without "Save Results" 349
Exercise 9: Creating a Virtual ZIPper 350

Chapter 7: DOS and Windows Under OS/2 Warp *353*
Virtual DOS Machines 353
DOS Sessions 354
Custom DOS Objects 355
    Creating a Custom DOS Object 355
DOS from Drive A: 361
    Real DOS 362
    DOS Images: The Virtual Floppy 363
Windows Sessions 365
    Separate Sessions 366
DOS and WIN-OS/2 Settings 366
Settings Reference Section 367

Chapter 8: OS/2 Warp Multimedia *389*
Installing Multimedia Support 389
Sample Digital Audio and Video Files 390
Using the Multimedia Objects 391
    Digital Video 392
    Compact Disc 394
    Digital Audio 395

Table of Contents

    MIDI 395
    Multimedia Install 396
    Multimedia Setup 396
    Multimedia with REXX 396
    Multimedia Data Converter 397
    Sound 397
    Volume Control 398
    Miscellaneous Folders 398

Chapter 9: DOS and OS/2 Command Lines 399

    DOS Full Screen 400
    DOS Window 401
    OS/2 Full Screen 401
    OS/2 Window 401
    Dual Boot 402
    Command Line Differences 402
    DOS and OS/2 Commands 403

Chapter 10: Advanced Warping 439

    Configuring OS/2 Through CONFIG.SYS 439
        What Is the CONFIG.SYS File? 439
        Base-Device Statements in CONFIG.SYS: 440
        Performance Statements in CONFIG.SYS 446
        Environment Variable Statements in CONFIG.SYS 455
    Extended Attributes 458
    Using the Print Spooler 459
        Printer Object Settings 460
            The Printer Driver 461
            The Printer Port 462
        The Print Queue 466

Chapter 11: Warping with REXX 469

    A Simple Programming Exercise 469
        Debugging Our Simple Program 470
        Using Return Codes 472
        Using the FOR Command 473
    Creating Command Files 475

REXX Programming.. 476
   Testing REXX Features 477
   Testing Your REXX Programs 477
   REXX and Extended Attributes 478
   REXX Basics 478
Putting REXX to Work.. 480
   Workplace Shell Open Command 481
   Go Wild Command 481

Chapter 12: When Things Go Wrong 489

The Magic Keystrokes.. 489
   Alt+F2: Device Driver Display 490
   Alt+F1: The "Recovery Choices" Display....................................... 492
      Option C: Command Line 493
      Option V: Standard VGA 493
      Option M: The Maintenance Desktop 494
      Option X: Original Desktop Archive 494
      Options 1, 2, and 3: Numbered Desktop Archives 494
      The OS/2 Desktop Archive.. 495
   Restoring Your Current Configuration 497
Resolving Resource Conflicts 500
   What Are Hardware Resources? 500
   The Resource Manager Utility (RMVIEW) 501
Disk Failure: Not IF, but WHEN!.. 502
CHKDSK: What and Why? 503
Errors, Traps, and IPEs 504
   Errors... 504
   Traps 507
   Internal Processing Errors (IPEs) 512

Appendix A: OS/2 Warp File Listing 515

Root Directory (C:\)... 516
The Desktop Directory (C:\Desktop\)... 517
The Templates Directory (C:\Desktop\Templates) 518
The IBMVESA Directory (C:\IBMVESA) 518
The LANLK Directory (C:\LANLK) 519
The Maintenance Desktop (C:\Maintenance Desktop)..................... 519

Table of Contents

The Multimedia Directory (C:\MMOS2) 519
The Multimedia DLL Directory (C:\MMOS2\DLL) 521
The Multimedia Help Directory (C:\MMOS2\HELP) 523
The Multimedia Install Directory (C:\MMOS2\INSTALL) 524
The Multimedia Macro Directory (C:\MMOS2\MACROS) 526
The Multimedia Movie Directory (C:\MMOS2\MOVIES) 526
The Multimedia Sounds Directory (C:\MMOS2\SOUNDS) 526
The Nowhere Directories (C:\Nowhere and C:\Nowhere1) 527
The OS/2 Directory (C:\OS2) 528
The OS/2 Applications Directory (C:\OS2\APPS) 532
The OS/2 Application DLL Directory (C:\OS2\APPS\DLL)... 533
The OS/2 Archive Directory (C:\OS2\ARCHIVES) 533
The OS/2 Installation Archive Directory
(C:\OS2\ARCHIVES\0X) 534
The OS/2 Installation Desktop Archive Directory
(C:\OS2\ARCHIVES\0X\DESKTOP) 534
The OS/2 Current Archive Directory
(C:\OS2\ARCHIVES\CURRENT) 534
The OS/2 Bitmap Directory (C:\OS2\BITMAP) 535
The OS/2 Electronic Book Directory (C:\OS2\BOOK) 536
The OS/2 Boot Directory (C:\OS2\BOOT) 537
The OS/2 DLL Directory (C:\OS2\DLL) 539
The OS/2 Null Printer Directory (C:\OS2\DLL\IBMNULL) ... 543
The OS/2 LaserJet Directory (C:\OS2\DLL\LASERJET) 543
The OS/2 PostScript Directory (C:\OS2\DLL\PSCRIPT) 544
The OS/2 Drivers Directory (C:\OS2\DRIVERS) 545
The OS/2 SOM Directory (C:\OS2\ETC) 545
The OS/2 C:\OS2\ETC\DSOM 546
The OS/2 Help Directory (C:\OS2\HELP) 546
The OS/2 Glossary Help Directory
(C:\OS2\HELP\GLOSS) 547
The OS/2 Tutorial Help Directory
(C:\OS2\HELP\TUTORIAL) 548
The OS/2 Install Directory (C:\OS2\INSTALL) 548
The OS/2 Installation Boot Disk Directory
(C:\OS2\INSTALL\BOOTDISK) 551
The OS/2 Installation VGA Directory
(C:\OS2\INSTALL\VGA) 552

xv

The OS/2 MDOS Directory (C:\OS2\MDOS) 553
The OS/2 WIN-OS/2 Directory (C:\OS2\MDOS\WINOS2) ... 555
The OS/2 Pointers Directory (C:\OS2\POINTERS) 555
The OS/2 System Directory (C:\OS2\SYSTEM) 556
The OS/2 System Trace Directory
(C:\OS2\SYSTEM\TRACE) 557
The Adobe Fonts Directory (C:\PSFONTS) 557
The OS/2 Printer Font Matrix Directory
(C:\PSFONTS\PFM) 558
The OS/2 Spool File Directory (C:\SPOOL) 559

Index *561*

Foreword

OS/2 Warp is the third generation of an operating system that was originally designed for large corporations and later refocused toward the personal-computer market. From its business-enterprise heritage, OS/2 brings robustness, reliability, and the technology to fully exploit PC hardware platforms. For the home user, OS/2 runs all the popular DOS, Windows, and OS/2 applications. The latest version of OS/2 Warp merges the information superhighway with multimedia technology on an object-oriented workplace desktop. It is the combination of business and consumer operating-system features that makes OS/2 Warp a unique experience.

Doug Azzarito is one of the OS/2 pioneers. First as a user, next as a teacher in Cyberspace and computer user groups, and currently as a member of the OS/2 development team. Doug's experience, knowledge, and enthusiasm has helped thousands of new users and OS/2 veterans. *The OS/2 Warp Survival Guide* is an excellent guide to help users exploit the power of OS/2 Warp.

Jack Boyce
IBM Senior Technical Staff Member—*Lead Architect: OS/2 Warp*

About the Authors

Doug Azzarito is an Advisory Programmer for IBM's Personal Software Products division in Boca Raton, Florida. He has been involved in the development of OS/2 since 1986, and is currently working on various aspects of the OS/2 kernel and file systems. A Certified OS/2 Engineer, Doug regularly demonstrates Warp to user groups and speaks at OS/2 conferences. Doug can be found in cyberspace, dispensing advice and technical information about OS/2 under the nickname, "The OS/2 Guy." Doug is also the founder of the TEAM OS/2 "SWAT" team, a volunteer army that provides OS/2 technical support at large computer trade shows.

David W. Green has been a technical author and editor, consulting to IBM and other major computer companies, for over ten years. In 1988, David received the Xerox Electronic Publishing Award (XEPA) for his design of computer software manuals. As president of CompuSoft, Inc., he successfully designed, developed, and marketed turnkey computer solutions for the commodity brokerage industry. His current ventures include the development of multimedia presentations and on-line tutorials. His multimedia works for Motorola and MobileComm has most recently been displayed at COMDEX and the Consumer Electronics Show.

Acknowledgments

We would like to acknowledge and sincerely thank the following people for their involvement in the development of this book.

Jim Donelson
George Fulk
Gary Lehnertz
Katharine Patoine
Mary Snedden

Trademark Acknowledgments

The following trademarks were compiled from several different sources. John Wiley & Sons, Inc., cannot guarantee that this information is completely accurate.

- CompuServe is a trademark of CompuServe Incorporated.
- FaxWorks is a trademark of SofNet, Incorporated.
- HyperACCESS Lite is a trademark of Hilgraeve, Incorporated.
- The PostScript logo is a registered trademark of Adobe Systems Incorporated.
- dBase III is a trademark of Borland International.
- IBM, Workplace Shell, Operating System/2, OS/2, Presentation Manager, WIN-OS/2, Multimedia Presentation Manager/2, IBM Works, Personal Information Manager, Multimedia Viewer, Video IN, Person to Person, and Ultimotion are trademarks of the International Business Machines Corporation.
- Intel, i750, ActionMedia, and Indeo are trademarks of the Intel Corporation.
- Lotus 1-2-3 is a registered trademark of Lotus Development Corporation.
- Microsoft and Microsoft Excel are registered trademarks, and Windows is a trademark of Microsoft Corporation.
- Pro AudioSpectrum 16 is a trademark of Media Vision, Inc.
- Sound Blaster is a trademark of Creative Labs, Inc.
- UNIX is a registered trademark of Unix System Laboratories, Inc.
- Xerox and XEPA are registered trademarks of the Xerox Corporation.

Warning and Disclaimer

The purpose of this book is to provide information about IBM's Operating System/2 (OS/2) Warp (version 3). Every effort has been made to ensure that this book is complete and accurate, but no warranty or fitness is implied.

The information is provided on an "as is" basis. The authors and John Wiley & Sons, Inc., shall have neither liability nor responsibility to any person or entity with respect to any loss or damages arising from the information contained in this book or from the use of the disks or programs that may accompany it.

Preface

Welcome to OS/2! OS/2 Warp is the first widely accepted, object-oriented operating system for IBM-compatible personal computers (PCs). As PC users begin to understand the power and simplicity of an object-oriented environment, the value of OS/2 becomes apparent.

Although the developers of DOS have done a great deal of work over the years to augment this tired old operating system, it was never meant to be the operating platform needed for today's powerful computers. This is one reason why the IBM-compatible PC market is so confusing, with all the patches to make DOS support increased memory, larger disk drives, faster video, and exotic new devices. OS/2 Warp was designed to inherently exploit the new generation of PC hardware.

Even though Windows provides a user-friendly interface to PCs, it stops short of being a true object-oriented environment. Windows is not an operating system; it's actually a DOS application program, and therefore has the same limitations as DOS. OS/2's user interface (the OS/2 Workplace Shell) is an OS/2 application program that works as an integral part of the operating system.

By developing Windows-NT, Microsoft acknowledged that today's computers have outgrown the DOS/Windows platform; but Windows-NT was a little late in arriving and a little short in function. When Windows-NT was released, existing OS/2 users were already enjoying functions that NT was supposed to provide, and OS/2 has many more years of development, testing, and use under its belt.

Because of the confused state of the PC market, IBM knew that OS/2 had to be—in a sense—"all things to all people." OS/2, therefore, must maintain compatibility with DOS and Windows, while providing a platform for the next generation of 32-bit, multitasking, computer software. All this had to be done without stretching the resources of today's computer hardware. OS/2 Warp accomplishes these goals splendidly.

You may have heard IBM's claims that OS/2 is a "better DOS than DOS" and a "better Windows than Windows." *The OS/2 Warp Survival Guide* provides you with information that will help you determine for yourself if these claims are true.

Who Should Read This Book

No matter what your level of experience with personal computers and operating systems, *The OS/2 Warp Survival Guide* will help you get the most out of OS/2 Warp and your computer.

New OS/2 Users

We didn't write this book thinking that whoever read it would be an OS/2 guru. Chapters 3, 4, and 5 assume you have little or no experience with OS/2. These chapters introduce you to the Workplace Shell, presenting the concepts of an object-oriented graphical user interface; show you how to access and use the many useful programs included with OS/2 Warp; and explain how you can customize the Workplace Shell so it looks and feels right for you. You'll also want to read Chapter 6; it provides exercises designed to help you get more function out of OS/2 Warp. After reading the information presented, you might end up knowing more about OS/2 Warp than many current OS/2 users.

Current OS/2 Users

Even if you've been using OS/2 for some time, you'll find explanations of the new tools and features provided with OS/2 Warp in Chapters 3, 4, and 5. You might also get something from Chapter 6. Believe it or not, some of the most seasoned OS/2 users are unaware of how to exploit OS/2's object-oriented advantages.

Preface

Throughout the book, we've sprinkled bits of previously undocumented information, clearly identified so you can find them quickly (see "Conventions Used in This Book" later in this Preface for details). This could prove reason enough for experienced OS/2 users to read *The OS/2 Warp Survival Guide*.

Advanced OS/2 Users

If you are a real power user, and think you know a lot about OS/2, you'll appreciate Chapters 9 and 10. These chapters present low-level OS/2 commands and their parameters (all of which are unique to OS/2 Warp and some of which are previously undocumented) as well as many advanced topics such as the print spooler, video device drivers, and system configuration. And if you want to try your hand at high-level programming under OS/2 Warp, Chapter 11 discusses using the REXX programming language.

DOS and Windows Users Migrating to OS/2 Warp

If you've been using DOS or DOS and Windows, and you want to give OS/2 Warp a try, *The OS/2 Warp Survival Guide* will help ease the transition. Throughout the book, we've provided tips and techniques that are specific to you. Having made the transition ourselves, we wanted to pass along our experiences and help you avoid some of the more common mistakes. Although you'll benefit from reading all the chapters in this book, Chapter 7 is especially for you. You'll see how you can "tweak" OS/2 to get the most out of your DOS and Windows programs running under OS/2 Warp.

The OS/2 Warp Survival Guide

How This Book Is Organized

To ensure that readers of this book—from novice to OS/2 expert—can find information easily we have organized the contents of this book into logical parts so that you can skip entire chapters if you feel they don't pertain to you.

- *Chapter 1: Prepare to Warp* — helps you get ready for the installation. This is where most people make their mistakes, starting the installation without adequate planning.

- *Chapter 2: Installing OS/2 Warp* — guides you through the installation process, answering questions that you might have along the way.

- *Chapter 3: Warping in the Workplace Shell* — helps you get acquainted with OS/2's graphical user interface, and explains some of the conceptual aspects of an object-oriented environment. This chapter introduces you to the basic types of objects found on the OS/2 Warp desktop.

- *Chapter 4: The OS/2 Warp BonusPak* — tells you how to install the BonusPak and introduces you to the applications it contains. It shows you how to access these software gems, and provides helpful operating tips.

- *Chapter 5: Customizing OS/2 Warp* — shows you how to use the OS/2 Settings Notebooks and System Setup objects so you can tailor OS/2's visual and operating characteristics.

- *Chapter 6: Getting Warped: Exercises in Virtual Reality* — provides an insightful discussion of "virtual" versus "real" objects in OS/2. This chapter also contains exercises you can perform within the Workplace Shell to help you become adept at operating your computer the object-oriented way.

- *Chapter 7: DOS and Windows under OS/2 Warp* — explains how OS/2 provides DOS and Windows sessions for your DOS and Windows programs, and shows you how to change their settings to improve performance.

Preface

- *Chapter 8: OS/2 Warp Multimedia* — provides a guided tour of the multimedia features of OS/2.

- *Chapter 9: DOS and OS/2 Command Lines* — shows you how to get to the DOS and OS/2 command lines through the Workplace Shell, and describes the differences between OS/2 Warp commands and their DOS counterparts.

- *Chapter 10: Advanced Warping* — discusses advanced features of OS/2 Warp, such as: the print spooler and adding printers, adding video device drivers, and configuring OS/2 through the low-level system files.

- *Chapter 11: Warping with REXX* — discusses using REXX in OS/2 Warp. We've provided a sample REXX program that you can tinker with. You might even find the program a useful addition to your software collection.

- *Chapter 12: When Things Go Wrong* — helps you interpret error messages and resolve problems that may arise while installing and using OS/2 Warp.

- *Appendix A: OS/2 Warp File Listing* — contains a listing of the files that are typically installed by OS/2 Warp, and describes their function within OS/2.

Conventions Used in This Book

Throughout this book, we've used several symbols to help you find the most useful bits of information that pertain to your needs and level of experience.

We'll use this symbol to point out *tips and techniques* and special notes that may prove helpful. Everyone should read the text printed next to this symbol.

The OS/2 Warp Survival Guide

 We'll use this symbol to *warn* you about possible pitfalls that could cost you time or aggravation. Don't worry, you won't see too many of these.

 The information printed next to this symbol is *undocumented*. You won't find this information in the IBM OS/2 manuals or in any other OS/2 manual.

 We've placed this symbol in places where there's an opportunity for you to skip certain sections based on your requirements (and patience— or lack thereof).

Special Information Icons

Find the symbol(s) below that best represents you; then look for your symbol(s) in chapter titles and next to paragraphs to find information specific to you.

 The information associated with this symbol is meant to be read by *new OS/2 users,* but is also for those who have no experience using a graphical user interface.

 The information associated with this symbol is meant to be read by *DOS users,* especially those who have experience using the DOS prompt.

 The information associated with this symbol is meant to be read by *Windows users*. This information should help with your transition to OS/2 Warp.

 The text printed next to this symbol is meant to be read by *advanced OS/2 users*. The information provided is of a more technical nature.

Preface

Typographical Conventions

To help you identify key elements of information in this book, we've used the following conventions.

Bold We'll use this typeface to identify key labels when telling you to press specific keys or key combinations. For example, "Press **Ctrl+Esc** to display the Windows List."

Italics We'll use the italic typeface to identify button and menu options. For example, "Click on the *OK* button." Or "Select the *Settings* menu option." Since these are proper names, they are also capitalized.

We also use italics the first time we introduce a word that might be unfamiliar to some readers. These words will not be capitalized.

`Monospace` We've used a monospaced font to simulate literal computer input or output, that is, things that you type into the computer or see displayed on the screen. For example, "Type the following command: `dir *.bmp /s /p`."

FULL CAPS We'll fully capitalize DOS and OS/2 command names and file names when referring to them in text. For example, "Use the FDISK command to create a partition."

Introduction

When IBM introduced the Personal Computer in 1981, it came with something called DOS, the Disk Operating System. With DOS, your computer could load files from disks, and store them back again. This might have been enough for the computer users of 1981, but the computer users of today need much more. DOS has evolved into a much larger product since its beginning, but even evolution isn't enough to keep pace with the needs of PC users. IBM and Microsoft first attempted to re-engineer DOS in 1987 when OS/2 Version 1.0 was released. Despite its power, OS/2 1.0 was not compatible with many existing DOS applications. Instead, OS/2 found itself limited to being used on network servers in large corporations.

After Microsoft abandoned OS/2, IBM continued development on their own, and in 1992 released OS/2 Version 2.0. A new user interface, enhanced DOS and Windows compatibility, and expanded hardware support made OS/2 2.0 extremely popular, but its resource requirements were better suited to a power-user's computer than the average desktop computer.

In 1994, IBM accelerated OS/2 computing to Warp speed. With the announcement of OS/2 Warp (version 3), users have a product that stands above the competition. OS/2 Warp has all the power of its predecessors, but its resource requirements are met by even the most basic systems sold today. OS/2 is IBM's first product that is based on the "Workplace" strategy. "Workplace" is IBM's vision of microcomputer operating systems for the future. To bring this vision to reality, the programmers who developed OS/2 set some incredible goals. First, OS/2 was designed to run nearly all existing DOS programs, and do so better than DOS. OS/2 must also run Windows applications, as well as 16- and 32-bit OS/2 applications. All these different programs would have to run *seamlessly* on the same display, under the control of a powerful, object-oriented, graphical interface. OS/2 also includes support for a wide variety of hardware devices, from CD-ROM drives to video capture adapters. The result of these goals is the most sophisticated operating system designed for personal computers.

You may have been using DOS for years, but you may not even know what an *operating system* (OS) is. DOS was created to help application software (such as word processing programs, spreadsheets, and computer games) communicate with the computer. Operating systems provide basic services to the applications we use; and until recently, they did little else. DOS was little more than a utility to load other programs. However, with the rapid increase in computing power and computer users' needs, operating systems have become much more. The most noticeable difference in OS technology is the *graphical user interface* (GUI). A GUI presents all information to the user in picture, or graphical, form. While not all pictures are worth a thousand words, the GUI does give us an easier way to view our data. Along with the GUI concept, the *Common User Access* or CUA standard defines a common method for operating programs. Once you learn to use one CUA program, you'll feel comfortable with any CUA program. This is a welcome change to anyone who has been lost in a DOS program, hopelessly looking for the "exit" key. The concepts of GUI and CUA allow operating systems to put pressure on application software to be easier to learn and use. How could any computer user disapprove of that?

OS/2 isn't just a GUI, it's a complete operating system. Everything from keyboard and mouse input to disk storage and printer output are under direct control of OS/2. Although OS/2 is the most complex operating system ever designed for personal computers, its complexity does not mean OS/2 is difficult to use. Once you become comfortable with the power of OS/2 (by reading this book, of course) you'll be able to do more with your computer, and do so easier than with DOS or Windows.

Introduction

What makes OS/2 different from other operating systems? Here's a quick list of OS/2 Warp's unique features:

- **Workplace Shell Interface:** This object-oriented, graphical user interface (GUI) provides an easy way to manage programs and files on your computer.

- **Pre-emptive Multitasking:** This allows many programs to run at the same time on your computer. OS/2 switches between programs automatically, even if the programs (such as older DOS programs) were not designed to multitask.

- **Multiple Virtual DOS Machines (MVDMs):** OS/2 can run many DOS and Windows programs at once, with each program running in what appears to be its own computer. DOS programs running in MVDMs do not have to compete for system resources with other programs and device drivers, so the "DOS 640K barrier" can be broken.

- **Installable File Systems:** DOS only supported one system for accessing files on disks. OS/2 allows you to add additional file systems as needed. The High Performance File System (HPFS) is an Installable File System (IFS) included with OS/2. HPFS features long file names, extended file attributes, and enhanced performance (disk fragmentation is practically eliminated). The CD-ROM File System (CDFS) allows you to access CD-ROMs the same way you access hard disk drives.

- **32-bit Architecture:** OS/2 is designed for the 80386 (and later) computer, which can process 32 bits of data at once. This means programs designed specifically for OS/2 will run faster, and can access more data.

- **DOS and Windows Compatibility:** Existing DOS and Windows programs will run seamlessly under OS/2, without modification.

- **Broad Device Support:** OS/2 automatically recognizes and configures itself for a wide range of devices, such as CD-ROM drives, sound cards, mice, video adapters, printers, and PCMCIA adapters.

To start using these features, you will have to survive the OS/2 installation. No part of the installation process is particularly difficult, but you might not be used to the flexibility and choices OS/2 gives you. The first two chapters of this book explain all these choices, and guide you through the task of getting OS/2 installed on your system. Once OS/2 is installed, you'll want to make OS/2 fit the way you work. Chapters 3 and 4 of this book describe many of the options available to customize OS/2. The remaining chapters describe the features of OS/2, and the many ways you can use them. By the time you finish reading this book, you'll be ready to leave DOS behind forever. So, bid farewell to the past, turn the page, and experience the future!

Chapter 1

Prepare to Warp

Congratulations! You just opened the OS/2 Warp package, and are now sitting in front of your computer staring at a tall stack of diskettes. Of course, you're so eager to install OS/2 Warp you've probably considered skipping the documentation and just start feeding the diskettes to your machine. That may work; but wouldn't you rather do it right the first time? Remember, OS/2 Warp has more options than any program you've ever seen. Your choices for many of these options depend on how you want to use OS/2 Warp, so you need to plan ahead. Take the time to install OS/2 Warp properly, and you won't have to start over later.

Your first decision is which option to buy. OS/2 Warp is available on diskettes and CD, and of course that decision depends on whether you have a CD-ROM drive. Whichever option you choose, remember, OS/2 Warp is an Operating System—you must be able to boot it from floppy in order to install it. If your A: drive is a 5.25" drive, you won't be able to install Warp (it is only offered on 3.5" diskettes). A computer store technician should be able to help you install a 3.5" A: drive.

OS/2 Warp comes in two models: the "Full Pack" (*Warp with WIN-OS/2*), and the "Without Windows" version. The only difference is the inclusion or exclusion of Windows support. If you already own a copy of Windows 3.1, 3.11, or Windows for Workgroups 3.11, you can purchase the "Without Windows" Pack. OS/2 Warp will use your existing Windows software to support any Windows applications you run. If you don't own a copy of Windows 3.1 or 3.11, and you want to run Windows programs, you should purchase *Warp with WIN-OS/2*.

Before we even talk about the installation process, let's discuss OS/2 Warp's computer hardware requirements. You may find that before you install OS/2 Warp, you need to take a trip to your local computer store for some hardware upgrades.

The OS/2 Warp Survival Guide

Hardware Requirements

According to IBM, OS/2 Warp requires the following minimum computer system:

- 80386 SX microprocessor,
- 4 megabytes of random access memory (RAM), and
- a 60 megabyte hard disk drive.

While OS/2 Warp will run on such a system, minor hardware upgrades can make the difference between sluggish and snappy system response.

Microprocessors

The *microprocessor* is the heart of the personal computer; this is where all the work takes place in the computer. You can rate the "power" of a computer based on the model and speed of its microprocessor. Different microprocessors have different capabilities. You should choose the microprocessor that best suits your computing needs. For example, if you plan to run programs that are math-intensive (such as CAD, graphic design, or spreadsheet programs), you should consider a microprocessor with a math *coprocessor* companion. Choosing the microprocessor speed is easy; faster is better, but more expensive. Generally speaking, you should buy as much power as you can afford.

OS/2 Warp was written specifically for the 80386-based computer. You may have seen OS/2 Warp described as a "32-bit" operating system. To run a 32-bit operating system, you need a 32-bit microprocessor. The following are 32-bit microprocessors and are compatible with OS/2 Warp:

- **80386 SX**—This is the least powerful, and least expensive microprocessor compatible with OS/2 Warp. While the 80386 SX has an internal 32-bit architecture, it only has a 16-bit external bus. This means that the microprocessor cannot communicate with other parts of the computer as quickly as a true 32-bit microprocessor.

However, you'll hardly notice the difference. Because of its 16-bit external architecture, the 80386 SX can only address 16 megabytes (millions of bytes) of RAM. If you have struggled with the DOS limitation of 640 kilobytes (thousands of bytes) of RAM, you probably think that 16 megabytes is more than you'll ever need. But when the first IBM Personal Computer was announced, 640 kilobytes of RAM was more than anyone could comprehend.

- **80386 DX**—The "DX" version of the 80386 is a true 32-bit microprocessor. Since the DX can move 32 bits of data internally as well as externally, there is no performance degradation when it communicates with other parts of the computer. The DX can address up to 4 gigabytes (billions of bytes) of RAM, although the support circuitry on most 386-based systems cannot support nearly that much.

- **80486 SX**—The 80486 SX microprocessor is compatible with the 80386 DX, but it contains advanced features to increase performance. An internal processor cache allows the 80486 to process instructions faster than an 80386. You don't have to understand these advanced features, just realize that an 80486 SX-based computer will have quicker system response than an 80386-based computer running at the same speed.

- **80486 DX**—Most "entry-level" computers come with an 80486 DX CPU. This microprocessor has all the functions of the 80486 SX, and has an additional internal Floating Point Unit (FPU—also known as a *math coprocessor*). The math coprocessor can be used by programs that do intensive mathematical calculations. Spreadsheets, CAD, and some graphic design programs are examples of programs that benefit from the presence of a math coprocessor. OS/2 Warp will emulate FPU instructions on computers that do not have an FPU; however, the internal FPU in the 80486 DX is many times faster than the emulator.

- **Pentium**—The current "king of the hill" is the Pentium, once called the 80586. The Pentium uses parallel processing and a 64-bit data bus to radically improve the performance of the microprocessor. The Pentium also contains built-in support for hardware redundancy.

By the time you read this, a new microprocessor may be available that offers better performance than the Pentium. But if history is any indicator, this new microprocessor will be compatible with existing microprocessors and, as such, will run OS/2 Warp without a problem.

> **Recommendation:** You need not agonize over the CPU decision. If you already have a computer capable of running OS/2 Warp, it is not necessary for you to upgrade your CPU. If you are buying a new computer for OS/2 Warp, let your budget pick the hardware for you.

System Architecture

The world of IBM-compatible computers is split into several segments, based on system architecture. The original IBM-AT architecture is now known as the *Industry Standard Architecture* (ISA). In 1987, IBM introduced a new architecture known as *Micro Channel*. In response to Micro Channel, several computer manufacturers created EISA, the *Enhanced Industry Standard Architecture*. Additionally, the *Video Electronics Standards Association* (VESA) introduced the VESA Local-Bus (VL BUS) standard, while Intel introduced the *Peripheral Component Interconnect* (PCI). These extensions to the bus architecture allow components to bypass the relatively slow system bus and communicate directly with the CPU. What does all this mean to an OS/2 Warp user? If you already own your computer, it doesn't mean much. OS/2 Warp will work on ISA, EISA, or Micro Channel computers. However, if you are buying a new computer to run OS/2 Warp, these facts may influence your decision.

ISA computers are the most popular and the least expensive. However, they do not communicate with peripheral devices (such as disk controllers and video adapters) as fast as an EISA or Micro Channel system. OS/2 Warp is very demanding of the system's architecture, and a slow ISA system may limit OS/2 Warp's performance. Both EISA and Micro Channel have advanced features that allow OS/2 Warp to run

Prepare to Warp

faster, and even survive a program that "crashes" the system. To improve system performance even more, VL-BUS or PCI slots are available in many computer systems. Local-bus video and disk controllers significantly improve OS/2 Warp's performance.

> **Recommendation:** Compare the performance of an EISA or Micro Channel computer to an ISA system. If you are on a tight budget, ISA may be the only choice. If possible, choose a system with local-bus video.

System Memory

IBM claims that OS/2 Warp will operate properly with 4 megabytes (MB) of random access memory (RAM). Previous versions of OS/2 Warp also made this claim, but didn't deliver. If your computer has only 4 MB of RAM, OS/2 Warp will work, but the more RAM you add, the more OS/2 Warp can do for you. The RAM is where the computer stores "active" programs and data. With more RAM, OS/2 Warp can do more things at once, without having to "put away" one program to make room for another. When OS/2 Warp runs out of RAM, it uses your hard disk as an extension to RAM (a technique known as *disk swapping*). This allows OS/2 Warp to run programs that require more RAM than is installed in your computer. The penalty is in performance. RAM is many times faster than your hard drive, so when OS/2 Warp starts swapping data to disk, there is a noticeable decrease in performance. If you don't have enough RAM, you might spend most of your time watching your disk light blink.

> **Recommendation:** Installing more RAM is the best thing you can do for your OS/2 Warp system. For most users, 8 megabytes of RAM is the best balance of price and performance for an OS/2 Warp system.

Hard Disk Drives

When DOS was first released, you could load the operating system and an application program on the same 180 kilobyte diskette. Today, DOS requires several megabytes of disk space. OS/2 Warp is even more demanding. To install the entire OS/2 Warp system, you will need over 45 megabytes of hard disk space. Installing the *OS/2 Warp BonusPak* will double that amount. That may seem like a ridiculous amount of storage for an operating system, but when you consider that OS/2 Warp includes DOS and Windows support, a myriad of system utilities, and on-line documentation, the space requirements are understandable. Inadequate hard disk space is a common problem facing new OS/2 Warp users.

Most computer systems have a hard disk large enough for OS/2 Warp, but the users have filled the hard disk with every program they can find. If "housecleaning" cannot reclaim enough space, you need to consider upgrading to a larger hard disk, or adding another hard disk to your system. Fortunately hard disk prices have steadily declined, so additional disk space is well worth the cost. When choosing a hard disk, remember that once you install OS/2 Warp, you will probably want to buy the new applications written for OS/2 Warp. These new applications are as hungry for hard disk space as OS/2 Warp is. You can never have too much disk space; so grab as much as your budget allows.

> Due to limitations in the standard computer BIOS, most systems can only access the first 504 MBytes (528 million bytes) on disk drives that use the IDE (Integrated Drive Electronics) interface. OS/2 Warp does not use BIOS, so it can work around this limitation and give you access to the entire drive. Since DOS is limited by BIOS, many drive manufacturers include software such as Ontrack Computer System's Disk Manager to overcome the limitation. OS/2 Warp can recognize disks that use Disk Manager, but if you have the original Warp (without Win-OS/2) you may need an upgraded OS/2 Warp disk device driver. Contact OS/2 technical support and obtain this update before you install Warp on a system that uses Disk Manager.

1 *Prepare to Warp*

> **Recommendation:** You can't have enough disk space. Before installing OS/2 Warp, you should have a minimum of 50 megabytes of free disk space. OS/2 Warp supports most hard disk drive interfaces, including MFM, RLL, IDE, ESDI, and SCSI.

Video Displays

You will do most of your work with OS/2 Warp on a graphical display. The quality of the display directly affects your productivity with OS/2 Warp. Almost all computers that can run OS/2 Warp are equipped with either VGA (Video Graphics Array) or *Super VGA* (SVGA) compatible displays. The VGA standard is adequate, but SVGA provides a better picture, with more room on the screen for application programs. Before selecting a display adapter, make sure a *device driver* exists for your display adapter—either in the OS/2 Warp package, or directly from the manufacturer of the display adapter. A device driver is a program that allows OS/2 Warp to communicate with the unique hardware on the display adapter. OS/2 Warp supports video adapters that use any of the following chip sets:

- ATI Technologies ATI28800 (VGA Wonder)
- ATI Technologies Mach8/32 and Mach64
- Cirrus Logic Accelerated 54xx
- Display Adapter 8514/A
- Extended Graphics Adapter (XGA)
- Headland Technology HT209
- IBM VGA 256c
- IBM/S3 864
- Super VGA (SVGA)
- S3
- Trident Microsystems TVGA8900
- Tseng Laboratories ET4000, W32, W32i, W32p
- Video Graphics Array (VGA)
- Weitek P9000, P9100
- Western Digital Imaging 90C11, 90C24-90C31, 90C33

Some IBM PS/2 computers have an 8514 or XGA display, which provides Super-VGA picture quality. Device drivers for these adapters come with OS/2 Warp. OS/2 Warp will work with the EGA and CGA graphics adapters, but these older video standards are not very pleasing to the eye.

> **Recommendation:** Select a Super-VGA display adapter from a manufacturer that provides OS/2 Warp display drivers or that supports one of the chip sets listed above. Make sure your video monitor can display everything your adapter can generate.

Pointing Devices

As discussed in the Introduction, OS/2 Warp provides a graphical user interface (GUI). Although you can use OS/2 Warp without a pointing device, most users would agree that a pointing device (such as a mouse or trackball) is essential in the GUI environment. Learning the many key-combinations required to use OS/2 Warp without a mouse is time consuming and awkward. If you are new to the idea of GUIs, you may feel that pointing devices are unnecessary. After using OS/2 Warp for a few days, your pointing device will be your most valuable possession.

> **Recommendation:** If you don't already own a mouse or trackball, buy one and install it *before* installing OS/2 Warp.

CD-ROM Drives

Many of today's computers come with Compact Disk-Read Only Memory (CD-ROM) drives. If you have a CD-ROM drive, we strongly suggest that you purchase OS/2 Warp in the CD-ROM format. The advantages to this format are:

- It includes "images" of the installation diskettes.
- You get more than 100 megabytes of multimedia samples.

Prepare to Warp

- Installation time is greatly reduced.
- It's often less expensive!

OS/2 Warp automatically recognizes the following CD-ROM drives:

- CD Technology T3301, T3401
- Chinon 431, 435, 535
- Creative Labs OmniCD
- Hitachi CDR-1650, 1750S, 1950S, 3650, 3750, 3750S, and 6750
- IBM CD-ROM I and II
- IBM ISA CD-ROM
- Mitsumi CRMC-LU002S, LU005S, FX001, FX001D, FXN01DE
- NEC Intersect 25, 36, 37, 72, 73, 74, 82, 83, 84
- NEC MultiSpin 3Xi, 3Xe, 3Xp, 38, 74-1, 84-1
- Panasonic CR-501, LK-MC501S, 521, 522, 523, 562, 563
- Philips LMS CM-205, 205MS, 206, 207, 215, 225, 225MS, 226
- Pioneer DRM-600 and 604X
- SONY CDU-31A, 33A, 55E, 531, 535, 541, 561, 6111, 6150, 6201, 6205, 6211, 6251, 7201, 7205, 7211, 7305, 7405, and 7811
- Texel DM-3021, 3024, 3028, 5021, 5024, and 5028
- Toshiba 3201, 3301, 3401, and 4101
- Wearnes CDD-120
- Generic IDE CD-ROMs

If your CD-ROM drive is not on this list, you might not be able to install OS/2 Warp in the CD-ROM format, unless you get a device driver for OS/2 Warp from the manufacturer of the CD-ROM drive. If you can't find a device driver, you can create a complete set of OS/2 Warp installation diskettes from the CD.

> **Recommendation:** If you do not already own a CD-ROM drive, now is a good time to buy one (make sure you get one that is on the list). If you do, purchase OS/2 Warp on CD-ROM instead of diskettes.

Multimedia Hardware

Computers are no longer silent boxes. Multimedia devices are popular not only for entertainment, but for business use as well. OS/2 Warp is capable of using multimedia adapters to add sound effects, music, and video capture to your computer's repertoire. OS/2 Warp supports the following multimedia hardware:

- AITech WaveWatcher
- Business Audio
- Compaq Business Audio
- Creative Labs Sound Blaster, Sound Blaster Pro, Sound Blaster 16, Sound Blaster AWE 32
- Creative Labs Video Blaster
- ESS AudioDrive
- Hauppauge Win/TV
- IBM M-Audio
- Media Vision Jazz 16
- Media Vision Pro Audio Spectrum 16
- New Media Graphics Super Video Windows
- Omnicomp M&M Basic
- Reel Magic Audio
- Reel Magic Video
- Samsung Video Magic
- Sound Galaxy NOVA-16
- IBM Thinkpad CS4231
- Toshiba T4700C and T6600C Business Audio
- Video Clipper

Miscellaneous Hardware

The explosive growth of the computer business has spawned some very strange and interesting hardware. Unique storage devices, modems, scanners, and other peripherals have come and gone. If any of your hardware is "non-standard," you may have trouble using it with OS/2

Prepare to Warp

Warp. A "README" file in the OS/2 Warp package describes many devices that need special configuration. In general, if your special hardware requires a device driver under DOS, you'll need an OS/2-specific device driver to make full use of this hardware with OS/2 Warp. If the manufacturer of your hardware is no longer in business, finding an OS/2 driver may be impossible. You might be able to coax limited function for your device from OS/2 Warp, or you might have to switch back to DOS when using that device. Fortunately, the popularity of OS/2 Warp will make sure that future "unique" hardware devices will be tested and supported under OS/2 Warp.

> **Recommendation:** Contact the manufacturer of any unique device you have in your computer, and inquire about its compatibility with OS/2 Warp.

Software Requirements

Unlike Windows, which requires DOS, OS/2 Warp is a complete operating system; it requires no other software to run. However, the job of an operating system is to allow you to run application software. You may already have a large collection of application software, and might be wondering how these programs will work once OS/2 Warp is in control of your system.

Existing DOS Software

Nearly every DOS program written will work with OS/2 Warp unmodified. However, some DOS programs take advantage of hidden or undocumented features of DOS, which may not be supported under OS/2 Warp. If a program requires a specific version of DOS to operate, OS/2 Warp will allow you to run genuine DOS under OS/2 Warp for that program (see "DOS from Drive

The OS/2 Warp Survival Guide

A:" in Chapter 7). DOS programs that control the computer hardware in unsupported ways might not work in OS/2 Warp. OS/2 Warp does not allow DOS disk utilities to manipulate the disk directly. DOS utilities that provide disk cache, RAM disks, and disk compression services will not work. However, many of these utilities are no longer needed since their functions are provided by OS/2 Warp. Some computer games that re-program system timers to create sound effects may not work. However, with the choices available in OS/2 Warp configuration, there will be a way to run almost any program that runs under DOS.

Existing Windows Software

OS/2 Warp can run most existing Windows 3.x applications, including 32-bit Windows (Win32s) programs. OS/2 Warp can even isolate Windows applications from each other, so Windows' famous "General Protection Faults" (GPFs) will not corrupt your entire system. The only types of Windows applications that are not supported under OS/2 Warp are those that require virtual device drivers (VXDs). Very few applications require VXDs, but if you rely on one of these, you will either have to switch back to DOS and Windows to use it, or upgrade to an OS/2 version of this program. An upgrade may be the best choice, since an OS/2 version of the application will provide the features of the Windows application, as well as many desirable features not available in Windows.

Existing OS/2 Software

If you are upgrading from a previous version of OS/2, you'll be happy to know that all your OS/2-specific applications will work under OS/2 Warp. This includes 16-bit OS/2 1.x programs, and 32-bit OS/2 2.x programs.

32-bit OS/2 Software: New OS/2 applications are now available that take advantage of OS/2 Warp's 32-bit architecture. You may have a DOS,

Prepare to Warp

Windows, or OS/2 16-bit version of these applications and wonder if it's worth the trouble to upgrade. 32-bit OS/2 applications can use OS/2 Warp's memory management, giving them easy access to megabytes of data. The multithreaded design of OS/2 programs means response time will be faster, and the graphical objects in OS/2 Warp will give the applications a standard look that will be easier to use. Although OS/2 Warp is designed to run DOS and Windows programs, you may want to contact the manufacturer of each DOS and Windows application you use, and ask about an upgrade to an OS/2 Warp-specific version. The increase in performance is often amazing!

Getting Ready for the Installation

Before you start to install OS/2 Warp, you need to make some decisions about how you want to use your computer. This section will help you make these decisions and show you how to plan your installation to get the most out of OS/2 Warp. In particular, you must decide:

- if you want to use multiple operating systems,
- how you want to set up your hard disk drive(s),
- if you want to use the OS/2 High Performance File System,
- which features of OS/2 Warp you do *not* want to install, and
- how you want to configure OS/2 Warp.

You'll also need to know what devices are attached to your computer, such as disk drives, printers, modem, and local area network (LAN).

 **Quick Start:** If you want to install OS/2 Warp without considering multiple operating systems, hard disk partitioning schemes, and file systems, and you have 30 to 45 megabytes of unused storage space on Drive C:, go to Chapter 2: "Installing OS/2 Warp."

Considering Multiple Operating Systems

OS/2 Warp allows you to have more than one operating system installed in your computer. Although you can run most DOS- and Windows-based programs under OS/2 Warp, you might want your computer to run real DOS with real Windows to ensure the integrity of your current system. You might be an application programmer and need to test your programs under different versions of DOS. You might want to run application programs that require some other operating system. OS/2 Warp lets you easily switch between different operating systems by giving you a few boot options.

Considering Your Boot Options

To run an operating system, you *boot* (or start) your computer with that operating system. If you decide to install multiple operating systems, OS/2 Warp helps you manage them with the following boot options:

Dual Boot: Lets you switch between running OS/2 Warp and real DOS when they are both installed on Drive C:. While running one of the operating systems, you can switch to the other by running the OS/2 program named BOOT.COM. To use Dual Boot, you must install OS/2 Warp on Drive C:, and use the FAT file system. If DOS is already installed on Drive C: before you begin the OS/2 Warp installation, the OS/2 Warp installation program will detect the presence of DOS and automatically set up your computer to use Dual Boot.

Boot Manager: Lets you choose from a menu of installed operating systems each time you start the computer. This is the most flexible way to install OS/2 Warp. You install the Boot Manager from the FDISK screen while creating your hard disk partitions.

OS/2 Warp does not help you install any other operating systems; you must use their installation programs. However, OS/2 Warp does

1 *Prepare to Warp*

help you set up your computer to accommodate additional operating systems through hard disk partitioning.

Hard Disk Partitions

If you want to install multiple operating systems, or if you want to use both the High Performance File System (HPFS) and the File Allocation Table (FAT) file systems, you need to understand *disk partitions*. When you partition a disk, you effectively divide it into two or more disk drives.

As in DOS, OS/2 Warp refers to disk drives by their *drive letter*. Drive letters consist of a single letter of the alphabet followed by a colon (i.e., A:, B:, or C:). Drive letters A: and B: are reserved for diskette drives while hard disk drives are identified as C:, D:, E:, and so forth. For example, you might have a 3.5-inch and a 5.25-inch diskette drive, and a 200 megabyte hard disk drive. You might configure OS/2 Warp so that it refers to these drives as A:, B:, and C:, respectively. Or you could partition your hard disk (floppy disks cannot be partitioned) so that OS/2 Warp refers to it as two (or more) *logical* drives (i.e., Drives C: and D:). Although you can change partitions after the installation, you can save yourself aggravation later by planning your partitions now.

If your computer already has DOS installed on it, you have at least one partition on your hard disk. If you plan to change this partition in any way, you must back up the data in that partition. You can't change an existing partition without erasing all its files.

Primary and Extended/Logical Partitions

Each physical hard disk can contain up to four partitions. OS/2 Warp allows you to create three kinds of hard disk partitions on a hard disk: Primary, Extended/Logical, and Boot Manager.

- *Primary Partitions*—The "standard" type of partition on a hard drive is the *Primary* partition. The most important feature of a primary partition is that your computer's BIOS (the program embedded in the hardware of your computer) can find a primary partition and load an operating system from it. You can have up to four primary partitions on each hard drive, but only one at a time can be "active" (see the *Advanced OS/2 Users* note below). If you already have DOS installed on your hard disk, you have at least one primary partition and OS/2 Warp will recognize it as Drive C:. When OS/2 Warp starts, it searches all your hard drives for primary partitions, and assigns drive letters (beginning with C:) to the active partition on each physical drive.

- *Extended Partition*—To increase the flexibility in hard disk storage, OS/2 Warp supports an *Extended* partition. While BIOS cannot load an operating system from the extended partition, OS/2 Warp's Boot Manager option can. The extended partition can be split into one or more "logical" drives, all of which are active at the same time. The only limit on the number of logical drives is the number of drive letters available. If you are familiar with the DOS FDISK program, you may realize that creating logical drives was a two-step process: Create an extended partition, and then create logical drives. The OS/2 FDISK program simplifies this. You specify the logical drives, and OS/2 Warp takes care of creating the extended partition. When OS/2 Warp starts, it assigns drive letters to *all* logical drives on the first physical drive (the drive letter assigned will depend on how many active physical partitions are found on all hard drives). Once all logical drives on the first hard drive are assigned, OS/2 Warp searches the next physical drive for logical drives.

- *Boot Manager Partition*—The Boot Manager is an OS/2 utility that makes it easy to install several operating systems on the same computer. When you install Boot Manager, your computer's BIOS loads the Boot Manager utility, which then allows you to select one of the operating systems installed on your hard drive.

Prepare to Warp

Primary partitions are commonly used to hold operating systems and their associated files (DOS can only be installed in a primary partition), while extended partitions are more commonly used to hold programs and data files. The following figure illustrates a disk drive that has one primary partition and an extended partition. The extended partition is further divided into three logical drives: Drive D:, Drive E:, and Drive F: (indicated by dashed lines).

 Advanced OS/2 Users: Since only one primary partition from each hard drive can be active at a time, all primary partitions on the same drive share a single drive letter. If you create more than one primary partition on a drive, you can use the FDISK or FDISKPM programs in OS/2 Warp to activate the desired partition.

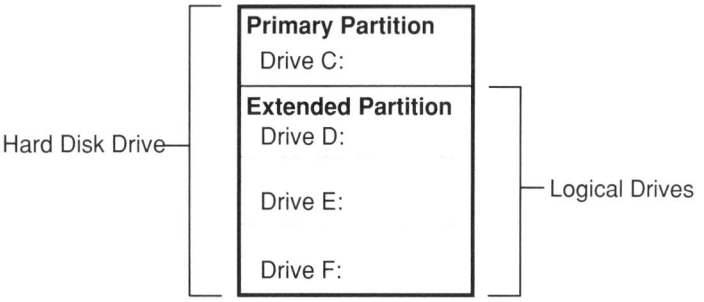

Figure 1.1   Partitions divide one hard disk into many drives.

You might be wondering why you would need more than one partition. One reason is to use more than one file system. You could use the FAT file system on C:, and HPFS on D:. It is also a good idea to separate operating system files from program and data files, which makes backing up and upgrading easier. So, why would you want more than one *Primary* partition on a hard drive? The main reason is to install multiple versions of DOS. For example, you could install DOS 5.0 on one primary partition and DOS 6.3 on another.

As mentioned before, your computer's BIOS can only start an operating system in the active primary partition. When you install the OS/2 Warp Boot Manager, OS/2 Warp can be installed on a logical drive. For multiple operating system installations, this means you can save your primary partitions for DOS or some other operating system by installing OS/2 Warp on a logical drive.

Dividing the extended partition into logical drives is helpful in allowing you to group related files. For example, you can keep all your critical data files on one logical drive, making them easier to back up with a single command. Our recommendations for partitioning schemes are provided on page 21.

Each primary and extended partition (or logical drive) can use one of two file systems: the File Allocation Table or the High Performance File System. When you format your partitions, OS/2 Warp asks you which file system you want that partition to use.

> **Recommendation:** Carefully plan your partitioning scheme, considering your requirements and your disk space. Use the following ground-rules:
>
> 1. Create a separate partition for OS/2 Warp. This will make modifying and upgrading your OS/2 Warp system easier, as you will even be able to format your OS/2 Warp partition without disturbing your applications and data. Make your OS/2 Warp partition at least 45 MB, larger if you have ample disk space.
>
> 2. Put HPFS partitions after all FAT partitions, so DOS will assign the same drive letters as OS/2 Warp.
>
> 3. If you have more than one physical drive, create primary partitions on the first disk only. Putting primary partitions on a second disk will cause a confusing drive-lettering scheme.

Choosing the Proper File System

The next decision you must make is which file system you want to use with OS/2 Warp: the File Allocation Table (FAT), the High Performance File System (HPFS), or both. A *file system* is a service that an operating system uses to read, write, and manage files on your disk drives. The FAT file system was introduced by DOS. OS/2 1.2 introduced the HPFS

1

Prepare to Warp

file system. OS/2 Warp understands both file systems. Both file systems manage their files in *directories* on your disk drives.

The File Allocation Table (FAT)

The FAT file system under OS/2 Warp is compatible with DOS, so DOS users upgrading to OS/2 Warp will probably be more comfortable with FAT. If you have a small partition on your disk (under 128 megabytes) FAT may be adequate, but you will be missing out on the performance benefits of HPFS. Among the drawbacks to FAT is *disk fragmentation.* As files are created, modified, and deleted under FAT, files tend to become fragmented. When a file is fragmented, it is split into sections and spread out over the disk, making disk reads and writes more time consuming. Disk fragmentation significantly affects the performance of your computer. Also, FAT file names are limited to 8 characters, with a 3-character extension. For large partitions, FAT can waste considerable space, because as the size of the partition grows, FAT increases the space allocated to each file (whether the file needs it or not). If these drawbacks concern you, consider using HPFS.

The High Performance File System

You can improve the performance and function of your computer by using the HPFS file system. HPFS uses sophisticated file allocation and lookup techniques to practically eliminate disk fragmentation while more efficiently using your hard disk space. HPFS can handle partitions up to 64 gigabytes in size, without wasting space due to increased allocation unit size. HPFS supports 254-character, mixed-case file names. If you are a DOS user, this might confuse you at first. There are no file name extensions in HPFS files. In fact the period that separates a DOS file name from its extension, is a valid character in HPFS file names, as are many other characters that are not valid under FAT. For example: Under HPFS, the following is a valid file name: "`End-of-Quarter Report for 03-31.`" As you can see, this is a huge advantage over FAT file names; you can describe the content of the file with its name. File names can be up to 254 characters long, including spaces and punctuation. HPFS also includes support for OS/2's *Extended Attributes*, which contain file-specific information such as file-type, association, icons, and comments. On FAT partitions, Extended Attributes are stored in a separate file, which wastes considerable storage. The OS/2 Warp system partition makes extensive use of Extended Attributes, so we recommend using HPFS for your OS/2 Warp system partition.

By putting your OS/2 *swap file* in an HPFS partition, you can reduce the effects of fragmentation, thereby improving the performance of your computer. However, don't create a separate partition for your swap file—put it on the partition with the most free space.

Partitions formatted using HPFS cannot be accessed when your computer is running real DOS. If you plan to start your computer with real DOS, plan to use FAT in at least one of your partitions. If you plan to use both HPFS and FAT, place the HPFS partitions after the FAT partitions; DOS will ignore any partition that has been formatted for HPFS. However, if you run DOS applications under OS/2 Warp, those applications can access HPFS files, as long as the HPFS file has a name that fits the 8.3 character format. HPFS also requires additional RAM, so if your computer only has 4 MB of RAM, HPFS performance will suffer.

HPFS expands the use of extended attributes. Each file under HPFS provides an area within the file where application programs can store file-specific information such as: a program's icon, last-revised date, owner's name, or previous file name. This is in addition to the normal file attributes such as: hidden, archive, read-only, and so forth.

1

Prepare to Warp

Disk Partitioning Examples

We developed the following scenarios that include the amount of disk space available, your comfort level with partitioning, and your need for real DOS.

 In the following examples, we will use 45 MB as the recommended size of the OS/2 Warp partition. The partition size required for OS/2 Warp can be much more, depending on the options you install. If you create a partition smaller than 45 MB, you will have to do without some OS/2 Warp features. If you have adequate disk space, consider creating an OS/2 Warp partition larger than 45 MB, which will give your OS/2 Warp setup room to grow.

Real DOS Users

We realize that you might not be comfortable with the idea of abandoning your existing DOS-based system. With that in mind, we developed the following list of recommendations. Find the scenario in the list that best matches your situation and consider the recommendation provided.

1. If your hard disk drive has 100 megabytes or less of storage space, or you do not want to create partitions (or change existing ones), and you have a limited need to boot real DOS, we recommend the following:

- Make sure you have at least 35 megabytes of free space (depending on the features you install) on your hard disk (Drive C:).

- Go to Chapter 2, "Installing OS/2 Warp," to begin the OS/2 Warp installation now.

The OS/2 Warp Survival Guide

2. If your hard disk drive has more than 100 megabytes of storage space, and you are willing to create new partitions (or change existing ones), we recommend the following:

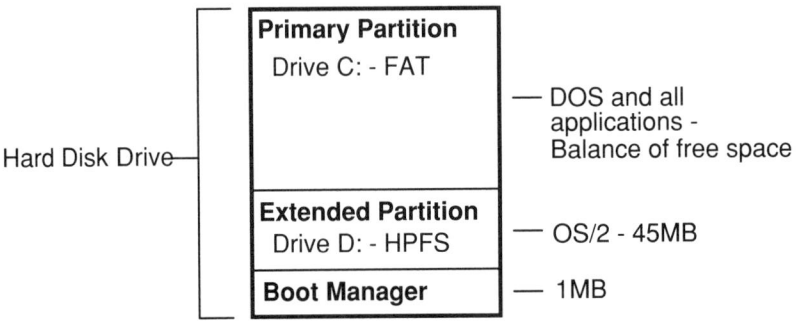

Figure 1.2   *One way you might partition a 100 to 200 MB hard disk drive.*

- Plan to install Boot Manager at the end of free space.

- Plan to create a 45 megabyte extended/logical partition for OS/2 Warp. Place the partition at the end of free space. This will be Drive D:.

- Plan to create a primary partition for DOS and all your application programs (DOS and OS/2 Warp). Use the balance of free space. This will be Drive C:.

3. If you routinely need to run different versions of DOS (to test software, for example), you may want to set up your hard disk partitions as follows:

 The shaded partition shown in the following figure is an optional primary partition, which you could use to hold a different operating system such as DOS version 6.

Prepare to Warp

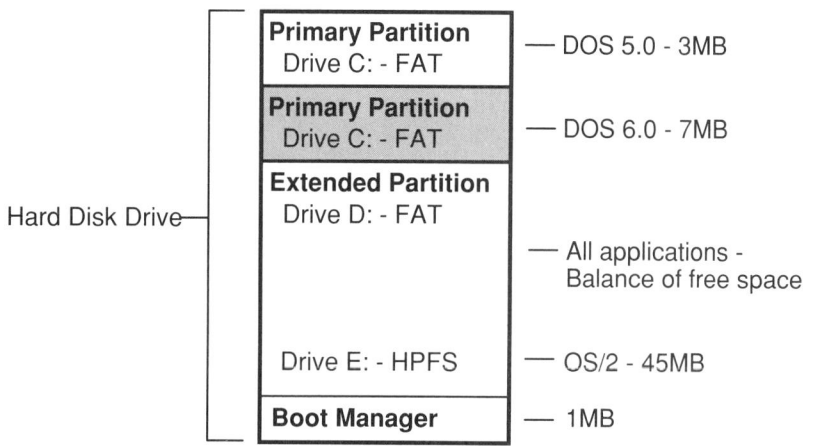

Figure 1.3   *This is one way you might partition hard disk drives to support several versions of DOS and OS/2.*

- Plan to install Boot Manager at the end of free space. If you have a large hard disk drive (more than 1024 cylinders), your system may not be able to start the Boot Manager from the end of free space. If you're not sure, place the Boot Manager at the beginning of free space.

- Plan to create a small primary partition (3–10 MB) for DOS. Place the partition at the beginning of free space. This will be Drive C:.

- Plan to create a 45 megabyte extended/logical partition for OS/2 Warp. Place the partition at the end of free space. This will be Drive E:.

- Optionally, plan to create a second primary partition for a second version of DOS or some other operating system. Place the partition at the beginning of free space. This will be a second Drive C: and will be inactive when the first Drive C: is active. See the *Advanced OS/2 Users* note on page 18 for more information.

23

The OS/2 Warp Survival Guide

- Plan to create an extended/logical partition for all your application programs (DOS and OS/2). Use the balance of free space. This will be Drive D:.

4. If you have more than one hard drive, your installation setup can be even more flexible. In this example, two hard drives are configured so that you can select between two versions of DOS, one version of UNIX, and several versions of OS/2. While you may not need this kind of flexibility, this example may give you an idea for your own configuration.

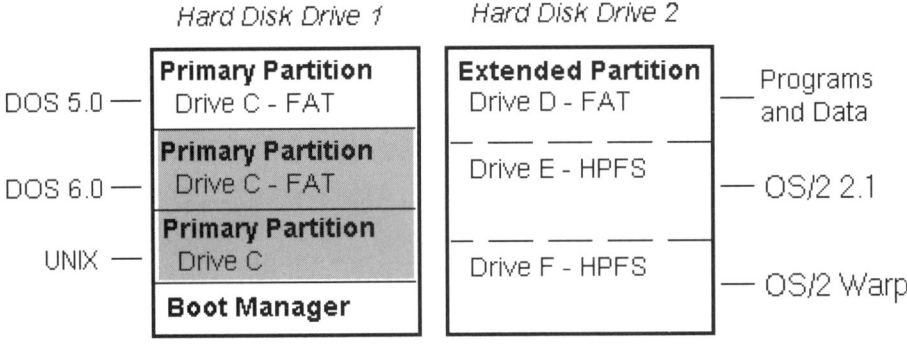

Figure 1.4   One way to partition two drives for multiple operating systems.

- Plan to install Boot Manager at the end of free space on Hard Disk Drive 1.

- Plan to create up to three primary partitions for DOS. These partitions will occupy the remainder of Hard Disk Drive 1. Each of these partitions will be Drive C:. Notice that since a hard drive can only have four primary partitions, you cannot allocate space for logical drives on this disk.

- Plan the number and sizes of the logical partitions you want on Hard Disk Drive 2 for your DOS and OS/2 application programs and data files. In our example, these would be Drive D:.

Prepare to Warp

 It's all right to install a second copy of OS/2 on one of these logical drives. In our example, OS/2 2.1 is installed on Drive E:. OS/2 Warp can be started from a primary or a logical partition.

- Plan to create a 45 megabyte logical drive for OS/2 Warp. Place the drive at the end of free space on Hard Disk Drive 2. In our example, this will be Drive F:.

Deciding Which OS/2 Warp Features to Install

The next decision you should make before starting the installation is which of the many OS/2 Warp features you want and which you do not want to install. Depending on your requirements from OS/2 Warp, you might be able to save a substantial amount of hard disk space by excluding some features.

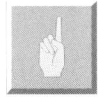 **Installation Note:** Many of the features are "luxury" items that are not required for basic operation. After the installation, you can add features at any time using the Selective Install program.

When you begin the OS/2 Warp installation, you will be asked if you want to perform the *Quick* or the *Advanced* installation. The *Quick* installation installs OS/2 Warp on Drive C:, and installs a pre-selected list of features. If you want to install OS/2 Warp on another partition, change partition sizes, or select the features to be installed, you should select the advanced installation.

Quick Installation

If you select the Quick installation, all other choices are made for you by the installation program. OS/2 Warp will be installed on Drive C:, and

25

you will need about 40 megabytes of hard disk space for this installation option. The other options can be installed later using the *Selective Install* option, so don't think this feature will lock you into a restricted setup.

Advanced Installation

This option allows you to customize the installation of OS/2 Warp features on your computer. You will be able to select the partition to contain OS/2 Warp, and you can select the file system for the OS/2 Warp partition. You will be presented with a hardware configuration screen, and a list of features with their descriptions and disk space requirements. As you include and exclude features from the list, OS/2 Warp shows you the total amount of disk space required for your selections, along with the amount of available disk space you have.

Considering Your OS/2 Warp Configuration

Your final consideration before starting the installation is your system configuration. This sounds more intimidating than it really is. During installation, OS/2 Warp "looks" at the hardware installed in your computer and configures itself appropriately. You probably will not need to change the configuration; however, the installation program displays a System Configuration *dialog box* that allows you to override these settings. The configurable items are:

- Country
- Keyboard
- Mouse
- Serial Device Support
- Primary and Secondary Displays
- Advanced Power Management
- PCMCIA Support
- CD-ROM Device Support

Prepare to Warp

- Printer
- Multimedia Device Support
- SCSI Adapter Support

Country

The characters displayed on your computer are based on the alphabet associated with the *Country* setting. You can change the set of characters used by your computer from a list of 31 countries.

Keyboard

The keys on computer keyboards are laid out differently in many countries to accommodate the alphabets used in their languages. You can change the selected layout of the keys on your keyboard from a list of 28 languages.

Mouse

If OS/2 Warp does not identify your mouse, you can change the mouse setting to one of the following:

- PS/2 Style Pointing Device
- Bus Style Mouse
- InPort Style Mouse
- Serial Pointing Device
- Logitech C-Series or M-Series Serial Mouse
- IBM Touch Device
- PC Mouse Systems Mouse
- Other Pointing Device for Mouse Port
- No pointing device support

Serial Device Support

If you have a serial communications device attached to your computer (such as a modem) you need to install this support. Otherwise, you can save some space on your hard disk and some of your computer's resources.

Primary and Secondary Displays

You can install two video adapters in your computer, one for graphics display, the other for text. You can select the device type for each.

If you have a high-resolution display adapter that is not shown in the list, you will need to install a special *device driver*. During installation you will be asked to insert a diskette containing the device driver. This diskette is provided by the manufacturer of your display adapter.

Advanced Power Management

If your computer supports Advanced Power Management (APM), installing this support will allow OS/2 Warp to monitor your system and shut off unused hardware to conserve power. APM support will also allow OS/2 Warp to display battery charge status on APM-compliant laptop and notebook computers.

PCMCIA Support

If your computer has PCMCIA expansion slots, installing PCMCIA support allows OS/2 Warp to control these slots. PCMCIA support includes *Plug and Play for PCMCIA*, OS/2 Warp's automatic PCMCIA

Prepare to Warp

configurator. With Plug and Play, OS/2 Warp can start selected programs whenever a PCMCIA card is inserted or removed.

CD-ROM Device Support

Many of today's computers have CD-ROM drives installed. If you have a CD-ROM drive, be aware of the make and model so you can verify that OS/2 Warp chooses the correct support during configuration. See "CD-ROM Drives" in this chapter for a complete listing of supported drives.

Printer

During configuration OS/2 Warp allows you to specify the type of printer you have connected to your computer. Be aware of the make and model of your printer so that you can specify the correct support. You also will need to know which printer port your printer is connected to (i.e., parallel ports 1, 2, or 3, or serial ports 1–4). Most printers use a parallel communications interface and are connected to parallel port 1 (also known as LPT1).

Multimedia Device Support

If you have a multimedia device in your computer (a sound card or a video capture adapter), this option will let you select and configure your multimedia device. Configuration options offered depend on the type of card in your computer.

29

SCSI Adapter Support

The small computer system interface (SCSI—pronounced "scuzzy") feature allows OS/2 Warp to access the devices you have attached to your computer through a SCSI adapter. SCSI devices are usually hard disk drives, CD-ROMs, or some other mass storage device. If you have a SCSI adapter in your computer, be aware of the make and model so you can verify that OS/2 Warp chooses the correct support during configuration.

Summary

You now should have a pretty good idea how you're going to install and configure OS/2 Warp for your computer. The most difficult part of the installation is hard disk partitioning. If you think you might need partitions (it's mandatory for multiple operating systems) and you do not have a partitioning scheme planned, return to "Hard Disk Partitions" now. Don't bother starting the installation without a partitioning scheme.

Chapter 2

Installing OS/2 Warp

This chapter contains step-by-step instructions for installing OS/2 Warp. These steps work for both diskette and CD-ROM installations. If you're installing from CD-ROM, keep in mind that after the first two diskettes, you won't have to continue to change diskettes during the installation.

 Don't start the installation procedure until you've backed up all program and data files on your hard disk drive. If you need to change existing partitions on your hard disk, your files will be erased. If you plan to use Dual Boot, and do not need to change your partitions, your files will not be erased.

Start

1 Insert the *OS/2 Warp Installation Diskette* into Drive A: and restart your computer.

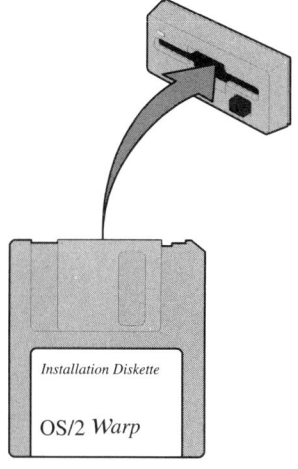

You can turn off your computer and then turn it back on, or you can press the **Ctrl**+**Alt**+**Del** key combination to restart your computer. But we strongly recommend that you turn it off and then back on so that all your hardware is properly initialized.

If your system has a disk translation utility (such as Ontrack Computer System's Disk Manager) it will ask if you want to boot from a diskette or install an operating system dur-

The OS/2 Warp Survival Guide

ing system startup. You must activate this feature before you insert the OS/2 Installation Diskette.

After a pause, which may take a minute, an introduction screen appears on your display, prompting you to replace the diskette in Drive A: with the diskette labeled *OS/2 Warp Diskette 1*.

OS/2 Warp requires two diskettes to complete the boot process—even if you are installing OS/2 Warp from CD. This first diskette contains only part of the system required to start the installation. Please note that OS/2 Warp will not install properly from Drive B:; the Installation Diskette *must* be in Drive A:.

If a problem exists, your system might stop (before the OS/2 Welcome screen appears) to display an error message such as "!!SYS2027." Turn your computer off and try to start the installation again, making sure the *Installation* diskette is in Drive A:. If you can't get past the error, consider calling IBM support. Your computer may not be compatible with OS/2 Warp. IBM support might have the answer, or at least be able to point you in the right direction.

2 **Remove the Installation Diskette, insert *Diskette 1*, and press Enter.**

The OS/2 Warp logo screen appears while the installation program identifies your computers hardware. This process can take several minutes, so don't give up too quickly. If you are installing from CD-ROM, make sure the OS/2 Warp CD is in the CD-ROM drive.

If the installation program prompts you to insert the CD even after you have inserted it, your CD-ROM drive may not be supported by OS/2 Warp. Check it against the list of supported drives in Chapter 1. If you have an unsupported drive, the drive manufacturer might have an OS/2 driver, which you can easily add to the installation diskette and try again.

If you can't get your CD-ROM to work with OS/2 Warp (but you can access it with DOS), you have two choices: you can make your own Warp installation diskettes, or you can install from diskette images that are provided on the CD. To make diskettes, boot DOS and run the `MAKEDSKS.BAT` file found in the root directory of the OS/2 Warp CD. This can take quite a bit of time, and requires a few boxes of blank diskettes. If you have enough free disk space on one of your hard drives (45 MBytes, not including the space it takes to install Warp), you might consider installing from image. Here's how:

- Boot DOS and insert the Warp CD.
- Copy the Warp installation image to a hard drive with at least 45 MBytes free. For example, if your CD-ROM drive is F:, and you have lots of free space on drive D:, use the command:

  `XCOPY F:\OS2IMAGE D:\OS2IMAGE /S /E`
- Find two blank 1.44MB diskettes, and run the `MAKEDSKS.BAT` program on the root directory of the Warp CD. Once you make the Installation diskette and Diskette 1, you can abort the program.
- Edit the CONFIG.SYS file on the newly made Diskette 1 and add the following line:

  `SET SOURCEPATH=D:\OS2IMAGE`
- If you copied the image to a directory other than D:\OS2IMAGE, substitute your drive and directory in that line.
- Save your CONFIG.SYS, and use the Installation diskette and Diskette 1 you created to install Warp. Rather than looking for the install files on floppy or CD-ROM, OS/2 Warp will look for them in your specified source path. Once the Warp installation is complete, you can drag the D:\OS2IMAGE directory to the shredder (deleting the files) to reclaim the 45 MBytes of space.

If all goes well, you should see the screen shown in the following figure.

The OS/2 Warp Survival Guide

```
                Installing Operating System/2

                     Welcome to OS/2!

   To begin the installation, select one of the following methods.
   Then press Enter.

   1. Easy Installation

   Easy Installation is intended for most users of OS/2.  The
   system makes decisions for you based on your current computer
   setup.  Press F1 now for more information.

   2. Advanced Installation

   Advanced Installation is intended for experienced technical
   users.  You must make decisions about your computer setup.
   Press F1 now for more information.


   Enter   F3=Command Prompt   F1=Help
```

Figure 2.1   Welcome screen indicates your computer has booted under OS/2 Warp.

Don't be intimidated by the option called *Advanced Installation*. This chapter will guide you through all the configuration options of the advanced installation, and you may learn something from the options you see.

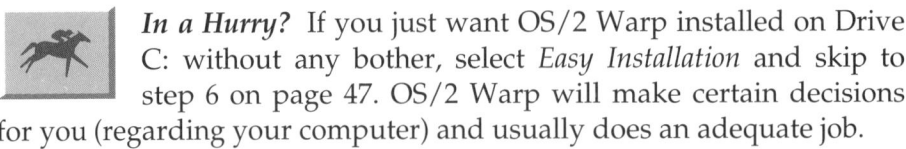 *In a Hurry?* If you just want OS/2 Warp installed on Drive C: without any bother, select *Easy Installation* and skip to step 6 on page 47. OS/2 Warp will make certain decisions for you (regarding your computer) and usually does an adequate job.

You can press F3 on the Welcome screen to suspend the installation program and display an OS/2 command prompt. From this command prompt, you can run OS/2 commands such as FORMAT, FDISK, and CHKDSK. These OS/2 commands are on the Installation Diskette and Diskette 1. To return to the installation program, type EXIT at the command prompt.

Installing OS/2 Warp

3 **Select Advanced Installation and press Enter.**

During this stage of the installation, you might see one or more "warning" screens. These screens alert you to situations that may need special attention. For example, OS/2 Warp may detect a compressed partition if you are using a disk-compression product (such as Stacker). Another warning screen appears if there isn't enough free disk space in the installation partition. Each warning screen will have a set of options to help you remedy the situation and continue with the installation. Once you satisfy any warnings, you should see the Installation Drive Selection screen (as shown in the following figure).

```
                    Installation Drive Selection

      If you want multiple versions of DOS, OS/2 or other operating
      systems on the same hard disk, refer to the OS/2 documentation
      for information on OS/2 hard disk management before continuing.

      If you have multiple primary partitions set up on your hard
      disk, select option 2 to verify that the correct partition is
      active.

      OS/2 will be installed on drive C :

      Select an option:

        1. Accept the drive

        2. Specify a different drive or partition

      If you select option 2, the FDISK screen is displayed.
  Enter   Esc=Cancel   F3=Exit   F1=Help
```

Figure 2.2   *Use this screen to select where you want to install OS/2 Warp.*

4 **Select the appropriate option on the Installation Drive Selection screen.**

The installation program selects Drive C: by default on this screen. You have two options: accept the drive, or specify a different drive or partition.

The OS/2 Warp Survival Guide

 ***In a Hurry?*** If you select option 1 on this screen (accept the drive) OS/2 Warp will be installed on the default drive. If you do not need to modify partitions and the default drive is where you want to install OS/2 Warp, select option 1, and skip to step 5 on page 45.

If you have a partitioning scheme planned for your hard disk drive, or if you want to install OS/2 Warp on a partition other than the default drive, select option 2 (Specify a different drive or partition). A screen appears warning you about modifying your partitions. Press **Enter** to continue to the FDISK screen.

FDISK Screen

Use the FDISK screen to make a different drive or partition "installable." To implement your partitioning scheme, you may need to first use this screen to create and manipulate hard disk partitions When the screen first appears, you'll see a box with a message in it stating that "a partition with at least 35 MBytes must be set installable." Press any key to remove the message, but remember, before you can exit FDISK, you must set a partition as *installable*. This is where the installation program will install OS/2 Warp.

If any partitions exist on your hard disk, they will be shown. If your hard disk has never been partitioned, the entire disk will appear as *Free Space* on the FDISK screen.

To use FDISK press the arrow keys to move the highlighted selection bar to a partition you want to change, and press the **Enter** key. A pop-up menu appears (as shown in Figure 2.3) with all the options you'll need to create new partitions, delete old partitions, set the installable partition, etc. This is called the FDISK Option menu. To find out more about an option on the menu, move the highlighted selection bar to the option and press the **F1** key.

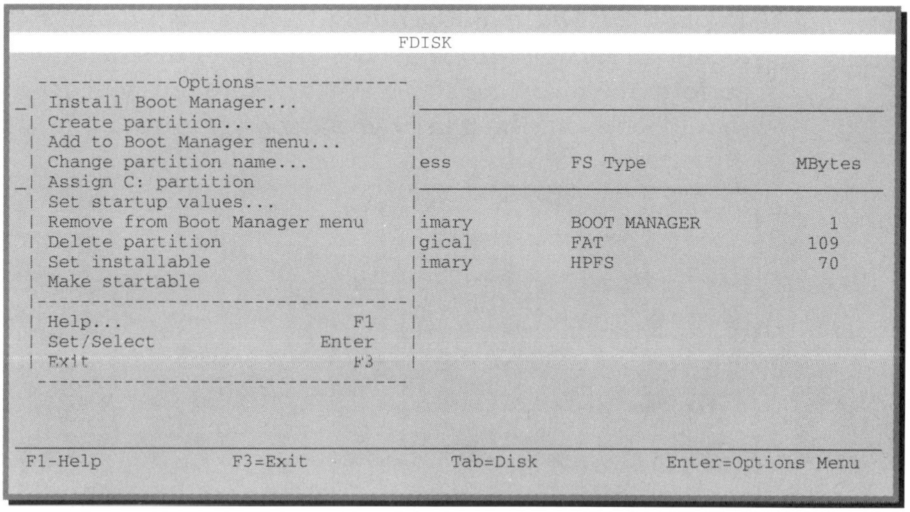

Installing OS/2 Warp

```
                              FDISK
      -----------Options--------------
  _| Install Boot Manager...        |
   | Create partition...            |
   | Add to Boot Manager menu...    |
   | Change partition name...       |ess        FS Type         MBytes
  _| Assign C: partition            |
   | Set startup values...          |
   | Remove from Boot Manager menu  |imary      BOOT MANAGER         1
   | Delete partition               |gical      FAT                109
   | Set installable                |imary      HPFS                70
   | Make startable                 |
   |--------------------------------|
   | Help...                    F1  |
   | Set/Select              Enter  |
   | Exit                       F3  |
   ----------------------------------

   F1-Help         F3=Exit          Tab=Disk         Enter=Options Menu
```

Figure 2.3   *FDISK lets you specify how to "divide" your hard drive and where you want your operating system(s) to reside.*

You may not have to use all the options on the pop-up menu to accomplish your partitioning scheme. Depending on your needs, you may have to create partitions, specifying whether they're primary or logical drives. If you're installing multiple operating systems, you should create a partition for the Boot Manager and add the partitions to the Boot Manager Menu to make them *bootable*.

The following pages contain examples of how you might partition your hard disk drive(s). You may want to find an example that is closest to your situation and perform the steps provided.

The OS/2 Warp Survival Guide

Example of Multiple Operating System Installations with a Single, Small (Under 200 MB) Hard Disk Drive: If this describes your system, perform the following steps. When you're finished, your FDISK screen should look something like the one shown below:

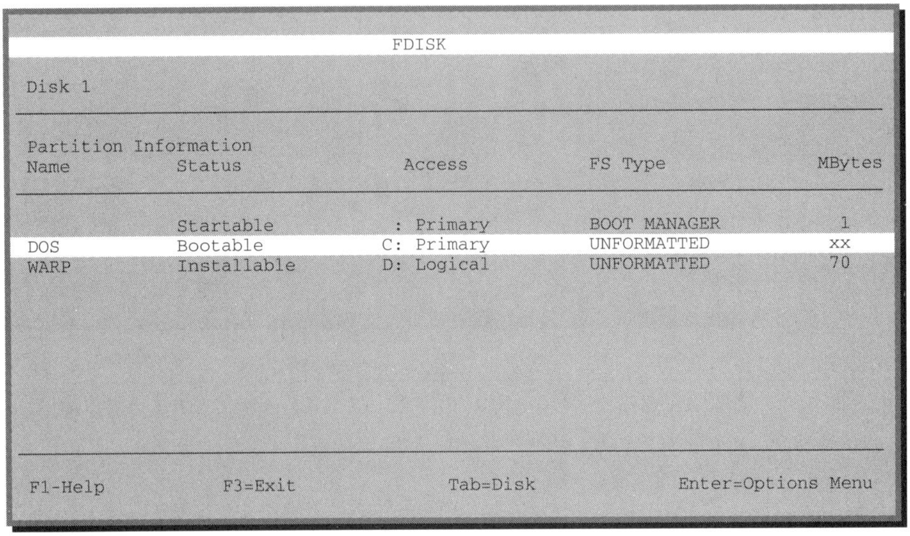

```
                                    FDISK

 Disk 1

 Partition Information
 Name         Status              Access           FS Type          MBytes

              Startable         : Primary         BOOT MANAGER         1
 DOS          Bootable          C: Primary        UNFORMATTED         xx
 WARP         Installable       D: Logical        UNFORMATTED         70




 F1=Help           F3=Exit              Tab=Disk           Enter=Options Menu
```

Figure 2.4   *FDISK for machines with smaller hard disk drives and multiple operating systems.*

   a. On the FDISK screen, press **Enter** to display the Option menu. Select *Delete Partition* to remove your old partition (if your hard disk has data on it, you should back up the hard disk before deleting any partition). If your hard disk had more than one partition on it, repeat this step to delete all partitions. The FDISK screen should show your entire disk as *Free Space*.

   b. Press **Enter** to display the Options menu. Select *Install Boot Manager* and press **Enter**. When asked where to place the Boot Manager partition, specify the beginning of free space. FDISK creates a small (usually 1 MB) partition and places it at the top of the list.

Installing OS/2 Warp

c. Highlight the *Free Space* line and press **Enter** to display the Options menu. Select *Create Partition* and press **Enter**. When asked for the size of the partition, enter your desired OS/2 Warp partition size. When asked if this is a primary partition or logical drive, specify *extended logical drive*. Place this partition at the *end of free space*. This will be your OS/2 Warp partition.

d. Highlight the *Free Space* line and press **Enter** to display the Options menu. Select *Create Partition* and press **Enter**. When asked for the size of the partition, enter the remainder of your hard disk space. When asked if this is a primary partition or logical drive, specify *primary partition*. This will be your second operating system's partition (i.e., DOS).

e. Highlight the primary partition (Drive C:) and press **Enter** to display the Options menu. Select *Add to Boot Manager* and press **Enter**. When asked to name the partition, type the name of the operating system (i.e., DOS) and press **Enter**.

f. Highlight the OS/2 Warp partition and press **Enter** to display the Options menu. Select *Set Installable* and press **Enter**. The Boot Manager will let you choose between DOS and OS/2 Warp when you start your computer.

g. Press **F3** to exit FDISK. Then select *Save and Exit* and press **Enter**.

If you have changed any partitions, OS/2 Warp will display a message saying that the system must be restarted so that the partitions can be recognized during system installation. Reinsert the Installation Diskette in Drive A: and press **Enter**. When prompted, insert Diskette 1 and press **Enter**.

The Installation Drive Selection screen reappears. This time, the partition you specified as being *installable* will be selected as the installation drive. Select option 1 (Accept the drive) and press **Enter**. Then skip to step 5 on page 45 to complete the installation.

The OS/2 Warp Survival Guide

Example of Multiple Operating System Installations with a Single, Large (over 200 MB) Hard Disk Drive: If this describes your system, perform the following steps. When you're finished, your FDISK screen should look something like the one shown below:

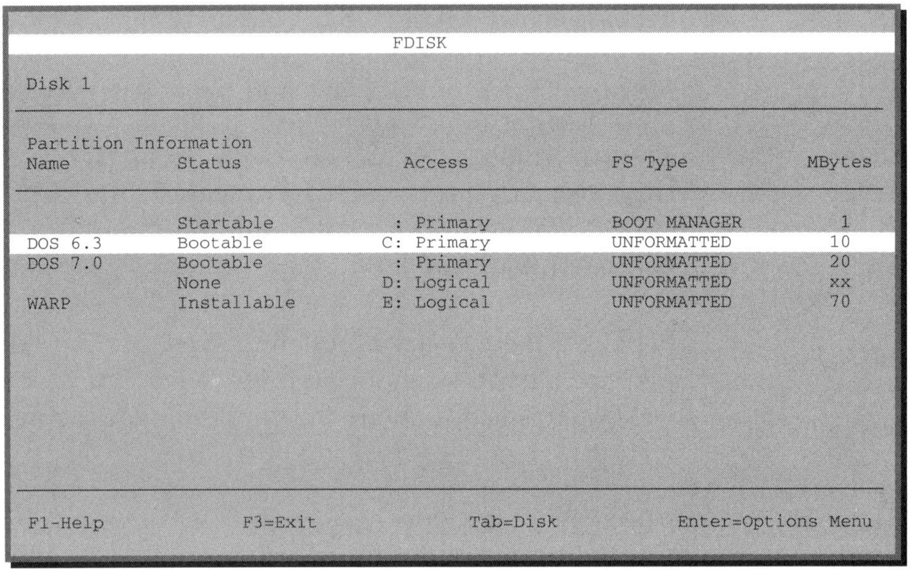

```
                              FDISK
Disk 1

Partition Information
Name          Status              Access         FS Type          MBytes

              Startable         : Primary        BOOT MANAGER         1
DOS 6.3       Bootable          C: Primary       UNFORMATTED         10
DOS 7.0       Bootable          : Primary        UNFORMATTED         20
              None              D: Logical       UNFORMATTED         xx
WARP          Installable       E: Logical       UNFORMATTED         70




F1=Help            F3=Exit           Tab=Disk          Enter=Options Menu
```

Figure 2.5   *FDISK for machines with three operating systems and Boot Manager.*

    a. On the FDISK screen, press **Enter** to display the Option menu. Select *Delete Partition* to remove your old partition (if your hard disk has data on it, you should back up the hard disk before deleting any partition). If your hard disk had more than one partition on it, repeat this step to delete all partitions. The FDISK screen should show your entire disk as *Free Space*.

    b. Press **Enter** to display the Options menu. Select *Install Boot Manager* and press **Enter**. When asked where to place the Boot Manager partition, specify the beginning of free space. FDISK creates a small (usually 1 MB) partition and places it at the top of the list.

c. Highlight the *Free Space* line and press **Enter** to display the Options menu. Select *Create Partition* and press **Enter**. When asked for the size of the partition, enter your desired OS/2 Warp partition size. When asked if this is a primary partition or logical drive, specify *logical drive*. Place this partition at the *end of free space*. This will be your OS/2 Warp partition.

d. Highlight the *Free Space* line and press **Enter** to display the Options menu. Select *Create Partition* and press **Enter**. When asked for the size of the partition, enter your desired DOS partition size. When asked if this is a primary partition or logical drive, specify *primary partition*. Place this partition at the *start of free space*. This will be your second operating system's partition (i.e., DOS Version 6.3).

e. If you want to install a third operating system, highlight the *Free Space* line and press **Enter** to display the Options menu. Select *Create Partition* and press **Enter**. When asked for the size of the partition, enter your desired DOS partition size. When asked if this is a primary partition or logical drive, specify *primary partition*. Place this partition at the *start of free space*. This will be your third operating system's partition (i.e., DOS Version 7.0).

To start your computer from either primary partition, select the partition from the Boot Manager menu. Once a primary partition is selected, it will remain the C: partition until you select the other primary. If you want to see the hidden primary partition from OS/2 Warp, run FDISK, highlight this partition, press **Enter** to display the Options menu, and select the *Assign C: Partition* option. The next time you start your computer, this partition will be the default visible primary partition.

f. Highlight the *Free Space* line and press **Enter** to display the Options menu. Select *Create Partition* and press **Enter**. When asked for the size of the partition, enter the remainder of your hard disk space. This partition will be known as Drive D:, where you could store all applications and data files for all your operating systems.

g. Highlight the first primary partition (Drive C:) and press **Enter** to display the Options menu. Select *Add to Boot Manager* and press **Enter**. When asked to name the partition, type the name of the operating system (i.e., DOS) and press **Enter**. Repeat this step for the other primary partition (if you created it).

h. Highlight the OS/2 Warp partition (Drive E:) and press **Enter** to display the Options menu. Select *Set Installable* and press **Enter**. The Boot Manager will let you choose between DOS and OS/2 Warp when you start your computer.

i. Press **F3** to exit FDISK. Then select *Save and Exit* and press **Enter**.

If you have changed any partitions, OS/2 Warp will display a message saying that the system must be restarted so that the partitions can be recognized during system installation. Reinsert the Installation Diskette in Drive A: and press **Enter**. When prompted, insert Diskette 1 and press **Enter**.

The Installation Drive Selection screen reappears. This time, the partition you specified as being *installable* will be selected as the installation drive. Select option 1 (Accept the drive) and press **Enter**. Then skip to step 5 on page 45 to complete the installation.

Installing OS/2 Warp

Example of Multiple Operating System Installation with 2 Hard Disk Drives (Disk 1): If this describes your system, consider the following FDISK screen. It shows how you might set up your partitions on the first hard disk drive.

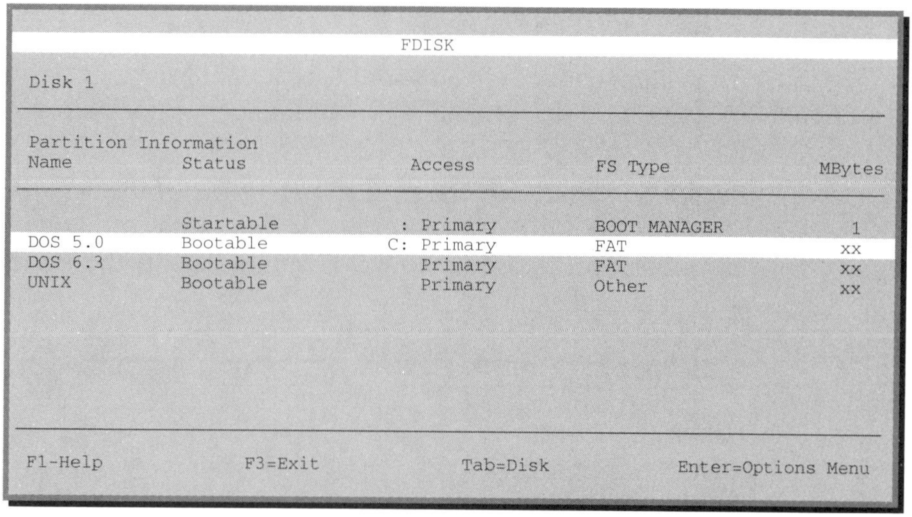

```
                                FDISK

 Disk 1


 Partition Information
 Name           Status                Access          FS Type             MBytes

                Startable           : Primary         BOOT MANAGER             1
 DOS 5.0        Bootable          C : Primary         FAT                     xx
 DOS 6.3        Bootable            Primary           FAT                     xx
 UNIX           Bootable            Primary           Other                   xx




 F1=Help            F3=Exit           Tab=Disk          Enter=Options Menu
```

Figure 2.6   *FDISK for machines with two hard disk drives and multiple operating systems (drive 1 of 2).*

If you want to keep your first hard disk drive as it is, you might want to install the Boot Manager on your second drive. This is not documented and is definitely *not* officially supported. However, the Boot Manager was designed to support this option, and it may work for you. Here's how:

- Disconnect your first hard drive, forcing your second hard drive to appear as the first hard drive. This may require jumper setting changes to your hard disk drive. If you don't understand jumper settings, don't try this.

- Boot the Warp installation disks, select "Advanced" installation, and choose to specify your partition. This gets you to FDISK. Install the Boot Manager on your drive and save the changes.

The OS/2 Warp Survival Guide

- Reconnect all your drives, and start the OS/2 installation. When you come to the "Easy or Advanced" installation, press **F3** to go to an OS/2 prompt.
- Type: FDISK /NEWMBR. This command changes the master boot record so it can find the Boot Manager
- Type EXIT and continue with your installation. If you've done everything correctly, you should see a Boot Manager partition on one of your hard drives, and all Boot Manager options are available to you.

Example of Multiple Operating System Installation with 2 Hard Disk Drives (Disk 2): If this describes your system, consider the following FDISK screen. It shows how you might set up the partitions on your second hard disk drive.

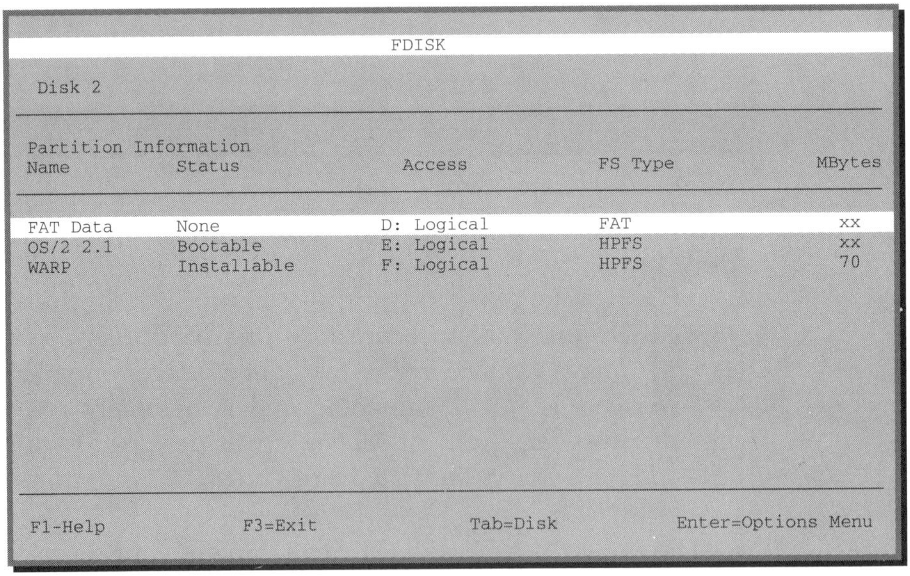

```
                              FDISK

 Disk 2


 Partition Information
 Name           Status            Access         FS Type        MBytes

 FAT Data       None              D: Logical     FAT            xx
 OS/2 2.1       Bootable          E: Logical     HPFS           xx
 WARP           Installable       F: Logical     HPFS           70




 F1=Help         F3=Exit          Tab=Disk       Enter=Options Menu
```

Figure 2.7   *FDISK for machines with two hard disk drives and multiple operating systems (drive 2 of 2).*

If none of these examples seemed appropriate for your system, you must have some unique requirements (and hopefully a planned partitioning scheme that you developed after reading Chapter 1 in this

Installing OS/2 Warp

book). Use the FDISK Option menu to implement your partitioning scheme. And remember:

A partition with at least 35 MBytes must be set *installable* before you exit FDISK. This is where the installation program will install OS/2 Warp; without this information, the installation cannot continue.

When you're finished defining your partitioning scheme, exit FDISK and continue the installation with step 5.

5 **When asked, remove Diskette 1, insert Diskette 2, and press Enter.**

If you are installing from a CD-ROM drive, you will not be asked for any more diskettes. You can still follow the installation steps provided here; the screens and procedures are similar to the diskette version.

If your installable partition is already formatted, the *Formatting the Installation Partition* screen appears next. If you are using Dual Boot, or you want to keep the data on the installable partition, select option 1 (Do not format the partition). Otherwise, select option 2 (Format the partition).

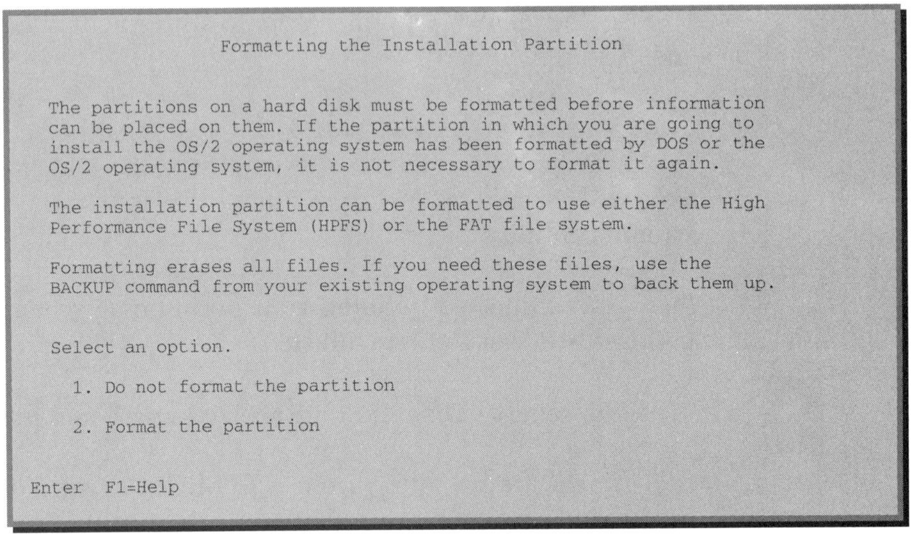

The OS/2 Warp Survival Guide

```
            Formatting the Installation Partition

The partitions on a hard disk must be formatted before information
can be placed on them. If the partition in which you are going to
install the OS/2 operating system has been formatted by DOS or the
OS/2 operating system, it is not necessary to format it again.

The installation partition can be formatted to use either the High
Performance File System (HPFS) or the FAT file system.

Formatting erases all files. If you need these files, use the
BACKUP command from your existing operating system to back them up.

Select an option.

   1. Do not format the partition

   2. Format the partition

Enter  F1=Help
```

Figure 1.8 *The FORMAT screen appears only if your installation partition is already formatted. Otherwise, OS/2 Warp asks you to select a file system to format the partition.*

When you select option 2, you will be asked if you want the partition formatted for the HPFS or FAT file system. Select the type of file system you want to use in the OS/2 Warp partition and press **Enter**. Unless your computer has only 4 MB of RAM, you will probably get better performance from HPFS on your OS/2 Warp partition.

When OS/2 Warp formats a partition, it uses a "fast format" method. This method can format any size partition in just a few seconds, but it does not test your entire partition for defects. Defect testing is usually unnecessary, but if you would like to test your partition for defects during formatting, use the command: FORMAT (drive): /L from the OS/2 command prompt.

After the partition is formatted, you'll see a message telling you that files are being transferred from Diskette 2. The installation program displays a meter to keep you informed of its progress. When the files are transferred, the system prompts you to insert the next diskette.

Installing OS/2 Warp

6 **Follow the instructions on the screen, changing diskettes when prompted.**

The installation program will prompt you for diskettes in succession; but long before you exhaust the supply of OS/2 Warp diskettes, you'll be prompted to re-insert the Installation Diskette, followed by Diskette 1. These diskettes must be re-inserted because the installation partition was selected after Diskette 2 was inserted. When the files from Diskette 1 have been copied, the system tells you to remove the diskette and press **Enter** to continue with the installation.

7 **Remove Diskette 1 and press Enter.**

At this point, enough of the OS/2 Warp files have been copied to your hard disk to start the computer on its own. When you press enter, the computer will reboot. This step is a common place for configuration problems to surface. If OS/2 Warp fails to start, consult Chapter 12, "When Things Go Wrong," for some suggestions. If all goes well, the OS/2 Warp Logo screen briefly appears, followed by the System Configuration screen, which begins the configuration phase of the OS/2 Warp installation.

The OS/2 Warp Survival Guide

OS/2 Warp System Configuration

The next phase of the installation is to configure OS/2 Warp so it knows what hardware is installed in your computer and how you want to use it. At this point, OS/2 Warp has "looked" at the devices in your computer and has made some configuration decisions for you. The System Configuration screen (shown in Figure 2.9) allows you to see how OS/2 Warp is currently configured and allows you to change things, if necessary.

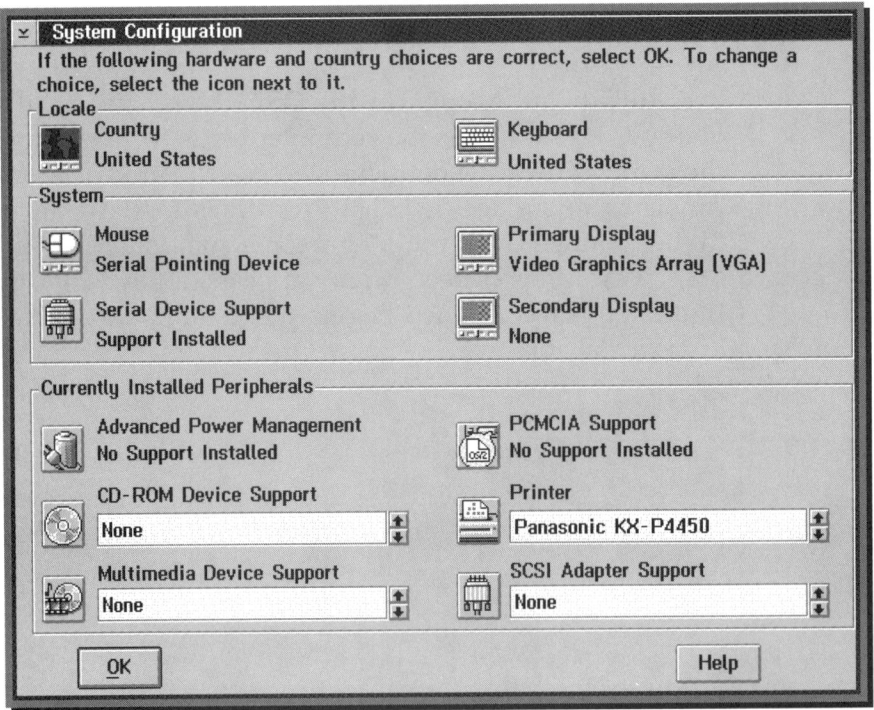

Figure 2.9 *The System Configuration screen shows you the devices OS/2 Warp thinks are installed in or attached to your computer.*

The installation program brings you to this screen automatically to give you the opportunity to verify the system's configuration before continuing with the installation. You can return to the System Configu-

Installing OS/2 Warp

ration screen any time after the installation to add new devices or modify certain device settings. You can refer to this section whenever you are using the System Configuration screen.

8. Make your configuration changes as appropriate.

To change an option's configuration, use the mouse to point to the icon next to the option and press (or click) the left mouse button. For each configuration option you select, a different screen will appear allowing you to make your desired changes. The following figures show the screens that appear when you click on the corresponding configuration icons. You can change the following configuration options, if they're applicable, for your computer system:

- Country
- Keyboard
- Mouse (Pointing Device)
- Serial Device Support
- Primary Display
- Secondary Display
- Advanced Power Management (APM) Support
- PCMCIA Support
- CD-ROM Device Support
- Multimedia Device Support
- Printer Support
- SCSI Adapter Support

In a Hurry? If you have no configuration changes to make or want to accept the default configuration for now, click on the *OK* button and skip to step 9 on page 64 to continue the installation. You can always return to the System Configuration screen at a later time to make any necessary changes.

The OS/2 Warp Survival Guide

Country

If you don't want to use the default country's character set (usually the United States) select the one you want in the list provided on the Country Information screen (as shown in Figure 2.10).

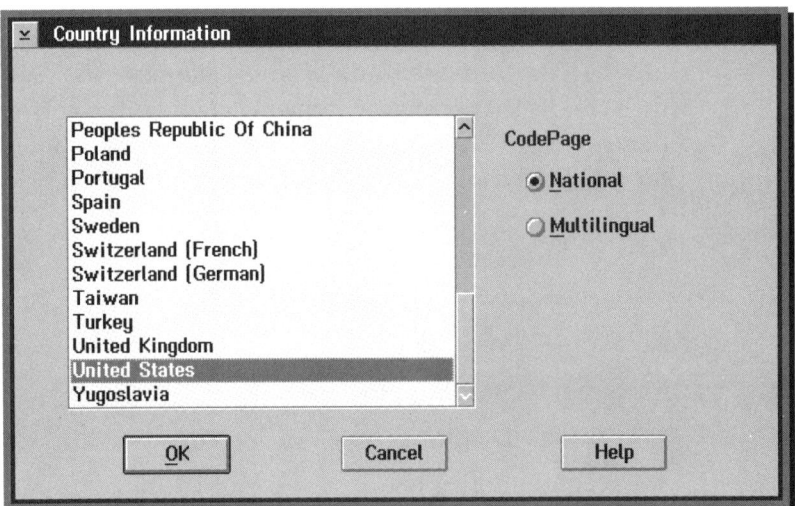

Figure 2.10 *The Country screen lets you select the character set used in a country's alphabet. These options affect the characters displayed on the screen.*

If the desired country is not visible, click on the up arrow to the right of the list to see more options. To view the multilingual countries, click on the *Multilingual* button. When you have selected the country you want, click on the *OK* button to continue.

2 *Installing OS/2 Warp*

This is the first screen you'll see that presents a *list box* (the area on the screen that contains a list of options from which you can select). Any time you're presented with a list box, you can click on the up and down arrow buttons, use the **Page Up** and **Page Down** keys, or use the up and down arrow keys to scroll through the options in the list. You also can type the first letter of the desired option to jump directly to options beginning with that letter. Options in list boxes are always alphabetically sorted and the currently selected option is highlighted.

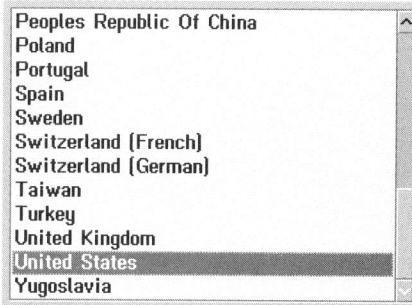

This also is the first screen that presents *radio buttons* (the little round buttons next to discrete options). Radio buttons are used for mutually exclusive options—when only one of the options can be active at a time. To select a radio button, either click directly on the button (or on the text next to the button), or press the key shown as the underlined letter in the button's text. A selected option's radio button will have a black circle on it.

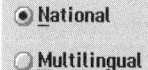

Keyboard

If you changed the Country setting, you'll probably want to change the keyboard layout to match. Select the desired keyboard layout in the list box on the Keyboard screen (as shown in Figure 2.11).

The OS/2 Warp Survival Guide

Figure 2.11   *The Keyboard screen lets you select the character set used in a language's alphabet. These options affect the characters generated by your keyboard.*

If the keyboard layout you want is not visible, click on the up arrow to the right of the list to see more options. When you have selected the keyboard layout you want, click on the *OK* button to continue.

Mouse (Pointing Device)

If you know that the wrong type of mouse is selected, click on the appropriate mouse device radio button (as shown in Figure 2.12). It's very rare that anyone needs to use this screen.

Installing OS/2 Warp

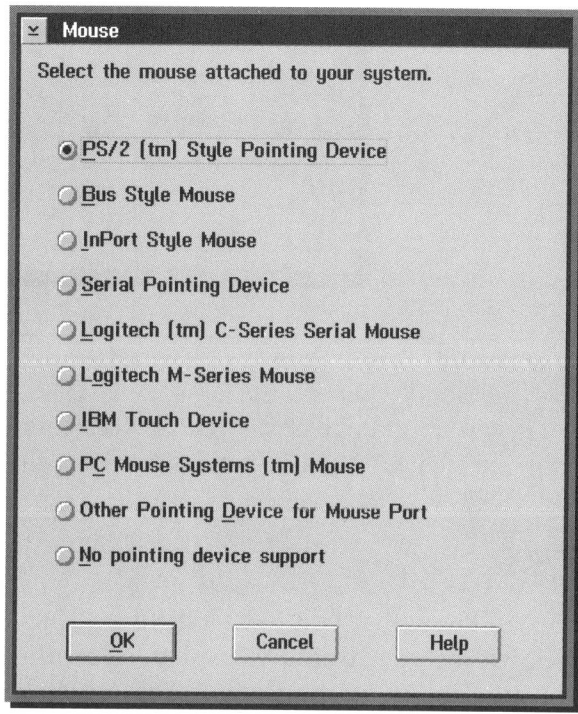

Figure 2.12   *The Mouse screen lets you select a different mouse device.*

If your mouse is not working, use the arrow keys to highlight your selection and press the space bar, or press the key indicated by the underlined letter in the radio button's text. Then press **Enter** to save your change. If your mouse is working, you probably don't need to change anything on this screen. Click on the *OK* button to continue.

Serial Device Support

If your computer has a serial device (such as a modem), make sure the *Install Support* radio button is highlighted on the Serial Support screen (as shown in Figure 2.13).

The OS/2 Warp Survival Guide

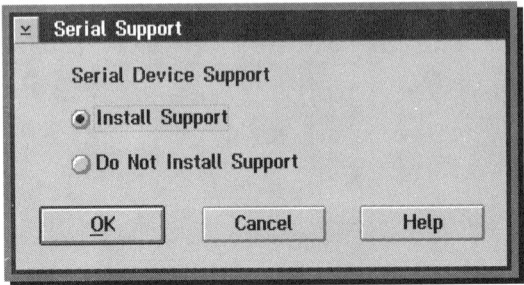

Figure 2.13   *The Serial Support screen lets you enable or disable support for serial devices.*

If you don't have any serial devices connected to your computer, disable this feature to save some memory.

Primary Display

If you know that you have a different display adapter than that shown for your primary display, select the appropriate adapter in the list box on the Display Drive Install screen (as shown in Figure 2.14).

Installing OS/2 Warp

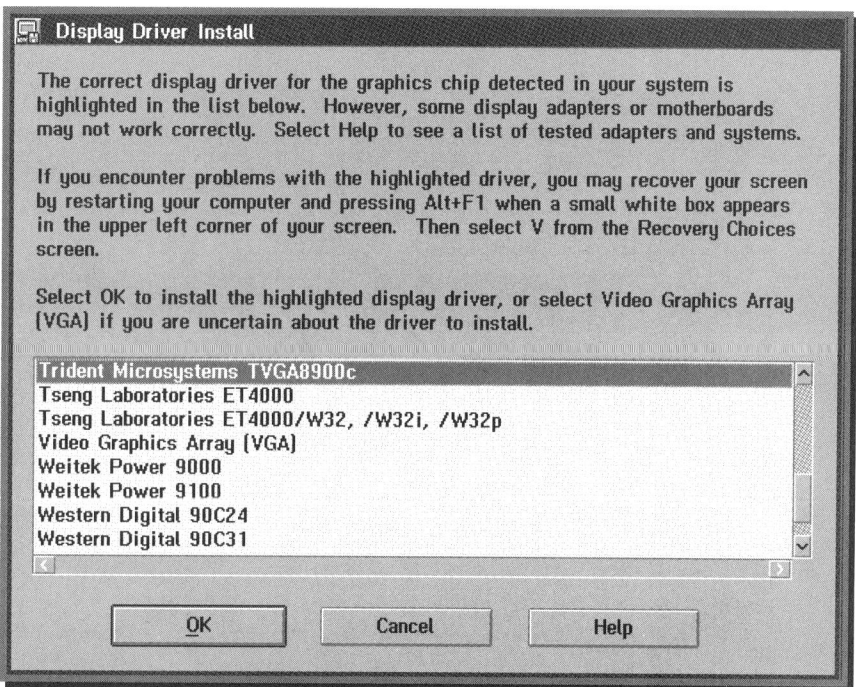

Figure 2.14 *The Display Driver Install screen lets you select a different device driver for your computer's display (monitor).*

Select the appropriate display driver in the list box, and click on the *OK* button to continue. To see a comprehensive listing of display adapters supported by these device drivers, click the *Help* button and select the "Supported Display Adapters and Systems" hypertext entry.

If you have a display adapter with its own device driver for OS/2, you can add the device driver after installing OS/2 Warp. If the device driver comes with a description (.DSC) file, placing this file in the \OS2\INSTALL directory allows the OS/2 Warp Selective Install utility to identify it and make it available on the list.

The OS/2 Warp Survival Guide

Secondary Display

If you have a second display attached to your computer, select the appropriate type of display adapter on the Display Driver Install screen (as shown in Figure 2.15). Then click on the *OK* button to continue.

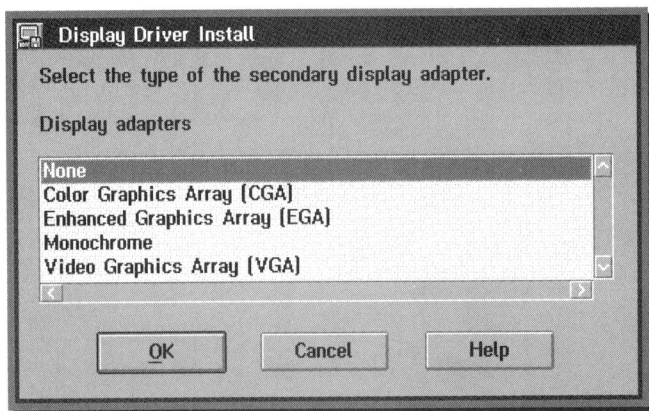

Figure 2.15   *Your selections are limited for the secondary displays.*

The devices available for a secondary display are limited to those adapters that can co-exist with the primary display. The secondary adapter is used for full-screen text displays only.

Advanced Power Management (APM) Support

If your computer has the APM feature, make sure the Install Support option is selected on the Advanced Power Management Support screen (as shown in Figure 2.16).

Installing OS/2 Warp

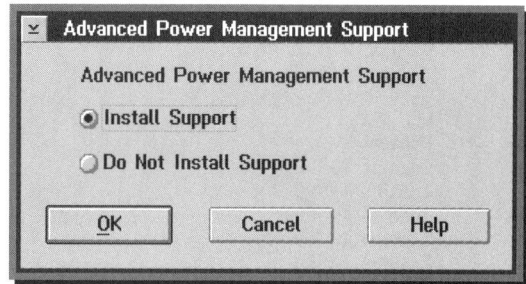

Figure 2.16 *The Advanced Power Management feature is usually available in battery-powered computers (such as notebooks and laptops).*

The APM support allows OS/2 Warp to reduce power to unused components (such as hard drives and displays) and monitor battery status.

PCMCIA Support

If your system provides a PCMCIA interface, select your computer make and model from the list box on the PCMCIA Support screen (as shown in Figure 2.17).

The OS/2 Warp Survival Guide

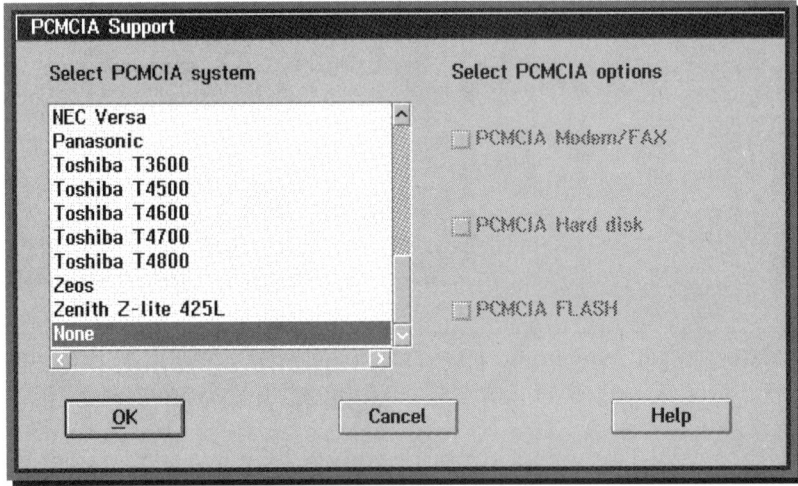

Figure 2.17   *OS/2 Warp recognizes many systems that support the PCMCIA interface.*

Installing PCMCIA support will allow you to use OS/2 Warp's *Plug and Play for PCMCIA* option to automatically configure PCMCIA devices when they're installed in your computer. Make sure the appropriate PCMCIA option check boxes (Modem/FAX, Hard Disk, and/or FLASH cards) are selected.

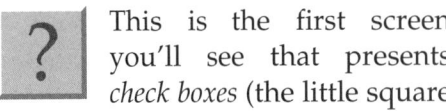 This is the first screen you'll see that presents *check boxes* (the little square 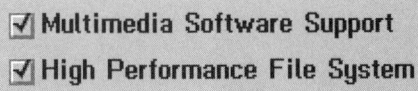 buttons next to options that you can toggle on or off). Unlike radio buttons, which are mutually exclusive when grouped together in a dialog box, you can select (turn on) as many check box options as desired within a dialog box. Selected check boxes contain a check mark. When you click on a selected check box, the check mark is cleared and the option turned off.

CD-ROM Device Support

If you have a CD-ROM drive installed, and OS/2 Warp has selected the wrong device type, select the correct make and model

Installing OS/2 Warp

from the list provided on the Select CD-ROM Device(s) screen (as shown in Figure 2.18). Click on *OK* to continue.

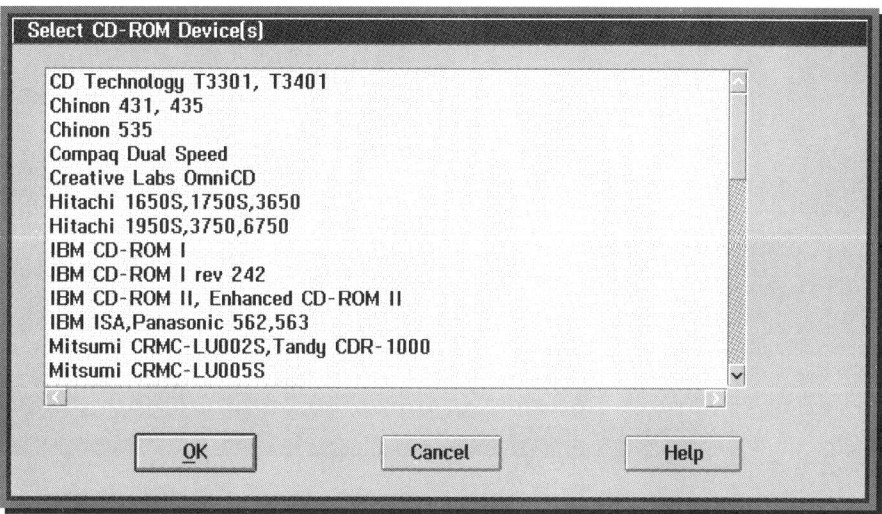

Figure 2.18 *The CD-ROM Device(s) screen lets you install CD-ROM device drivers.*

If your CD-ROM drive is not in the list, contact the manufacturer of your CD-ROM drive and ask if they have an OS/2 device driver. You could also check with IBM Support; they might be able to help you acquire an OS/2 device driver. Device drivers are usually provided without cost.

Printer Support

If you have a printer attached to your computer, now is the time to tell OS/2 Warp what kind it is. Find and select the correct printer in the list provided on the Select System Default Printer screen (as shown in Figure 2.19).

The OS/2 Warp Survival Guide

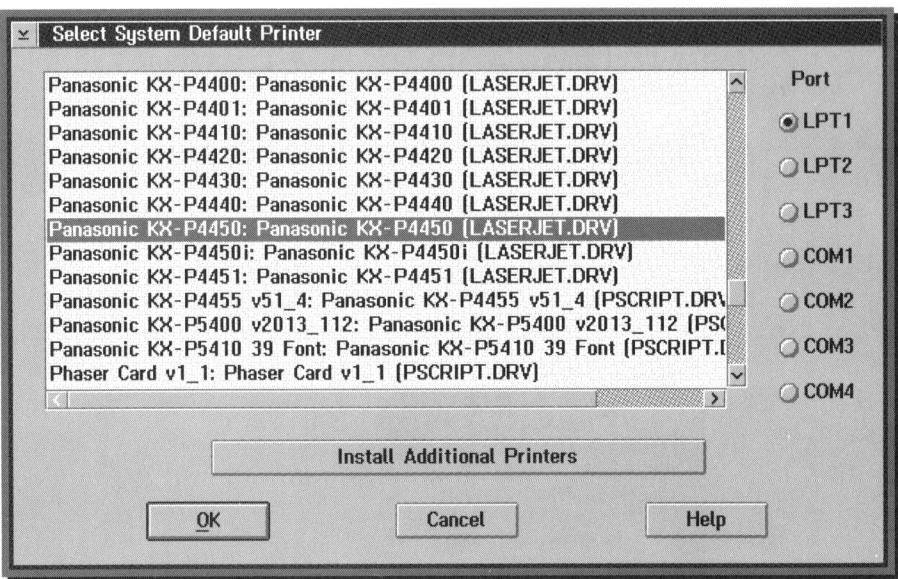

Figure 2.19 *Use the Select System Default Printer screen to install the device driver for your primary printer and tell OS/2 Warp which communications port it's connected to.*

You can use the down arrow to scroll through the list, or you can type the first letter of the manufacturer's name to jump to that section of the list. If you don't see your printer, find out what types of printers it emulates (look in the manual that came with the printer under "Printer Emulation") and select that printer from the list.

Select the communications port to which the printer is connected by clicking on the appropriate button along the right side of the list. OS/2 Warp supports printers connected to one of three parallel ports (LPT1 through LPT3) or one of four serial ports (COM1 through COM4). Click on *OK* to continue.

Multimedia Device Support

If you have a Multimedia device (sound or video capture adapter), select it from the list of supported multimedia devices on the left side of the Multimedia Device Support screen (as shown in Figure 2.20), and click on the *Add >>* button.

Installing OS/2 Warp

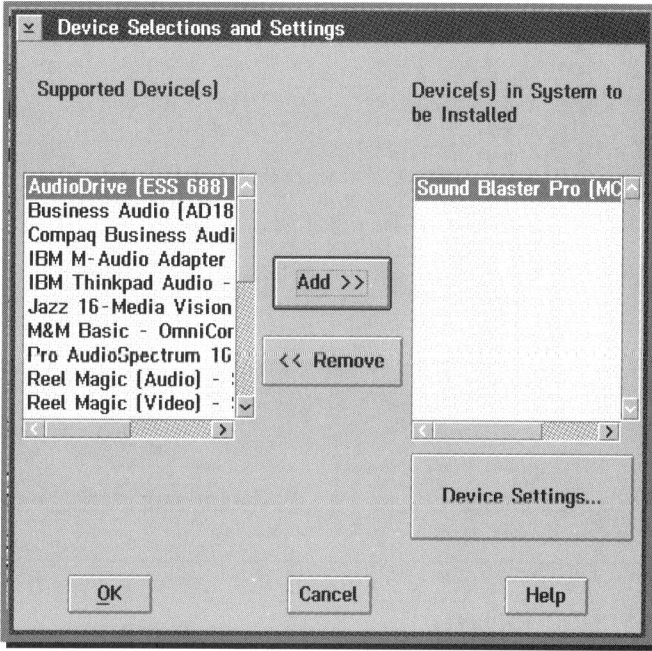

Figure 2.20 Use the Device Selection and Settings screen to install the device driver(s) for your multimedia device(s).

When you select a device from the list on the left and click on *Add*, the device is moved into the list on the right. Continue selecting and adding each device that you have installed in your computer (if you have multiple devices).

Some adapters have additional configuration options, which you can set by clicking on the *Device Settings...* button. When all the appropriate devices are added, click on the *OK* button.

SCSI Adapter Support

If you have a SCSI adapter installed, and OS/2 Warp has incorrectly identified it, select the correct make and model from the list provided on the Select SCSI Adapter(s) screen (as shown in Figure 2.21). Click on *OK* to continue.

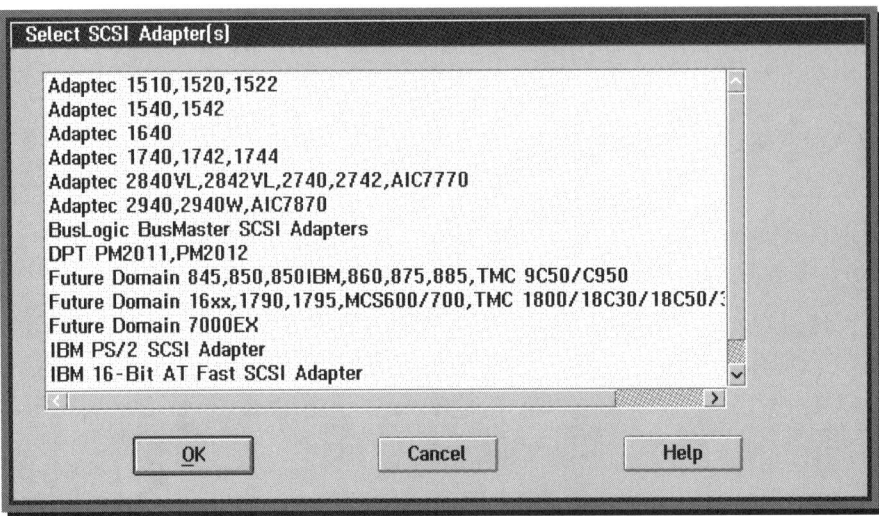

Figure 2.21   Use the Select SCSI Adapter(s) screen to install the device driver(s) for your SCSI adapter(s).

After changing the configuration options as required, you'll need to click on the *OK* button on the System Configuration screen to continue with the installation.

Because an incorrect display driver selection can cause a big problem, OS/2 Warp will present you with the Display Driver Install screen for primary video. This is your last chance to make sure your video selection is correct.

If you didn't select a printer on the System Configuration screen, OS/2 will present you with the "Select System Default Printer" screen, allowing you to specify your printer now. If you don't have a printer, select the "Do not install default printer" option in the list box.

The OS/2 Setup and Installation screen will then appear, marking the beginning of the Selective Feature Installation phase of the OS/2 Warp installation.

2

Installing OS/2 Warp

Selective Installation

After completing the System Configuration phase, the installation program allows you to dictate which features of OS/2 Warp you want to install using the OS/2 Setup and Installation screen (shown in Figure 2.22).

If your system has a relatively small hard disk drive, you might want to exclude certain features from the OS/2 Warp installation. Certain features are simply included or excluded, and some may not apply to your computer. However, OS/2 allows you to specify exactly which items you want to include or exclude within "feature groups." The feature groups you can "tweak" are:

- Documentation
- Fonts
- Optional System Utilities
- Tools and Games
- OS/2 DOS Support
- WIN-OS/2 Support
- Multimedia Software Support

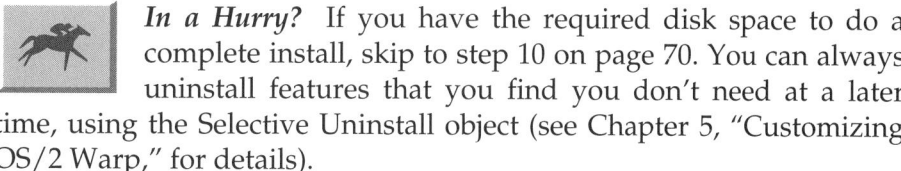

In a Hurry? If you have the required disk space to do a complete install, skip to step 10 on page 70. You can always uninstall features that you find you don't need at a later time, using the Selective Uninstall object (see Chapter 5, "Customizing OS/2 Warp," for details).

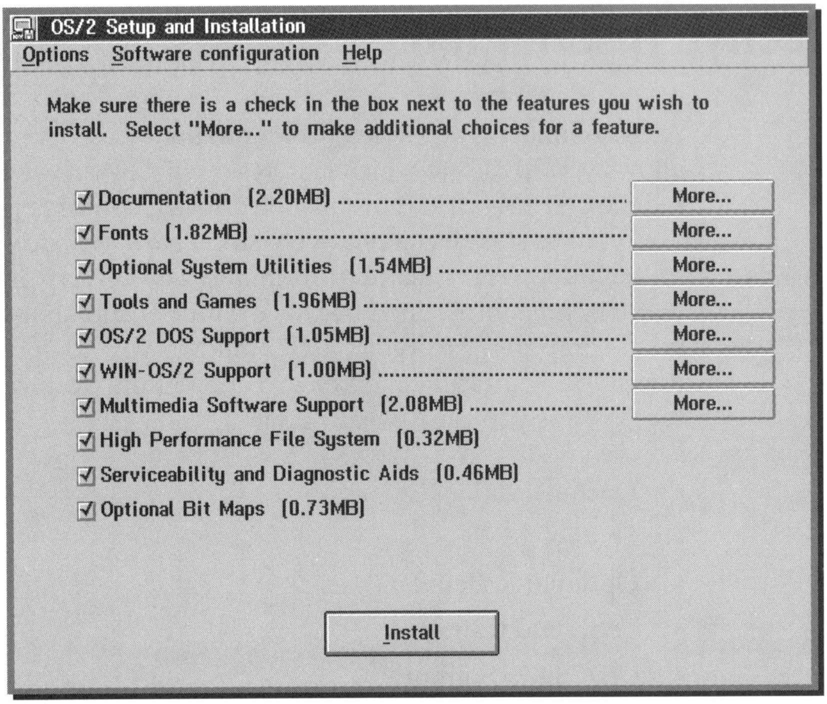

The OS/2 Warp Survival Guide

Figure 2.22   *The OS/2 Setup and Installation screen lets you tailor the installation to fit your needs and available disk space.*

The installation program brings you to this screen automatically, but you can return to it at any time to install (or uninstall) any of the features.

9 **Select the features you want to install from the OS/2 Setup and Installation screen.**

Make sure that only the features you want to install are selected on the OS/2 Setup and Installation screen. You can install any of these features at a later time, so don't think you have to install everything now. Notice the *More...* buttons beside the first several features. If you click on one of these buttons, a second screen appears allowing you to exclude specific parts of the feature. For example, you might want the documentation, but you might not want the OS/2 Tutorial. In that case,

Installing OS/2 Warp

click on the *More...* button next to *Documentation* and de-select the *OS/2 Tutorial*.

From this point on, during installation, you can display an OS/2 command prompt by pressing **F3** on any screen. Why would you need a command prompt during installation? If you find that you don't have enough disk space, you can use the command prompt to move files to make more room on the installation partition.

The OS/2 Setup and Installation screen also provides two useful pull-down menus that you might want to use before you continue with the installation. These pull-down menus are called the *Options* menu and the *Software Configuration* menu. The tasks you can perform using these menu options are discussed on the following pages.

Options Menu

If you have partitions (other than the installable partition) that need to be formatted, you can use the *Options* menu on the OS/2 Setup and Installation screen. This menu contains the *Install*, *Format*, and *Command Prompt* options. The *Install* 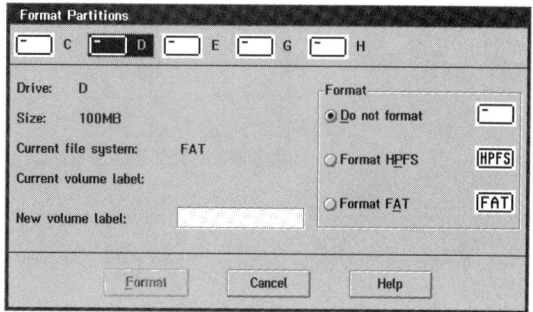 option is the same as clicking on the *Install* button on the OS/2 Setup and Installation screen. The *Format* option displays the screen shown here, allowing you to format partitions on any valid hard disk drive. The *Command Prompt* option starts a new OS/2 session in a window, providing you with a command prompt where you can enter OS/2 commands.

The OS/2 Warp Survival Guide

Software Configuration Menu

This pull-down menu lets you change OS/2 and DOS session parameters. The screen shown in Figure 2.23 is displayed when you select *OS/2 Configuration* from the OS/2 Setup and Installation screen.

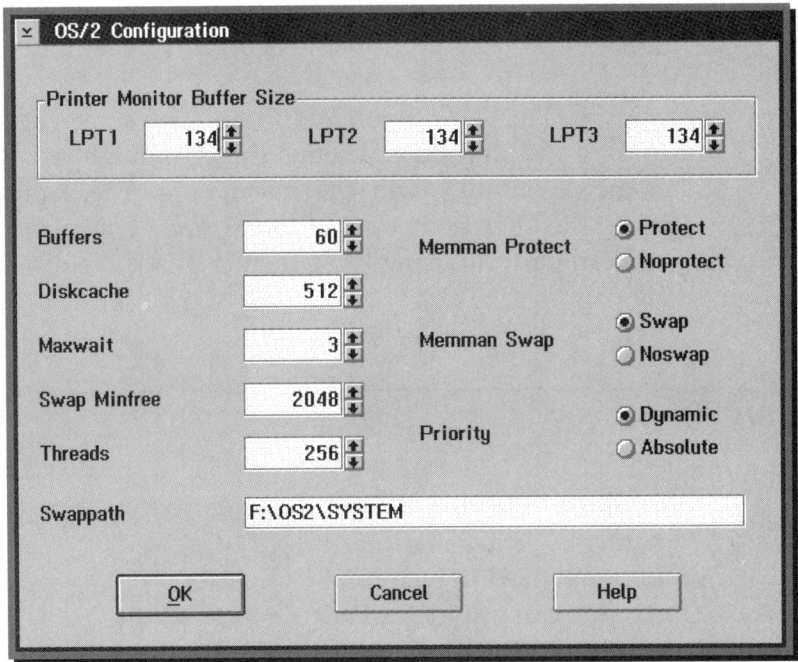

Figure 2.23   *The OS/2 Configuration screen sets parameters in CONFIG.SYS that deal with OS/2-specific options.*

All of these options are specified in the OS/2 CONFIG.SYS file. You can manipulate these settings now, or you can manually edit the CONFIG.SYS file later to set these options. The meaning of the configuration options on this screen are:

- *Print Monitor Buffer Size:* If you use a printer character monitor (a program that manipulates data sent to the printer port), this option

Installing OS/2 Warp

sets the size of the buffer for each port. For most systems, this option can be ignored.

- *Buffers:* When OS/2 Warp is asked to read/write disk data less than 512 bytes in size, these buffers are used. Increasing this amount can improve performance if your system performs many simultaneous disk operations. Each buffer consumes 512 bytes of RAM.

- *Diskcache:* This option stores recently-used disk data in RAM, so that it can be retrieved much faster. This cache is for FAT-formatted partitions only (HPFS and CD-ROMs have their own cache). The size specified is in KBytes (cache is required, the minimum is 64K).

- *Maxwait:* This parameter controls how OS/2 Warp allocates CPU time. Normally, OS/2 Warp gives CPU time to programs in order of priority. If higher-priority programs use all the CPU time, some low-priority programs may stall. The Maxwait setting will give stalled programs a priority boost after the specified number of seconds. Setting this value to a low number will make sure all programs get CPU time, but will hurt overall performance.

- *Swap Minfree:* The OS/2 Swap file grows as your applications allocate more RAM. This value sets the point at which a disk-space warning will appear. When the amount of free space on the swap drive drops below the amount specified (in KBytes), OS/2 Warp will warn you that the swap drive is nearly full. If you do not close applications or delete files to free more space, OS/2 Warp will halt (die) when the swap drive is completely full.

- *Threads:* A thread is an executable unit. Each program that executes in your computer has at least one thread (multithreaded OS/2 programs can have several). OS/2 Warp itself creates several dozen threads to process your requests. Decreasing this number can save some RAM (the minimum number is 128), but if you receive an error that says OS/2 Warp can't start a program because it is out of resources, you should increase this setting. The maximum number of threads is 4095.

- *Swappath:* This option sets the drive and path for the OS/2 *swap file*. If your programs need more RAM than your computer has available, the swap file uses disk space to satisfy the request. The swap file should be placed on the drive with the most free space, and if you have more than one physical drive, place the swap file on the fastest drive. You can move the swap file by editing CONFIG.SYS, but you must reboot the system for the change to take effect.

- *Memman Protect:* This option allows Dynamic-Link Libraries (DLLs) to allocate data in a protected region, so it cannot be accessed by another 32-bit program. There should be no reason to disable this setting.

- *Memman Swap:* This option activates the allocation of a disk swap file. If you set this option to *swap*, the swap file is available. If you set it to *noswap*, programs can only allocate as much memory as is physically available. Setting noswap can improve performance on systems where a known set of applications are run. Normally, swap should be enabled.

- *Priority:* This option controls OS/2 Warp's ability to modify process priority. When set to *Dynamic*, OS/2 Warp will modify the execution priority of programs, in order to improve overall performance. When set to *Absolute*, OS/2 Warp will not change priorities, and will allocate CPU time based on the priority set by each program. This setting should normally be set to Dynamic.

If you select the *DOS Configuration* option from the Software Configuration pull-down menu, the screen shown in Figure 2.24 appears.

Installing OS/2 Warp

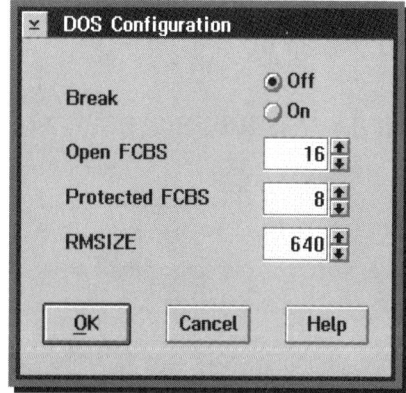

Figure 2.24 *Use the DOS Configuration screen to set CONFIG.SYS parameters specific to DOS.*

You can change the following settings on the DOS Configuration screen:

- *Break:* Enabling this option increases the number of times OS/2 checks for a **Ctrl+Break** key press while in DOS sessions. Disabling this option will increase the performance of DOS programs.

- *Open FCBs:* An FCB is a File Control Block, an obsolete method of performing disk I/O by DOS programs. If you use old DOS programs, they may require FCBs, and increasing this number may be required to make them run. Decreasing this number will increase the amount of RAM available to DOS programs.

- *Protected FCBs:* If DOS programs use all available FCBs, they are recycled. This option "protects" the first FCBs allocated, so they won't be recycled. This may increase performance for DOS programs that use many FCBs.

- *RMSIZE:* This is the default size of the conventional memory for DOS programs. Most DOS programs don't need the maximum (640 KBytes), and you can save RAM by decreasing this amount. You can

The OS/2 Warp Survival Guide

set the RMSIZE on each DOS program individually, but this option sets the default.

10 **Click on the Install button in the Setup and Installation screen.**

After selecting the features you want to install, click on the *Install* button to proceed with the installation. You'll see the Advanced Options screen (as shown in Figure 2.25).

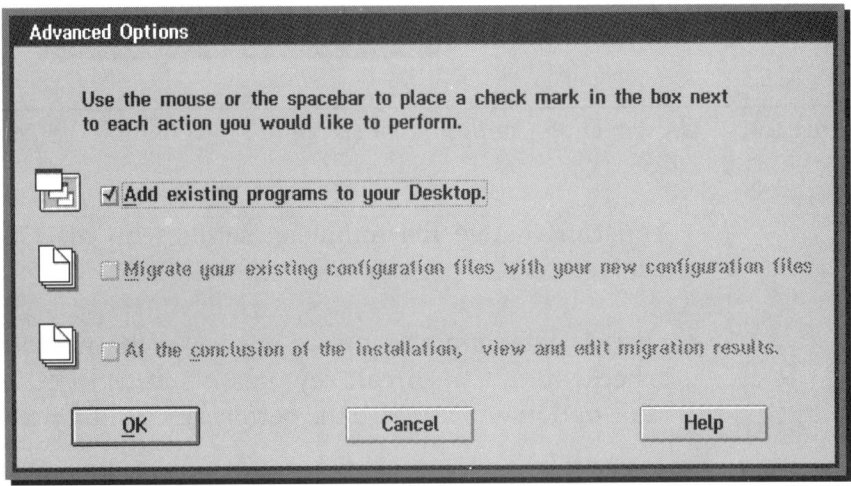

Figure 2.25   *The Advanced Options screen lets you easily make OS/2 aware of programs that exist on your system.*

The first option, *Add existing programs to your Desktop* instructs OS/2 Warp to search all your drives for DOS, Windows, and OS/2 programs. It will then create "Program Objects" for all programs it finds. This step can be done at any time, by using the *Add Programs* object (in the System Setup folder). The next options are only shown if OS/2 Warp finds an existing CONFIG.SYS file. When selected, these options instruct OS/2 Warp to read the existing CONFIG.SYS file, and add appropriate statements to the new CONFIG.SYS file it creates. You can also view/edit the results of this process by selecting the third option on this screen.

Installing OS/2 Warp

When you have selected the appropriate options, select **OK** to continue the installation.

11 Follow the instructions on the screen, inserting diskettes as required.

A screen appears to inform you that files are being transferred. This screen shows you which diskette is being copied, and a progress meter shows you what percentage of the diskette has been copied. If you are installing from CD-ROM, no diskette numbers are displayed.

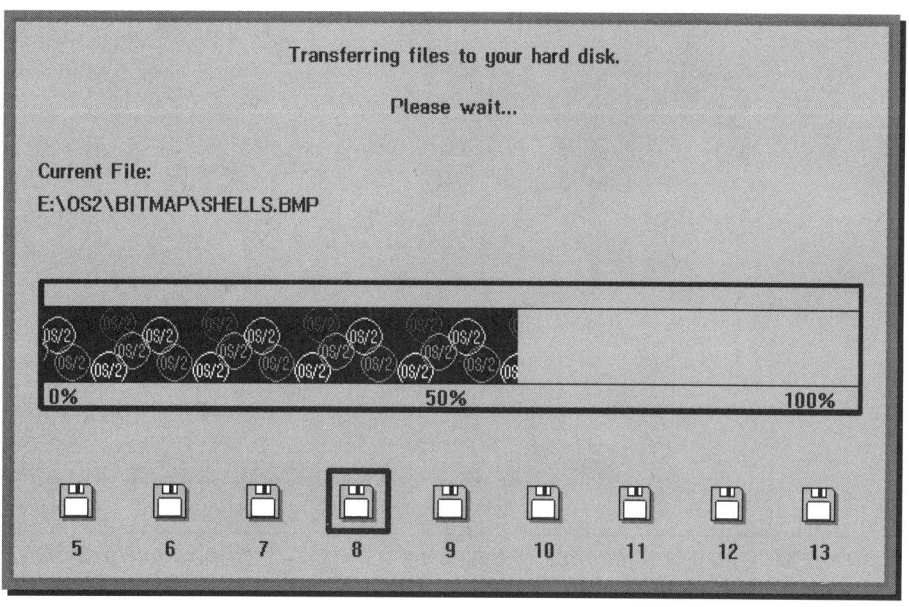

Figure 2.26   *You can watch the progress of the OS/2 Warp installation as it copies files to your hard disk.*

Perform this step for the remaining diskettes. Don't be alarmed if the installation program doesn't ask for all the diskettes. Depending on the features you selected, some diskettes may not be required.

The OS/2 Warp Survival Guide

If you've nothing better to do during the file transfer, you can minimize the window and access folders on the OS/2 Warp desktop. This might be a good time to look at the README file and/or the Master Help Index in the Information folder. The README file contains some last-minute information that's not in the manual, as well as some tips for configuring certain application programs. If you do minimize the File Transfer window, it'll be a challenge to find your way back. (*Hint:* Look for the Minimized Window Viewer.)

During the File Transfer, you might see the following screen:

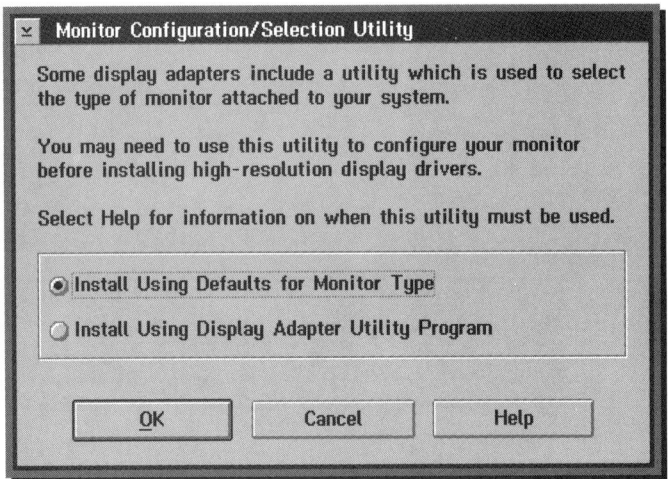

Figure 2.27   *If your monitor comes with a special configuration program for the operating system, use this screen to "teach" OS/2 its capabilities.*

At this point, OS/2 Warp is going to attempt to determine the capabilities of your primary video adapter. For most users, you can select OK using the default, but if your monitor came with configuration utilities for high-resolution use, you may need to select "Install Using Display Adapter Utility Program." When you select OK, the screen will go blank for a few seconds as OS/2 Warp determines the video capabilities.

Installing OS/2 Warp

If Windows 3.x was on your computer before you began the OS/2 Warp installation, you will be asked to insert several of your existing Windows diskettes. This is so OS/2 Warp can copy the proper Windows font files to match your OS/2 Warp display resolution, and will only happen if you purchased Warp without WIN-OS/2 support.

Depending on your configuration, other warnings or prompts may appear during installation. When you have completed all installation steps, you will see the following message:

Figure 2.28   *OS/2 Warp installation is complete when you see this screen.*

Congratulations! Your installation is complete. When you select OK, the system will shut down automatically. If you select Cancel, you will see a blank "Maintenance Desktop." This is a simple OS/2 Warp Desktop that you can use during installation, but it doesn't have all the same objects as the complete OS/2 Warp desktop.

The OS/2 Warp Survival Guide

 If you want to make custom configuration changes to your system, you can use the maintenance desktop to do so before you reboot. If you want to configure the desktop itself, wait until after you shut down and reboot, as OS/2 Warp will start using the complete desktop after you reboot.

First Boot

After completing the installation, your computer must be restarted. If you've installed the Boot Manager, you should see a menu appear after your computer finishes its self-test. This menu contains a list of installed operating systems from which you can choose to start running. Select the OS/2 Warp partition, and watch the first boot. This will take longer than subsequent reboots, as OS/2 Warp does quite a bit of "clean-up" work during the first boot. Files that are only used during installation are deleted, and OS/2 Warp takes some time to "build" your first object-oriented desktop.

If OS/2 Warp Doesn't Seem to Start

If you don't see the Boot Manager menu, the OS/2 Warp Logo screen, or any apparent system activity (watch the hard disk drive access light) within five minutes of restarting your computer, you've got a problem. We suggest the following procedure:

1. Try performing a "cold start." Turn off your computer, wait a minute or two, and then turn it back on. Sometimes the hardware is not fully initialized by a "warm start" (where the system is restarted while the power is still on).

2. If the problem still exists, refer to Chapter 12, "When Things Go Wrong," and perform the steps listed under "The Magic Key-

Installing OS/2 Warp

strokes." If your system "hangs" while a driver is being loaded, the problem might be with the device associated with that driver.

3. If the problem persists, contact the IBM Technical Support Group at the phone number listed in the OS/2 Warp Customer Service and Support pamphlet that was included in the original package.

The OS/2 Tutorial

If you installed the OS/2 Tutorial, it will appear during the first boot. You can begin using the tutorial even while OS/2 Warp completes the clean-up process (one of the benefits of multitasking).

Figure 2.29   *If you take the time to run the OS/2 Tutorial, you might learn some interesting ways to use OS/2 Warp.*

The tutorial contains several exercises that will help you familiarize yourself with the Workplace Shell. You'll probably learn something from the tutorial, but you don't have to complete it now. It's available for use at any time.

The tutorial supports two undocumented parameters: -r (Return) and -m (Minimize). The Return parameter causes the tutorial to resume at the point in the tutorial where you left off the last time you ran it. The Minimize parameter allows you to minimize the tutorial without closing it. Refer to Exercise 2 on page 330 to see how to add parameters to a program object.

Chapter

3

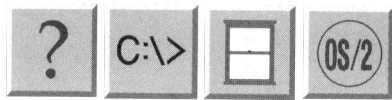

Warping in the Workplace Shell

Each time you start OS/2 Warp, you'll see a screen similar to the one shown below in Figure 3.1. This is called the *Workplace Shell* (you may have heard it referred to as the *desktop*). As you'll see in this chapter, this is an easy way to work with OS/2 Warp. We think you'll find the Workplace Shell an efficient workplace.

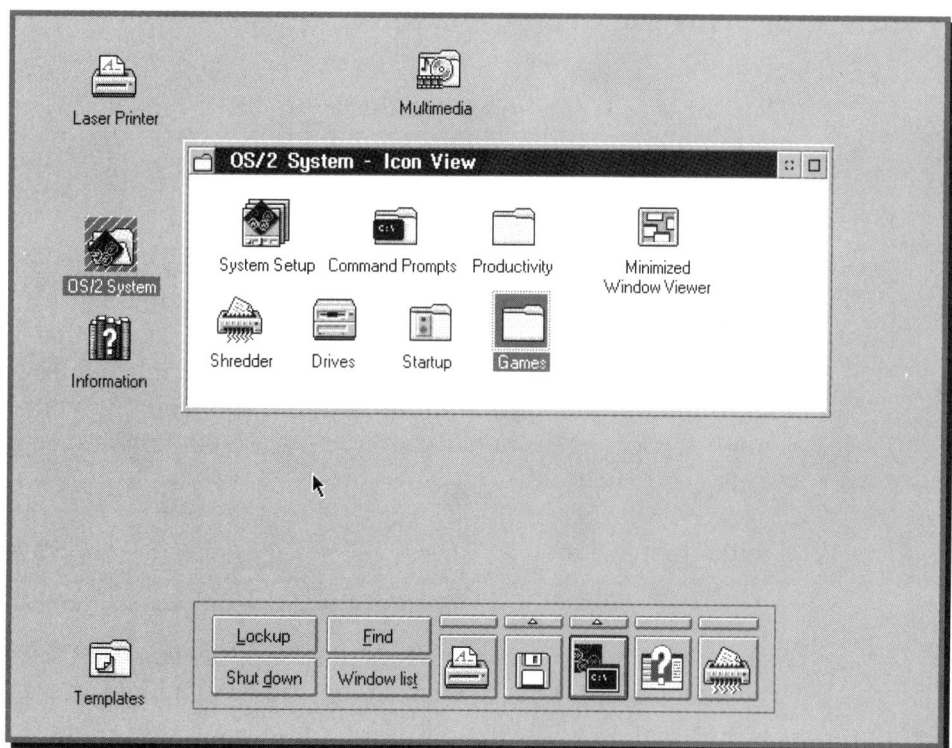

Figure 3.1.   *The first time you see the Workplace Shell, it looks something like this.*

77

Although you can use OS/2 Warp from a command prompt (much like the DOS command prompt) the easiest way to use OS/2 is through the Workplace Shell. It's the graphical user interface (GUI) for OS/2 Warp, and it shields you from the complexities of the operating system. With the Workplace Shell, you use your computer by pointing to and manipulating graphical objects (or icons) with a mouse instead of typing cryptic commands. These icons represent objects in your computer like programs, data files, disk drives, and so forth.

This chapter describes the objects you'll see in the Workplace Shell and tells you how to use them. To help you get the most out of the Workplace Shell, we'll also give you some tips about customizing your OS/2 Warp working environment.

What's New with the Warp Workplace?

For those of you who are familiar with OS/2 version 2.x, here are some of the new features you should look for with OS/2 Warp.

LaunchPad

OS/2 Warp brings a welcome new object to the Workplace Shell: the LaunchPad. It's a special device object that can make your life much easier on the desktop. It provides virtual "drawers" and buttons for your desktop. As you might expect by its name, the LaunchPad lets you launch (or start) objects (and their associated programs) with a single mouse click. You can place program, data file, and device objects on the LaunchPad in drawers or as buttons for convenient access. Objects placed on the LaunchPad are automatically shadows of their parent objects.

3
Warping in the Workplace Shell

BonusPak

The BonusPak is full of bonuses. Here's a complete listing of what's on the BonusPak CD-ROM. We'll introduce you to these programs in Chapter 4, "The OS/2 Warp BonusPak."

- **Internet Access Kit (IAK)**—The IBM Information Superhighway is paved with Internet goodies such as:
  - *Gopher Client*
  - *TelnetPM*
  - *Ultimail*
  - *FTPPM*
  - *World Wide Web (WWW) Browser*
  - *NewsReader/2*
- **IBM Works**—These applications replace the personal productivity applets that were in OS/2 version 2.1.
  - *Word Processor*
  - *Spreadsheet*
  - *Chart*
  - *Database*
  - *Report Writer*
  - *Personal Information Manager (PIM)*—This suite of software includes the following integrated applications:
    ] Appointment Book
    ] Monthly Planner
    ] Calendar
    ] To-Do List
    ] Phone Book
    ] Contact List
    ] Notepad
- **FaxWorks for OS/2**—For sending, receiving, and managing faxes
- **HyperACCESS Lite**—A 32-bit modem communications program
- **Person to Person**—Amazingly interactive network communications
- **Multimedia Extensions**
  - *Ultimedia Video IN for OS/2*
  - *Ultimedia Viewer*

Pickup Feature

To help you perform drag-and-drop operations on the desktop, OS/2 Warp provides a new "pickup" feature. It allows you to virtually pick up an object, "attaching" it to your mouse pointer. Your mouse is then free to open a destination folder where you'll have the option of dropping a copy of the object, moving the object, dropping a template of the object, or canceling the pickup. This is especially useful when your destination folder is obscured or inside another folder.

Default Folder Views

With previous versions of OS/2 you could only change your default folder view (Icon View, Tree View, or Details View) on a folder-by-folder basis. With OS/2 Warp, you can now change the default view for *all* folders, on a system-wide basis (see "System Setup Objects" in Chapter 5).

Other Desktop Enhancements

OS/2 Warp adds features that make the desktop more usable:

- Automatic folder close and "parent open" helps stop desktop clutter
- Transparent backgrounds so your text is always visible
- Archive your desktop so you can return to your favorite desktop
- Make your desktop read-only—no one can rearrange your desktop
- Animated icons let you know whether an object is closed or open
- The modifiable cursor and "Comet Cursor" features help you keep track of the pointer. Great for portable computers with LCDs.

Changes to the Context Menus

- *Settings* is now a primary option on each object's context menu
- An *Unarrange* (Undo Arrange) option has been added

3

Warping in the Workplace Shell

Warp Basics

The *desktop* is the foundation of the Workplace Shell. Just like a real desktop, it's where you place the objects you want to work with. The desktop itself is always in the background, filling the entire screen. All other objects are contained within the boundaries of the desktop. It can be any color you like, or it can be a graphic image.

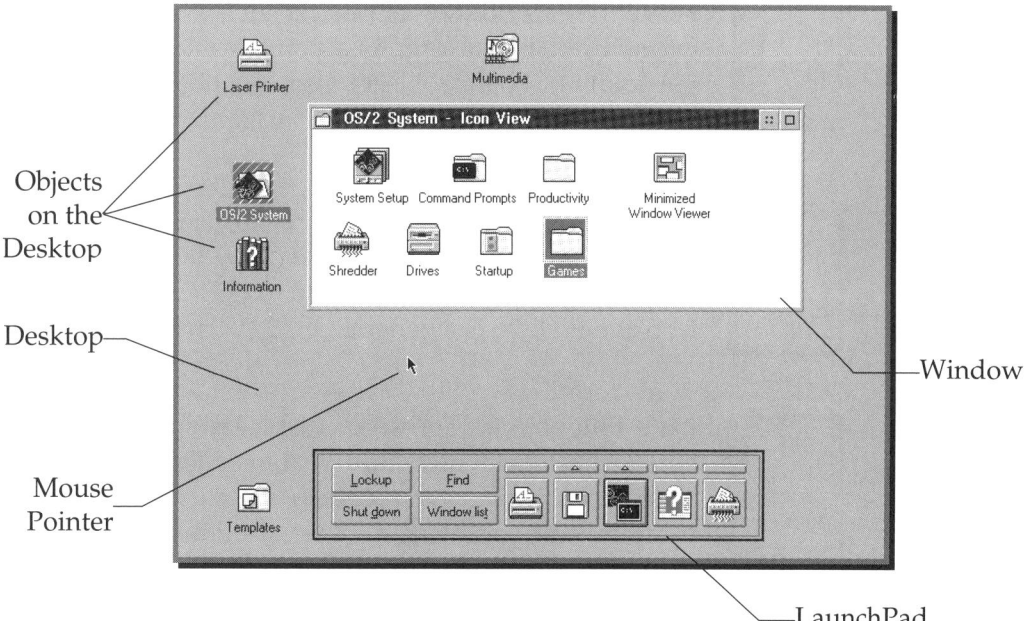

Figure 3.2.   *The Workplace Shell appears as a desktop with objects on it.*

The *objects* on the desktop are your working tools. You can accomplish all tasks on your computer using the mouse and keyboard to manipulate these objects. Working with your computer in this manner is called an *object-oriented* interface. For example, if you wanted to print a file, you would point at the file object and drag it to the printer object. This one simple action tells the operating system to open the file, read it, and send its contents to a printer that is attached to your computer. We'll discuss the object-oriented operations in more detail after we introduce you to the types of objects you'll see in the Workplace Shell.

Workplace Shell Objects

The Workplace Shell contains four basic types (classes) of objects: *folders*, *programs*, *data files*, and *devices*.

Folder objects hold other objects such as data files and programs to help you organize your desktop (much like real file folders). Folder objects also can hold other folder objects, allowing you to highly organize objects on your desktop.

Program objects represent the DOS, Windows, and OS/2 application programs installed in your computer. Each program can have a unique icon to help you identify it. The icon shown here is a generic OS/2 Warp program object.

Data File objects represent work files such as documents, spreadsheet data files, and graphic files. However, OS/2 Warp uses this icon to represent any file on your disk that it can't identify as being a folder, program, or device object.

Device objects represent physical devices such as printers, disk drives, and fax machines. Device objects also represent *virtual devices* such as the document shredder and the OS/2 Warp LaunchPad.

You'll encounter other kinds of objects, but they're generally variations of these basic object types. It's not always obvious what type of object a particular icon represents, especially considering that OS/2

3

Warping in the Workplace Shell

Warp lets you change any object's icon. If you're not sure what an object is, open it to find out. Don't be shy, this is one of the best ways to explore and learn the features of OS/2 Warp. To *open* an object, point to it with the mouse, then press and release the left mouse button twice in quick succession (double-click). When you open an object, the resulting action depends on the object type. In general, you can expect the following:

- When you open a folder object, a window appears showing you the objects it contains.
- When you open a program object, the program starts to run.
- When you open a data file object, different things happen depending on the type of file it is. If OS/2 recognizes the file as belonging to an application program, it will start the program and "tell" the program to open the data file. For example, if the data file is a file that contains text, OS/2 will open the file with the OS/2 System Editor, allowing you to edit (or change) the contents of the data file.
- When you open a device object, several things can happen depending on the type of device it is. For example, if you open a printer object, a window appears showing you the documents (if any) that it's printing.

 You should think of folder objects as subdirectories on your disk drive. Program objects represent the .EXE, .COM, and .BAT files. Data file objects represent all other files on your system.

You can think of folder objects as Windows Groups; however, OS/2 folders are not as restrictive. For example, in Windows you can't place Groups inside other Groups. And you can't place Groups on the desktop. These are both valid operations in the Workplace Shell.

There is another object type called a "shadow" object. A shadow is a virtual copy of the original object. All objects can have shadows. We'll discuss shadow objects more in a minute.

The OS/2 Warp Survival Guide

Getting Object-Oriented with the Mouse

Although you can use the keyboard alone with OS/2 Warp, it makes much more sense to use a pointing device (such as a mouse). To work with most objects on the desktop, you *point* at the object with the mouse and *click* (or press) a mouse button. As you move the mouse, the *pointer* (an arrow on the screen that looks like the one shown here) follows your movements to show you where you're pointing.

When you've positioned the pointer anywhere over an object, you can use the mouse buttons to perform several operations. You can click, double-click, drag, and chord. We'll discuss the meanings of these operations in a minute.

First, you need to know how to perform them. To *click*, point to an object, then press and release a mouse button. To *double-click*, press and release mouse button 1—two

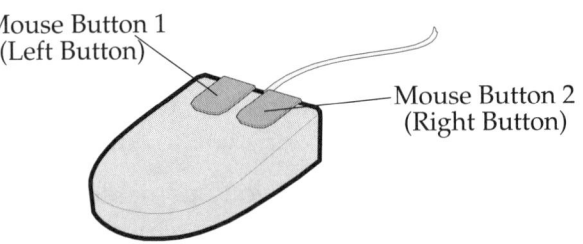

times in quick succession. To *drag*, press and hold down mouse button 2, then move the mouse until you've "dragged" the object to the position you want, and release the mouse button. To *chord*, press and release both mouse buttons in unison. The chord has only one function in OS/2: to open the Window List (see "The Window List" on page 101 to learn about the Window List); but some applications programs may support this operation.

IBM refers to the mouse buttons as button 1 and button 2. For simplicity, we'll call them the left and right mouse buttons, respectively. OS/2 Warp allows you to swap mouse buttons, or completely redefine the mouse actions to suit your needs. By default, if you click the left mouse button, you'll select the object. If you double-click the left mouse button, you'll open or launch the object. If you click on an object with the right mouse button, you'll open the object's context menu.

3

Warping in the Workplace Shell

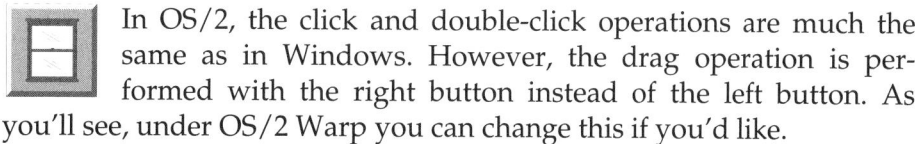
In OS/2, the click and double-click operations are much the same as in Windows. However, the drag operation is performed with the right button instead of the left button. As you'll see, under OS/2 Warp you can change this if you'd like.

The next several topics tell you how to perform certain object-oriented operations. The benefits of the object-oriented nature of OS/2 Warp will become apparent once you understand how to perform these operations. You can accomplish most tasks using the point, click, and drag-and-drop mouse techniques. You also can perform many of these object-oriented operations using the object context menus. See "Using the Pop-Up Controls" on page 99 for a discussion of the context menus.

Throughout this book, we provide mouse instructions based on the default mouse button assignments. OS/2 Warp allows you to change the functions of the mouse buttons through the mouse device settings (see Chapter 5, "Customizing OS/2 Warp"), which you might want to do if you're left-handed or if you're used to different mouse button assignments.

Selecting an Object

Before you can work with an object, you must select it. To select a single object, point to the object and click the left mouse button. To perform one operation (such as copy or move) on more than one object, select the objects using one of the following multiple-selection techniques:

- *Swipe-select:* Point to one of the objects, then hold down the left mouse button and drag the mouse to touch the other objects you want to select.

- *Marquee-select:* Place the mouse pointer just outside an object, then hold down the left mouse button and drag the mouse to draw a box around the objects you want to select. The box must completely enclose an object to select it.

The OS/2 Warp Survival Guide

- *Control-select:* Select one of the objects, then hold down the **Ctrl** key while selecting additional objects. You can also use the control-select technique to deselect individual objects.

When you select objects, they're highlighted to show that they're selected. This highlighting causes the object to appear somewhat like a negative image of itself, and is always quite noticeable.

Starting a Program Object

To start (or run) a program, point at the program icon and double-click with the left mouse button. OS/2 Warp is a multitasking operating system; so you can run more than one program at a time. Starting a program is also known as *launching* the program.

Opening a Folder Object

Point at the folder icon and double-click with the left mouse button. When you open a folder, a window appears showing you the objects it contains. Folders can contain any type of object, including other folders.

Moving an Object

To move an object, point to it with the mouse and drag it to its new position by holding down the right mouse button. When the object is in its new position, release the mouse button. If the destination for the move (i.e., a folder) is not visible on the desktop, you can use the *pickup* feature, which we'll discuss in a minute.

Unlike Windows, OS/2 Warp is a true object-oriented operating system. For example, in OS/2 you can move objects out of folders and onto the desktop. Be aware that if you do this, you're actually moving the file (or files) associated with the object into the subdirectory called `Desktop`. See Chapter 6, "Getting Warped: Exercises in Virtual Reality," for more insight into the object-oriented nature of OS/2 Warp.

3

Warping in the Workplace Shell

Copying an Object

To copy an object, point to it, hold down the **Ctrl** key, and drag it to a new location on the screen. The original object remains where it was. If the destination for the copy (i.e., a disk drive) is not visible on the desktop, you can use the *pickup* feature, which we'll discuss in a minute.

During the operation, the appearance of the object changes to indicate whether you're performing a move or a copy. During a move, the object is opaque. During a copy, the object is translucent.

Creating a "Shadow" of an Object

To create a shadow of an object, point to it, hold down the **Ctrl** and **Shift** keys, and drag it to a new location on the screen. When you create a shadow, the original object remains intact, and the shadow object appears in the target location. A shadow is a "virtual" object. It isn't real, but it acts just like the original object. As you drag to create a shadow, a line will connect the original object and the shadow. If the destination for the shadow (i.e., a folder) is not visible on the desktop, you can use the *pickup* feature, which we'll discuss next.

Picking Up an Object

With the release of OS/2 Warp (version 3) there's a new feature for drag-and-drop operations. It's called *pickup*, and it's most useful when your destination object (i.e., a folder or drive) for a copy, move, or shadow operation is not visible. With pickup, you can virtually pickup an object and keep it "attached" to your pointer while you perform other operations (such as opening a folder) with the mouse. The object will stay attached to your pointer until you're ready to drop it, allowing you to go find the destination object.

To perform a pickup, hold down the **Alt** key and right-button click on the object you want to drag. The pointer will change to an arrow with a briefcase attached, indicating that the object is attached to your pointer. You can now let go of the mouse button without dropping the object!

This frees up your mouse (and finger), letting you prepare the desktop for the drop.

When you are ready to drop the object, place your pointer over the destination object (the desktop, a folder, or another object) and click the right mouse button. The destination object's context menu will appear with a *Drop* option listed. Click on the *Drop* option's right arrow button (as shown here) and then select the type of drop you want from the cascade menu: *Copy*, *Move*, *Create shadow*, or *Cancel drag*.

Deleting an Object

To delete an object, point to it and drag it to the Shredder. You can use another technique as well: Select the object and press the **Del** key. This technique might not be as much fun as dragging the object to the shredder, but it does the job. Still another technique for deleting an object is to open its context menu (click on it with the right mouse button) and select the *Delete...* option on the menu.

Drag-and-Drop

This operation is what makes an object-oriented, graphical user interface so much fun to use. Many of the tasks you perform with your computer can be done with drag-and-drop. The copy and move tasks are one type of drag-and-drop operation; but the "drag-and-drop" concept really means more than that. For example, when you want to print a file, you can drag the file object to the printer object and release the mouse button to "drop" the file on top of the printer.

Obviously, it wouldn't make sense to drag-and-drop the printer onto the shredder (unless you really wanted to delete the printer object); but that's the kind of power you get in an object-oriented environment.

The task performed with a drag-and-drop depends on the object types involved, and whether the target object knows what to do with the object being dropped. Here are some examples:

- When you drop something on a device object, some physical action takes place (as in our printer example above). For example, if you drop a folder object on a diskette drive object, OS/2 copies all files contained in the folder to the diskette in the drive.

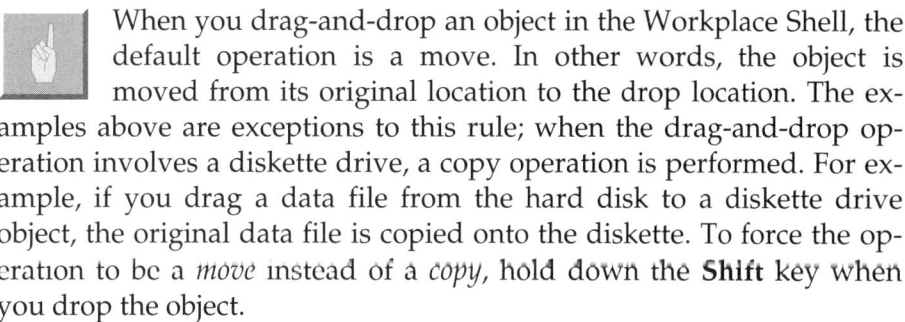

When you drag-and-drop an object in the Workplace Shell, the default operation is a move. In other words, the object is moved from its original location to the drop location. The examples above are exceptions to this rule; when the drag-and-drop operation involves a diskette drive, a copy operation is performed. For example, if you drag a data file from the hard disk to a diskette drive object, the original data file is copied onto the diskette. To force the operation to be a *move* instead of a *copy*, hold down the **Shift** key when you drop the object.

- When you drop a file object on a program object, OS/2 Warp assumes you want the program to start running and opens the file so you can work with it.
- When you drop a folder object on another folder object, all objects in the folder being dropped are moved into the target folder. Behind the scenes, the files associated with the objects are moved to the target folder's subdirectory.

Using an object-oriented operating environment is easy—far easier than entering cryptic commands at a DOS prompt. However, you should be aware of certain actions that take place "behind the scene" when you perform tasks in the Workplace Shell. See Chapter 6, "Getting Warped: Exercises in Virtual Reality," for more information about the inner workings of OS/2 Warp's object-oriented GUI.

With the release of OS/2 Warp (version 3) there's a new feature for drag-and-drop operations. It's called *pickup*, and you can find out how to use it under "Picking Up an Object" earlier in this chapter.

Exiting OS/2 Warp (Shutdown)

When you want to turn off your computer (or boot a different operating system) you must first exit OS/2 Warp. This is called a system *shutdown*.

There are a couple of ways to shut down OS/2 Warp. The default LaunchPad configuration contains a button labeled *Shut down* which, when pressed, starts the shutdown process. Or, if the LaunchPad is unavailable, you can shut down OS/2 by pointing to a clear area on the desktop and clicking the right mouse button. The desktop's context menu appears. Then click on the *Shut Down...* menu option. If you have any open windows (running programs) OS/2 will ask if you're sure you want to exit, reminding you to save any changes you might have made to your data files.

When you exit OS/2 Warp, you'll notice some activity with your hard disk drive. OS/2 is saving the changes you made to the desktop so it can "remember" how you had your objects arranged. The next time you run OS/2 Warp, your desktop will look just as it did when you left!

 If you turn your computer off without performing a system shutdown, the changes you made to your desktop will not be saved. OS/2 does other housekeeping tasks as well during the shutdown, which will not be performed. At the end of a shutdown, OS/2 displays a message telling you to press the **Ctrl+Alt+Del** key combination. When this message appears, it's safe to turn off your computer.

Basic Window Controls

Windows are rectangular areas on the screen through which you enter or retrieve information. When you start a program object or open a folder or device object, a new window opens on the desktop to let you interact with the object. As you open new windows, they appear to stack up on the desktop (as shown in Figure 3.3). Since you can run multiple programs and open multiple folders, you can quickly find yourself with lots of open windows on your desktop.

3

Warping in the Workplace Shell

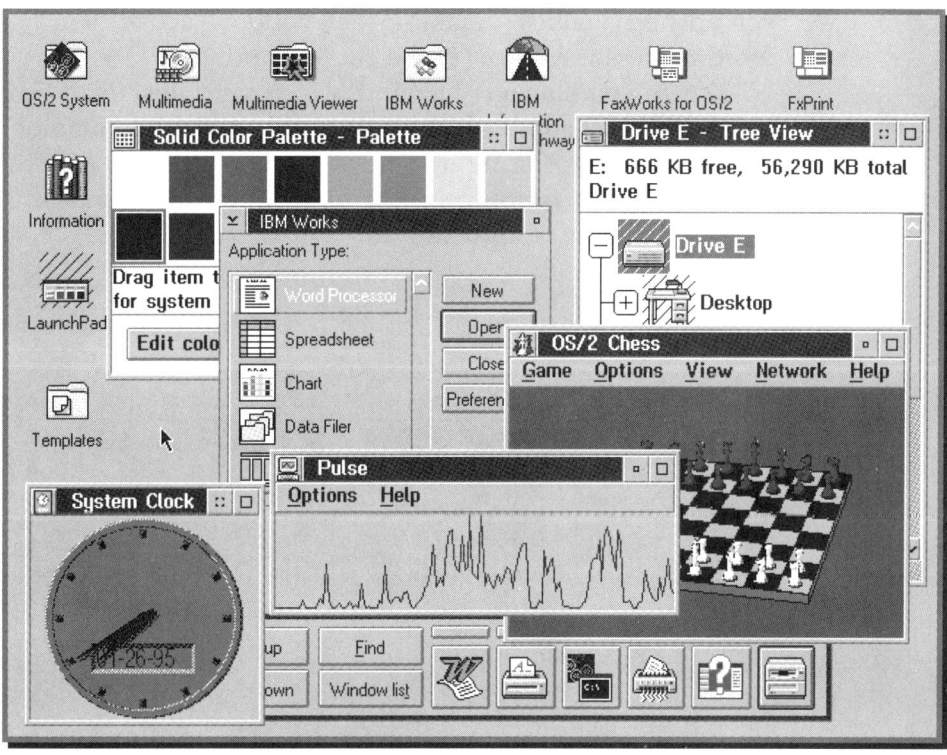

Figure 3.3. *A busy desktop can get quite cluttered.*

Although you can have several windows open at once, you can only interact with one window at a time. This is called the active window. OS/2 places the active window in the foreground, on top of other objects so you can interact with it. In the figure above, the Pulse monitor is the active window.

Understand, however, that the programs in the inactive windows continue to operate (or run) in the background while you're focusing on the window in the foreground. For example, you might start a spreadsheet program and tell it to recalculate or print a file. While it's busy with your file, you could start your word processor program and begin typing a letter. While you're working on the letter, the spreadsheet program continues to recalculate or print. If you wanted to check the progress of your spreadsheet, you could click on any visible portion of the

The OS/2 Warp Survival Guide

spreadsheet window, making that window active, which places your word processor window in the background.

To help you manage the windows on your desktop, OS/2 Warp provides a consistent set of controls that you'll find common to all windows. The following figure shows a single window with the Enhanced Editor program running in it, and identifies the controls and features that are common to all windows.

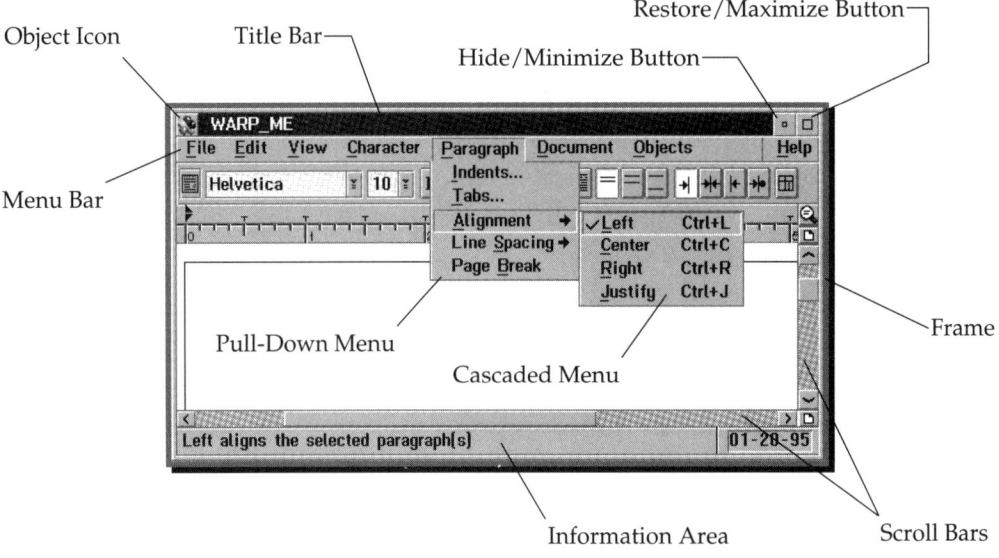

Figure 3.4.   *The contents of open windows can differ, but they all have the same controls.*

As previously mentioned, you can only interact with an active window. If you have multiple open windows, you control which window is active by clicking on any visible part of the window.

If you can't see any part of a window that you want to make active, you can use the Window List to select the window (see "The Window List" on page 101). Or you can rotate through all open windows by pressing the **Alt**+**Esc** key combination on the keyboard.

3

Warping in the Workplace Shell

Object Icon

This is a button control. It has a picture of the object's icon on it—the same icon that represents the object when it's in a folder or on the desktop. When you click on this button in non-application windows, the object's context menu appears. See "Using the Pop-Up Controls" on page 99 to learn about the context menu. When you click on this button in an application window, the window menu appears.

 You can close any window by double-clicking on the object icon button (in the upper-left corner of the window).

Title Bar

This area of the window contains the title of the program that is running in the window. When applicable, this area also shows the name of the data file the program is using. When the window is not active, this bar changes color and the title is de-emphasized (or grayed out). You also use the Title Bar to move a window to a new location on the screen. To move a window, point to the Title Bar and drag the window to its new location.

You can *maximize* a window by double-clicking on its Title Bar. A maximized window fills the screen. If you double-click on the Title Bar while a window is maximized, it will be restored to its original size.

93

Hide/Minimize Button

Depending on a global system setting, this button is either a minimize or hide button. The hide button is a small square made of dashed lines, and the minimize button is a small square made of solid lines. The difference is just cosmetic; you can choose whichever looks best to you. When you click on this button, the window is reduced (minimized) to its icon view. Depending on the object's settings, OS/2 will place the minimized window (icon) on the desktop, in the Minimized Window Viewer folder, or it will hide it from view. To bring a hidden window back into view, use the Window List. See "Window List" on page 101 for more information.

Maximize/Restore Button

Click on this button to enlarge (maximize) the window so that it fills the entire screen. You won't be able to see the desktop or any other windows while a window is maximized, and the maximize button changes to a restore (shown here on the right) button. If you click on this button while the window is maximized, the window is restored to its original size.

Menu Bar

This area of the window contains the primary menus for the program running in the window. In almost all windows, you'll see at least the *File*, *Edit*, and *Help* menus. To use a menu in the menu bar, click on the word or press the underlined letter in the word while holding down the **Alt** key.

Frame

The frame is the outermost border of the window (see Figure 3.4). You can stretch the frame to change a window's size and shape. When you place the mouse pointer over the frame, the pointer changes shape to indicate that you can stretch the frame at that point. Drag the frame to reduce or enlarge the window to suit you. You can drag horizontally or vertically using the sides of the frame, or you can drag diagonally using any of the four corners of the frame.

When you manually size a window that contains a program written for the Workplace Shell, OS/2 remembers the new size. Even after turning off your computer, the next time you open the window it will be the size you set it to. If you want OS/2 to remember the new size of a window that contains a non-Workplace Shell program (a text-mode window), hold down the **Shift** key while sizing the window. Be aware that OS/2 uses this new size for *all* non-Workplace Shell program windows.

Information Area

When a program needs to inform you of something, it displays an informational message in this area of the window. It is often used to display messages that clarify the meanings of pull-down menu items.

Scroll Bars

When an application program has more information than can be displayed in the current window size, scroll bars appear allowing you to scroll left and right or up and down to view the additional information. There are two sets of scroll bars: one for vertical scrolling and one for horizontal scrolling. To scroll in fine increments, click on the appropriate arrow button (up, down, left, or right). As you scroll, the slider button (located between the arrow buttons) moves a proportionate amount. You can scroll in larger increments by dragging the slider button to the desired point in the scroll bar.

Using Menus and Option Controls

There are several different types of menu-item and option-selection features in OS/2 Warp; they all allow you to select from a list or group of options. This section describes these features, including pull-downs, cascaded menus, dialog boxes, radio buttons, etc.

Generally speaking, to select a menu item or option, point to the item and click the left mouse button.

Pull-Down Menus

When you click on an option in the menu bar, a pull-down menu appears, allowing you to select from a list of actions associated with that option (see Figure 3.4). For example, the *File* menu typically contains the *Open*, *Save*, and *Print* options. To select a menu item, click on the word or press the underlined letter in the word.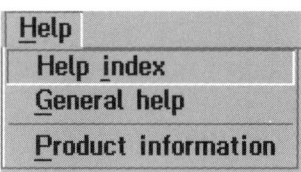

 After starting most application programs, you'll have to use the menu bar to open a file that you want to work with. To do this you would click on the *File* menu (in the menu bar) and then click on the *Open* menu item.

Cascade and Conditional Menus

When a second menu is available for an item on a pull-down menu, you'll see a right-pointing arrow (not on a raised button) next to the menu item. When you click anywhere on this menu item, you'll see the *cascade* menu, where you must select an option. The arrow for a *conditional cascade* menu appears on a raised button.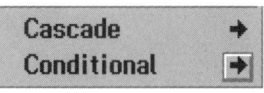

If you click anywhere on the menu item (except on the arrow button), a default choice is made for you automatically, and the cascade menu doesn't appear. If you click on the arrow button, the menu will open like a normal cascade menu. A check mark next to one of the items in a conditional cascade menu indicates that it's the default choice.

3

Warping in the Workplace Shell

To select an item on a cascaded menu, click on the word or press the underlined letter in the word.

Dialog Boxes

As you're working in a window, the system may need to ask you for more information about a task you're performing. Application programs ask for this information through dialog boxes. Figure 3.5 shows a typical dialog box that might appear when you tell a program to open a file.

Note the differences between a window and a dialog box; you don't have the same controls (such as the minimize and maximize buttons) in a dialog box. Although you can move dialog boxes, you can't resize them. Dialog boxes don't have pull-down menus.

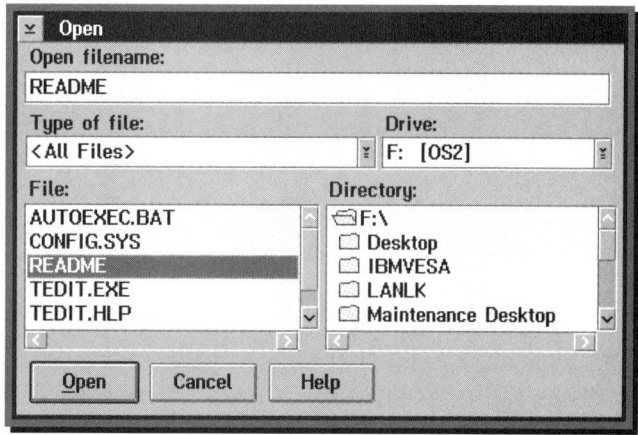

Figure 3.5.   *The Open File dialog box is probably the most common.*

Dialog boxes contain *input fields* where you enter the requested information much like you would fill out a form. Whenever possible, input fields will provide drop-down list buttons or spin buttons to make it more convenient for you to fill in the fields. The dialog box shown above contains drop-down list buttons for the *Type of File* and *Drive* fields.

The OS/2 Warp Survival Guide

Radio Buttons

You will sometimes see a list of options that are mutually exclusive; that is, only one of the options can be selected at a time. To make a selection, point at the button and click. Any other option that was selected will be deselected.

Drop-Down Lists

When a list of possible selections exists for an input field, you'll see a small button icon to the right of the field. When  you click on this icon, a drop-down list appears, allowing you to make a selection for the input field. Click on the item to select it.

Check Box

When OS/2 presents you with options that you can turn on or off, it places a square three-dimensional box next to the option. When the option is off, the box is empty. To turn the option on, click on the option; a check mark appears in the box.

Push Buttons

These are the most common button type. You have already used the ones labeled *OK*, *Cancel*, and *Help* during the installation of OS/2 Warp. Push buttons can also be labeled with graphic illustrations that represent the action they perform. You simply click on them when you want to perform their labeled action.

Spin Buttons

When an input field has a finite list of possible selections, you'll see up and down button icons to the right of the field. When you click on them, the items in the list are displayed in the input field. You can scroll through the selections in either direction.

3
Warping in the Workplace Shell

Using the Pop-Up Controls

To help you control your desktop, OS/2 Warp provides two unique tools: the *context menus* and the *Window List*. These tools are referred to as "pop-ups" because they're always available to you at the click of a mouse button (or two).

Context Menus

Each object in OS/2 Warp (including the desktop itself) has a context menu that you can "pop up" for the object. This menu allows you to open the object's settings or perform certain object-related tasks. The context menu options change based on the object for which they appear. For example, *Print* is an appropriate option for text file objects, but you wouldn't print an executable program, so *Print* doesn't appear on executable programs' context menus. You can customize context menus for individual objects through their Settings notebook.

To open the context menu for an object, point to the object and click the right mouse button. The object is enclosed in a dashed-line box to show you which object the context menu belongs to.

The OS/2 Warp Survival Guide

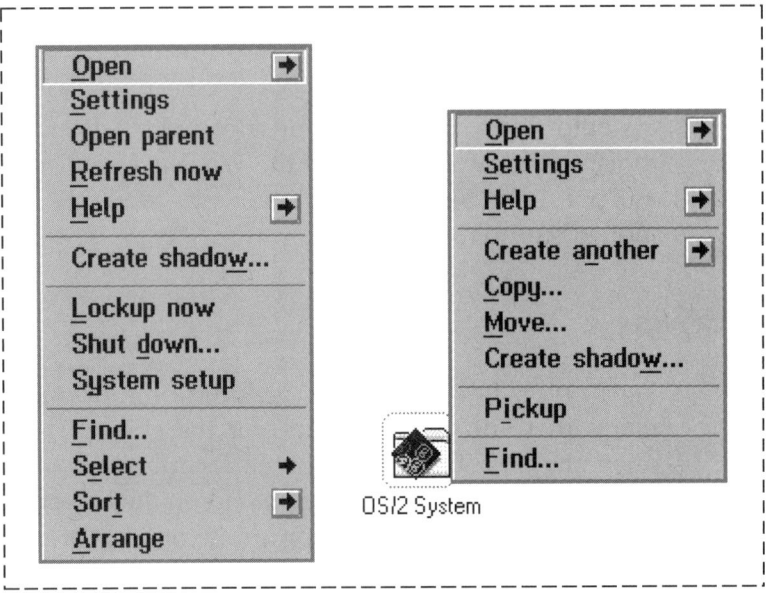

Figure 3.6.   *All OS/2 Warp objects have a context menu.*

Figure 3.6 contains examples of context menus. The one on the left belongs to the desktop. To pop up the desktop's context menu, point to any clear area on the desktop and click the right mouse button. The menu on the right belongs to the OS/2 System folder object. As you can see, context menus contain different options—options that are appropriate for the object to which the menu belongs. Hence the term context menu.

All context menus provide certain standard options. For example, the *Open* and *Help* options always appear on a context menu, and most context menus include the *Copy*, *Move*, *Delete*, and *Close* options.

> You can add items to any context menu through the object's settings (see Chapter 5, "Customizing OS/2 Warp"). You might want to place frequently used tasks on the desktop's context menu, since it is readily available. For example, you might add a DOS command prompt to the menu so you can quickly enter DOS.

Warping in the Workplace Shell

The Window List

When working with multiple windows on your desktop, inactive windows can become partially or totally obscured by other windows. The Window List allows you to switch your focus to any open object, making that object's window the active window.

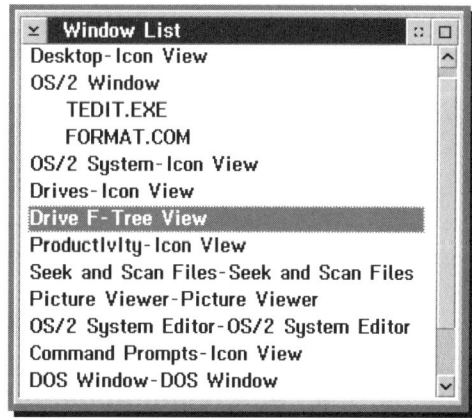

Figure 3.7. *The Window List lets you see all open windows, in list form.*

To pop up the Window List, point to a blank space on the desktop and chord the mouse buttons (simultaneously press then release both mouse buttons). If you can't see the desktop, or if you prefer keyboard controls, you can also open the Window List by pressing the **Ctrl+Esc** key combination. The list shows you all open programs, in the order in which they were started.

To make a window active, simply double-click on the title of the window in the Window List. The Window List will disappear and your selected window will come into the foreground as the active window.

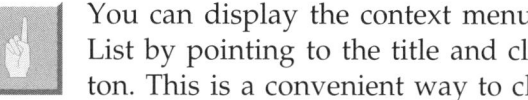You can display the context menu for objects in the Window List by pointing to the title and clicking the right mouse button. This is a convenient way to close or maximize a window that you can't see.

Visual Clues in the Warp Workplace

OS/2 keeps you informed about your session using several visual indicators in the Workplace Shell. These indicators include the use of:

- Colors and Shading,
- Hatch Lines and Borders, and
- Cursor Shapes.

Colors and Shading

OS/2 Warp uses colors to indicate which window is active and which are inactive. An active window's title bar contains white text on a green background, while an inactive window's title bar contains dark gray text on a light gray background. With the exception of shadowed object titles, OS/2 uses light gray to indicate that an action or menu item is not available or not appropriate.

When you select an object (point to it and click) OS/2 places a gray background behind the object so you know it's selected. You must select an object before you can perform an action on it.

Of course, the colors we've discussed here are the default OS/2 Warp colors; you can change the color combinations to be anything you like using the Color Palette object.

Hatch Lines and Borders

When you open an object, its window appears and OS/2 places hatch lines around the original object (in its background area) to show you that the object is open. Notice also that the icon itself changes to produce an animated effect (i.e., folders appear to open). If the object's window becomes obscured, and you want to use the object, you might try to reopen the object. The hatch lines serve to remind you that you have already opened the object. In this case, you might want to use the Window List to select the open window.

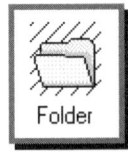

3
Warping in the Workplace Shell

Objects on the desktop that are minimized windows have a border around them to indicate that they are in fact minimized windows and not the original object. Double-click on a minimized window object to re-open its window on the desktop.

Cursor Shapes

OS/2 Warp uses the *cursor* to convey certain information to you. Most of the time, the cursor is a black arrow, which allows you to perform most point-and-click operations.

When the cursor changes to a clock, OS/2 is telling you that it's busy and your point-and-click operations will not be immediately processed. When the cursor is shaped like a capital "I" OS/2 is telling you that you can type into that area of the screen. These areas are called *input fields*, where you can specify information directly to the program running in that window. To type information into input fields, point to the field. When the cursor changes to a capital I, click the left mouse button. A text cursor (straight vertical line) is placed in the input field. You can use the keyboard (including left and right arrows, **Del**, **Home**, **End**, and backspace keys) to change the contents of the input field.

A Look Inside the OS/2 Warp Folders

With OS/2 Warp, objects are stored in folders. The default icon for a folder object looks like a manila file folder, but folders can look like anything. For example, the icon for the OS/2 Information folder looks like a set of books.

When you start OS/2 Warp, you are opening the first folder; the desktop itself is a folder that holds *all* objects in the Workplace Shell. While you are running OS/2, the Desktop folder is open. (You can prove this to yourself by looking in the Drives folder of your OS/2 boot drive for the Desktop folder, as shown above. It appears with hatch lines through it, indicating that it's open.) When you exit OS/2 Warp, you close the Desktop folder.

The OS/2 Warp Survival Guide

Once inside the Desktop folder, you'll see four main folder objects (on your desktop). They are the OS/2 System folder, the Templates folder, the Information folder, and the Multimedia folder. The best way to start "getting warped" is to find out what's inside each of these folders.

 **OS/2 System Folder:** This folder contains the objects you'll need to access most of the OS/2 Warp system functions. The bulk of this chapter discusses these objects.

 **Templates Folder:** This folder contains *templates* for various types of objects. You'll use templates to create new objects under OS/2 Warp. We'll discuss each Template object in this chapter.

 **Information Folder:** This folder contains the reference information for OS/2 Warp. The documents in this folder are "electronic books" that are meant to be read on your computer. They describe many aspects of OS/2 Warp.

 **Multimedia Folder:** If your system has multimedia capabilities, this folder contains objects that can take advantage of those capabilities, such as sound, music, and even full-motion video.

The OS/2 System Folder

The OS/2 System folder contains most of OS/2's system utilities. When you open the OS/2 System folder, a window appears showing you the following objects:

3

Warping in the Workplace Shell

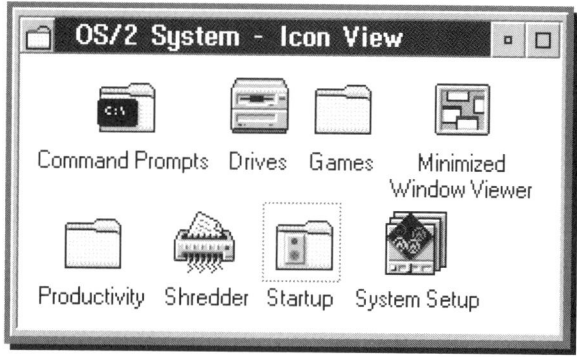

Figure 3.8.   *The OS/2 System folder contains a variety of tools.*

As you can see, some of the objects in the OS/2 System folder are also folders, some objects are programs, and some objects are devices.

Command Prompts Folder

This folder contains objects that give you access to OS/2, DOS, and Windows prompts, allowing you to "get below" the Workplace Shell and enter operating system commands directly.

When you open the Command Prompts folder, you'll see a window similar to the one shown in Figure 3.9.

105

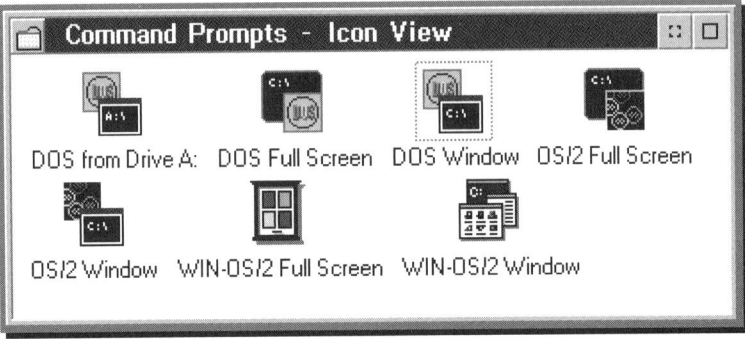

Figure 3.9. *The Command Prompts folder contains an object for just about every kind of prompt you might want.*

If you installed OS/2 Warp with Dual Boot, the "Dual Boot" object is also located in this folder. You can use it to restart your computer so that it boots from your original DOS partition.

Refer to Chapter 9, "DOS and OS/2 Command Lines," for an in-depth discussion about the command prompt objects in this folder.

Drives Folder

This folder contains an object for each diskette, hard disk, and CD-ROM drive attached to your computer. To look at the files on a drive, you would open this folder (a window similar to that shown in Figure 3.10 appears) and then open the desired drive object (Drive A:, Drive B:, Drive C:, etc.).

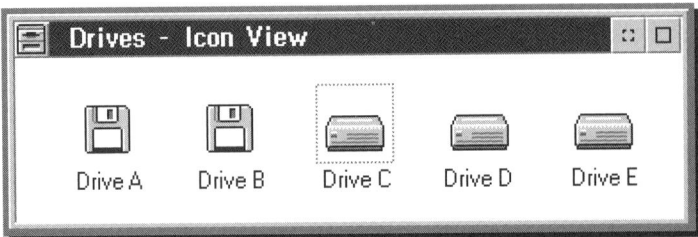

Figure 3.10. *The Drives folder holds all your disk drives together in one container.*

3

Warping in the Workplace Shell

When you open one of the disk drive objects, the contents of that drive appear in a window for you to see (as shown in Figure 3.11).

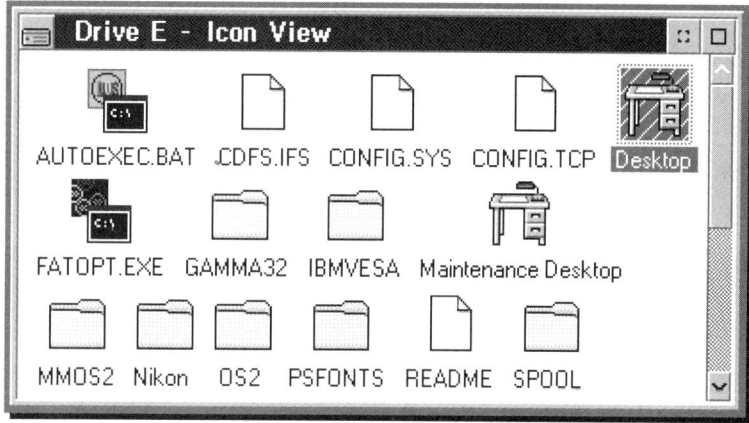

Figure 3.11.   *A drive object contains objects that represent the files on a disk drive.*

Notice that each file on the drive is represented with an icon, accompanied by the file's name. This is called the *Icon View*. By default OS/2 is set up to show files in Icon View. If you prefer to see files in a more traditional format, you can change to either the *Tree View* or the *Details View* using the window's context menu (as shown below).

The OS/2 Warp Survival Guide

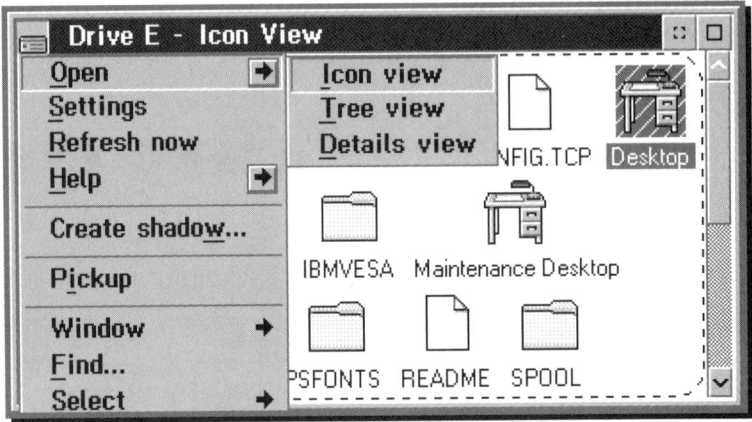

Figure 3.12. *You can change a window's view with the Open option on the context menu.*

To change to a different view, open the context menu for the drive window (right-click on the Object Icon in the upper-left corner), click on the arrow next to the *Open* option, and select *Tree View*. A new window similar to the following appears.

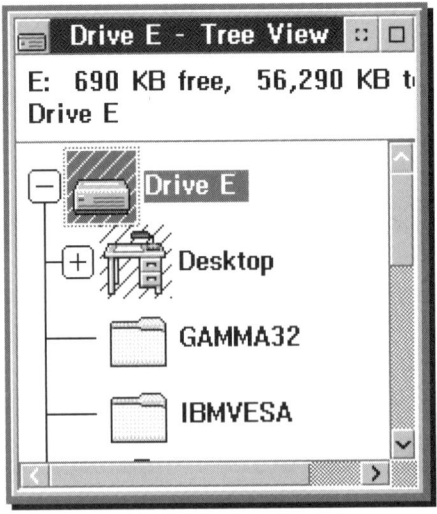

Figure 3.13. *The Tree View contains objects that represent the folders on your drive.*

3
Warping in the Workplace Shell

Of course, the Tree View only shows folder objects. This would be useful if you want to perform file operations at the folder level (for example, moving an entire folder and its contents to a new drive). But for detailed file management work, you'll need a different view.

Now try Details View. Again, open the context menu for the drive window, click on the arrow next to the *Open* option, and select *Details View*. A new window similar to the following appears.

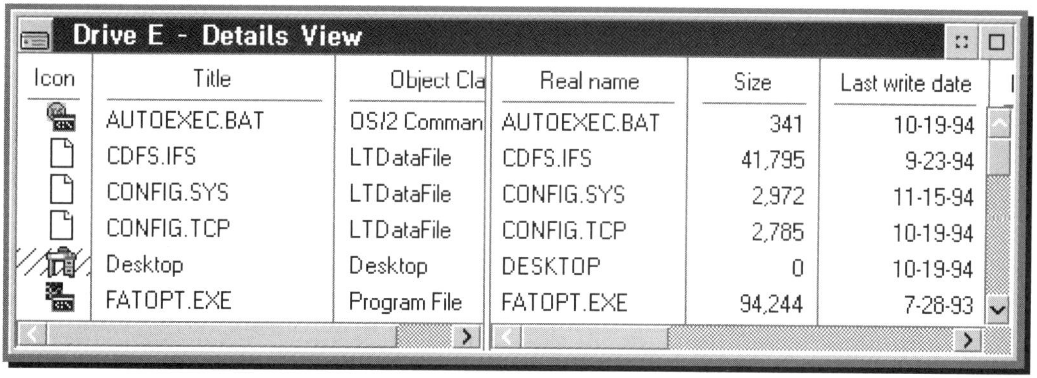

Figure 3.14.   *The Details View shows you much more about the files on a drive.*

The Details View allows you to see more files at once, and shows you much more information about each file. You can customize the format of the information presented, and you can still use drag-and-drop techniques to manipulate files in the Details View. If you prefer a view other than the view that OS/2 uses by default, refer to Chapter 5, "Customizing OS/2 Warp," for more information about permanently setting your view preferences.

Games Folder

If you installed the OS/2 Warp games, this folder contains everyone's favorites: Solitaire, OS/2 Chess, and Mahjongg Solitaire. To play one of these games, first open the Games folder. You'll see the following window. Then *launch* a game.

The OS/2 Warp Survival Guide

Figure 3.15. *The Games folder is rather sparse, but it does contain some classic games.*

Minimized Window Viewer

When you first start OS/2, this folder is empty. When you minimize an open object (or window) its window disappears and its icon will either be hidden, placed on your desktop, or placed in the Minimized Window Viewer folder, depending on the object's settings.

If you are a power user who runs several programs or uses several windows at the same time, you might find this folder to be particularly useful. When you minimize open windows, their icons are placed in this folder rather than on the desktop. The intent is to keep your desktop from becoming cluttered.

When you open the Minimized Window Viewer folder, a window appears showing you the objects that are minimized. To restore an object's window, double-click on the object.

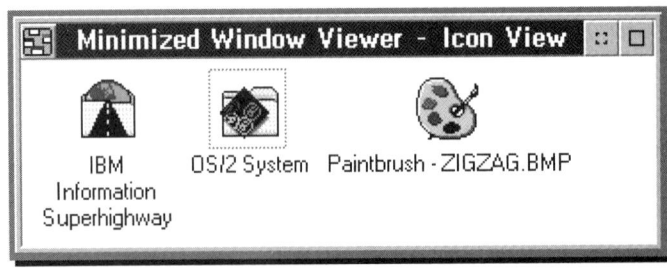

Figure 3.16. *The Minimized Window Viewer can hold DOS, Windows, and OS/2 objects.*

3

Warping in the Workplace Shell

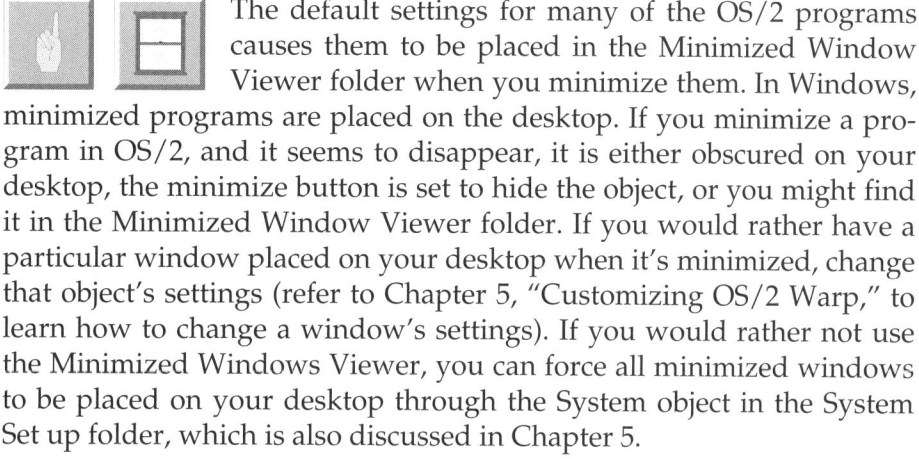The default settings for many of the OS/2 programs causes them to be placed in the Minimized Window Viewer folder when you minimize them. In Windows, minimized programs are placed on the desktop. If you minimize a program in OS/2, and it seems to disappear, it is either obscured on your desktop, the minimize button is set to hide the object, or you might find it in the Minimized Window Viewer folder. If you would rather have a particular window placed on your desktop when it's minimized, change that object's settings (refer to Chapter 5, "Customizing OS/2 Warp," to learn how to change a window's settings). If you would rather not use the Minimized Windows Viewer, you can force all minimized windows to be placed on your desktop through the System object in the System Set up folder, which is also discussed in Chapter 5.

Productivity Folder

This folder holds some useful tools, including: the Clipboard Viewer, two text editors, the Icon Editor, the Picture Viewer, a "pulse" monitor for your system, and the Seek and Scan file finder. When you open this folder, the following window appears.

Figure 3.17.   *The Productivity folder contains system utilities that you should be aware of.*

You're probably thinking "Where did all the old OS/2 applets go?" IBM decided to release some new (hopefully better) OS/2 applications in the BonusPak. The BonusPak applets replace

The OS/2 Warp Survival Guide

those old applets such as *To-Do List* and *Daily Planner*. The only thing that's sorely missed is the *Calculator*. If you want to keep using those old applets, they should migrate easily into OS/2 Warp. See Chapter 5, "Customizing OS/2 Warp," for instructions on how to install application programs.

Clipboard Viewer

The Clipboard Viewer lets you look at the current contents of the clipboard. The clipboard is where the system stores data when you use the *Edit* menu options: *Cut*, *Copy*, and *Paste* from any OS/2 application. When you open the Clipboard Viewer object, a window similar to the following appears.

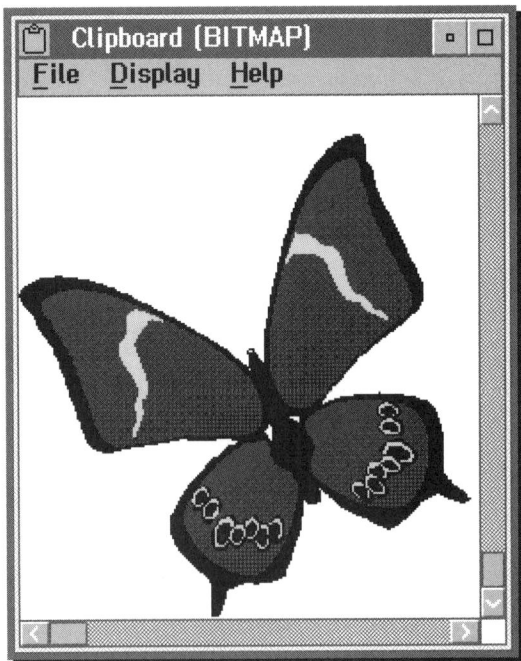

Figure 3.18.   *The Clipboard Viewer lets you see what's on the clipboard, whether it contains text or graphics.*

3
Warping in the Workplace Shell

All OS/2 applications can share data through the clipboard (see Chapter 6, "Getting Warped: Exercises in Virtual Reality," for an example of using the clipboard).

You can share data between Windows applications and OS/2 applications through the clipboard, as long as either the `WIN_CLIPBOARD` or `WIN_DDE` setting is ON in the WIN-OS/2 settings notebook. These are both set to ON by default. See Chapter 5, "Customizing OS/2 Warp," for details.

By now you might have noticed that most applications have an *Edit* pull-down menu on their menu bar. The *Cut*, *Copy*, and *Paste* options on the *Edit* menu work with the clipboard. The *Cut* option removes selected data (text or graphics) from its original location and places it on the clipboard. The *Copy* option copies selected data from its original location to the Clipboard. The *Paste* option copies the data from the clipboard to your current application and places it wherever your cursor is located. Notice the keyboard shortcuts for these options (**Shift**+**Delete**, **Ctrl**+**Insert**, and **Shift**+**Insert**).

Edit	
Cut	Shift+Delete
Copy	Ctrl+Insert
Paste	Shift+Insert

You don't need to use the Clipboard Viewer to use the clipboard. The clipboard is always available; whenever you use the *Cut*, *Copy*, and *Paste* options, you're using the clipboard. But if you're not sure what's on the clipboard, you can see its contents with the Clipboard Viewer.

A nice feature of the Clipboard Viewer is that you can save the contents of the clipboard to a file using the *File* menu. Because the clipboard can contain only one object at a time, you might want to use this feature if you need to cut or copy multiple objects from one source to another.

OS/2 Warp provides a feature called *Dynamic Data Exchange* (DDE—a.k.a. *Paste Link*). This feature lets you paste objects that maintain a link with the original object so that, when the original object changes, the pasted object will reflect those changes. This is most useful for pasting objects such as spreadsheets, which have a tendency to change a lot.

Enhanced Editor

The Enhanced Editor is a full-screen text editor with some interesting capabilities. Although it can't be considered a professional word processing program, it does have many of today's sophisticated word processing features. When you open the Enhanced Editor object, a window similar to the one shown in Figure 3.19 appears.

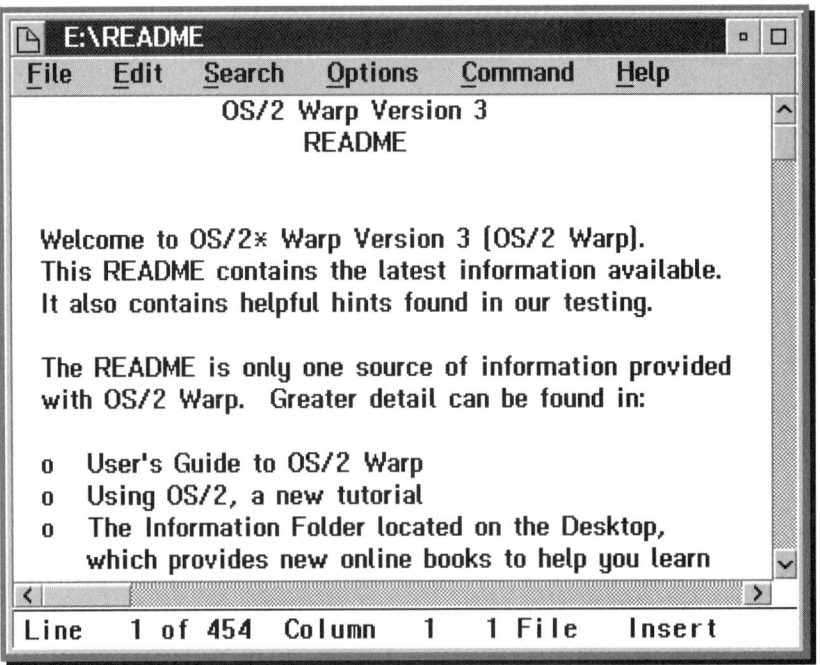

Figure 3.19.   *The Enhanced Editor is more powerful than the OS/2 System Editor.*

With its roots in the IBM Internal Use Only circles, the Enhanced Editor brings you some nifty search-and-replace features; supports bookmarks, file rings, and powerful block manipulation features; and it even provides an internal macro programming language. It's ideal for creating REXX programs. If you're serious about full-screen editors, we think you'll like this one. Give it a try!

Icon Editor

The Icon Editor allows you to create or modify graphic image files (with a file name extension of .ICO) that can be used as icons for objects in the Workplace Shell. When you open the Icon Editor object, a window similar to the following appears:

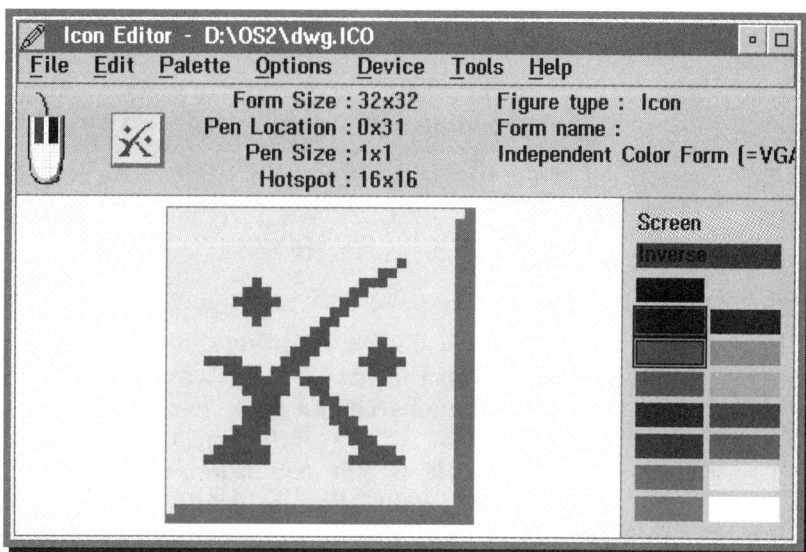

Figure 3.20. *The Icon Editor is a bitmap editor that lets you make your own icons.*

The Icon Editor works a lot like a paint program. By default, it's set up to create perfect icon-size images, but is automatically associated with OS/2 bitmap files. If you double-click on an OS/2 bitmap file, OS/2 will launch the Icon Editor and open the bitmap file, allowing you to edit it.

If you create an icon (with a .ICO file name extension), and name it the same as an executable on your hard disk that doesn't have an icon, you can get OS/2 to automatically use your icon for that program. Make sure you save it in the folder where the executable resides and name it the same as the executable. OS/2 will associate your icon with that executable.

The OS/2 Warp Survival Guide

OS/2 System Editor

This application is a full-screen text editor. It allows you to create and modify the contents of data files that contain text. It is not a word processing program, although you could create and print a document with it. It's more appropriate for creating or modifying batch program files and system files such as AUTOEXEC.BAT and CONFIG.SYS. When you open the System Editor object, a window similar to the following appears:

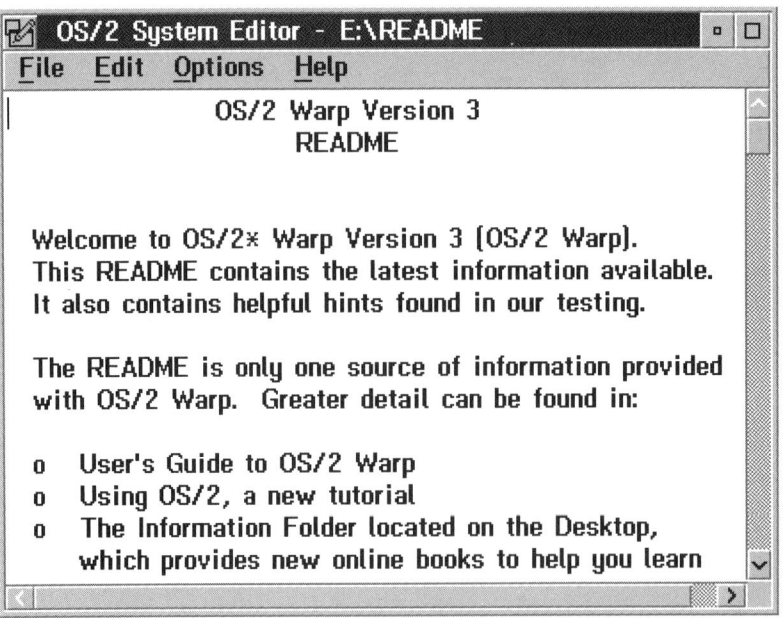

Figure 3.21. The System Editor is a simple full-screen text editor.

Using the options on the pull-down menus, you can open, close, and print files; perform cut-and-paste operations; change fonts; and search for specific text.

The System Editor is really a very basic editor; you might want to use the Enhanced Editor for more sophisticated document processing.

3 — Warping in the Workplace Shell

Picture Viewer

The Picture Viewer object allows you to view files that contain graphics in the metafile (MET) or Picture Interchange File (PIF) format. You also can use the Picture Viewer to work with Spool File Support (SPL) files. You can place spooled print jobs on hold while you view their contents through the Picture Viewer. When you open the Picture Viewer object, a window similar to the following appears:

Figure 3.22. The Picture Viewer lets you look at certain image files, including spooled print jobs.

Using the options on the pull-down menus, you can open, print, cut-and-paste, convert formats, and specify a viewing sequence for multiple files.

The OS/2 Warp Survival Guide

Pulse

The Pulse application is a simple utility whose only function is to track your computer's microprocessor utilization while you're running the OS/2 Workplace Shell. When you open the Pulse object, a window similar to the following appears:

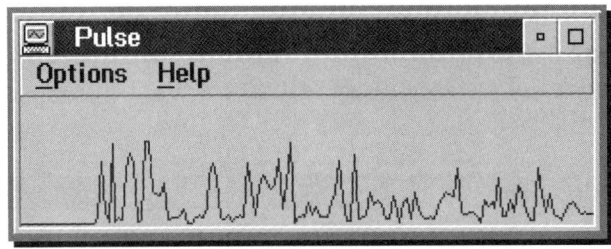

Figure 3.23. *Pulse gives you an idea of how busy your computer is.*

With the Pulse application running, you can watch a continuous graph that tracks your microprocessor. It can reveal some interesting things about your computer utilization. For example: If, after starting a program, you've ever found yourself wondering if your computer was still working, Pulse gives you positive feedback when you observe no other apparent activity.

Seek and Scan Files

You'll find the Seek and Scan Files application to be a very useful tool. It lets you quickly search entire disk drives for a specific file. If you've ever misplaced a file, you'll appreciate the seek feature of this program. Seek and Scan has a second, very powerful feature—it can search (or scan) through files for a specific text pattern. This is very helpful if you can't remember the name of a file you need, but you can remember some unique sentence or word that you know is in your desired file.

When you open the Seek and Scan Files object, a window similar to the following appears:

3

Warping in the Workplace Shell

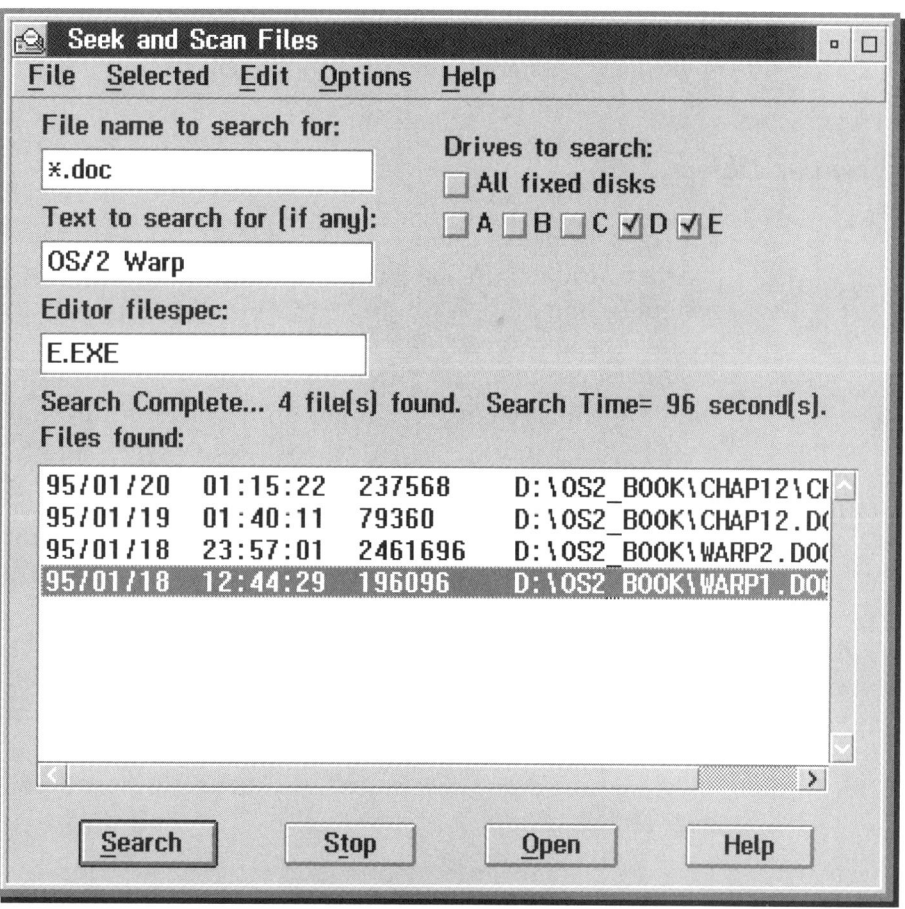

Figure 3.24.   The Seek and Scan program is a great way to find files on any disk drive.

The uses for this program may not be obvious at first. Of course, you use it to find files using wildcard characters (* and ?) like DOS. But you also can use it to create a list of files on which you want to perform some action. For example, you might need to change the text in all files that contain a specific string of characters. You can get OS/2 to open and process all or selected files that meet the search criteria you specify. Or you can get OS/2 to perform a command on files in the resulting list. You can even save the list of files to a document file. See the Help menu for detailed instructions.

The OS/2 Warp Survival Guide

> This concludes our tour of the objects in the Productivity folder. We'll now pick up where we were with the objects in the OS/2 System folder.

Shredder Object

This object deletes other objects. Drag any object (data file, program, folder) on the shredder and it will be deleted. A system option allows you to be prompted before the objects are deleted, to prevent "accidental" shredding.

When you open the Shredder object, its Settings notebook appears, allowing you to change the name and/or icon for this object.

Startup Folder

When you start the OS/2 Workplace Shell, the objects in this folder are started or opened. This folder is similar to the DOS AUTOEXEC.BAT file and the Startup Group in Windows. If you place a program object in this folder, it automatically starts to run when you start OS/2 Warp. When you no longer want a program to automatically start, simply delete it from the Startup folder.

When you place objects in the Startup folder, they are shadows of their real objects.

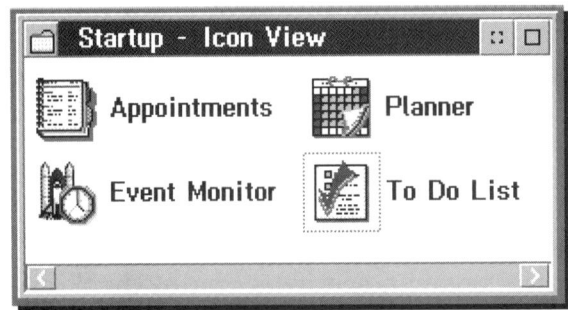

Figure 3.25. Objects you place in the Startup folder are shadows that will be automatically started when you start OS/2 Warp.

3 Warping in the Workplace Shell

System Setup Folder

This folder contains tools that allow you to customize OS/2. You can change the color scheme, system fonts, operating characteristics, and mouse and keyboard settings; and you can selectively install or uninstall OS/2 features and new device drivers using the tools in this folder.

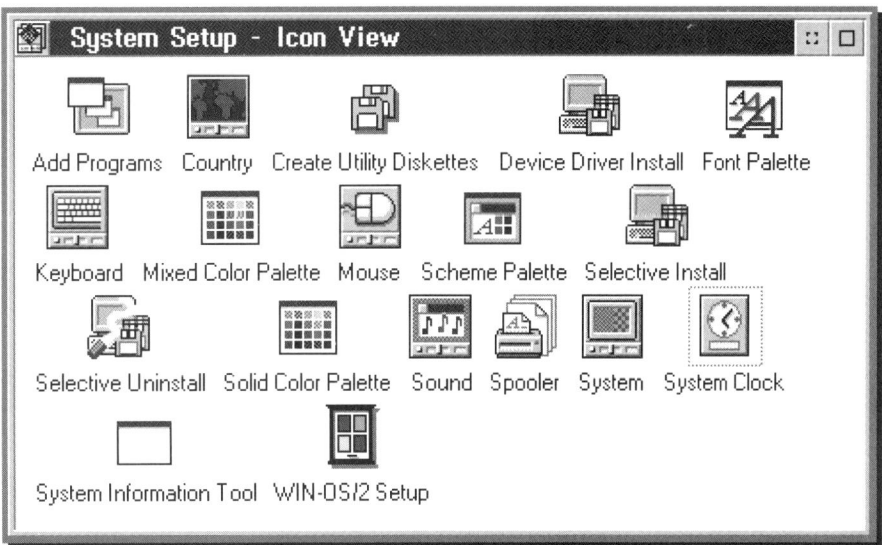

Figure 3.26. *The System Setup folder is where you'll find most of the OS/2 Warp customization and optimization utilities.*

Because the objects in this folder are used primarily for customizing OS/2 Warp, we won't discuss each of them here. Refer to Chapter 5, "Customizing Warp," for all the details.

> This concludes our tour of the objects in the OS/2 System folder. We'll now pick up where we were with the standard folders on the desktop.

The Templates Folder

This folder contains a special type of object: *templates*. The template objects provide a convenient way to create new objects. When you open the Templates folder, a window appears showing you the following objects:

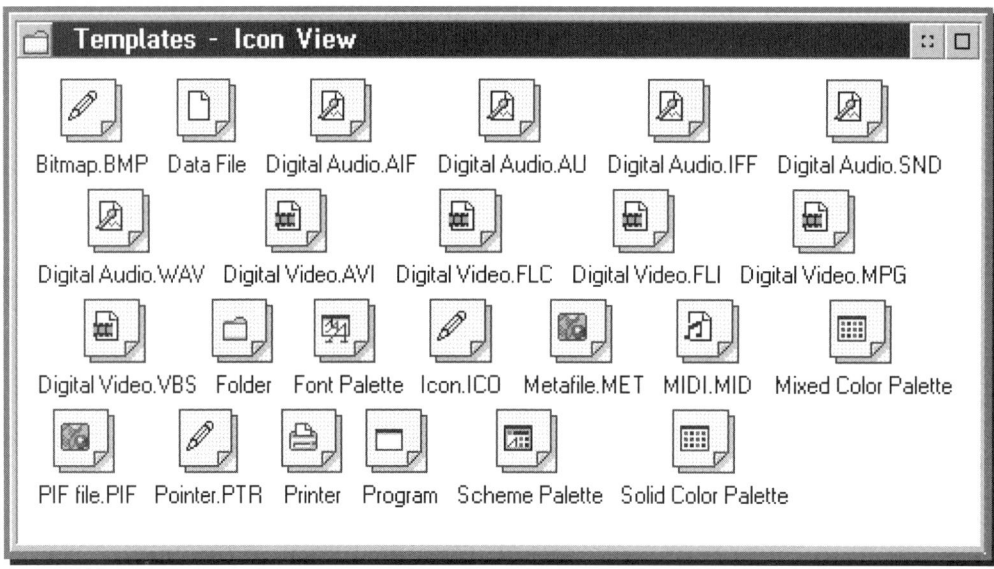

Figure 3.27. Use the objects in the Templates folder to create new objects.

To create a new object, point to the appropriate template object and drag it to the desktop (or to another folder). The new object (a copy of the template object) will appear on your desktop as if you peeled off a sheet from a little yellow sticky pad. You can then modify the settings for the new object, assigning a name, an icon, and so forth. See Chapter 5, "Customizing OS/2 Warp," for details.

Although you can create new objects by copying existing ones, the Templates folder provides all object types in one convenient place, and template objects have default settings that may be more appropriate for your new object. You can create your own template objects, and some OS/2 applications may create new ones for you.

3 — Warping in the Workplace Shell

Not all templates shown here may be available to you, depending on your hardware configuration. For example, if you have no audio adapter (sound card) installed, OS/2 will not install the audio file templates. The templates that you might see are listed below.

Bitmap.BMP

Use this template to create a new bitmap image-file object. OS/2 automatically associates these files with the Icon Editor and the Windows Paintbrush program (if you have migrated Paintbrush into OS/2 Warp).

Mixed (and Solid) Color Palettes

Use these templates to create a unique color palette object. Once created, you can open the new palette and modify the colors. You could then use the object to apply your unique colors to other OS/2 objects.

Data File

You can create new data file objects with this template, although your OS/2 application programs will create their own data file objects for you as needed.

Digital Audio.WAV

Use this template (as well as the other digital audio templates) to create empty digital audio files that conform to a specific format (i.e., .WAV, .AU, and .SND). The three-letter extension shown under the title of the icon indicates the format (i.e., WAV).

Folder

When you want to create a new folder to hold related objects, use this template. A new subdirectory is created on your hard disk. Assign the name of the folder and its other properties through its settings.

Font Palette

Use this template to create a unique font palette object. Once created, you could open the new palette and change the fonts. You could then use the object to apply your unique fonts to other objects in OS/2.

Icon.ICO

Use this template to create a new icon object. OS/2 automatically associates the Icon Editor with the new object. If you open the object, the Icon Editor starts and saves any changes you make to the new object. You could then associate your new icon object with other objects.

Metafile.MET

Use this template to create a new metafile. OS/2 metafiles are graphics files that can be interchanged between graphics application programs under OS/2. For example, if you create a drawing in one program, you can export it as a metafile to be imported into some other drawing program. All attributes of the drawing (line weights, colors, fill patterns, etc.) are contained in the metafile. You can view metafiles with the OS/2 Picture Viewer (found in the Productivity folder).

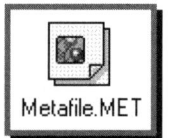

PIF File.PIF

This template creates new Picture Interchange Format (PIF) files. Like metafiles, PIF files can be exchanged by drawing programs that run in the Workplace Shell.

Pointer.PTR

Using this template, you can create a new graphical image for the mouse pointer. The OS/2 Icon Editor can create and edit pointer files.

Warping in the Workplace Shell

Printer

This template allows you to create a new printer object. Use this template when you want to install a printer on your computer. When you use the template, the Create a Printer window appears allowing you to tell OS/2 everything it needs to know to use the printer.

Program

Use this template to create a new program object in the Workplace Shell. Open the Settings for the new object to give it a name, set up its associations, and change its icon.

Scheme Palette

Use this template to create a new color scheme that you can apply to other windows. You can modify the colors in an existing color scheme with the OS/2 Scheme Palette application. See Chapter 5, "Customizing OS/2 Warp," for information about changing the color schemes for your desktop.

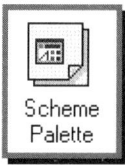

 In addition to the template objects listed above, the OS/2 Warp BonusPak applications create their own templates. These templates are specific to the BonusPak applications, which change depending on the BonusPak you received.

Chapter 6 contains exercises that teach you how to use template objects. Refer to that chapter for more information about the virtues of template objects.

The Information Folder

As its name implies, this folder contains information about OS/2 Warp. The information it contains ranges from a glossary, to programming reference manuals, to the OS/2 Tutorial. Most of these objects are "electronic books" that provide automatic tables of contents, hypertext links, searches, and indexes. If you've never used an electronic book before, give these a look. They're very easy to use. When you open the Information folder, a window appears showing you the following objects:

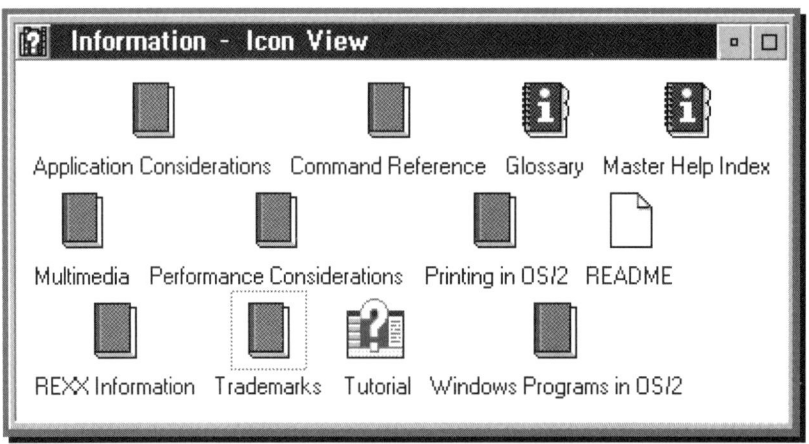

Figure 3.28.   *The objects in the Information folder can be quite helpful.*

Electronic Books: These are objects that look like the book shown here. They all operate the same; just click on the plus and minus buttons next to entries in the table of contents to reveal or hide subtopics. Then click on the desired topic. If you don't see your topic, try the *Search* and/or *Index* buttons.

Electronic Indexes: These objects share the features of electronic books, but also provide tabs along the right edge of the pages, allowing you to jump directly to a letter in the alphabet.

3   *Warping in the Workplace Shell*

Application Considerations

This is an electronic book that contains information about compatibility issues between your non-OS/2 applications and OS/2 Warp. If you are having compatibility problems, you might consider looking in this information resource for clues.

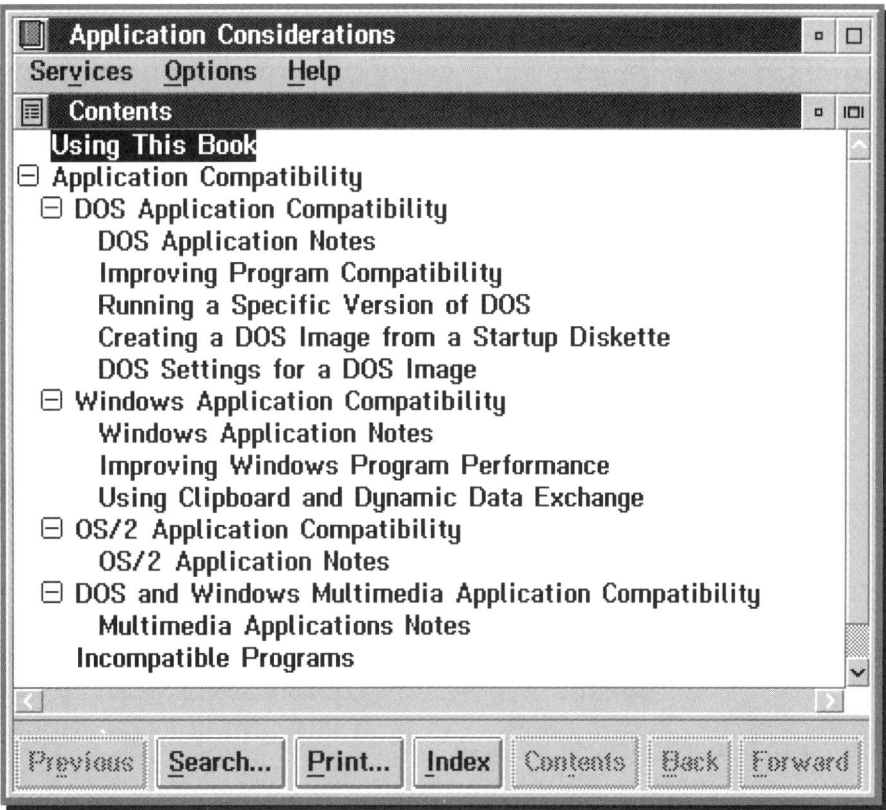

Figure 3.29.   The Application Considerations *book could help you resolve incompatibility issues for your DOS, Windows, and even OS/2 programs.*

The OS/2 Warp Survival Guide

Command Reference

If you opted to install the Command Reference, it appears in the Information folder. This electronic book contains information about OS/2 commands that you can use at the OS/2 command prompt. Refer to Chapter 9, "DOS and OS/2 Command Lines," for some interesting and undocumented command options.

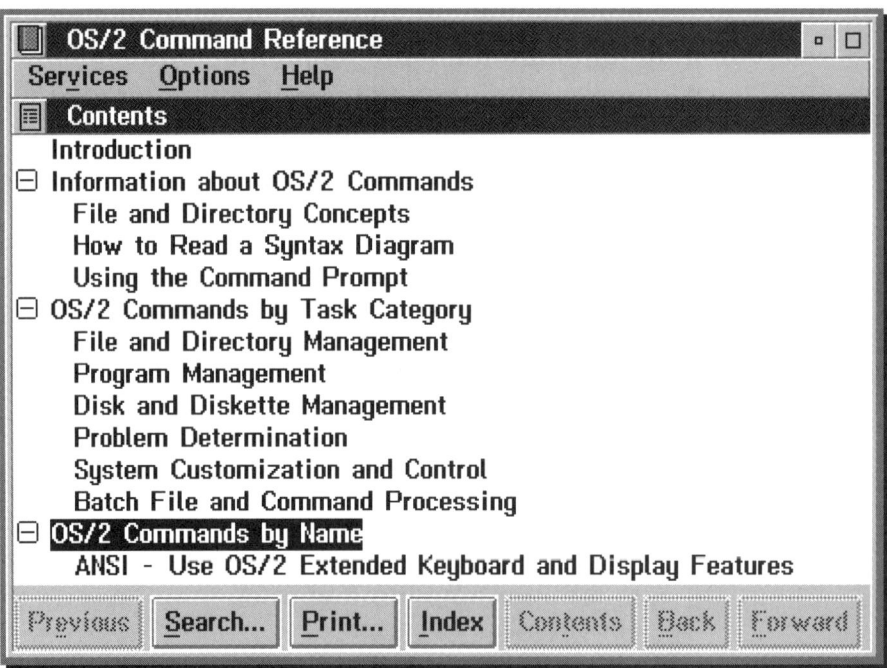

Figure 3.30. You'll find a complete listing of OS/2 commands with their syntax in the Command Reference.

The commands are listed two ways: by task categories in case you know what you want to do, but don't know which command will do it; or alphabetically by command name in case you know the command you want but forgot some of the command options.

3
Warping in the Workplace Shell

Glossary

This electronic book contains definitions for terms used in OS/2 and the Workplace Shell. To use it, simply double-click on the Glossary object; the window shown in Figure 3.31 will appear.

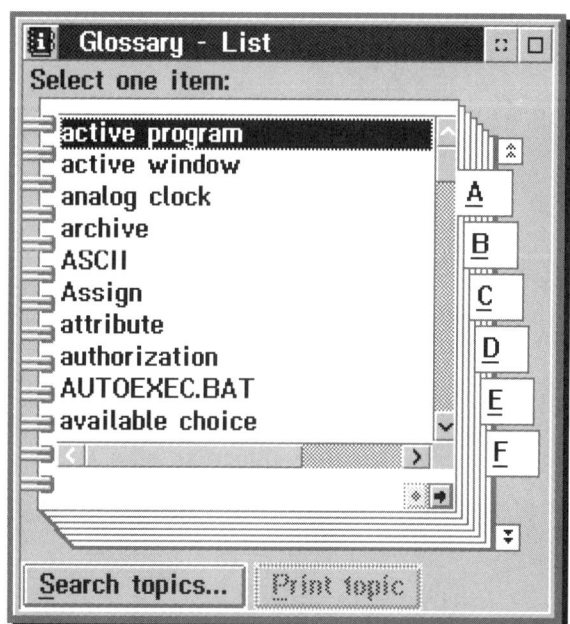

Figure 3.31. *If you've never used an electronic glossary, you've got to try the* Glossary *object.*

You can simply type the first letter of the term you're looking for. The list of terms scrolls to the words that start with the letter you typed. Or you can scroll to the word for which you want a definition using the scroll bars, arrow keys, or **Page Up** and **Page Down** keys. You can also jump directly to a letter of the alphabet using the tabs on the edges of the "pages."

When you see the term you're looking for, double-click on it to see its definition. A window will appear with the definition.

The OS/2 Warp Survival Guide

Master Help Index

This object is an electronic index that contains the OS/2 on-line help information. The help index contains information that is not published in the printed OS/2 Warp manuals, and is a pretty good source for step-by-step instructions.

Figure 3.32. *The* Master Help Index *provides access to all OS/2 help screens.*

To view the help for an index entry, double-click on the entry. A window will appear with the information you requested. To find the index entry you're interested in, you can use the scroll bars, the arrow or **Page Up**/**Page Down** keys, the index tabs, or the *Search topics* push button. The *Print topic* push button lets you print out the text for a selected index entry.

3

Warping in the Workplace Shell

Multimedia

This electronic book contains useful information about the multimedia capabilities of OS/2 Warp. If you're into multimedia, you might want to read this information before jumping into the Multimedia folder.

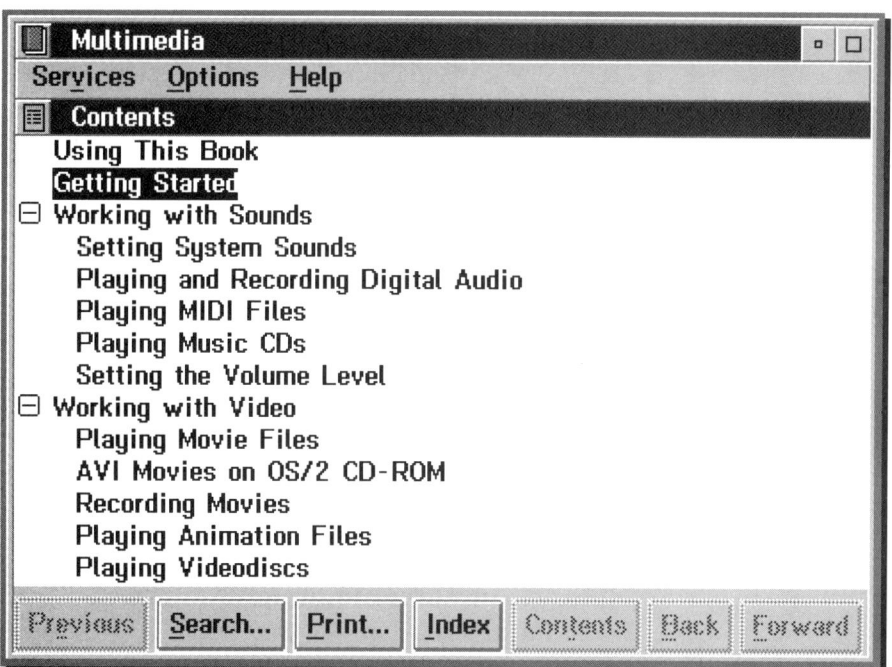

Figure 3.33. *The* Multimedia *book tells you how to work with sound and video in OS/2 Warp.*

Hardly a definitive source for the new multimedia craze, this book does help you get started warping with audio and video. A little reading now could help you avoid misconceptions about the *ins* and *outs* of multimedia.

The OS/2 Warp Survival Guide

Performance Considerations

With all the money you spent on that fast new computer, you owe it to yourself to at least glance at this electronic book. It contains tips for getting even better performance from your DOS, Windows, and OS/2 programs while running under OS/2 Warp.

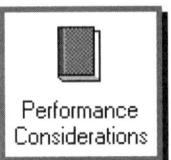

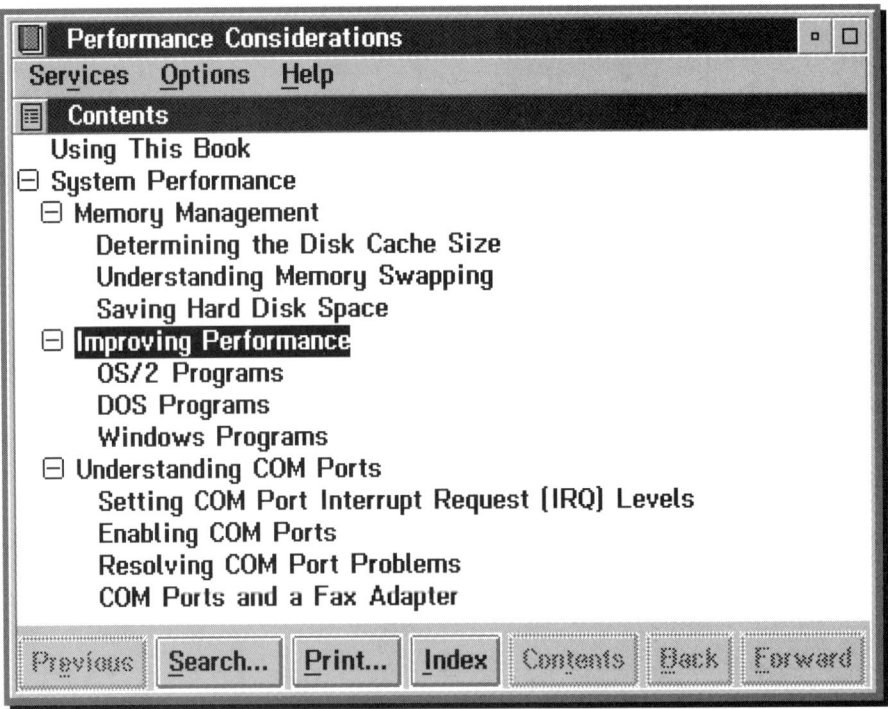

Figure 3.34.   Even the most seasoned OS/2 gurus can learn something about tweaking their DOS, Windows, and OS/2 sessions in the System Performance *book.*

You might also want to refer to Chapter 7, "DOS and Windows Under OS/2 Warp," where you'll find additional, undocumented information on the subject.

Printing in OS/2

Printing and printer management is a primary requirement from any operating system. You haven't truly learned to Warp until you've mastered this task. "Printing in OS/2" brings you closer to that goal.

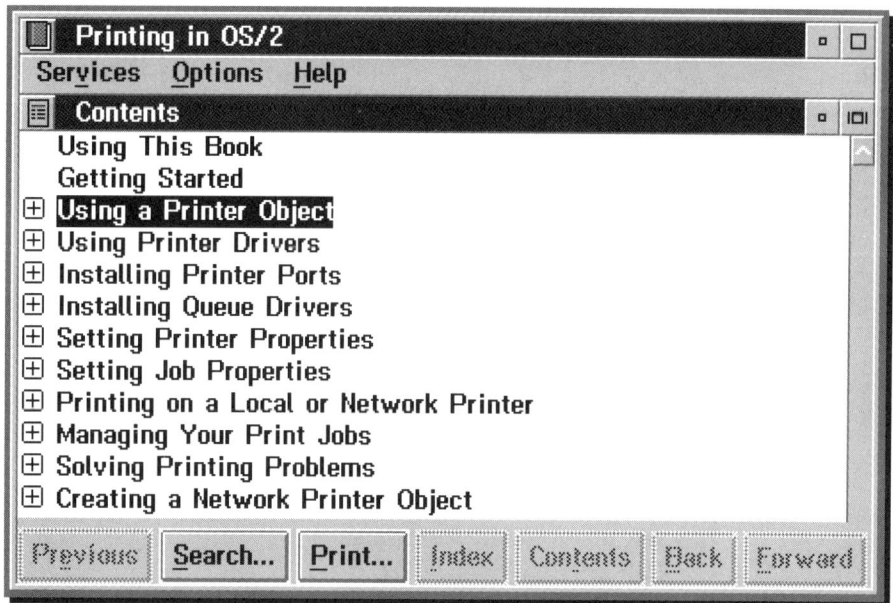

Figure 3.35. *The* Printing in OS/2 *book discusses all aspects of printing—from printer objects and device drivers to print queues and print job management.*

READ.ME

This object contains information that could not be incorporated into the OS/2 documentation at the time OS/2 Warp was released. You should open this object to see if any of the last-minute information applies to you and your computer.

REXX Information

This electronic book contains information about using the REXXprogramming language. You can use REXX in OS/2 Warp to create batch programs (much like .BAT files in DOS). But REXX is a much more powerful language than the DOS batch commands.

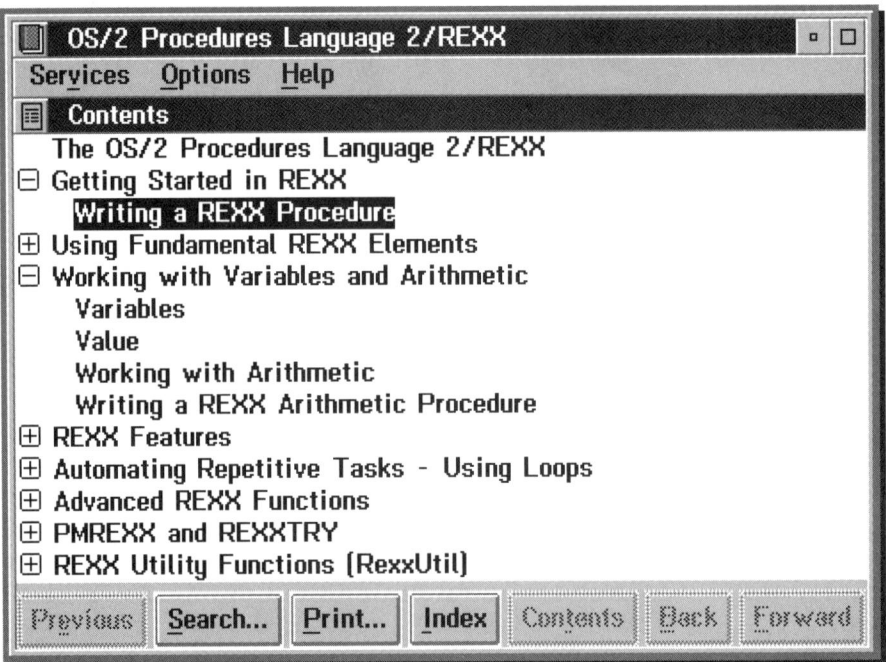

Figure 3.36. *If you'd like to try your hand at high-level programming under OS/2 Warp, you'll need to refer to the* REXX Information *book.*

In addition to this information resource, take a look at Chapter 11, "Warping with REXX." You'll find some interesting tips and previously undocumented functions and parameters.

3

Warping in the Workplace Shell

Tutorial

Any time you want to run the OS/2 Warp Tutorial, double-click on this object. This is the same tutorial you saw right after you finished the installation (if you installed it). If you didn't install the tutorial, consider using the Selective Install object (found in the System Set up folder) to do so.

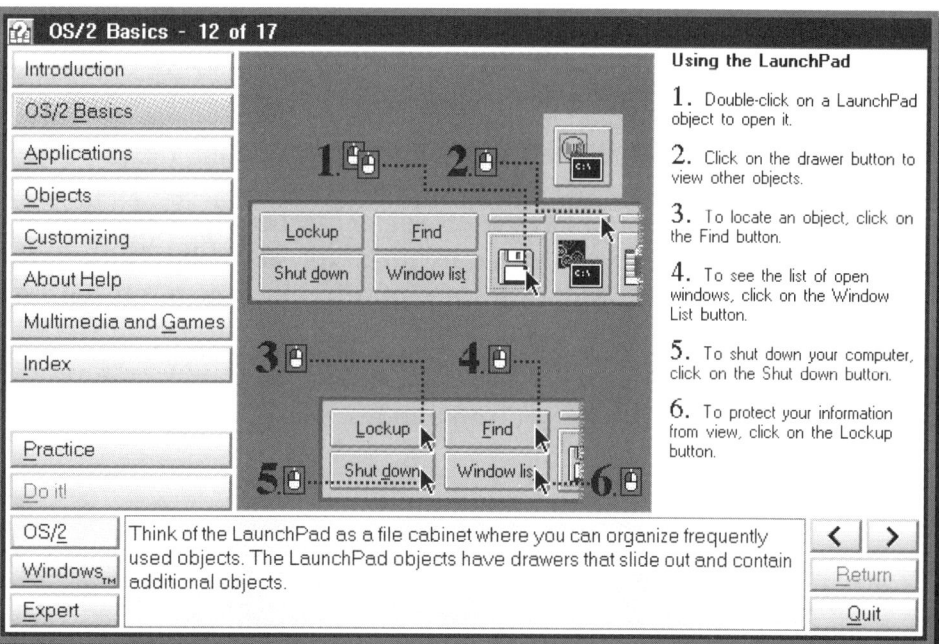

Figure 3.37. *The* OS/2 Tutorial *has been greatly enhanced for OS/2 Warp, featuring a slick new user interface.*

A big feature of the tutorial is the fact that, for each topic, you can select the type of information that's appropriate for you: OS/2, Windows, or Expert. You'll also want to try the *Practice* and *Do It!* buttons; they help make this object a true tutor.

To use the tutorial, click on the desired topic (go through them sequentially the first time) and use the arrow buttons to view additional pages of information. Use the Index to find specific topics.

Virtual Desktop Devices

Not all the objects on your desktop are folders. A standard OS/2 Warp installation will place some special-purpose objects on your desktop. This section discusses these objects.

The LaunchPad

The LaunchPad is a special type of device object that improves the accessibility of objects on your desktop. It provides virtual "drawers" and buttons that you can customize to hold the objects and actions that you most frequently need. You can launch (or start) objects (and their associated programs) with a single mouse click. Objects on the LaunchPad are shadows of their parent objects.

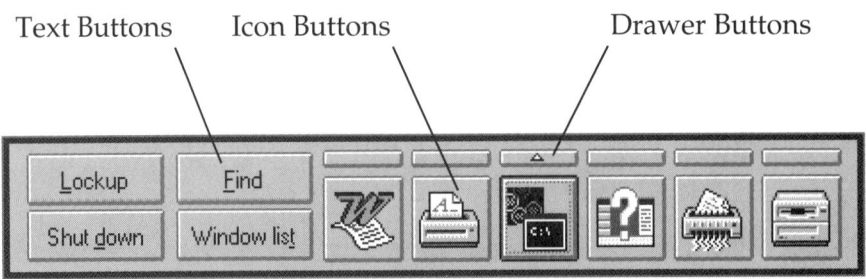

Figure 3.38.   *The LaunchPad provides a variety of button types that you can configure any way you like.*

3
Warping in the Workplace Shell

The Printer Object

This is a device object that represents a printer connected to your computer. When you open the printer object, a window appears showing you the status of the items that are being printed (as shown below in Figure 3.39). These items are print job objects, and their appearance is your first clue as to their status.

Figure 3.39. *The Printer object shows its print jobs as objects being processed by the printer.*

In Figure 3.39, the first print job has a "hold" status (as indicated by the black bar between the document and the printer), the second print job is being spooled into the print queue (note the arrow pointing into the document), the third job is being printed (as indicated by the arrow pointing from the document into the printer), and the forth job is not printing due to a problem with the document or the printer. But that's just the beginning of what you find out about each print job.

 If you change the window to *Details View* (using the *Open* cascade menu) you'll see the job IDs, document names, date, time, status, and owner information.

Since the print jobs are treated as objects, you can open a context menu for them just as you can with any other object in OS/2 (right-button click on the object). To see more details about the print job, select the *Settings* option on the job's context menu. You'll see a settings notebook for the print job!

137

The OS/2 Warp Survival Guide

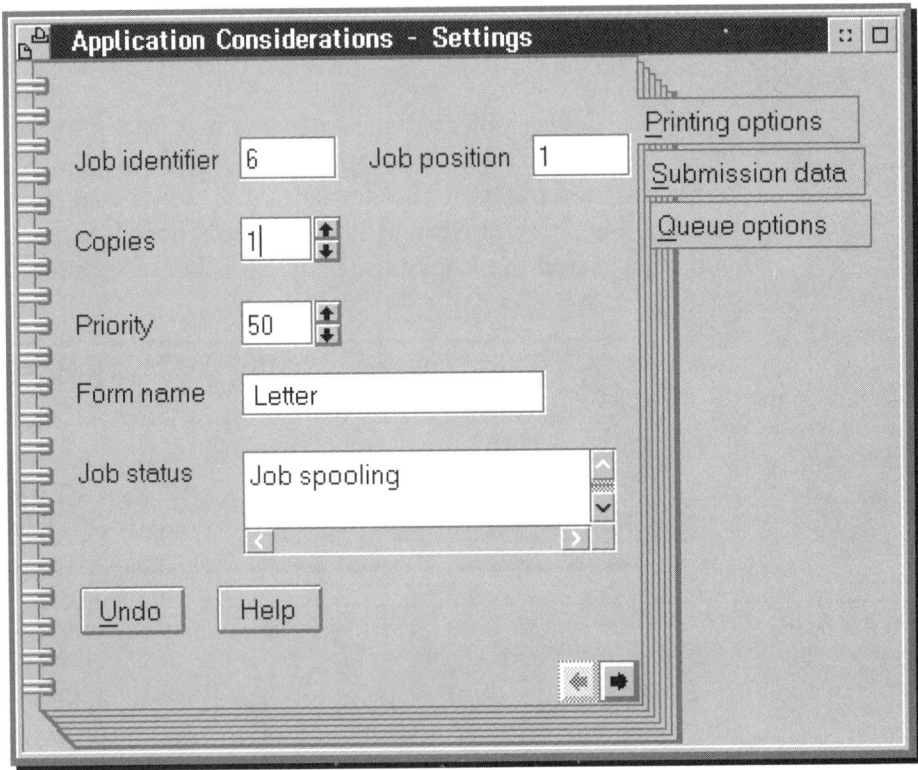

Figure 3.40. Even print jobs have a settings notebook where you can control properties of the print job, printer, and print queue.

In addition to viewing information for a print job, you can use the settings notebook to change the number of copies to print, the job's priority, and other printer and queue options.

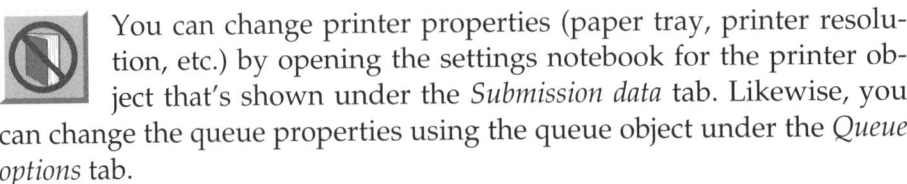 You can change printer properties (paper tray, printer resolution, etc.) by opening the settings notebook for the printer object that's shown under the *Submission data* tab. Likewise, you can change the queue properties using the queue object under the *Queue options* tab.

The OS/2 Warp printer objects also let you view the contents of print jobs. (That's right, you can preview the printed output right on your screen!) To view the contents of a print job, double-click on the print job object. The Picture Viewer object will appear and automatically display the print job.

You will originate most of your print jobs from within your application programs, but you can also print the object-oriented way with drag-and-drop. To print using this technique, drag the object you want to print to the printer and drop it. Of course, it wouldn't make sense to print some objects. For example, you can't print a program object. You can only use this drag-and-drop technique for plain text files, or files that contain printer-specific data; that is, data in a format that the printer will understand.

The Shredder Object

This object gives you an easy way to delete unwanted objects. To delete an object, drag it to and drop it on the shredder. This is a great example of the object-oriented operation of OS/2 Warp. When you drag an object to the shredder, OS/2 will ask if you're sure you want to delete the object.

If you become aggravated with OS/2 for asking you if you're sure you want to delete something, you might want to disable the *confirm on delete* feature through the System Set up object. Refer to Chapter 5, "Customizing OS/2 Warp," for more details about the System Set up object.

When you open the Shredder object, its settings notebook appears, allowing you to change basic properties of the object.

If you accidentally shred (or delete) an object, you can use the UNDELETE UNDELETE command at the OS/2 command prompt. Open an OS/2 Command Prompt object and type HELP UNDELETE for instructions.

Chapter

4

The OS/2 Warp BonusPak

The BonusPak is so chock-full of surprises, it deserves a chapter to itself. In this chapter, we'll tell you how to install the BonusPak and then take you on a tour of the programs it contains. Some of the programs and utilities are grouped into related folders to make up software suites, some are stand-alone programs. The bonus software consists of the following:

- **Internet Access Kit (IAK)**—The IBM Internet connection for OS/2

- **IBM Works and Personal Information Manager (PIM)**—These applications replace the personal productivity applets that were in OS/2 version 2.1.

- **CompuServe Information Manager for OS/2**—The CompuServe connection provides easy access and information management.

- **FaxWorks for OS/2**—For sending, receiving, and managing faxes

- **HyperACCESS Lite**—A 32-bit modem communications program

- **Person to Person**—Amazingly interactive network communications

- **Multimedia Extensions**—Consisting of the Multimedia viewer and Video IN for OS/2

 The *IBM Works* and *Personal Information Manager* programs replace the personal productivity applets that were found in the Productivity folder with OS/2 Version 2.1.

Installing from the BonusPak Diskettes

The OS/2 Warp BonusPak consists of many programs on several diskettes. You can install all the programs, or just the ones you're interested in trying. These procedures assume that you're installing from diskette Drive A:. If you're installing from Drive B:, substitute that letter in these steps.

1. With OS/2 Warp running, insert the *BonusPak Installation Utility* diskette into Drive A:.
2. Open the *OS/2 System* folder.
3. Open the *Command Prompts* folder.
4. Start an *OS/2 Window*.
5. Type **A:INSTALL** and press Enter.
6. Using your mouse, select the programs you want to install from the list provided.
7. Click on the *Install* button and follow the instructions on the screen. You'll be prompted to insert additional diskettes.

Installing from the BonusPak CD-ROM

If you have the CD-ROM version of the OS/2 Warp BonusPak, you must install the programs from one of fifteen subdirectories on the CD that correspond to fifteen countries. You can install all the programs, or just the ones you're interested in trying. These procedures assume that you're installing from a CD-ROM drive known as E:. If you're installing from a different drive, substitute that letter in these steps.

1. With OS/2 Warp running, insert the *BonusPak CD-ROM* into the CD-ROM drive.
2. Open the *OS/2 System* folder.
3. Open the *Command Prompts* folder.

The OS/2 Warp BonusPak

4. Start an *OS/2 Window*.

5. Type **E:** and press Enter.

6. Change to the directory that represents the appropriate country or language by typing the following:

   CD *two-letter code* (and press Enter)

   where the *two-letter code* is one of the following (US for English):

BR=Brazil	**SV**=Sweden	**NL**=Netherlands
FR=France	**UK**=United Kingdom	**PO**=Portugal
IT=Italy	**US**=English	**SU**=Finland
NO=Norway	**DK**=Denmark	**CF**=Canadian French
SP=Spain	**GR**=Germany	**LA**=Latin America

7. Type **INSTALL** and press Enter.

8. Using your mouse, select the programs you want to install from the list provided.

9. Click on the *Install* button and follow the instructions on the screen. You'll be prompted to insert additional diskettes.

IBM Information Superhighway: The Internet Access Kit (IAK)

If you'd like to get started using the Internet, you'll want to install this suite of programs. When installed on a computer with a modem, you have everything you need to "surf the net" (explore the information resources on the Internet). This folder has several objects in it that relate to accessing, navigating, sending, and receiving (as shown in the following figure).

The OS/2 Warp Survival Guide

Figure 4.1.   *The IBM Information Superhighway folder contains your window to the world.*

You can think of the folders in this window as different "arteries" of the "information superhighway"—the collective, worldwide communications network. We'll cover each of these folders in the order they appear in this window: *CompuServe, HyperACCESS Lite*, and *IBM Internet Connection for OS/2*.

CompuServe

This folder contains everything you need to use CompuServe, even if you don't have an account with them. CompuServe provides you with access to thousands of products and services, open discussion forums, and even news retrieval. When you open the CompuServe folder, a window similar to the one shown in the following figure appears.

Figure 4.2.   *The CompuServe folder makes connecting an easy task.*

This folder contains the *CompuServe Information Manager (CIM) for OS/2*, and a special new-member signup object. If you want to try CompuServe and you are not a current member, open the *Member Signup* object. For subsequent (and existing member) connections, open the *CIM for OS/2* object. New members and existing members alike should open the *Read Me* object before trying to connect.

CIM for OS/2

This is the primary CompuServe connection program, which was developed by CompuServe specifically for OS/2. Open this object to start a session. You'll see a window similar to the one shown in the following figure.

Figure 4.3. CIM for OS/2 offers a wealth of tools designed to assist you with specific on-line tasks.

Whether you want to browse the forums, retrieve files, peruse the news, or send e-mail, this folder has the right tool for the CompuServe information service.

The OS/2 Warp Survival Guide

Member Signup

If you don't already subscribe to CompuServe, double-click on this icon to get started. Then follow the instructions on the screen; they'll walk you through a simple registration process.

HyperACCESS Lite

This modem communications program was developed specifically for OS/2 Warp, and takes full advantage of the 32-bit operating system's object-oriented design. Although this is the "lite" version of the well-known product, HyperACCESS Lite allows you to explore several on-line "worlds."

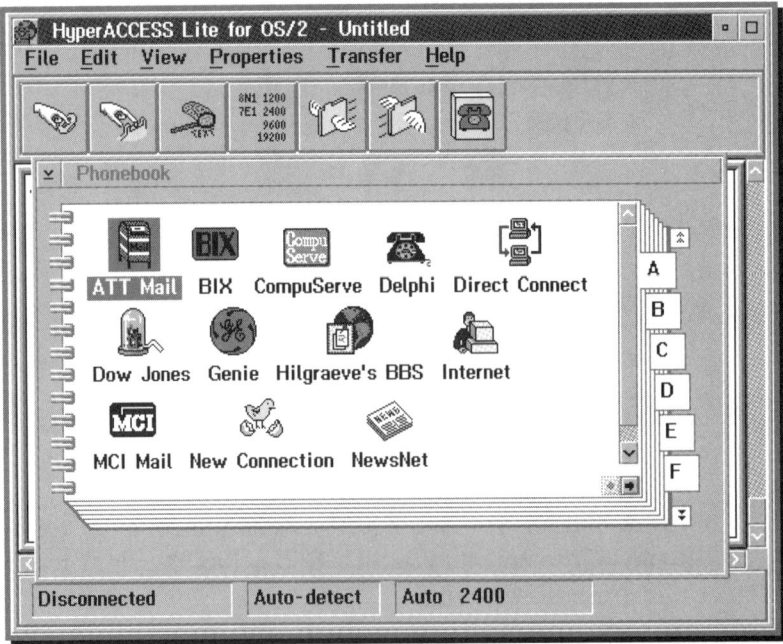

Figure 4.4. *HyperACCESS Lite is an interface to several networks.*

The OS/2 Warp BonusPak

IBM Internet Connection for OS/2

This folder is IBM's collection of Internet connection and information access tools. The Internet is the world's fastest-growing network, which consists of millions of computers connected worldwide. With its roots in colleges and universities, the Internet is a wealth of information, and a formidable challenge for even experienced "net surfers." But with all the free services, software, and information available, you should rise to the challenge!

Figure 4.5.   *The IBM Internet Connection folder contains tools to help you tame the Internet "monster."*

All Internet users must register with a service provider, who will provide an Internet-access telephone number, a registered ID (with password), and an Internet address for you. Use the *IBM Internet Dialer* to gain access to your service provider. First-time users will have the opportunity to register with the IBM Internet Connection Services.

You should read the *READ ME FIRST* and *Introduction to the IBM Internet Connection* objects before starting your first Internet connection.

The OS/2 Warp Survival Guide

There are also several great Internet books available in your local bookstore. We recommend that you refer to one of them for a better source of information about using the Internet.

Introduction to the IBM Internet Connection

This object is an electronic book, much like the books provided in the Information folder. You might save yourself some time and aggravation by reading the information provided in this "book."

IBM Internet Dialer

If you want to use the IBM Internet Connection Services, this is the tool you use to physically connect to the Internet. This *Dialer* program has been programmed and configured appropriately for the IBM Internet Connection. If you don't want to use the IBM service, use the *Dial Other Internet Providers* dialer (found in the Internet Utilities folder).

The first time you start this program, you're prompted to register with the IBM service provider. During the registration process (which will ask you for a credit card number) you'll be prompted to select from a list of local-access telephone numbers. Select a number within your local calling area (if available).

Each time you subsequently start this dialer, you'll be prompted to register (until you click on the *Already Registered* button) and the Dialer will dial your local access number.

The following figure shows the Dialer's connection management window and the Internet Logon screen.

The OS/2 Warp BonusPak

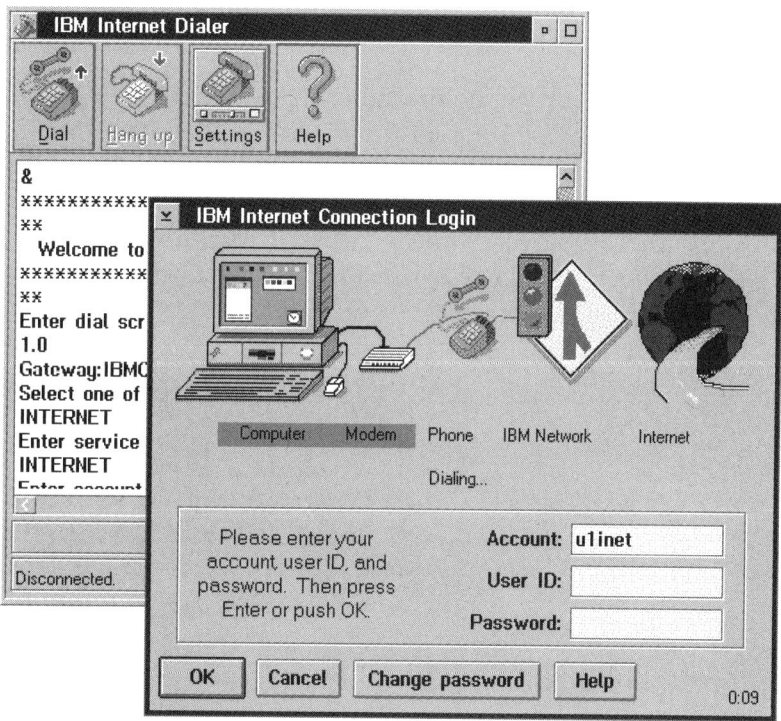

Figure 4.6.   *The IBM Internet Dialer is configured to automatically dial the IBM Internet Connection Services' access number.*

Click on the *Dial* button and watch for the status of your connection. Once your Internet connection is established, you can use the other tools in the *IBM Internet Connection for OS/2* folder to perform specific tasks on the Internet. For example, if you want to go exploring, open *Gopher*. If you want to read news items, open *NewsReader/2*. If you want to read or send e-mail open *Ultimedia Mail/2*.

When you're finished using the Internet, click on the *Hang Up* button in the Dialer's connection management window.

Retrieve Software Updates

This might be the first Internet tool you'll want to use. You can use it to get *free* software. It accesses a list of available packages from which you can select. This list is frequently updated, so you're likely to find new packages every time you use it. When you open this object, you'll see a window similar to the one shown in the following figure.

Figure 4.7. Use the software retrieval tool to download free packages and software updates.

When you select a package and click on the *Install* button, the system will automatically download and install the package on your computer.

If you didn't get it with your BonusPak, one of the first packages you'll want to retrieve is the *WebExplorer*. This will be one of the most useful pieces of software you'll use on the Internet for serious surfing.

 You've really got to hand it to IBM. OS/2 Warp must be the first operating system that gives the tools and services to automatically upgrade your software, virtually for free!

4

The OS/2 Warp BonusPak

Gopher

The *Gopher* is an inter-computer, hypertext interface to the Internet that helps you find, view, and transfer information contained on any of the millions of computers connected to the Internet. This is the easiest tool for exploring the net. After establishing your Internet connection (with one of the *dialers*), double-click on the gopher. You'll get a window similar to the one shown in the following figure.

Figure 4.8.   *The Gopher is your friendly Internet companion. He'll help you get to all the resources available on the Internet.*

Probably named after his real-life counterpart—the office "go-fer," whose job is to "go fer" this and "go fer" that—the Gopher will search for and retrieve information and programs. There are many other gophers available on the Internet, most of which have very specific "go-ferring" jobs. You can even use Gopher to find other gophers.

Notice the different types of items listed in our example above. When you double-click on an item, you launch the action that's appropriate for the item. For example:

 When you double-click on a document, that document opens, allowing you to view its contents. You can use the *File* menu to save or print the document on your computer.

 When you double-click on a gopher item, you're instantly taken to that gopher's server machine (perhaps in Hong Kong) to view the resources available there.

 When you click on these items you launch a search program that's usually dedicated to searching a specific information repository.

 When you click on a program item (a binary file) you're prompted as to where you want to save the file on your computer.

You'll encounter other objects as well. When in doubt, double-click! These objects also support the right-button click to display a context menu, which offers you the options that are appropriate for that object.

WebExplorer

The *WebExplorer* comes in the BonusPak when you buy OS/2 Warp with WIN-OS/2. If you didn't get the WebExplorer, use the *Retrieve Software Updates* tool to retrieve it from the Internet. Once you connect, using one of the dialers, you can access *Web Pages* all over the world. When you open the WebExplorer, you're presented with the window shown in the following figure.

4

The OS/2 Warp BonusPak

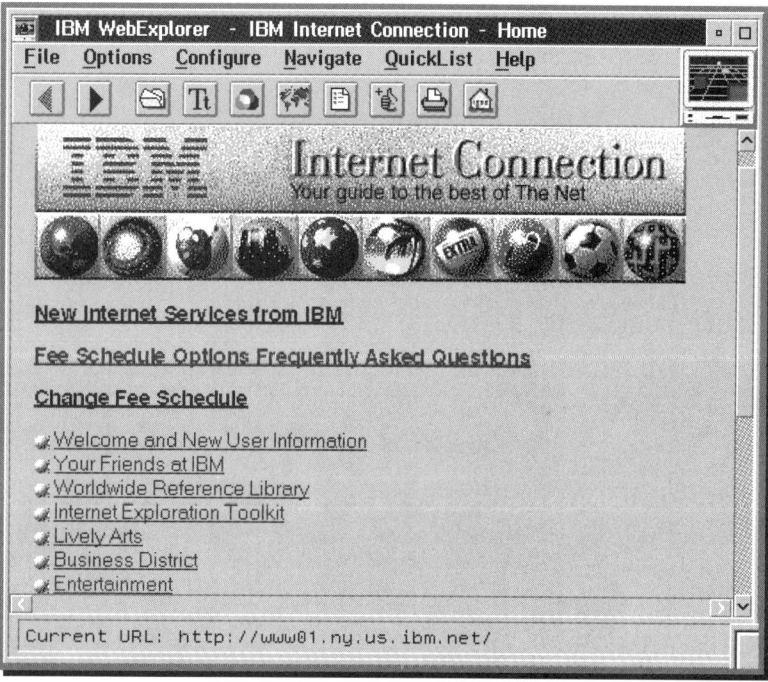

Figure 4.9. *The WebExplorer allows you to "surf the net" with a graphical user interface.*

Don't be afraid to get wet. Anyone can surf the net like a pro with this easy-to-use web page browser. More and more people on the net are providing web pages—some with sound. With WebExplorer you can experience these multimedia web pages if you have a multimedia computer and have installed the *Multimedia Viewer* with support for AU/SND sound files (which comes with the BonusPak).

NewsReader/2

The NewsReader/2 is a special-purpose Internet utility that lets you access USENET news groups. Using NewsReader/2, you can read and reply to open discussions on special-interest topics. The following figure illustrates a typical NewsReader/2 session, showing how you simply point-and-click in a series of windows to display items of interest to you.

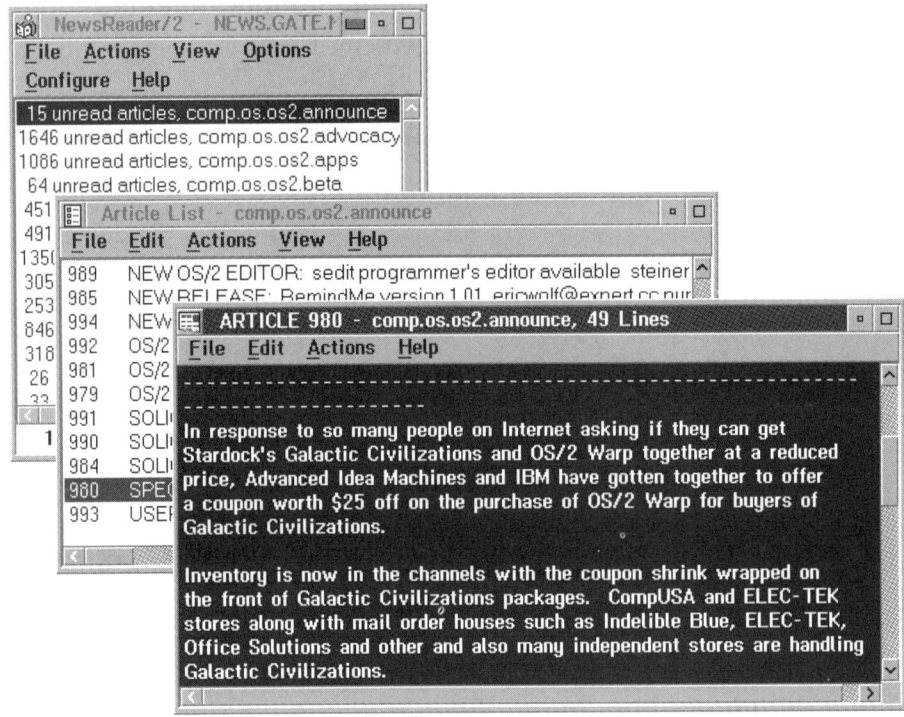

Figure 4.10.   Point-and-click your way to USENET news groups around the world with NewsReader/2.

Ultimedia Mail/2 "Lite"

Even though this isn't the full-blown version of the product, the Ultimedia Mail/2 folder contains all you'll need to create, send, and receive electronic mail (e-mail). As shown in the following figure, you get an In-basket, a Mail Cabinet, an Address Book, and a Mail Processor.

The OS/2 Warp BonusPak

Figure 4.11. With everything you get in the Ultimedia Mail/2 "Lite" folder, you may not need the full-blown version of this product.

Use the *In-basket* to read your incoming e-mail. Use the *Mail Cabinet* to manage the storage and retrieval of your e-mail. You can use the *Names and Addresses* object to automatically provide addressing information for your outgoing e-mail. And the *New Letter* object lets you create, print, and send outgoing e-mail like a pro.

Figure 4.12 shows an Ultimedia Mail/2 session in which a new letter has been created, with an attached image object, in response to a letter that was in the user's In-basket.

The OS/2 Warp Survival Guide

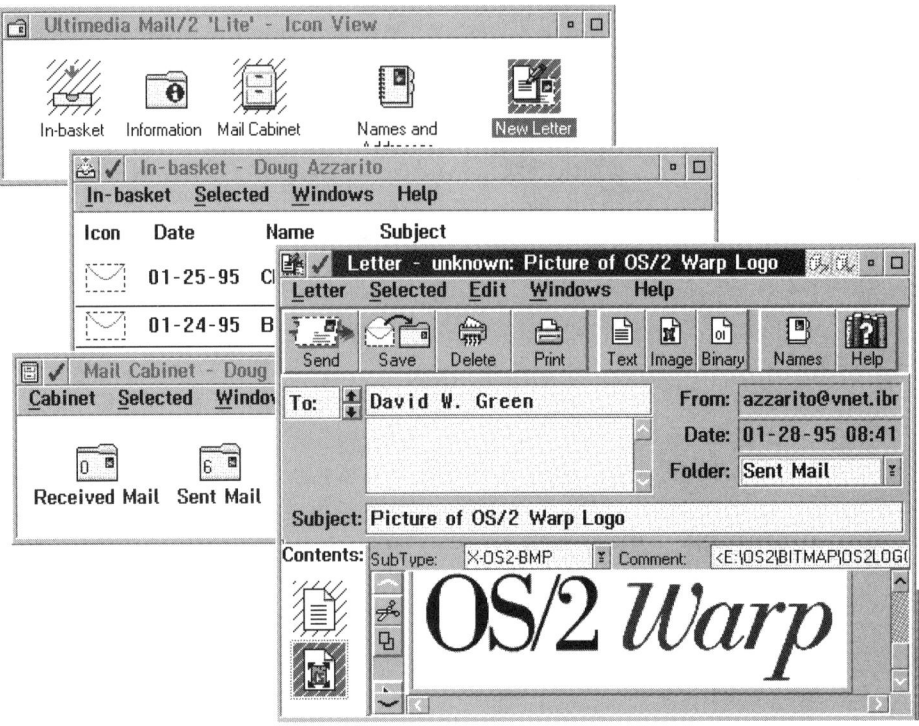

Figure 4.12. *You can use Ultimedia Mail/2 "Lite" to attach anything, including multimedia objects, to your e-mail.*

Ultimedia Mail/2 not only lets you send and receive e-mail, it also lets you attach objects such as data files, programs, documents, and multimedia objects (images, videos, and sound) to your outgoing e-mail.

Internet Utilities

This folder contains some special-purpose utility programs to help you connect to other Internet service providers and retrieve, distribute, and share information with other on-line computer users. When you open the Internet Utilities folder, a window similar to the one shown in the following figure appears.

4

The OS/2 Warp BonusPak

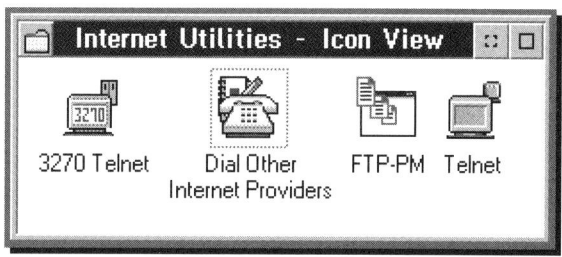

Figure 4.13. The Internet Utilities folder is where you'll find the generic Internet dialer, Telnet-PM, and FTP-PM.

3270 Telnet

This program lets you connect directly to other computers over a modem, using the 3270 Telnet protocol. It's used for communicating with mainframe computers that support 3270 type terminals. If you don't know what 3270 is, you won't need this.

Dial Other Internet Providers

If you opt not to register with the IBM Internet Connection Services, you can use this dialer program to access other service providers. Of course, you must be registered with a service provider and have configured this dialer to access the appropriate telephone number. When you double-click on this icon, the window shown below in the following figure appears.

The OS/2 Warp Survival Guide

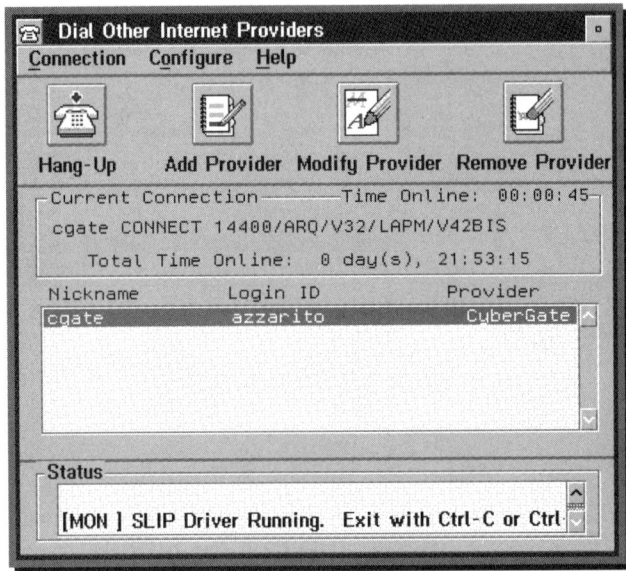

Figure 4.14. *This dialer can be configured to automatically dial your Internet service provider.*

To configure this dialer, click on the *Add Provider* button. You'll be greeted with a multipage settings notebook that will thoroughly confuse you. Make sure your Internet service provider can tell you exactly how to fill in the information requested in the settings notebook. You'll need to provide information such as:

- the provider's access number,
- the subnet mask, and
- the names of the provider's default servers.

FTP-PM

FTP-PM stands for File Transfer Protocol-Presentation Manager. This program lets you connect directly to other computers and transfer files using the FTP protocol. FTP has long been the file transfer method of choice for thousands of Internet power users. With FTP, you can virtually share storage resources with other FTP sites (any computer on the

4

The OS/2 Warp BonusPak

Internet with FTP capability) as if their hard disk drives were physically located in your computer!

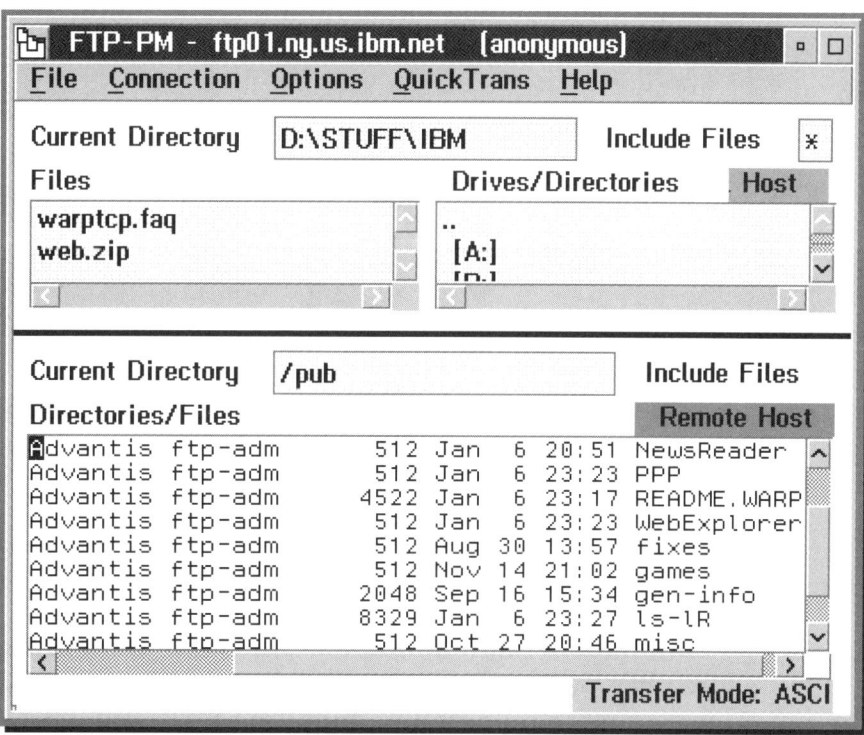

Figure 4.15.   *FTP-PM allows you to transfer files between your computer and other computers on the Internet.*

Telnet

This program lets you log onto another computer on the Internet. If you have access to a remote computer, you can use Telnet to connect to that computer and you'll see a command session (a DOS session, an OS/2 session, or even a UNIX session, depending on what operating system is running on the remote computer).

The OS/2 Warp Survival Guide

IBM Internet Customer Service

Use the objects in this folder to find out how to call IBM's Internet Customer Service group, and to register with the IBM Internet Connection Services. When you open this folder, the window shown in the following figure appears.

Figure 4.16.   *Use the Internet Customer Services folder to call for help or to register*

If you haven't already registered with the IBM Internet Connection Services (through the IBM Internet Dialer) you can do so with the *Registration* object. The actual service provider is *Advantis*. IBM contracted with them because they offer local access in almost every city in the country, and three free hours for every OS/2 Warp user. However, if you don't travel a lot, you might be able to find a better rate through a local service provider.

Customer Assistance

When you open the Customer Assistance object, the system displays the window shown in the following figure. This window actually gives you access to the Internet registration and account-management services, as well as the customer assistance phone numbers.

4

The OS/2 Warp BonusPak

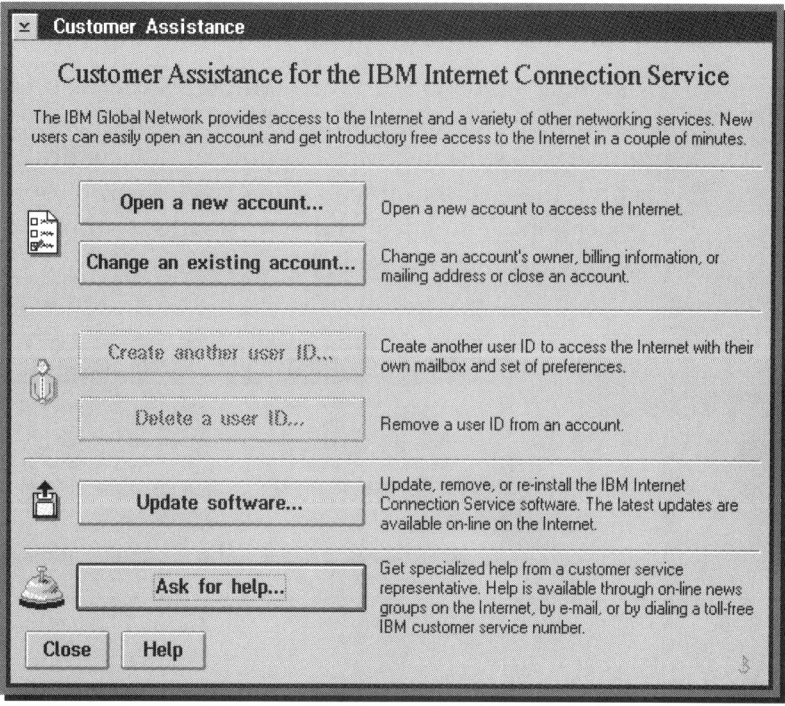

Figure 4.17.   Use the Customer Assistance window to access Internet account-management tools, or to get help.

If you need help, click on the *Ask for help...* button. You'll be presented with a list of telephone numbers for various types of assistance. Use these numbers when you need to speak to a human being.

Registration

Use the Registration object any time to register for the IBM Internet Connection Services. This is the same procedure you're presented with when you open the IBM Internet Dialer object. When you open the Registration object, you're presented with a registration form that will ask you for a credit card number.

161

The OS/2 Warp Survival Guide

Application Templates

This folder holds OS/2 Warp templates that you can use to create specific 3270 Telnet, FTP-PM, and Telnet communications sessions, each capable of automatically connecting to a different computer. When you open the Application Templates folder, a window similar to the one shown in the following figure appears.

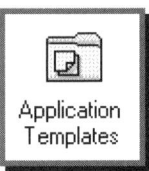

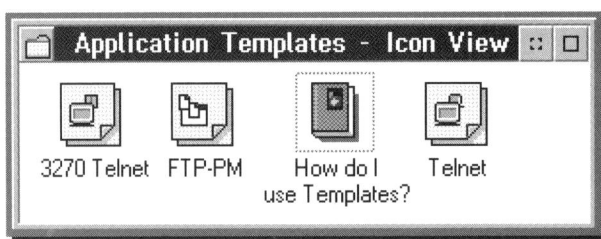

Figure 4.18. Use the Application Templates to create custom communications sessions.

The Telnet templates allow you to set up sessions in which you want to log onto other computers connected to the Internet, where you can access files as if they were in your own computer. The FTP-PM template allows you to use FTP (the File Transfer Protocol) on the Internet, which gives you direct file-manipulation abilities with other computers (if they have granted you permission to do so). For example, with FTP you can copy a file from your computer directly to another computer's disk drive, almost as if you were copying a file from your diskette drive to your hard disk.

4

The OS/2 Warp BonusPak

IBM Works and the Personal Information Manager

The next major bonus in the BonusPak is IBM Works and the Personal Information Manager (PIM). These 32-bit OS/2 applications provide your virtual desktop with a complement of object-oriented tools. As you'll see, these tools offer a high degree of integration. When you open the IBM Works folder, a window similar to the one shown in the following figure appears.

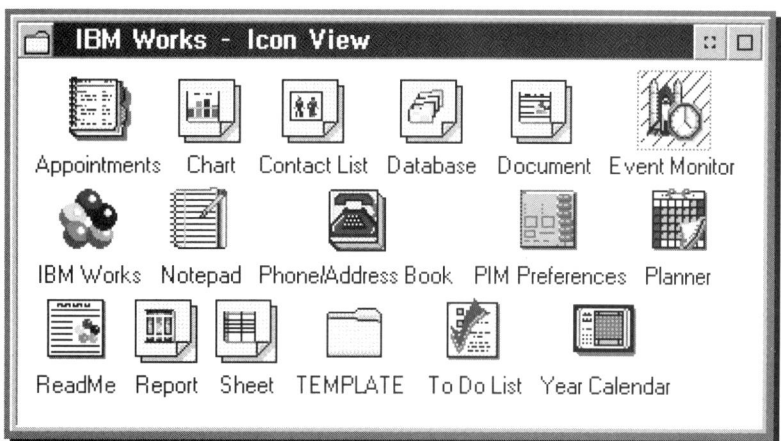

Figure 4.19. *The IBM Works folder contains both the IBM Works and PIM applications.*

Personal Information Manager is a suite of integrated, activity-management applications that are spread throughout the folder. The following objects are considered to comprise the PIM:

- Appointments
- Planner
- Phone/Address Book
- To-Do List
- Event Monitor
- Year Calendar
- Contact List
- Notepad

163

You might be wondering "What are integrated applications?" In simpler terms, these are separate programs that know how to share related information. In this case, the PIM applications all deal with personal information and activity management. Where appropriate, these applications can share information, and you can even use drag-and-drop techniques to copy data between applications. In theory, this should let you efficiently manage your activities without redundant data entry.

For example, you can drag contact names from the *Phone/Address Book* or the *Contact List* and drop them in the *Appointments* book or *Planner* to create an appointment with that person.

Appointments

The first (and probably most important) personal activity-management tool you should know about is the *Appointments* book. This is where you'll "micro-manage" your daily appointments and activities. As you enter activities, you're automatically updating a database that the *Planner*, *Event Monitor*, and *To-Do List* applications can share.

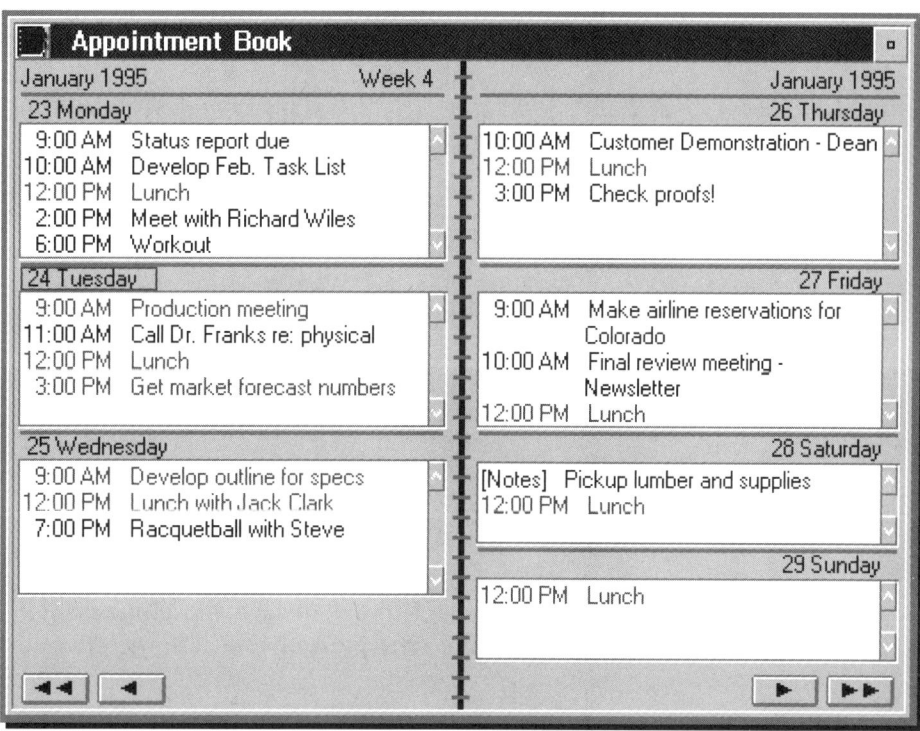

Figure 4.20. *The Appointments application has the appearance of a typical, spiral-bound appointment book.*

This electronic appointment book is also integrated with the *Contacts List* in that you can drag a contact name to a date in the appointment book, and drop it to schedule an appointment on that day with that contact. A meeting is automatically set up with the contact (at the default appointment time of 9:00 A.M.) and his or her name and phone number become the title of the appointment.

The more conventional way to add an activity is to double-click on a blank area in the appointment book for the day you want. You'll see a dialog box that allows you to enter details for the appointment (as shown in the following figure). To change or view the details of an existing appointment, double-click on that appointment. This same dialog box will appear.

The OS/2 Warp Survival Guide

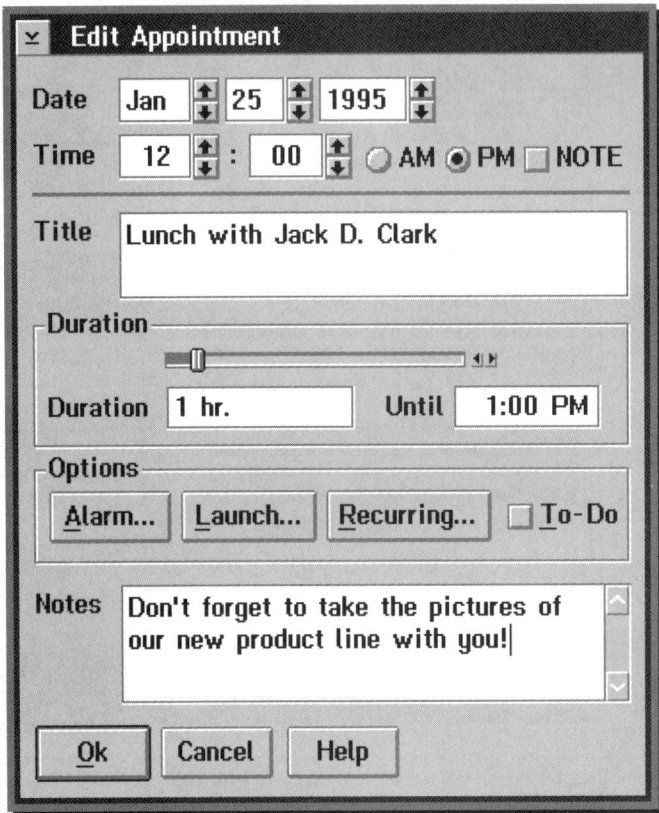

Figure 4.21. *All details for a specific appointment are entered, viewed, and changed in the New/Edit Appointment dialog box.*

Most of the fields and controls in the this dialog box are obvious. Of special note are the *To-Do*, *Alarm*, *Launch*, and *Recurring* features. When you click on the *To-Do* check box, this appointment is automatically added to the To-Do List. Alarms, Launches, and Recurring events are a bit more involved.

 Now's probably a good time to point out that the PIM application windows don't have menu bars! They're not really necessary. In this book, we'll describe the object-oriented procedures for performing certain tasks. If you prefer to use menus, you can perform most procedures (such as add, update, print, etc.) through the context menus for each PIM application.

Alarm...

If you want the computer to get your attention when the time for a scheduled appointment arrives (or is approaching), use the *Alarm* feature. When you click on the *Alarm...* button in the New/Edit Appointment dialog box, the dialog box shown in the following figure appears.

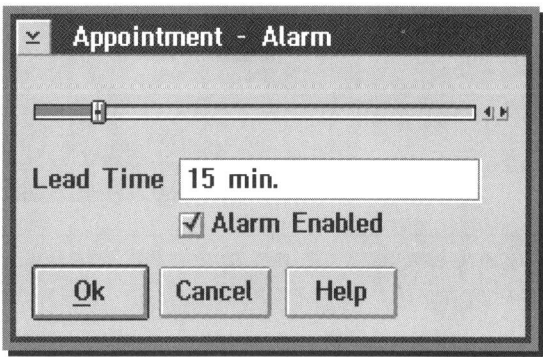

Figure 4.22. *The Appointment Alarm dialog box lets you enable/disable alarms and set the lead time for the appointment's alarm.*

Drag the slider to set the desired lead time for the alarm (the amount of time before the scheduled event in which you want the alarm to sound). When the alarm time arrives (appointment time minus the lead time) the system sounds an alarm (through the PC speaker or using a multimedia audio player) and displays an Appointment Alarm window, which contains the title of the appointment. You can clear the alarm by clicking on the OK button, or delay the alarm with the Snooze button (just like a real alarm clock).

Launch...

If you want the computer to launch (load and start running) a program when the time for a scheduled appointment arrives, use the *Launch* feature. When you click on the *Launch...* button in the New/Edit Appointment dialog box, the dialog box shown in the following figure appears.

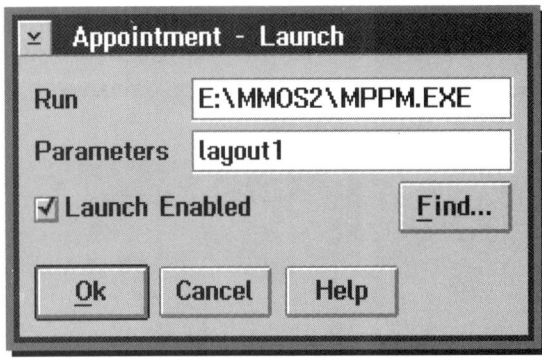

Figure 4.23. *The Appointment Launch dialog box lets you enable/disable the launch feature and specify the program to launch for the appointment.*

In the *Run* field, enter the drive, path, and file name of the program you want the system to launch when the appointment time arrives. If you're not sure of the location and/or file name of the program, use the *Find* button to search for the file. You can optionally enter Parameters that will be "passed" to the program when it starts.

For example, if you wanted to begin updating a report named "STATUS.DOC" that you maintain with WordPerfect, you might enter `C:\WP\WP.COM` in the *Run* field and `C:\WP\STATUS.DOC` in the *Parameters* field. This would cause the system to automatically start WordPerfect and have it open your status report document when the appointment time arrives.

If you're not sure where to begin looking for the file name of the program you want to launch, try using the *Program* or *File* tab in the Settings notebook of the program object to find out its drive, path, and *real* file name. See Chapter 5, "Customizing OS/2 Warp," for more about Settings.

The OS/2 Warp BonusPak

Recurring...

If you have appointments that re-occur on a daily, weekly, monthly, or even yearly basis, you'll want to use the *Recurring* feature for those appointments. When you click on the *Recurring...* button in the New/Edit Appointments dialog box, the window shown in the following figure appears.

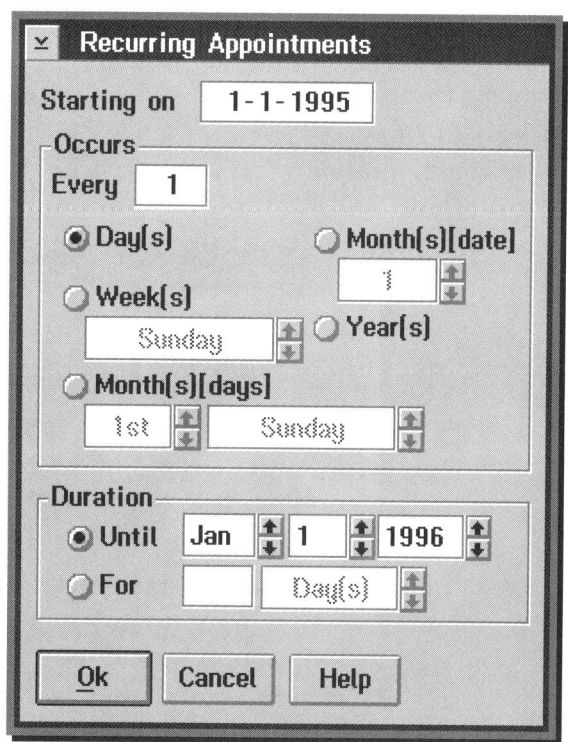

Figure 4.24. The Recurring Appointments dialog box lets you set up regularly scheduled appointments.

This feature is great for events such as lunch (daily), the bowling league (weekly), paying your bills (monthly), and birthdays (yearly).

Event Monitor

The Event Monitor is not really an application in that it has no user interface. It is automatically loaded by OS/2 whenever there are alarms or launch events scheduled in your appointment book. When you set an alarm, or launch an event for an appointment, the Event Monitor is responsible for "watching the clock" and triggering those events at the specified time.

The Event Monitor is also responsible for reminding you when alarms for events in the past have not yet been cleared, and when items on a To-Do List are overdue. Every time you open a PIM application in those situations, the Event Monitor displays the window shown in the following figure, allowing you to specify the disposition of those events.

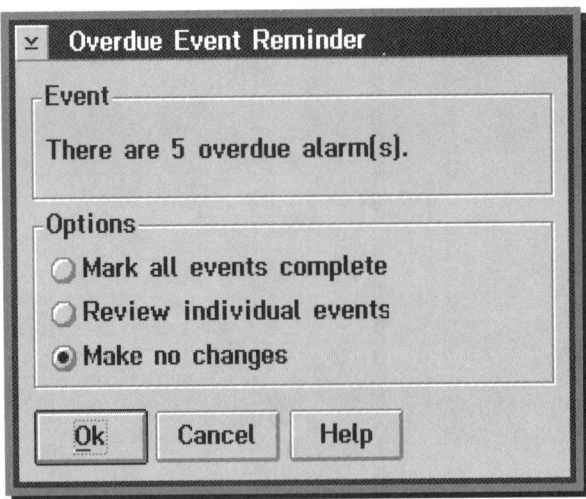

Figure 4.25.   *The Overdue Event Reminder can become a nuisance if you get in the habit of not clearing alarms and marking To-Do List items as completed.*

Normally, you would clear alarms and mark To-Do List items as being completed as they occur. But don't worry; if you forget, the system will keep reminding you. You can clear all overdue events at once or review and clear individual events from the Overdue Event Reminder window.

Of course, the Event Monitor must be loaded and running so it has an opportunity to "watch the clock" and trigger alarms and launch events. Something to keep in mind in case you find yourself searching for a way to close this object.

Planner

The Planner is an application that helps you manage your activities on a monthly basis. The Planner shares the data that you enter through the appointment book. You cannot directly modify activities with the Planner; it simply lets you view your appointments in a month-at-a-glance format.

When you open the Planner, a window similar to the one shown in the following figure appears.

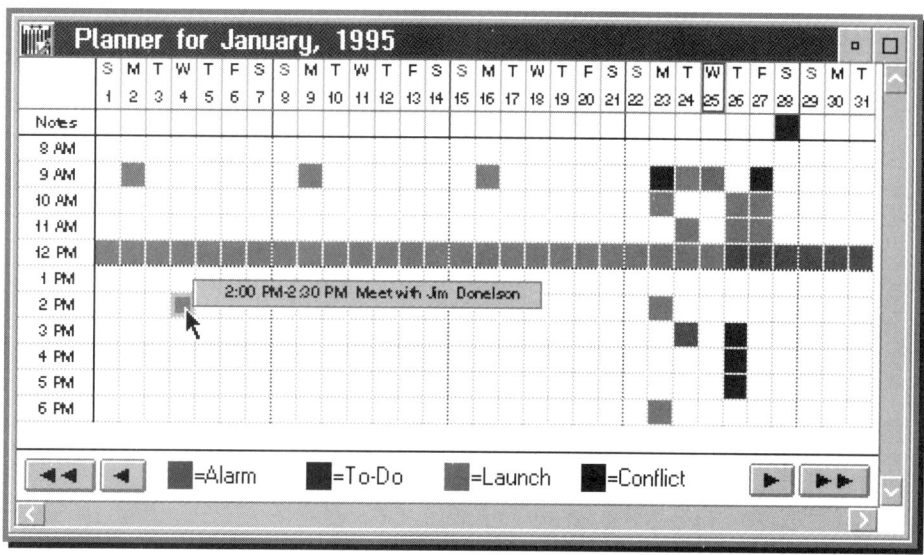

Figure 4.26.   *The Planner gives you a broader view of the days that have scheduled activities.*

Cells with appointments are color-coded to remind you of the type of event each one is. Gray cells are appointments in the past. Red cells are appointments with alarms. Blue cells are items that are also on a To-Do List. Green cells are appointments with launch events. Black cells are cells whose start/end times conflict.

Although you *cannot* reschedule appointments in the Planner using direct drag-and-drop techniques (as advertised and expected) you can see the time, duration, and title of an appointment by clicking the left mouse button on the appointment's cell.

You can also add new appointments through the New/Edit Appointment dialog box by double-clicking the left mouse button while pointing to an empty cell on the Planner. However, you *cannot* edit an existing appointment by double-clicking on the appointment's cell (again as advertised and expected).

The Planner does demonstrate its object-orientedness by allowing you to drag-and-drop a contact from the Phone/Address Book and/or Contacts List to any cell on the Planner.

Year Calendar

The Year Calendar serves two functions: It shows you the entire year (current, past, or future) in a single window, and it provides direct access to the *To-Do List*. When you open the Year Calendar object, a window similar to the one shown in the following figure appears.

4

The OS/2 Warp BonusPak

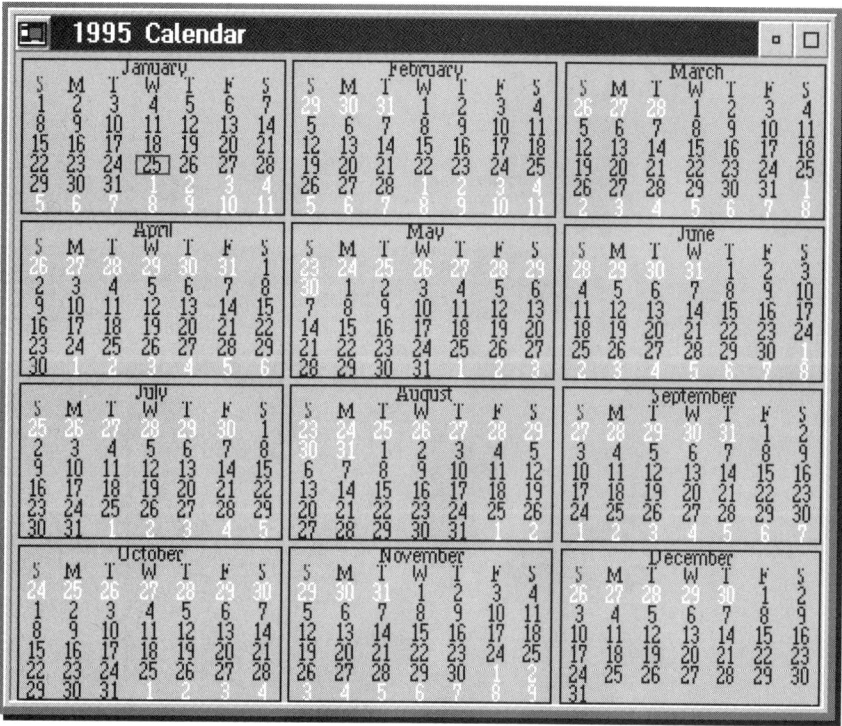

Figure 4.27.   *The Year Calendar lets you access the To-Do List for any day of the year.*

To view the To-Do List for any particular day, double-click on that day with the left mouse button. The To-Do List window will appear, showing you the things you're supposed to do (if any) for that day.

To-Do List

The *To-Do List* provides an easy way for you to keep track of your "things to do." It's integrated with the appointment book in that when you click on the To-Do List check box in the New/Edit Appointment dialog box, that appointment's title is added to the To-Do List for that day.

And, if you edit a To-Do List item (through the To-Do List application) the appointment book is automatically updated.

The OS/2 Warp Survival Guide

When you open the To-Do List object, the To-Do List Launcher appears followed by the To-Do List itself (as shown in the following figure).

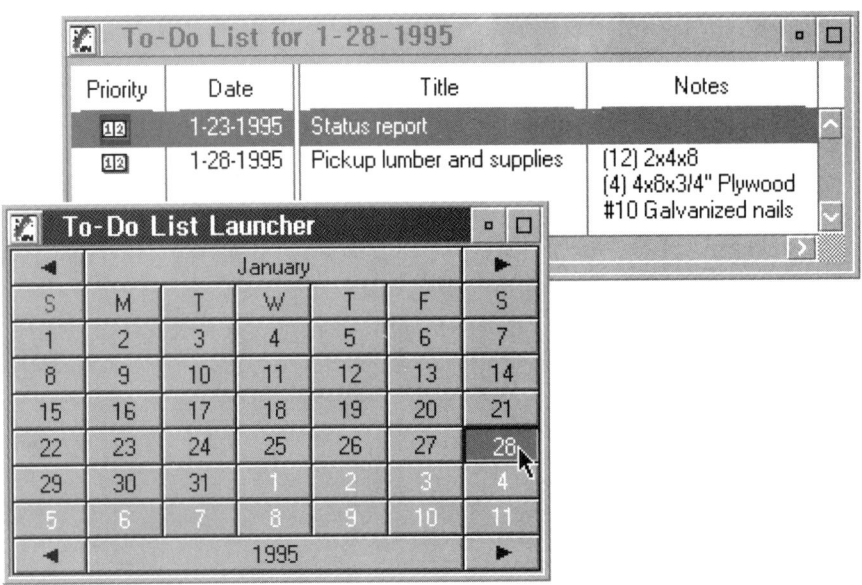

Figure 4.28.   *The To-Do List has a Launcher that lets you directly access the list for a specific date.*

To add an item to a To-Do List through the To-Do List application, click on the desired date in the To-Do List Launcher. Then double-click in a blank area of the list. The To-Do Item Information dialog box will appear (as shown in the following figure). To change or view the details of an existing item, double-click on that item in the To-Do List. This same dialog box will appear.

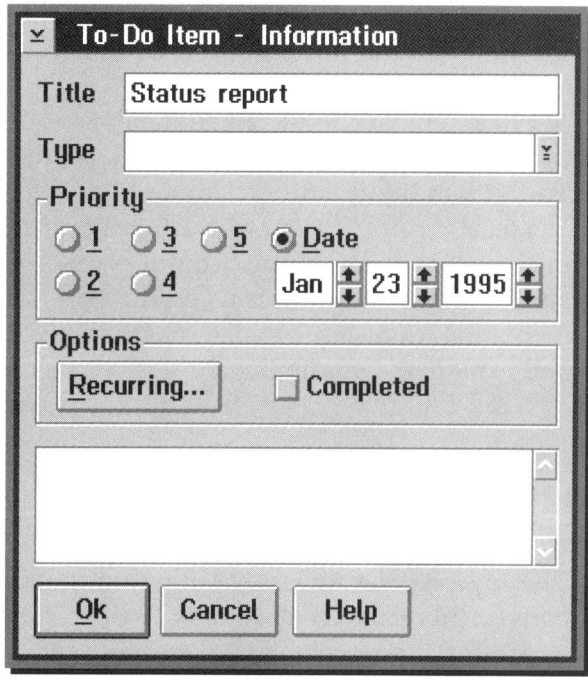

Figure 4.29. Use the To-Do Item Information dialog box to add, view, or change the details of a To-Do List item.

Using this dialog box, you can set/change an item's priority from 1 to 5 (1 being most important) or you can set a due date for the item. The option you select in this portion of the dialog box is reflected on the To-Do List (in the Priority column). This column also shows other status information for each item, as follows.

The symbols ❶ through ❺ appear, indicating the item's priority.

The 🗓 symbol appears for items that have a due date set.

The 🗓 symbol appears for overdue items (not marked as completed).

The symbols 🗵 and 🗙 appear for items that have been completed.

The OS/2 Warp Survival Guide

If you have items that you must do on a regularly scheduled basis, use the *Recurring* feature. It works much like the Recurring feature for appointment book entries.

When you've completed an item on a To-Do List, display the list and double-click on the item. Then click on the *Completed* check box in the To-Do Item Information dialog box.

You can print To-Do Lists using their context menus, or by using the drag-and-drop technique. You also can sort tasks by priority or type, and change other choices using the options on the To-Do List's context menu. Just right-button click on the To-Do List or on an item in the list, and explore the possibilities.

Address/Phone Book

The *Address/Phone Book* application gives you a convenient place to store and retrieve the names, addresses, and phone numbers (as well as other important information) for the people in your life. It also supports automatic *Dialing* and a *Log Book* feature that helps you manage your phone calls like a professional.

Although this application is primarily dedicated to managing phone numbers and phone calls, it is integrated with the other PIM applications. You can drag-and-drop or cut-and-paste (with *paste-links* if desired) from this application to all the other PIM applications. You can also launch the *Appointments* and *To-Do List* applications during a phone call to take information about the current call to those applications. When you launch the *Phone/Address Book*, the Phone Book window appears (as shown in the following figure).

The OS/2 Warp BonusPak

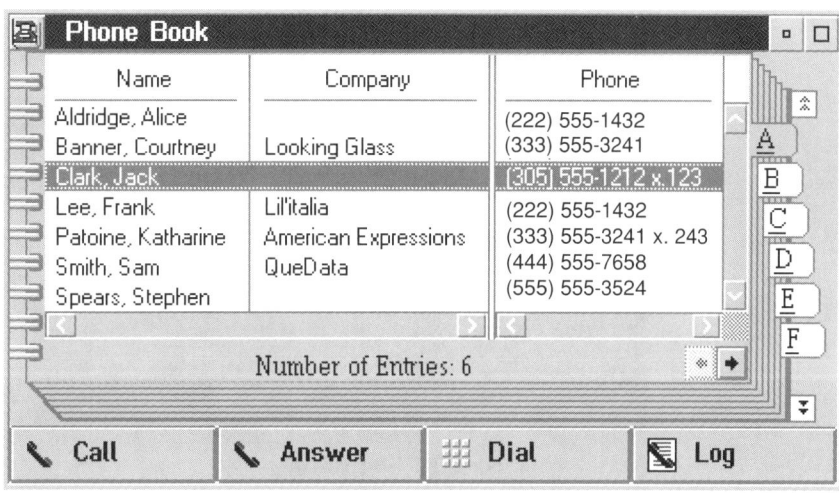

Figure 4.30.   *The Phone Book is set up like a spiral-bound, electronic rolodex with automated dialing and call logging capabilities.*

In the Phone Book, as with the other PIM applications, you can add by double-clicking on a blank area of the list, or by using the *Create another* option on the context menu.

To view or modify existing records, double-click on the entry in the list. The Phone Book's Personal Profile notebook will appear, as shown in the following figure, allowing you to add, view, or modify Phone Book records.

The OS/2 Warp Survival Guide

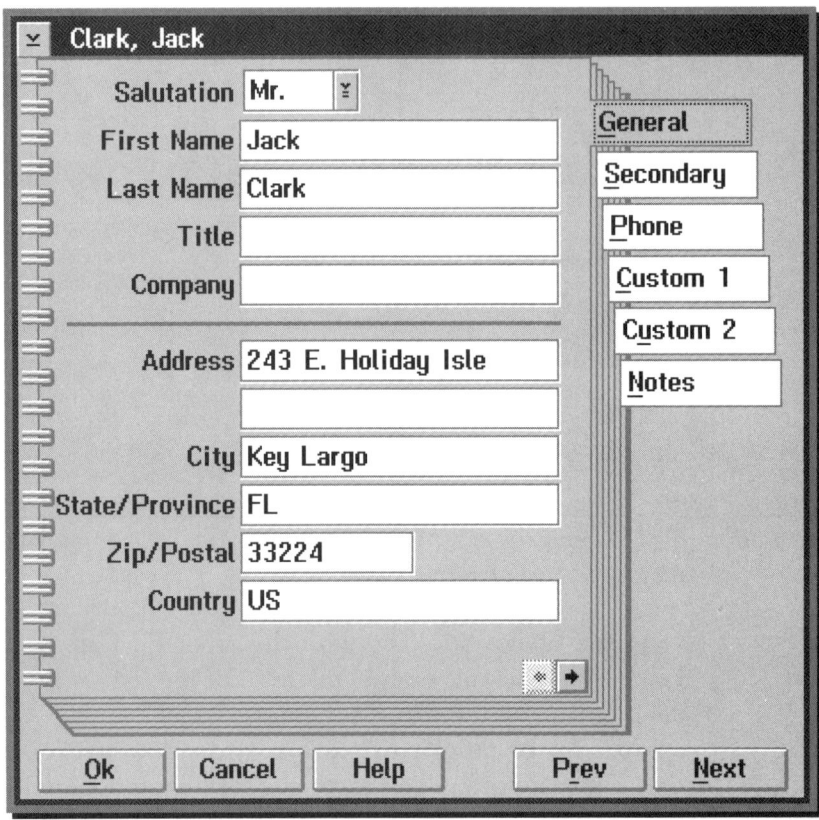

Figure 4.31.   *Use the Phone Book's Personal Profile notebook to add, view, or update entries.*

The index tabs in this notebook-style window let you enter a detailed name, two addresses, and up to eleven phone numbers (for everything from business and home numbers to FAX, cellular, and pager numbers). The minimum information you must enter for a Phone Book record, is a name (use the *General* tab) and a phone number (use the *Phone* tab).

This notebook provides two *Custom* tabs, allowing you to design and store specialized information for each contact. And the *Notes* tab gives you a place to store notations about the contact.

When you have your contact names and phone numbers entered, you must select an entry when you want to perform a Phone Book function on it. To retrieve and select an entry, you can type the first letter of the last name, click on the alphabetic tabs, and/or scroll through the list until the entry is displayed. Then click on the entry to select it.

Outgoing Calls

Once you select an entry you can use the *Call* function button at the bottom of the window to automatically dial and keep track of the call. Or you can drag the entry to many of the other PIM applications to begin creating a new Appointment, To-Do List item, or Contact List item.

When you click on the *Call* button, the window shown in the following figure appears, allowing you to correct the number (if required) and enable the modem for automatic dialing.

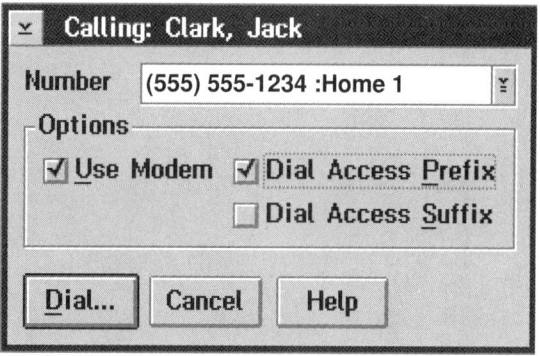

Figure 4.32.   Use the Calling dialog box to enable/disable the modem and activate dialing prefixes and suffixes.

If you want to use the modem, activate the *Use Modem* check box. If the number is long distance or your phone system requires that you dial a number to access an outside line, enable the *Dial Access Prefix* check box. The dialing prefixes and suffixes are stored and maintained in the PIM Preferences notebook. This is also where you configure your modem for the PIM applications.

If you don't want to use the automatic dialer function, clear the *Use Modem* check box. You can still use the call tracking feature even if your computer doesn't dial the number for you. Click on the *Dial* button when you're ready to begin the call. The window shown in the following figure will appear.

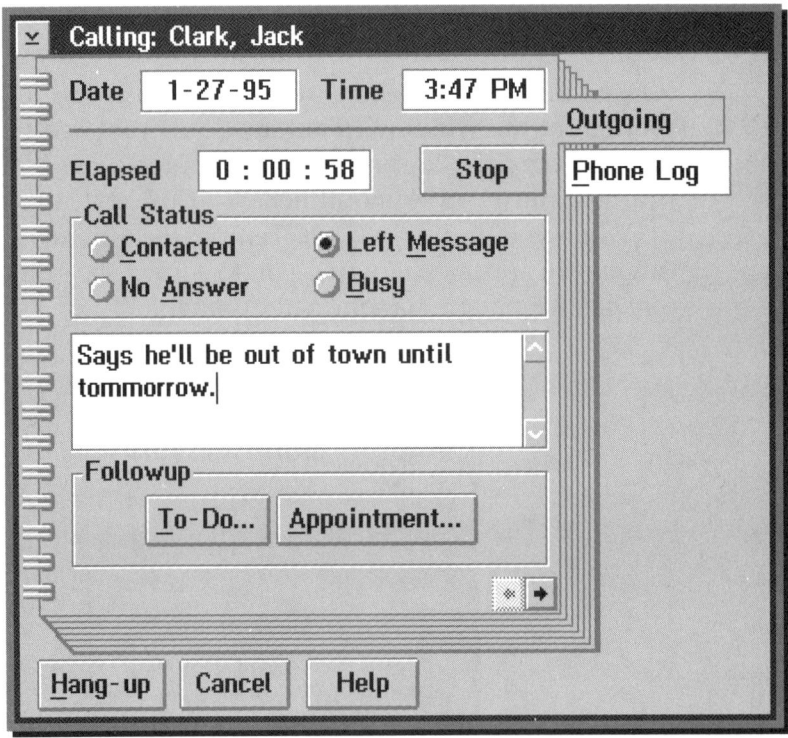

Figure 4.33. *The Calling notebook lets you record date, time, duration, status, and messages for an outgoing call.*

Use the Calling notebook to record all the details you want about the current call. There's a call timer, which you can start and stop on demand, Call Status radio buttons, and an area to jot notes about the call.

Note that you can launch the *To-Do List* and *Appointment* applications to automatically create follow-up events for those programs. While you're making the call, you can use the *Phone Log* tab to look at the details for previous calls made to this contact.

The OS/2 Warp BonusPak

When you're finished with the call, click on the *Hang-up* button. The Phone Log is automatically updated with this outgoing call record.

Incoming Calls

The application works the same way for incoming calls, except that you retrieve the contact name after answering the phone (obviously) either through the Phone Book or a Contact List (we'll discuss this in a minute). You would then click on the *Answer* button in the Phone Book (or Contact List) to automatically start tracking and logging the call.

Phone Dialer

When you click on the *Dial* button in the Phone Book, you'll get the Phone Dialer window, as shown in the following figure.

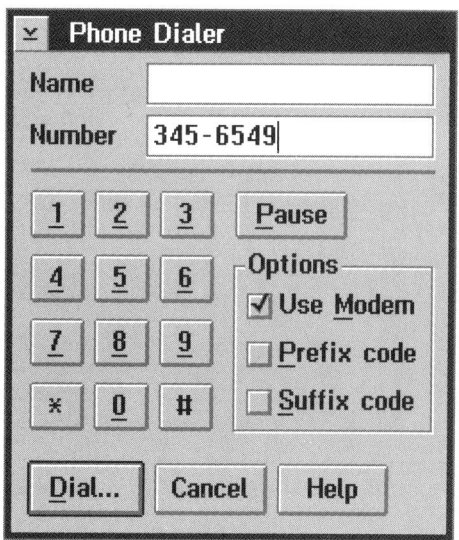

Figure 4.34.   *You can use the Phone Dialer to make spontaneous calls or to impress your friends with your virtual telephone keypad.*

Enter the numbers by typing directly into the Number field, or by clicking on the keypad buttons. Click on the *Dial* button when you're ready to place the call.

Phone Log

The Phone Log is a valuable feature if your phone time is billable, or even if you just want to keep track of who said what, when. When you click on the *Log* button in the Phone Book, the Phone Log appears, as shown in the following figure.

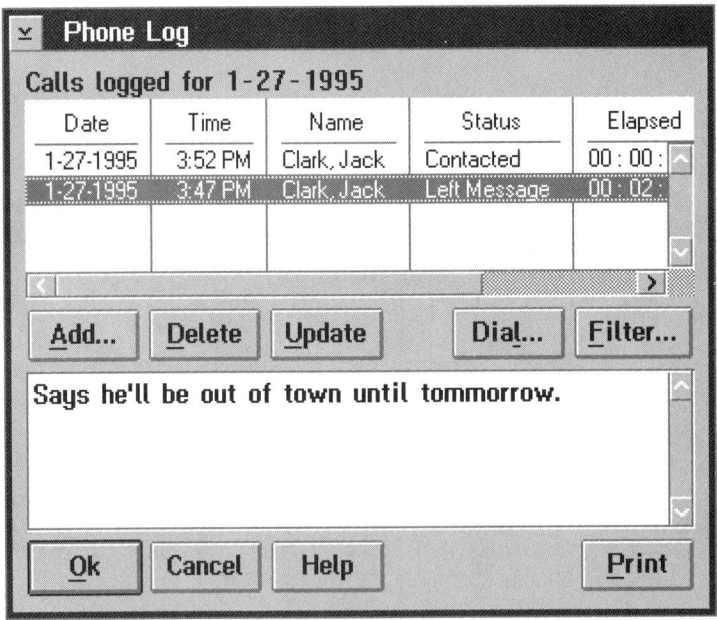

Figure 4.35.   *You'll be amazed at the detailed Phone Log records you get.*

Use the Phone Log to view details of processed calls, or to manually enter calls that you may have made away from your computer. You can also edit existing records. Just click on the *Add...* or *Update* button (as appropriate) to access the Calling notebook window where you can add or modify a record.

4

The OS/2 Warp BonusPak

Contact List

Closely related to the *Address/Phone Book* application, the *Contact List* provides a convenient way for you to create lists of people to call on a given day, for a specific project, or just your most frequently contacted people. Using the drag-and-drop or cut-and-paste techniques, you can place specific contacts on a Contact List. Then you can close the Phone Book and leave just the Contact List on your desktop (which can use much less desktop space).

To create a Contact List, drag the Contact List template object to your desktop. A new Contact List will be created, and a window similar to the one shown in the following figure will appear.

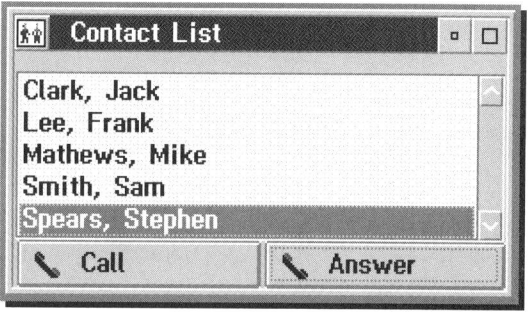

Figure 4.36.   *The Contact List templates give you a convenient way to process your calls.*

To retrieve and select a name on the list, you can type the first letter of the last name and/or scroll through the list until the name is displayed. The *Call* and *Answer* buttons function the same here as they do in the Phone Book. You can also access the Phone Book's profile notebook by double-clicking on a name, where you can view or modify that contact's record.

The Contact List's context menu contains options for printing, launching other PIM applications, etc. And you can drag-and-drop names from the Contact List to the other PIM applications, taking the contact's profile information with you to the new application.

The OS/2 Warp Survival Guide

Notepad

The Notepad is an electronic index that lets you store categories of related information in structured "chapters." You might find it useful for storing things such as "How To" notes to remind yourself how to perform a procedure, or just as a place to store quick, free-form notes. The Notepad is not limited to text; it can hold graphic images as well. You can insert files that are bitmap (*.BMP) or metafile (*.MET) format. When you open the Notepad, a window similar to the one shown in the following figure appears.

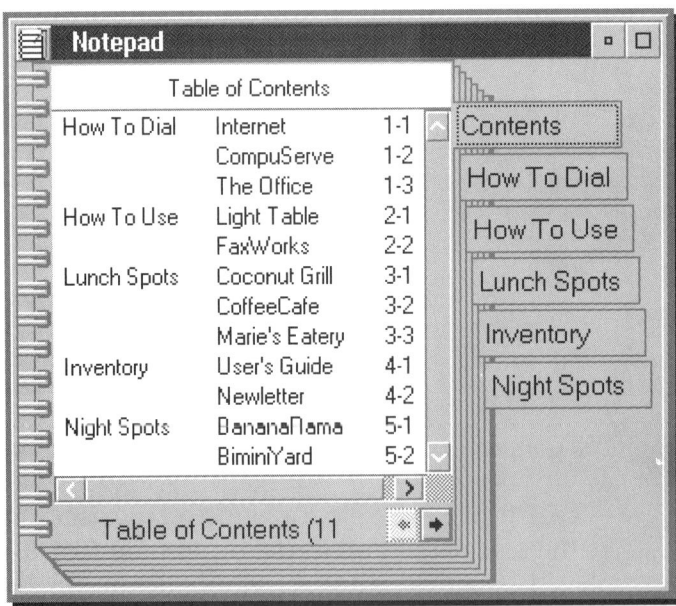

Figure 4.37.   *The Notepad lets you organize notes that might otherwise be fragmented.*

The first page of the Notepad is an automatic table of contents. The first time you see it, it's blank. As you add pages and chapters, the Table of Contents page and index tabs are updated to reflect the new information.

The OS/2 Warp BonusPak

To create a page and/or chapter, double-click anywhere on the Table of Contents page. The dialog box shown in the following figure will appear.

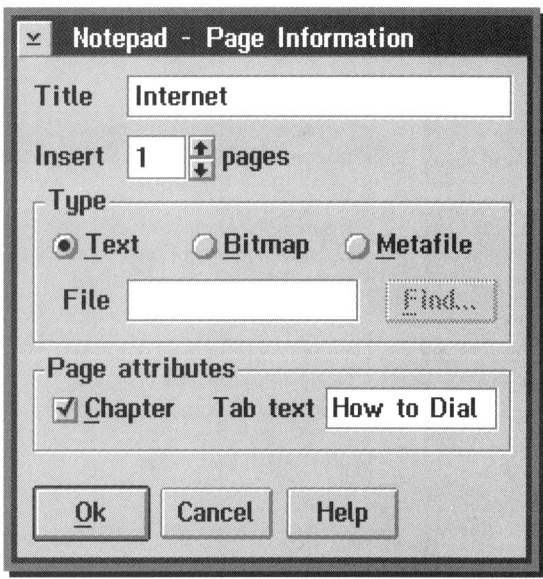

Figure 4.38. Use the Notepad Page Information dialog box to set up chapters and pages within chapters.

In our example, "How to Dial" is the name of the first chapter in the notebook, and "Internet" is the name of the first page in that chapter. Notice in our example how these titles were entered to create the chapter and first topic.

If you want to insert a graphic image on this new page, click on the *Bitmap* or *Metafile* radio button (as appropriate) and enter the drive, path, and name of the graphic file. You can use the *Find* button to help locate your desired graphic file.

 Each page is only capable of holding 4 KBytes of information. For text, that's quite a lot, but graphic files chew up memory quickly. You won't be placing large graphic images on the

The OS/2 Warp Survival Guide

pages of Notepad. If that is your need, try the Light Table (see "Ultimedia Viewer (The Light Table)" later in this chapter).

When you finish setting up the page information, click on *OK* and you'll be returned to the Table of Contents page. Now double-click on the new topic to access its page, as shown in the following figure.

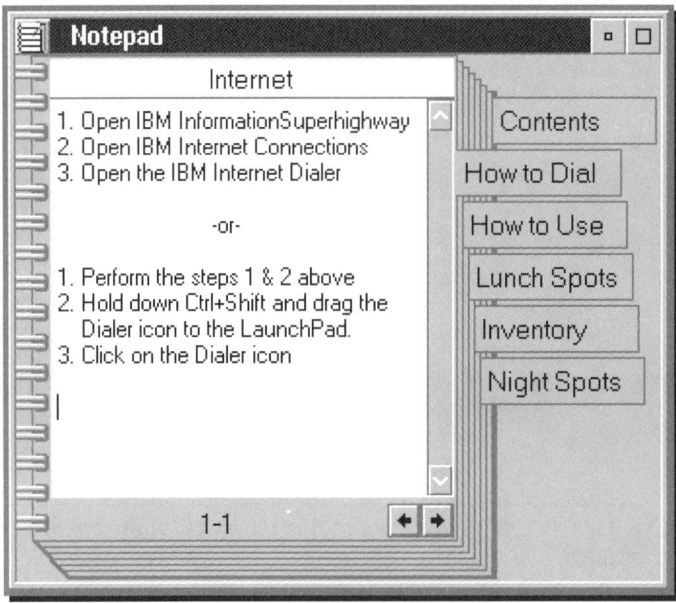

Figure 4.39.   *Access a page in the Notepad by double-clicking directly on its Table of Contents entry.*

Review or add the text you want to store under this title. As with all of the PIM applications, you don't have to perform a "save" operation. The information is automatically saved when you leave the page or close the Notepad.

If you want to reorganize pages in the Notepad, simply use drag-and-drop techniques on the Table of Contents page. And don't forget to explore the Notepad's context menu. That's where you'll find options such as *Search* and *Print*.

4 — The OS/2 Warp BonusPak

> This concludes our tour of the PIM applications. We'll now cover the tools that comprise IBM Works.

IBM Works is a suite of integrated software products that provides you with additional office-automation tools, including: a Word Processor, a Spreadsheet program, a Charting program, a Database manager (with a Forms Designer), and a Report Writer program. As with the PIM  tools, these applications can share information with each other. When you open the IBM Works object (shown here) a menu window appears (as shown in the following figure) allowing you to launch any of these programs.

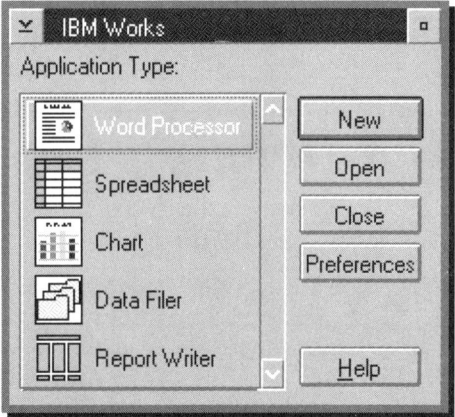

Figure 4.40. The IBM Works menu lets you launch any of the IBM Works applications with a new or existing file.

To start any of the applications, you can simply double-click on its application button. This will start the application with a new data file. Or you can single-click on the application button, and then click on the *New* button if you want a new data file, or click on the *Open* button if you want to work on an existing document.

To set your system preferences (units of measure, etc.) click on the *Preferences* button to access IBM Works' Preferences notebook.

Word Processor

The first offering in the IBM Works software suite is the Word Processor. At first glance, it looks a lot like Word for Windows; but, after using it for  a short time, we're not fooled. Although it's a full-featured word processor with complex tables, mail merge, import filters, support for graphics, and spell checking, its performance seems a bit clumsy at times. The following figure shows the Word Processor.

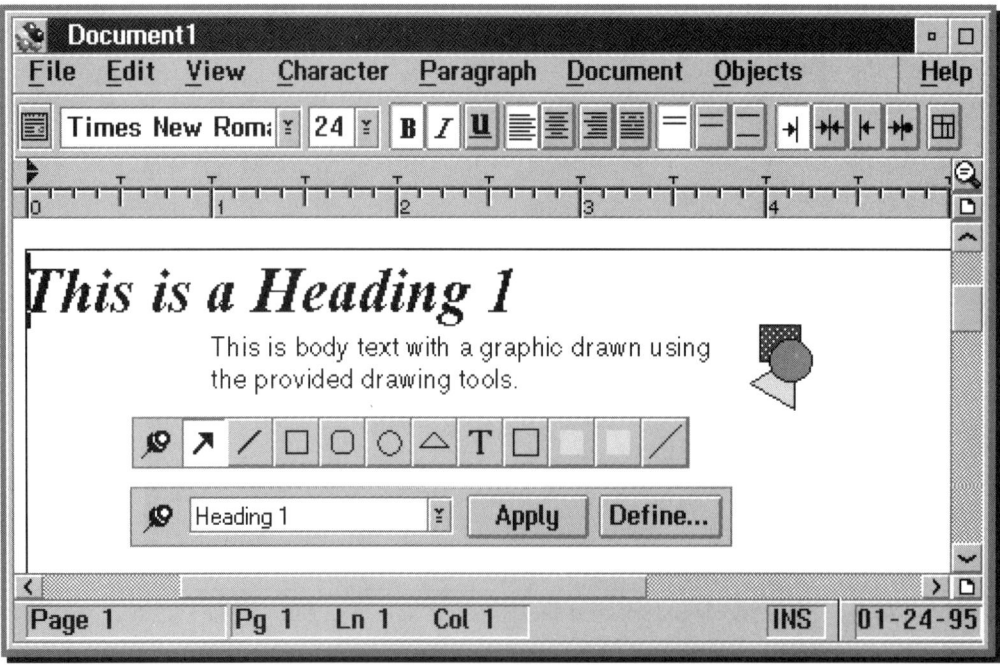

Figure 4.41. *If you cross your eyes slightly when you look at the Word Processor, you'll think you're running Word for Windows 2.0.*

With its named styles, formatting toolbar, a horizontal ruler, and macros, this application does seem to be fashioned after Word 2.0. If you're familiar with that product, you won't have much trouble with the Works Word Processor. You will, however, notice big differences in the location of menu options, and some slight differences in text-selection techniques.

One interesting difference between Word and Works is the use of "pin-up" palettes. You'll find the Drawing palette and the Style palette. These "global" tools are available for all Works applications; they don't belong just to the Word Processor. In fact you can "pin" 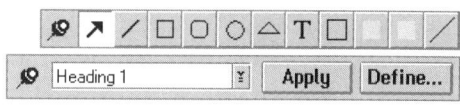 them to the desktop and they'll stay put while you close one application and start another. They also hold their properties (as you define them) between applications. So Heading 1 style is the same everywhere you go. To close a pin-up palette, double-click on its push-pin icon.

The level of integration with the other IBM Works applications is surprisingly good. You can grab data from the Spreadsheet application, and insert charts from the Chart program. And you can design forms and manage databases for mail-merges with the Database application.

Our problems started when we tried to open a small Word for Windows 2.0 document. After a few minutes, we noticed that the pointer was clock-shaped everywhere we moved it, keeping us from doing any other work while we waited. This is an indication that the program might not be multithreaded—a definite "no no" in OS/2 programming.

All in all, we found this to be a useful tool. And it's probably the *best* word processor to ever accompany an operating system, free of charge!

Spreadsheet

The IBM Works Spreadsheet application is far and away superior to the spreadsheet program that was included with OS/2 version 2.1. This  sophisticated application features comprehensive cell formatting, support for complex formulas, import filters for Lotus and Excel, and macros. It is tightly integrated with the Chart program, which can chart your spreadsheets at the "click of a button." When you launch the Spreadsheet, a window similar to the one shown in the following figure appears.

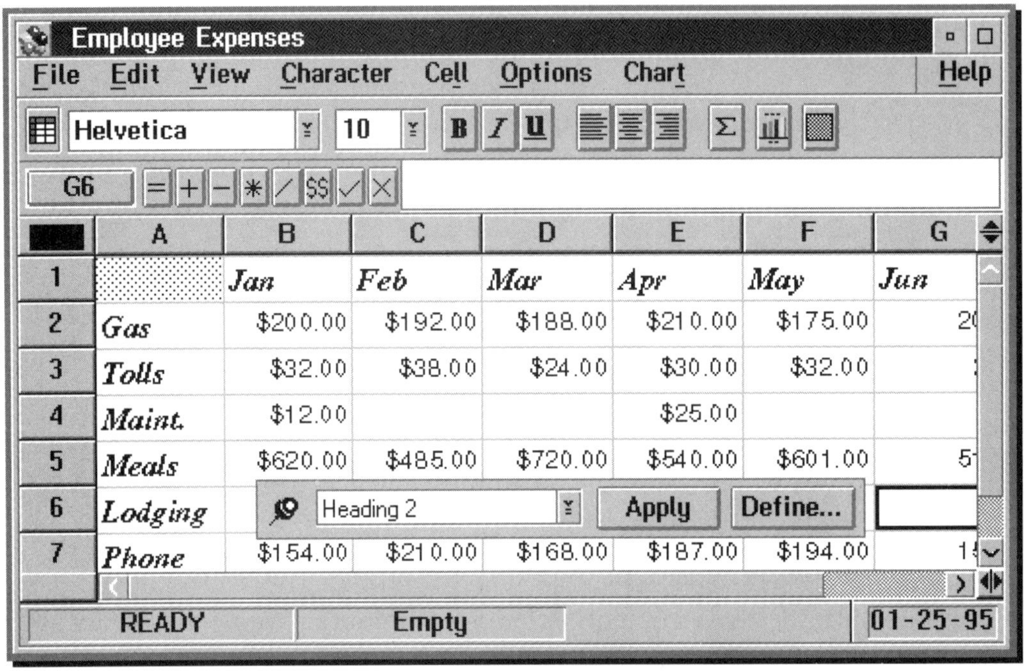

Figure 4.42. The Spreadsheet is well-suited for both small and large projects.

There is no virtual limit to the number of rows and columns your spreadsheet can have. Cells are formed where the columns and rows intersect, and each cell is identified by its column letter(s) and row number. For example, the cell in the upper-left corner of the spreadsheet (the first column of the first row) is called A1.

Each cell can contain text, numbers, or a formula. To enter any of these elements in a cell, point-and-click anywhere in the cell and start typing. Enter a formula to have the Spreadsheet automatically place the results of a calculation (performed with other cells) in your selected cell.

Notice the Style palette pinned to our sample spreadsheet in the preceding figure. This makes the job of formatting text cells a snap. To access the Style palette from within Spreadsheet, select the *Style* option on the *View* pull-down menu.

To create a spreadsheet, enter your text, numbers, and formulas in the appropriate cells and save the spreadsheet using the *Save* option on the *File* menu. To retrieve an existing spreadsheet, select the *Open* option on the *File* menu and specify the drive, path, and file name of the existing file. After you click on *OK*, the spreadsheet data will appear in the Spreadsheet window.

The default file name extension for Spreadsheet files is `.LSS`. The Spreadsheet automatically knows about files with this extension. If you use a different file name extension you'll lose the association between Spreadsheet and your spreadsheet file.

To Chart the data on your spreadsheet (or any part of it) drag the pointer over the cells you want to chart. Start in the upper-left corner and include the column or row label cells. Then click on the *Chart* button, or select *New* from the *Chart* pull-down menu. The program prompts you to draw a rectangle to indicate where you want the chart placed on the spreadsheet. The charts are scaleable, so you can resize them after they're placed.

To modify the chart with the Chart application, double-click anywhere in the chart. This launches Chart, loading it with your new chart.

Chart

The IBM Works Chart program offers a variety of pre-defined charting and graphing formats that you can use to graphically represent a series of  numeric data. The data for your charts can come from the Spreadsheet application, or you can manually enter data into Chart's Data Input sheet. And since this is a PIM application, you have access to the Drawing and Style palettes, so you can decorate and annotate your charts. The following figure shows the Chart application window.

The OS/2 Warp Survival Guide

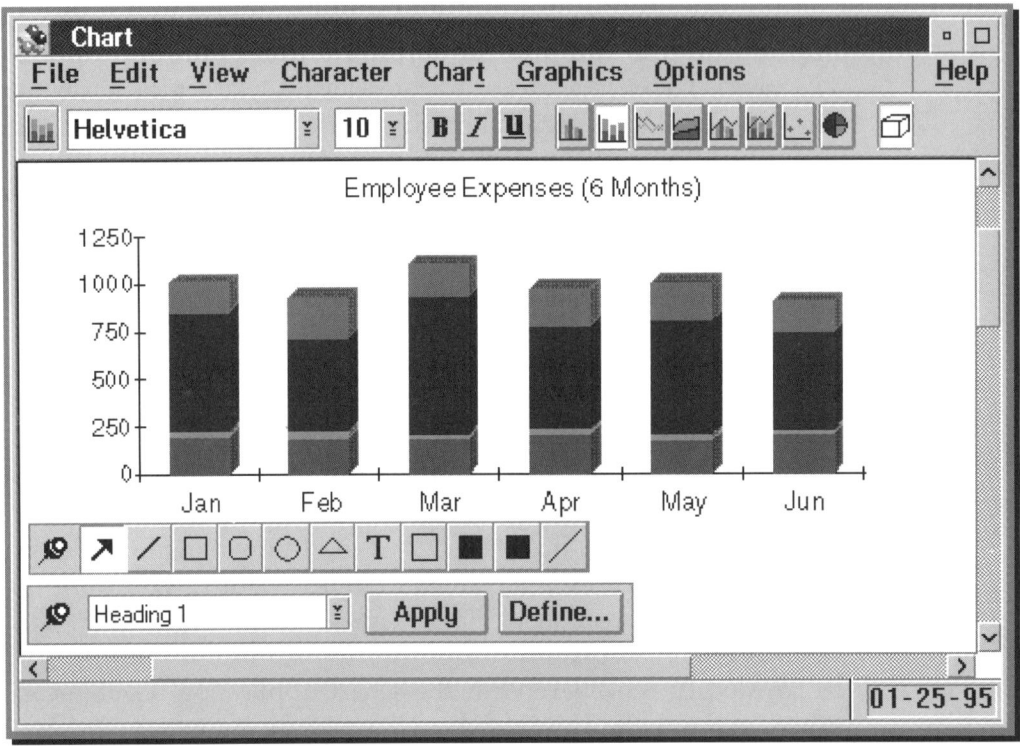

Figure 4.43. *The Chart application makes it easy to develop the right style of chart to best visualize your data.*

When you first start the Chart program, the Data Input dialog box appears, prompting you to enter data for charting. The best way to enter data for a chart is through the Spreadsheet application (as described earlier). After plugging data into Chart, it presents the data graphically in the default chart style. To experiment with different chart styles, click on the style buttons on the toolbar. The program will redisplay your data using the current style, either Bar, Stacked Bar, Line, Area, Bar/Line, Stacked Bar/Line, Scatter, or Pie. For each of these styles, you can enable and disable their perspective (3D) views with the cube button (at the end of the toolbar).

You can copy your finished charts to the Spreadsheet application and/or to the Word Processor, where you might want to embellish your presentation with data and words to bolster it.

4

The OS/2 Warp BonusPak

Data Filer (Database)

The Data Filer application is a simple database management system (DBMS) that allows you to create and modify your personal databases. It in-
cludes a *form designer*, which allows you to design input forms that are linked to a database. The following figure shows the Data Filer application window, which doubles as a form designer and data-entry window. The window shown below is in its default form-design mode, with an open form. The shadowed boxes are input fields on the form, which contain their name and size information while the Data Filer is in form-design mode.

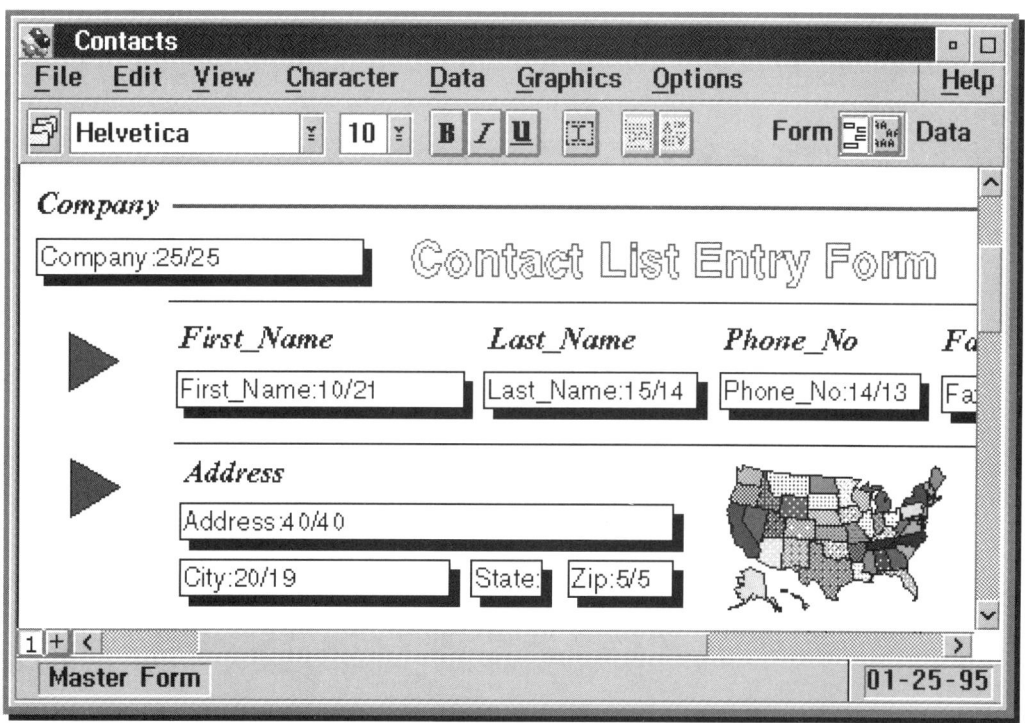

Figure 4.44. *The Data Filer application is a basic database manager with a neat, built-in form designer.*

The OS/2 Warp Survival Guide

The Data Filer is not meant to replace professional-strength database management programs. It does work well as a personal database manager with its relatively easy database-design process. As you design the form that will be used to enter data into the database, you're simultaneously designing the database itself!

You'll also use the Data Filer to create databases when you want to perform a mail-merge with the Word Processor. Refer to the IBM Works Help for step-by-step mail-merge instructions.

Creating a New Database

There are a couple of different ways to create a new database. You can drag a Database template into a folder and open it. Or you can select the *New* button on the IBM Works menu when starting Data Filer. Either way, the Insert Field dialog box will appear (as shown in the following figure).

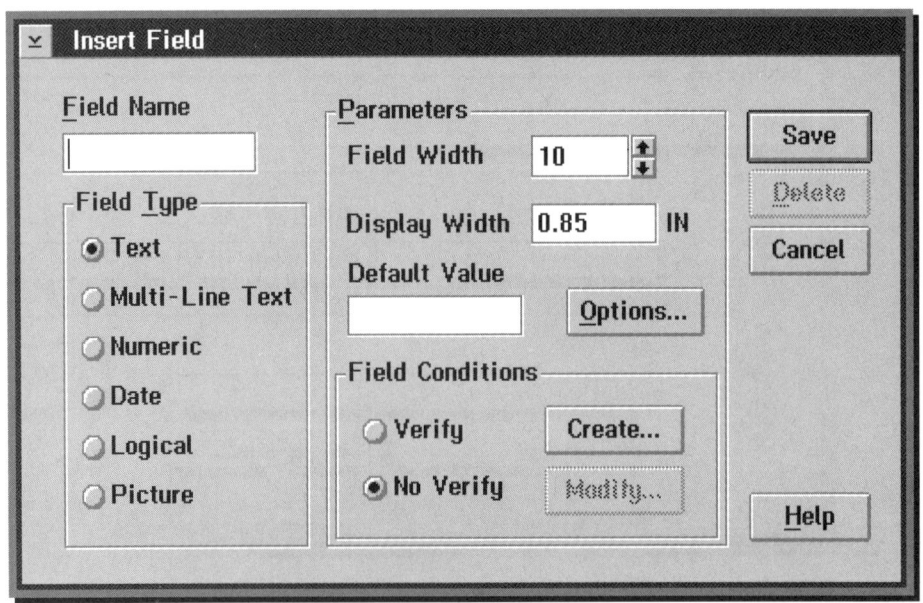

Figure 4.45. *The Insert Field dialog box lets you define form and database fields.*

Use this dialog box to define the fields that will go on your form. You can specify the type of data the field is allowed to contain, its length, default value, and certain field edits (conditions to be verified at data-entry time). And as you define a field for your form, you're also defining a field for the database.

When you finish defining a field in the Insert Field dialog box, click on the *Save* button. You'll return to the Data Filer window where your form is waiting, with the field "attached" to your pointer. Click on the area of the form where you want to place the field. The system places two objects on the form: the field name and the field itself. You can use point-and-click and drag-and-drop techniques to move and resize these objects, and to otherwise design the form.

Designing the Form

The primary form-design tool is the Insert Field dialog box. This is where you create the fields for the form. To insert a new field, click on the *Insert Field* button on the toolbar (it has the appearance of a text pointer) or select the *Insert* Field option on the *Data* menu. Then define the field and place it on the form (as described above). Repeat this process until you've placed all the fields you need on the form.

The Data Filer provides a variety of additional form-design tools. Using the options on the pull-down menus, you can:

- Import graphics (most formats) ....File, Import Picture...
- Add frames around objects............................Edit, Object Properties
- Define and apply named styles.......................View, Style Palette
- Add text and draw graphics...........................View, Draw Palette
- Change fonts and typefaces...........................Character
- Change colors and fill patterns ....Graphics
- Set the size of the form   ....Options, Page Set up...
- Change the data-entry field order ....Options, Entry Order
- Align objects on the form ....Options, Alignment

The Style and Draw palettes are the same ones we introduced you to in the Word Processor. You can use the palettes to beautify your form.

Entering Data

After designing your form, you'll want to test it. First, you should save your form using the *Save* option on the *File* menu. Your new database is now ready to accept data. To add a record to your new database, you must switch the Data Filer application window into Data-Entry mode. To do this, click on the Form/Data button on the right side of the toolbar. The form fields clear and the cursor is placed in the first input field, ready to accept data. Enter the appropriate data and press the Tab key to go to the next input field. Repeat this process to fill in each field on the form. When finished, press the **F2** key to add this record to the database.

If you've been following along on your computer, you now have a database that contains one record—not much of a database. To add more records, simply continue to fill in the fields with information, pressing F2 (Add) each time you get to the end of the form. Go ahead and add a few records to your database.

Viewing Your Database

Now that you have some records to work with, you might want to explore the database management options on the pull-down menus (the menu bar and toolbars change in Data-Entry mode).

With the Data Filer in Data-Entry mode, click on the *Cancel* button in the toolbar. The Data Filer switches into View mode, the record shuffle buttons appear, and some new menu options become active.

You can use the record shuffle buttons (arrows pointing left and right) to go to the first record, previous record, next record, or last record. Using the pull-down menu options, you can:

- Import data files (from dBase IV, etc.) ....File, Import Data File...
- Select certain records and fields for update ..Record
- Change and use sort orders ....Organize, Change Sort
- Create and use indexes ....Organize, Create Index
- Access Report Writer ....Report
- Perform miscellaneous file management.......Options

4

The OS/2 Warp BonusPak

Printing Your Database

To printout your database, you can use the *Print* option on the *File* menu. You can print the currently selected record or all records in the database. You can even set up elaborate conditions for selecting records to print. But there's a more comprehensive way to print records in a database: the Report Writer.

Report Writer

The Report Writer is tightly integrated with the Data Filer. When you select the *List* View option on the Data Filer's *Report* pull-down menu, the
Report Writer is launched and "told" to display a listing of all fields in all records. But, as you'll see, it can do much more than that! When you launch the Report Writer, a window similar to the one shown in the following figure appears.

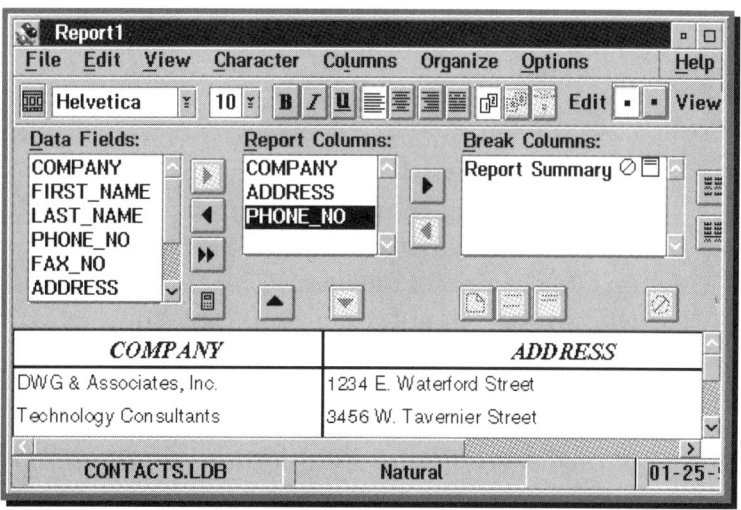

Figure 4.46.   *The Report Writer window has two modes of operation: Edit mode and View mode.*

197

For new reports the Report Writer appears in Edit mode, allowing you to select the fields you want and the order you want them to appear on the report. This is similar to the Data Filer, in that you first edit (design) your report, then you view (or print) it.

Editing a Report

With the Report Writer in Edit mode, select a field you want on the report from the *Data Fields* list box. Then click on the right arrow button (between the *Data Fields* and *Report Columns* list boxes) to transfer the field to the *Report Columns* list box. This tells the Report Writer to place that field on the report. Repeat this process until all the fields you want are listed in the *Report Columns* list box. If you want all fields, click on the double-arrow button.

Notice that a sample of the report is displayed at the bottom of the window as you select fields. If you want to change the order of the columns, click on the fields in the *Report Columns* list box, and use the up and down arrow buttons to change the order of the fields. The field at the top of the list is the first column of the report.

If you want the report to contain a summary at the end, click on the *Report Summary* item in the *Break Columns* list box, and then click off the button with the international "no" symbol (circle with a line through it) to enable the summary feature. If you want a record-group summary (such as a subtotal) whenever a key field changes, select the field that you want to trigger the summary from the *Report Columns* list box, and transfer it to the *Break Columns* list box. Then click on the *Group* button (just to the right of the *Break Columns* list box) to define the type of calculation(s) you want for the summary. You can define three such summaries, usually for sort or index fields.

The buttons below the *Break Columns* list box let you choose whether the next group of records should start on a new page, two lines down, or on the next line after the subsummary.

Of course, as always, there's the Style palette, the formatting toolbar, and pull-down menu options to help you jazz-up your report. And the *Organize* menu contains options similar to the Data Filer, allowing you to manage the database with custom sorts and indexes, as well as record selection criteria. The *Options* menu lets you set up a title, running headers and footers, and a page layout for the report.

Viewing and Printing a Report

When you're finished editing and designing your report, you'll want to look at it in all its splendor. You have a couple of options here. You can switch the Report Writer window into View mode with the *Edit/View* button (in the upper-left corner). This causes the list boxes to be replaced with a bigger report viewing window, where you can scroll up and down or left and right to view the entire report.

When you're satisfied that this is the report you want to commit to paper, first save your work using the Save option on the File menu. The use the Print option on the File menu to generate hard copy. The next time you want to print this report, open it and reprint it. Any changes made to the database since the last printing will be reflected in the report.

> This concludes our tour of the *IBM Works* applications. We'll now cover the balance of the BonusPak: *FaxWorks for OS/2*, *Person to Person*, and the *Multimedia* extensions.

FaxWorks for OS/2

Why buy a fax machine? You virtually have one in the form of *FaxWorks for OS/2*. This valuable addition to your virtual office lets you send, receive, and manage faxes. This OS/2 device object works a lot like the printer object, in that you can drag a fax document from a folder and drop it on FaxWorks to initiate the fax. Or you can double-click on FaxWorks to open its window (as shown in the following figure).

The OS/2 Warp Survival Guide

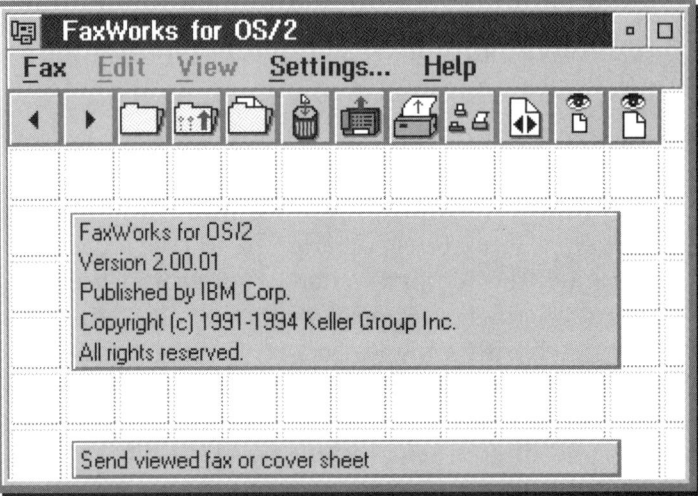

Figure 4.47.   *FaxWorks for OS/2 is more than a virtual fax machine; it helps you manage your faxes.*

There are several ways you can send a fax. The best way depends on the source of the information you want to fax. The FaxPrint object brings drag-and-drop faxing to your desktop. Think of it as a printer object that sends its output to your modem to be printed on the fax machine (or someone else's computer running fax software) at the other end of the phone line.

The OS/2 Warp BonusPak

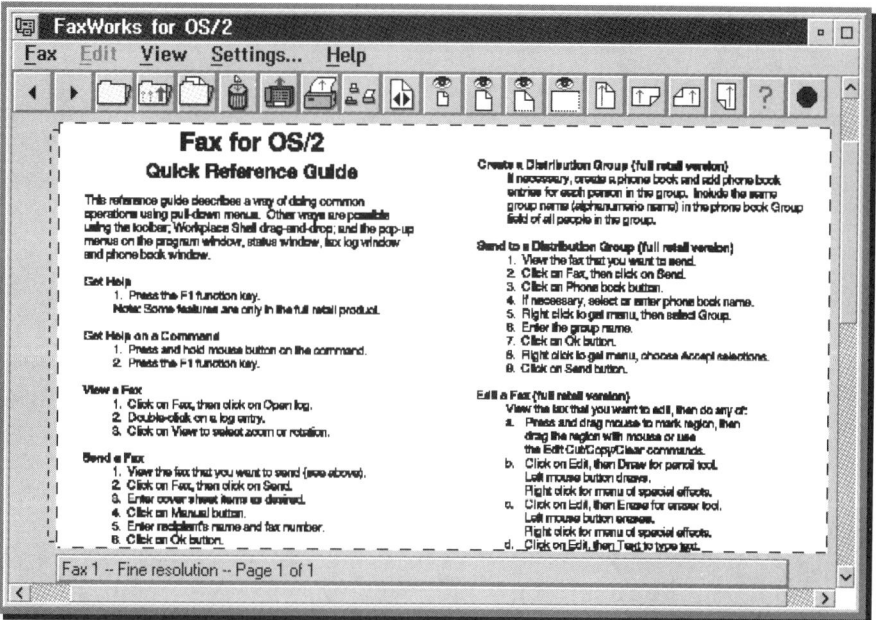

Figure 4.48.   You can send, receive, file, and print faxes in the FaxWorks environment.

Refer to the on-line help provided for FaxWorks to learn exactly how to prepare, send, and receive faxes.

Person to Person/2

This amazingly useful tool will surprise you with what it can do. The capabilities that it adds to OS/2 Warp are unprecedented in the operating systems market. With Person to Person (P2P), you can hold your own "teleconference" with other computer users via LAN, a modem, or the internet. If you can connect to other Warp users, you will want to install P2P and give it a try.

When you install P2P, you will see a new folder on your desktop that contains the objects shown in the following figure.

The OS/2 Warp Survival Guide

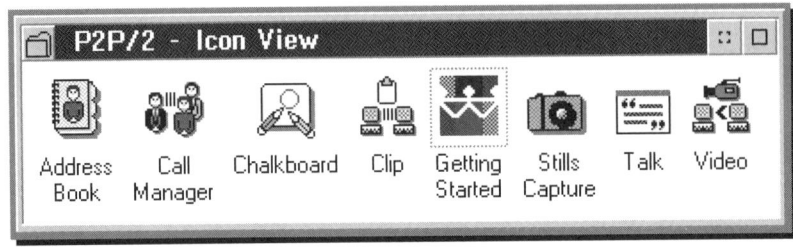

Figure 4.49. *The P2P folder contains all the objects you'll need to run Person to Person.*

Before you dive into P2P (or after you run into trouble), open the *Getting Started* object. This contains information and "how-to" details on all P2P objects.

The Address Book

The first thing you'll need to do to start using P2P is add some names and numbers to the Address Book. Figure 4.50 shows you what the Address Book looks like.

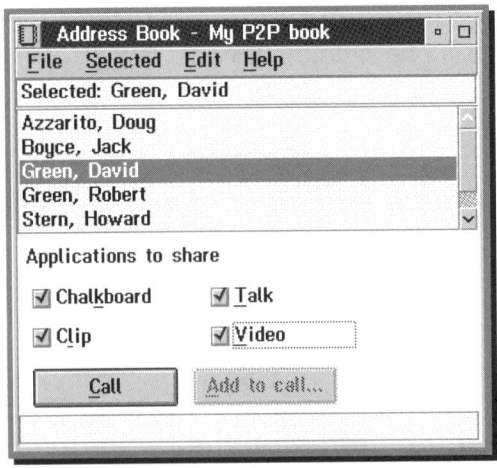

Figure 4.50. *The P2P Address Book keeps track of other P2P users you can call.*

You can create more than one address book, if you have different groups of people you need to call. When you add entries to the Address

202

Book, use the *File* pull-down and save the book. You can also give your address book a "user-friendly" name, separate from the file name. In this example, the book is called *My P2P Book*. When you make a call, you select the person (or persons) to connect, the applications to use for the call, and then click on the *Call* button. You must start the Call Manager before placing or receiving a P2P call. Once you have a call established, you can add people to the call by selecting them from the address book and clicking on the *Add to Call* button.

The first thing you'll need to do is add users to your P2P book. Select the *Edit* pull-down and add a user (as shown in the following figure).

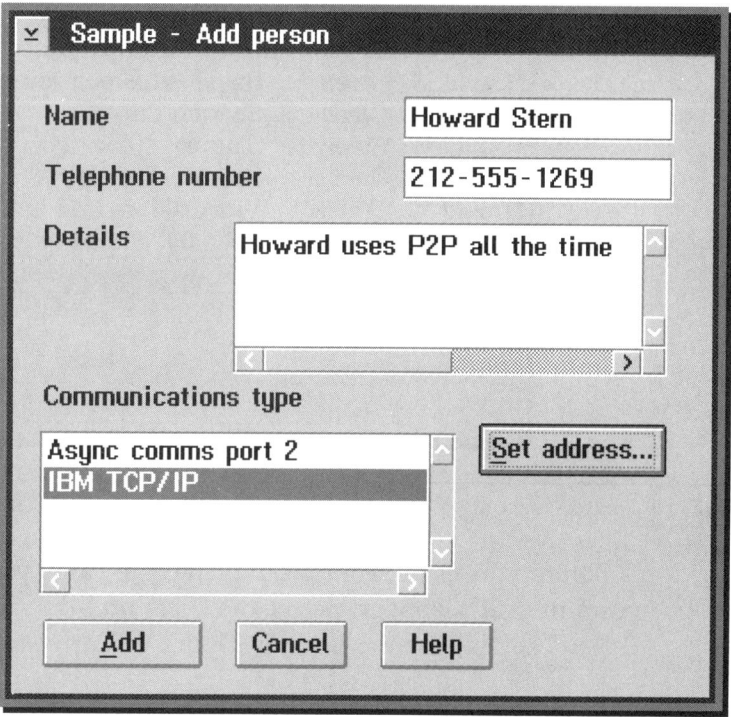

Figure 4.51.   *Use the Add User option to add a person's name, phone number and communications parameters.*

You cannot make the call until you have started and configured the Call Manager, so that will be your next task.

The OS/2 Warp Survival Guide

The Call Manager

The Call Manager is the control center for P2P. Without Call Manager running, you cannot place or receive P2P calls. You configure your communications parameters with Call Manager, so it knows how to connect to the other P2P users. An active Call Manager screen is shown in the following figure.

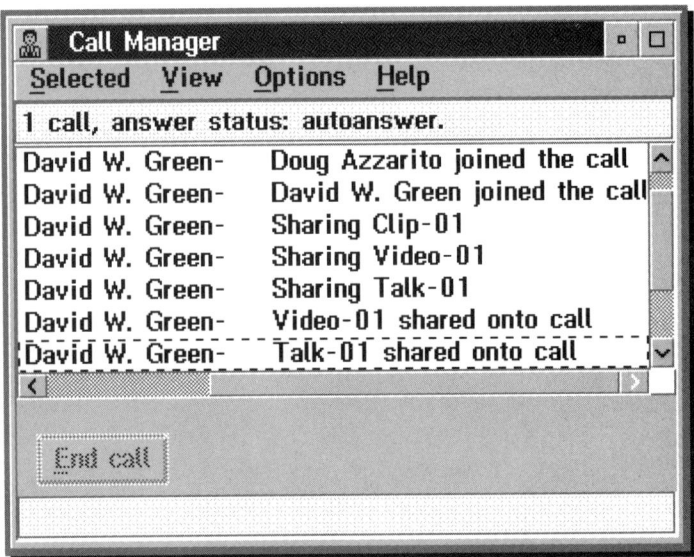

Figure 4.52. *The Call Manager is the main control center for P2P communications.*

Before you use P2P to place or receive calls, you must configure the ports in Call Manager. Select the *View* pull-down, and select *Configure Ports*. The dialog box shown in Figure 4.53 appears.

The OS/2 Warp BonusPak

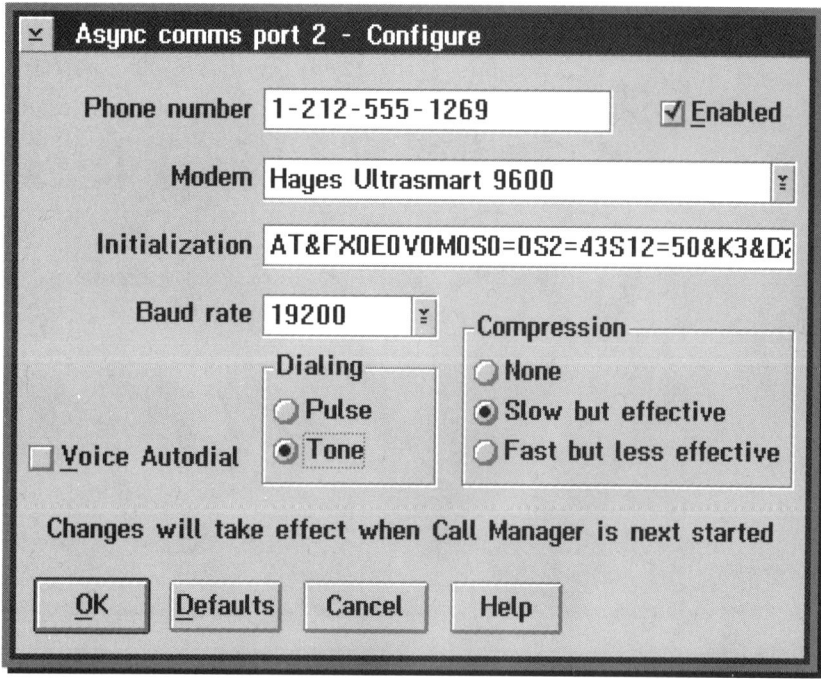

Figure 4.53. *The Configure Ports option on the View pull-down menu lets you set up your communications defaults.*

You can activate LAN connections, serial ports (modems), or TCP/IP (internet) ports. You can also set P2P for automatic or manual answer. Once Call Manager is configured, you must close it and re-launch. Configuration changes do not take effect until you restart. When a call comes in, you will see it on Call Manager. If you place a call, you will also see it here. Any change of status (adding/deleting of people/applications) will be reflected on the Call Manager display.

The Chalkboard Application

The chalkboard can be used to "draw" on a screen that other P2P users can see. You can also "mirror" an application from your desktop to the chalkboard, so others can see what it looks like.

The OS/2 Warp Survival Guide

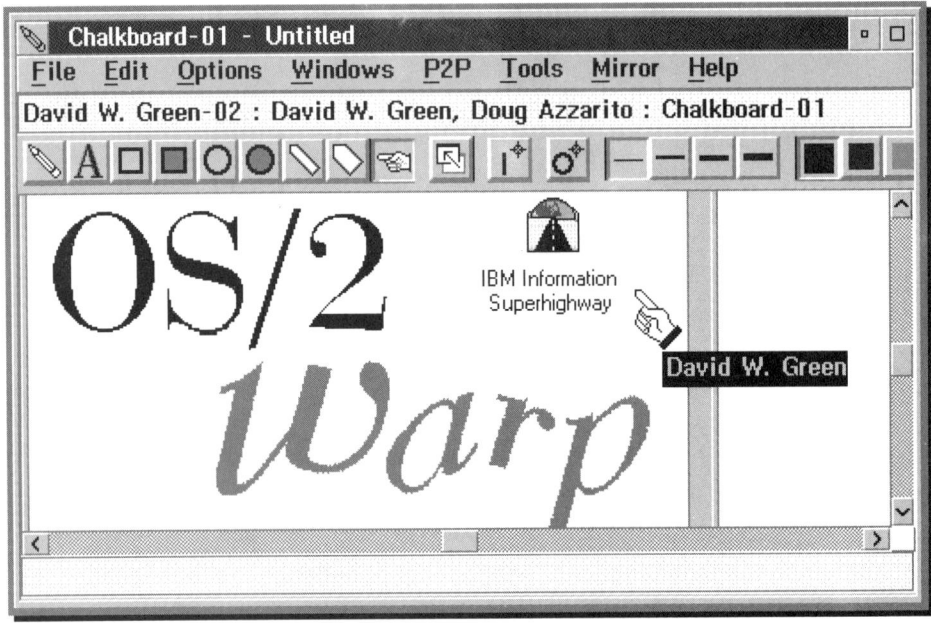

Figure 4.54.   *The Chalkboard allows you to draw and show your desktop to other users.*

When you start a chalkboard, it will be blank. You can use the tools on the chalkboard toolbar to draw, write text, erase, or "point." You can see someone "pointing" to something in the preceding figure. If you want to show other P2P callers an application on your desktop (or even your whole desktop), use the mirror function. Mirror allows you to take a snapshot of a selected program (only programs that are visible on the desktop can be mirrored), and display that snapshot on the clipboard. If your application changes appearance regularly, you can also set up a timed mirror, where snapshots are sent at regular intervals.

The Clipboard Manager

The Clip application allows you to share the OS/2 clipboard with P2P callers. If you share clipboards, one P2P caller can use a CUT or COPY operation in any program, and another P2P caller can PASTE that item into another program.

4

The OS/2 Warp BonusPak

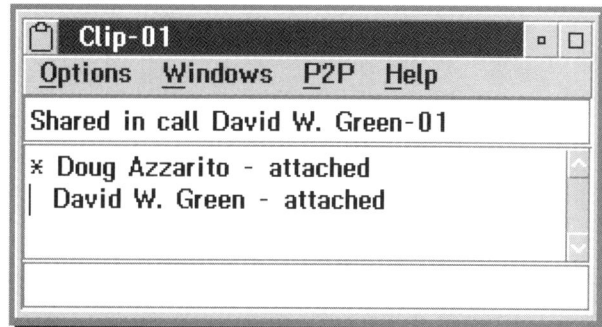

Figure 4.55. *The Clip application allows you to share your OS/2 clipboard with others.*

This is a great way to transfer small graphics or text passages to another user. Just remember, the "public" clipboard acts just like your regular OS/2 clipboard—only one item at a time can be in the clipboard, so only one person at a time can do a CUT or COPY.

The Talk Application

It doesn't really talk, but it does allow you to type back and forth with other P2P callers. If you have used an on-line chat facility on an electronic bulletin board, or other on-line service, you will feel comfortable with Talk.

The OS/2 Warp Survival Guide

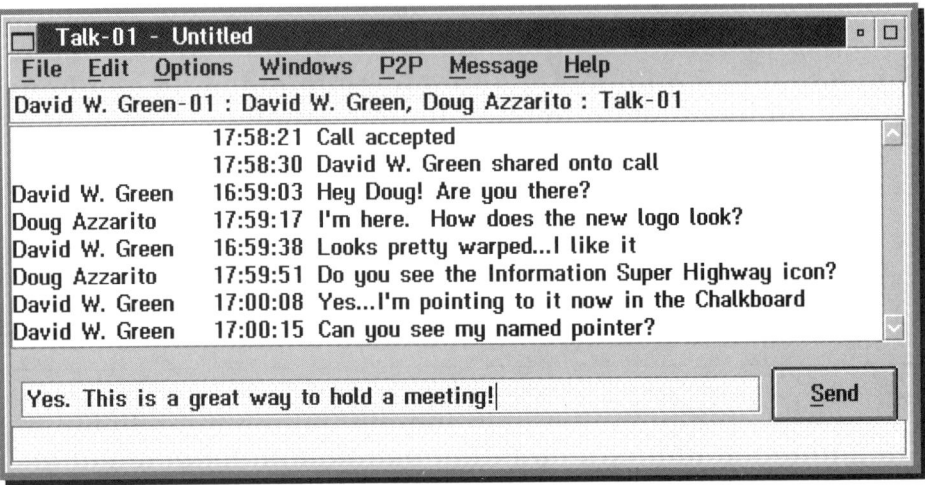

Figure 4.56. *The Talk application lets you type messages for other P2P users to see.*

The combination of a Chalkboard and a Talk session works well for P2P sessions that can't be used in combination with a voice connection. Once you get used to using Chalkboard and Talk, electronic meetings will seem quite natural.

The Video Application

For those P2P users with high-speed communications, and fancy video hardware, the Video application can let you see other P2P callers in real-time. The Video application requires the IBM *ActionMedia II* adapter to capture video, but if you don't have that hardware, you can use a still image for video (a scanned image of a photograph will work).

4

The OS/2 Warp BonusPak

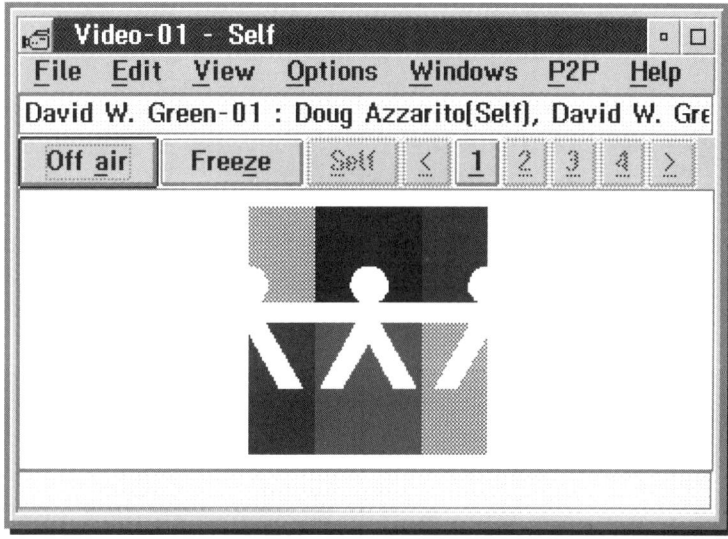

Figure 4.57. *The Video application lets you send and receive video images or still pictures.*

When you share a Video session, you can select which P2P user's video you want to watch (or you can select your own video). You can also go *Off Air*, which prevents other P2P users from seeing your video.

Stills Capture

The Stills Capture application is used to capture images from a P2P video session. It is only useful if you have the IBM ActionMedia II adapter. You can save still images to separate files or place them on the clipboard, where they can be shared by every you're connected to.

Multimedia Extensions

The BonusPak introduces two new stars to the multimedia show. If you have the right hardware, properly configured, you can enjoy state-of-the-art video capture with the *Ultimedia Video IN for OS/2*. If you've been looking for a better way to visually catalog all those bitmaps, audio

The OS/2 Warp Survival Guide

clips, or even full-motion video and animations, take a look at the *Ultimedia Viewer* (a.k.a. *the Light Table*).

Ultimedia Video IN for OS/2

If you're a serious multimedia buff, you're probably at least looking into full-motion video capture. To capture full-motion video into your computer, all you need is a video source (such as a camcorder, laser disk player, or video cassette player) and a video capture adapter. You've already got the software you'll need: *Ultimedia Video IN for OS/2*.

Figure 4.58.   *The controls in the Ultimedia Video IN window are intuitive.*

The controls provided function just like the transport controls on any real-world, tape-based recorder/playback machine. The upper-half of the window operates as a playback-only deck, while the lower-half of the window provides full recording capabilities. But watch out, you're going to need a lot of disk space to do any serious recording!

Ultimedia Viewer (The Light Table)

Its nickname, the Light Table, evokes visions of a paste-up artist, hard at work with a loupe and razor blade. That's not too far-fetched from how you can use this virtual, artist's light table: the *Ultimedia Viewer*. It's a special folder that can hold thumbnail "slides" of the following objects:

- Bitmap images of all forms (such as .bmp, .pcx, .tif,. .gif, .dib, .ico)
- Wave, MIDI, and AVC audio files
- Ultimedia Builder/2 and AVC story files
- Plain text and document (.txt / .doc) files
- Ultimedia Video (.avi) and DVI (.dvi / .avs) full-motion video files

When you installed the BonusPak, the *Light Table* template was added to your Templates folder. To create a light table, drag the template to your desktop. Change its title to something meaningful, and start creating *Light Table References* for the objects you want on the table.

To create a Light Table (LT) Reference of an object, open its context menu and select the *Create LT Reference* option. A window will appear asking you which folder you want the reference object placed in. Locate and select your new light table and click on *OK*. A reference of the object (not the actual file) is placed in the light table.

Although you can also just drag-and-drop objects into the Light Table folder, the method described above is preferred. Why? Because a reference object will stay in the light table, even if the original file is moved or deleted (unlike shadows). This is especially useful for clip-art libraries on CD-ROM. You can make a light table that represents a CD, and

The OS/2 Warp Survival Guide

place thumbnail references in it from the CD. The CD does not need to be loaded to see the thumbnails.

> Before you open your new light table to look at its contents, we suggest you open its settings notebook and turn on the "Always maintain sort order" option. You might even want to change the default folder sort attribute to *Type* while you're there.

The following figure shows what a finished Light Table folder might look like after a few different types of multimedia objects are placed in it.

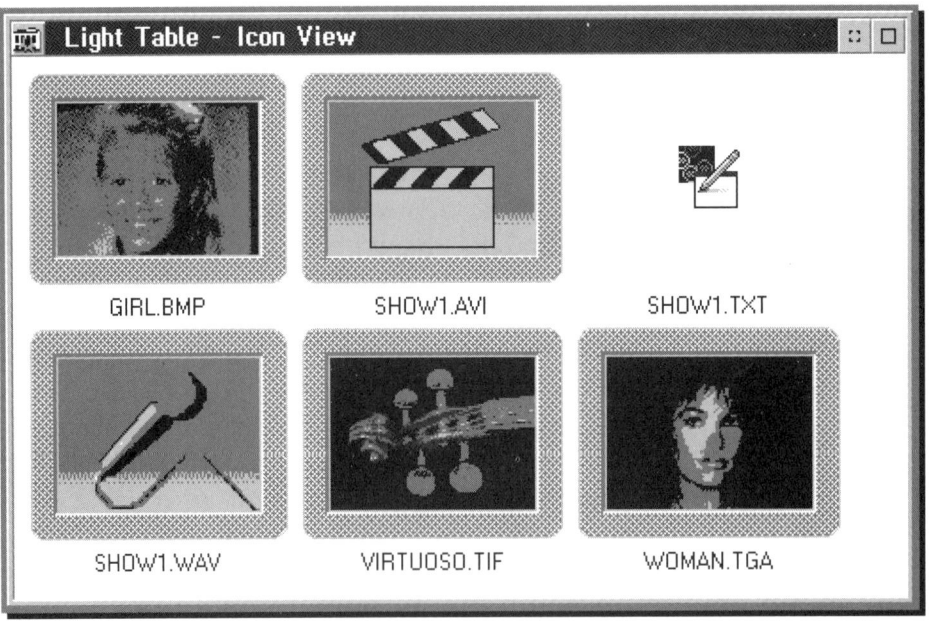

Figure 4.59.   Light Tables can hold thumbnail views of images, along with references to sound, video, and text objects.

Notice the frames around objects in the light table. These are not just for decoration. When you double-click on an object's frame, you'll launch the appropriate browser for that object, either the Image, Audio, or Video/Animation browser. When you click inside the frame, you'll launch the application that is associated with that type of object (i.e., bitmap editor for bitmap files, etc.).

Summary

This concludes our tour of the BonusPak for OS/2 Warp. We saw some very useful features and some radical new approaches to object-oriented computing. We also saw some rather disappointing shortcomings. But these programs are among the first of true 32-bit OS/2 Warp applications. As more people discover the power of this operating system, and software developers become more Warp-aware, we expect OS/2 applications to get more elegant. And when you consider the cost of the BonusPak (free), you can hardly complain!

However, we do have one major complaint. Since the operating system is not being shipped with a calculator (as of this printing), we were expecting to see one in the BonusPak. None was to be found! Is this an oversight, or are we missing something? Don't tell us we have to use the Spreadsheet to perform quick math problems!

Chapter

5

Customizing OS/2 Warp

In this chapter, we'll show you how to "personalize" OS/2 Warp so the Workplace Shell is a more comfortable and productive place for you to work. As OS/2 Warp is delivered (in its default configuration) you can find yourself double-clicking a lot, and watching a seemingly endless supply of open folders stack up on your desktop. This chapter shows you several ways you can refine folders to be more usable. You might even want to make your desktop more visually appealing in the process.

You can change many characteristics of the Workplace Shell—from simple things like colors and type styles (fonts), to more complex things like object behavior and program associations. You'll learn how to change virtual objects (folders, programs, and devices) through their *settings notebooks*, and how to make system-wide changes through the *System Setup* object. Refer to Chapter 6, "Getting Warped: Exercises in Virtual Reality," for some interesting examples of how to customize your virtual workplace.

What Can I Customize?

Look in the following table for the types of changes you would like to make. It refers you to the appropriate topic in the reference sections of this chapter.

Customization Activity	Reference Topics
Just getting started	Using the Settings Notebooks
Changing your desktop	Folder Object Settings System Setup Objects
Changing the way objects appear	*Folder Object Settings* - View Tab - Include Tab - Sort Tab - Window Tab - General Tab *System Setup Objects* - System (Window Tab)
Changing the way objects disappear	*Folder Object Settings* - Include Tab - Window Tab
Changing colors	*Folder Object Settings* - View Tab - Background Tab *System Setup Objects* - Mixed Color Palette - Solid Color Palette - Scheme Palette
Changing fonts	*Folder Object Settings* - View Tab *System Setup Objects* - Font Palette
Changing titles and icons	*Folder Object Settings* - General Tab

5

Customizing OS/2 Warp

Customization Activity	Reference Topics
Changing the resolution of your screen	*System Setup Objects* - System (Screen Tab)
Changing your system hardware	*System Setup Objects* - Selective Install
Changing the order of things	*Folder Object Settings* - View Tab - Include Tab - Sort Tab - Menu Tab
Changing the behavior of things	*Folder Object Settings* - Window Tab - Program Tab *Program Object Settings* - Session Tab - Association Tab *System Setup Objects* - Keyboard - Mouse
Find out about the components in your computer	System Information Tool

Using the Settings Notebooks

As you may have already gathered from the earlier chapters, the settings notebook is an important part of OS/2 Warp. Each object in the Workplace Shell has a settings notebook—even DOS and Windows objects that you've migrated into OS/2.

The OS/2 Warp Survival Guide

There are two basic types of settings notebooks: one for Folder objects and one for Program objects. You can customize and configure an individual object through its settings notebook. To open any object's settings notebook, perform the following simple steps.

1. Click on the object with the right mouse button. Its context menu appears, and the object is enclosed in a box with dashed lines to show you which object the menu belongs to (see Figure 5.1).

 The object can be in any of its forms when you click on it (minimized, maximized, or even shown in a directory listing). If you can see an object, you can open its context menu.

2. Click on the *Settings* option in the context menu.

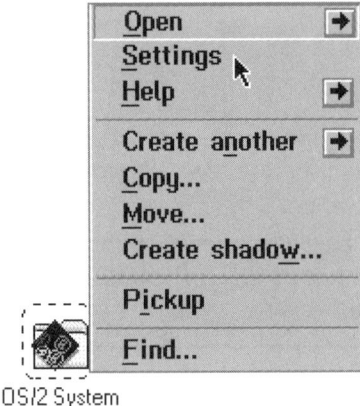

Figure 5.1. *Open the settings notebook for an object through its context (pop-up) menu.*

Even the desktop has a context menu, and a settings notebook (it's a folder that's always open). To access the context menu for the desktop, right-button click on any blank area of the desktop.

When you click on the *Settings* option of a context menu, a window similar to the one shown in Figure 5.2 appears. This is a settings notebook. Our example is the *OS/2 System* folder. All folder objects have a similar settings notebook. Notice the index tabs along the edge of the "notebook-style" pages.

Figure 5.2.   *The settings pages are presented in notebook form with index tabs.*

To access the different settings available in the notebook, click on the index tab that corresponds to the type of setting you want to view or change.

The notebook settings are dynamic. As you make changes in the notebook, they are immediately applied to the object. If, after making a change, you don't like what you see, use the *Undo* button to reverse the change before you close the notebook. Some notebook pages have a *Default* button, which allows you to undo changes you've made even after saving the changes (return the settings to their default values).

Some index tabs have multiple pages of settings (such as the View tab shown in Figure 5.2). To turn pages in a notebook, click on the left or right arrow buttons at the bottom of the page (next to the page number). If there is no page number displayed, clicking the arrow buttons will take you to the previous or next tab.

The settings notebooks make extensive use of all OS/2 Workplace Shell controls, such as radio buttons, check boxes, list boxes, push buttons, and dialog boxes. You'll use these controls to enable and disable features, and to change various attributes of the object belonging to the notebook.

After making the desired changes in a settings notebook, simply close its window by double-clicking on the object icon (in the upper-left corner) or by selecting the *Close* option on the window's menu. You won't find a *Save*, *Quit*, or *Close* button on any of the notebook pages. But don't worry, you can close notebooks from any page and all your changes (for all pages) will be saved and applied to the object.

Most objects share two common index tabs in their settings notebook: Window tabs and General tabs. There are other tabs that are common to both folder and program notebooks. These common tabs have the same settings, and they generally work the same way.

This chapter covers the Folder notebook settings first. Then we'll discuss the Program notebook settings. Since the desktop is the folder you see most of the time, we'll use its settings notebook as an example, but you can make these same changes to all folders.

5

Customizing OS/2 Warp

Folder Object Settings

Although the settings shown in this section modify the characteristics of the desktop object, the discussions apply to any folder object. The settings notebooks for program objects contain some of the same index tabs as are available for folder objects. Learning to navigate through the folder settings will be time well-spent in pursuit of *getting warped*.

When you open a folder's settings notebook, a window appears with the notebook open to the first index tab: the View tab.

View Tab

The View tab is available in the settings notebook of all folder objects. It lets you control how the folder's contents are presented. You can change the way the icons appear; the text's font type, size, and color; and various operating characteristics.

The following figure illustrates the settings under the View tab in the desktop's settings notebook.

The OS/2 Warp Survival Guide

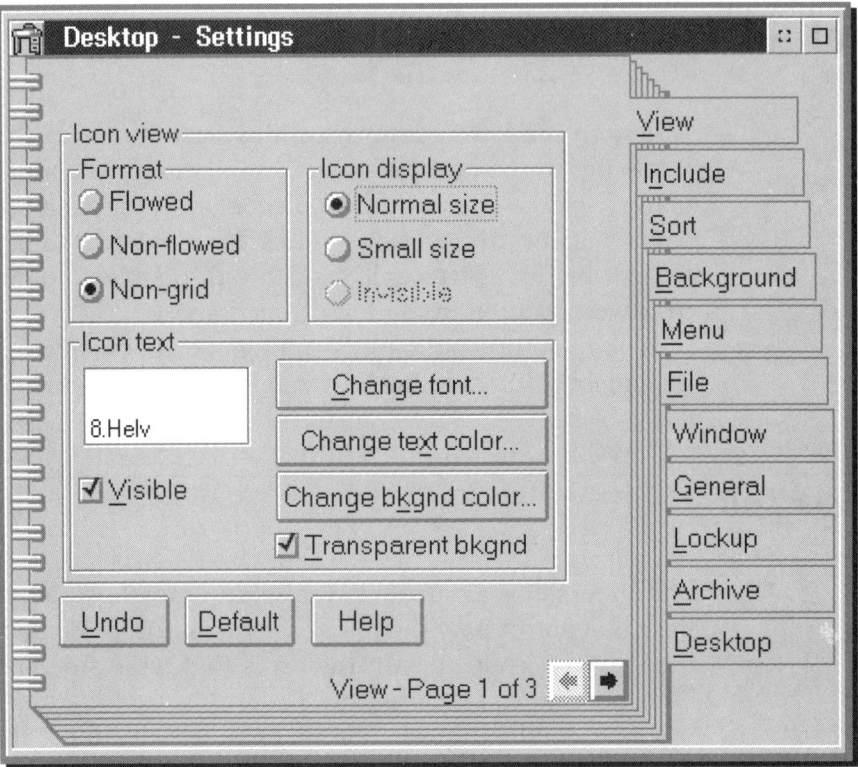

Figure 5.3. *The View tab in the desktop's settings notebook lets you change how the objects are presented on the desktop.*

There are three "views" for any folder, all of which you can access through the *Open* option of the folder's context menu (see Figure 5.1). You can select from the *Icon* View, *Tree* View, or *Details* View. These options are listed on the *Open* cascade menu, which appears when you click on the *Open* option (see "Using the Pop-Up Controls" in Chapter 3 for details).

The View tab in the settings notebook lets you customize each of these views. When you first open the settings notebook, it's open to page 1 (of 3) for the View tab. For each view, there is a separate page in the settings notebook. Page 1 is for the *Icon* View settings. The *Tree* View settings are on page 2, and page 3 contains the *Details* View settings. To change pages, click on the left or right arrow buttons next to the page number reference.

To change a folder's default view, use page 3 of the *Window* tab in the *System* object. See "Window Tab" under "System Setup Objects" later in this chapter for more information.

Icon View

The *Icon* View is the default view for all folders (including the desktop). The first time you saw the OS/2 Desktop, it was shown in its Icon View (and probably still is). You can customize this view using page 1 of the View tab in a folder's settings notebook. For example, the following figure illustrates a portion of the desktop with the *Flowed* setting selected. Notice that the titles move to the right of their objects.

Remember: Although we're using the desktop as our example folder, these options are available, and perform the same way for *all* folders.

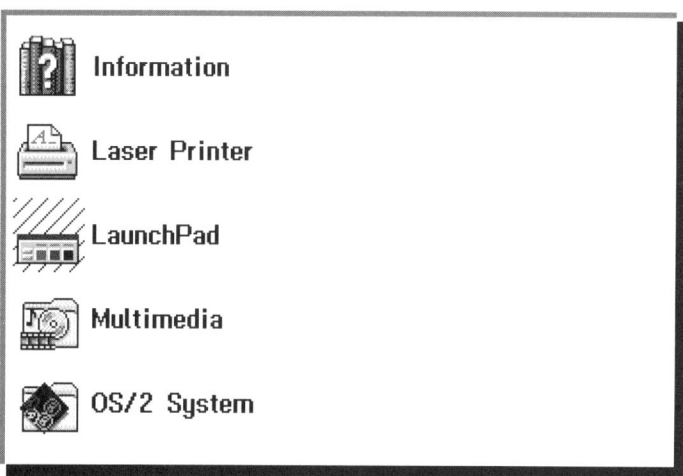

Figure 5.4. *Objects can be "flowed" into neat columns if you don't like the default "Non-grid" setting.*

You can also change the size of the objects' icons (*Normal size*, *Small size*, or *Invisible*). You can change the font used in the object's title by clicking on the *Change font* button, and you can change the color of the title's text. And if the color or font you've selected isn't working well against the folder's background color or image, you can opt to change the background color for the text or make the background opaque.

The following figure illustrates a portion of the desktop with small icons and a smaller font. We're using a white folder background to help you see the objects.

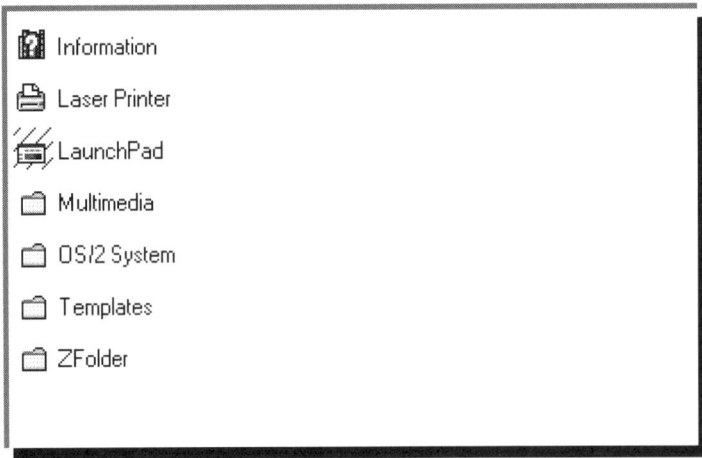

Figure 5.5.   *Objects inside folders can be viewed with their* Small *icons and smaller fonts to conserve space.*

With all the background, color, and size options available, you can create some really ugly folders. But if you experiment with these options (in conjunction with the options under the Background tab) you can create some attractive combinations.

Customizing OS/2 Warp

Tree View

The *Tree* View displays the contents of a folder in a "directory tree" format. In this view, an open folder shows only the hierarchy of its folders (subdirectories). All program and data objects are *excluded* from this view. For example, if you were to open the Tree View of the desktop, you would see a desktop similar to the one shown in the following figure.

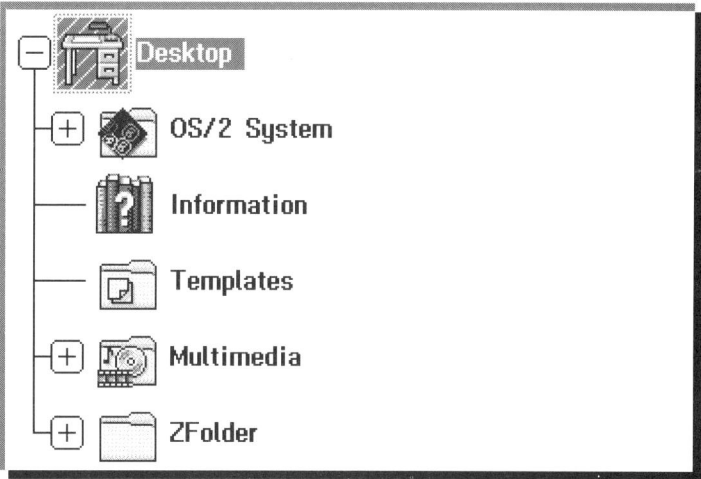

Figure 5.6. *When you open a folder in Tree View, you'll only see its folder objects, shown in a directory-tree structure.*

In this view, you'll notice buttons with plus or minus signs in them, next to some folders. Each button lets you *expand* (plus) or *collapse* (minus) one level of the tree structure under its corresponding folder. When you expand the tree (click on a plus button), you see more levels.

To change the Tree View settings for a folder, click on the right arrow button to display page 2 of the View tab. The window shown in the following figure appears.

The OS/2 Warp Survival Guide

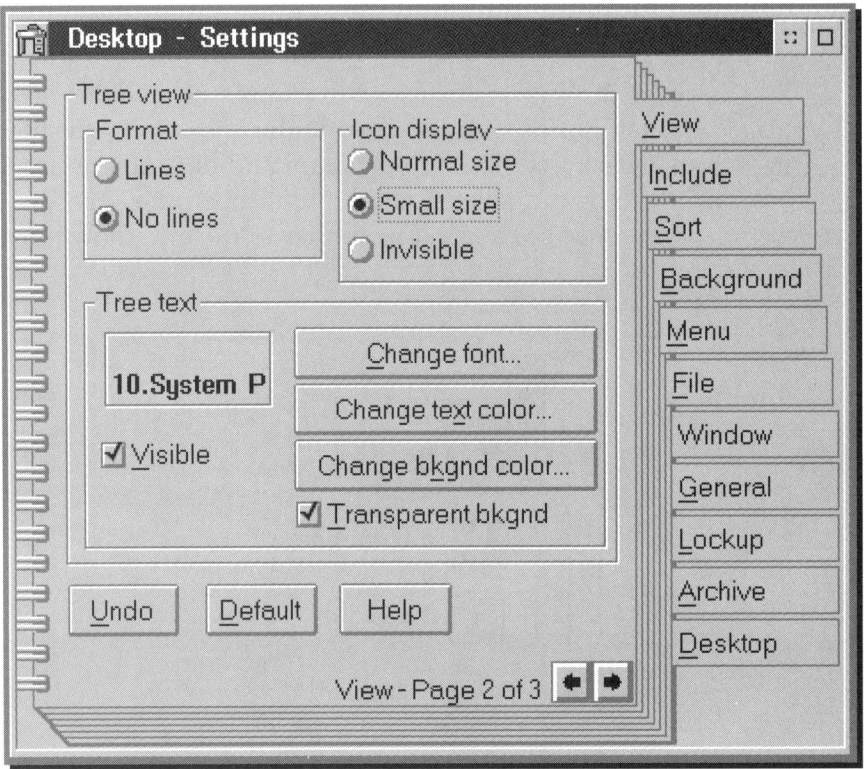

Figure 5.7.   *Use page 2 of the View tab to customize the Tree View.*

As with the Icon View settings, you can select to view the small size icons, and you can change the font used for the objects' titles. In addition, you can eliminate the lines that connect the objects in Tree View. For example, the following figure illustrates the Tree View of the desktop with the "No lines" and "Small size" icon settings selected.

5

Customizing OS/2 Warp

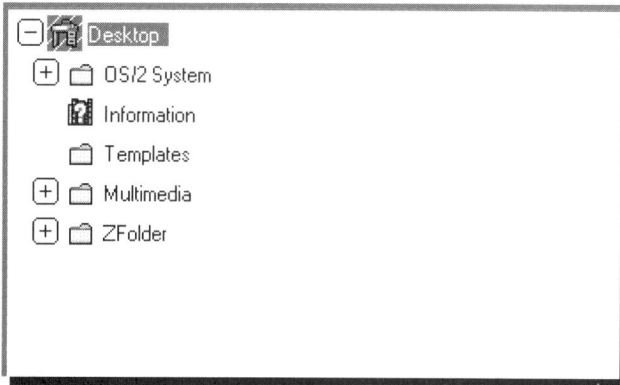

Figure 5.8. *The Tree View of a folder with "No lines" and "Small icons."*

Details View

The *Details* View provides just what its name implies: lots of detail. When in Details View, each object in the folder is shown with details about the file's creation date and time, its flags, its icon (shown in small size), and much, much more (if you want it). The following figure illustrates a portion of the desktop shown in its Details View.

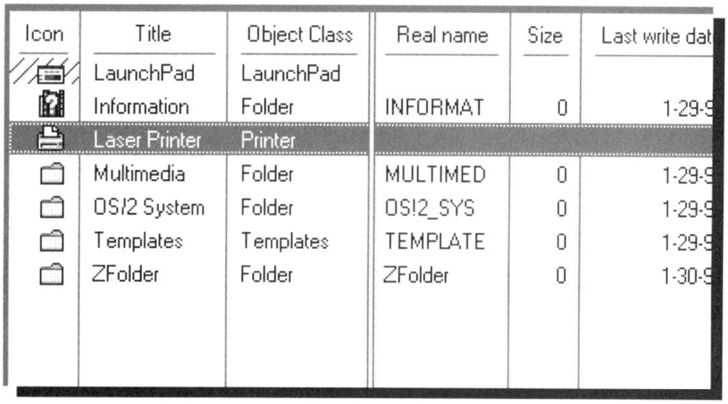

Icon	Title	Object Class	Real name	Size	Last write dat
	LaunchPad	LaunchPad			
	Information	Folder	INFORMAT	0	1-29-9
	Laser Printer	Printer			
	Multimedia	Folder	MULTIMED	0	1-29-9
	OS/2 System	Folder	OS2_SYS	0	1-29-9
	Templates	Templates	TEMPLATE	0	1-29-9
	ZFolder	Folder	ZFolder	0	1-30-9

Figure 5.9. *A folder's Details View shows* all *file details by default.*

The OS/2 Warp Survival Guide

To change the Details View settings, click on the right arrow button in the settings notebook to display page 3 of 3. The window shown in the following figure appears.

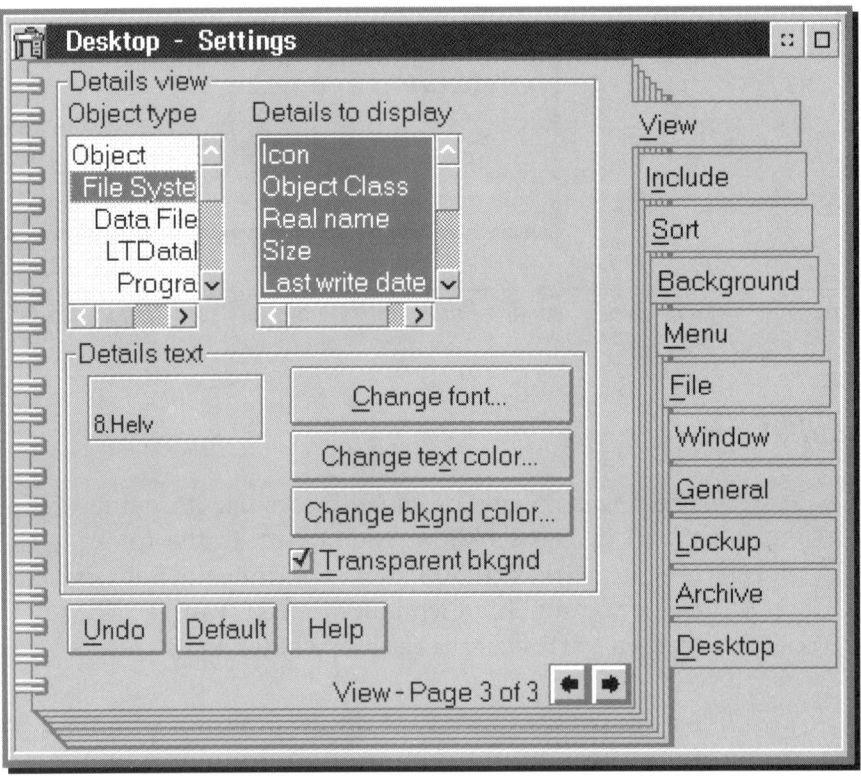

Figure 5.10.   *Use Page 3 of 3 under the View tab to customize the Details view.*

The first field on the screen (*Object type*) contains a list of every conceivable type of object that can exist under OS/2. Notice that *File System* is selected by default, causing the Details View to show file-system type information. The second field (*Details to display*) contains a list of the detailed information that can be displayed for each object. Notice that all details are selected by default. As with the other views, you can use the *Change font*, *text color*, and *background color* buttons to change the way the object titles appear in the Details View.

Customizing OS/2 Warp

The following figure illustrates a portion of the desktop shown in Details View with some File System details excluded.

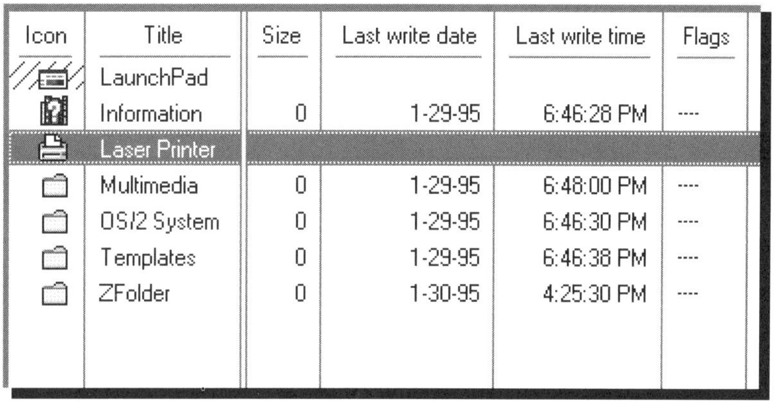

Icon	Title	Size	Last write date	Last write time	Flags
	LaunchPad				
	Information	0	1-29-95	6:46:28 PM	----
	Laser Printer				
	Multimedia	0	1-29-95	6:48:00 PM	----
	OS/2 System	0	1-29-95	6:46:30 PM	----
	Templates	0	1-29-95	6:46:38 PM	----
	ZFolder	0	1-30-95	4:25:30 PM	----

Figure 5.11. *You can customize a folder's Details View to show only the information you're interested in.*

You might be wondering why OS/2 has provided so much control over how objects are presented. You'll probably want to work mostly with Icon views; but sometimes you might wish you could see a folder's files in a traditional file list format, with dates and file sizes.

Because you can customize the settings for individual objects, each of your folders can use the view that's best for it. Best of all, since OS/2 is a true object-oriented operating system, you can still use drag-and-drop techniques on objects—regardless of the view being used.

Include Tab

The *Include* tab lets you include (or exclude, depending on how you look at it) particular types of objects for presentation within a folder. For example, you might want a folder to show only its data files even though it actually contains program files *and* data files.

The following figure illustrates the settings under the Include tab in the desktop's settings notebook.

The OS/2 Warp Survival Guide

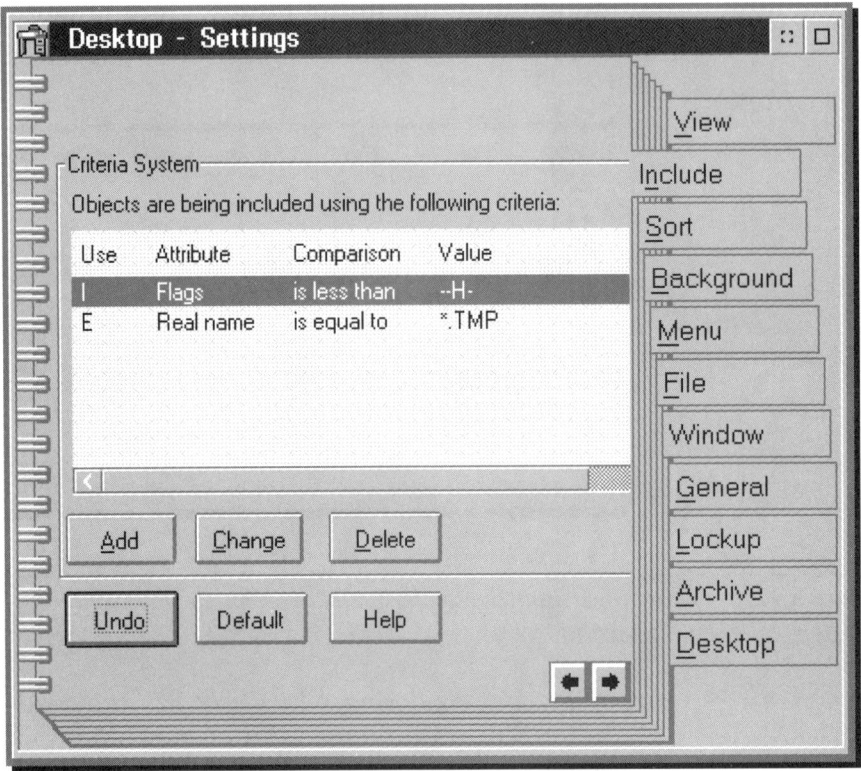

Figure 5.12.   *The Include tab lets you decide which objects are shown in an open folder.*

By default, the folders are set up to include all objects whose *flags* are less than an "H" (hidden files)—meaning that if a file has the *hidden* flag set, it will not be displayed. All other objects will be displayed.

In our example, we wanted to exclude real files whose file name extensions are .TMP. To accomplish this, we used the *Add* button to set up an *exclude* condition through the Add/Change Criteria dialog box (as shown in the following figure).

Customizing OS/2 Warp

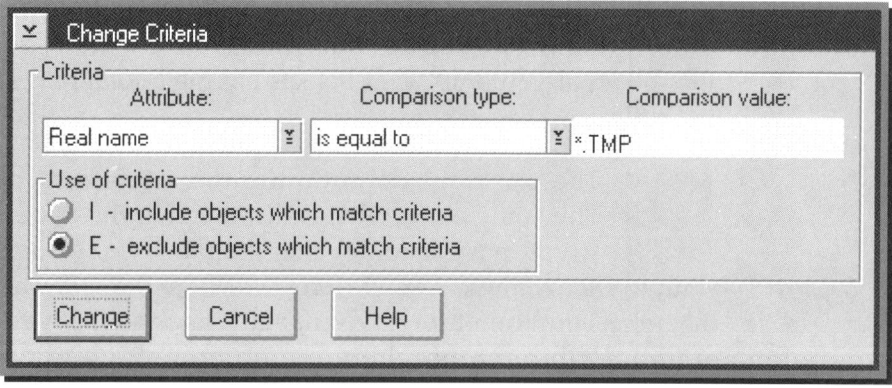

Figure 5.13.   *Use the Add/Change Criteria dialog boxes to specify file system attributes that you want OS/2 to consider when including or excluding files in an open folder.*

You can use this dialog box to set up include or exclude criteria based on the options you select in the three list boxes: *Attribute*, *Comparison type*, and *Comparison value*. In our example above, we've told OS/2 to:

"Exclude any object whose Real name is equal to *.TMP"

Using the *Attributes* list box, you can set up include/exclude conditions based on qualities such as: Real name, Creation date, and File size. Almost all OS/2 object attributes are available in this list.

The options available in the *Comparison type* list box change according to the attribute you select. Generally, your options are comparisons such as: less than, greater than, and not equal to.

The *Comparison value* field changes based on the type of comparison you select. You'll sometimes be able to select from a list of options, and sometimes be able to type in your comparison (as with file names).

If you are setting up a comparison based on a file name, you can use the wildcard character (*) in place of any character(s) in the name. In our example, we used an asterisk because we don't care what the first part of the file name is.

Don't forget to specify whether you want to use the defined criteria as an *include* or *exclude* condition. Click on the appropriate radio button in the *Use of Criteria* field.

The OS/2 Warp Survival Guide

You can add as many comparisons as you want. Each entry is logically *and*-ed to the criteria. For example, you might specify that you only want objects having a Real name equal to *.TXT *and* a file size greater than 1024 KBytes.

These settings do not affect the actual contents of the folder. They only affect what is displayed in the folder when it's open. If you have a folder that contains lots of objects, you might want to change these settings temporarily to make it easier to work with the objects. But don't forget to change it back so that you'll be able to see everything that's in the folder.

Sort Tab

The *Sort* tab lets you specify what sort options will appear on the folder's context menu, and which one will be the default

The following figure illustrates the settings under the Sort tab in the desktop's settings notebook.

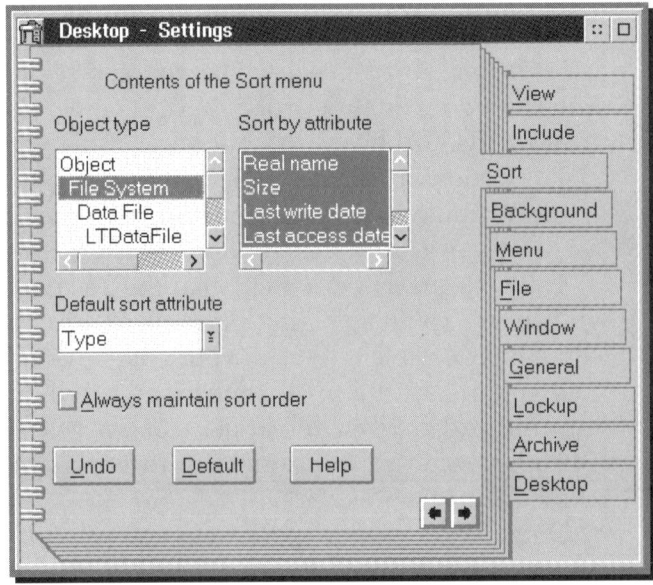

Figure 5.14.   *The Sort tab lets you select the sort options for a folder's context menu.*

Customizing OS/2 Warp

Using the *Object type* field, you can specify different sort criteria for different types of objects. Specify these sort criteria in the *Sort by attribute* field. You can select multiple attributes to get multiple-level sorts.

The *Default sort attribute* field allows you to specify which attribute will be selected on the pop-up menu by default.

If you click on the *Always maintain sort order* check box, the contents of the folder will always be sorted (using the default sort attribute). As you bring a new object into the folder, it will be sorted automatically.

Background Tab

The *Background* tab lets you customize the look of a folder's background (the area in which all objects within the folder appear). You can select a simple background, such as a solid color, or a more extravagant background such as a bitmap image—several of which are included with OS/2. Your background image can even be a bitmap of a full-color, scanned photograph.

Since the desktop is a folder, you can use this tab to change the look of your desktop, which *is* the background of the desktop folder. The following figure illustrates the settings found under the Background tab in the desktop's settings notebook.

The OS/2 Warp Survival Guide

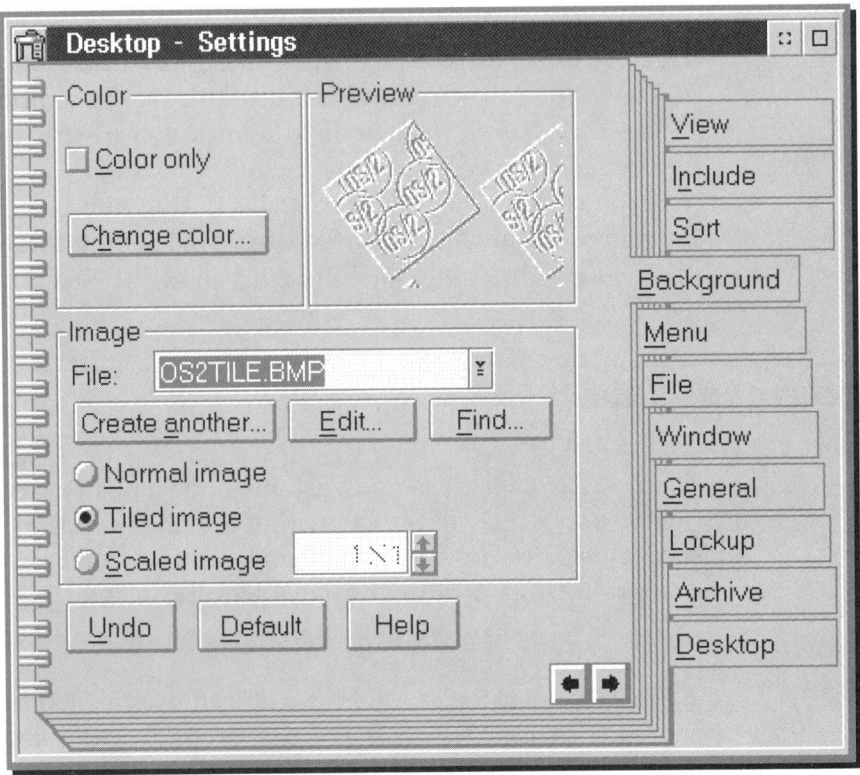

Figure 5.15. The Background tab lets you add interesting backgrounds to the folder.

Your first decision is whether you want to use a *color* or an *image* as the folder's background.

Background Images

If you want to use an image, remove the check mark from the *Color only* box. The *Image* field becomes active, allowing you to specify the file name of a bitmap file. You can use the *Find...* button to locate bitmap files. Several bitmaps come with OS/2 Warp and are available through the *File* list box. The *Create another...* and *Edit...* buttons take you to the Icon editor, where you can create or edit small bitmap files.

234

Use the radio buttons to control how the image is displayed. If the bitmap is smaller than the full screen, you might want to use the *Tiled* or *Scaled image* options to fill the screen. A scaled image is repeated on the screen as many times as you specify in the field next to the option.

 Experiment with these options to find the background that best suits you. Most of the bitmaps that come with OS/2 are meant to be tiled or scaled. Even though the *Change color...* button is active while you're using an image, you cannot change the color of the bitmap image.

Color Backgrounds

If you choose to use a color background, make sure the *Color only* check box is selected and click on the *Change color...* button. The Edit Color dialog box will appear, allowing you to select the color you want (as shown in the following figure).

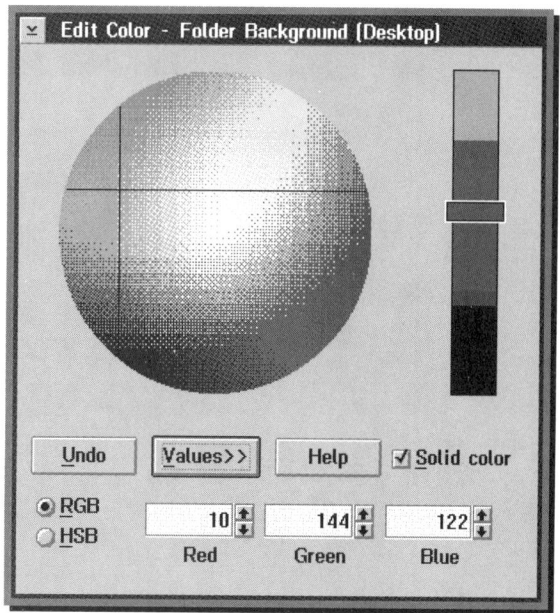

Figure 5.16. *The Edit Color dialog box lets you select colors three ways.*

The OS/2 Warp Survival Guide

To select a color, point-and-click directly on the color in the color wheel (the circular, multicolored area). You can then adjust the tint in the color slider bar to the right of the color wheel. If you select the Solid color check box, the number of possible colors is limited to only those that do not produce a *dithering* pattern (a visible mixing of different colored pixels to achieve an apparent tint).

The *Values>>* button provides access to the RGB and HSB color selection values. You can mix your own color using the red, green, and blue (RGB) values or the hue, saturation, and brightness (HSB) values.

Menu Tab

The *Menu* tab lets you customize the folder's context menu. You can add options and create new cascade or conditional menus, and you can change some existing options, including options on the *Open* cascade menu. The following figure illustrates the Menu settings for the desktop's context menu.

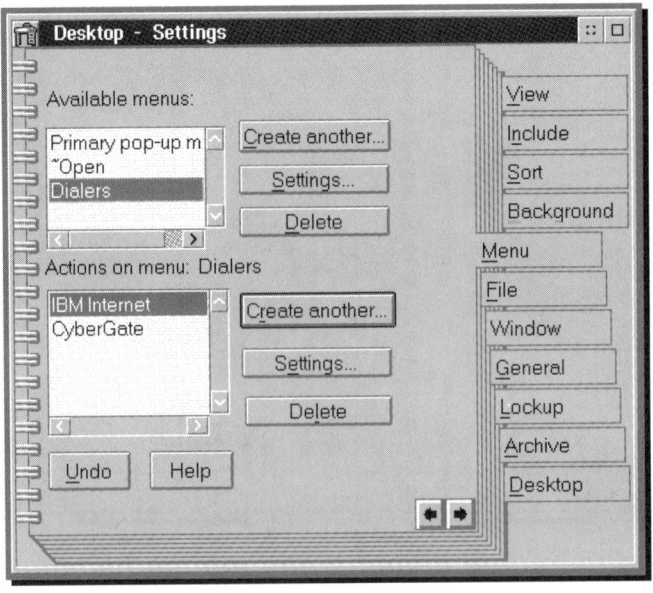

Figure 5.17. *The Menu tab lets you change certain options for a folder's context menu.*

Customizing OS/2 Warp

Notice that the *Available menus* field contains three items: *Primary pop-up menu*, *~Open*, and *Dialers*. The *Dialers* entry is a custom cascade menu

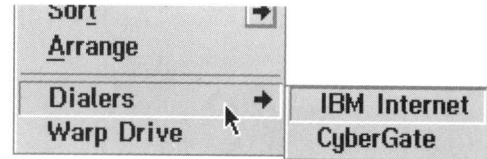

that we created. It's currently selected so that we can see the items (actions) defined for it in the *Actions on menu* field. The settings shown in Figure 5.17 created the cascade menu shown here. The user interface is quite confusing, so we'll show you by example how we accomplished this task.

This custom cascade menu was created using the buttons next to the *Available menus* and *Actions on menu* fields, using the following procedure (refer to Figures 5.17 and 5.18).

Click on *Primary pop-up menu* and then click on the *Create another...* button (adjacent to the *Available menus* field). The Menu Settings dialog box appears. Type the name of the cascade menu (Dialers) and select the type of cascade menu you want. Click on *OK*.

Now click on *Dialers* in the *Available menus* field and then click on the *Create another...* button adjacent to the *Actions on menu* field. The Menu Item Settings dialog box appears. Type the name of the first cascade menu item and the name of the program you want that option to launch. You can use the *Find program...* button to locate the executable program. Click on *OK* when you're finished.

Repeat step 2 for the second item on our custom cascade menu.

The OS/2 Warp Survival Guide

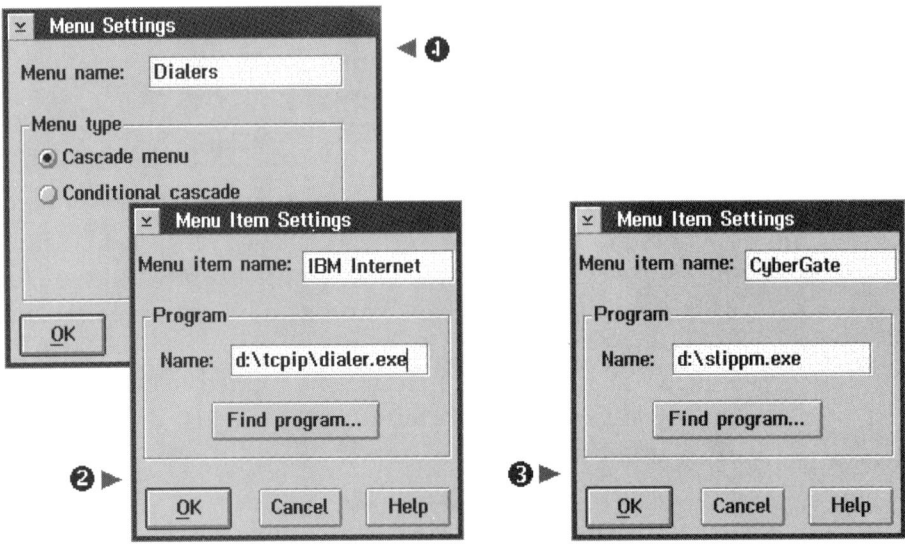

Figure 5.18. *The Menu Settings and Menu Item Setting dialog boxes let you add or modify cascaded menus and menu options.*

After defining the cascade menu, you can return to the Menu Settings dialog box to specify which option you want OS/2 to use as the default option. Use the *Default action* list box to select from the list of defined menu items.

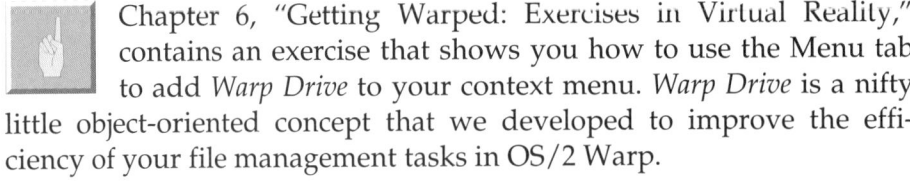

Chapter 6, "Getting Warped: Exercises in Virtual Reality," contains an exercise that shows you how to use the Menu tab to add *Warp Drive* to your context menu. *Warp Drive* is a nifty little object-oriented concept that we developed to improve the efficiency of your file management tasks in OS/2 Warp.

File Tab

The *File* tab lets you view or change the drive and subdirectory names that are associated with a folder. It also lets you view statistical information about a folder, and it lets you turn a folder into a Work Area.

The File tab contains three pages of settings. The following figure illustrates the settings on page 1 for the desktop folder.

Customizing OS/2 Warp

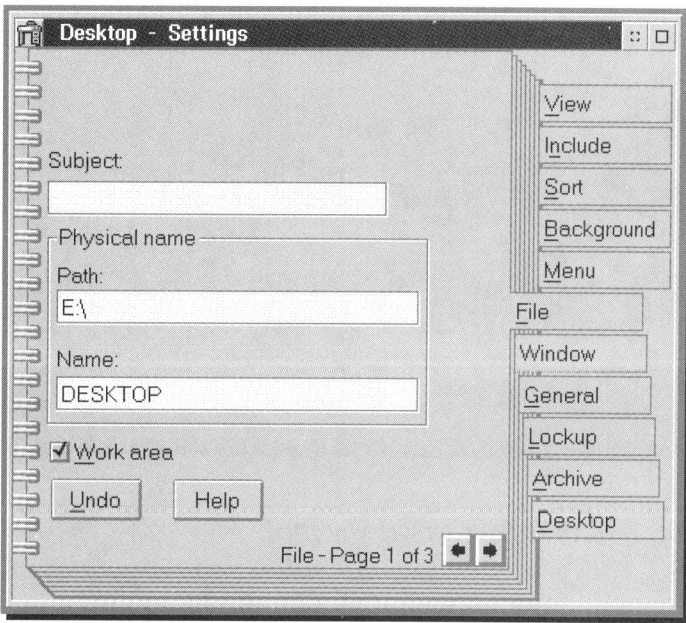

Figure 5.19. *Page 1 of the File tab lets you add a descriptive Subject for the folder and (if desired) turn the folder into a Work Area.*

The *Subject* field is an optional field. If you enter something in this field, it may be used by other OS/2 application programs for special purposes.

The *Physical name* field contains the drive and real subdirectory name associated with the folder. You cannot change these specifications.

Below the fields is a check box labeled *Work area*. If you select this option, the folder becomes a *Work Area*. Work Areas are great for holding project-oriented applications and data files. We used the following Work Area folder during the development of this book. It's a good example of how you can customize a folder.

The OS/2 Warp Survival Guide

Figure 5.20. *Work Area folders let you group your tools for a particular project.*

This example Work Area folder contains Windows programs, OS/2 programs, and OS/2 shadow objects. It has a bitmap image as its background, with small size icons, and an italicized font.

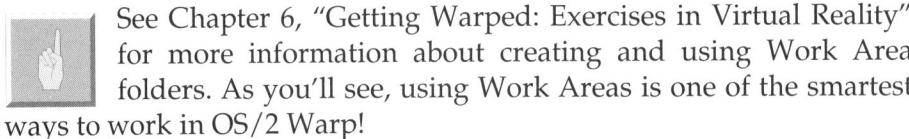 See Chapter 6, "Getting Warped: Exercises in Virtual Reality" for more information about creating and using Work Area folders. As you'll see, using Work Areas is one of the smartest ways to work in OS/2 Warp!

Page 2 of the File tab lets you view certain details about the folder, and it lets you set or clear the flags (normal file attributes) associated with the folder's real subdirectory file. The following figure illustrates the settings on page 2 of the File tab for the desktop folder.

5

Customizing OS/2 Warp

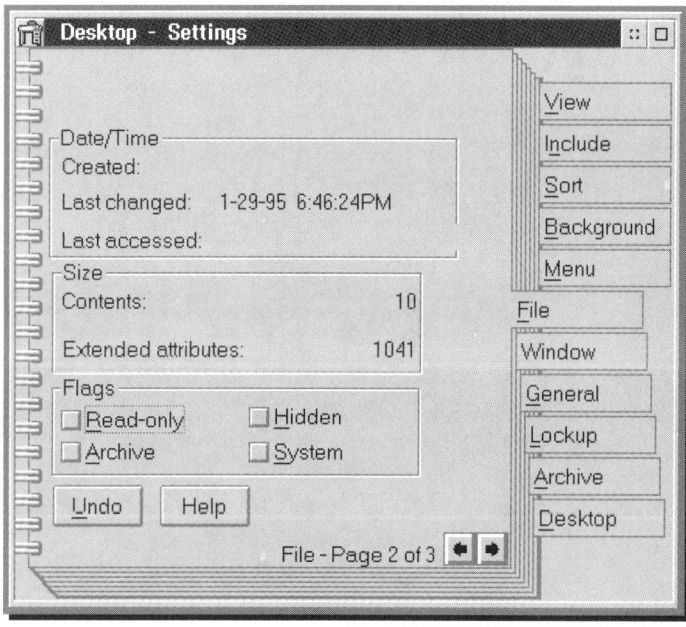

Figure 5.21. *Page 2 of the File tab shows you file details for the folder (subdirectory).*

On this page, you can see the *Date* and *Time* the folder (subdirectory) was *Created*, *Last changed*, and *Last accessed* (if that data exists). It also shows you the file's *Size* and the size of its *Extended attributes*.

In the *Flags* field, you can change the flag attributes for the folder (subdirectory). These flags are the same as the traditional DOS file attributes.

- *Read-Only:* Select this flag to keep the contents of the folder from being changed. You might use this flag to protect archived data files from being accidentally altered.

- *Hidden:* Select this flag to hide the folder in the file system. By default, hidden objects cannot be seen in any folders on the desktop.

- *Archive:* Set or clear this flag to set or clear the folder's archive attribute. Many programs use the archive attribute to perform automatic backup. The file system automatically sets this flag ON when the contents of a file are changed.

- *System:* This flag is for files that are part of the operating system.

The OS/2 Warp Survival Guide

 If you select the read-only, hidden, and system flags for a folder, that folder will seem to have disappeared the next time you start the operating system.

Page 3 of the File tab presents certain information from the *extended attributes* of the folder. The following figure illustrates the settings on page 3 of the File tab for our *OS/2 Book* Work Area folder.

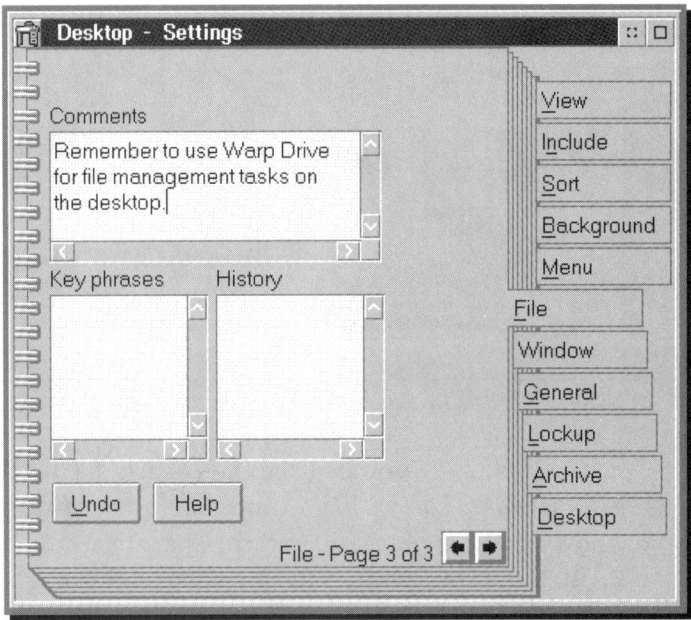

Figure 5.22. Page 3 of the File tab settings shows certain extended attributes for the folder.

You can type anything you want about the selected folder in the *Comments* and *Key Phrases* fields. The *History* field displays a chronological record of the folder; you cannot type anything in this field.

These fields are optional; you don't need to have anything in these fields. You might find the comments field a useful place to attach your own notations about the object.

The information on this page of the settings notebook is part of the extended attributes for the folder. Programs written for OS/2 can use this information, although only a few applications currently take advan-

Customizing OS/2 Warp

tage of this feature. For example, a word processor program might categorize files according to the information in these fields. See Chapter 10, "Advanced Warping," for more information about extended attributes.

Window Tab

The *Window* tab is common to most objects' settings. It allows you to control how the object appears and behaves when opened. The following figure illustrates the page that appears for the Window tab.

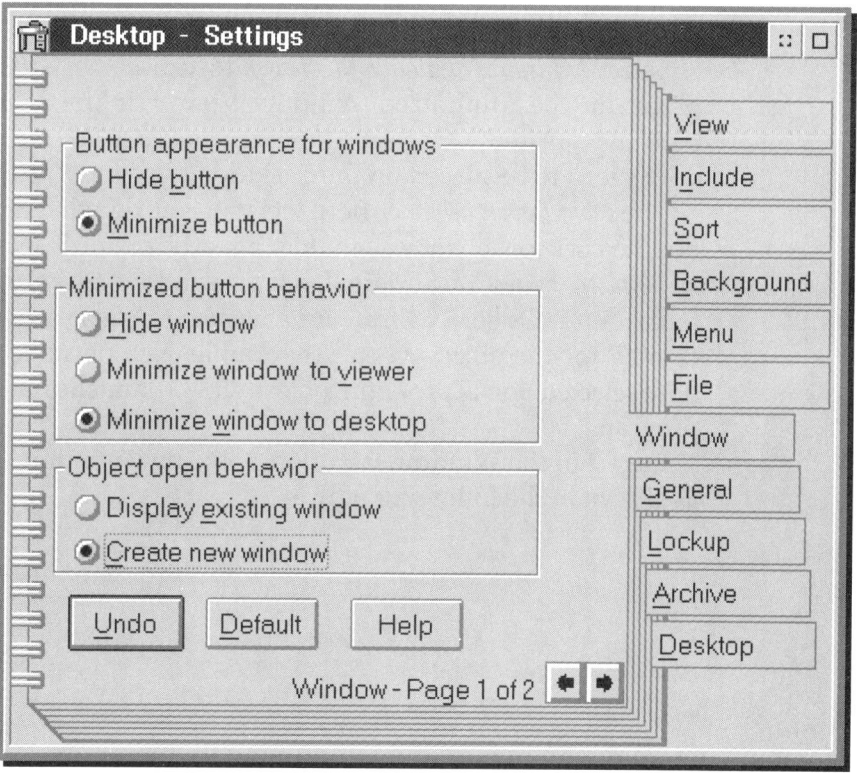

Figure 5.23.   *Page 1 of the Window tab lets you change the appearance and behavior of a folder object.*

The *Button appearance for windows* field lets you choose between whether the *Hide* or *Minimize* button appears in the upper-right corner of the window when it's open.  The *Hide button* and *Minimize button* options simply change the appearance of the minimize button (as shown above).

If you selected *Minimize button* in the *Button appearance for windows* field, the options in the *Minimized button behavior* field are available. Select *Hide window* to cause the window to be hidden when the minimize button is pressed. To restore a hidden window, select it from the Window List (click the left and right mouse buttons simultaneously on any portion of the desktop to get the Window List).

Select *Minimize window to viewer* to cause the window's icon to be placed in the Minimized Window Viewer folder when the minimize button is pressed. Or select *Minimize window to desktop* to cause the window's icon to be placed on the desktop.

The *Object open behavior* field lets you control what happens when you double-click on an object that is already open. Select *Display existing window* to cause the original object window to become active in the foreground. Or select *Create new window* to cause a new window to be created for the object when you double-click on its icon. With this option selected for a program object, OS/2 launches a new copy of the program.

Page 2 of the Window tab offers some new window behavior options, as shown in the following figure.

Customizing OS/2 Warp

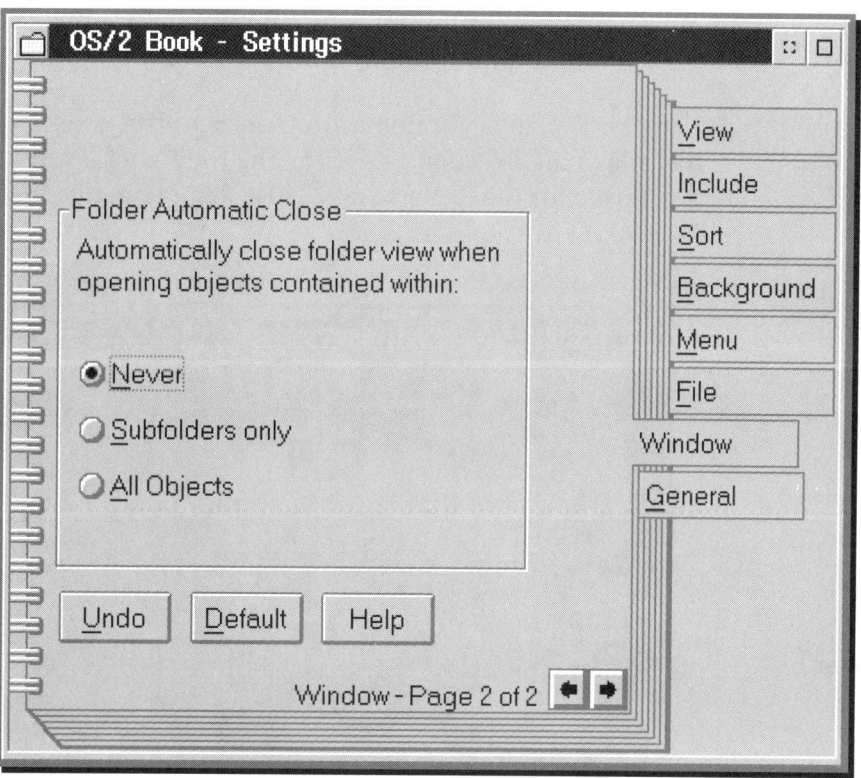

Figure 5.24. *Page 2 of the Window tab lets you enable the new Folder Automatic Close feature of OS/2 Warp.*

If you find yourself constantly closing windows to get back to your desktop, you might want to try this feature. As you open objects in a folder, the folder closes automatically, keeping your open-window count to a minimum.

The *Never* radio button disables the feature. The *Subfolders only* option causes the folder to close automatically whenever you open another folder contained in this folder. The *All Objects* option causes the folder to close whenever you open an object it contains.

General Tab

The *General* tab is common to all objects. These settings let you change the title of an object and its icon. The following figure illustrates the settings page for the General tab. This example happens to be for our *OS/2 Book* Work Area folder.

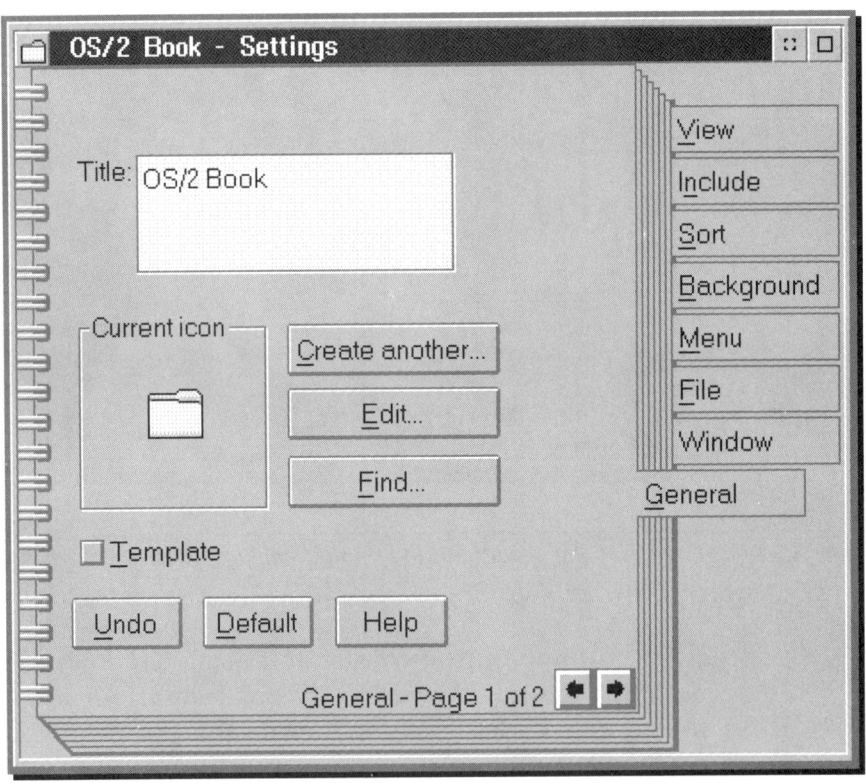

Figure 5.25.   *Page 1 of the General tab lets you change an object's title and icon.*

If you want to change an object's title, type the new text in the *Title* field. The actual title (adjacent to the object's icon) changes as soon as your cursor leaves the field.

Customizing OS/2 Warp

There's an easier way to change an object's title. Just hold down the **Alt** key and click anywhere in the text adjacent to the icon. A text box will open with the current title inside it, allowing you to change the text at will. You can even press Enter to create multiple line titles. Click outside the box to complete the change.

If you want to change the icon associated with the object, you can use the *Create another...* button, *Edit...* button, or the *Find...* button. The *Create another* and *Edit* buttons take you to the OS/2 Icon Editor, where you can create your own icon. The *Find* button presents you with a Find dialog box, allowing you to search your subdirectories for icon files. When you find the icon you want, select it and click on *OK*. The new icon will appear in the *Current icon* field of the General tab's settings page, and anywhere else it's currently being displayed.

This is the icon that represents the object in its "closed state" (object not open or running). If you change this icon, you'll probably also want to change the "open state." This icon is available on page 2 of the General tab, as shown in the following figure.

The OS/2 Warp Survival Guide

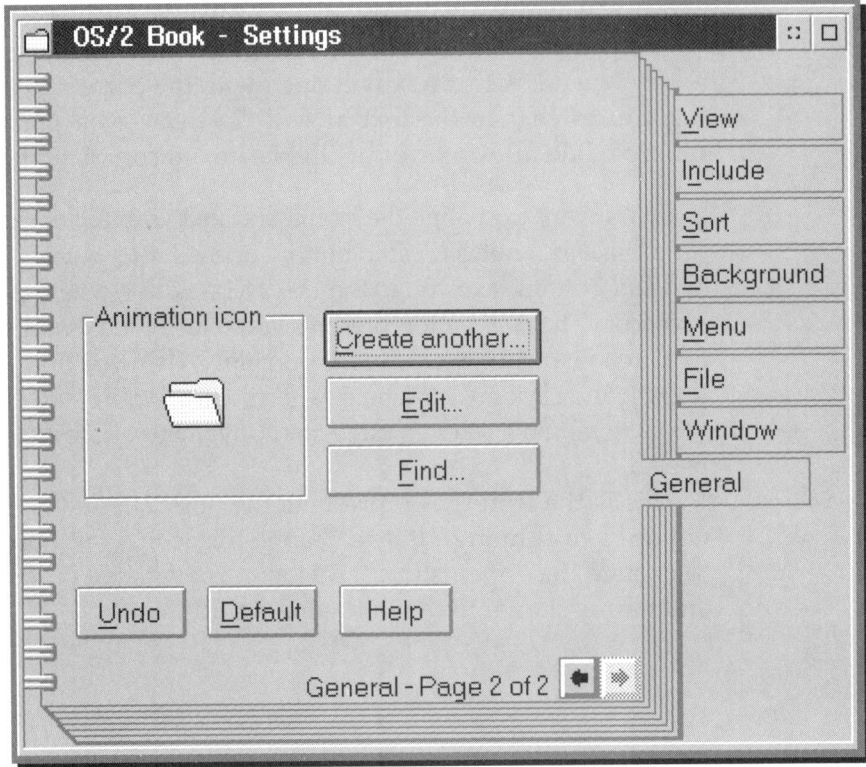

Figure 5.26.   *Page 2 of the General tab lets you specify which icon should be used to represent the folder when it's open.*

IBM calls this their *animated icon* feature. Well, that might be stretching it a bit. The animation consists of two icons: one for when the folder is closed, and one for when the folder is open. If you want to see a better example of an animated icon in OS/2, run the *WebExplorer* and watch the upper-right corner of the window while you're surfing the net.

5

Customizing OS/2 Warp

Lockup Tab

This tab is only available for the desktop folder. It lets you set the OS/2 Lockup security feature. When enabled, OS/2 will hide the contents of your screen and lock the keyboard after a specified amount of inactivity. To unlock OS/2, you must type a password.

The Lockup tab has three pages associated with it. The following figure illustrates the settings found under page 1 of the Lockup tab.

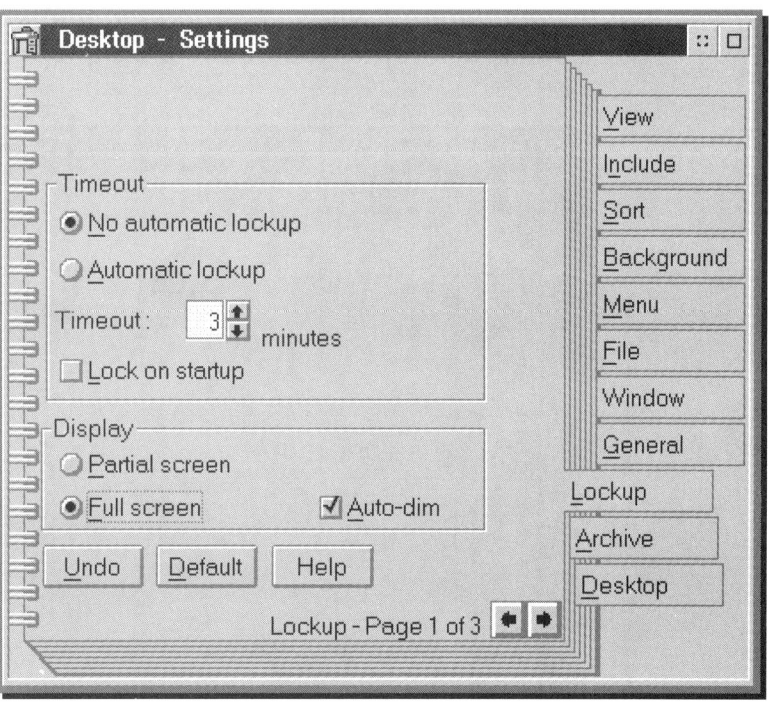

Figure 5.27. *The Lockup tab lets you control how and when your computer locks itself.*

To enable the Lockup feature, select the *Automatic lockup* button. The *Timeout* value tells OS/2 when to lock up. After the specified number of minutes elapses without anyone touching the keyboard or mouse, OS/2 will lock up. If this value isn't what you want, click on the up or down arrows to adjust it.

The OS/2 Warp Survival Guide

If you select the *Lock on startup* option, OS/2 will lock up as soon as it starts, forcing you to enter your password before you can access the desktop.

The options in the *Display* field let you use the full screen to display the image or limit the image to a portion of the screen. You can also select the *Auto-dim* feature to enable the padlock screen saver. With Auto-dim on, the screen will blank after a time and the floating padlock icon appears. This helps protect your screen from phosphor burn by constantly changing what's being displayed.

The settings on page 2 of the Lockup tab let you select a color or image that will appear when OS/2 locks up. It works exactly like the Background tab for specifying colors or images.

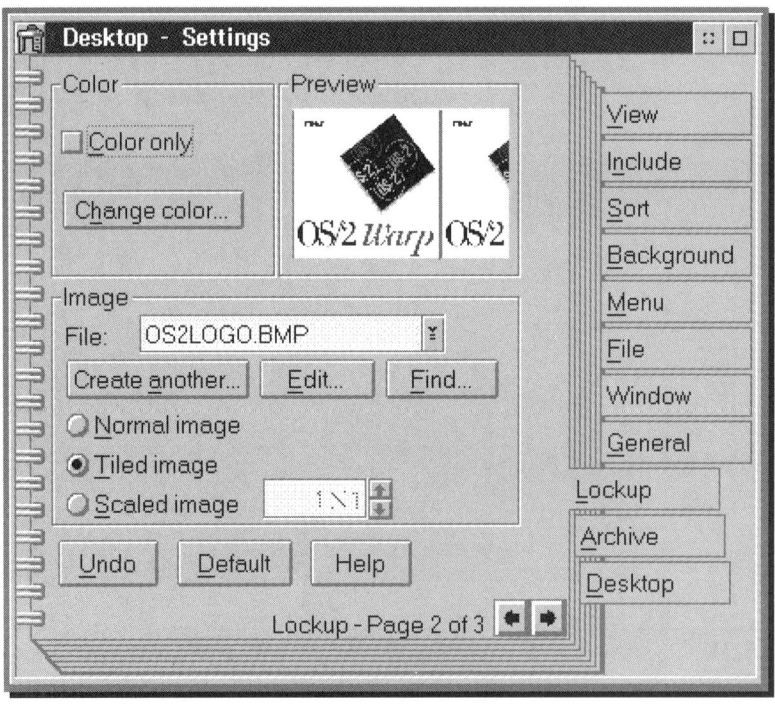

Figure 5.28.   *Page 2 of the Lockup tab lets you specify the image that appears when OS/2 Warp is locked up.*

Customizing OS/2 Warp

If you don't specify an image file name, you won't see an image when OS/2 locks up. Instead you'll see a blank screen with a padlock icon floating around the screen to indicate the system is locked. The *Create another...* and *Edit...* buttons take you to the Icon editor where you can create or edit small bitmap files.

Use the sizing buttons to control how the image is displayed. If the bitmap is smaller than the full screen, you might want to use the *Tiled* or *Scaled image* options. A scaled image is repeated on the screen as many times as you specify in the field next to the option.

The setting on page 3 lets you establish or change your password. This is the password that must be typed to unlock OS/2 Warp.

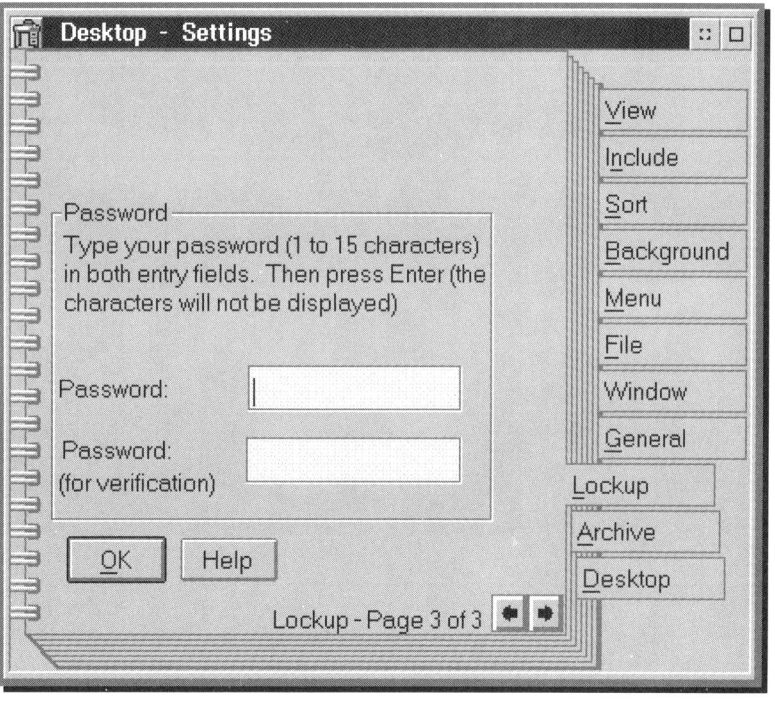

Figure 5.29.   *Use page 3 of the Lockup tab to set your security password.*

Because the characters you type are not displayed, you'll need to type your password in both fields to assure that you didn't make a typing mistake.

The OS/2 Warp Survival Guide

Archive Tab

The Archive tab is only available for the Desktop folder. It lets you specify how you want OS/2 Warp to archive your system files—the minimum group of files required by OS/2 to start the Workplace Shell in the event of a system failure. This tab also lets you specify whether or not OS/2 should display the new system recovery choices at startup. When you click on the *Archive* tab, the notebook page shown in the following figure appears.

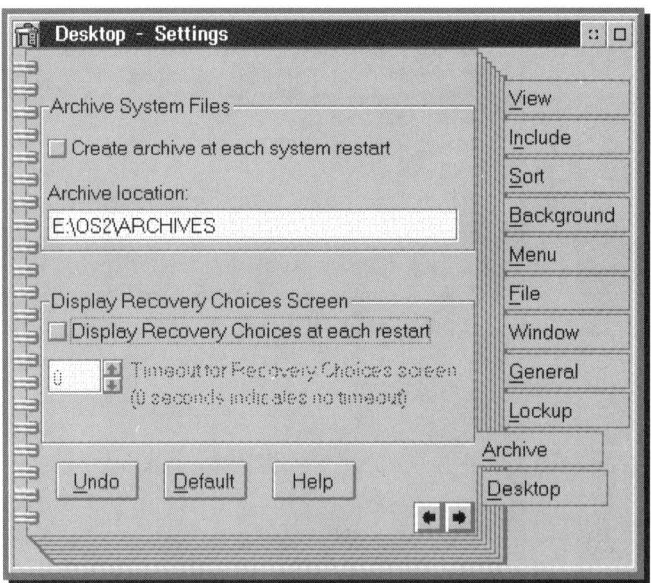

Figure 5.30. Use the Archive tab to enable/disable the new Archive and Recovery Choices features.

When you installed OS/2 Warp, an original archive was made of the system files (in \OS2\ARCHIVES). If you want OS/2 to create a new archive every time you successfully start OS/2, click on the *Create archive at each system restart* check box. If you want the archive to be stored in a different location, specify a path in the *Archive location* field.

Customizing OS/2 Warp

The *Recovery Choices* feature is an optional menu that you can have displayed when OS/2 Warp is starting up. This menu offers the following choices:

- Restore archived system files
- Go to a command line
- Reset the primary display to VGA
- Start the Maintenance Desktop
- Start the system using a customized CONFIG.SYS file

If you want this menu to appear each time OS/2 starts, select the *Display Recovery Choices at each restart* check box, and specify an amount of time that the system should wait before automatically leaving the menu and opening the desktop.

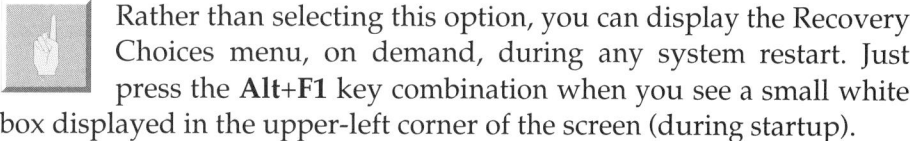
Rather than selecting this option, you can display the Recovery Choices menu, on demand, during any system restart. Just press the **Alt+F1** key combination when you see a small white box displayed in the upper-left corner of the screen (during startup).

Desktop Tab

This tab is only available for the Desktop folder. It controls the Save Desktop settings feature. This feature allows you to specify whether or not you want OS/2 to "remember" how your desktop is arranged when you shut down.

After you get your desktop arranged the way you want it, you might want to select this feature and then shut down OS/2 to save the settings. Then, the next time you start OS/2, turn this feature off so that each time you subsequently start OS/2, you'll get your saved desktop back.

The OS/2 Warp Survival Guide

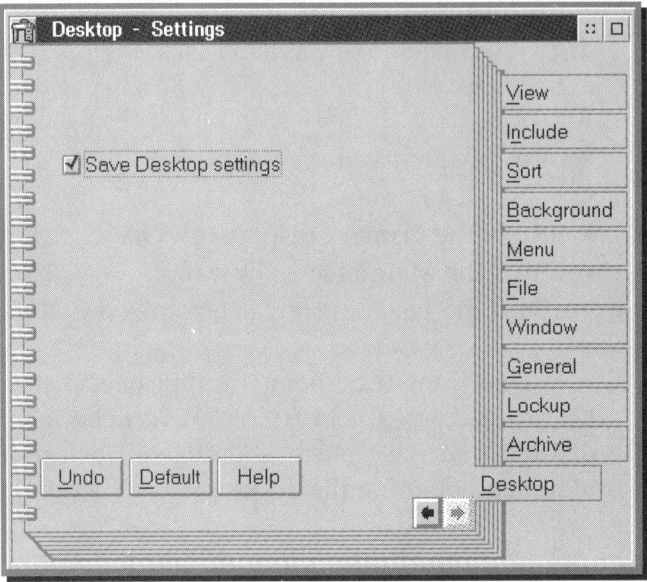

Figure 5.31.   *Use the Desktop tab to enable/disable the Save Desktop feature.*

If you want this feature enabled, select the Save Desktop setting check box. Otherwise de-select it. This feature is like the *Save Settings On Exit* option in Windows.

Folder Settings Summary

When you're finished changing the settings, close the notebook either by double-clicking on the object icon button (in the upper-left corner of the window) or by selecting the *Close* option on the context menu. All your settings will be saved, regardless of which tab or page you're on when you close the notebook.

Program Object Settings

The settings notebooks for program objects are similar to the settings notebooks for folders, in that they can have the *Window, Menu, File,* and *General* tabs, just like the settings notebooks for folders. But that's where the similarity ends. This section discusses the unique index tabs pro-

Customizing OS/2 Warp

vided for program objects. For discussions of the common tabs, refer to the settings notebook for folder objects earlier in this chapter.

To help explain the settings notebook for program objects, we'll use *Paint-Brush* as an example program. We've chosen PaintBrush to make a point: OS/2 provides seamless support for Microsoft Windows applications.

If a program is properly installed under OS/2, it will have two objects: a *program object* (the virtual object that references the actual program file) and a *program file object* (the "real" program file). Each of these objects has its own settings notebook. The following figure shows both settings notebooks for the PaintBrush program object.

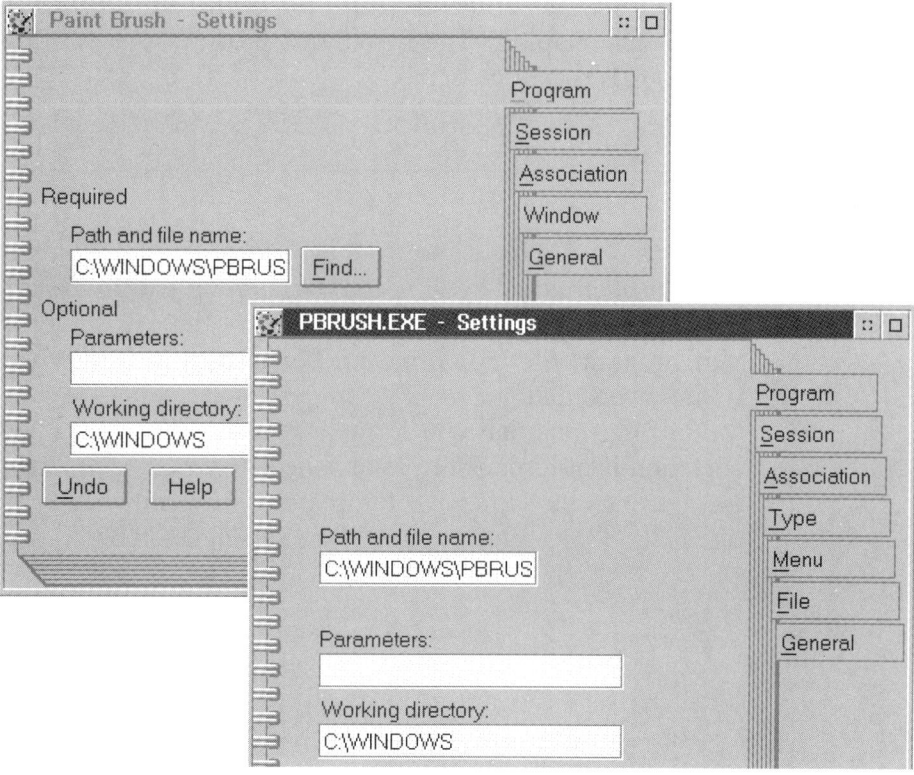

Figure 5.32. *There are two objects for most programs: the Program Object and the Program File Object.*

The first notebook (titled *Paint Brush–Settings*) is for the program object—the virtual object. The second notebook (titled *PBRUSH.EXE - Settings*) is for the program file object—the real file. Notice that the *Paint Brush* notebook has a *Window* tab and the *PBRUSH.EXE* notebook has a *Type* tab and a *File* tab. This is one way you can tell whether you're changing settings for a virtual or real object. Another way is the title of the object (Paint Brush vs. PBRUSH.EXE). This distinction is covered more comprehensively in Chapter 6, "Getting Warped: Exercises in Virtual Reality."

When you open the settings for a program object, a window appears containing that object's settings notebook. (If you need instructions to open the settings notebook, refer to "Using the Settings Notebook" earlier in this chapter.) The first index tab in a program object's settings notebook is the *Program* tab.

Program Tab

The *Program* tab lets you specify where the executable program file resides. For program objects, this is where the association is made to the real program file. For program file objects, this is where the real file name is specified.

For programs that you formally install or migrate into OS/2, this association is automatically established. If you create a new program object (using the *Program* template) you will have to specify this association through this page of the settings notebook.

Customizing OS/2 Warp

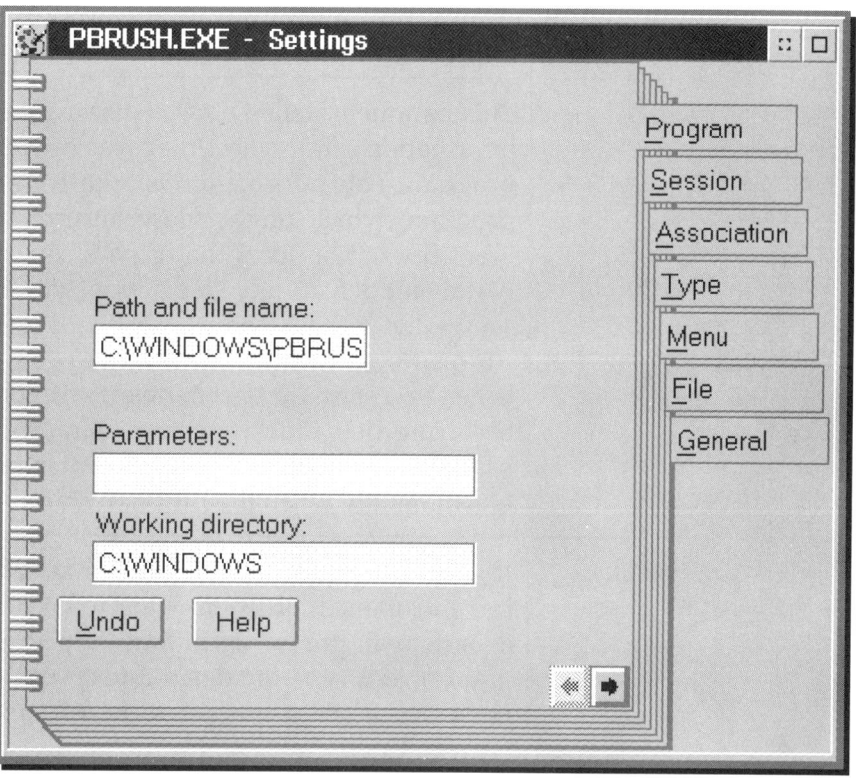

Figure 5.33.   *The Program tab is where the object is linked to the executable program file.*

There are two optional fields: *Parameters* and *Working directory*. Whatever you type in the *Parameters* field is passed to the program when it starts to run. If your program requires or supports parameters, you should refer to its documentation to determine what you can specify.

For example, an editor might support passing the name of the file you want to edit as a parameter. You could type the name of the file in the parameters field and the editor will automatically open that file when you launch the program object.

There are other special parameters supported by OS/2. They let you do the following:

Parameter	Description
%	This parameter tells OS/2 to discard the file name information of an object that was dropped on this program. This information is otherwise sent to the program, which might cause an error if the program doesn't support that type of operation. This parameter defeats any associations you might have set up under the Association tab.
[ ]	When you start a program object with this parameter string (left bracket, space character, and right bracket) you'll be prompted to enter the parameters manually when the program starts.
[text]	If you want a particular phrase or set of characters to be displayed, or if you want to be prompted by a particular phrase each time you start the program object, type the desired text within brackets. For example, if you want to be prompted by the words "Good day...enter a file name:" type [Good day...enter a file name:] in the *Parameters* field.
%*	This parameter lets you add drag-and-drop support for starting the program object. It causes the drive letter, path, and file name of the object you dragged onto the program object to be sent to the program.
%**P	Passes the drive and path information without the last backslash (\).
%**D	Passes the drive letter with a colon (:).
%**N	Passes only the file name (without an extension).

Parameter	Description
%**F	Passes the full file name (with the extension, but without the path).
%**E	Passes only the file name extension (without the leading dot or period). In HPFS, the extension always comes after the last period.

For example, we have a data file named TEMPLATE.TXT. We want to use drag-and-drop to edit this file with the MYEDIT.EXE editor program and save the edited file as MYFILE.TXT in the NEW subdirectory on Drive D:. To accomplish this, we would type the following into the *Parameters* field for the MYEDIT.EXE program object:

%* C:\NEW\MYFILE.%**E

When we drag the TEMPLATE.TXT object and drop it on the MYEDIT.EXE object, the MYEDIT editor program starts and opens the file named TEMPLATE.TXT. When we exit the MYEDIT program, it saves the modified file as C:\NEW\MYFILE.TXT.

The *Working directory* field lets you specify a directory name that you want to be the current directory when the program starts.

Session Tab

The *Session* tab lets you specify whether the program runs in a window or uses the full screen. You can also force the program to run in its own separate session and select how the window behaves when it opens and when you exit the program.

The following figure illustrates the page that appears under the Session tab of the settings notebook.

The OS/2 Warp Survival Guide

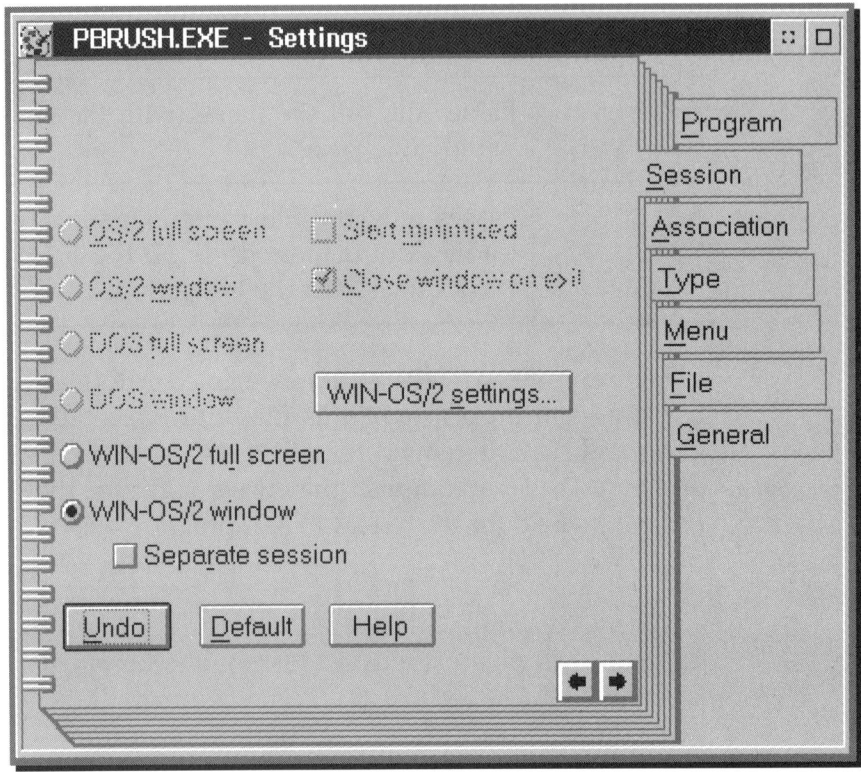

Figure 5.34. *The Session tab lets you select how the program will run under OS/2.*

Select the appropriate window or full-screen setting. For OS/2 programs, only the *OS/2* options are available. For DOS programs, only the *DOS* options are available. For Windows programs, only the *WIN-OS/2* options are available. For DOS and Windows programs, the *DOS* or *WIN-OS/2 Settings* button appears, allowing you to "fine-tune" your session. When you click on these buttons, you'll see the corresponding dialog box for selecting settings to change, as shown in the following figure.

Customizing OS/2 Warp

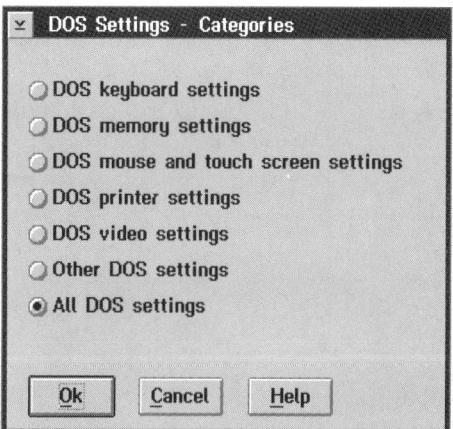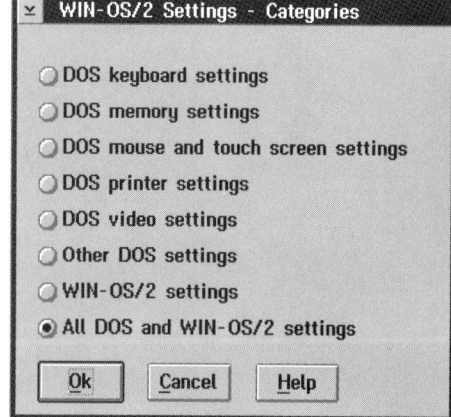

Figure 5.35. *When you click on the DOS or WIN-OS/2 Settings button, the corresponding dialog box appears, letting you choose which settings you want to change.*

Select the type of settings you want to change and click on *OK*. The corresponding DOS or WIN-OS/2 Session settings window will appear. Refer to Chapter 7, "DOS and Windows Under OS/2 Warp," for details about changing these settings to "fine-tune" your DOS and Windows sessions.

Select the *Start minimized* option on the Session tab if you want the program to minimize itself when it's opened. Select the *Close window on exit* option if you want the window to close automatically when you exit the program. This is a default setting for program objects.

Association Tab

The *Association* tab is where you set up links between your programs and data files based on data file types and/or file names. Associations allow you to start the program by double-clicking on an associated data-file object.

The following figure illustrates the Association tab settings for Paint-Brush.

The OS/2 Warp Survival Guide

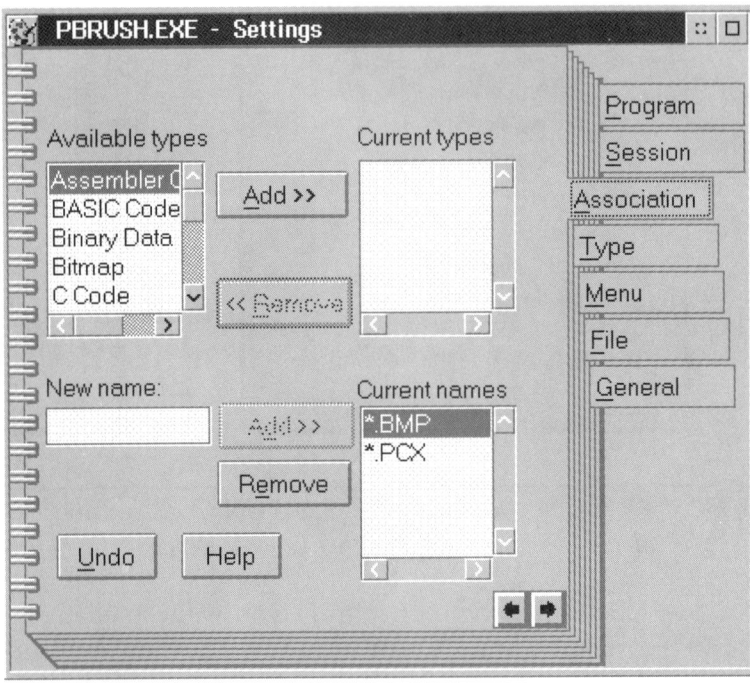

Figure 5.36.   *The Association tab lets you associate data-file objects with the program object.*

To establish an association, either click on the appropriate object type in the *Available types* field and click on the *Add>>* button, or type a file specification in the *New name:* field and click on the *Add>>* button to add it to the list of *Current names*.

For example, you might want to set up an association between all files with an extension of .ZIP and PKWare's PKUNZIP.EXE program. To accomplish this, first you would create a program object for PKUNZIP.EXE. Then, in that object's settings notebook, type *.ZIP in the *New name:* field and click on the *Add>>* button. Then, whenever you double-click on a data-file object with a file name extension of .ZIP, OS/2 will start PKUNZIP in its own DOS session and pass along the name of the .ZIP file.

 If you set up the *Parameters* field properly on the Program tab, you could also drag the .ZIP to and drop it on the PKUNZIP object to decompress it.

5

Customizing OS/2 Warp

Type Tab

The *Type* tab lets you add new object types to the *Available types* list, and set up an association between the program and data files based on object type.

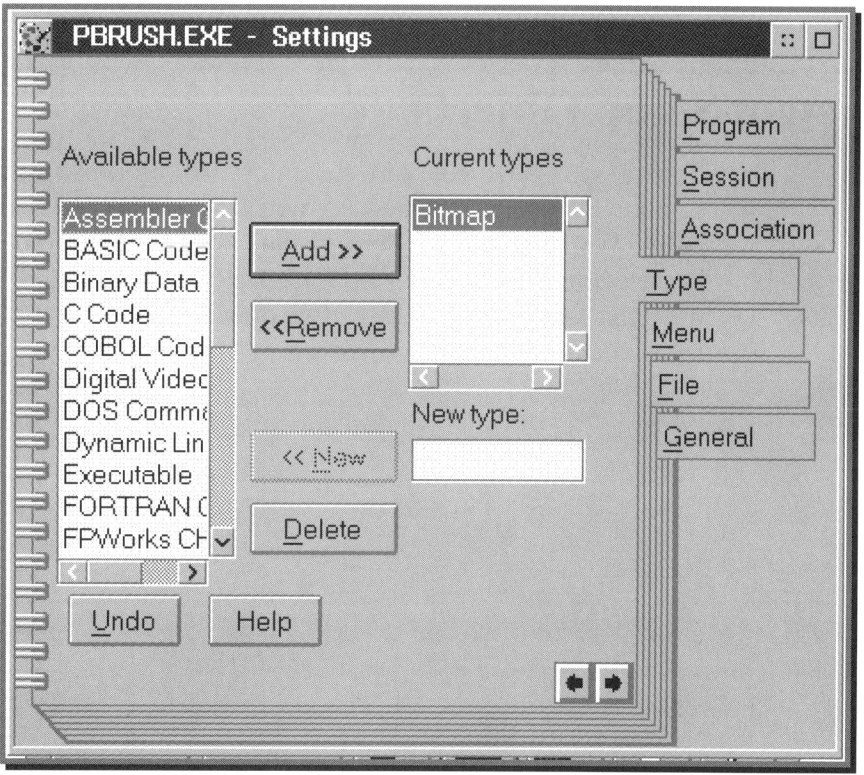

Figure 5.37. Use the Type tab to set up associations with types of data files for the program.

This concludes the Program Object Settings section of this chapter. For information about the *Window*, *Menu*, and *File* tabs, refer to the Folder Object Settings section.

Program Settings Summary

As with the folder settings, when you are finished changing the program settings, close the notebook either by double-clicking on the object icon button (in the upper-left corner of the window) or by selecting the *Close* option on the context menu. All your settings will be saved, regardless of which tab or page you're on when you close the notebook.

System Setup Objects

You've seen how you can customize the Workplace Shell through the settings notebooks. Another way you can customize the Workplace Shell is through the *System Setup* objects. The System Setup folder is in the OS/2 System folder. When you open the System Setup folder, a window similar to the following appears:

5

Customizing OS/2 Warp

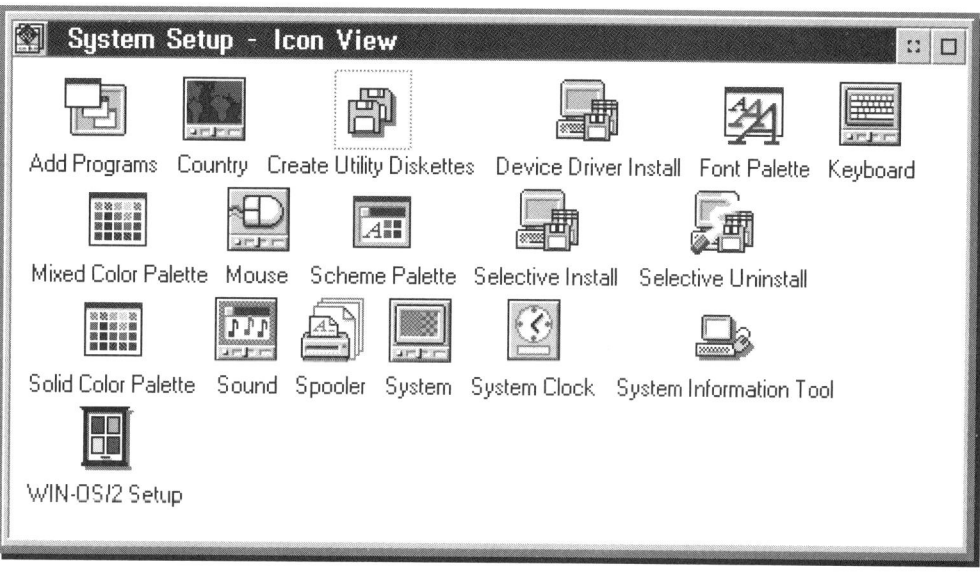

Figure 5.38. *The System Setup folder contains objects that let you customize many aspects of the Workplace Shell.*

In this section, we'll present each of these objects, starting with Add Programs and ending with WIN-OS/2 Setup.

Add Programs

The *Add Programs* object assists you in two ways: First it helps you find DOS, Windows, and OS/2 programs that are already on your system. Then it sets them up properly under OS/2 Warp, creating the appropriate program objects based on information in a migration database (included with OS/2). When you open this object, the following window appears:

The OS/2 Warp Survival Guide

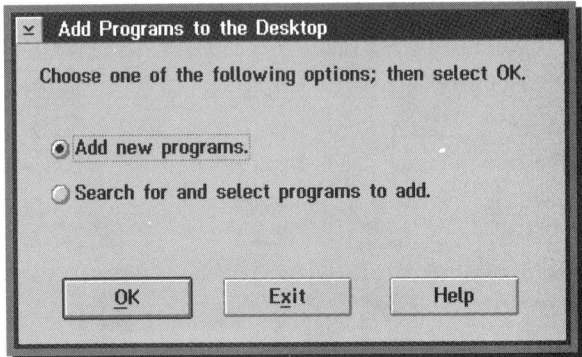

Figure 5.39. *If you select the Add new programs option, OS/2 won't ask you any more questions about adding programs. It just does it!*

Unless you're sure that you want *all* your DOS, Windows, and OS/2 programs automatically added to and set up under OS/2 Warp, select the *Search for and select programs to add* option. When you click on *OK*, the following window appears:

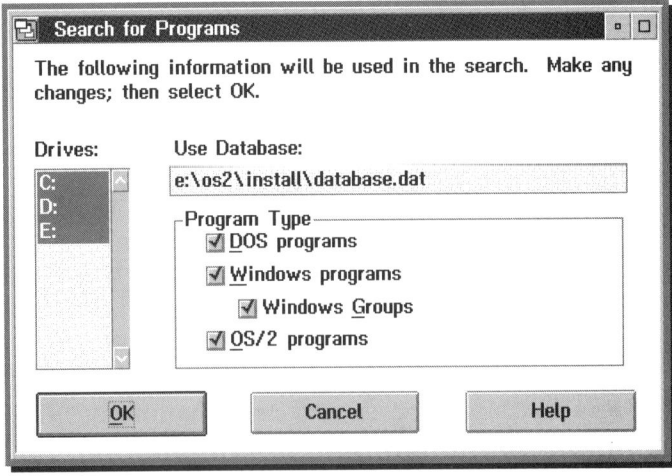

Figure 5.40. *By default, the Add Programs object is set up to search all drives and subdirectories for all DOS, Windows, and OS/2 programs.*

Customizing OS/2 Warp

Select the drives and program types you want OS/2 to search for. When you click on *OK*, OS/2 will search according to your selections, and display its findings in a new window. Follow the instructions on the screen to select only the ones you actually want added, and click on *OK*. OS/2 Warp will proceed to build program objects that it places on your desktop in the *DOS Programs*, *Windows Programs*, and *Additional OS/2 Programs* folders. Open these folders and run each one to test the migration. If a program gives you trouble, refer to Chapter 7, "DOS and Windows Under OS/2 Warp," for tips about "fine-tuning" these program objects.

Country

The *Country* object lets you set up your system for operation in one of several countries. You can change character sets and measurement systems, date and time formats, and the formatting of currency numbers. When you launch this object, the following settings notebook appears:

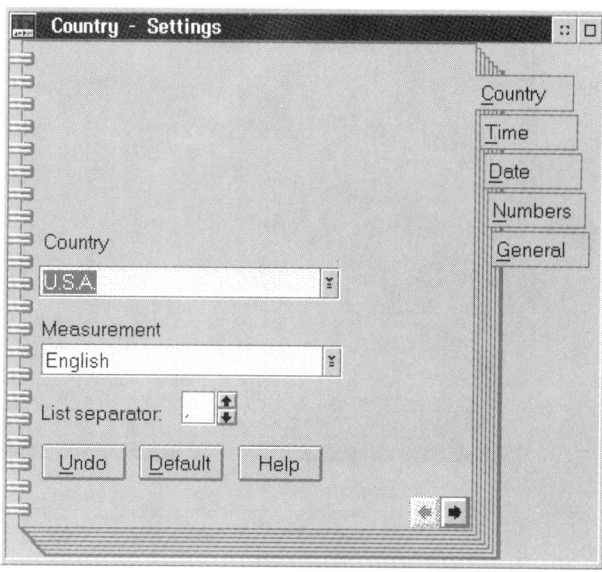

Figure 5.41. *You can modify certain "language"-based options through Country settings.*

The OS/2 Warp Survival Guide

The notebook opens up to the *Country* tab. Use this tab to select the appropriate country. This selection effects the character set (code pages) that the system will use. If you want your system to present units of measure in metric or the picas-and-points systems select your option in the *Measurement* list box.

Time Tab

When you click on the *Time* tab, the following notebook page appears:

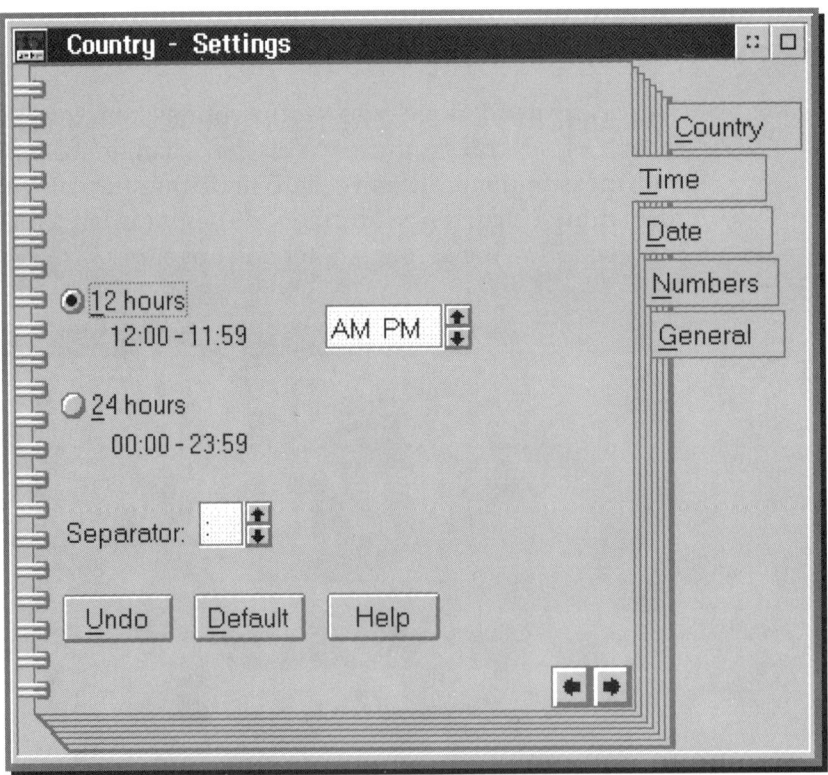

Figure 5.42.   *Use the Time tab to specify how times are to be presented.*

You can select the *12-hour* or *24-hour* time format, and you can specify the character to *separate* hours, minutes, and seconds. For the 12-hour time format, you can also specify how the abbreviation for before and after noon should look (*AM* and *PM*, *am* and *pm*, or none).

Date Tab

When you click on the *Date* tab, the following notebook page appears:

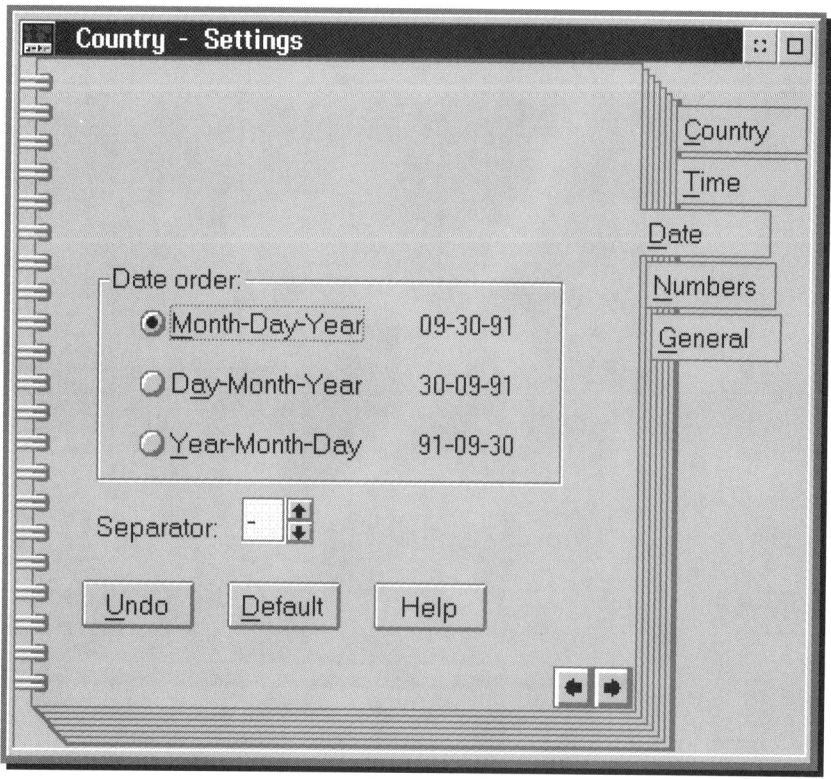

Figure 5.43.   *Use the Date tab to specify the system date format.*

Everyone has a preferred way to show dates. Some of us would write July 4, 1995 as *07-04-95*, while others would write *04/07/95*, and others (perhaps just to be different) would write *95.07.04*. Whatever your preference, select it here.

The OS/2 Warp Survival Guide

Numbers Tab

When you click on the *Numbers* tab, the following notebook page appears:

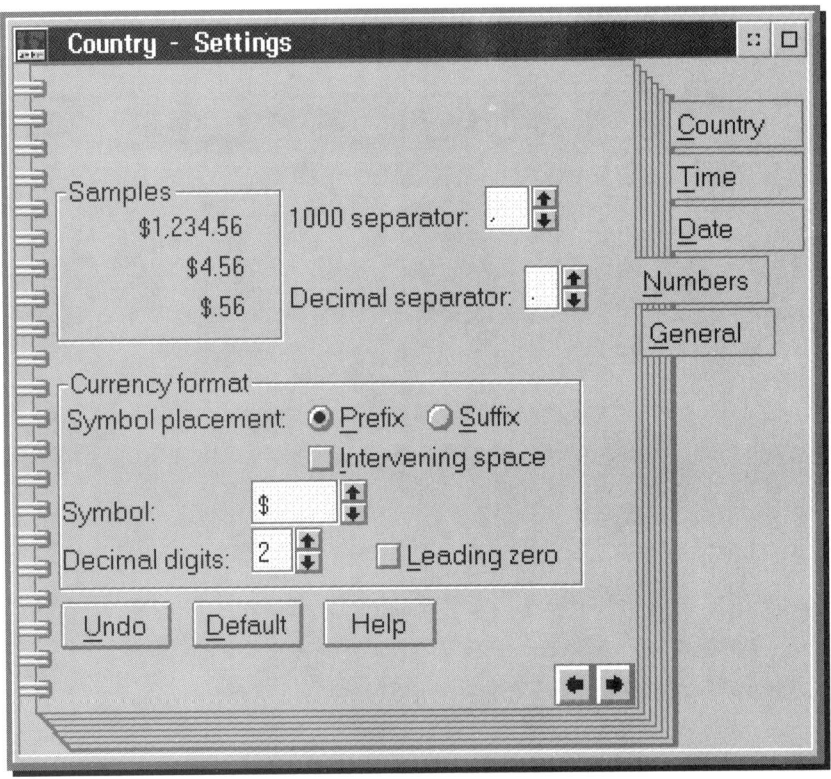

Figure 5.44.   *Use the Numbers tab to choose your preferred currency format.*

If you don't care for the default currency formatting of *$1,234.56*, you can give it a variety of different looks using the combinations provided on the Numbers tab. As you make changes, they're reflected in the *Samples* area of the notebook page.

When you're finished changing or viewing the Country settings, close the notebook by double-clicking on the object icon (upper-left corner). Your changes (if any) will be saved and start taking effect immediately.

Customizing OS/2 Warp

Create Utility Diskettes

The Create Utility Diskettes object lets you create a set of emergency system-recovery diskettes that you might be able to use to restore your system in the event you have a hard disk failure. When you launch this object a window appears, prompting you for a destination drive letter where you want to create the diskettes. You'll need three high-density diskettes, which will hold the following:

- A bootable diskette so you can start OS/2 from diskette
- Tools that can check your hard disk for errors
- Utilities that can back up and restore OS/2 directories

Device Driver Install

The *Device Driver Install* object lets you install device drivers that are distributed on *Device Support Diskettes*. This program is not for installing individual device drivers that are on normal diskettes. Device Support Diskettes contain *profile control files*, which OS/2 uses to learn about and properly install the device drivers. If you try this method for installing device drivers that are not on a Device Support Diskette, you'll get an error message. Use the Selective Install object in these cases to install your device driver.

Font Palette

The *Font Palette* object lets you reassign (change) the fonts being used for various text objects in OS/2 Warp. You can reassign the font for a particular window, for a text group (all text of a certain type), or for the entire system. When you launch the Font Palette, the following window appears:

271

The OS/2 Warp Survival Guide

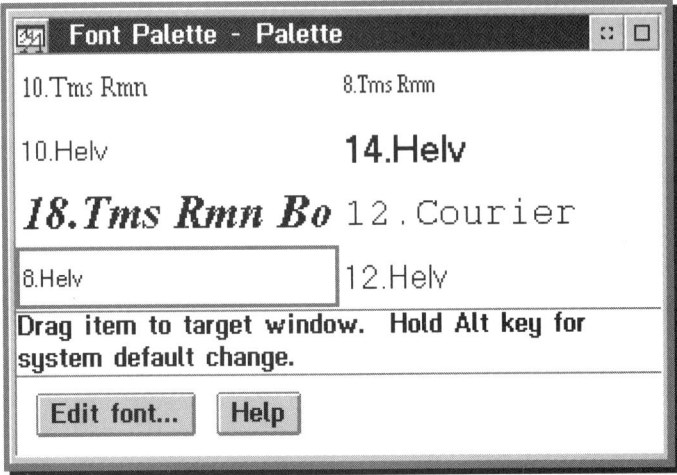

Figure 5.45. *The Font Palette lets you drag-and-drop your font selections to change the appearance of your desktop.*

Each entry on the palette is a field object that you can select and drag just like any other object in OS/2.

Changing Fonts

To change the font for a particular text object, drag the font name from the Font Palette to that object and drop it. To change the font for all objects of a particular type, hold down the **Alt** key when you drag the font to one of those types of objects.

For example, if you want to change the title-bar text for a particular window, drag the font and drop it anywhere in the title bar of that window. If you want to change the title-bar text for all windows, drag the font and drop it anywhere in the title bar of any open window. This technique works for most text objects in the Workplace Shell, including:

- Icon text
- Window title bars
- Button labels
- Input fields

If the font you want is not shown in the Font Palette, click on the *Edit* button. The Edit Font dialog box will appear.

Adding and Editing Fonts

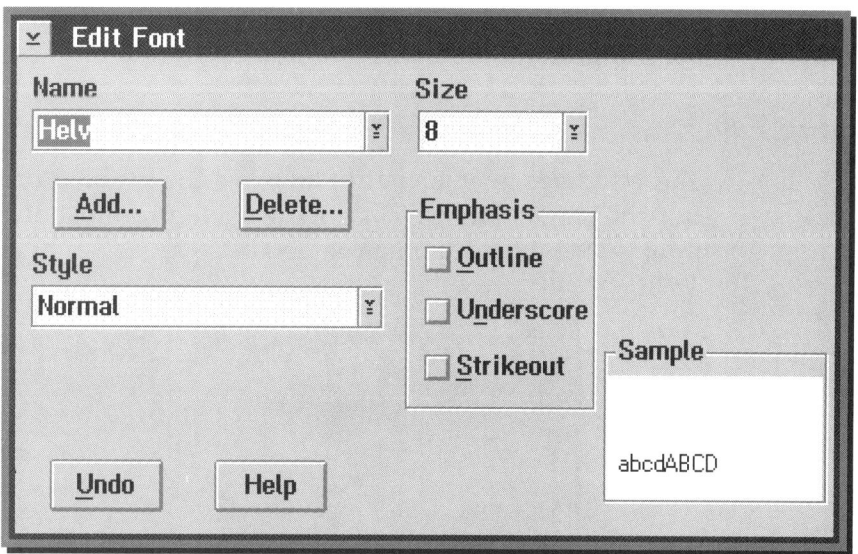

Figure 5.46.   *Use the Edit Font dialog box to change or add fonts in the system and to change the samples available on the Font Palette.*

Click on the *Add...* button to bring new fonts into the system. You'll be prompted to insert a diskette containing the new font. To change a font sample on the Font Palette, select that font before accessing the Edit Font dialog box. Then select the new font *name*, *size*, and *style* using those list boxes. You can also change the style of emphasis placed on the font using the *Outline*, *Underscore*, and *Strikeout* check boxes.

As you make changes, you can see them reflected both in the Sample window and on the Font Palette (if it's visible). If you don't like what you've done, click on the *Undo* button. When you're ready to leave the

The OS/2 Warp Survival Guide

Edit Font dialog box, double-click on the button in the upper-left corner of the dialog box.

Keyboard

The *Keyboard* object lets you set keyboard options such as repeat rate, cursor blinking rate, and the keystroke assignments for various keyboard shortcuts. When you launch the Keyboard object, the Keyboard settings notebook appears, open to the Timing tab.

Timing Tab

These settings let you control how fast the keyboard responds and how fast the cursor blinks. The following figure illustrates the Timing tab from the Keyboard settings notebook.

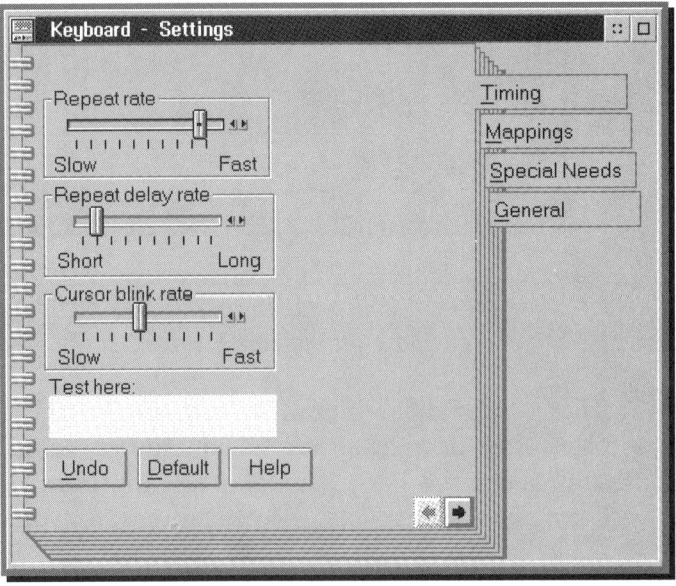

Figure 5.47. *The Timing tab lets you control the response rates of the keyboard.*

Customizing OS/2 Warp

These settings affect the rate at which your keyboard repeats key presses when you hold down keys (*Repeat rate*), and the amount of delay before this repeating occurs (*Repeat delay rate*). It also lets you set how rapidly the cursor blinks (*Cursor blink rate*).

To change a setting, drag its slider arm in the desired direction for shorter or faster rates. You can test the new setting in the *Test here* field.

Mappings Tab

The settings under this tab let you reassign the keystroke combinations associated with certain keyboard shortcut operations. When you click on the *Mappings* tab, the following page appears in the settings notebook.

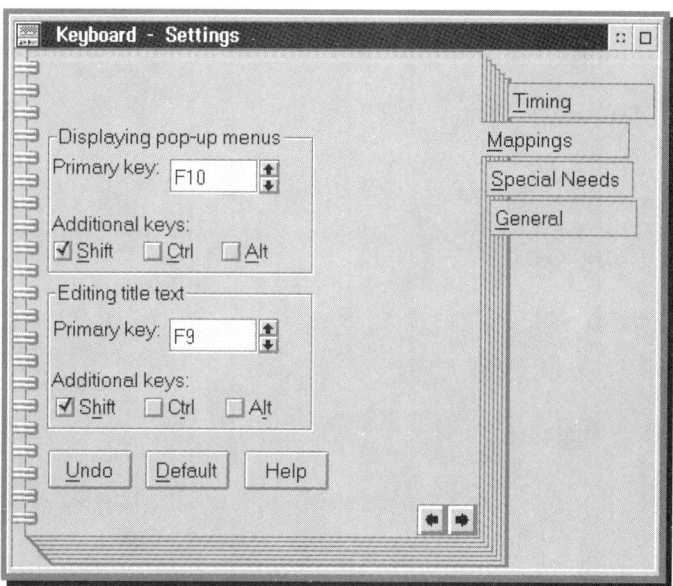

Figure 5.48. *The Mappings tab lets you customize certain keyboard shortcut operations.*

Using these settings, you can change the key combination used to display an object's context (pop-up) menu. By default, this key combination is **Shift**+**F10**, but you can change it to any key listed in the *Primary key* field (use the spin buttons [up and down arrow keys] to change the assignment). The default key combination for *Editing title text* is **Shift+F9**.

If you want the setting to include a key combination in addition to the primary key, select one or more keys from *Additional Keys* (*Shift*, *Ctrl*, and *Alt*).

Special Needs Tab

The settings under the *Special Needs* tab can make the keyboard easier to use for those with special requirements. When you click on the Special Needs tab, the following page appears in the Keyboard settings notebook.

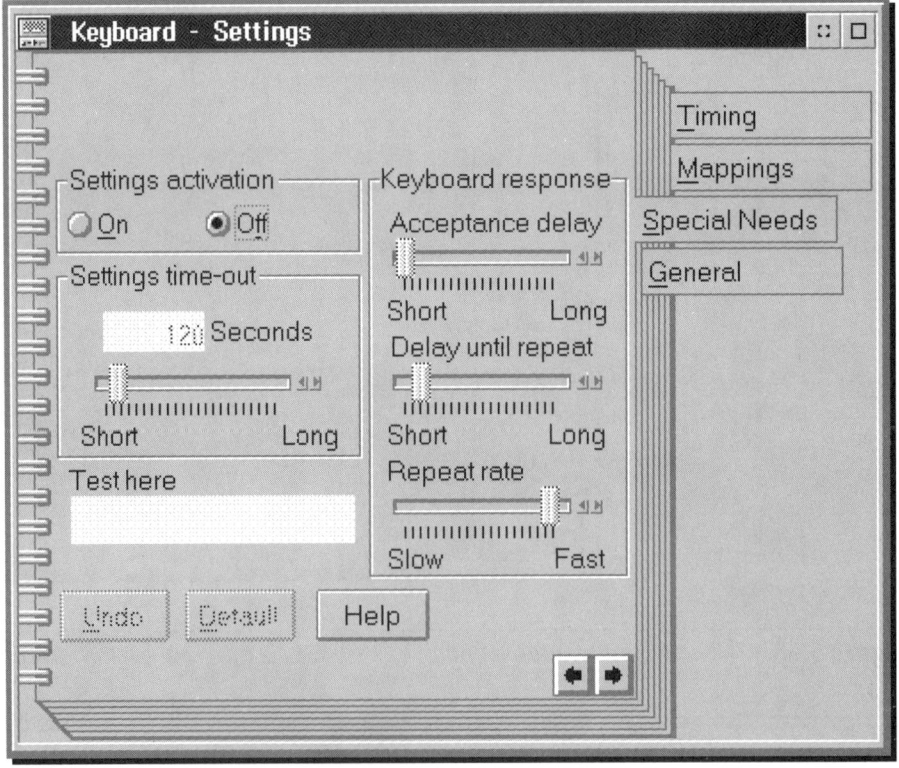

Figure 5.49. *The Special Needs tab provides keyboard controls for unique user requirements.*

Customizing OS/2 Warp

If your computer is shared by someone who would rather not use the special needs settings, the settings can be turned off and on as required via the *Settings activation* radio buttons. They can also be set to turn off automatically with the controls in the *Settings time-out* field.

You can adjust the *Acceptance delay*, which is how long a key must be held down before it's recognized as a keystroke; the *Repeat rate*, which is the rate at which the key will repeat when held down; and the *Delay until repeat*, which is how long a pressed key must be held down before it begins repeating.

General Tab

The *General* tab in the Keyboard settings notebook is the same as the General tab in any settings notebook. See the *Folder Object Settings* for details about the General tab.

Mixed Color Palette

The *Mixed Color Palette* object lets you change the color of things in the foreground or background of a window. You can reassign the colors for a particular window, for an element group (all elements of a certain type), or for the entire system. If you want to use a color that appears on the palette, simply point at the color and drag it to the desired window. The window's background will change to that color (unless the window is set up to have an image as its background). When you launch the Mixed Color Palette object, the following palette appears:

The OS/2 Warp Survival Guide

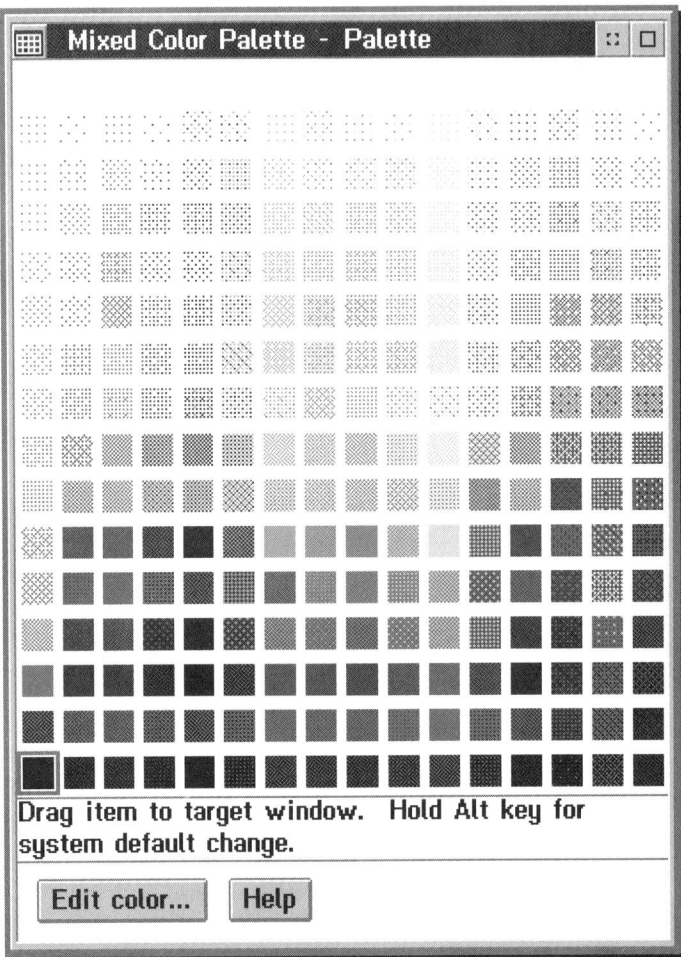

Figure 5.50. The Mixed Color Palette lets you drag-and-drop your color selections to change the appearance of your desktop.

Each color swatch on the palette is an object that you can select and drag just like any other object in OS/2.

Customizing OS/2 Warp

Changing Colors

To change the color for a particular object, drag the desired color swatch from the *Color Palette* to that object and drop it. To change the color for all objects of a particular type, hold down the **Alt** key when you drag the font to one of those types of objects.

For example, if you want to change the title-bar color for a particular window, drag the font and drop it anywhere in the title bar of that window. If you want to change the title-bar color for all windows, drag the color and drop it anywhere in the title bar of any open window. This technique works for most objects in the Workplace Shell, including:

- Text
- Window title bars
- Buttons
- Input fields
- Folder backgrounds

If the color you want is not shown in the Mixed Color Palette, click on the *Edit color...* button. The Edit Color dialog box will appear.

Editing a Color

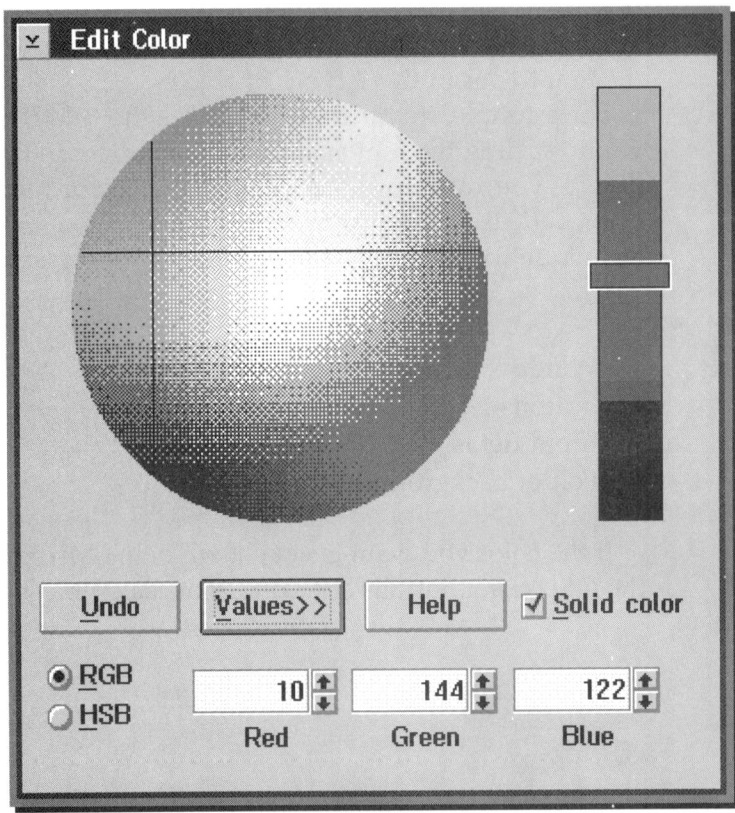

Figure 5.51. Use the Edit Color dialog box to change the color swatches available on the Mixed Color Palette.

To select a color, point-and-click directly on the color in the color wheel (the circular, multicolored area). You can then adjust the tint in the color slider bar to the right of the color wheel. If you select the *Solid color* check box, the number of possible colors is limited to only those that do not produce a *dithering* pattern (a visible mixing of different colored pixels to achieve an apparent tint).

Customizing OS/2 Warp

The *Values>>* button provides access to the RGB and HSB color selection values. You can mix your own color using the red, green, and blue (RGB) values or the hue, saturation, and brightness (HSB) values.

As you make changes, you can see them reflected both in the sliding bar area in the dialog box and on the Color Palette (if it's visible). If you don't like what you've done, click on the *Undo* button. When you're ready to leave the Edit Color dialog box, double-click on the button in the upper-left corner.

Mouse

The *Mouse* object lets you control how your mouse operates, such as the click rate and tracking speed. It also lets you change the default button assignments. When you launch the Mouse object, the Mouse settings notebook appears, open to the Timing tab.

Timing Tab

These settings let you control how fast the mouse responds to double-clicks and how fast the pointer follows your mouse movements. The following figure illustrates the Timing tab page in the Mouse settings notebook.

The OS/2 Warp Survival Guide

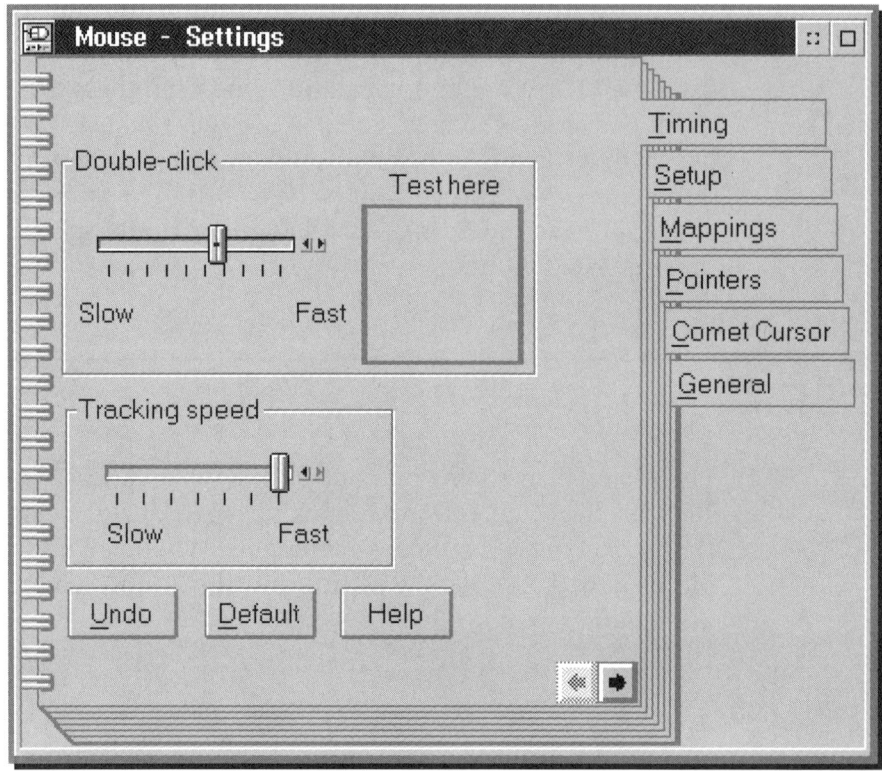

Figure 5.52.   *The Timing tab lets you control how responsive the mouse is.*

Drag the *Double-click* and *Tracking speed* sliders to the desired positions. You can use the *Test here* field to sample the settings as you change them.

Setup Tab

These settings let you set up the mouse for left-handed or right-handed use. When you click on the *Setup* tab, the page shown in the following figure appears.

Customizing OS/2 Warp

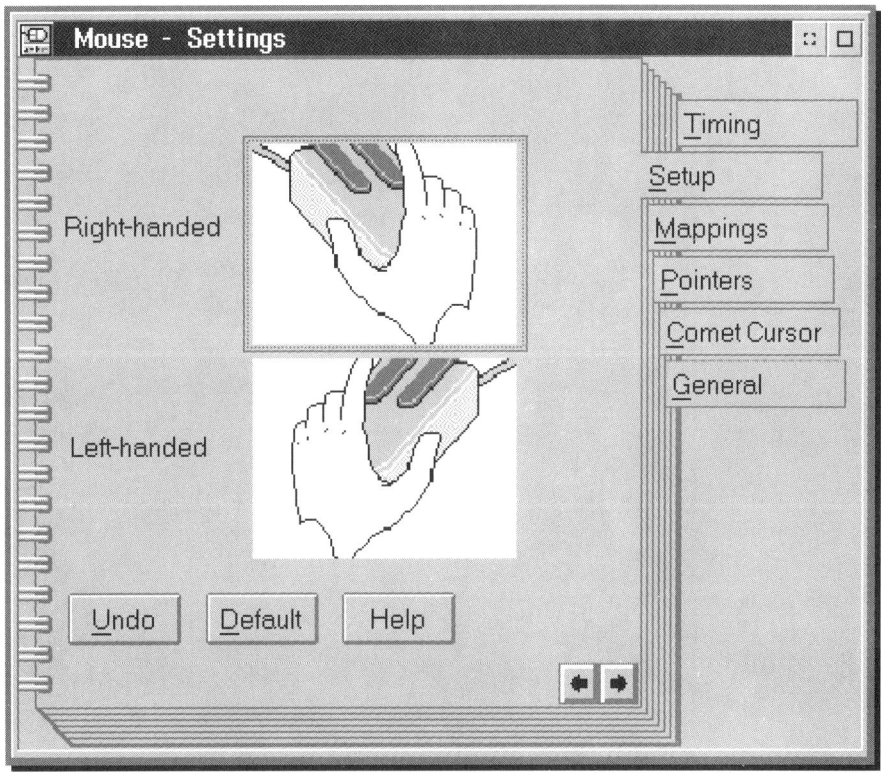

Figure 5.53. *The Setup tab lets you select between a left-handed or right-handed mouse.*

On a left-handed mouse, Mouse Button 1 is the right button, and Mouse Button 2 is the left button. On a right-handed mouse, Mouse Button 1 is the left button, and Mouse Button 2 is the right button.

To make your selection, click on the appropriate picture.

Mappings Tab

These settings let you reassign the mouse controls for performing certain mouse operations, such as dragging, opening the Window List, and opening an object's context menu. When you click on the *Mappings* tab, the following page appears in the Mouse settings notebook.

The OS/2 Warp Survival Guide

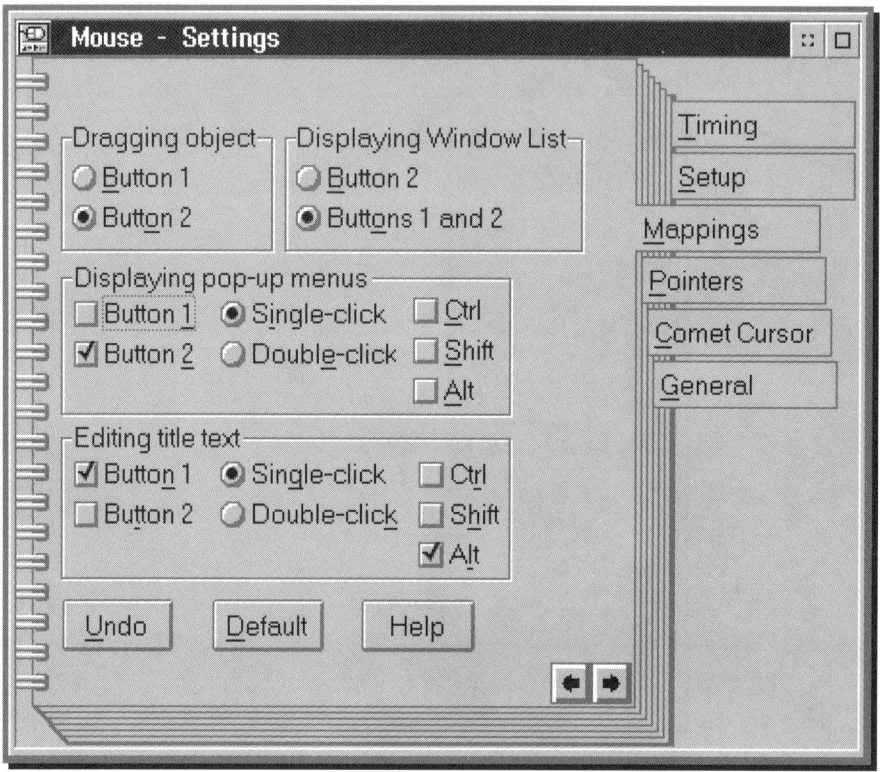

Figure 5.54. *The Mappings tab lets you change the mouse button assignments for certain mouse operations.*

These settings let you change mouse button assignments to whatever you prefer. With all the options available, you should be able to suit yourself.

 If you change these settings, remember that the OS/2 help screens and the OS/2 Tutorial refer to the default button assignments (not to mention this book).

Windows users might want to change the *Dragging objects* operation to use Button 1 to make OS/2 operate more like Windows.

If you change the *Displaying Window List* operation, you'll also have to change the *Displaying pop-up menus* operation so the two operations don't conflict. You can force the Displaying pop-up menu operation to require a *Ctrl*, *Shift*, or *Alt* key in addition to the mouse button press.

By default, the *Editing title text* operation is **Alt**+*Button-1 single-click*, allowing you to change the text in the title of an object. You can also change this if you like.

Pointers Tab

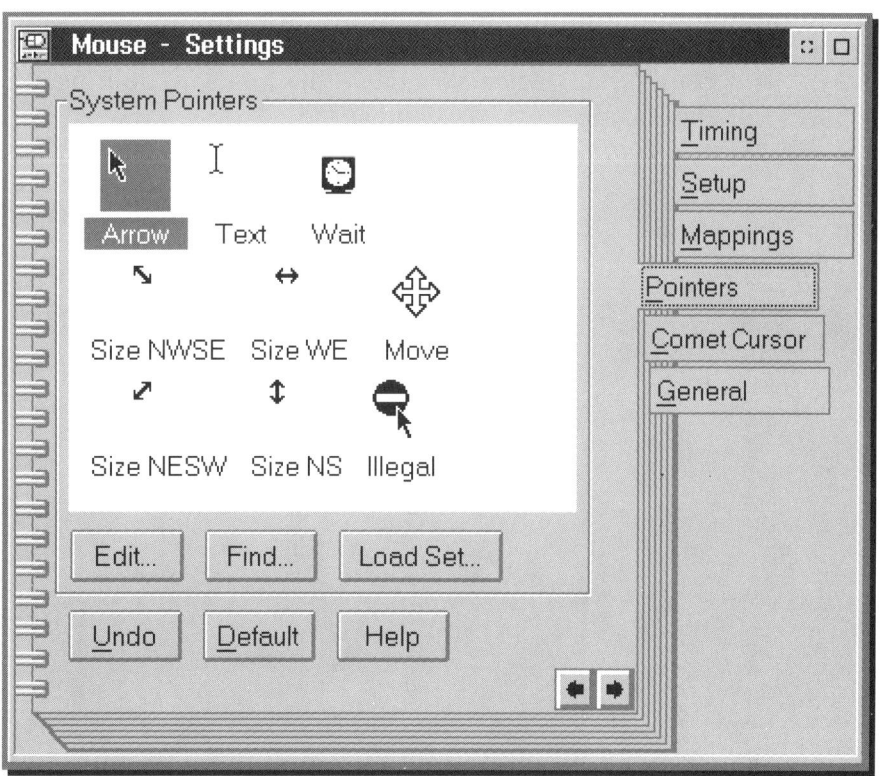

Figure 5.55.   *Use the Pointers tab to set the various mouse pointers used in OS/2.*

To change a pointer, select it from the *System pointers* area, and click on the *Edit...* or *Find...* button. The *Edit...* button takes the currently selected pointer to the Icon Editor where you can modify it. The *Find...* button

The OS/2 Warp Survival Guide

lets you search the system for other bitmap images that you might want to turn into the pointer.

But before you go editing the pointers, take a look at the other pointer sets available via the *Load Set...* button. It gives you access to pre-designed families of pointers that might be closer to what you're looking for.

Comet Cursor Tab

The Comet Cursor is a new feature included with OS/2 Warp. When you enable Comet Cursor, the pointer produces "trails" (much like a comet's tail) when you move the mouse. You'll use this tab to control the comet's color, size, and speed.

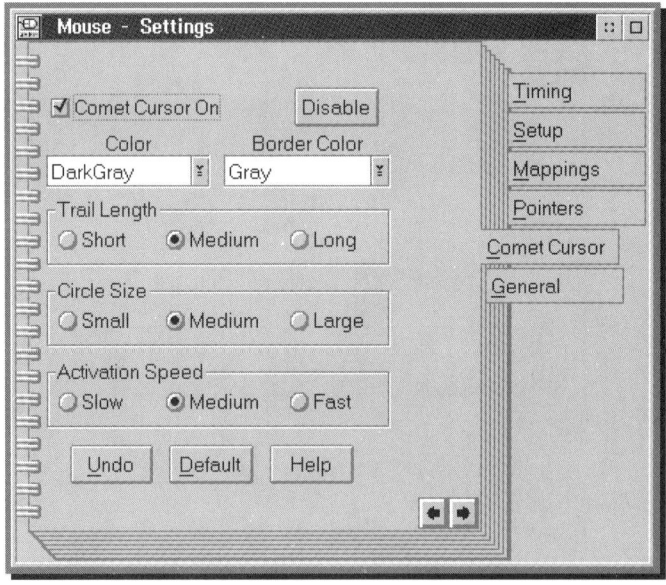

Figure 5.56.   *Use the Comet Cursor tab to enable/disable this new feature.*

This feature is most useful on laptop and notebook computers, to help you find the cursor on slower LCD displays. The trails make the cursor highly visible. When you enable Comet Cursor, you'll have to

Customizing OS/2 Warp

restart OS/2 to see the effect. However, you can disable the Comet Cursor without having to restart the operating system.

General Tab

The *General* tab in the Mouse settings notebook is the same as the General tab in any settings notebook. See "Folder Object Settings" for details about the General tab.

Scheme Palette

The *Scheme Palette* lets you change both the fonts and colors (as well as some other characteristics) of objects on your desktop. As with the other palettes, you can reassign the scheme of a particular window or the entire system. If you want to use a scheme that appears on the palette, simply point at the scheme and drag it to the desired window. When you launch the Scheme Palette object, the following palette appears:

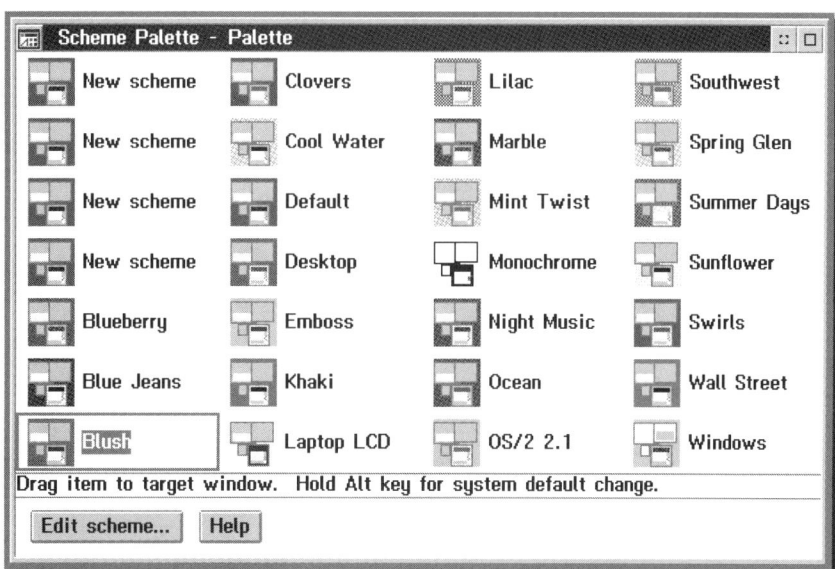

Figure 5.57.   *Use the Scheme Palette to make font and color changes at once.*

The OS/2 Warp Survival Guide

Each scheme on the palette is an object that you can select and drag like any other object in OS/2.

Changing Schemes

To change the scheme for a particular window, drag the desired scheme from the Scheme Palette to that window and drop it. To change the scheme for the entire desktop, hold down the **Alt** key and drag the scheme to any visible area on the desktop.

If you don't like any of the schemes provided on the Scheme Palette, click on one of the New Schemes and click the *Edit scheme...* button. The Edit Color dialog box will appear.

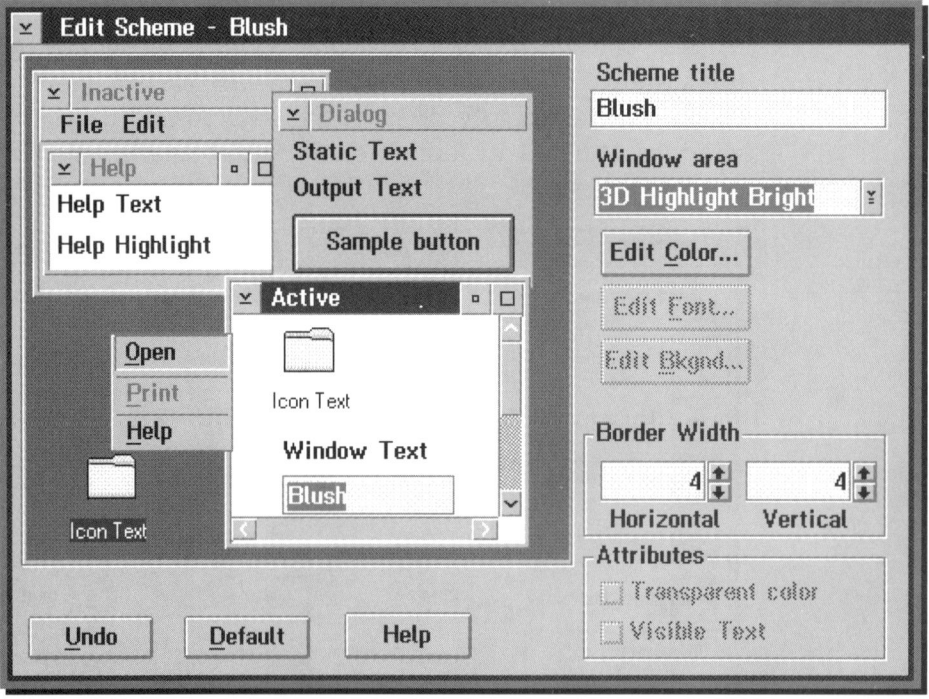

Figure 5.58. Use the Edit Scheme window to design your own scheme for the Workplace Shell.

Editing a Scheme

Using the Edit Scheme dialog box, you can change the fonts and colors for most elements of the windows and screens. Examples of these elements are shown in the sample viewer to help you identify them.

Most of the window elements are changed via the *Window area* field. Select an element in the Window area list box, and click on the *Edit Color*, *Edit Font*, and/or *Edit Bkgnd...* buttons (if applicable) to modify that element. These buttons take you to the Edit Color, Edit Font, and Edit Background dialog boxes, all of which have already been discussed in this chapter.

In addition to the elements listed in the *Window area* field, you can change the Border width of windows and background transparency attributes.

As you make changes, you can see them reflected in the sample viewer area of the Edit Scheme dialog box. If you don't like what you've done, click on the *Undo* button. When you're ready to leave the Edit Scheme dialog box, double-click on the button in the upper-left corner.

Selective Install

You've already seen the windows and dialog boxes associated with the *Selective Install* object. It's the same program you ran during installation to configure and install various features of OS/2 Warp. Use this object when you want to add OS/2 Warp features that you opted not to include during your original installation. When you launch this object, the System Configuration window appears, marking the beginning of Selective Install.

The OS/2 Warp Survival Guide

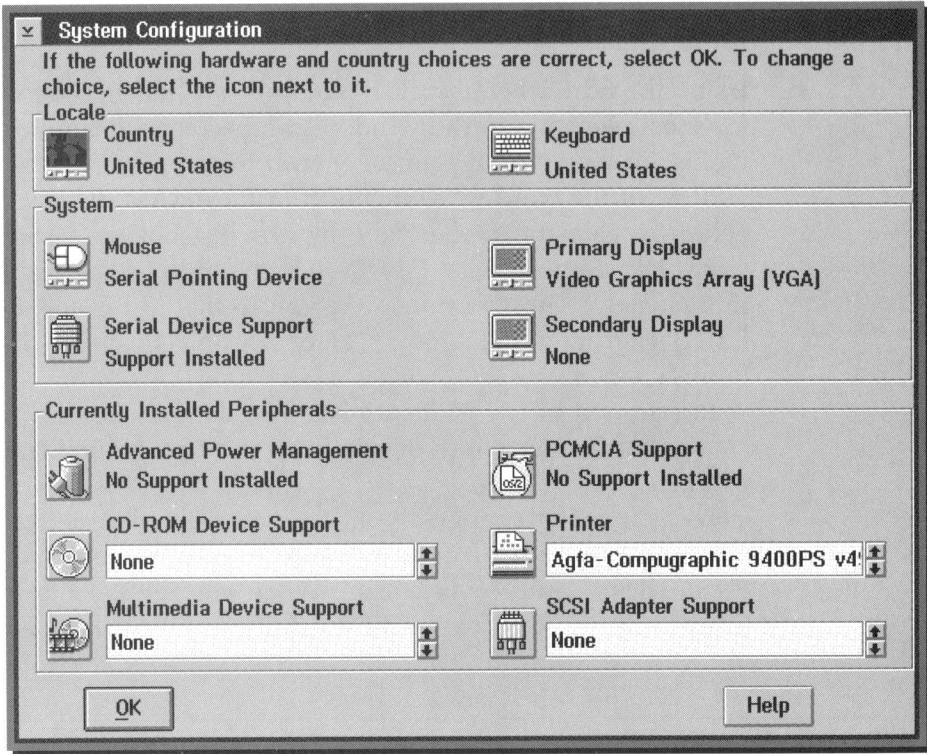

Figure 5.59. *The System Configuration window that appears for Selective Install is the same window you saw during your original installation.*

You can use the options on this screen to reconfigure your system when you add or remove hardware components. Refer to "OS/2 Warp System Configuration" in Chapter 2 for instructions on using the options in this window. When you've finished (or if you have no configuration changes to make) click on the *OK* button. The OS/2 Setup and Configuration window will appear, just as it did during installation. Refer to "Selective Installation" in Chapter 2 to learn about the options presented in this window.

5
Customizing OS/2 Warp

Selective Uninstall

As you might have guessed, the *Selective Uninstall* object is the opposite of the Selective Install object. If you installed features of OS/2 Warp that you no longer need or want (or if you're running out of hard disk space) use this object to remove those features from your computer. When you launch the Selective Uninstall object, the following window appears:

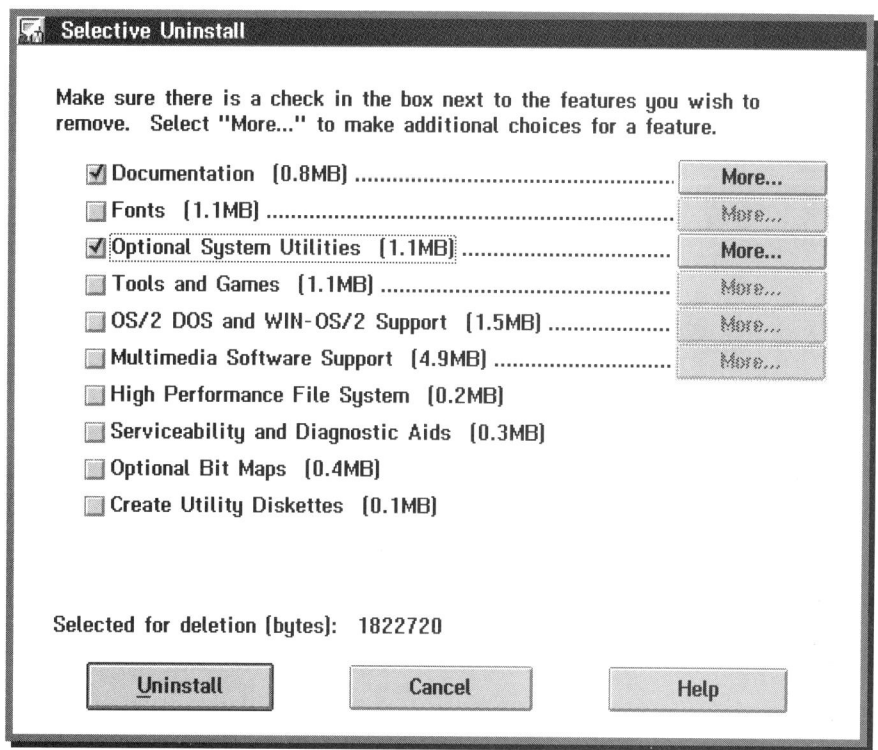

Figure 5.60. *The Selective Uninstall window lets you decide which features of OS/2 you want to remove from your computer.*

This window functions much like the OS/2 Setup and Configuration window, except that it works in reverse. Instead of selecting features you want to install, you select the features you want to remove. Refer to

The OS/2 Warp Survival Guide

"Selective Installation" in Chapter 2 to learn about the options presented in this window.

Solid Color Palette

The *Solid Color Palette* works the same as the Mixed Color Palette. The primary difference between the two is the number of colors available. You'll notice that the Solid Color Palette is much smaller; it can only hold 16 colors. And it contains only solid colors—colors that don't require a *dithering* pattern to create.

"Dithering" is the pattern of different colored dots that are mixed to produce subtle variations of tints and shades. Depending on the color and resolution capabilities of your video subsystem, dithering patterns can be less than subtle. The Solid Color Palette allows you to create a more attractive desktop when your display is operating in a 16-color video mode (such as standard VGA).

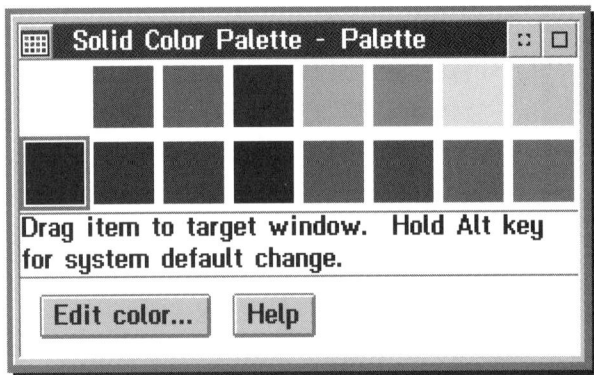

Figure 5.61. Use the Solid Color Palette to change the colors of objects on your desktop.

As with the other palettes, drag the desired color swatch to and drop it on an object to change just that object. You can change groups of object types (such as *all* title bars and *all* folder backgrounds) by holding down the **Alt** key while dragging and dropping the color.

Customizing OS/2 Warp

The *Edit color...* button provides the same editing options as the other palette objects. If you need help with the Edit Color dialog box, refer to the "Mixed Color Palette" section in this chapter.

 If you clear the *Solid Color* check box in the Edit Color dialog box, you will effectively change the Solid Color Palette to a small mixed color palette.

Sound

The *Sound* object lets you control sounds used by your computer. The degree of control you have depends on the hardware available in your computer to make sounds. When you open the Sound object, its settings notebook appears. If your system does not have multimedia capabilities, you'll only have one tab in this notebook: the *Warning Beep* tab.

Sound Tab

The Sound tab only appears if you have installed the OS/2 Multimedia features. Its settings let you associate sounds with certain system events, such as the Alarm clock, beginning a drag operation with the mouse, and closing a window.

The OS/2 Warp Survival Guide

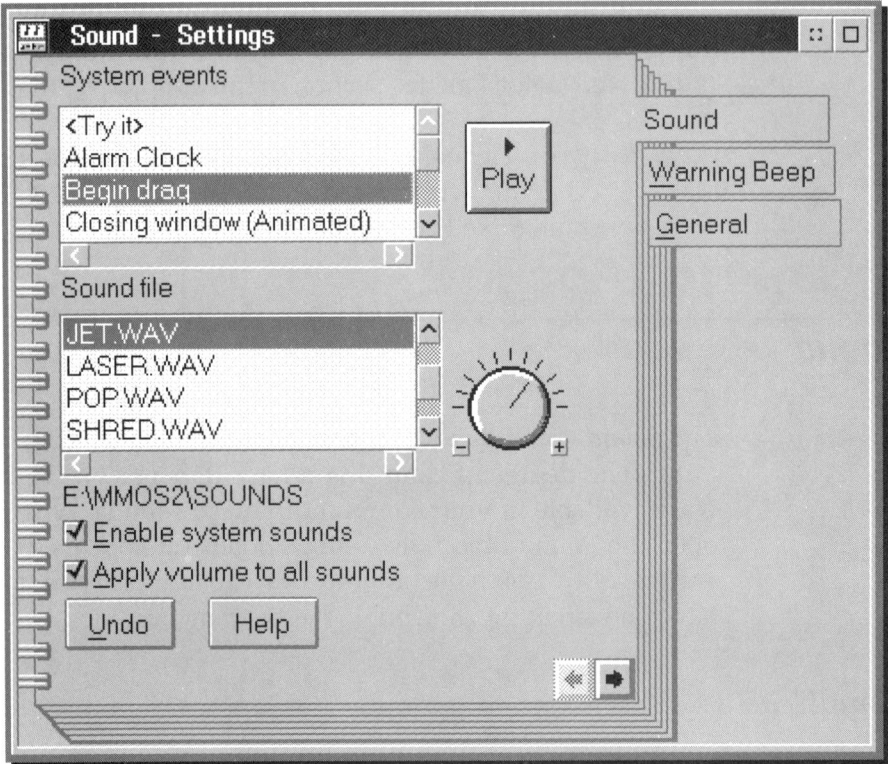

Figure 5.62. *The Sound tab lets you assign sound files to System Events.*

The *System events* field contains a list of system events for which you can assign sounds. The Sound file field contains a list of .WAV (pronounced "wave") files that you can associate with any of the supported system events. Each system event already has a sound file associated with it, but you can change these default assignments to any file listed.

First click on the system event for which you want to assign a sound. Then click on the appropriate sound file. Repeat these steps for each system event you want to change. When you close the notebook, the new settings will take effect.

The volume knob lets you control how loud OS/2 will play the sound. You can set a volume for each system event, or make the volume setting apply to all sounds (using the check box at the bottom of the window). To turn the knob, drag the line to the desired setting, or click on the plus or minus button. If you get tired of all those system-event sounds, you can disable them by clearing the *Enable system sounds* check box.

Warning Beep Tab

This is a pretty simple tab (and not even worth showing). Its only setting (a single check box) allows you to enable or disable the warning beep.

Spooler

The *Spooler* object lets you specify the path where you want OS/2 Warp to store the system *spool files*. It also lets you change the priority factor for your system's print jobs. Spool files are temporary files that hold your print jobs on their way to a printer. OS/2 Warp *spools* print jobs to release your application from the task of interacting with a real printer. Since disk drives are much faster than printers, spooling can improve the speed at which application programs process your print requests. When you launch the Spooler object, its settings notebook appears.

Spool Path Tab

This is where you specify the drive and subdirectory (path) to be used for system spool files.

The OS/2 Warp Survival Guide

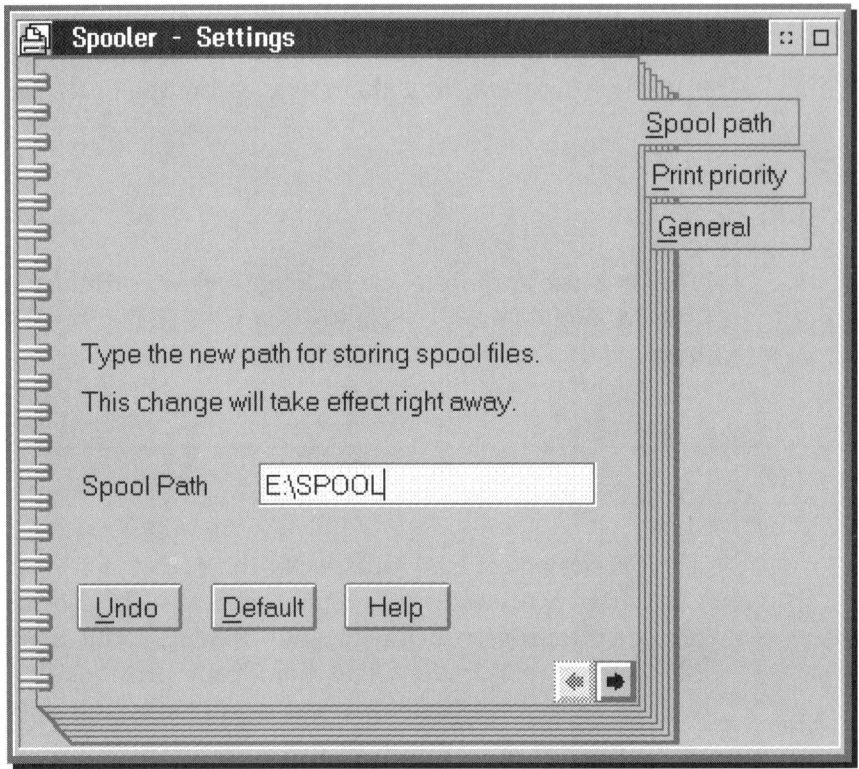

Figure 5.63.   *Use the Spool Path tab to tell OS/2 where you want printer spool files stored.*

By default, OS/2 stores spool files in the \SPOOL subdirectory of your OS/2 installation partition (the disk drive where you installed OS/2 Warp). If you had just enough space in your installation partition for OS/2, and you do a lot of printing, you might consider changing this setting.

Print Priority Tab

The Print Priority tab lets you change the priority setting for your print jobs. This setting forces OS/2 to spend more or less time concentrating on spooled print jobs when you're performing other tasks on your computer.

Customizing OS/2 Warp

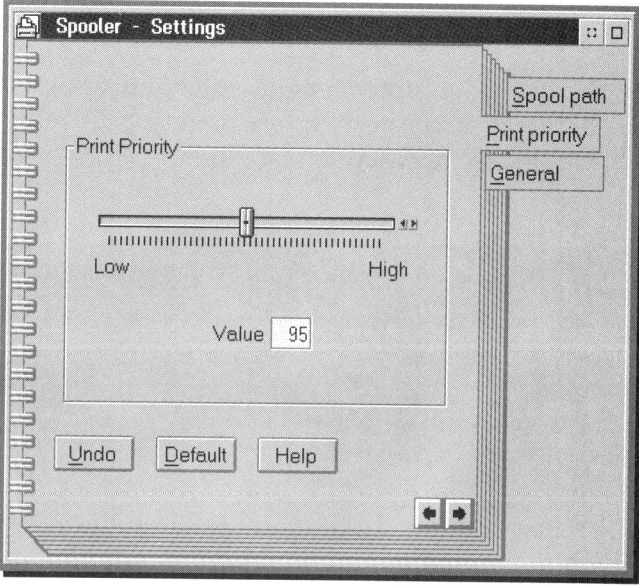

Figure 5.64. *Use the Print Priority setting to adjust the importance of printing on your system.*

This control is conveniently available for you to make dynamic changes to the print priority, based on the current importance of printing. For those times when your printing requirements have top priority, set the print priority value to a higher number.

System

The *System* object lets you customize certain system-wide settings such as video resolution, window appearance and behavior, deletion confirmations, and how to handle title clashes. When you open the System object, the System settings notebook appears. This notebook contains some tabs that you have not yet seen in this chapter.

The OS/2 Warp Survival Guide

Screen Tab

If your video subsystem (adapter and display) is capable of operating at different screen resolutions under OS/2 Warp, you can use the Screen tab to select a different resolution.

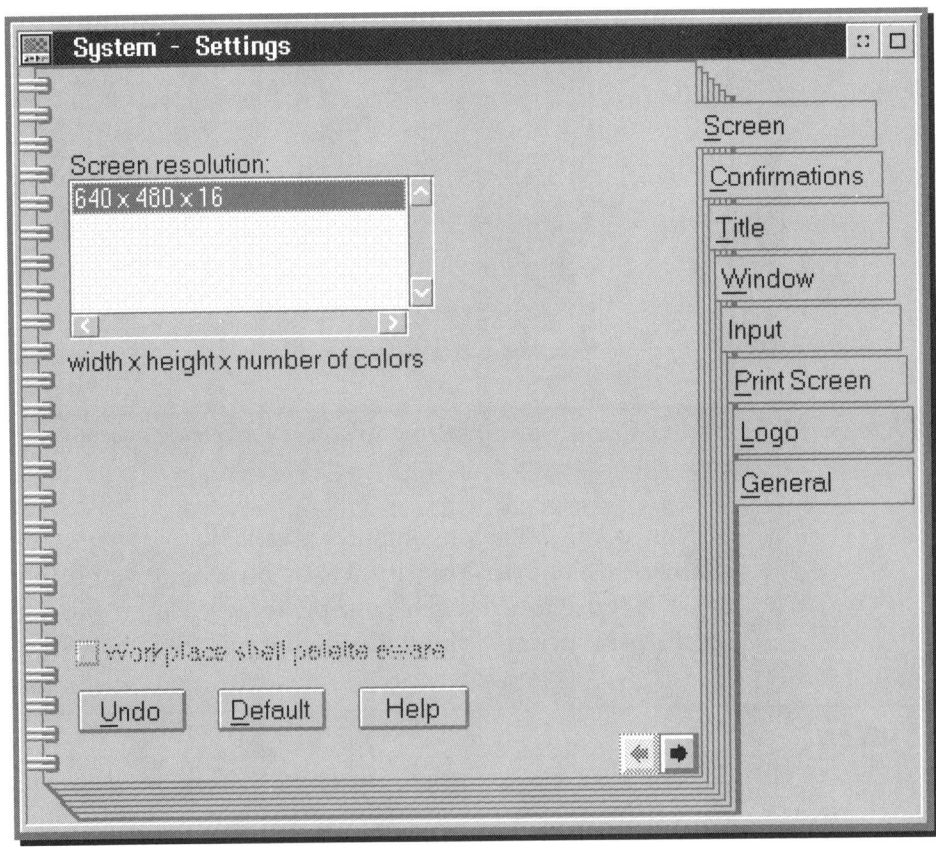

Figure 5.65.   *Use the Screen tab to change the resolution of your video subsystem.*

OS/2 Warp comes with the appropriate device drivers for several video (or display) adapters. If you're lucky enough to have a video adapter that's fully supported by OS/2, you might have more than one entry in the *Screen resolution* list. The only resolution you can count on for all video adapters is standard VGA (640 × 480 × 16).

Customizing OS/2 Warp

If you have only one resolution listed, and you know your video subsystem is capable of higher resolutions, you probably have to install a new device driver. First, find out if there's a device driver for OS/2 that supports your desired resolution. Start by contacting IBM. They may tell you to contact your place of purchase or even the video adapter's manufacturer, or they might tell you how you can get it from their bulletin board service. When you get the device driver, use the *Selective Install* or *Device Driver Install* object to install it.

Most people seem to think IBM should be responsible for automatically supporting all features of every video adapter known to man (or at least the one in *their* computer). If you stop to think about it, this is a virtually impossible expectation. It's actually up to the manufacturers of video adapters to provide device drivers for OS/2 Warp. *They* have the intimate knowledge required to develop device drivers for *their* hardware—not IBM. At best, it's a shared responsibility.

To change resolution, select the desired *screen resolution* from the list provided. You'll have to restart OS/2 (when you close the notebook) in order to see the new resolution; OS/2 must load the appropriate device driver.

If your video subsystem supports multiple simultaneous palettes, the *Workplace Shell palette aware* check box will be available. With this option enabled, certain bitmap images might have a better appearance.

If you change from a higher to lower screen resolution, some of your windows might extend beyond the visible desktop (off the screen). To fix this condition, find the window in the Window List (chord-click on the desktop) and then select the *Tile* or *Cascade* option on the window's context menu. The window will be repositioned to fit on the desktop.

The OS/2 Warp Survival Guide

Confirmations Tab

These settings let you control how often OS/2 asks if "you're sure" you want to perform operations such as deleting, copying, and moving objects.

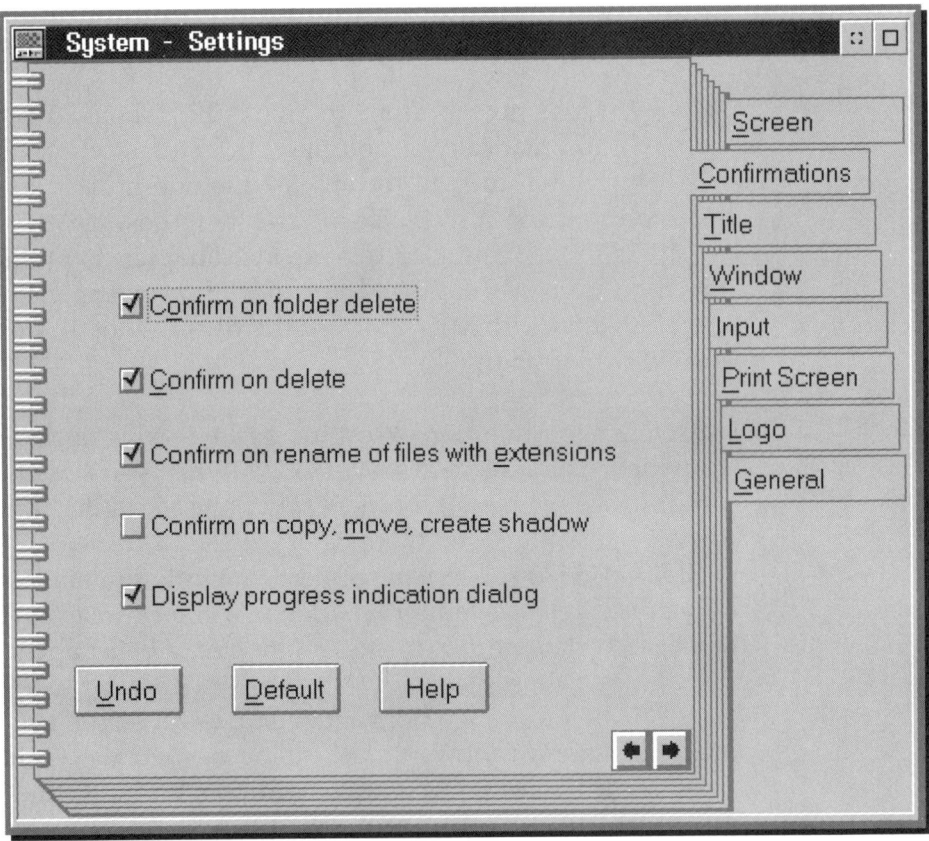

Figure 5.66.   *The Confirmations tab lets you decide how you want OS/2 to react when you ask to delete objects.*

Select or de-select the options according to your level of comfort with your own delete, copy, and move requests. When you get tired of OS/2 asking you to confirm that you actually want to delete objects, it might be time to turn off some of these options.

Customizing OS/2 Warp

Title Tab

These settings let you control what happens when two objects' titles clash due to a copy, rename, or move operation. When you click on the *Title* tab, the following settings page appears:

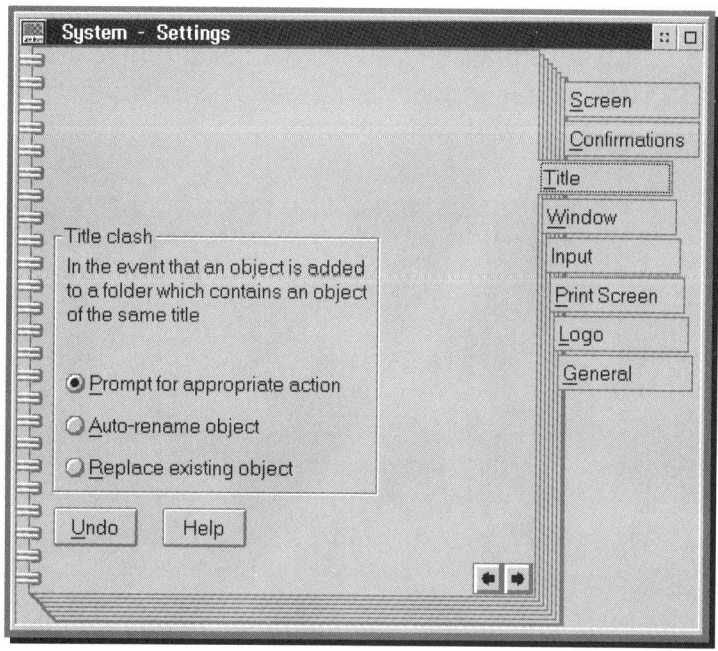

Figure 5.67. *The Title tab lets you handle naming clashes gracefully.*

A title clash occurs if you create, copy, rename, or move an object into a folder that already has an object with that same name. Use these settings to specify how OS/2 should react to a title clash:

- Select *Prompt for appropriate action* to have the system display a message with choices to determine system behavior for dealing with object title conflicts.
- Select *Auto-rename object* if you want OS/2 to rename the new object by adding a colon and a number to the end of the original name. For

The OS/2 Warp Survival Guide

example, a duplicate object named My File would be renamed to My File:1.
- Select *Replace existing object* if you want OS/2 to always replace the existing object with the new one.

Window Tab

These settings let you set the default appearance and behavior of windows on a system-wide basis. When you click on the *Window* tab, the following settings page appears:

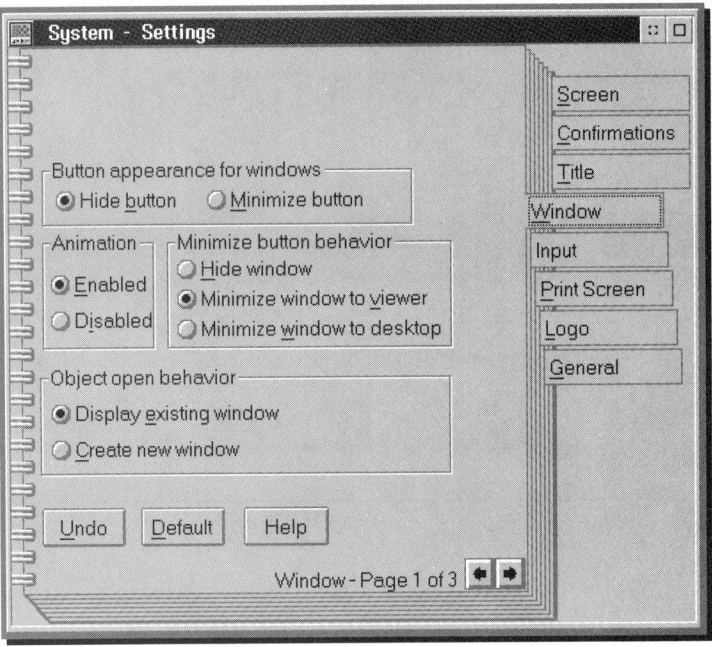

Figure 5.68.   *The settings under the Window tab let you change the system-wide default settings for windows.*

The options on *page 1* and *page 2* are the same as the Window tab found in any folder's settings notebook (see "Window Tab" under "Folder Object Settings" earlier in this chapter) with one exception: the *Animation* option.

Customizing OS/2 Warp

With *Animation Enabled*, you'll see traces of squares that simulate movement on the screen as you open and close objects. When opening an object, these traces expand outward from the object's icon to the outline of its window. When you close a window, these traces collapse from the outline of the window to its icon. This option somewhat slows system performance. When the novelty of this feature wears off, disable it.

Page 3 of Window Tab: This page lets you set the default open folder view on a system-wide basis. Using the options on this page, you can tell OS/2 to open folders in their *Icon View*, *Tree View*, or *Details View* when no other view is specifically requested.

Changing the default folder views to *Details* will help you work with files more efficiently in the drives folders, but you might not like all folders to appear this way. If you do enable this option, you can explicitly set the view back to *Icon* for individual folders (such as OS/2 System, Productivity, etc.).

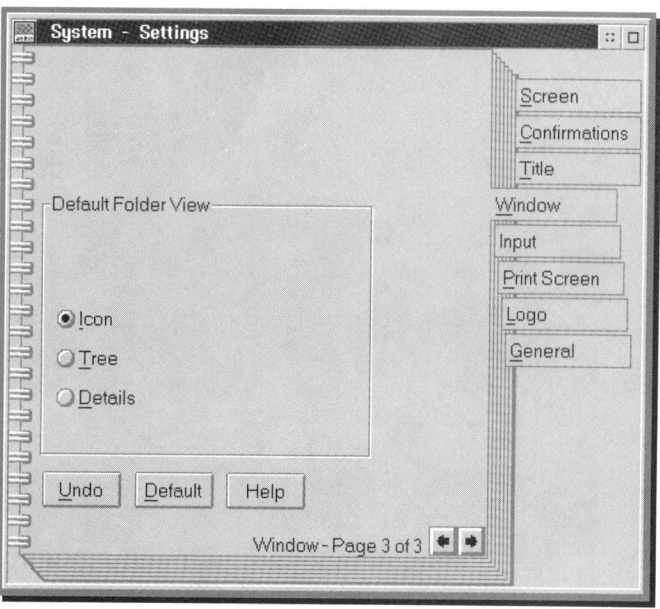

Figure 5.69. Use page 3 of the Window tab to set the default open folder view.

The OS/2 Warp Survival Guide

This setting affects all folders on the desktop, except for the ones you have specifically set through the Menu tab in their own settings notebook.

Input Tab

The Input tab lets you enable or disable the type ahead feature. With this feature enabled, the system will accept input from the keyboard even when the *wait* pointer (the little clock) is being displayed to indicate that the system is busy.

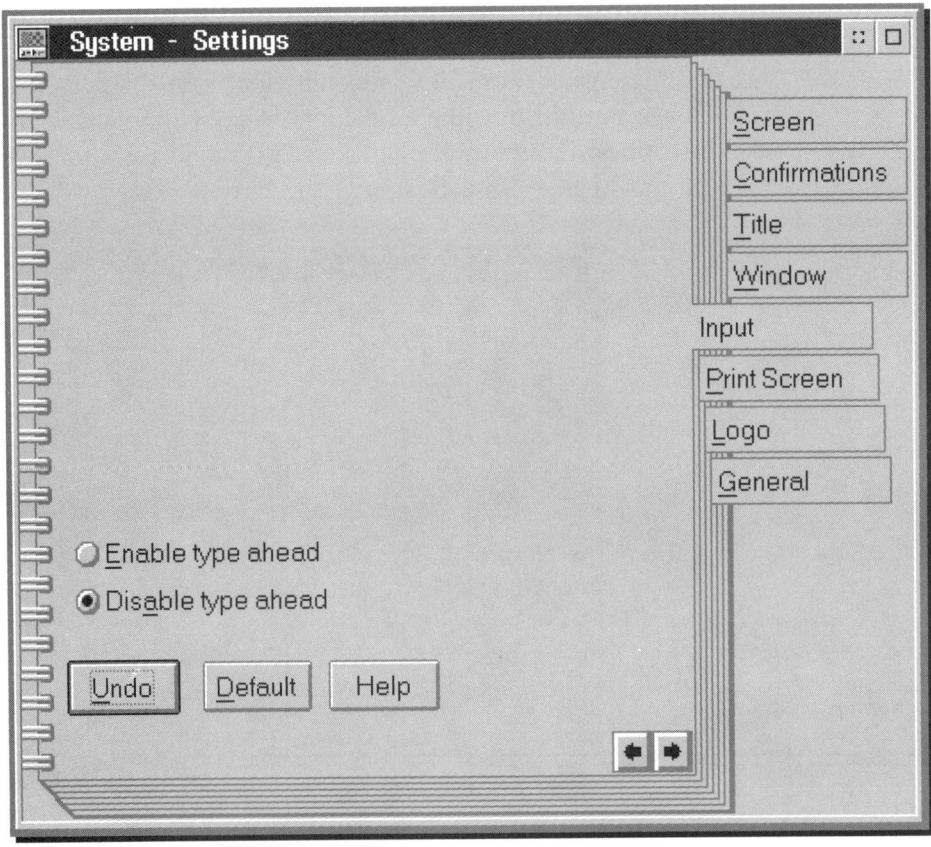

Figure 5.70. *Use the Input tab to turn on or off the keyboard type ahead feature.*

Customizing OS/2 Warp

Print Screen Tab

The settings on the Print Screen tab let you turn the print screen feature *on* or *off*. The following figure illustrates this page of the System settings notebook.

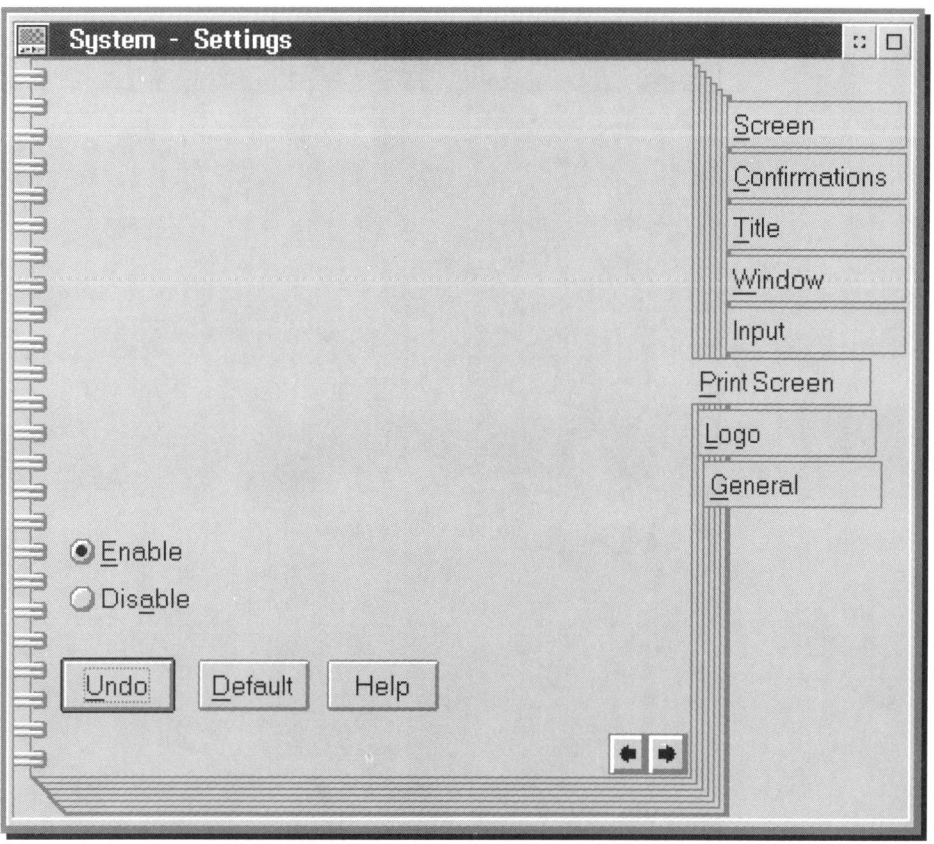

Figure 5.71. *The Print Screen tab lets you enable or disable the print screen feature.*

Select the desired setting. When enabled, the current contents of the screen will be sent to the default printer when you press the Print Screen key. When disabled, no action will take place when you press the Print Screen key.

The OS/2 Warp Survival Guide

Logo Tab

These settings let you control how long the introductory (logo) screen remains on the screen when a program starts to run. When you click on the *Logo* tab, the following page appears in the System settings notebook.

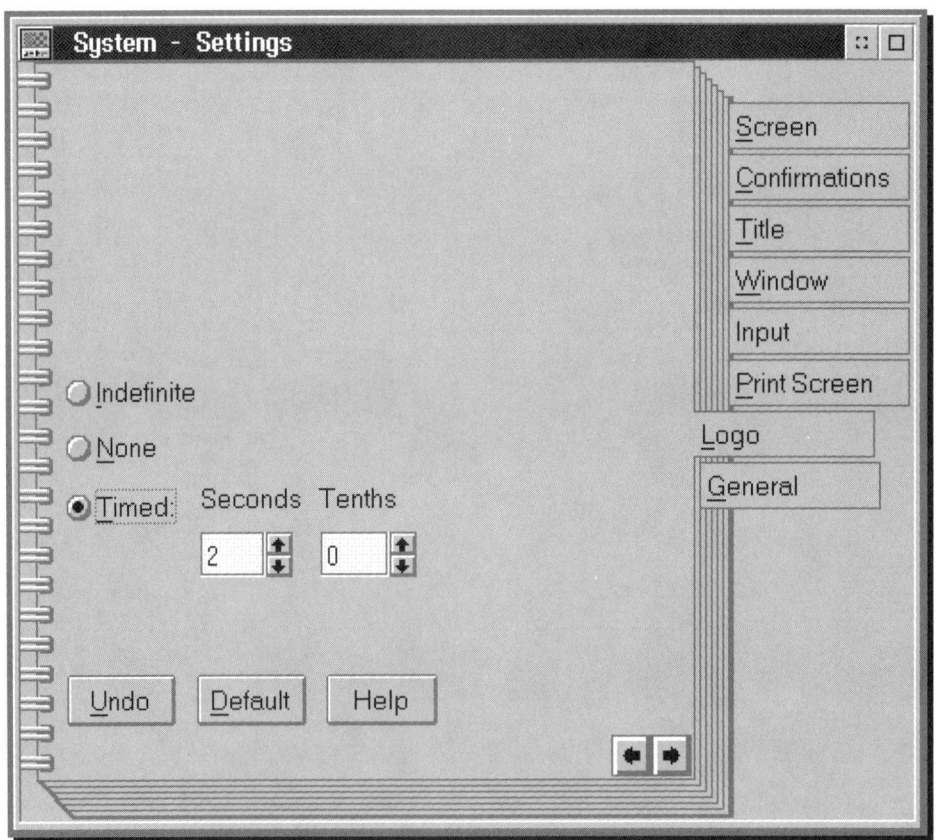

Figure 5.72. The Logo tab lets you control how long logos are displayed.

Many OS/2 programs display an introductory screen while the program loads and initializes. Using the settings on this page, you can have the logo displayed indefinitely, never displayed, or displayed for a specific amount of time.

Customizing OS/2 Warp

General Tab

The General tab for the System settings notebook is the same as the General tab for any settings notebook. See "Folder Object Settings" earlier in this chapter for details about these settings.

System Clock

The *System Clock* is a useful little object. It serves three functions: tell the date and/or time, set the system date and/or time, and provide an alarm clock for the desktop. When you launch the System Clock, a window appears with a clock in it (just what you might expect).

Figure 5.73. *Use the System Clock to view or set the date and time. It's also an alarm clock.*

To perform the other functions available through the System Clock, you must open its settings notebook. Right mouse-click on the object icon (in the upper-left corner of the window).

Date/Time Tab

Use the Date/Time tab to set the system date and time through the spin buttons provided.

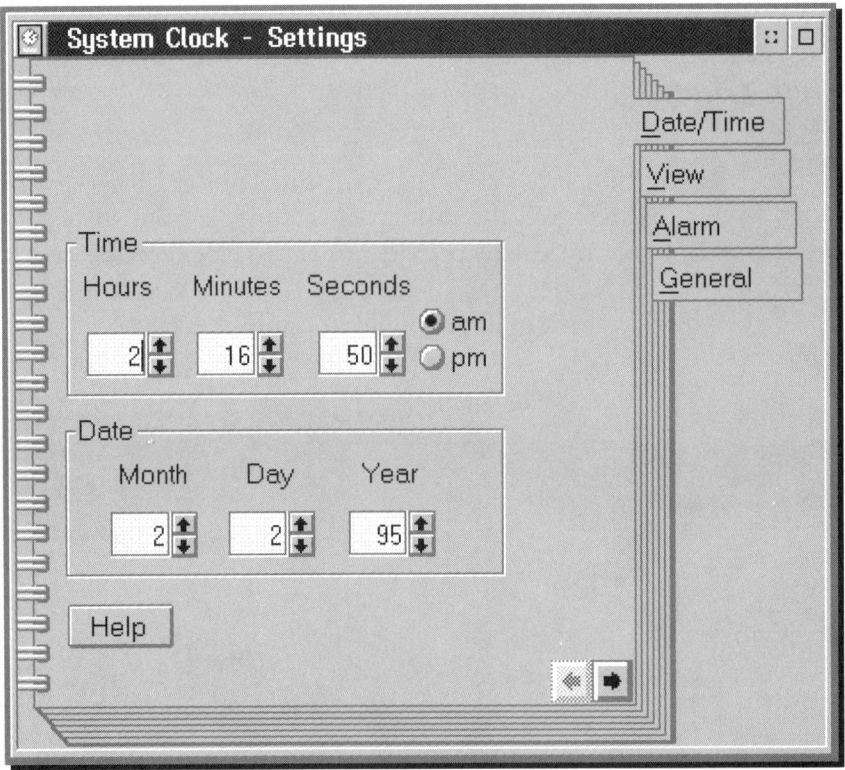

Figure 5.74. Use the Date/Time tab to correct the system's date and/or time information.

View Tab

Use page 1 of the View tab to set the System Clock's view settings. You can choose between time, date, date and time. You also have the option of using a digital or analog clock face.

Customizing OS/2 Warp

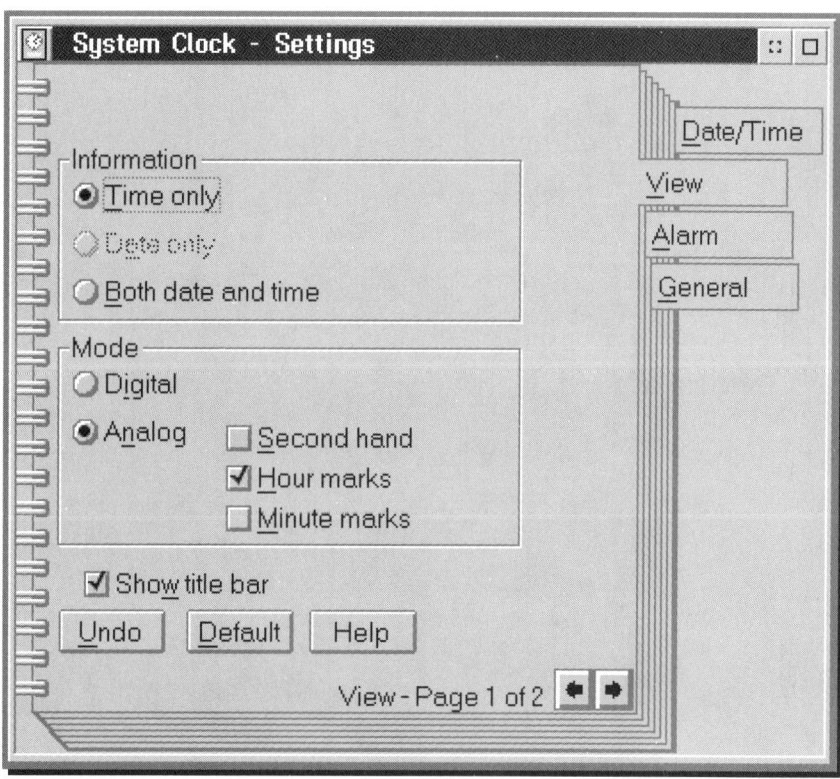

Figure 5.75.   *Use page 1 of the View tab to change the face of the clock.*

Page 2 of the View tab lets you set the colors and fonts used in the face of the clock. You can change colors independently for the background, face, hour marks, and hour and minute hands. The Date and Time numbers can be different fonts.

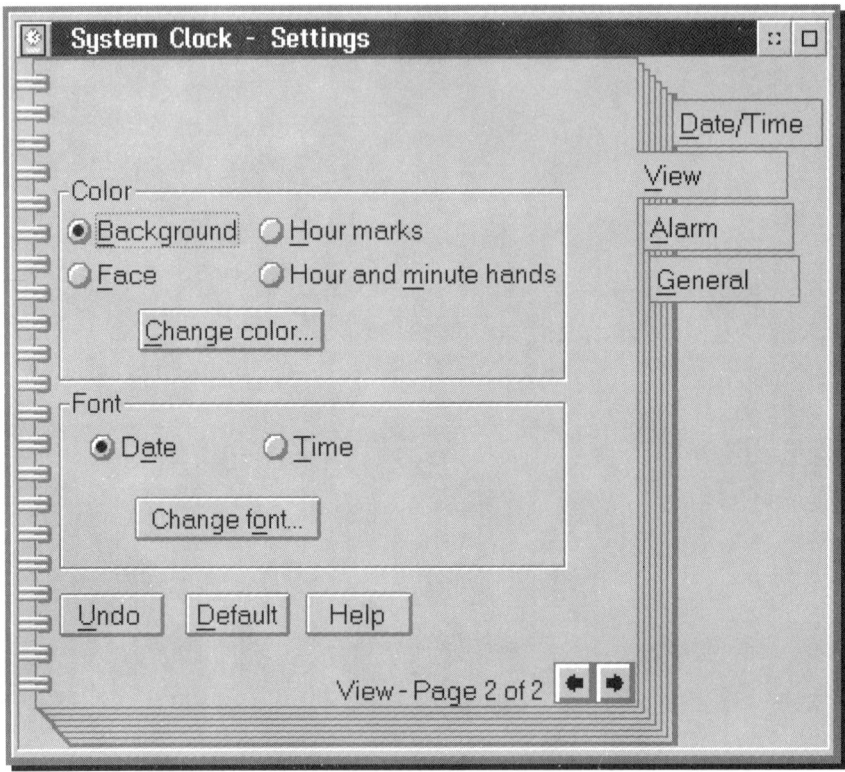

Figure 5.76.   *Use page 2 of the View tab to change the System Clock's colors and fonts.*

Alarm Tab

The Alarm tab lets you set audible alarms and messages for specific times and dates.

Customizing OS/2 Warp

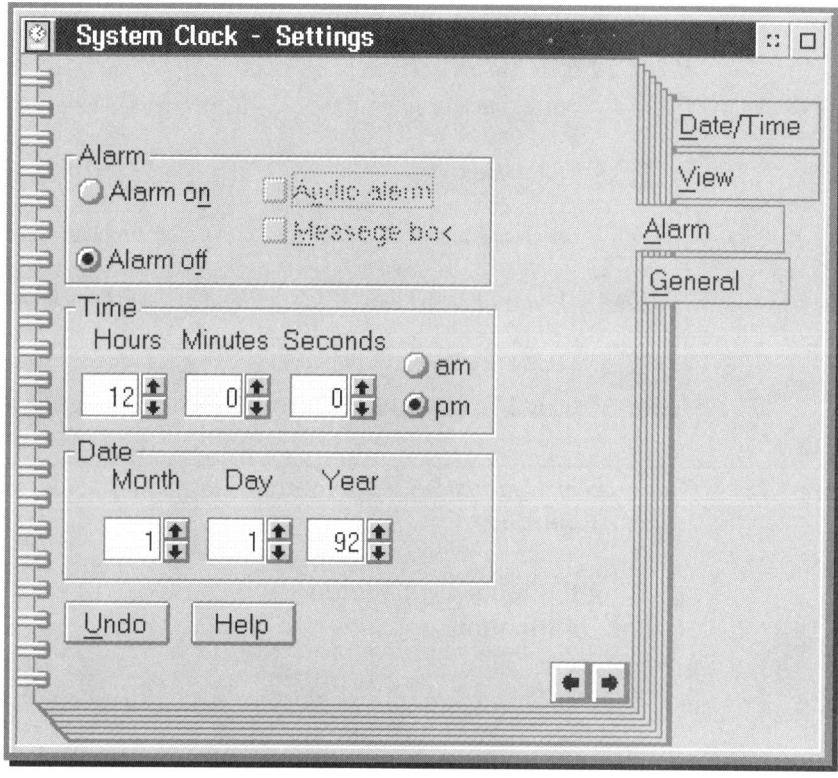

Figure 5.77.   *Use the Alarm tab to set alarms in the System Clock.*

When you set an alarm, you can specify whether you want an audible alarm and/or have the system send a message to the message box.

System Information Tool

The *System Information Tool* is a welcome new feature of OS/2 Warp. It allows you to interrogate various components of your computer for status, type and model, performance, and settings. When you launch the System Information Tool, the window shown in the following figure appears.

The OS/2 Warp Survival Guide

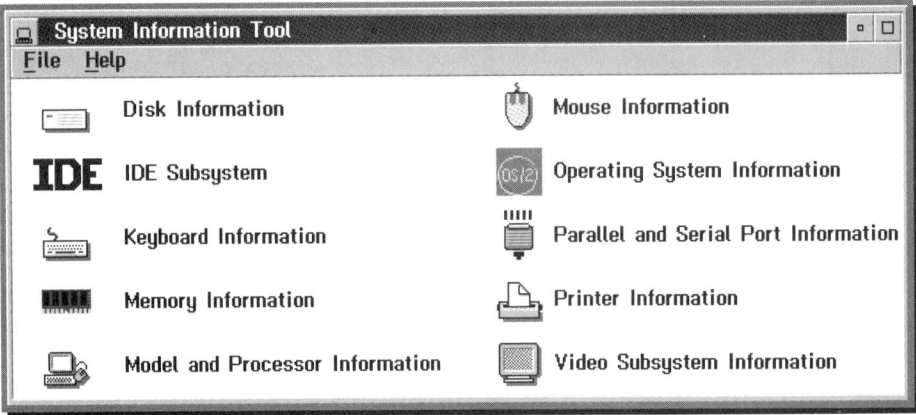

Figure 5.78. *The System Information Tool reports information about your system's hardware and software.*

Using the tools in this folder, you can find out the following types of system information:

- *Disk Information:* Gives you an inventory of your drives (physical and logical) and their storage capacities.

- *Mouse Information:* Tells you the type, port assignment, sensitivity, and scaling factor settings.

- *IDE Subsystem:* Shows you information about this type of disk drive interface (if installed).

- *Operating System Information:* Fills you in on certain specifics about the operating system being used on your computer (OS/2 Warp).

- *Keyboard Information:* Shows the keyboard's type, country code, code page, and typematic rates.

- *Parallel and Serial Port Information:* Gives you the physical and logical information about your serial and parallel ports.

- *Memory Information:* Shows the recognized memory address ranges and the amount of memory installed.

Customizing OS/2 Warp

- *Printer Information:* Lists the printer models, device drivers, queue names, and port assignments for the printers installed in your computer.

- *Model and Processor Information:* Tells you the processor type(s), internal cache status, model, BIOS, and interrupt request level assignments.

- *Video Subsystem Information:* Displays specifications for the primary and secondary video adapters in your computer (as reported by OS/2 Warp).

WIN-OS/2 Setup

The *WIN-OS/2 Setup* object lets you set up certain operating characteristics and session settings for your Windows 3.1 application programs. When you launch the WIN-OS/2 Setup object, a settings notebook appears.

3.1 Session Tab

The Session tab in the WIN-OS/2 Setup notebook lets you set up the default session settings for new Windows 3.1 applications. You can specify full-screen, or windowed operation, and you can access the WIN-OS/2 settings.

The OS/2 Warp Survival Guide

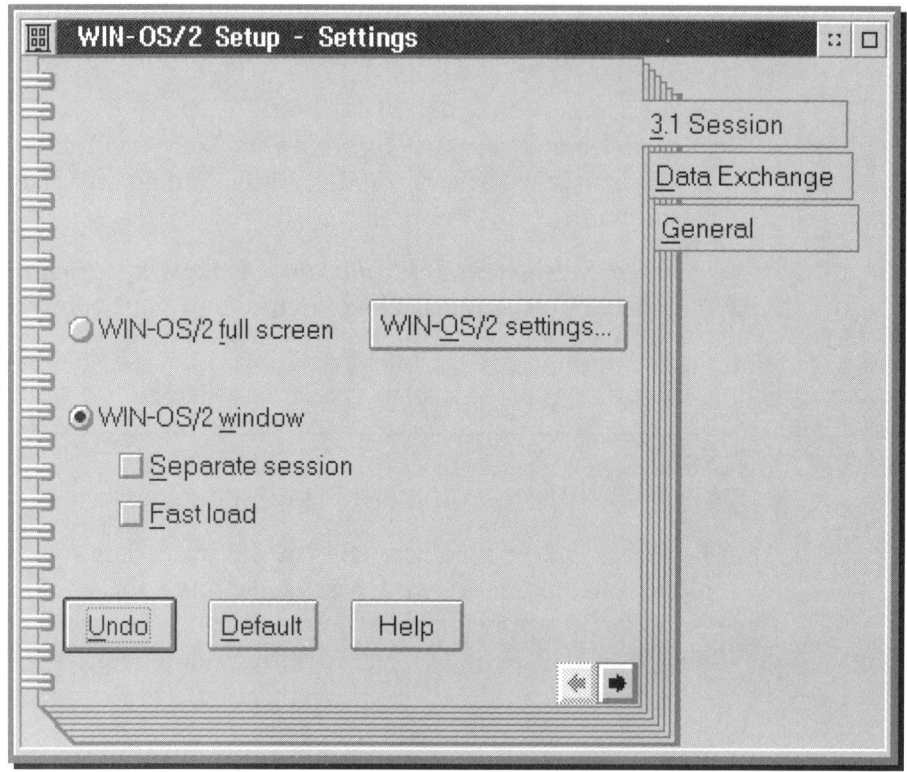

Figure 5.79. Use the "3.1 Session" tab to specify the default Windows session settings.

Refer to Chapter 7, "DOS and Windows Under OS/2 Warp" for descriptions of the WIN-OS/2 settings you can change.

Data Exchange Tab

If you're an advocate of cutting and pasting and Dynamic Data Exchange (DDE) or Object Linking and Embedding (OLE), this tab's for you!

Customizing OS/2 Warp

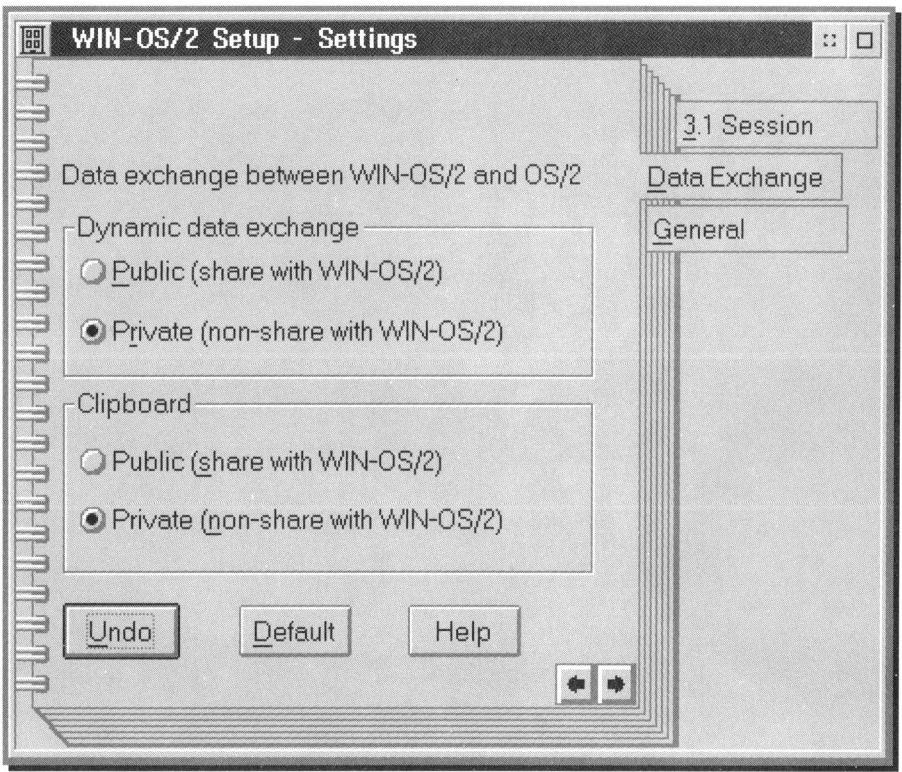

Figure 5.80. *Use the Data Exchange tab to allow/disallow your Windows programs to share DDE and Clipboard functions with OS/2 programs.*

We recommend that you set the *Clipboard* option to *Public*. If you use Dynamic Data Exchange links in your Windows applications, set its option to *Public*.

When you're finished changing the settings, close the notebook either by double-clicking on the object icon button (in the upper-left corner of the window) or by selecting the *Close* option on the context menu. All your settings will be saved, regardless of which tab or page you're on when you close the notebook.

Chapter 6

Getting Warped: Exercises in Virtual Reality

The phrase "getting warped" doesn't refer simply to the act of buying and installing OS/2 Warp. You're not truly warped until you understand how to fully utilize this object-oriented, virtual workplace. After your first look at the Workplace Shell, you might think "I know how to use this . . . I've used Microsoft Windows!" Although there are many similarities on the surface, the Workplace Shell runs much deeper; it's an integral part of the operating system. One of the first differences you might notice is how interactively OS/2 Warp works with you. For example, as you change visual options in settings notebooks, your changes are immediately reflected on the desktop. This is a small clue as to just how powerful OS/2 Warps' Workplace Shell really is.

You've seen how the Workplace Shell can greatly simplify your interaction with your computer over DOS. If you follow the exercises in this chapter, you'll learn how to get more out of OS/2, and you'll avoid some common pitfalls experienced by new users. So far we've shown you enough about the Workplace Shell to make you somewhat dangerous. Before you get too carried away with the power of this object-oriented interface, you should *truly* understand the concept of virtual reality in the Workplace Shell, and what's going on "behind the scenes."

The OS/2 Warp Survival Guide

Virtual Reality in the Workplace Shell

We're not just using the phrase "virtual reality" as a cute gimmick; OS/2 Warp is full of examples of what we mean. At the highest level, there are the real-world analogies, such as: a desktop, push button controls, disk drives, and printers. Then there's the lower-level analogies such as folders (subdirectories) and files. The following figure illustrates the concept of virtual reality at its highest level.

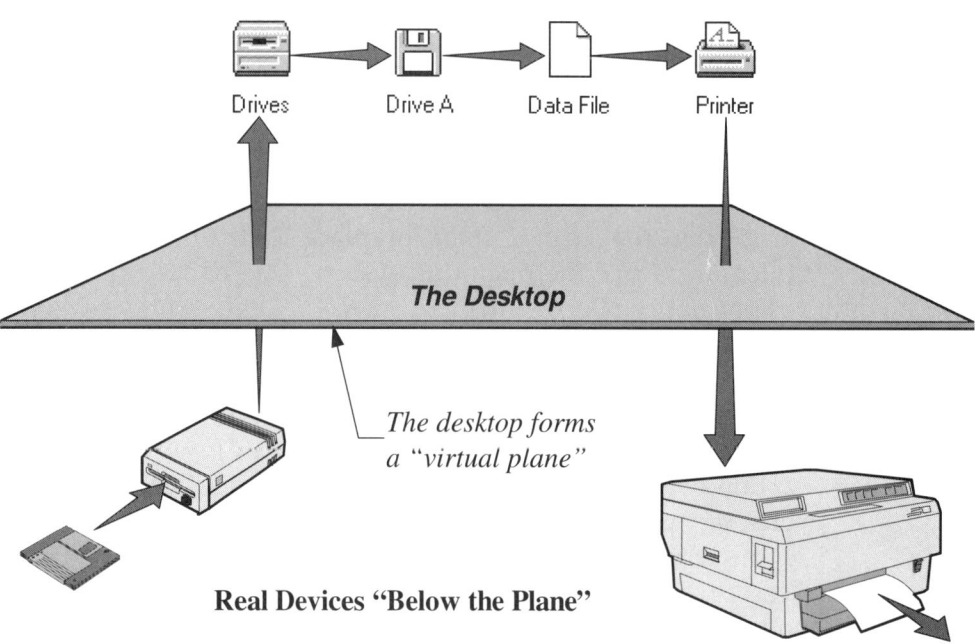

Figure 6.1. *The desktop separates the "real" from the "virtual."*

You've probably already realized some of the concepts shown above. You can think of the desktop as a "plane" that separates real objects (such as disk drives, printers, and files) from OS/2's virtual objects (in this case, the corresponding Device objects).

6

Getting Warped: Exercises in Virtual Reality

What you might not have realized, is that a similar analogy exists for subdirectories, program files, and data files. Files and subdirectories on your disk drives are "real" objects that are also represented by virtual objects on the desktop. We call these the File System Objects.

File System Objects

Let's take a look at how OS/2 Warp represents the elements of the file system. Remember the following rules:

- *Folder Objects* represent subdirectories.
- *Program File Objects* represent executable files.
- *Data File Objects* represent all other files on a disk drive.

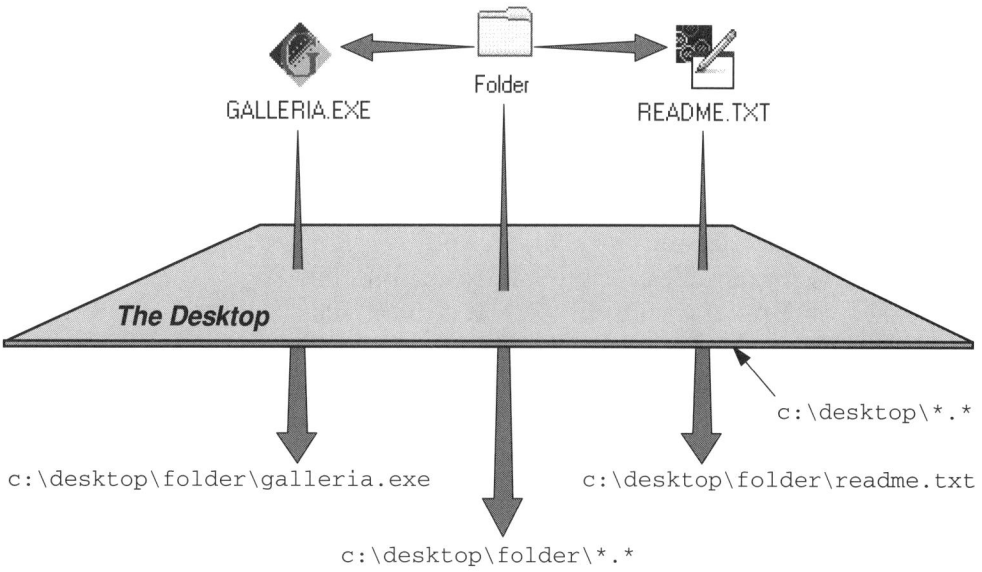

Figure 6.2.   *Elements of the file system under the desktop (real subdirectories and files) are represented by folder and file objects.*

The OS/2 Warp Survival Guide

In Figure 6.2, the files GALLERIA.EXE and README.TXT are *real* files contained in the desktop. If you only learn one thing from this chapter, it should be that doing this is a *bad idea*! Since the desktop is the plane that separates the real from the virtual, only virtual objects should be contained in the desktop. If you only learn two things from this chapter, the second will be how to create virtual objects on the desktop that make it easy for you to find, access, and manipulate your real objects.

Folder Objects

In Figure 6.2, you'll notice the desktop (itself a folder) is a virtual object that represents the `c:\desktop` subdirectory in the real world. The folder shown in Figure 6.2 sits on top of the desktop, making its real-world counterpart the `c:\desktop\folder`  directory. In fact every folder on your desktop is a subdirectory of the `desktop` directory. Of course, folders can have *any* icon associated with them; they don't always look like manila file folders. For example, the *Information* object is a folder that looks like a library of books.

Just like their real-world counterparts, folders are intended to hold related objects, helping you organize your projects (programs and data files).

File Objects

The files on your disk drives fall into two basic classes: *program files* and *data files*. Program files include all executable files (*.BAT, *.CMD, *.EXE, and *.COM files for DOS, Windows, and OS/2). Data files include all other files.

In Figure 6.2, "GALLERIA.EXE" is a program file object, and "README.TXT" is a data file object. Both objects are stored in the folder, which means that their real files are stored in the `c:\desktop\folder` subdirectory on the hard disk drive. Since these are file objects, they're directly linked with their real files: `GALLERIA.EXE` and `README.TXT`. If you were to drag either of these objects out of the folder and drop it on the desktop, you would literally be moving its real file to the `c:\desktop` subdirectory on the disk drive.

In the Workplace Shell, file objects can also be represented by *reference* objects. Reference objects are *virtual* copies of file objects; they're not di-

6 Getting Warped: Exercises in Virtual Reality

rectly linked to their real files, but still give you access to those files. This concept is at the foundation of the Workplace Shell design. The reference objects for program files are called *Program Objects*.

Program File Objects versus Program (Reference) Objects

You need to understand the distinction between these two types of objects. Consider the following illustration.

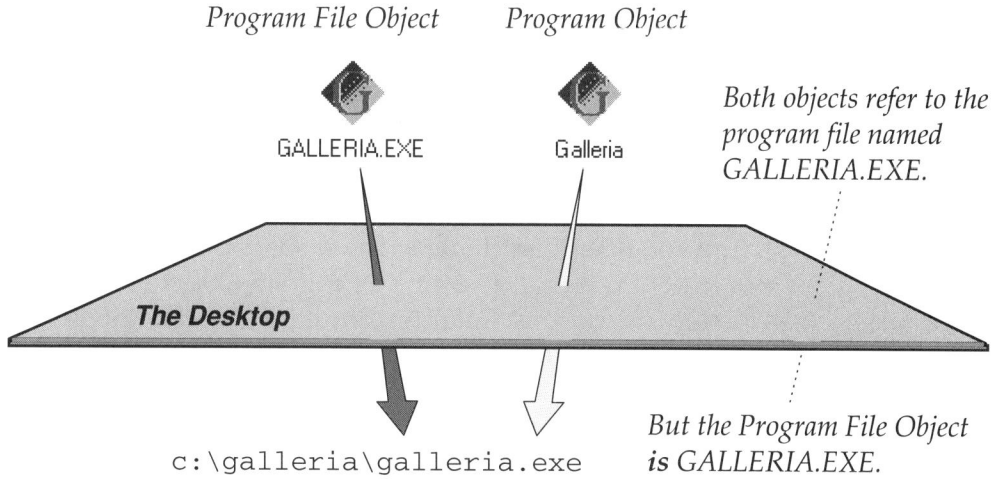

Figure 6.3.   *Executable files are represented in the Workplace Shell by Program File Objects and Program Objects.*

    A program object acts just like its program file object in that the same program will launch when you double-click on either of these icons. The **big** difference between these two objects is that a program file object is *real*. A program object is virtual—it is just a way to specify attributes for the corresponding program file object.

    Program objects let you get creative when designing your working environment in the Workplace Shell. A program file can have multiple program objects associated with it, each with its own settings. This means you can create program objects that launch a program with different start up and operating characteristics. For example, you might want a full-screen version and a windowed version of the same program. Or, you might want to set up a Work Area folder for a particular spreadsheet project. You could create a program object that automatically opens the project spreadsheet. And since program objects are reference objects, you can move them around on the desktop or to other folders without moving their real files.

If you are going to launch programs from the desktop, you should have program objects for each one. Don't drag a program file object out of your Drives object and drop it on your desktop, and don't create a shadow of the program file object. Either of these actions could cause your program to stop running. Creating program objects is easy. The Warp install does it for you when you select *Add Programs*, but if you install a new program and want to create just a single program object for it, open the Templates folder and drag a Program template to a folder (or the desktop). The settings notebook box will appear, allowing you to associate the object with the program file (executable), customize its startup and operating characteristics, specify a title, and even change the icon. See "Exercise 2: Creating a Program Object" in this chapter for step-by-step instructions. Refer to "Program Object Settings" in Chapter 5 for the specifics about folder settings.

If you want your newly created program object to be visible in more than one place, you can copy the program object, or create a shadow of the program object. Remember, avoid creating shadows of program file objects, but shadows of program objects are no problem. The difference between copying the program object and creating a shadow is that the copies allow you to make independent changes to their settings. If you create shadows, changing the settings of a shadow will change the settings for the program object, and vice versa.

Reference Objects for Data File Objects

When you install an application, it often creates its own data files, or it specifies a directory where it expects to find the data files. If you move the data files out of this directory, the application may not be able to find them. On your system, you may have created directories to hold specific data files (a subdirectory for all of February's receipts, for example). Balancing between the requirements of your applications, and your desire to store data files logically can be a chore under DOS. The virtual reality of the Workplace Shell will give you the freedom to put data files where *you* think they should be. You could even make a data file appear to exist in more than one location. For example, the file C:\ACCT\DATA\PAYROLL2.95 could appear in the "95 Payroll" folder, while also appearing in the "Feb Accounting" folder. Another view of the file could be in the "Back-up today" folder. If you access any of these files, you will actually be accessing the C:\ACCT\DATA\PAYROLL2.95 file, but you don't have to be concerned with the physical location of the file.

Shadows allow you to make files appear where you need them. If you find it inconvenient to have to: 1) open the Drives folder, 2) open the appropriate drive, 3) open the desired folder object, and 4) access the data file, create a shadow object for often-used data files in a convenient location. Of course, if you like where your data files are, you can access them directly, without shadows. Direct manipulation of data files is the only way to delete, copy, or move them. Deleting, moving, or copying a shadow of a data file *does not disturb* the data file itself.

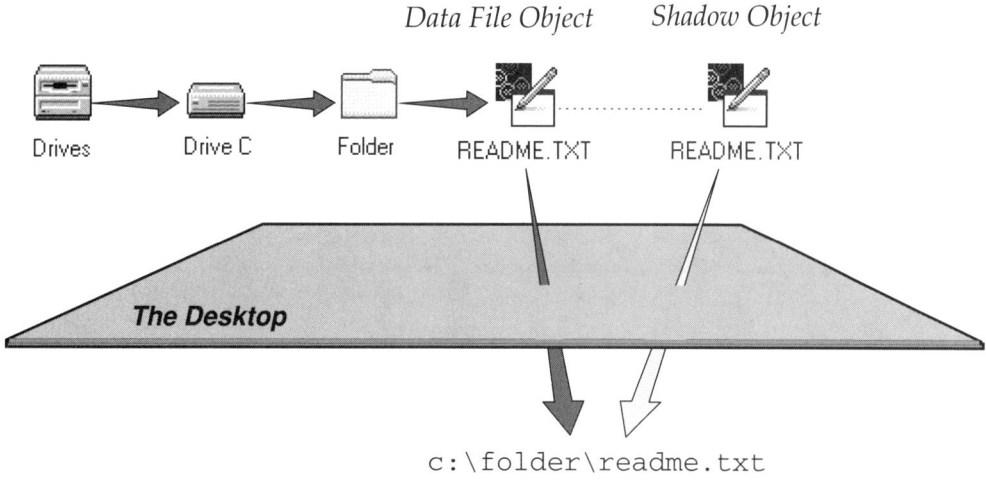

Figure 6.4.   *You can create shadow objects as references to data file objects.*

OS/2 Warp provides two types of reference objects for data files: *Shadow* objects and *Light Table (LT) Reference* objects. See "Shadow Objects" later in this chapter for more about shadows, and refer to "Ultimedia Viewer (The Light Table)" in Chapter 4 for details about LT References.

Device Objects

Device objects are called "abstract" objects in the Workplace Shell. They're virtual objects representing abstract concepts such as printing. For example, a printer object represents all the hardware and software required to transfer the contents of a document file to a printed page.

Device objects are virtual in that they don't directly represent real files on your disk drives. When you copy a printer object, you don't end up with two copies of the same file on your disk drive (and, unfortunately, you don't end up with two printers either). You're simply creating two references to the abstract idea of "printing." Consider the following illustration.

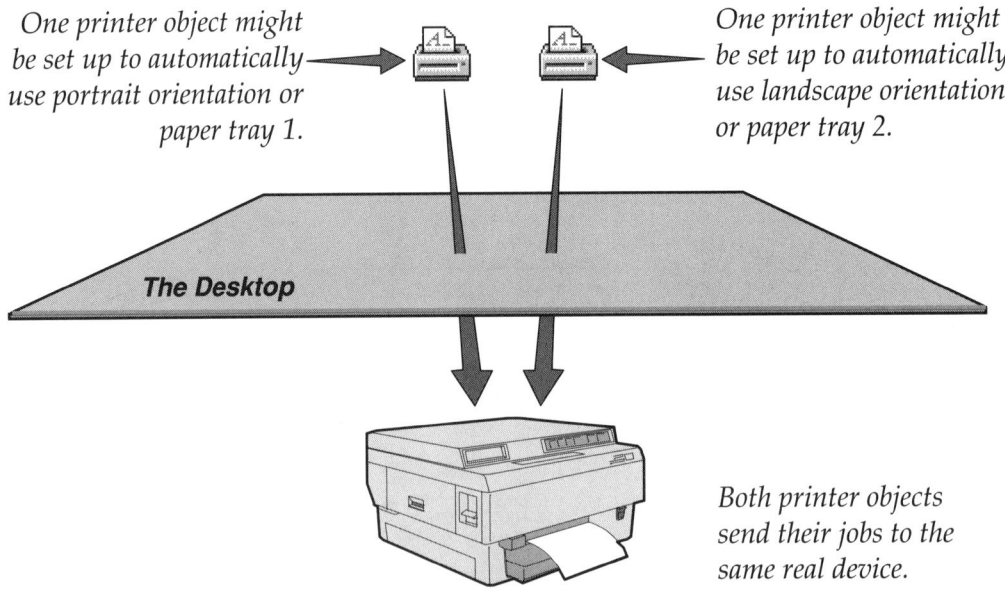

Figure 6.5.   *Device objects are abstract objects that represent abstract ideas.*

6　　Getting Warped: Exercises in Virtual Reality

Shadow Objects

Sometimes you might want an object to be conveniently available on your desktop or in a frequently used folder. To avoid making you copy or move the real object (which would affect the file on your disk drive) OS/2 lets you create shadow objects. For example, the default OS/2 installation places shadows of the Drives folder on your desktop (in the LaunchPad). The real Drive A: object is in the Drives folder. The shadow lets you see the contents of a diskette without first having to open the Drives folder.

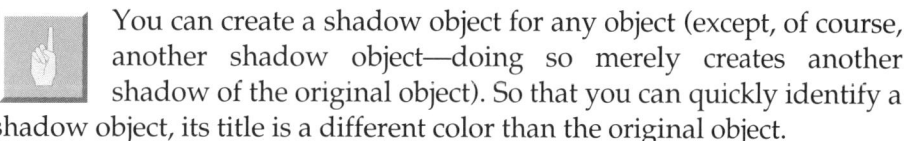
You can create a shadow object for any object (except, of course, another shadow object—doing so merely creates another shadow of the original object). So that you can quickly identify a shadow object, its title is a different color than the original object.

To create a shadow object, open the folder that contains the original object. While holding down the **Shift+Ctrl** keys, drag the object to its destination (another folder or the desktop). A "rubber-band" line connects the original object with its shadow while you're dragging it. Re-

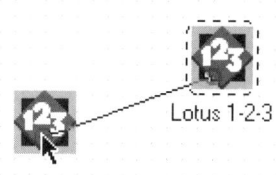

lease the mouse button to drop the shadow at its destination. If holding the **Shift**+**Ctrl** keys is too cumbersome, hold the **Alt** key and click on the object with the right mouse button. This "picks up" the object. You can release the **Alt** key, and locate the folder where you want the shadow. Open the context menu for the Destination folder, and select the arrow next to *Drop*, and then select *Create Shadow*. You can also use the Create Shadow option on an object's context menu to accomplish the same thing through dialog boxes, but that's not nearly as much fun.

OS/2 uses shadow objects extensively. For example, the folder that OS/2 creates as a result of using the *Find* function contains shadows of the files that match the find criteria.

Keep "Real" Objects off Your Desktop

One of the most common mistakes for new (and even experienced) users is to drag a program file object from the Drive A: object to the desktop in an attempt to install that program. In doing so, one is copying the real file to the c:\desktop subdirectory. Although there's nothing to stop you from doing this, you should keep objects that represent real files off your desktop. Here are a few reasons why:

- For the sake of organization, you should place related file objects in their own folders (subdirectories) just as you would place related papers into a manila file folder.

- You probably installed OS/2 in a hard disk partition that's just big enough for the operating system. If you store file objects on the desktop, their real files will be placed in the \desktop subdirectory within the OS/2 partition. You won't be able to store too many files there.

- If you copy a file object to the desktop from a folder, you end up with two copies of the real file on your disk drive. If that wasn't your intention, you can quickly become confused about which version of the file you want.

- You might forget that the object is real, and do something foolish with it, like drag it to the shredder.

This is not to say that you can't have objects on your desktop that represent programs and files. If you really want to place an object on your desktop, use a *shadow* of the real object. For programs, you can use a *program object*.

All of this might sound like we're making things more complicated than they need to be, but as you'll see, working with the concept of virtual reality in the Workplace Shell is more efficient and a lot more fun! Besides, when you shred shadow objects and program objects, you don't actually erase any real files.

6 — Getting Warped: Exercises in Virtual Reality

Exercises in Virtual Reality

This section contains some useful and interesting exercises designed to help you understand the virtual workplace. If you perform these exercises on your computer you'll be well on your way to getting warped.

- *Exercise 1:* Copying a Program File Object
- *Exercise 2:* Creating a Program Object
- *Exercise 3:* Creating a Work Area
- *Exercise 4:* Using the Virtual Clipboard
- *Exercise 5:* Creating a Desktop Window
- *Exercise 6:* Building a File Manager (Warp Drive)
- *Exercise 7:* Controlling the Virtual with the Real
- *Exercise 8:* Using the Find Utility
- *Exercise 9*: Creating a Virtual ZIPper

The OS/2 Warp Survival Guide

Exercise 1: Copying a Program File Object

In the following example, we'll demonstrate the wrong way and the right way to copy a program object from a diskette to your hard disk using various object-oriented techniques. Although most application programs come with an installation program that properly copies and installs the program files, you may need to do it manually sometime. Go ahead and try the steps on your computer while following the example.

The Wrong Way

This is how *not* to copy a program from a diskette to your computer's hard disk drive.

1. Place a diskette containing at least one executable file (`*.EXE` or `*.COM`) in Drive A: of your computer.

2. Open the Drives object.

3. Open the Drive A object.

4. Drag the program object from the Drive A window to the desktop.

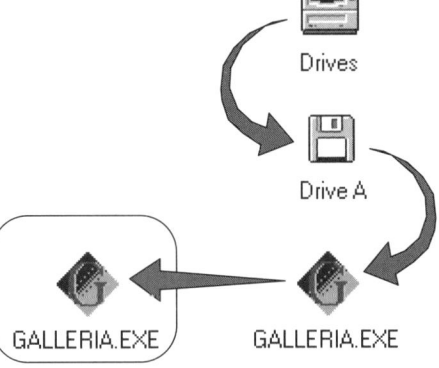

If you're following along on your computer, you just copied the executable file from the diskette drive to the \desktop subdirectory of your hard disk drive. To prove it to yourself, open an OS/2 Window (in the Command Prompts folder of the OS/2 System object) and look for the file in the \desktop subdirectory using the DIR command. Now move or resize your OS/2 Window so that you can see the program object on your desktop. Using the DEL command in the OS/2 Window, delete the executable file from the \desktop subdirectory. Watch the program object disappear from the desktop!

6
Getting Warped: Exercises in Virtual Reality

If you had already thought of using the steps listed above to copy the file, you're using object-oriented thinking—and that's great. But take the time to consider the right way.

The Right Way

This is how you should install program files to your computer's hard disk drive.

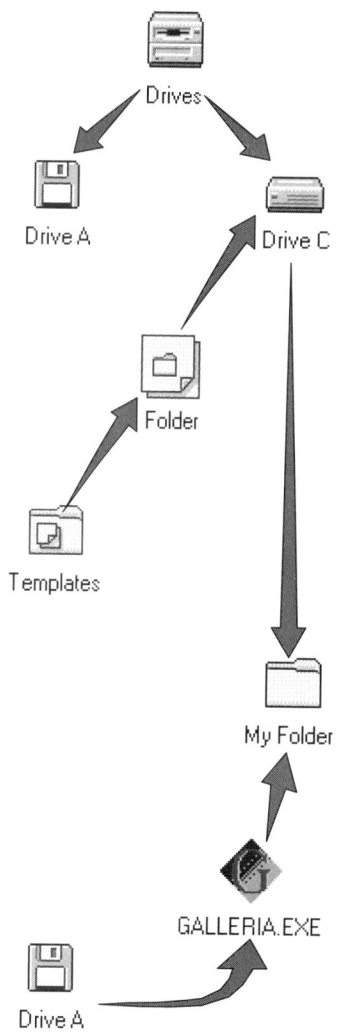

1. Place a diskette containing at least one executable file (*.EXE or *.COM) in Drive A: of your computer.

2. Open the Drives object.

3. Open the Drive A object, and open the Drive object where you want the program to reside.

4. Create a new folder:
   a. Open the Templates folder and drag a Folder template to the directory tree in the Drives window. Drop it on the Drive icon if you want the folder in the root directory, or drop it on another Folder object if you want to create a subdirectory.
   b. Find your new folder in the directory tree and rename it (**Alt**-click on the title, edit the title, and click outside the title area when finished).

5. Drag the program object from the Drive A window to your new folder. In doing so, you've just copied a program file ("GALLERIA.EXE" in our example) from the diskette to a new subdirectory ("My Folder" in our example) on your hard disk.

The OS/2 Warp Survival Guide

 Although the number of steps required for the right way seems to far outweigh the wrong way, you'll be happier in the long run for using the right way.

You could start this new program by double-clicking on its program file object, but it's better to create a program object for this program, as shown in Exercise 2.

Exercise 2: Creating a Program Object

After copying an executable (program) file to your hard disk, you should create a virtual object for it in the form of a program object. You'll be able to modify the settings for the new object and move it around your desktop without affecting the original program file object.

1. Open the Templates folder and drag a Program template to the desktop or another folder where you want to store the new object. The settings notebook will open for this new object.

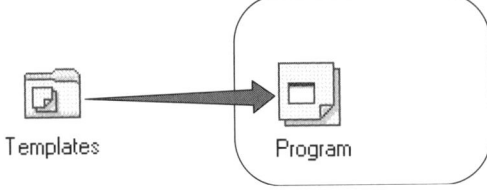

6
Getting Warped: Exercises in Virtual Reality

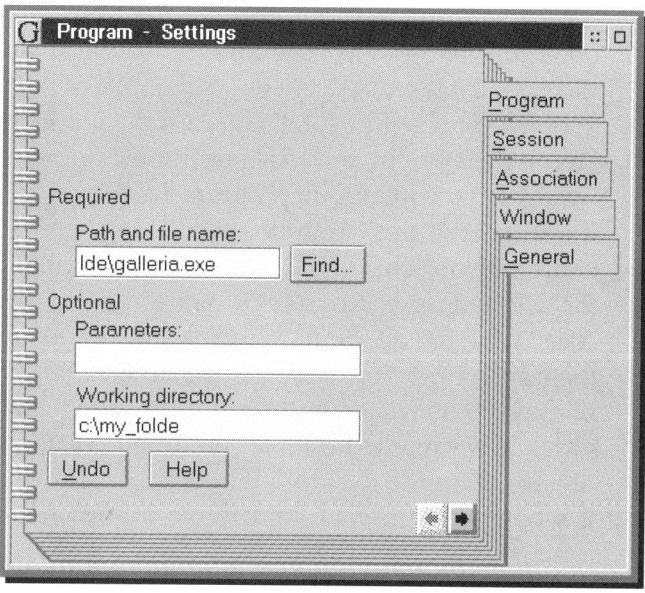

Figure 6.6. *The settings notebook appears when you drop a program object template.*

2. Type the path and file name of the program file object in the field provided on the *Program* tab of the settings notebook. You can use the *Find* button to search drives and subdirectories for the program file. If you want to pass any parameters to the program at launch time, type them into the Parameters field. See "Program Object Settings—Program Tab" in Chapter 5 for a list of possible parameters. If you want the program to think it is starting from a directory other than where the program file is located, type the path into the Working directory field.

3. If desired, use the *Association* tab to set up associations between this program object and other types of objects. Use the *General* tab to change the title of the program object to something meaningful to you. See "Program Object Settings" in Chapter 5 for a complete discussion of what you can set up using the tabs in the settings notebook.

You're now free to move this new program object to a folder, leave it on the desktop, or place it on the LaunchPad—wherever it will be more convenient for you to access. In the next exercise, we'll show you another idea about where you might want to place the program object: in a *Work Area* folder.

Before we continue, let's discuss the consequences of doing things the "wrong" way. In our first example, doing things the "wrong" way would have copied our program file object to the c:\desktop directory. If you launch this program, everything seems to work, but try this: Rename this object by holding the **Alt** key and clicking on the name with the left mouse button. Let's name the object "My Favorite Program." After you change the name, click on a blank area of the desktop to save the new name. You have just renamed the *real* executable file, which is probably not what you want (it can even cause programs to stop running). The same would happen if you created a shadow of the program file object on the desktop. If you create a program object, you can name it whatever you want, and move it anywhere, and the program file is not disturbed.

Exercise 3: Creating a Work Area

This exercise shows you how to create and employ one of OS/2's most useful features: *Work Areas*. In the previous exercise, you learned how to create a program object. You could just leave it floating around your desktop, but we'd like to show you another way to store and launch your programs.

Let's say you have a project you're working on that requires a spreadsheet program, a graphics editor, and a text editor program. Rather than opening the different folders that contain these programs and your project data files, you can create a special Work Area folder and place program objects and shadow objects in it. Your original objects (and their files) stay where they are, safely tucked away in their appropriate folders while being conveniently available as a group in your Work Area folder.

6

Getting Warped: Exercises in Virtual Reality

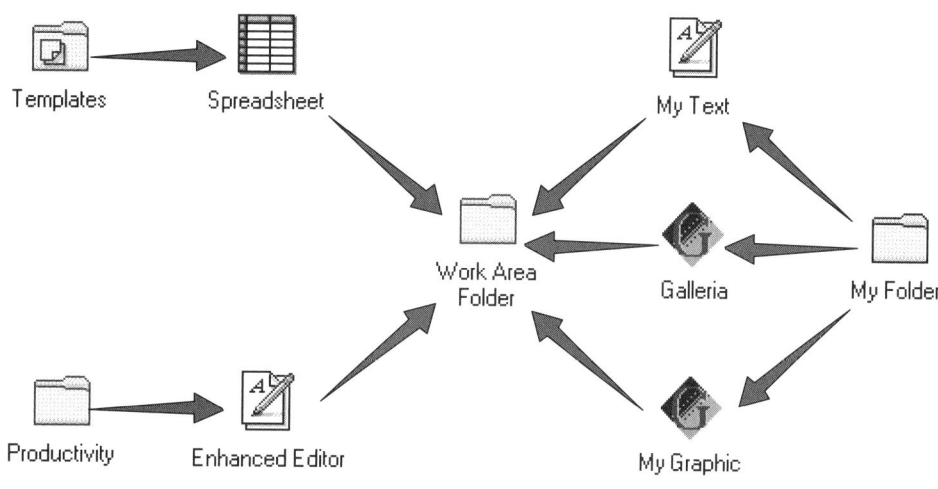

Figure 6.7.   *Collect virtual objects into your Work Area folder.*

To create a Work Area folder, perform the following steps:

1. Create a new folder and make it a work area:

    a. Open the Templates folder and drag a Folder template to the desktop. You can drop it on another Folder object if you want to create a subdirectory.

    b. Rename the new folder (**Alt**-click on the title, edit the title, and click outside the title area when finished). We'll call it "Work Area Folder" for the sake of this exercise.

    c. Open the settings notebook for the new folder (click the right mouse button while pointing at the folder, and click on the *Settings* option). Click on the *File* tab, and select the *Work area* option. Type a description of the project in the *Subject* field, and close the settings notebook.

The OS/2 Warp Survival Guide

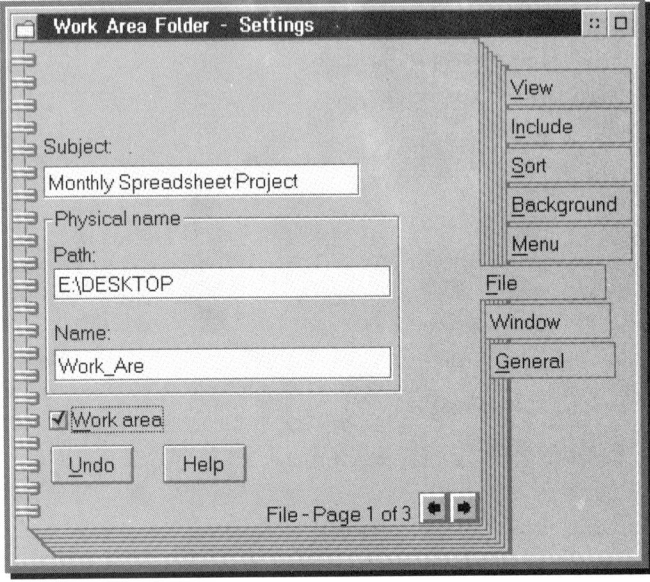

Figure 6.8. *The Work Area option is under the File tab of the folder's settings notebook.*

2. Create a program object and set up its association with the graphics editor program. In our example, this is the Galleria program.

    a. Drag a Program template from the Templates folder and drop it on the new Work Area folder. The settings notebook will appear for the new program object.

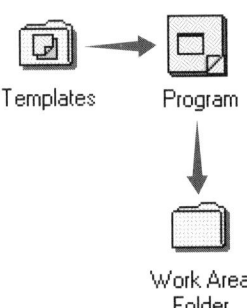

6
Getting Warped: Exercises in Virtual Reality

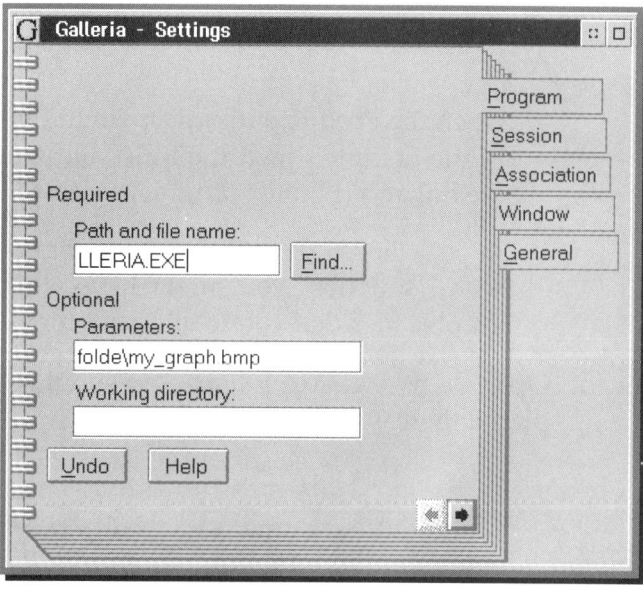

Figure 6.9. *Use the Program tab to associate your program object with its program file.*

    b. Enter the drive, path, and file name of the executable file (C:\MY_FOLDE\GALLERIA.EXE in our example). This sets up the association between our program object and the program file object.

    You can use the *Find* button to locate the file if you're not sure where it is, or if you're too lazy to type the information.

    To take full advantage of the program object, you can make it automatically open a data file when it starts to run. To do this, enter the drive, path, and file name of the data file in the Parameters field (as we did in our example).

    c. Click on the *General* tab in the settings notebook, and change the Title of the object. You can also change the icon that displays for the object. Close the settings notebook when you're finished.

3. Create a new IBM Works Spreadsheet data file for the Work Area. Open the Templates folder and drag the Spreadsheet template object to the Work Area folder.

The OS/2 Warp Survival Guide

4. Create shadow objects for the other items you want in the Work Area:

   a. Open the Productivity folder (found in the OS/2 System folder). While holding down the **Shift** and **Ctrl** keys, drag a shadow of the Enhanced Editor program object to the Work Area folder.

   b. Repeat this step for your text and graphic file objects. In a real-world situation, you might have already created some text, or graphic files that you want to use for the project.

5. Open the Work Area folder. You should see all the objects you just placed there.

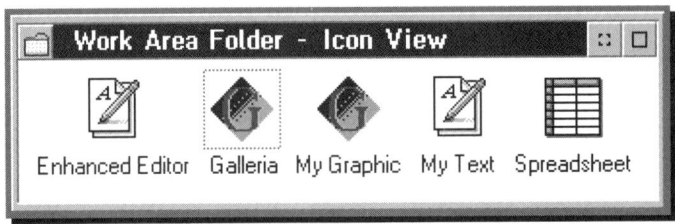

Figure 6.10.   *The Work Area folder looks like any other folder, but it has one important difference—automatic object open and close.*

Open the program objects you want to be automatically started. Then move and size them as desired to set up your working screen.

6

Getting Warped: Exercises in Virtual Reality

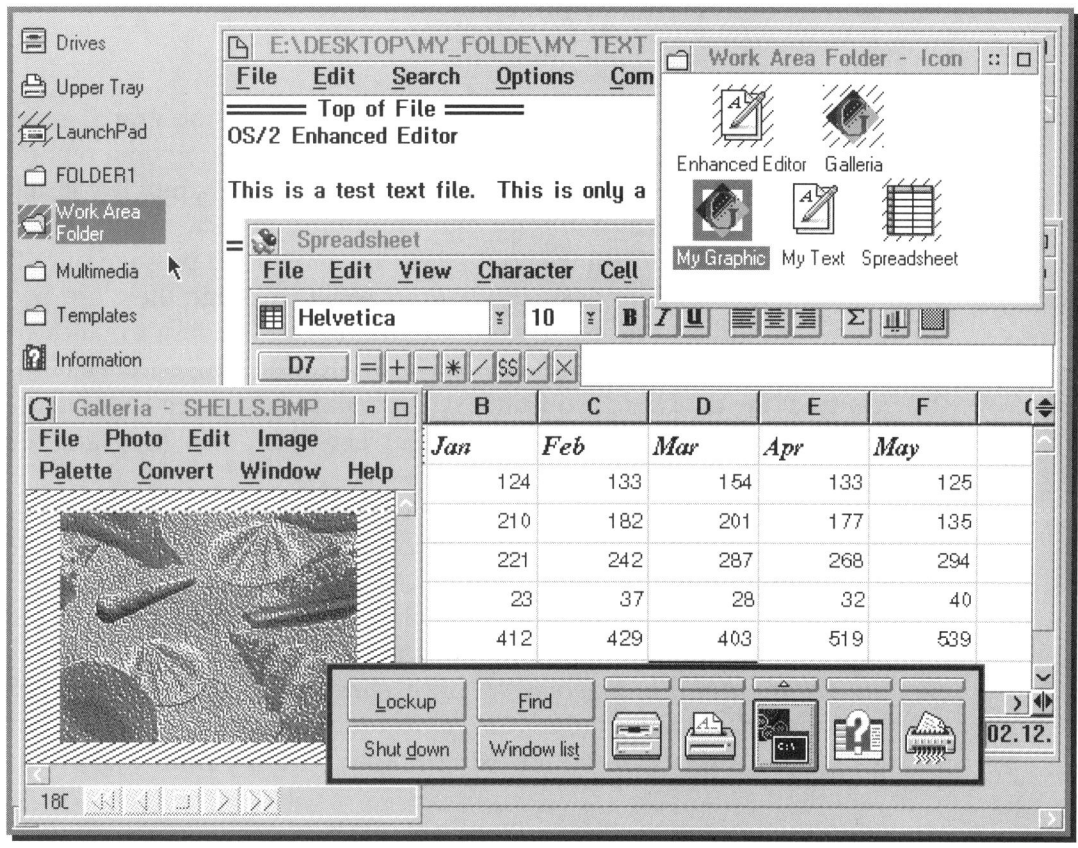

Figure 6.11.   *Work Areas are useful for project-oriented tasks.*

When you close the Work Area folder, OS/2 Warp closes all of the folder's open objects. OS/2 "remembers" what was open and the size of each window. The next time you open the Work Area folder, the screen will look as it did when you left it, and you're ready to start working again. This is the only difference between a Work Area and other folders: Closing a Work Area automatically closes all objects contained in the Work Area. And re-opening a Work Area automatically re-opens objects in the Work Area that were open when it was last closed.

When you're finished with the project, you can drag the Work Area folder to the Shredder. Since the folder only contains reference and shadow objects, the actual files are unaffected by the Shredder.

337

Exercise 4: Using the Virtual Clipboard

The clipboard is useful for moving and copying text and graphics from one place to another. For example, you might be creating on a report in which you want to quote a passage from a letter or memo. If you have the letter or memo as a file in your computer, you can open that file with an appropriate editor and *copy* or *cut* (move) the passage onto the virtual clipboard, then paste it into your report through the word processor program you're using to create the report. It doesn't matter that the text wasn't created with the same application program. That's the beauty of the clipboard; you can exchange data between *all* applications running under OS/2 Warp—even between Windows programs and DOS programs.

The clipboard can copy graphic data as well as textual data. Let's say you drew a nifty logo with your favorite drawing program, and you want to place it at the top of a letter you're creating in your word processor. After drawing the logo, you find out that the format of your graphic file is not supported by your word processor. Take heart, you can always use the clipboard! (You can even cut graphics from DOS programs that don't provide *Cut*, *Copy*, and *Paste* options, by running them in a DOS window and using *Mark* and *Copy* from the window menu.)

In our exercise, we'll copy a graphic from the Windows PaintBrush program to the clipboard, and from the clipboard into the IBM Works Charting program.

1. Open the Windows PaintBrush program and create a small graphic image. If you migrated your Windows programs into OS/2, you can find PaintBrush in the Windows Programs folder. Otherwise, look in the WIN-OS/2 Groups folder for the Accessories group. If you cannot find PaintBrush, refer to "Add Programs" in Chapter 5.

Paint Brush

6

Getting Warped: Exercises in Virtual Reality

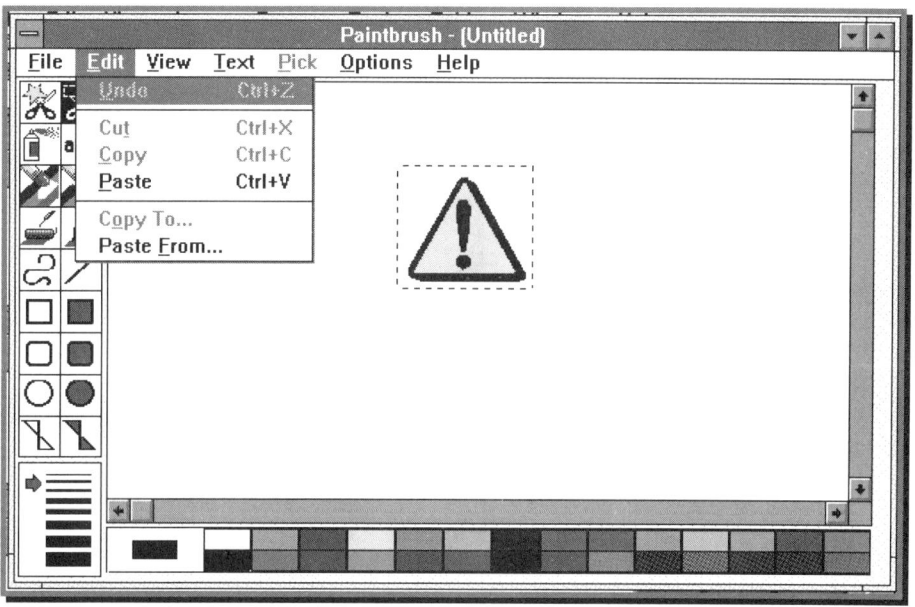

Figure 6.12. *Create a bitmap image and copy to the clipboard using PaintBrush's Edit menu.*

Select the image using the cut tool (the scissors tool) and select the *Copy* option on the *Edit* pull-down menu.

2. Just to make sure the image is on the OS/2 Clipboard, open the Clipboard Viewer (found in the Productivity folder within the OS/2 System folder). You should see the image you that you copied from PaintBrush. If not, your Windows clipboard may be set to *Private.* Check the Win-OS/2 Settings for the PaintBrush object.

The OS/2 Warp Survival Guide

Figure 6.13. *The Clipboard Viewer shows you the current contents of the clipboard, automatically adapting between textual and graphic objects.*

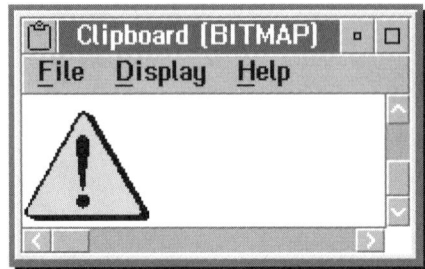

3. Open a new chart with the IBM Works Chart program (found in the IBM Works folder). Enter some charting data (or just click on the *Cancel* button) to get to the chart workspace. Select the *Paste* option from the *Edit* pull-down menu. You should see the image placed in the Chart window, with a frame around it. You can now move and place the image within Chart.

6

Getting Warped: Exercises in Virtual Reality

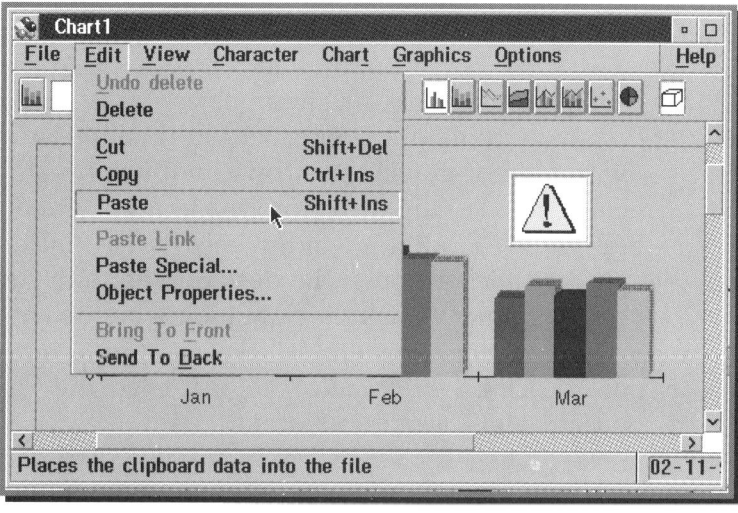

Figure 6.14.   *Open another application (Windows or OS/2) and use the Paste option on its Edit menu to copy the graphic image from the clipboard.*

As you might imagine, the virtual clipboard can be a very handy tool when you want to copy or move text or graphics from one application to another. To copy or move text, the steps are the same as the exercise you just performed:

1. Select the text you want in the source application.

2. Select the *Cut* or *Copy* option from the *Edit* pull-down menu.

3. Open the target application and select the *Paste* option from the *Edit* pull-down menu.

You can use the clipboard in even more unusual ways. Let's assume you are reading an on-line manual in a DOS windowed session. On the screen, the manual gives you an example of a command to type. Rather than typing the command yourself, select *Mark* from the window menu of the DOS and mark the command (you can mark several lines at once, if you wish). Then select *Copy* from the system menu. Now go to another DOS window and select Paste from the system menu. The command you copied will be "typed" into this session.

Exercise 5: Creating a Desktop Window

Sometimes you might want an object that's on your desktop, but your desktop is buried under stacks of open windows. You could start minimizing or moving windows until you find the object, or you could open a *new* desktop (in a window) to reveal the objects that are on your desktop. We'll call this window the *Desktop Window*.

Before you can open the desktop window, you have to modify the desktop settings. Click the right mouse button anywhere on the desktop to open its context menu. Click on *Settings* to open the settings notebook. Click on the *Window* tab and select the *Create new window* radio button under *Object open behavior*.

Now whenever you select the *Open* option on the desktop's context menu, a new window appears showing a replica of your desktop—without any open windows on it. This feature can be extremely convenient when your desktop is covered with programs.

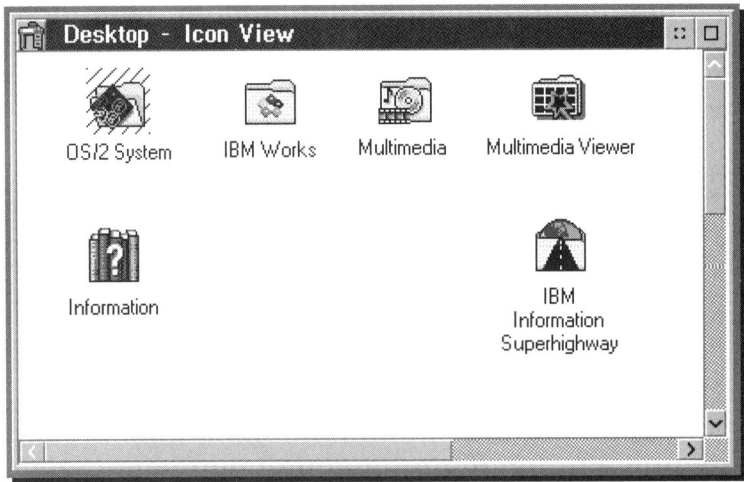

Figure 6.15. You can open a desktop window to see closed objects on your desktop.

Once you've opened a desktop window, you can open the objects contained in the window as if you were opening them from the original desktop.

6

Getting Warped: Exercises in Virtual Reality

Exercise 6: Building a File Manager (Warp Drive)

If you're a Windows user, you might be wondering "Where's my File Manager?" File management in OS/2 Warp is typically accomplished through the Drives folders. This technique can sometimes seem clumsy, especially when you find yourself opening and managing folders on multiple drives. We have a suggestion that will make file management more efficient in these (and maybe all) circumstances.

Warp Drive

This exercise shows you how to create a special folder that will automatically open multiple drives in Tree View, and then open subsequent subfolders in Details View. This technique lets you perform file management functions more like you would in the Windows File Manager.

1. Create a Work Area folder (call it *Warp Drive*). See Exercise 3 for detailed instructions to create a Work Area folder.

2. Drag shadows of the drive objects you want *Warp Drive* to automatically open (i.e., Drive A:, Drive C:, and Drive D:) and drop them in the Warp Drive folder. If necessary, refer to "Shadow Objects" earlier in this chapter for instructions.

3. Open the settings notebook for each drive object in the Warp Drive folder and make the following changes:

  a. Set the *Icon Size* option to *Small* on the Tree View page (page 2) of the View tab (see "View Tab" in Chapter 5).

  b. Set the *Default sort attribute* to *Name* and enable the *Always maintain sort order* option under the *Sort* tab (see "Sort Tab" in Chapter 5).

  c. Set the *Default folder view* to *Details* (see "Menu Tab" in Chapter 5).

  d. Set the *Folder Automatic Close* option to *Never* under page 2 of the Window tab (see "Window Tab" in Chapter 5).

4. Select all drives in the Warp Drive folder, open the context menu of one of these drives, and select the *Open* cascade menu (click on the

The OS/2 Warp Survival Guide

arrow button). Then select the *Tree View* option to open Tree View windows for all of your drives.

5. Position and size each window as desired. You might want to tile them next to each other and make them the same size.

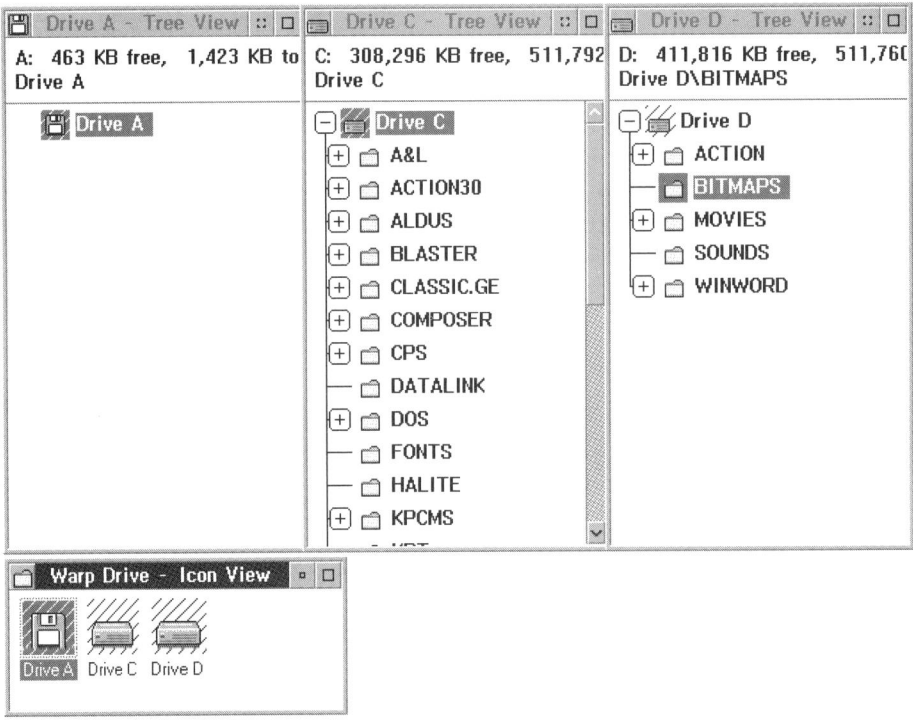

Figure 6.16.   *Warp Drive gives you an interface to the file system similar to File Manager.*

Now, when you open folders in the drive windows, you'll get windows in Details View. This view is often more useful for file management; it shows file dates and sizes. When you no longer need a window, close it.

 Don't close the individual drive windows (the ones in Tree View). Close the Warp Drive folder instead. If you forget this rule and close a drive window, you'll have to perform step 4 again for that drive object when you next use Warp Drive.

Getting Warped: Exercises in Virtual Reality

6. Close the Warp Drive folder. OS/2 Warp will close all open drive windows, remembering their positions and sizes.

If you'd like, you can add the *Workplace Shell Open* program object to the Warp Drive folder. We developed this program to provide a drag-and-drop object opener; it lets you drop folders on it and have them open in Icon View or Tree View. See Chapter 11, "Warping with REXX," for details about this program. The programming code is provided there with instructions for its use.

Exercise 7: Controlling the Virtual with the Real

This exercise attempts to demonstrate the link between the virtual objects and their real-world counterparts in your computer.

1. Close all open windows on the desktop, and open an OS/2 Command Prompt window (*OS/2 Window* object in the Command Prompts folder).

2. Change to the desktop directory with the following command:
   `cd \desktop`

3. Create a new subdirectory (folder) by entering the following command:
   `md folder2`

   Watch the desktop; a new folder will appear titled FOLDER2! Depending on the configuration of your desktop, you might have to move the OS/2 Command window in order to see the new folder.

4. Refer to Figure 6.17. We created a folder titled *Folder1*. This folder is open on the desktop, containing a data file object and a shadow of that data file. In the OS/2 Command window, we changed to that subdirectory (folder) and requested a directory of the files contained there. Notice that the results of the DIR command indicate that there is only one file in the directory. The shadow object isn't real.

The OS/2 Warp Survival Guide

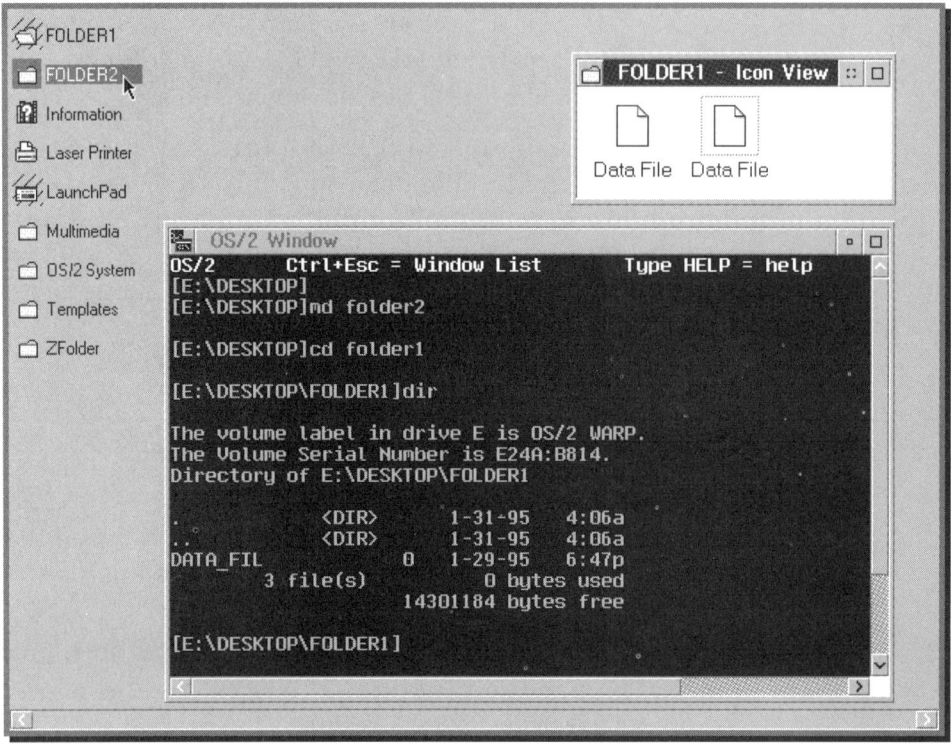

Figure 6.17. The link between real and virtual works both ways: You can make objects come and go on the desktop by entering OS/2 Command Line commands.

In your OS/2 Command window, enter the following command to remove the folder we created in this exercise: `rd folder2`. Watch the folder disappear from the desktop.

Exercise 8: Using the Find Utility

At first, it might not be obvious how powerful the *Find* utility can be. Sure, it finds files on your disk drives; but it also lets you quickly manipulate files in different drives and directories, or create folders full of related shadow objects. By using the *Save Results* option, the results window becomes a folder full of shadows, giving you

6 Getting Warped: Exercises in Virtual Reality

a convenient way to access virtual groupings of files such as documents, bitmaps, and music files.

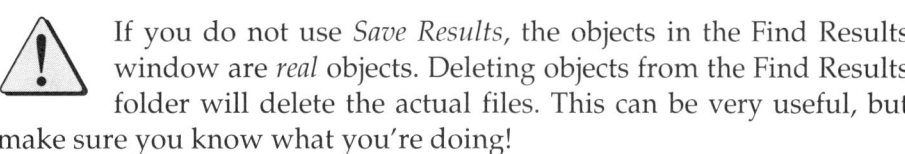 If you do not use *Save Results*, the objects in the Find Results window are *real* objects. Deleting objects from the Find Results folder will delete the actual files. This can be very useful, but make sure you know what you're doing!

1. Launch the Find utility. You can find it as a button on the default LaunchPad, and it's an option on almost every context menu in OS/2 Warp. You'll see the following dialog box.

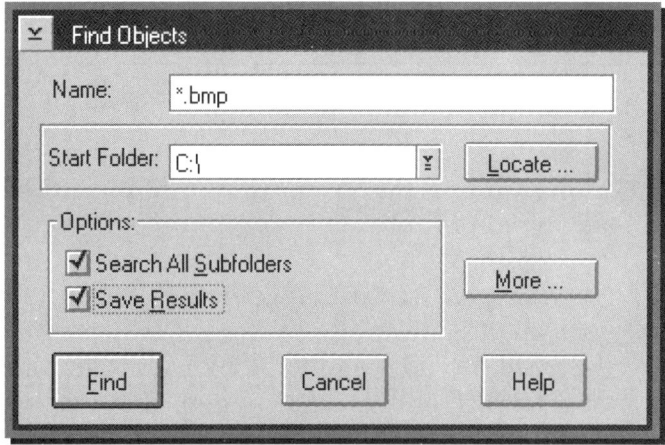

Figure 6.18. Use the Save Results option of Find to create folders containing shadows of files that match your search criteria.

2. Enter `*.BMP` in the *Name* field, and specify your OS/2 installation drive in the *Start Folder* field. Then click on the *Search all Subfolders* option and click on the *Save Results* option. The *More...* button lets you specify additional include/exclude search criteria.

3. Click on the *Find* button when you're ready to start the search. The results of the Find will appear in a window.

The OS/2 Warp Survival Guide

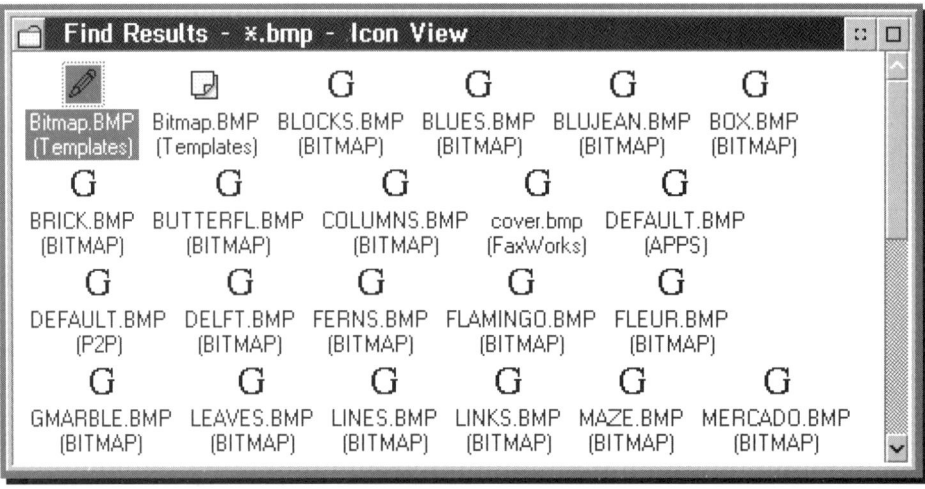

Figure 6.19. *The Find Results folder contains shadows of the files matching the search criteria.*

You can keep this folder around to provide convenient access to all bitmap images that came with OS/2 Warp. This concept works well for any type of file object.

When you start a find operation, only one folder is searched, but if you select *Search all subfolders*, all folders within the "start" folder are searched. If you'd like to be more specific about where you search for objects, click on the *Locate* button. This will open a notebook with several ways to specify the "start folder" for the search.

6   Getting Warped: Exercises in Virtual Reality

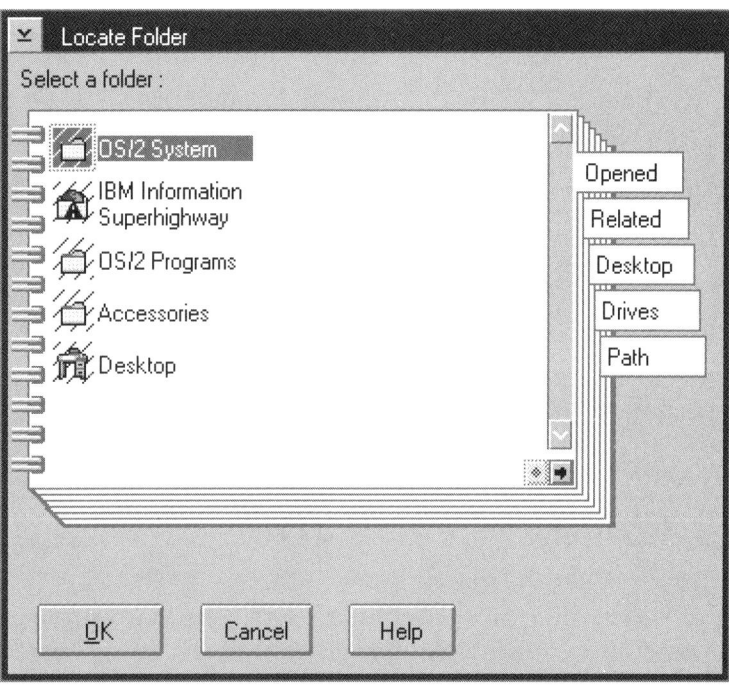

Figure 6.20.   *The Locate button displays other ways to specify the start folder for a find.*

Select the *Opened* page to select from the list of all opened folders. The *Related* page will display a Tree View of folders adjacent to the object from which Find was started. The *Desktop* page displays a Tree View of the Warp desktop. The *Drives* page displays Tree Views of all drives, and the *Path* page allows you to type a starting folder.

Once you start a search, you will see a progress dialog. You can press the *Cancel* button at any time to stop the search, and display the objects that were found so far.

Using Find Without "Save Results"

When you do not select the *Save Results* check box, the Find utility creates a folder with the real objects rather than the shadows. This can be useful for disk clean up functions. For example, to delete all files with the .TMP extension (temporary files), do the following:

1. Launch the Find utility as you did in the previous example.

2. Enter *.TMP in the *Name* field, and select *All Drives* from the *Start Folder* drop-down menu.

3. Select *Search all Subfolders*, and de-select *Save Results*.

4. Click on the *Find* button when you're ready to start the search. The Find utility will search for all .TMP files on all drives. When the search is complete, a *Find Results* window will appear. If you want to delete all the .TMP files, select all the objects in the *Find Results* window and drag them to the shredder.

Exercise 9: Creating a Virtual ZIPper

If you are like most computer users, your hard drive isn't big enough to hold all your files. You've probably been using some kind of file compression utility to store more files in the limited space available on your system. One popular method of compressing files is the ZIP utility, created by PKWARE, Inc. You may also be used to a fancy front-end to the ZIP utility, so you don't have to remember the command syntax. There are several OS/2 front-end utilities that put a graphical face on the ZIP utility, but until you find one you like, you can use the following procedure. In our example, we will be using the InfoZIP utility, which is compatible with PKZIP 2.x, and offers native OS/2 support (as well as many other operating systems). The InfoZIP utility is free, and can be downloaded from any BBS or Internet FTP site where OS/2 files are found. To integrate ZIP with the Workplace Shell, do the following:

1. Create a batch command file named C:\ZIPVIEW.CMD containing the following statements:

   ```
   ECHO Contents of %1 > C:\$$ZIPTMP.TMP
   UNZIP.EXE -v %1 >> C:\$$ZIPTMP.TMP
   TEDIT C:\$$ZIPTMP.TMP
   ```

The `C:\$$ZIPTMP.TMP` file is a temporary file used to save the list of files in the target ZIP file. The first line of the command writes the name of the target ZIP file to a temporary file. The second line tells `UNZIP.EXE` to place a ZIP directory of the target ZIP file in the same temporary file, and the last line uses `TEDIT.EXE` to display the temporary file containing the ZIP list.

2. Create a program template for this CMD file (refer to exercise 2). On the *Association* page, add an association for *.ZIP. On the *General* page, rename this object ZIP Viewer. See "Program Object Settings" in Chapter 5 for detailed instructions.

3. Create another program template. In the *Program* field, enter the complete path and name for `UNZIP.EXE`. In the *Parameters* field, enter "`%* -d [enter destination directory]`". On the *Association* page, add an association for `*.ZIP`. On the *General* page, rename this object to unZIPper.

You now have two Workplace Shell objects. The first is the ZIP Viewer. This one was the first object associated with `*.ZIP`, so it should be the default association for ZIP files. If you drop a ZIP file on this object (or just launch any ZIP file from a Drives object), the `UNZIP.EXE` program will create a ZIP directory of that ZIP file and save it as `C:\$$ZIPTMP.TMP`. Then TEDIT will start, and display the `$$ZIPTMP.TMP` file, allowing you to view the contents of the ZIP.

The second object will unzip all files in a ZIP file to a directory you specify. When you drop a ZIP file on this object, OS/2 will ask the question specified inside the square brackets on the Parameters field. When you type in a path, `UNZIP.EXE` will receive the name of the ZIP (from the `%*` in the parameters) and the target directory (from what you type). It will then unzip the dropped ZIP file into that directory.

Two simple objects and a few lines of batch programming now allow you to view and unzip ZIP files using drag-and-drop, as well as direct manipulation. If you have the DOS PKZIP instead of InfoZIP, you can do the same thing, but your ZIP VIEW program would be a .BAT instead of a .CMD, and you'd need to use `QBASIC /EDIT` instead of `TEDIT`.

Chapter 7

DOS and Windows Under OS/2 Warp

Using DOS and Windows programs under OS/2 Warp may at first seem complicated, but when you realize how flexible your choices are and how powerful, you might agree with the claim that "OS/2 Warp is a better DOS than DOS" and a "better Windows than Windows."

This chapter will help you optimize your DOS and Windows programs when running under OS/2 Warp. You don't have to understand the concepts presented here. In fact, you don't have to do anything special to run DOS and Windows programs under OS/2 Warp. But, if you find that one of your programs doesn't seem to run like it used to, this chapter may prove to be quite useful.

Virtual DOS Machines

When you use real DOS, the files CONFIG.SYS and AUTOEXEC.BAT define the DOS environment in which all your DOS programs will run. This forces you to make some compromises; a DOS environment that's perfect for one application might be less than perfect for another. OS/2 Warp eliminates this restriction by letting you set up a different environment for each DOS program. When you run several DOS programs at the same time under OS/2 Warp, each one is running in its own *Virtual DOS Machine* (VDM). You can think of each VDM as a separate computer, with its own environment. OS/2 does have a CONFIG.SYS file that defines settings common to *all* DOS sessions. There is also an AUTOEXEC.BAT file that lets you configure the environment of DOS sessions. You can probably run most of your DOS programs from this single environment, but if you need or want more flexibility, each DOS session can have its own `AUTOEXEC.BAT` file, and load device drivers specific to that DOS session.

If all that sounds too complex, don't worry. In its simplest form, Warp's DOS support lets you run more than one DOS session at the same time. The default settings for `CONFIG.SYS` and `AUTOEXEC.BAT` are usually sufficient to run any DOS program, but if you are interested in maximum performance, you'll want to "tune" your sessions to fit the programs they run.

DOS Sessions

In the Command Prompts folder you'll find the *DOS Full Screen*, *DOS Window*, and *DOS from Drive A:* objects. If you launch the *DOS Full Screen* and *DOS Window* objects, you'll have two separate DOS sessions running. The only difference is in how they initially appear. A DOS Window session runs in a virtual screen, which appears in a window on the OS/2 desktop. A DOS Full Screen session uses the entire screen, much like a real DOS program. You can switch between windowed and full-screen DOS by using the **Alt+Home** key combination. The *DOS from Drive A:* object is a bit different. Rather than using OS/2 Warp's built-in DOS support, it allows a specific version of DOS to run under OS/2. This means you can boot any bootable DOS floppy without leaving OS/2 Warp. Even a DOS 1.0 diskette can boot under OS/2 in this way. We'll discuss this support for *Specific DOS* sessions later in this chapter.

 If you open the Settings notebook for these objects, you may notice that the *Object open behavior* on the *Window* page is set to *Create new window*. Normally, objects are set to *Display existing Window*. By selecting *Create new window*, you'll be able to start more than one session from the same object. Each time you want to start another

DOS program, just launch this object, which opens a new DOS command prompt, and you can run another program. With proper tuning, you might be able to run as many as 100 DOS sessions at the same time. (Most systems will run out of resources by the time the 100th simultaneous DOS program is started.)

Custom DOS Objects

If you want to use multiple DOS prompts, and are comfortable with that concept, you're ready to experiment with custom DOS objects. Using a custom object for each DOS program is the best way to tune each DOS application for maximum performance. When you install OS/2 Warp, it creates custom DOS objects for every DOS program it finds on your hard drive (using the "add programs" function). When you use a custom DOS object, you don't see a DOS command prompt. OS/2 Warp will start a DOS session and automatically run the program associated with the object. For example, in the \OS2\MDOS subdirectory, you can find QBASIC.EXE, which is a DOS program. This program can be used as a text editor by starting it with the /EDIT option. To run the program, you could open a DOS command prompt session and type: OS2\MDOS\QBASIC /EDIT, or you could create a custom DOS object.

Creating a Custom DOS Object

To create a custom DOS object, drag a Program template from the Templates folder and drop it on your desktop. The Settings notebook will appear for this new object.

The OS/2 Warp Survival Guide

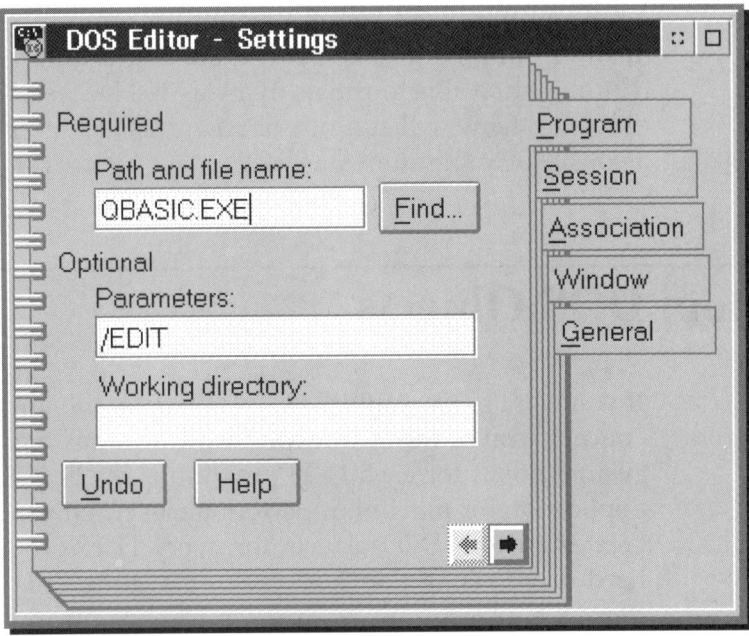

Figure 7.1.   *The Settings notebook lets you customize your DOS session*

Now let's turn this DOS object into a DOS session that runs QBASIC in its Editor mode. Type \OS2\MDOS\QBASIC.EXE in the Path and File name field. Press **Tab**, and OS/2 Warp looks through an application database to see if it recognizes this program. In this case, OS/2 Warp recognizes QBASIC.EXE, so it changes the object title, and adds the /EDIT parameter as shown in Figure 7.1. If OS/2 did not recognize the application, you could name the object and set any parameters manually. This object will tell OS/2 to start QBASIC.EXE in the DOS session, and pass the /EDIT parameter to the program. This object will even support drag-and-drop mouse operations. If you drop a file on this object, the fully qualified file name for the dropped file will be appended to the parameter line. If you want the file name to be placed elsewhere, put %* in the parameter field where you want the file name to be placed.

Now click on the *Session* tab of the settings notebook. A screen similar to the following appears:

7 DOS and Windows Under OS/2 Warp

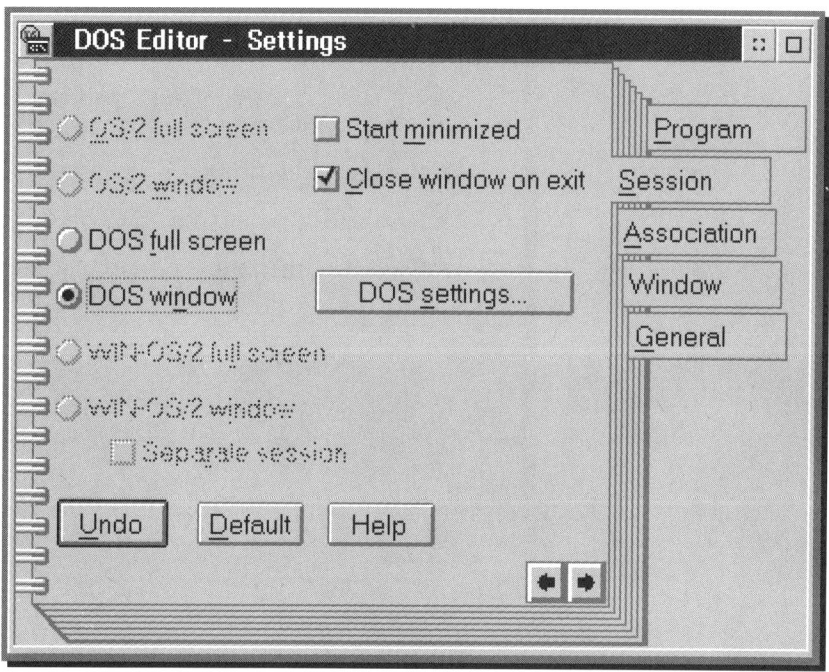

Figure 7.2. Use the Session tab to specify whether you want the DOS session to use a window or full screen.

Notice that the *DOS window* setting is selected, and the only other available option is *DOS Full screen*. The OS/2 and WIN-OS/2 Settings are disabled, because OS/2 Warp has already determined that the program you chose was a DOS program. Notice also the button labeled *DOS settings...*. By clicking on this button, you can tune this particular object for optimum performance.

The OS/2 Warp Survival Guide

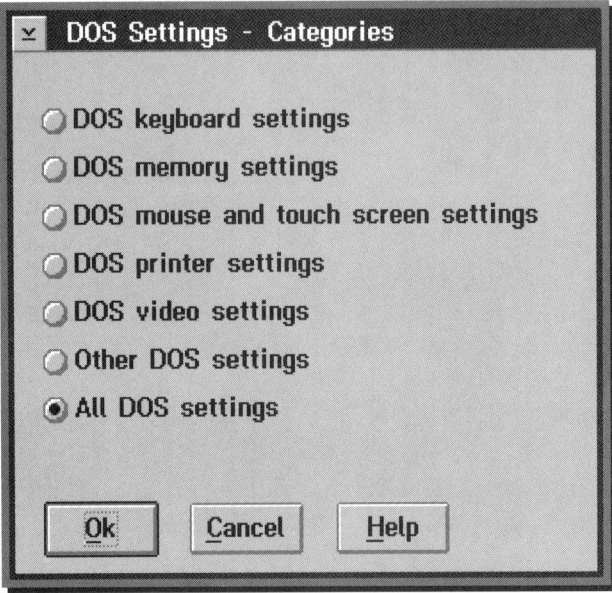

Figure 7.3. *The DOS settings button reveals a menu of options for tuning your DOS session.*

You can select one of the buttons to display only a certain category of options, or select *OK* with *All DOS settings* selected to see them all at once. The long list of settings may scare you at first, but remember, the defaults should be adequate for most programs. You only need to change the settings if your program has an unusual need for some resource. The list of DOS settings you can change is presented as follows:

7
DOS and Windows Under OS/2 Warp

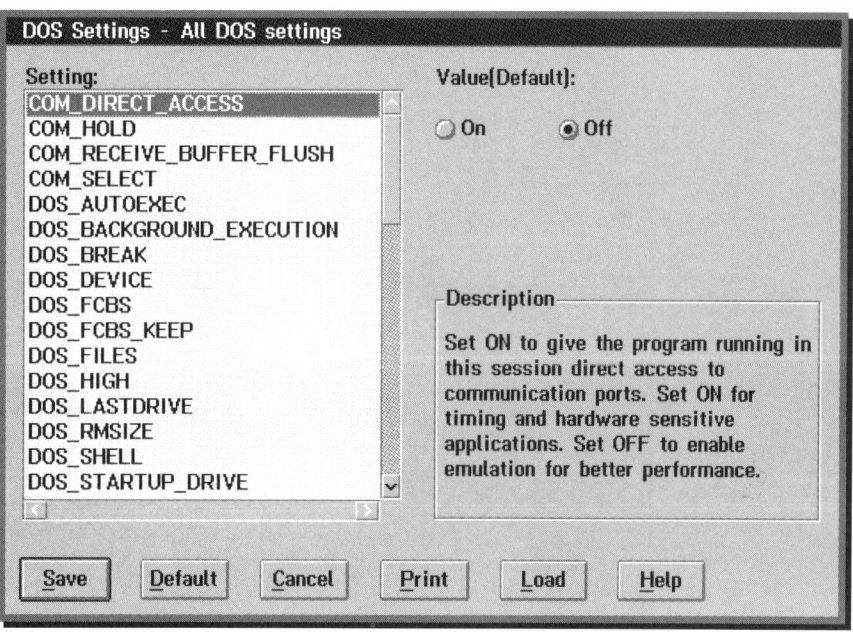

Figure 7.4. *The DOS Settings dialog allows you to customize all the attributes of the DOS session.*

Which setting you change will depend on the application you are configuring. For example, the QBASIC editor does not need EMS or XMS memory, and it does not need processor time if it is not the *active* program. When OS/2 Warp recognized this application, it configured defaults that work for this program, but feel free to experiment with these settings. You can review all the DOS settings for this object and change them, without affecting the environment of other DOS programs you run.

Now click on the *General* tab of the settings notebook. A screen similar to the following appears:

The OS/2 Warp Survival Guide

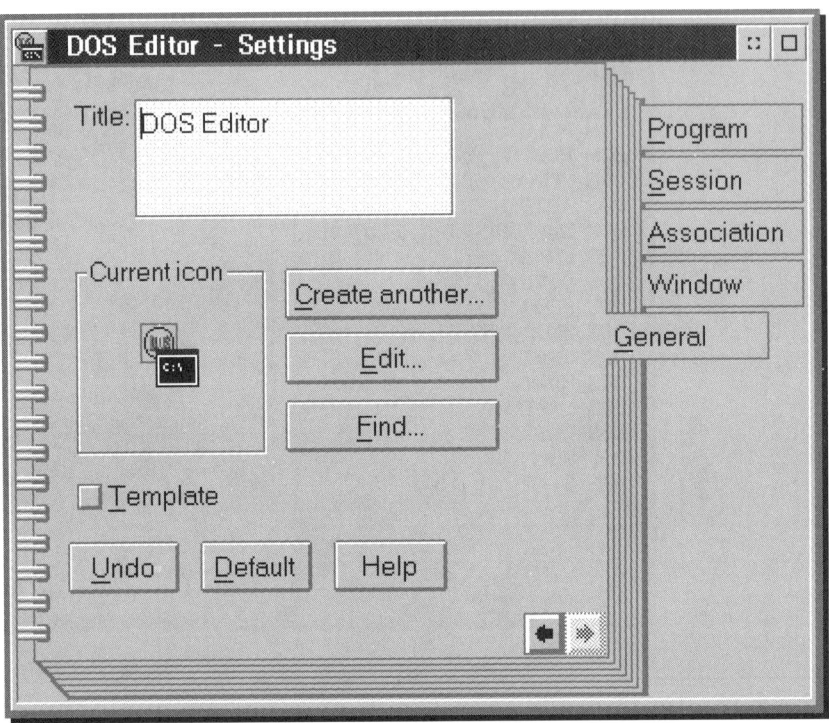

Figure 7.5. Use the General tab to change the title and icon associated with your new DOS object.

You can give this object a new title, and also assign or create a custom icon for the DOS program. Once you save the DOS object, you can start a DOS session and start the editor in that DOS session with a single mouse-click. To test it, open your Drives object, and open the root directory folder. Find the AUTOEXEC.BAT data file. Drag it from the directory folder and drop it on your newly created object. OS/2 Warp will start QBASIC using the /EDIT parameter, and the editor will load AUTOEXEC.BAT. Was using a DOS editor ever this easy?

If you followed everything so far, you now realize how powerful DOS support under OS/2 really is. However, you might be wondering how you can create custom objects for *all* your DOS applications. It's easier than you think. When you installed OS/2 Warp, you were asked if you wanted to "add programs." If you did, you already have custom objects for the programs OS/2 Warp found. You can use the "add programs" object (in the System Setup folder) at any time to search for newly-installed programs.

The Add Programs utility uses a database of DOS, Windows, and OS/2 applications with custom settings for each one. Add Programs will search all your hard drives for known programs, and create custom objects for each. If some of your programs are not in the database, the Add Programs utility lets you create objects for them as well. The *Other Programs* button (displayed after you search for known programs) lets you create a custom object for any executable program (even your DOS .BAT files), but you may have to spend some time tuning the settings for these programs.

DOS from Drive A:

Inside the Command Prompts folder is an object titled *DOS from Drive A:*. This object can show you how to get even more use out of the DOS compatibility built into OS/2 Warp.

The OS/2 system has a "DOS emulator" that allows you to run most DOS programs. However, there are some programs that make use of undocumented features in a specific release of DOS. Such programs might not run if OS/2 Warp's DOS emulator does not exactly duplicate these undocumented features. To solve this, you can actually run a real version of DOS under OS/2 Warp, complete with any of the features specific to that version (all DOS versions, beginning with PC-DOS 1.0 will work in this way). If you are developing DOS applications, it might be helpful to be able to run your program on different *Specific DOS* sessions at the same time to compare results. Doing this is easy with OS/2 Warp.

Real DOS

To run real DOS under OS/2 Warp, you must first prepare a DOS boot disk. This can either be a floppy, or (if you installed OS/2 Warp using the "Boot Manager" option) your computer's C: drive. As an example, we will use a typical DOS 6.3 boot floppy. The CONFIG.SYS for this floppy might look like this:

```
device=himem.sys
device=emm386.exe auto 4096 ram
devicehigh=ansi.sys
dos=high,umb
files=20
buffers=20
shell=a:\command.com a:\ /p
```

This configuration loads an XMS driver (HIMEM.SYS), an EMS driver (EMM386.EXE), a screen driver (ANSI.SYS), and loads DOS into the High Memory Area (DOS=HIGH). Upper Memory Blocks are allocated (DOS=UMB), and the ANSI.SYS driver is loaded into a UMB (via the DEVICEHIGH statement).

The drivers loaded by DOS will not all work under OS/2 Warp, because they attempt to take complete control of the computer. However, replacements for all of these functions are provided by OS/2 Warp. In the \OS2\MDOS subdirectory, you will find a HIMEM.SYS, an EMM386.SYS (note that the DOS version is called EMM386.EXE), and an ANSI.SYS. The OS/2 version of ANSI.SYS is not required, but it will use less memory than the one that comes with DOS. In addition, the driver FSFILTER.SYS is required to give DOS access to OS/2-controlled hard drives.

If you copy the OS/2 replacement drivers from \OS2\MDOS into an \OS2 subdirectory of the DOS boot floppy, you can change the CONFIG.SYS as follows:

```
device=a:\os2\himem.sys
device=a:\os2\emm386.sys auto 4096 ram
devicehigh=a:\os2\ansi.sys
devicehigh=a:\os2\fsfilter.sys
```

7
DOS and Windows Under OS/2 Warp

```
dos=high,umb
files=20
buffers=20
shell=a:\command.com a:\ /p
```

The only changes are to access the OS/2 versions of these files, and to add the `FSFILTER.SYS` driver, so DOS can read and write to the hard drives. Before you boot this floppy under OS/2 Warp, you'll want to create an object for it. The *DOS from Drive A:* is suitable for this, but you may want to make some configuration changes to it. Under DOS, all available RAM is converted to XMS by `HIMEM.SYS`. Under OS/2, the DOS setting "XMS_MEMORY_LIMIT" controls how much XMS memory is available. Under DOS, the amount of EMS is specified by the parameter on the `EMM386.EXE` statement (in this case, 4096K, or 4MB). Under OS/2, the DOS setting, "EMS_MEMORY_LIMIT" controls this. If you try to load `EMM386.SYS` when "EMS_MEMORY_LIMIT" is set to 0, DOS will generate an error.

Once you have made any changes to the DOS Settings of the DOS from Drive A: object, you can insert the modified DOS boot floppy and open the object. DOS should start and initialize, but OS/2 Warp is still running. You can return to the Warp desktop at any time by pressing **Ctrl+Esc**. You can also run this copy of DOS in a window by pressing **Alt+Home**. The session looks and acts like any other DOS session under OS/2, but in this case it is *real* DOS. Try the DOS `VER` command to prove this. About the only difference you may notice between "real" DOS under OS/2 and emulated DOS is that the `EXIT` command does not close a real DOS session. To accomplish this, you will find `EXIT_VDM.COM` in \OS2\MDOS. This program will close a real DOS session, so you might want to put it on your floppy for easy access. This program works in all DOS sessions, so if you need a way to close a DOS session from a batch file, `EXIT_VDM.COM` is the answer.

DOS Images: The Virtual Floppy

Once you have set up a DOS boot floppy for use under OS/2 that you want to use often, you can make an image of the diskette using the

VMDISK.EXE program. An image allows you to boot the DOS session without using the floppy itself. To create an image, insert the DOS boot diskette in Drive A:, open an OS/2 session, and type:

```
VMDISK A: C:\mydos.img
```

This will create the file, MYDOS.IMG in the C:\ directory. You no longer need the diskette. Open the settings for the DOS object you use to start the DOS session, and edit the DOS setting, "DOS_STARTUP_DRIVE." Change it from A: to C:\MYDOS.IMG and save the setting. Now when you open this object, DOS will start, and will use the image file as an A: drive. The image boots much faster than the floppy drive, and your A: drive is available for other sessions. When you type: DIR A: in the DOS session, you will not be accessing the floppy drive, you will access the image. If you need to access the actual A: floppy drive, the program FSACCESS.EXE in \OS2\MDOS can help. From the DOS session, type:

```
FSACCESS Z=A
```

This will tell OS/2 Warp to route any request in the DOS session for Z: to the physical A: drive. Once you type this command, try DIR Z: with a diskette in the A: drive. You don't have to use drive Z:, you can specifiy any unused drive letter when re-assigning drive A:.

The VMDISK program can be used to create images of any type of floppy. If you don't need much space on the boot image, create a 360K bootable floppy and make an image of that. Also, you can create an image from B:, so if you have a bootable 5.25" DOS floppy, and your A: drive is 3.5", you can modify the disk as previously described and create an image, without ever booting the actual diskette.

7
DOS and Windows Under OS/2 Warp

Windows Sessions

Configuring OS/2 Warp to run your Windows programs is a lot like setting up your DOS applications under OS/2. The WIN-OS/2 Full Screen object in the Command Prompts folder looks much like Windows under DOS. When you open the  WIN-OS/2 object, OS/2 Warp starts a DOS Full Screen session and runs either its internal version of Windows (WIN-OS/2), or the Windows system you installed separately (this is governed by the "flavor" of OS/2 Warp you installed). In either case, you'll see the Windows Program Manager. This allows you to run your Windows programs just like you would under DOS and Windows alone. In fact, WIN-OS/2 is so similar to Windows 3.1 that you might forget you're actually running OS/2. If you want to remember where you are (and get more use out of OS/2), you can launch the Windows WIN-OS/2 Window object.

When you launch *WIN-OS/2 Window*, the Windows Program Manager will start, but it will be on your OS/2 Warp desktop. Running Windows this way allows you to see OS/2 and Windows programs at the same time. This is known as "seamless" win-  dows support, because windows programs are running alongside OS/2 on the same screen. There's an easier way yet. Both of the previous examples start the Windows Program Manager, which allows you to start other Windows programs. Why not just start the Windows program itself from the OS/2 desktop? The "Add Programs" object will look for previously installed Windows software, and create OS/2 objects for them. You can also create your own "custom Windows" objects, using the same method you use to create a custom DOS object (described earlier in this chapter). Your custom Windows objects can be set to run in either *WIN-OS/2 full screen* or *WIN-OS/2 window* via the *Session* page in the settings notebook.

 Some video drivers may not support seamless Windows, making this technique unavailable. If your video driver does not allow this technique, contact your video adapter manufacturer to see if an upgrade exists for your video adapter.

Separate Sessions

Another option you can use is *Separate Session*. This instructs OS/2 Warp to open a different DOS VDM and run another copy of Windows for this program. Normally, if you already have a Windows program running, OS/2 will start subsequent Windows programs in the same session (just as in real Windows). By selecting Separate Session, you can actually run more than one copy of Windows at the same time. When you start a DOS object, a separate session is *always* created. For windows objects, a separate session is only created if you select "Separate Session." This also affects how the custom settings are used. If you tune the DOS settings in an object, they are used to start that session. However, the Windows session's environment is determined by the *first* Windows object that is started. If you want to customize your default Windows environment, you can modify the settings of the WIN-OS/2 Setup object in the System Setup folder.

Using separate sessions does consume quite a bit of extra resources, but if you have one Windows program that tends to crash often, you can run it in a separate session so it cannot corrupt your other windows programs. You may also need to use separate sessions to run two resource-hungry Windows programs at the same time. Windows is limited to providing only 64 KBytes of resources for *all* Windows programs. Often, two programs will compete for these resources and exhaust them. If you run them in separate sessions, they'll each receive 64 KBytes of resource memory, which will allow them both to run. This is definitely "a better Windows than Windows."

DOS and WIN-OS/2 Settings

Now that you know everything you need to create custom DOS and Windows objects, you'll want to understand what all the tuning parameters mean. This section explains the DOS and WIN-OS/2 settings you might consider modifying. Some of these options are only available

7

DOS and Windows Under OS/2 Warp

for Windows objects; others are only for DOS. If you load a virtual device driver, it might add options to this list.

AUDIO_ADAPTER_SHARING

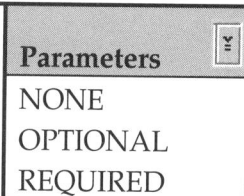

Parameters
NONE
OPTIONAL
REQUIRED

If you install Multimedia hardware, this setting controls access to your audio adapter in DOS sessions. Select NONE if the DOS session does not use the audio card. Select OPTIONAL if the DOS session can use the audio adapter, but exclusive access is not required. Select REQUIRED if the DOS session cannot run unless it has exclusive access to the audio card.

COM_DIRECT_ACCESS

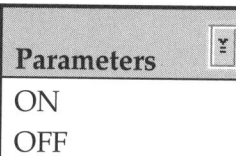

Parameters
ON
OFF

This setting allows the DOS session to access the communications hardware directly. This should only be used for timing-specific communications programs. Normally, this setting should be OFF, which allows OS/2 Warp to emulate communications hardware, and control access to it.

COM_HOLD

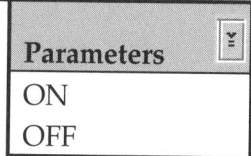

Parameters
ON
OFF

This setting is used to hold a communications port for the duration of a session. With this setting OFF, if a program in one session closes a comm port, another session can claim it. If you set this to ON, the first session to open a comm port will keep it, even if the program subsequently closes the port.

COM_RECEIVE_BUFFER_FLUSH

Parameters
ALL
RECEIVE DATA...
SWITCH TO...
NONE

This setting controls when the communication buffer is emptied. The default is NONE, which means the buffer will never be automatically emptied. You can select RECEIVE DATA INTERRUPT ENABLE to flush the buffer any time the DOS program activates the RECEIVE DATA INTERRUPT. You can select SWITCH TO FOREGROUND to flush the buffer any time you bring the DOS session into the foreground. You can select ALL to flush the buffer in both cases. Normally, flushing the communications buffer will result in communications errors, so leave this setting at NONE unless you really understand the communications software you are using.

COM_SELECT

Parameters
ALL
COM1
COM2
COM3
COM4
NONE

This setting allows you to "hide" communications ports from your DOS session. The default is ALL, which allows the DOS session to see all communications ports. If you have a DOS program that "touches" all ports, even though it never uses them, you can use this setting to hide all but a single port from the session. If the program in the session does not require access to communications ports, you can select NONE, which will prevent the session from touching any of the ports.

DOS_AUTOEXEC

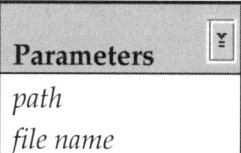

This setting specifies the `batch file` to be used when starting this DOS session. Normally, a DOS session will execute `\AUTOEXEC.BAT` when starting, but if you have commands that are only needed by a specific DOS application, you can create a separate `.BAT` file, and specify it in this setting.

 You can pass paramters to the `AUTOEXEC.BAT` file using this setting. The parameters can be used in the `AUTOEXEC.BAT` file the same way all batch files use parameters (%1, %2, etc). You can use this feature to create a single `AUTOEXEC.BAT` file that handles custom setups for more than one DOS object.

DOS_BACKGROUND_EXECUTION

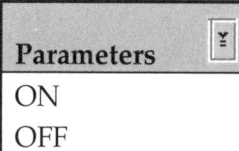

With this setting OFF, OS/2 Warp will suspend the operation of a DOS application when it's in the background. Word processors, games, and some other applications don't need processor time if they're not the active program. Setting this option to OFF for those DOS programs will give overall system performance a slight boost.

DOS_BREAK

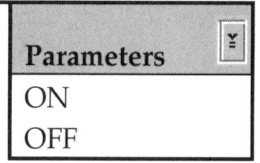

This setting activates break handling in the DOS session. The default is OFF. If you set `DOS_BREAK` to ON, the system will check for Ctrl-C and

Ctrl-Break in the DOS session more frequently. BREAK=ON|OFF in the CONFIG.SYS file will set the default for all DOS sessions.

DOS_DEVICE

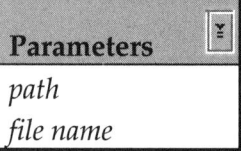

Parameters
path
file name

This setting allows you to load device drivers for a single DOS session. For example, if a DOS session needs ANSI terminal support, you can add: \OS2\MDOS\ANSI.SYS to the DOS_DEVICE setting. If every DOS session needs a certain DOS device driver, you should add it to your CONFIG.SYS with a DEVICE=\OS2\MDOS\ANSI.SYS statement.

 Loading Device Drivers into Upper Memory Blocks (UMBs): If you set DOS_UMB to ON, you may have enough space to load the device into UMBs. This is similar to the DEVICEHIGH= statement in CONFIG.SYS. To load a device driver into UMBs via the DOS_DEVICE setting, use the format: SIZE=xx *drivername* where *xx* is the number of bytes (in hexadecimal) of RAM in addition to the size of the driver itself that the driver needs to load. For example, SIZE=0 \OS2\MDOS\ANSI.SYS tells OS/2 to load ANSI.SYS into a UMB. The SIZE=parameter can be left at 0, but if a device driver needs more space at load time than the size of the file itself, specify the amount in the SIZE= paramter. Some device drivers need more memory to load than they do to run, so the SIZE= helps OS/2 find a UMB that is large enough. If an area of the required size cannot be found, OS/2 loads the device driver into low memory. You can use the MEM program to determine if a driver is loading high or low. Open a DOS command prompt without the driver, and type MEM. Record the "largest executable program size" value. Then add the DOS_DEVICE to the object, re-open it and type MEM. The "largest executable program size" value will be smaller; the difference is the size of the driver. Now add the SIZE=0 to the beginning of the DOS_DEVICE setting, save the change, and open the DOS setting again. When you type MEM, the "largest executable program size" should be as large (or nearly as large) as it was without the driver loaded at all. If not, there may not have been enough room for the driver, or you may need to specify a load size (consult the driver's documentation about its ability to load in UMBs).

DOS_FCBS

Parameters: 0 *to* 255

An FCB is a File Control Block, which is used in older DOS programs to control access to files. If more than the specified number of FCBs are requested by a DOS program, old ones are closed to make room for new ones. OS/2's DOS sessions do not need FCB's, as the OS/2 file system keeps track of open files. However, using this setting will create the appearance of FCB tables for DOS applications that look for them. The statement FCBS=x,y in `CONFIG.SYS` (where x is the number for DOS_FCBS and y is the number for DOS_FCBS_KEEP) sets the default setting for all DOS sessions.

DOS_FCBS_KEEP

Parameters: 0 *to* 255

This setting specifies how many of the FCBs should not be re-used to make room for new FCB requests. When a DOS session runs out of FCBs, it will "recycle" them. This setting allows you to "protect" the first few FCBs from recycling. This number should not be greater than the `DOS_FCBS` setting.

DOS_FILES

Parameters: 20 *to* 255

This setting allocates a file handle table for the DOS session. The File handle method has replaced the FCB method for opening files, and most newer programs will use file handles instead of FCBs. If you do not allocate enough handles in a session, a DOS program that accesses many files at once may fail. Often, DOS programs will specify how many handles they require in their installation instructions. The statement FILES=x in CONFIG.SYS will specify the default number of files to allocate for each DOS session.

DOS_HIGH

Parameters
ON
OFF

This setting allows you to load portions of the DOS operating system above the normal 1MB memory area. Doing so will free up more of RAM for the DOS program. This is usually not required, but some large DOS applications may benefit from the extra RAM provided by this setting. Rather than using the CONFIG.SYS DOS=HIGH statement, you can turn DOS_HIGH on in just those DOS sessions that require it. If you have disabled XMS memory in a session, DOS_HIGH will not work.

DOS_LASTDRIVE

Parameters
A *to* Z

This setting specifies what "logical" drive letters are available to the DOS session. Certain DOS programs (SUBST, for example) can create a logical drive. This setting sets the last drive letter available for such programs. If set to Z, any logical drive letter can be used. Under "real" DOS, more memory is required to allocate space for these drive letters (even if you don't use them), but not under Warp.

DOS_RMSIZE

Parameters
128 *to* 640

This setting defines the memory size for the DOS session. If you are defining a DOS session for a program that does not require much memory,

DOS and Windows Under OS/2 Warp

you can reduce this setting to save RAM. Since OS/2 consumes less space in DOS sessions than real DOS, you can often run DOS programs in less than the maximum 640K. If you reduce this setting too much, you may see the error "program too big to fit in memory."

DOS_SHELL

Parameters
path
file name

This setting defines which command processor file will be used for the DOS session. The normal command processor file is \OS2\MDOS\COMMAND.COM, but if you have an alternate command processor (such as 4DOS), you can specify it here. The syntax of this command is the same as the SHELL= command used in a DOS CONFIG.SYS, except the /P parameter should not be used here.

DOS_STARTUP_DRIVE

Parameters
drive,
path, and
file name

This setting is used to start a specific DOS session from another drive, or from a disk image. If you specify a drive, OS/2 will expect to find a bootable DOS system on that drive. If you boot OS/2 from D:, and you have DOS loaded on C:, you can specify C: to boot real DOS while still inside OS/2. If you have a bootable DOS floppy, you can use the VMDISK utility to create a DOS image, and then specify the path and name of that image (for example, C:\IMAGES\DOS5.IMG) in this setting to run the image.

The OS/2 Warp Survival Guide

DOS_UMB

This setting controls access to UMBs (Upper Memory Blocks). UMBs are in the area of memory between 640K and 1MB in the DOS session. When set to ON, DOS controls the UMBs, and can use them for LOADHIGH and DEVICEHIGH statements. When set to OFF, DOS will not control the UMBs, but if your DOS program can access UMBs directly, it can place data in these areas. This setting should be left ON unless you know a specific program makes use of UMBs.

DOS_VERSION

This setting allows you to "lie" to DOS programs when they inquire about the version of DOS that is running. OS/2 will normally tell a program that it is running under DOS version 20.30. Some programs will refuse to run if they don't recognize the DOS version. For example, if your program, SAMPLE.EXE, reports "incorrect DOS version," but it will run under DOS 6.30, you can add the line: SAMPLE.EXE,6,30,255 to the DOS_VERSION setting. The first item on the line is the program that does the version inquiry. The second item is the Major DOS version. The third item is the Minor DOS version, and the last item is the number of times OS/2 should "lie." Setting the last item to 255 will make OS/2 lie every time.

7

DOS and Windows Under OS/2 Warp

DPMI_DOS_API

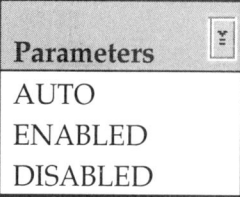

Parameters
AUTO
ENABLED
DISABLED

This setting controls DPMI (DOS Protected Mode Interface) translation. This is only used if your DOS program can use DPMI to access memory above 1MB. If set to DISABLED, the program will not be able to use DPMI memory. If set to ENABLED, OS/2 will always translate DPMI addresses. If set to AUTO, DPMI is available, and OS/2 will determine if address translation is required. Leaving this set to AUTO uses less memory than ENABLED. Most DPMI programs can work with AUTO, but if they do not, select ENABLED.

DPMI_MEMORY_LIMIT

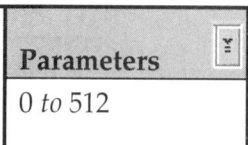

Parameters
0 *to* 512

This setting selects the amount of DPMI memory (in megabytes) available to the DOS session. If the DOS program attempts to use more DPMI memory than is physically available on your computer, OS/2 will create "virtual" memory using free hard disk space.

DPMI_NETWORK_BUFF_SIZE

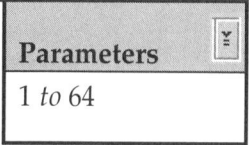

Parameters
1 *to* 64

This setting allocates memory (in kilobytes) for a DPMI network buffer. If your DPMI DOS program uses a network to communicate with other programs, increasing this buffer may improve performance.

EMS_FRAME_LOCATION

Parameters
NONE
AUTO
(address)

This setting controls the location of the four 16KB EMS Page frames (64KB total). EMS is the "Lotus, Intel, Microsoft Expanded Memory Specification." This specification allows DOS programs to access memory outside the normal 1MB address range. Programs that use EMS require page frames somewhere in the 1MB range so they can "see" the EMS memory. If you set this to NONE, EMS will be disabled. Set it to AUTO, and OS/2 will find a 64K area for the page frames. If your program requires the page frames to be at a specific location, you can specify the starting address here.

EMS_HIGH_OS_MAP_REGION

Parameters
0 *to* 96

This option sets the amount of additional EMS page-frame memory that the program can create. Normally, EMS programs only use four 16K page frames, but if an application can allocate and use a larger frame, this settings allows it.

EMS_LOW_OS_MAP_REGION

Parameters
0 *to* 576

This option controls the remapping of conventional RAM. If your EMS program can remap conventional memory (as additional pages for EMS access), this setting controls how much memory (in KBytes) it can use. Only Windows 2.x applications use this when there is no UMB space available.

EMS_MEMORY_LIMIT

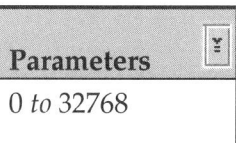

Parameters
0 *to* 32768

This setting defines the maximum amount of EMS memory (in KBytes) that the DOS session can allocate. Most programs that use EMS will only access the EMS memory they need, so you can set this setting generously. However, some programs may "test" all EMS memory, which means OS/2 will have to allocate it just so the application can test it. In this case, allocating too much EMS memory will hurt performance.

HW_NOSOUND

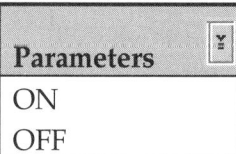

Parameters
ON
OFF

This setting controls access to the system speaker. If you set this to ON, certain DOS programs will not be able to use the system speaker to make sounds.

HW_ROM_TO_RAM

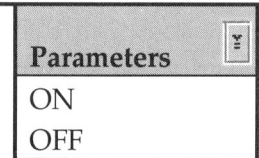

Parameters
ON
OFF

This setting allows the computer's system ROM to be copied to RAM. The system ROM is where the BIOS program resides, and many DOS programs make frequent use of BIOS calls. By copying the ROM to RAM, the DOS session can access the BIOS program quicker, which will improve performance.

HW_TIMER

Parameters
ON
OFF

This setting controls access to the hardware timer. Some programs (usually games) require access to the system timer to operate. If a timing-sensitive program does not seem to operate correctly in a DOS session, try turning this setting ON. The default is OFF, which should be sufficient for most DOS programs.

IDLE_SECONDS

Parameters
0 *to* 60

This setting defines how long a program must be in an "idle" state before OS/2 reduces its priority. OS/2 constantly monitors DOS sessions to determine if they are just wasting time (waiting for a keystroke, for example). Once this determination is made, OS/2 can reduce the priority of the DOS session, which allows more processor time to be given to "active" programs. This setting should be left at 0 unless a specific program should not be lowered as soon as it appears idle.

IDLE_SENSITIVITY

Parameters
1 *to* 100

This setting controls how OS/2 determines a DOS session is "idle." OS/2 monitors the DOS session's "polling" activity (how often the DOS session checks for input from various devices). If the DOS session polls often, OS/2 will consider the session "idle" and will lower the session's priority. The IDLE_SENSITIVITY sets the percentage of polling for the idle determination. Setting this value to a low number means the program would be considered idle even if it did not poll often. If you set this number high, the program would have to poll almost constantly before it were considered idle. Set this number to 100, and the program will never be considered idle. Experimentation with this setting (and using the Pulse applet) is the only way to determine a DOS program's idle setting. By tuning a DOS program for proper idle sensitivity, you can increase overall performance dramatically.

INT_DURING_IO

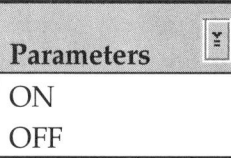

Parameters
ON
OFF

This setting allows the DOS session to process interrupts during an I/O operation. Normally, DOS programs are "single-threaded," and can only do one thing at a time. By setting INT_DURING_IO, you can actually gain some of the benefits of "multithreading" in a DOS program. Multimedia and communications programs can benefit from this setting, as they often need to process interrupts while they are doing disk I/O. Most other programs will not benefit from this setting.

KBD_ALTHOME_BYPASS

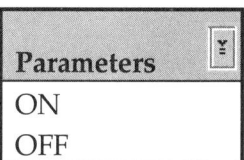

Parameters
ON
OFF

This setting controls the **Alt+Home** key sequence. If this setting is OFF, **Alt+Home** will cause the session to switch from Windowed to Full-Screen and back. If this setting is ON, the keystroke will be passed to the DOS session with no special handling by OS/2. You can set this to ON for programs that do not run in a window, or programs where **Alt+Home** is a valid keystroke.

The OS/2 Warp Survival Guide

KBD_BUFFER_EXTEND

Parameters
ON
OFF

This setting allows the DOS session to benefit from OS/2's enhanced keyboard buffer. If set to OFF, the DOS session will only use the standard DOS 16-character keyboard buffer. When set to ON, the DOS session will be able to buffer up to 128 keystrokes.

KBD_CTRL_BYPASS

Parameters
NONE
Alt+Esc
Ctrl+Esc

This session prevents OS/2 from handling either the **Alt+Esc** or **Ctrl+Esc** keystrokes. The default setting, NONE, allows OS/2 to use both keystrokes. If your DOS program uses either of these keystrokes, you can restrict OS/2's use of one of them, in which case the keystroke will be given to the DOS program to handle. You cannot disable both keystrokes, as you will need one of them to switch between a full-screen DOS program and other OS/2 tasks.

KBD_RATE_LOCK

Parameters
ON
OFF

This setting will prevent the DOS session from changing the key-repeat rate. If set to ON, no changes are allowed. When set to OFF, the DOS session is free to change the key-repeat rate.

MEM_EXCLUDE_REGIONS

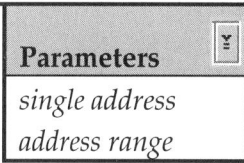

Parameters
single address
address range

This setting allows you to exclude regions in the 640K–1MB range from being filled with UMBs or EMS page-frames. You can specify a single address to exclude a 4K area, or you can specify the beginning and ending addresses (e.g., C0000–C8000). This setting is not normally required. OS/2 will not fill areas that are needed for adapter ROMs, but if you believe there is a conflict, you can explicitly exclude addresses.

MEM_INCLUDE_REGIONS

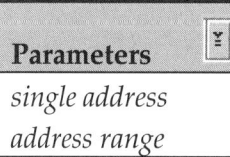

Parameters
single address
address range

This setting allows you to explicitly include regions for use by EMS/XMS. If OS/2 automatically excludes a region, but you would like to use it for EMS (for example, an area used by adapter ROM, but the adapter is not used in this session), enter the addresses in this setting. Enter the starting address only to include a 4K area, or specify the starting and ending addresses.

MOUSE_EXCLUSIVE_ACCESS

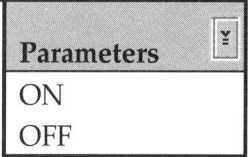

Parameters
ON
OFF

This setting controls mouse access when this session is in a window. If the DOS program uses standard mouse commands, this setting can be left OFF, and the OS/2 mouse cursor can be used for mouse commands in the window. Some programs use non-standard mouse controls, and require exclusive use of the mouse. In this case, you will usually notice a second mouse cursor when using this program in a window. Set MOUSE_EXCLUSIVE_ACCESS to ON, and when you click the mouse in this program, the OS/2 mouse disappears. The DOS program has exclusive use of the mouse until you press **Ctrl+Esc** or **Alt+Esc** to switch away from the DOS program.

PRINT_SEPARATE_OUTPUT

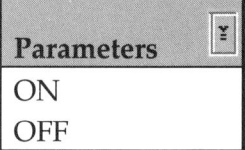

If two programs in the same DOS session print to the same printer port, this setting can be used to separate the output into different print jobs.

PRINT_TIMEOUT

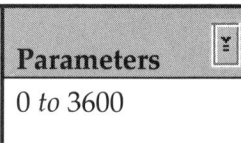

This setting specifies the time (in seconds) of idle time that must elapse before OS/2 forces a print job to finish. Many DOS programs don't close a printer port when the print job is complete. Since OS/2 will not print a job until it is complete, this time-out will force the job onto the printer. If you set this value too low, your print job may be broken into pieces. If you set it too high, you will have to wait for your print job to show up on the printer.

SESSION_PRIORITY

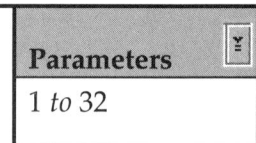

This setting specifies the relative priority of a DOS session. The higher the priority, the better the chance that the DOS session will get access to the CPU. If you increase this session, you may cause other DOS sessions to be "starved" because the high-priority session consumes all available CPU time.

VIDEO_8514A_XGA_IOTRAP

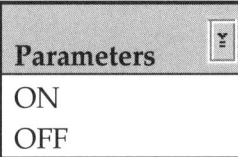

Parameters
ON
OFF

This setting allows programs to access video hardware directly on 8514A and XGA systems. When set to ON, OS/2 controls access to the video hardware. If you set this to OFF, the DOS session can bypass OS/2, and write directly to the hardware. OS/2 will release the 1MB video RAM buffer when this setting is OFF, but if you switch away from the DOS session, the video image may be distorted when you switch back (you can use `VIDEO_SWITCH_NOTIFICATION` to correct this). Also, you won't be able to copy data to the clipboard when this setting is OFF.

VIDEO_FASTPASTE

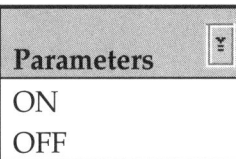

Parameters
ON
OFF

This setting selects the speed of text transfers from the clipboard. If you use the clipboard to cut text, and then use PASTE to "type" it into a DOS program, setting `VIDEO_FASTPASTE` to ON will increase this operation. However, some programs may not be able to keep up with the fast speed, and characters will be lost.

VIDEO_MODE_RESTRICTION

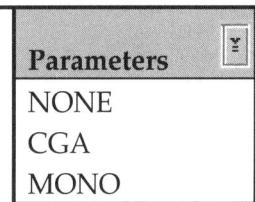

Parameters
NONE
CGA
MONO

This setting restricts the DOS session to using only specific video graphic modes. The default is NONE, which allows the DOS session to use any mode supported by your video hardware. If you set this to CGA, the DOS session can only use CGA graphic modes. If you set this to MONO, the DOS session can only use the text modes of a monochrome video adapter. This setting can be used to increase DOS memory size. If you restrict the video mode to CGA, allocate XMS memory, and allow DOS to control UMBs, OS/2 will extend the DOS memory area from 640K to 735K. Using MONO can increase the DOS memory area to 703K.

VIDEO_ONDEMAND_MEMORY

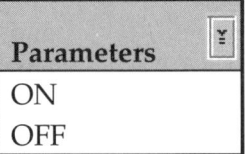

Parameters
ON
OFF

This setting controls when OS/2 allocates memory for a video buffer. A video buffer is needed to save a full-screen DOS graphic screen if you switch away from the full-screen DOS session. When this setting is ON, OS/2 will not pre-allocate the video buffer memory. If you set this to OFF, OS/2 will allocate this memory as soon as you start the DOS session. Pre-allocating the memory makes the DOS session take longer to start, and consumes memory that may never be needed, but it ensures that there is enough space for the buffer when it is needed. This setting should usually be left ON.

VIDEO_RETRACE_EMULATION

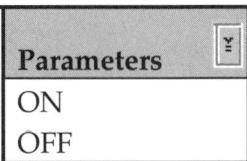

Parameters
ON
OFF

This setting controls the video retrace. When set to ON, OS/2 controls the re-drawing of the video screen. Some graphics programs may run faster if video retrace emulation is disabled, but doing so may cause video corruption when switching away from the DOS session. Most DOS sessions should use the default, ON.

VIDEO_ROM_EMULATION

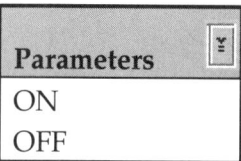

This setting allows OS/2 to emulate certain text-mode video functions. The OS/2 emulation is usually faster than the functions provided on the video ROM. However, if your video card provides enhanced text-mode functions, you may have to turn VIDEO_ROM_EMULATION off.

VIDEO_SWITCH_NOTIFICATION

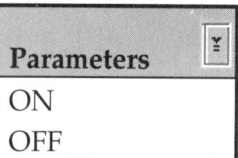

Some video modes can automatically redraw an image when switching from another session (Windows programs use this feature). If this session is not able to automatically redraw the screen after a session switch, leave this setting at the default, OFF.

VIDEO_WINDOW_REFRESH

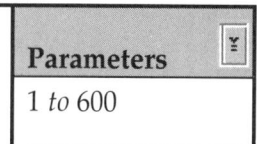

This setting controls how often (in tenths of seconds) the DOS session's screen is redrawn. Setting this to a higher value will increase overall performance (less-frequent refreshes means OS/2 can spend more time on other tasks), but it may make the screen hard to read. Experimenting with this setting may boost performance, if you can tolerate less-frequent updates.

WIN_ATM

This setting allows Windows programs to use Adobe Type Manager support. If this setting is OFF, OS/2 will disable the built-in ATM support. This can save memory and increase performance in Windows programs that don't use ATM fonts.

WIN_CLIPBOARD

This setting allows Windows programs to share clipboard data with OS/2 programs and other Windows sessions. If this setting is OFF, the Clipboard is private, and can only be shared between Windows programs in the same session.

WIN_DDE

This setting allows Windows programs to share DDE (Dynamic Data Exchange) information with OS/2 programs and other Windows sessions. If this setting is OFF, DDE information can only be shared between Windows programs in the same session.

WIN_RUN_MODE

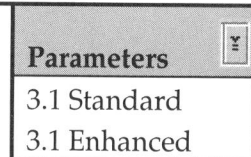

Parameters
3.1 Standard
3.1 Enhanced

This setting is only available to Windows programs. It defines the mode to be used by the Windows program. Normally, Standard mode is sufficient, and will provide the best performance. If you use a Windows program that requires "enhanced" or "386" mode, you should select "3.1 Enhanced Compatibility."

XMS_HANDLES

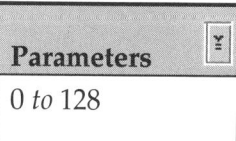

Parameters
0 *to* 128

This setting allocates handles for XMS memory use. Each separate allocation of XMS memory requires a handle. Reducing this number will free more memory and increase performance, but if a program in the DOS session allocates many separate XMS regions, you may need to increase the number of handles.

XMS_MEMORY_LIMIT

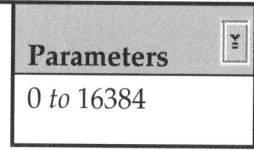

Parameters
0 *to* 16384

This setting determines the maximum amount of XMS memory (in KBytes) available in the DOS session. XMS (eXtended Memory Specification) is a method by which DOS programs can access memory above 1MB. If the DOS program attempts to use more XMS memory than is available in your system, OS/2 will allocate "virtual" memory using free hard disk space.

XMS_MINIMUM_HMA

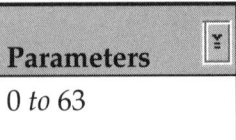

Parameters
0 *to* 63

This setting sets the minimum request size (in KBytes) for access to the HMA (High Memory Area). The HMA is the first 64K of XMS memory, and can be used by only one program in the DOS session. By setting this number to a high value, you are ensuring that a program will not request the HMA, but then only use a small piece of it. Often, DOS uses the HMA (if `DOS_HIGH=ON`, DOS will use the HMA), so this setting is not applicable. However, if you do not load DOS into the HMA, this setting can control what other program receives HMA access.

Chapter

8

OS/2 Warp Multimedia

With the release of OS/2 Warp, the Multimedia Presentation Manager/2 (MMPM/2) is installed as part of the main OS/2 Warp installation. Previously sold as a separate product, MMPM/2 allows you to play digital music, sound effects, and even watch full-motion video on your desktop. The power of a multimedia desktop must be seen and heard, so if you haven't explored multimedia, you owe it to yourself to give it a try.

MMPM/2 now supports the MPEG, .FLC, and .FLI digital video file formats in addition to .AVI files. And its performance over the OS/2 2.1 iteration is noticeable.

Installing Multimedia Support

Installation of multimedia support is an option during the OS/2 Warp installtion process, or you can install it at a later time. On the *System Configuration* screen (the first screen you see when you run "Selective Install"), you can choose and configure your multimedia hardware devices. This includes sound cards, video capture and playback adapters, and laser-disc controllers.

You can install support for one or more audio adapter. However, installing support for an audio adapter that you don't have physically installed in your computer can cause problems when working with audio files and can cause error messages when booting OS/2 Warp. If you are planning to install an adapter that is on the list, wait until the adapter is actually in your computer before you install the support for it.

On the "OS/2 Setup and Installation" screen, you can choose the software options for multimedia support. If you install a multimedia adapter, the software support is automatically installed. You can, however, choose to install just the base multimedia support, or add support for software motion video.

Sample Digital Audio and Video Files

You'll find a bonus in the number of sample digital audio and video files included on the CD for use with the multimedia features. These files are *not* automatically copied to your hard disk during installation (they take up considerable disk space). Before you copy all these samples to your hard disk, finish reading this section.

You can find additional sound (digital audio) files on the CD in the \MMPM2\SOUNDS subdirectory. You can find additional "movie clip" (digital video) files on the CD in the following subdirectories:

- \MMPM2\MOVIES\ULTIMOTN\8BITAUD\STANDARD\320X240
- \MMPM2\MOVIES\ULTIMOTN\8BITAUD\STANDARD\160X120
- \MMPM2\MOVIES\ULTIMOTN\8BITAUD\HIGHPERF\320X240
- \MMPM2\MOVIES\ULTIMOTN\16BITAUD\STANDARD\320X240
- \MMPM2\MOVIES\ULTIMOTN\16BITAUD\STANDARD\160X120
- \MMPM2\MOVIES\ULTIMOTN\16BITAUD\HIGHPERF\320X240
- \MMPM2\MOVIES\INDEO\320X240
- \MMPM2\MOVIES\INDEO\160X120

The video clips contained in the ULTIMOTN and INDEO subdirectories were processed using Ultimotion and Indeo compression technologies, respectively. Ultimotion video compression was developed by IBM, and Indeo compression was developed by Intel.

The sound files in the 8BITAUD and 16BITAUD subdirectory are for Ultimotion movie clips, and were recorded using either 8-bit or 16-bit PCM audio, respectively. The 16-bit PCM audio files generate a higher-quality sound, but really require a sound card capable of 16-bit audio playback. All video soundtracks were recorded using a 22 KHz sampling rate.

8 *OS/2 Warp Multimedia*

The movies in the STANDARD subdirectory were recorded at a data rate less than 150 KB per second. You can play these movies directly from a standard CD-ROM drive. The movies in the HIGHPERF subdirectory were recorded at higher data rates and must be played either on a double-speed (300 KB per second) CD-ROM drive, or from a hard disk.

Files contained in the 160X120 and 320X240 subdirectories were recorded using a 160-by-120 pixel window or a 320-by-240 pixel window, respectively.

Within these subdirectories, you can interpret the individual file names as follows:

- xxxxxx05.AVI — These movies play at 5 frames per second.
- xxxxxx15.AVI — These movies play at 15 frames per second.
- xxxxxx24.AVI — These movies play at 24 frames per second.

Obviously, the more frames per second a movie contains, the higher the quality of the video. But, the higher the quality of the video, the higher-performing computer you need to adequately play them.

Using the Multimedia Objects

After completing the multimedia installation, a new folder object (the Multimedia folder) will appear on your desktop. The Multimedia folder contains objects that allow you to use and control Multimedia Presentation Manager/2 (MMPM/2). When you open this object, a window similar to the following appears:

The OS/2 Warp Survival Guide

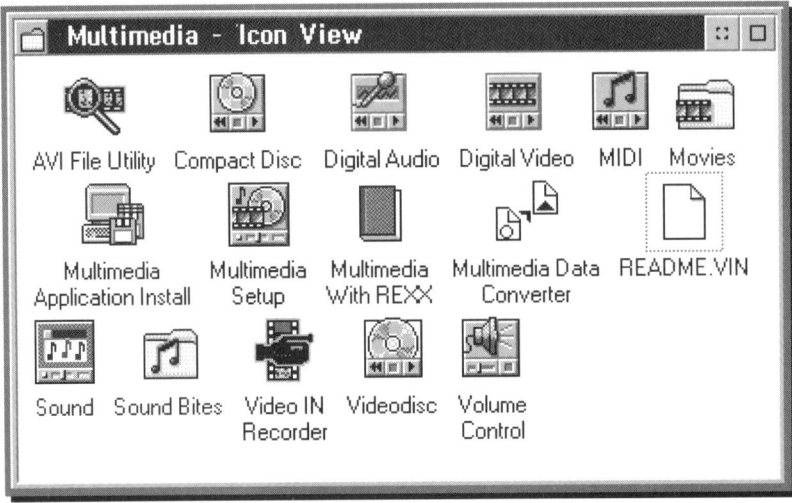

Figure 8.1.   *The Multimedia folder groups all the multimedia features.*

Each of the objects contained in the Multimedia folder are described below (with the exception of the README.VIN file, Movies folder, and Sound Bites folder).

Digital Video

This feature allows you to play "movies" on your computer screen. It is called *software motion video* because no special hardware is required to see the movies. If you have a supported sound adapter in your computer, you will also be able to hear the movies' soundtracks through your computer.

Software motion video is a major breakthrough in computer use, especially in the area of user training. Soon, you'll be able to buy a CD-ROM with full-motion videos, showing you everything from how to repair your car to what you'll see on your next vacation.

If you purchased OS/2 on CD, you'll find a good collection of videos on the CD (see "Sample Digital Audio and Video Files" earlier in this chapter for details). There are samples in both Ultimotion and Indeo format. If you purchased OS/2 on diskettes, you will only have a small video clip as a sample. When you open the Digital Video object, a window similar to the following appears:

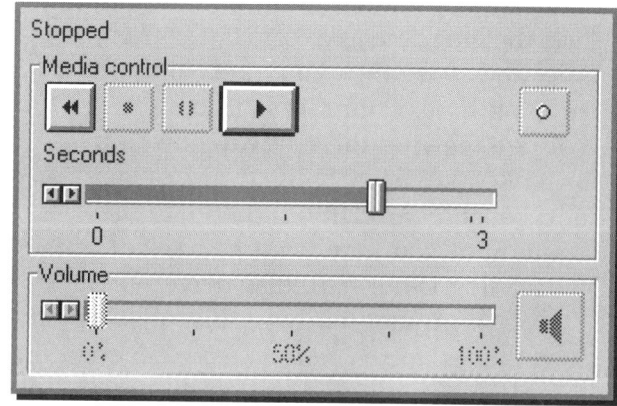

Figure 8.2. *The Digital Video player provides rewind, stop, pause, and play buttons to control playback of a digital video file.*

Like all OS/2 applications, the options on the menu bar let you open files and select options. You can also drag a digital video program object to this application, and drop it to load the video. In addition, this window contains push button controls similar to a video cassette recorder (VCR). There's also a volume control that lets you control the volume of the soundtrack associated with the video clip.

When you open a video (.AVI) file with the player, a video window appears. This window looks a lot like a television screen, and it's where the video clip will be displayed when you press the play button in the Digital Video player window. The video window displays the file format (either Intel Indeo or IBM Ultimotion) in the title bar.

When the video window is the active window, you can select from one of three sizes: Half-size (press shift-F1), Normal-size (press shift-F2), or Double-size (press shift-F3). You can also use the drag method to resize the window to any size. The quality of the video after you resize it may be degraded. That is because Warp is using software techniques to either add or remove pixels. The best quality and performance will always be the "normal size" display.

The quality of the video is based on the frame rate and the recorded frame size. Press shift-F4 to display image information for the video. This display lists the file name and format, the frame size and rate, the data rate, and the running time. Data rate is important if you are viewing the files directly from a CD-ROM. Some CD-ROM drives may not be able to deliver the data fast enough, so you may want to transfer a video clip to your hard disk drive.

Your computer hardware also plays a part in the quality of the video. If your desktop is not at least 256 colors, the display quality will be poor. If your system is not fast enough, MMPM/2 will not be able to process the video and display it completely. In this case, MMPM/2 drops frames from the video in order to maintain proper timing. Losing a frame every once in a while is usually not noticeable, and is much better than having the video stall or stop.

If the system is severely under-powered, the audio will stop completely. Running the videos at half-size will improve performance. The MMPM2\MOVIES folder on the OS/2 CD contains video clips of varying frame rates and frame sizes, so you can determine the limits of your own system.

If you spend some time experimenting with the Digital Video program, you may notice that it has "record" capabilities. If you have a video capture adapter, you can explore these capabilities.

Compact Disc

If your CD-ROM drive can play music CDs, this program will allow you to play a music CD and control it from your desktop. Insert a music CD and open the Compact Disc object. You'll see the Music CD player program. You can select a track, play, rewind, and even name your CD from this program. If you name a CD, the player will remember this name and display it if you insert this same CD later.

8

OS/2 Warp Multimedia

Digital Audio

If you installed support for an audio adapter, this object allows you to play, record, and edit sound-clip files. The program uses the .WAV file format, so if you have .WAV files from another program you can work them using this program.

You also can download .WAV file collections from many Bulletin Board Services (BBSs) and Internet sites. And there are several companies that market digital sound files in the .WAV format.

When you open the Digital Audio object, a window appears that is very similar to the Digital Video window. This is called the Player/Recorder view, which shows you controls similar to a standard tape recorder, including Play, rewind, fast-forward, record, pause, and stop. There is also a timer and a volume control.

If you select the View pull-down menu, you can change to the Editor View. When you load a .WAV file in the Editor View, you'll see a graphical representation of the sound. This makes it easier to select a portion of the sound to manipulate. You can cut pieces out of one sound and add them to another, add echo or reverb to pieces of a sound-clip, or change the volume of the clip. You can also record a new sound from a microphone, a line-input, or even from a music CD.

MIDI

This object lets you play Musical Instrument Digital Interface (MIDI) files. A MIDI file is different from Digital Audio. Digital Audio is just like a tape recorder. It records the sounds just as it hears them. MIDI doesn't record sound, it records the actions performed on a MIDI instrument. For example, on a MIDI keyboard, each key press and release is recorded.

When a MIDI file is played, these actions are combined with sound signatures from a musical instrument to create music. You could combine the key actions on a MIDI keyboard with the sound signature of a violin, a guitar, or any instrument. Several MIDI songs are provided for your listening pleasure.

When you open the MIDI object, a window similar to the Digital Video window appears. It contains the same type of controls, such as rewind, stop, and play. Use the File Open menu option to open a MIDI file so you can play it.

Multimedia Install

This object is used to install options for the multimedia support. If you installed the Multimedia viewer or Video In options in the Warp BonusPak, you have already used this program. Other multimedia options may be released by IBM or other companies, and can use this program to provide a standard installation interface.

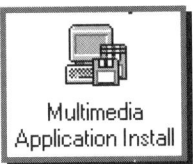

Multimedia Setup

This object sets certain parameters for MMPM/2. In it you will find settings pages for each MMPM/2 device, which allow you to set file associations and default devices. You can also turn on *Captioning*, which is used by certain Multimedia programs to provide visual text when any spoken words are played.

Multimedia with REXX

This help document explains how you can use Multimedia capabilities in your REXX programs. If you develop your own REXX programs, you might want to explore this document to see how you can add sound to your programs.

8

OS/2 Warp Multimedia

Multimedia Data Converter

This object lets you convert certain video and audio files to other formats. For example, if you have Sound Blaster .VOC files, you can convert them to .WAV files so they can be used as System Sounds clips. To convert a file, open the Data Converter, and click on the *Include* button. Select the format(s) you wish to convert from, and choose the *selected formats only* option. You can then find and select the files you want to convert. You can view selected graphic files using the *Preview* button. When you're ready to start the conversion process, click on the *Convert* button.

During the conversion process, you'll be able to select the target format for each video and/or audio file you selected. You can also select the target directory for the converted files. Once you have converted the files, you can use one of the MMPM/2 player programs to play the converted file.

Sound

This object is a *shadow* of the Sound object in your System Setup folder. Once you install MMPM/2, the Sound object changes significantly. The first page of the Sound settings controls the OS/2 System Sounds. MMPM/2 allows you to attach sound-clips to OS/2 events. For example, every time your system starts, it can play a specific sound effect (the default sound is a trumpet call). You will see a list of events, and another list of available sound-clips. You can add new sounds and even create your own if you have a supported audio adapter. If you decide you don't want your OS/2 system making noise, you can disable System Sounds as well through this object.

397

Volume Control

This object provides you with a master volume for all MMPM/2 sounds. Each MMPM/2 object has a separate volume control, so you can set any program to a comfortable level, but you may find a situation where you have sounds coming from several sources, and you have to stop them all at the same time (for an incoming phone call, perhaps).

When you open the Volume Control object, a window similar to the following appears:

Figure 8.3.   *The Volume Control object serves as a master volume.*

The volume control can mute all MMPM/2 sounds with one mouse-click (on the button with the picture of a speaker), or you can change the master volume with a twist of the volume knob. To turn the knob, drag the knob in the appropriate direction, or click on the plus and minus buttons to increase or decrease the volume.

Miscellaneous Folders

In addition to these objects, there are folders containing sample sounds and movies. Since all MMPM/2 objects have built-in associations, you can open these folders and select any sound or movie file, and the appropriate MMPM/2 program will start and load the selected file. Or, you can drag a sound or video clip to an open player program, and the player will load the sound clip for you.

Chapter

9

DOS and OS/2 Command Lines

The power of OS/2's Workplace Shell is impressive; but for computer users who have spent years learning their way around the DOS command prompt, OS/2 offers a variety of ways to get the "DOS look and feel." Inside the Command Prompts folder, you'll find five objects that give you access to the "old-fashioned" command prompt.

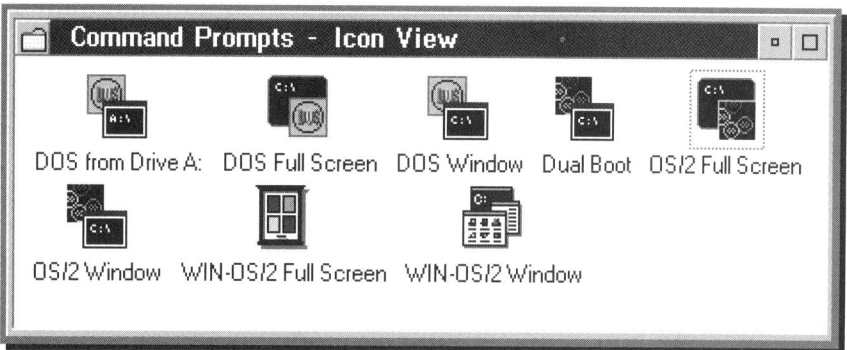

Figure 9.1.   *The Command Prompts folder gives you an assortment of OS/2, DOS, and Windows command prompt views.*

The *OS/2 Full Screen*, *OS/2 Window*, *DOS Full Screen*, *DOS Window*, and *DOS from Drive A:* objects give you the look and feel of DOS, but there is much more power under the covers. Each time you open one of these objects, you are opening a new command *session*. You can open several sessions at once, and start programs in each session. You can then switch from one session to another, keeping more than one program active at a time. You can even start other sessions from the sessions you have already started. It may take some time to get used to this power, but once you've used it, the single command session you had in DOS will never be good enough again.

You may wonder why there are so many different types of sessions. They are there for flexibility. You can decide how you want each program to look, and what type of session to run it in. For DOS programs, you'll select either DOS Window or DOS Full Screen (and, in fact, you can easily switch any DOS session from windowed to full screen with the **Alt+Home** key combination). Full Screen sessions look more like DOS, and usually offer better performance.

Windowed sessions allow you to see more than one program at a time, and allow you to change fonts and sizes easily. If you have OS/2 programs, you can use the OS/2 Window and OS/2 Full Screen sessions. A description of the session types follows.

DOS Full Screen

This object acts almost exactly like DOS 5.0. Open this object, and the screen changes to that familiar black background with nothing but the DOS prompt and a blinking cursor. DOS users shouldn't notice any difference between this session and true DOS. This object can be used when DOS compatibility is important. Even DOS graphics programs will run in this session. The difference between real DOS and a DOS session is that while you are using the DOS Full Screen object, any other programs you have running in other sessions can continue to run. You can switch away from the DOS Full Screen object by pressing **Ctrl+Esc** (which returns you to the desktop and brings up a Window List), or by pressing **Alt+Esc** (which switches to the next program in the Window List). When you switch away from the DOS Full Screen, any program running in that session can continue to run in the background. If you press **Alt+Home**, the session will change to a DOS Window object.

9   DOS and OS/2 Command Lines

DOS Window

This object is nearly identical to the DOS Full Screen object, except that by default, it opens in a window. The DOS display screen is "virtualized" by OS/2, which allows you to size the window to your liking. You can see the entire DOS screen, or just a part of it, by using the window Size and Scroll functions. Running DOS sessions in a window allows you to see more than one session at a time, and also allows you to cut-and-paste data from one session to another. The "virtualization" of the screen does incur a performance penalty, but you can use **Alt+Home** to switch the session to Full Screen at any time.

OS/2 Full Screen

This object may seem similar to the DOS Full Screen object, but there are significant differences. This object is not meant to be a DOS clone. The programs you run from this session are not DOS programs, but are protected-mode OS/2 programs. If you run a DOS program from an OS/2 session, OS/2 starts a separate DOS session for the DOS program. Since the OS/2 command prompt does not attempt to maintain DOS compatibility, the commands available can be greatly enhanced. The bulk of this chapter describes the differences between DOS commands and OS/2 commands.

OS/2 Window

This object is similar to the OS/2 Full Screen object, but it opens in a window on the desktop. OS/2 Window sessions cannot be switched to OS/2 Full Screen using **Alt+Home**, as DOS sessions can. The underlying functions are different between full-screen and windowed sessions. Some OS/2 programs are written only for full-screen sessions; if you run them

401

The OS/2 Warp Survival Guide

in an OS/2 Window, OS/2 opens a full-screen session for that program, and returns you to the windowed session when the program completes.

Dual Boot

This object is used to switch between OS/2 Warp and native DOS. It is only available if you installed OS/2 Warp on Drive C:, when Drive C: is formatted as a FAT drive. If DOS was installed on Drive C: before you installed Warp, the Dual Boot function is set up automatically. If DOS was not installed, launching the Dual Boot object will allow you to install DOS. Launching this object is the same as typing BOOT /DOS from either a DOS or OS/2 command session.

Command Line Differences

Normally, standard DOS commands work in DOS and OS/2, in both windowed and full-screen sessions. Rather than document every command and all their options (switches) we will only discuss commands that are significant due to their little-known or undocumented switches, or their differences from the DOS counterparts. If you need the full description of a command, use the electronic (on-line) Command Reference manual found in the Information Folder.

For each command, we tell you if it's *Internal* or *External*, and whether it works in DOS, OS/2, or both. Internal commands are part of the operating system, and are always loaded and available to run. External commands are disk files that the operating system must be able to find either in the current drive and directory, or through the *path*.

To save space when showing syntax examples, we have used the term *filespec* to mean the drive letter, path, and file name of a file. This is also known as a *fully qualified* file name. We have used *d:* to represent drive letters.

9

DOS and OS/2 Command Lines

ANSI

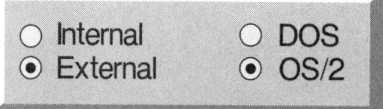

```
ANSI [ON|OFF]
```

In an OS/2 session, type `ANSI ON` to activate ANSI screen and keyboard functions. `ANSI OFF` disables this support, and `ANSI` with no options reports the current status of ANSI support.

ARCRECOV

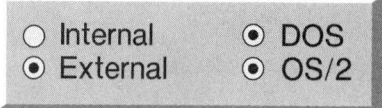

```
ARCRECOV 1 | 2 | 3 | X
```

Restores a Desktop archive. This is the function provided in the "Recovery Choices" screen. The parameter specifies the archive number (X is the initial install archive). This command restores the desktop and system files from the archive, and places the current desktop and system files in \OS2\ARCHIVES\CURRENT.

ASSIGN

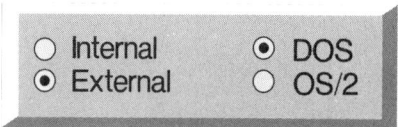

```
ASSIGN [d:=d:|/S]
```

You can use `ASSIGN` with the `/S` switch to display the current assignment status. This switch is not documented for OS/2, but works as it does in DOS 5.0.

BACKUP

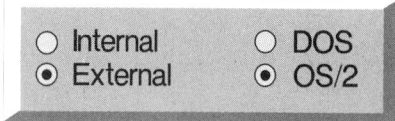

BACKUP *d:\path\file d:*

Similar to the DOS BACKUP, but supports EAs and long file names. It is only available in OS/2 Window and OS/2 Full Screen sessions.

BOOT

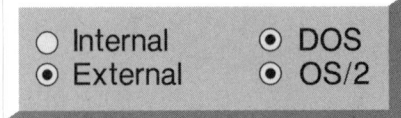

```
BOOT /DOS|OS2 [/N]
BOOT /Q
```

Activates the Dual Boot feature. If you installed OS/2 on the C: drive, formatted as FAT, Dual Boot is available. `BOOT /DOS` prepares Drive C: to boot DOS and restarts your computer. `BOOT /OS2` prepares Drive C: to boot OS/2 and restarts your computer.

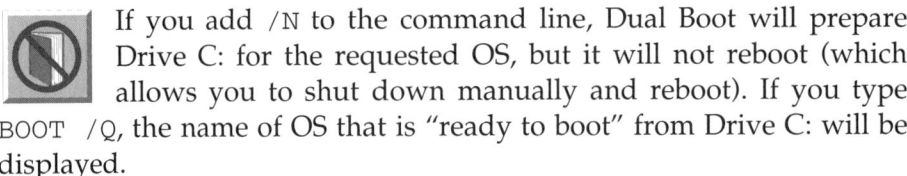

If you add `/N` to the command line, Dual Boot will prepare Drive C: for the requested OS, but it will not reboot (which allows you to shut down manually and reboot). If you type `BOOT /Q`, the name of OS that is "ready to boot" from Drive C: will be displayed.

If you type `BOOT /DOS` on a system that does not have DOS installed, you will be asked if you want to install it. To install DOS, continue with Dual Boot, and shut down OS/2. Insert a DOS boot floppy and reboot. Install DOS according to the DOS instructions. When DOS is properly installed, make the following changes:

- Add a line to the DOS CONFIG.SYS file that reads:

    `SHELL=C:\DOS\COMMAND.COM C:\DOS /P`

- Move the COMMAND.COM file from the root directory to the C:\DOS directory.

  To return to OS/2, type: `C:\OS2\BOOT /OS2`.

CACHE

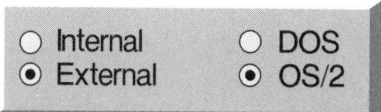

CACHE [/*switches*]

Sets parameters for HPFS cache memory. This command is only available if you installed an HPFS file system. If you type CACHE without any switches, the current cache settings are displayed. Valid switches include:

- /LAZY:ON|OFF turns on/off lazy-write. Lazy-write allows disk writes to be held in the cache instead of being immediately written to disk. This increases performance, but a power loss without a proper shutdown may cause data loss.

   LAZY cannot be used with other switches. CACHE does not return to the command prompt if you specify /LAZY:ON (until lazy-write is subsequently turned off). To turn on LAZY, type: DETACH CACHE /LAZY:ON

- /MAXAGE:*time(ms)* Any cached write that is older than this age is immediately scheduled for write to disk. Default is 5000 (5 sec).

- /DISKIDLE:*time(ms)* specifies the amount of time in which an inactive disk should be considered "idle." The default value is 1000 (1 second).

- /BUFFERIDLE:*time* specifies the age (in milliseconds) of buffers that will be written to disk when the disk is considered idle. When the disk becomes idle, buffers that are this age or older are written to disk. Default is 500 (1/2 second).

- /WRITECACHE:*size(bytes)* specifies the maximum size of writes to be cached. If a write request is larger than this size, it isn't cached; the write is immediate. Default is 65536 bytes (64K); maximum is 65536.

- /DIRTYMAX:*buffers* specifies how many unwritten buffers can be held before writes MUST occur. The default is 65535 (64K -1) and the maximum is also 65535.

CALL

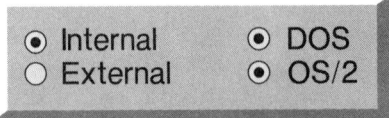

CALL [/Q] *filespec*

Functions as in DOS, except for the undocumented /Q switch. As used in OS/2 .CMD files (CALL /Q does not work in DOS), CALL /Q calls the specified program without letting it write messages to the screen. For example:

ONE.CMD:
```
@ECHO OFF
ECHO Watch This!
CALL /Q TWO.CMD
ECHO Did you see that?
```

TWO.CMD:
```
ECHO You can't see this!
```

If you run ONE.CMD, you will see:
```
Watch This!
Did you see that?
```

CHDIR, CD

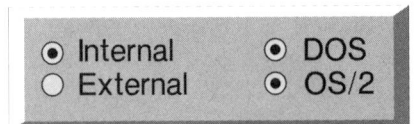

CD [..] [\]*directory name*

In OS/2 sessions, the specified directory can be enclosed in quotes. You must use quotation marks around HPFS directory names that contain spaces. For example: "My Project Files".

9

DOS and OS/2 Command Lines

CHKDSK

CHKDSK [*d*: /*switches*]

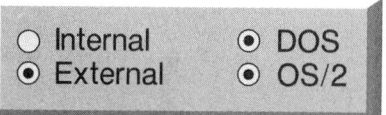

Only OS/2 sessions can perform a CHKDSK for an HPFS partition. The new switches for HPFS are:

- /C repair only if HPFS was not shut down properly.
- /F:*x* specifies the level of repair, where *x* can be:
  - /F:0 = no repair (same as leaving off /F)
  - /F:1 = only repair file system structures
  - /F:2 = scan for space in use but not claimed (same as CHKDSK /F)
  - /F:3 = scan unused space for lost file system structures

Lost data on HPFS partitions is put in a subdirectory named FOUND.*nnn*. Recovered file data is put in files named FILE*nnnn*.CHK and lost directories are named DIR*nnnn*.CHK where *nnnn* is a serialized number in the format 0001, 0002, and so forth. The syntax: CHKDSK [*path*\ ]*filename* is only available on FAT partitions.

CMD

CMD [*d*:*path* /*switches*]

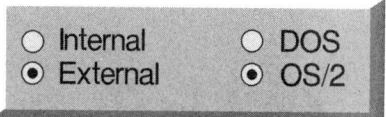

Starts an OS/2 command processor, much like the COMMAND function does in DOS.

- /Q suppresses echo to the command line.

- /S turns off the **Ctrl+C** signal handler.

- /C "*string*" starts a new OS/2 command process, passes *string* to the new process, and returns to the calling OS/2 command process upon completion.

The OS/2 Warp Survival Guide

- /K *"string"* starts a new OS/2 command process, passes *string* to the new process, and remains in the new command process upon completion.

COMMAND

COMMAND [*drive:path*]

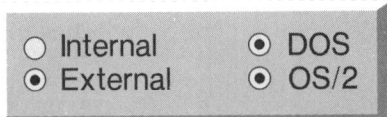

From within a DOS session, this command works as it does in DOS 5.0. From within an OS/2 session, COMMAND will start a DOS session. The DOS 5.0 /MSG switch is not needed, nor is it supported under OS/2.

COMP

COMP *filespec_a filespec_b*

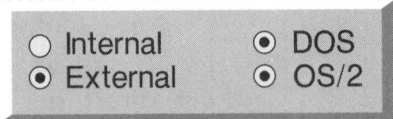

 DOS 5.0 switches /D, /A, /L, and /C are not supported. The /N switch is not supported, but COMP will ask if it should continue when the files are different sizes.

COPY

COPY *filespec_a filespec_b*

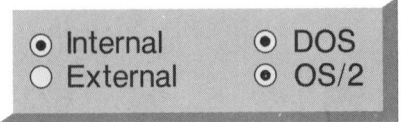

Same as DOS 5.0 with one additional switch. The /F switch causes the copy to fail if the file being copied contains extended attributes, and the destination drive does not support extended attributes. Without the /F switch, the file will be copied without its extended attributes.

DATE

DATE *mm-dd-yy*

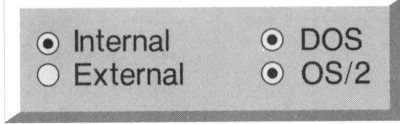

9 DOS and OS/2 Command Lines

Same as DOS 5.0, with one additional undocumented switch.

 `DATE /N` displays the current system date without prompting you to enter a new date.

DEL, ERASE

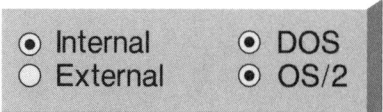

`DEL` *filespec* [*switches*]

Deletes (erases) files meeting your filespec. Some examples of the more interesting switches are:

- `DEL * /N` — Deletes all files, with *no* prompt, even if you delete all files in a subdirectory.

 `DEL * /F` — Deletes all files, and does *not* save the files in the UNDELETE subdirectory (folder).

DETACH

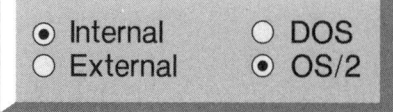

`DETACH` [*program* | *command*]

Executes programs without keyboard or screen access. If a program does not need any interaction, it can be started with the DETACH function (which will use less resources than a separate screen session). Redirection can be used to provide basic input/output to detached programs, for example:

`DETACH DIR C: > DIR.TXT`

DIR

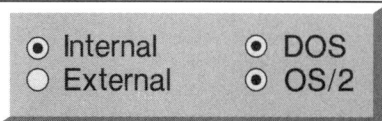

`DIR` [*filespec* /*switches*]

409

Displays a listing of files matching the filespec you specify. If you type DIR without a *filespec* or any *switches*, all files in the current directory are displayed.

 Since few people know all the switches for DIR, we'll explain them all—not just the ones that are new in this release of OS/2.

- /F displays "fully qualified" file names (filespec). Only the drive and path information is displayed for each file. The standard headings, file sizes, dates, and times are not included. This switch is great for passing file information to a batch file for processing. This switch is not available in DOS 5.0.

- /B displays files without headers and statistics. This switch is like /F without the drive and path information.

- /W displays file names in the "wide" format. Displays file names only, in five columns (invalid when combined with /F or /B).

- /N displays files in "new" style.style. File names are on the right hand side, and the extended attribute size is displayed. This is the default for HPFS drives in OS/2 sessions. This switch is not available in DOS 5.0.

- /R includes the *long name* for each file. The long name is the Title of the file, as set on the General page of the object's settings. This switch is not available in DOS 5.0, and can only be used in OS/2's DOS sessions.

- /P tells DIR to pause after each screenful.

- /A:*attributes* displays only those files that have the attributes you specify: H = hidden, S = system file, D = directory, A = archive, and R = read-only.

DOS and OS/2 Command Lines

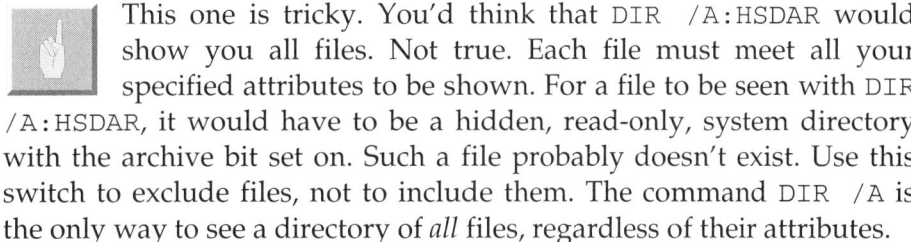

This one is tricky. You'd think that `DIR /A:HSDAR` would show you all files. Not true. Each file must meet all your specified attributes to be shown. For a file to be seen with `DIR /A:HSDAR`, it would have to be a hidden, read-only, system directory with the archive bit set on. Such a file probably doesn't exist. Use this switch to exclude files, not to include them. The command `DIR /A` is the only way to see a directory of *all* files, regardless of their attributes.

- `/A-D` shows files only, no directories or subdirectories are displayed.

- `/O[x]` sorts (orders) the files. The *x* modifier specifies the sort order. With no modifier, it shows directories first (alpha sort) followed by files (alpha sort). The valid sort modifiers are:

    - `/ON` sorts by file name in ascending order.
    - `/OE` sorts by file name extension in ascending order.
    - `/OD` sorts by file date in ascending order.
    - `/OS` sorts by file size in ascending order.
    - `/OG` lists directories first.

  The default is to sort in an ascending manner. To request a descending order place a minus sign (–) in front of the switch. For example, `/O-N` sorts the directory by file name in a descending order.

  You also can request multilevel sorts by specifying more than one sort order switch. The first switch specified is the "major" sort key, and subsequent options are "minor" sort keys.

- `/S` includes files in all subdirectories under the current directory.

- `/L` converts file names to lowercase.

Wildcards: In DOS, the "*" and "?" are very simple. When you put a "*" anywhere in a file name, DOS ignores anything else in the filename. This is not true in OS/2, so you could use `DIR A*B*C`, which would look for files whose file names start with an A, end with a C, and have at least one B in the middle. Under DOS 5.0, `DIR A*B*C` would find all files that start with A.

411

Also, in DOS, `DIR ABC` means the same as `DIR ABC.*`. This is only true in the DOS `DIR` command, which can lead to trouble. For example, `DIR ABC` would show `ABC.`, `ABC.XYZ`, and `ABC.BAT`. Now type `DEL ABC`, and only `ABC.` will be deleted. OS/2 makes sure that `DEL` will delete all the files that `DIR` shows you, given the same wildcard.

Here's what happens under OS/2: `DIR ABC` will only find a file named `ABC`, not `ABC.BAT`. Also note that `DIR ABC*` and `DIR ABC.*` are different. `DIR ABC*` would find `ABC.BAT`, and `ABCXYZ.BAT`. `DIR ABC.*` would find `ABC.BAT`, but not `ABCXYZ.BAT`. Since HPFS does not treat a period (.) as a special character, neither does OS/2. The only exception is when you type `DIR *.*`. That *should* mean: Find all files with a period (.) somewhere in their file names, but to satisfy old DOS habits, HPFS will even display files without a period (.) in their name.

DISKCOMP

`DISKCOMP d: d: [/switch]`

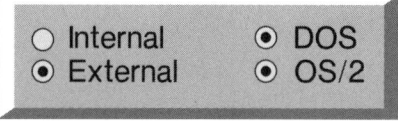

Compares the contents of the diskettes in the designated diskette drives. The DOS 5.0 switches `/1` and `/8` are not supported.

DISKCOPY

`DISKCOPY d: d: [/switch]`

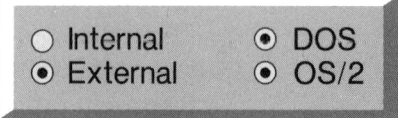

Copies entire diskettes. The DOS 5.0 `/V` switch is not supported.

DOSKEY

`DOSKEY`

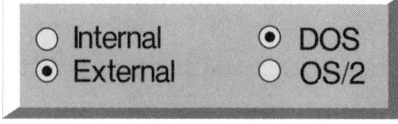

Adds the keyboard command retrieval feature to DOS sessions. To retrieve a previously entered command, press the up arrow key. You can use the left and right arrow keys to move the cursor through the characters in a retrieved command, allowing you to edit the command string. Use the KEYS command to add this feature to OS/2 sessions.

EAUTIL

○ Internal   ● DOS
● External   ● OS/2

EAUTIL *filespec* [*eafile*] /S [/R] [/P]
EAUTIL *filespec* [*eafile*] /J [/O] [/M] [/P]

Allows you to split the extended attributes from a file and save them in a holding file. You also can re-attach or restore the extended attributes to a file using this command. Some applications do not recognize extended attributes and can, therefore, corrupt them. This command allows you to get around this problem. To save extended attributes, type:

EAUTIL *filespec* [*eafile*] /S [/R] [/P]

- *filespec* is the name of the file to split.

- *eafile* is the name of the file that will hold the extended attributes. If you don't specify *eafile*, EAUTIL makes a subdirectory named "EAS" and creates a file in that subdirectory with the same file name as specified in *filespec*.

- /S specifies that you want to save extended attributes.

- /R forces EAUTIL to replace the *eafile*. If you do not specify /R, and the *eafile* exists, EAUTIL returns an error.

- /P preserves the extended attributes in *filespec* (does a copy instead of a move).

To restore extended attributes (re-attach them to the file) type:

EAUTIL *filespec* *eafile* /J [/O| /M] [/P]

The OS/2 Warp Survival Guide

- /J specifies that you want to restore (join) the extended attributes (in *eafile*) for *filespec*.

- /O specifies that you want to overwrite. Any extended attributes already on the file will be deleted before the saved extended attributes are joined with the file.

- /M merges any existing extended attributes with the saved extended attributes.

- /P preserves the *eafile*. If not specified, the *eafile* is deleted once the extended attributes are re-joined.

You might be wondering why you would want to split and join extended attributes for your files. The following examples show you some possible uses for EAUTIL.

- If you have a DOS-based BACKUP program, and you need to preserve extended attributes, you can split them, and save the *eafile* with the file.

- Many operations you can perform in OS/2 attach extended attributes to files, using up valuable space (especially on FAT drives). For example: Any file you edit with the OS/2 system editor will have extended attributes attached to it. DIR /N will show you these files. You may want to split unnecessary extended attributes to save disk space. Just don't remove extended attributes from OS/2 system files! All OS/2 executables have extended attributes; *leave them alone*!

EDIT

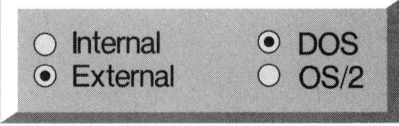

EDIT [*filespec*]

Starts the DOS Full Screen editor as in DOS 5.0.

Actually, in DOS 5.0, EDIT.COM just starts QBASIC.EXE with the /EDIT switch. There is no EDIT.COM in OS/2, but there is an EDIT macro defined in the OS/2 AUTOEXEC.BAT file that

9   *DOS and OS/2 Command Lines*

does the same thing. As shipped, however, this macro is disabled. To enable it, edit `AUTOEXEC.BAT`, and remove the `REM` from the line that reads: `REM DOSKEY EDIT=QBASIC /EDITOR $*`.

EDLIN

`EDLIN` [*filespec*]

○ Internal	● DOS
● External	○ OS/2

Same as DOS 5.0, unfortunately! `EDLIN` commands are not documented in OS/2; maybe because anyone who has ever used this command probably thought "I'll never use this again!" EDLIN is a simple, line-oriented editor that is virtually unchanged since DOS 1.0.

ENDLOCAL

`ENDDLOCAL`

● Internal	○ DOS
○ External	● OS/2

Restores the OS/2 environment variables to the values they were set to using the `SETLOCAL` command. See `SETLOCAL` for details.

EXIT

`EXIT`

● Internal	● DOS
○ External	● OS/2

Exits the current `CMD.EXE` or `COMMAND.COM` session and returns you to the calling OS/2 or DOS session. If you `EXIT` the last command processor in a session, the session is closed.

The last command processor in a Specific DOS session does *not* close the session (since it's real DOS, it doesn't don't know about sessions). The `EXIT_VDM.COM` program is supplied for that purpose. `EXIT_VDM` can be used from any DOS session, and will *always* close the session, even if there are several command processors running in that session (whereas EXIT will exit only one command processor at a time).

EXTPROC

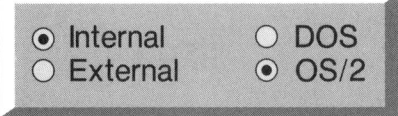

EXTPROC *filespec*

Installs a custom batch processor for .CMD files. This statement must be the first line in a .CMD file, and specifies the name of a custom batch processor. If anyone ever uses this function, I'll probably faint!

FDISK

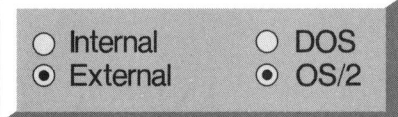

FDISK [/*commands*]

Normally, FDISK (or FDISKPM) is specified without parameters. However, several command line options are available. FDISK /HELP displays a summary of these options. The following are FDISK commands:

- /QUERY displays the partition table. The following are examples of using options with the FDISK /QUERY command:

    - /QUERY /SIZE:200 /DISK:1 shows any 200MB partitions on disk 1

    - /QUERY /BOOTABLE:1 shows all partitions on the Boot Manager menu

    - /QUERY /BOOTABLE:0 /FSTYPE:HPFS shows all HPFS partitions that are not on the Boot Manager menu

- /CREATE:*name* creates a partition on the specified disk, with the specified partition name. If you specify a *name* for the partition, it is added to the Boot Manager menu. If you don't name the partition,

FDISK will create a name based on the location of the partition. Consider the following examples:

- `/CREATE:OS2BOOT /DISK:2 /VTYPE:2 /SIZE:40 /FSTYPE:HPFS /START:T /BOOTABLE:1` creates a 40MB logical partition at the beginning of free space on disk 2, and adds it to the Boot Manager menu. It is marked as an HPFS partition, but it must still be formatted.

- `/CREATE /BOOTMANAGER /START:B` installs Boot Manager at the beginning of the free space on disk 1 (only disk 1 can have Boot Manager).

- `/DELETE:`*name* deletes the named partition. To delete all partitions on a disk, use `/DELETE:ALL /DISK:`*n*.

- `/SETNAME:`*name* adds a name to a partition, and adds it to the Boot Manager menu. For example:
  `/SETNAME:OS2BOOT /NAME:00000820`.

- `/SETACCESS` makes a hidden primary partition visible (after rebooting the computer).

- `/STARTABLE` marks the startable partition. This must be a primary partition (either C:, or the Boot Manager).

- `/FILE:`*name* reads `FDISK` commands from the named file and processes them. This is useful for automatic partition setup.

The most useful command is `FDISK /QUERY`. A printout of this screen could be used to restore your system in the event of a catastrophic disk failure.

For all commands (except `FILE`), you can specify optional parameters that control the action of the command. These are:

- `/NAME:`*partition name* acts only on the named partition.

- `/DISK:`*n* acts only on the specified disk number.

- /FSTYPE:*string* acts only on the specified type of file system (not used in SETACCESS command). If you know the hex code for the desired type, you can use /FSTYPE:H*xx*. For example, HPFS is file system type 07. The string can be DOS, FAT, HPFS, FREE, or OTHER.

- /START:*x* specifies a partition's starting point, where *x* can be T for top (or beginning) of free space, or B for bottom (or end) of free space.

- /SIZE:*n* sets the size of the partition where *n* is specified in megabytes.

- /VTYPE:*n* specifies the type of partition (not used in SETACCESS or STARTABLE commands) where *n* can be:

  ```
  0 = acts only on free space
  1 = only primary partitions
  2 = only extended/logical partitions
  ```

- /BOOTABLE:*n* specifies whether or not the partition is on the Boot Manager menu, where *n* can be:

  ```
  0 = not on the Boot Manager menu
  1 = on the Boot Manager menu
  ```

- /BOOTMGR specifies the Boot Manager partition.

FOR

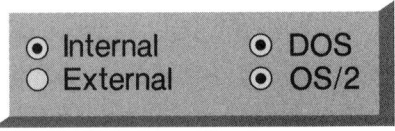

FOR %*var* IN (*set*) DO *command*

Lets you repeat a command; same as DOS 5.0. This is a *very* powerful yet underused command, so we'll describe it. The FOR command lets you repeat commands based on a list of files or names. For example:

DOS and OS/2 Command Lines

- `FOR %x in (*.EXE *.COM) DO ATTRIB +R %X` marks all `.EXE` and `.COM` files with the READ-ONLY attribute.

- `FOR %x in (DEVICE BASEDEV IFS) DO FIND /i "%x=" \CONFIG.SYS` displays all lines in `CONFIG.SYS` that contain `DEVICE=`, `BASEDEV=`, or `IFS=`.

When using the `FOR` command in a batch file, use `%%x` instead of `%x` (because the percent sign is a reserved character in batch files)

FORMAT

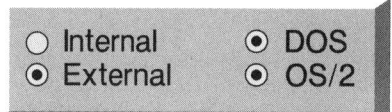

`FORMAT d: [/switches]`

Formats hard disks and diskettes. Under OS/2, this command differs from DOS in the following ways:

- `/1` (single sided floppy) is not supported
- `/8` (force 8 sectors/track) is not supported
- `/Q` (quickformat) is the default for FAT and HPFS hard drives
- `/B` (reserve room for system files) is not supported
- `/U` (save unformat information) is not supported

The following are supported only under OS/2; they are not available under DOS 5.0:

- `/ONCE` cancels the "Format another?" prompt.

- `/FS:type` specifies a file system where *type* is either `HPFS` or `FAT`.

- `/L` specifies the *long* format. For optical disks, or FAT and HPFS hard drives (overrides the /Q default).

`/NOF` Obsolete—For HPFS drives, this is the same as /Q (which is now the default for HPFS and FAT partitions on hard drives).

FSACCESS

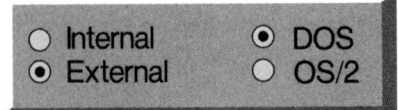

`FSACCESS` *driveletter*

This command specifies how each disk is accessed in a Specific DOS session. Normally, DOS will access floppies directly, and OS/2 will control access to hard drives. `FSACCESS` can modify this scheme. This function is available only when the `FSFILTER.SYS` driver is loaded in the Specific DOS session's `CONFIG.SYS` file. All Specific DOS sessions should load the driver named `FSFILTER.SYS`.

Here are a couple of scenarios for using the `FSACCESS` command:

- You have booted from a disk image. Drive A: is the image, so you don't have access to the physical drive A:. To gain access, you would enter:

  `FSACCESS Q=A`

  This tells OS/2 that any DOS requests for Drive Q: should be sent to physical Drive A:.

- You have a program on an OS/2-controlled drive that must use the DOS `SETVER` function. `SETVER` is activated when the program is read from disk, and if OS/2 is processing the read, DOS `SETVER` isn't activated. For example: if `C:\MSCDEX.EXE` requires the DOS `SETVER` function, you could use the following commands:

  1. `FSACCESS !C` The exclamation point (!) means to turn off OS/2 control of Drive C:.

  2. `\MSCDEX` This loads `MSCDEX` through DOS.

  3. `FSACCESS C` This allows OS/2 to regain control of Drive C:.

 If you turn off OS/2 control of hard drives, the Specific DOS session *cannot* see the drive if it is formatted as HPFS. On FAT drives, DOS can see the drive, but will have READ-ONLY ac-

cess until OS/2 is allowed to regain control. This use of FSACCESS can be activated on several drives at once, as in:

- FSACCESS !C-F turns off OS/2 control for Drives C:, D:, E:, and F:.

- FSACCESS C-F returns control for Drives C:, D:, E:, and F:.

FSFILTER.SYS

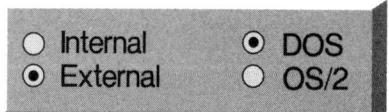

DEVICE=FSFILTER.SYS

This device driver allows Specific DOS sessions to use OS/2's file system. Without this device driver, which is loaded via the DOS CONFIG.SYS file, the Specific DOS session cannot access any OS/2-controlled drive. This driver is *not* needed in the OS/2 CONFIG.SYS or the DOS_DEVICE setting of DOS objects. It is only for Specific DOS sessions.

HELP

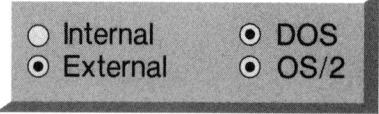

HELP *command*

Provides help on DOS and OS/2 commands, system error messages, and lets you view any .INF file.

For OS/2 sessions, HELP.CMD is used. For DOS sessions, HELP.BAT is used.

- HELP with no parameters gives you some basic instructions.

- HELP=ON adds the "help text" to the top line of the session's screen.

- HELP=OFF removes the "help text" from the top line of the session's screen. The help text is provided by the $I parameter in the session's PROMPT, so HELP=ON simply creates a prompt with $I.

The rest of the Help functions actually use the `HELPMSG.EXE` program. `HELP.BAT` and `HELP.CMD` both call `HELPMSG.EXE` to perform the help functions.

- For help on a DOS or OS/2 command, type `HELP` followed by the command. For example: `HELP DIR` would show you a summary of the `DIR` command and its options.

- For help on a system message, type `HELP` followed by the message number. For example: if you see the message `SYS0039`, you can type `HELP 39` to find out you tried to write to a write-protected disk.

- Optional system utilities and applications you install can also use the help system to provide information on error messages. For example, messages explaining REXX error codes are supplied in the file `REXH.MSG`. To see the error message for REXX error 26, type `HELP REX0026`.

- The HELP command will also load an .INF (hypertext help) file and display a help topic. For example, if you need help on the REXX `SAY` command, type `HELP REXX SAY`. This loads `REXX.INF`, and displays help on `SAY`.

KEYB

○ Internal   ○ DOS
● External   ● OS/2

`KEYB` *country* [*codepage*]

Loads the keyboard layout for specified *country* and *codepage*. For example:

- `KEYB UK 168` loads the United Kingdom layout from codepage 168.

- `KEYB IT 142` loads the Italian keyboard layout from codepage 142.

9
DOS and OS/2 Command Lines

KEYS

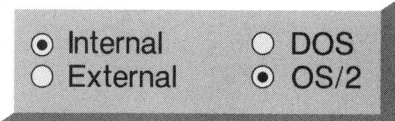

`KEYS=ON|OFF|LST`

Activates command line retrieval and editing features, much like the DOS `DOSKEY` command.

- `KEYS` reports current status (`ON` or `OFF`).
- `KEYS=ON` activates the features.
- `KEYS=OFF` deactivates the features.
- `KEYS LIST` lists commands in buffer.

With `KEYS=ON`, OS/2 Full Screen and windowed command prompts allow retrieval of commands with the up and down arrow keys, and editing of commands with the left and right arrow and home and end keys. This feature is similar to the `DOSKEY` statement in DOS.

MAKEINI

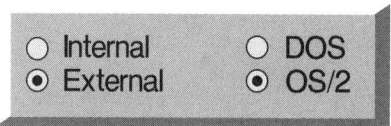

`MAKEINI` *ini-filespec source-filespec*

Re-creates the OS/2 System and User `.INI` files. These files hold configuration information about the OS/2 system and programs.

`MAKEINI` creates new `.INI` files if the originals become damaged, or if you would like to re-configure your system. The `.INI` and the files used to create the `.INI` files (`.RC` files) are located in the `\OS2` subdirectory. To create a new `.INI`, use the commands:

- `MAKEINI \OS2\OS2.INI \OS2\INI.RC`
- `MAKEINI \OS2\OS2SYS.INI \OS2\INISYS.RC`

 OS/2 can be re-configured for an OS/2 1.3, 2.0, or Windows 3.x "look-and-feel." To do this, enter `ATTRIB -R -S \OS2\OS2.INI` (so `MAKEINI` can update the `.INI` file) and then one of the following:

423

- `MAKEINI \OS2\OS2.INI OS2_13.RC` for the OS/2 1.3 look-and-feel.
- `MAKEINI \OS2\OS2.INI WIN_30.RC` for the Windows look-and-feel.
- `MAKEINI \OS2\OS2.INI OS2_20.RC` for the OS/2 2.0 look-and-feel

MODE

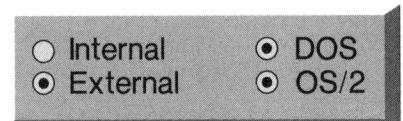

MODE *device arguments*

Controls various characteristics of devices connected to your computer. Consider the following:

- `MODE /status` is not supported.

- `MODE LPTx:` is the same as DOS, except only option P of RETRY is supported.

- `MODE COMx:` is the same as DOS, except only option P of RETRY is supported.

- `MODE COMx:` with no parameters displays the current status of the communications port. The following additional parameters can be supplied in a `MODE COMx:` statement:

    - `TO=ON|OFF` sets infinite time-out ON or OFF. The default setting is OFF.

    - `XON=ON|OFF` sets software flow control ON or OFF. The default setting is OFF.

    - `IDSR=ON|OFF` input hardware handshaking using DSR. The default setting is OFF.

    - `ODSR=ON|OFF` output hardware handshaking using DSR. The default setting is OFF.

- OCTS=ON|OFF output handshaking using CTS. The default setting is OFF.

- DTR=ON|OFF status of Data Terminal Ready. The default setting is ON.

- RTS=ON|OFF|HS|TOG status of Request To Send. The default setting is ON. HS = use RTS for Handshaking, TOG = toggle RTS during transmit.

- BUFFER=ON|OFF|AUTO configures the hardware buffer. AUTO allows the buffer to be set based on other parameters.

- MODE LPTx=COMx is not supported. The SPOOL command provides this function.

- MODE ... CODEPAGE is not supported.

- MODE *display*,*rows* sets the display to monochrome or color, sets the number of columns (40, 80, or 132), and sets the number of rows (25, 43, or 50). In OS/2 windowed sessions, the rows can be any value from 1 to 102.

- MODE DSKT VER=ON|OFF activates diskette read-back verification. The default setting is OFF.

MOVE

MOVE *source destination*

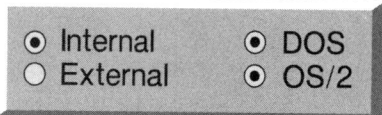

Moves files from one directory to another on the same drive. If *source* is a directory, MOVE relocates the entire directory (including any subdirectories) into the destination directory. If *source* is a file (or wildcard filespec) and *destination* is a directory, MOVE relocates the source file(s) in the destination directory. If *source* is a file, and *destination* is a filespec,

MOVE relocates the source file to the directory specified in *destination*. The file will be renamed to the destination name.

 If the *destination* file already exists, MOVE will *not* move the file. If the *destination* is not specified, the current directory on the drive where the source files reside will be used for the *destination*.

An extension of the RENAME function, MOVE can relocate files from one directory to another. The data in the file is not touched, only the directory information. Because of this, MOVE is *much faster* than COPY, but it will *not* move files to another drive.

PATCH

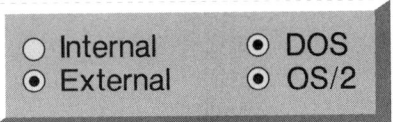

PATCH *filespec* [/A]

Applies IBM-supplied patches to OS/2 system files. Needed only if you receive a Patch file, although you can use the PATCH program to create patches for your own files. The /A option specifies "automatic" mode, in which the specified *filespec* refers to a supplied patch file. Without /A, PATCH runs in "interactive" mode, in which the specified *filespec* is the actual file to patch. You will be prompted for the specific bytes to patch.

 A PATCH file contains one or more groups of the following commands: *filename*, VER *offset data*, or CHA *offset data*. The *filename* command specifies the file to be patched. The VER command specifies that the original file should have the specified bytes at the specified location. This is used to verify the file being patched is correct. The CHA command changes the bytes at the specified offset to new values. The *offset* parameter specifies a byte offset (in hexadecimal) within the file (starting at 0). The *data* option specifies a string of bytes (in hexadecimal) to be verified or changed.

9

DOS and OS/2 Command Lines

PMREXX

`PMREXX [/T]` *filespec args*

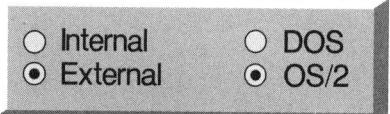

Provides a Presentation Manager interface for interacting with REXX programs.

`/T` starts REXX in trace mode, allowing you to step through the program one line at a time. This feature is very useful for debugging your REXX programs.

- *filespec* is the name of the REXX program file.

- *args* are parameters that are passed to the REXX program.

PROMPT

`PROMPT` *text*

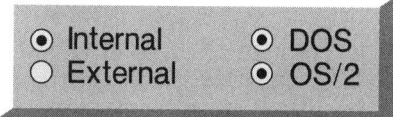

Sets the content of the command prompt. The command prompt can contain textual messages mixed with special characters and indicators. The following special characters are in addition to the ones supported by DOS 5.0:

- `$A` adds the ampersand character (&) to the prompt.
- `$C` adds the left parenthesis character "(" to the prompt.
- `$F` adds the right parenthesis character ")" to the prompt.
- `$I` adds the help text line (see `HELP`).
- `$R` adds the return code from the last function.
- `$S` adds the space character to the prompt.

An example of a "programmer's" prompt might be:

`PROMPT $D $T$H$H$H$_rc=$R [$P]`

This displays the date and time (time without the hundredths of seconds), the return code, and the current path. Displaying the return code is helpful when writing .BAT and .CMD files that need to check the value of ERRORLEVEL when a program fails.

PSTAT

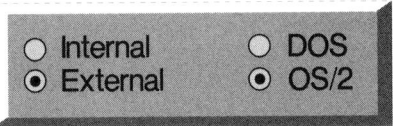

`PSTAT [/switches]`

Displays process-statistical information. By default (without any switches), PSTAT displays information as if you had entered PSTAT /C /S /M /L. The following optional switches are supported:

- /C displays information on processes and threads.
- /S displays information on semaphores.
- /L displays information on dynamic-link library usage.
- /M displays information on shared memory.
- /P:*id* displays information on the specified process. The argument *id* is the desired process ID.

READLINE

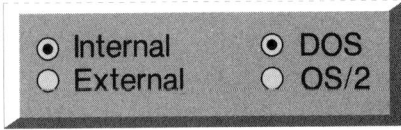

`READLINE [/V]`

Used in .BAT files, READLINE reads a line of text from the keyboard and places it in the batch parameter variables. READLINE /V converts all input to uppercase. Try the following example:

```
ECHO Type something (I'll make it upper case):
READLINE /V
CLS
ECHO You typed: %0 %1 %2 %3 %4 %5 %6 %7 %8 %9
```

9

DOS and OS/2 Command Lines

REN, RENAME

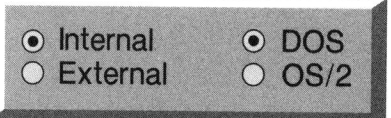

REN [/S] *filespec filespec*

 You may have thought that the REN and RENAME commands didn't allow you to rename subdirectories in a DOS session. The undocumented switch /S allows you to do this. For example, REN /S ABCDIR XYZDIR renames "ABCDIR" to "XYZDIR"

In OS/2 sessions, you can rename directories without using the /S switch.

RMVIEW

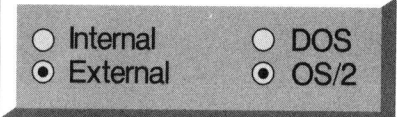

```
RMVIEW [/D | /D1 | /L | /P | /P1] [/R]
RMVIEW [/DMA | /IO | /IOA | /IRQ | /MEM] [/SO]
```

 Displays OS/2 Resource Manager information. The Resource Manager is a service that allows OS/2 device drivers to register the resources they need, in order to avoid conflicts. RMVIEW allows you to see the resources that have been claimed by Resource Manager-aware device drivers. The switches that are available are:

- /D   Display driver view.
- /D1   Display driver view with chipset information.
- /L   Logical view.
- /P   Physical view.
- /P1   Physical view with chipset information.
  - /R   (Used with above switches, display in raw mode.)
- /DMA   Display DMA channel use.
- /IO   Display used I/O ports above 100 hex.
- /IOA   Display all used I/O ports.
- /IRQ   Display IRQ level use.
- /MEM   Display memory regions used.
  - /SO   (Used with above switches, display items sorted by owner.)

The OS/2 Warp Survival Guide

The RMVIEW command can assist in configuring new peripheral devices. If you are going to add a new device to your system, and the installation instructions ask you to choose a DMA channel, IRQ level, or I/O port, you can use RMVIEW to see what choices are not used by other ports.

SET

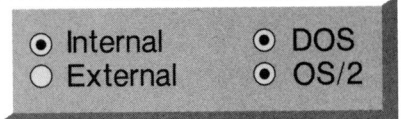

SET [/S] [*var_name*[=*value*]]

In DOS sessions, the SET /S command displays the size of the environment. This option is not available in OS/2 sessions, as the environment size is dynamic.

- SET /S displays the size of the current environment DOS sessions only).
- SET *var_name* displays the current value of the variable you name.
- SET *var_name=value* sets the variable to the specified value.

SETBOOT

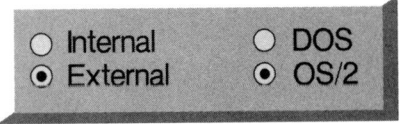

SETBOOT [/*switches*]

Allows you to configure the Boot Manager menu without running FDISK. The following switches are supported:

- /T:*x* sets the Boot Manager time-out to *x* seconds.
- /T:NO disables the Boot Manager time-out feature.
- /M:*n* sets the Boot Manager to *normal* mode.
- /M:*a* sets the Boot Manager to *advanced* mode.
- /Q queries the current Boot Manager settings.
- /B shuts down OS/2.
- /IBA:*n* shuts down OS/2 and starts the *n* partition.
- /IBD:*d* shuts down OS/2 and starts drive *d*.

- /X:*n* selects *fallback mode* partition (*n* = 1, 2, or 3).
- /0:*name* sets the *name* partition as the default partition.
- /1:*name* sets the *name* partition as *fallback* partition 1.
- /2:*name* sets the *name* partition as *fallback* partition 2.
- /3:*name* sets the *name* partition as *fallback* partition 3.

Normally, Boot Manager displays a menu that allows you to select which partition to boot from. If you set a time-out (SETBOOT /T:*x*), Boot Manager automatically boots the last-booted partition if you don't select another one before the time-out expires. If you set a default partition (SETBOOT /0:*name*), Boot Manager boots the default partition after the specified time-out.

If you set a *fallback* partition (SETBOOT /X:*n*), OS/2 boots the specified fallback partition, and then decrements the fallback partition number. This feature is used for automatic fallback to another boot partition. For example, if you issue the following commands:

```
SETBOOT /3:PRIMARY
SETBOOT /2:SECONDARY
SETBOOT /1:EMERGENCY
SETBOOT /X:3
```

Boot Manager boots the PRIMARY partition. If the PRIMARY partition starts normally, a program should issue SETBOOT /X:3 again, so the PRIMARY partition will boot the next time. If this is not done (because PRIMARY does not start properly), Boot Manager boots SECONDARY and then EMERGENCY unless either of those partitions issues the SETBOOT /X:3 command. The SECONDARY and EMERGENCY partitions can be designed to perform maintenance on the PRIMARY partition, and then reboot to re-start the other partitions.

SETLOCAL

SETLOCAL

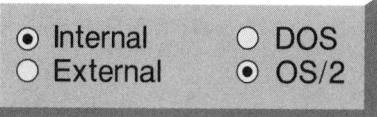

Used in batch (.CMD) files, SETLOCAL saves the current drive, directory, and environment variables. The command ENDLOCAL restores these values. This can be used in batch files that perform disk operations, and then returns to the same drive and subdirectory where it was started.

SHUTDOWN

`SHUTDOWN`

Shuts down OS/2 from a command prompt session. This command performs the same function as the "Shut down" choice from the Desktop context menu or the LaunchPad. You can use it in .CMD files to initiate an orderly shutdown, but remember, any DOS or Windows sessions running will cause the Workplace Shell to display an "are you sure" pop-up.

SPOOL

`SPOOL /D:`*input* `/O:`*output*`]`

Provides redirection for printer devices (similar to the DOS `MODE LPT:`*x* command).

- *input* is the device name the application will use to print: (`PRN`, `LPT1`, `LPT2`, or `LPT3`).

- *output* is where you want the output to be sent: (`PRN`, `LPT1-3`, `COM1-4`).

The `SPOOL /Q` invocation displays the current redirection settings.

START

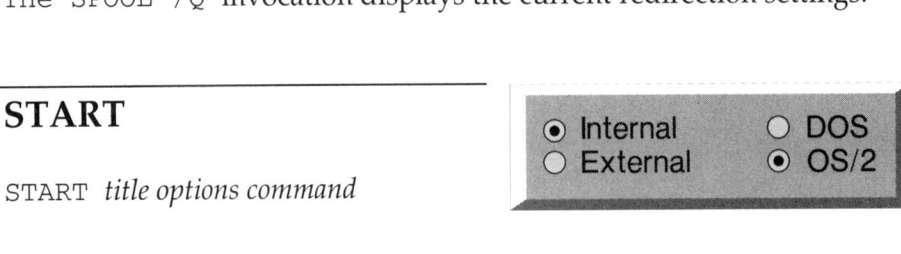

`START` *title options command*

Starts a program in another session where *title*, if specified, is used to identify the program in the task list (the program name will be used if no *title* is specified). START supports the following options:

- `/K` keeps the session running, even after the program completes (default for non-Presentation Manager programs).

- `/C` terminates the session after the specified program completes.

- `/N` runs the program directly, without a command processor. This option cannot be used to start Internal commands, and is the default for Presentation Manager programs.

- `/F` makes the session the new FOREGROUND session.

- `/B` starts the session in the BACKGROUND.

- `/FS` starts a full-screen session.

- `/WIN` starts a windowed session.

- `/DOS` forces the application to start in a DOS session.

- `/PM` starts a Presentation Manager session.

- `/MIN` starts the session Minimized (Presentation Manager applications might ignore this option).

- `/MAX` starts the session Maximized (Presentation Manager applications might ignore this option).

- `/I` causes the session to inherit the environment as defined in `CONFIG.SYS`, rather than the current environment of the session issuing the START command.

You tell START the name of the program you want to run using the *command* argument. If you specify redirection symbols, enclose *command* in quotes.

Examples:

- `START` starts an OS/2 Window session in the background.

- `START /FS CHKDSK` starts `CHKDSK` in a foreground OS/2 Full Screen session.

- `START "Window" /win /f` starts an OS/2 Window named "Window" in the foreground.

- `START /C "DIR > DIR.TXT"` runs the command: `DIR > DIR.TXT` and then exits.

SYSINSTX

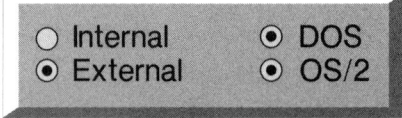

`SYSINSTX d:`

 Makes a drive bootable by copying the OS/2 Warp boot files to the target drive. This command would be required if you wanted to format a drive, then restore a bootable OS/2 drive from backup. This is the same as the DOS command SYS. If the target drive is formatted for a file system other than FAT, the IFS utility `DLL` must be in the current `LIBPATH`. For example, to run `SYSINSTX` on an HPFS drive, the `UHPFS.DLL` file must be in the `LIBPATH`. The `SYSINSTX.COM` file can be found in `\OS2\INSTALL\BOOTDISK`, which is not normally in the path.

SYSLEVEL

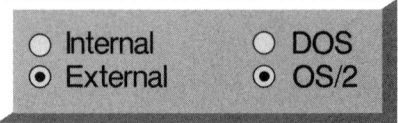

`SYSLEVEL`

Displays version information for installed products. This command searches your system for known products, and displays the current version level for each.

TEDIT

TEDIT *filespec*

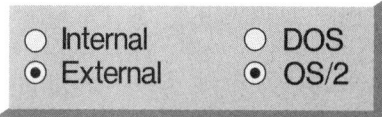

This full-screen editor is stored in the root directory of the installation partition and in the OS/2 subdirectory. It's also on Diskette 1 of the Installation set. It works great for doing emergency edits to CONFIG.SYS or AUTOEXEC.BAT. It can run in an OS/2 window, and works with file "rings."

TIME

TIME *hh*:*mm*:*ss*:*cc*

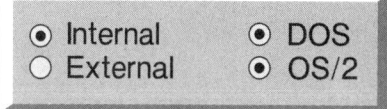

 Same as DOS 5.0, with an additional undocumented switch: /N. In DOS sessions, TIME /N displays the time, without prompting you to enter a new time.

TRUENAME

TRUENAME *filespec*

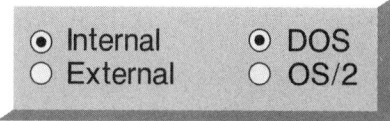

 Displays the "true" name of a file, resolving any relative path information. For example: From \OS2\MDOS if you type TRUENAME ..\CMD.EXE, OS/2 would show you C:\OS2\CMD.EXE.

UNDELETE

UNDELETE [*filespec*/*switches*]

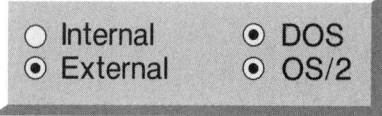

Recovers files that were previously deleted. UNDELETE supports the following switches:

- `/L` lists file names that can be undeleted.
- `/S` includes files in subdirectories.
- `/A` undeletes *all* files without prompting.
- `/F` removes files from the UNDELETE area so they cannot be recovered.

The UNDELETE area is only available if you add the `SET DELDIR` command to the `CONFIG.SYS` and `AUTOEXEC.BAT` files. By default, this command is preceded by a `REM`, making it inactive. Once `DELDIR` is active, files that are deleted are placed in a holding area. You can use `UNDELETE` to recover files from the holding area. The size of the holding area is defined in the `DELDIR` command.

UNPACK

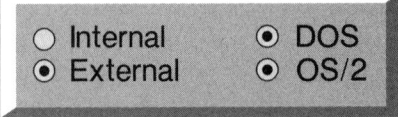

UNPACK

Uncompresses files from the OS/2 installation diskettes. UNPACK also allows you to view the contents of a compressed file on an OS/2 installation disk. Most of the files contained on these disks are compressed into "bundle" files, and must be uncompressed before they can be used. Type:

- UNPACK *filespec* `/SHOW` to view the contents of a compressed file.

- UNPACK *filespec* [*path*] [/V] [/F] [/N:*filename*] to retrieve files from the compressed file, where:

    - [*path*] if specified, is the drive and directory where the uncompressed files should be placed. The compressed files have standard path information in them, and in most cases, only the drive should be specified. If the path is not specified, UNPACK will place the files in the standard directory on the current drive.

    - /V verifies the file after uncompressing.

- /F omits files with Extended Attributes if the target drive does not support EAs.

- /N:*filename* only uncompresses the named file. If /N is not specified, all files in the compressed file will be uncompressed.

VER

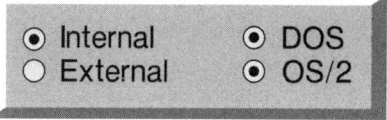

VER [/R]

The VER command displays the OS/2 version number. This command works just as in DOS, but if you use the command: VER /R from an OS/2 or DOS command prompt, it will display the "internal" version of OS/2.

VIEW

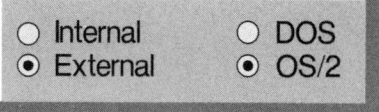

VIEW *filespec* [*topic*]

Displays OS/2 information (.INF) files.

- *filename* is the name of the .INF file.

- *topic* is a topic in the .INF file. If not specified, the table of contents is displayed for the .INF file.

The .INF files are *hypertext* help files which contain on-line documentation for OS/2 and other installed applications.

The VIEW program (which is already associated with all .INF files) is a Presentation Manager program that displays these files.

VMDISK

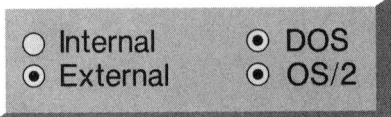

`VMDISK`

`VMDISK` will read a DOS boot disk, and create an "image" file which can be started as an OS/2 object. Image files are useful when you have a DOS program that requires a specific boot disk to run, but you do not want to keep the boot disk in your computer.

To use `VMDISK`, you must first prepare the boot disk for use with OS/2. Usually, this is as simple as copying `FSFILTER.SYS` from `\OS2\MDOS` to the floppy, and then adding the command `DEVICE=A:\FSFILTER.SYS` as the first line in the `CONFIG.SYS` of the boot floppy. You can test the boot disk by using the "DOS from Drive A:" object in the Command Prompts folder. When you are satisfied with the boot disk, use `VMDISK` to create an image file. Use the command:

- `VMDISK` *drive filename*

    - *drive* is the drive where the boot disk is (usually Drive A:).

    - *filename* is the name of the image file you wish to create.

Once the image is created, you can make a copy of the *DOS from Drive A:* object, and change the `DOS_STARTUP_DRIVE` setting to the path and filename of your newly created image. When you open this object, the image file will boot, without having the boot floppy in Drive A:.

Chapter

10

Advanced Warping

This chapter discusses the more advanced aspects of using OS/2. It contains many tips and techniques that you might find useful and interesting. We'll discuss the following topics:

- Configuring OS/2 through CONFIG.SYS
- Understanding Extended Attributes
- Using the Print Spooler

Configuring OS/2 Through CONFIG.SYS

For most OS/2 users, the CONFIG.SYS file is the most frightening file on the computer. This file is filled with the most unintelligible technospeak ever seen, and any attempt to tame this file can cause your entire system to come to a halt. Fortunately, most of us don't even need to look at the CONFIG.SYS file. However, if your curiosity can't be controlled, and you just have to wander into the depths of CONFIG.SYS, the following section will help you make the journey safely.

What Is the CONFIG.SYS File?

The OS/2 CONFIG.SYS file directs the initialization of OS/2. Without this file, OS/2 could not even load. All the pieces of OS/2 that communicate with hardware, control performance, and define the look and feel of the system are defined in the CONFIG.SYS file. The CONFIG.SYS file is created according to the observations made by the installation program. If you change your system's hardware, the change will be noted in CONFIG.SYS.

Since OS/2 automatically creates a working CONFIG.SYS, you may be wondering why you'd even want to look inside this file. The best reason is performance. If you are interested in tuning the performance of OS/2, you will do so by editing CONFIG.SYS. Knowing what to modify (and what to leave alone) can make a big difference in how your system operates. You may be wondering why performance tuning is even necessary. If OS/2 is such an advanced operating system, why doesn't it tune itself? That would be ideal, but there isn't a single "best way" to tune OS/2. Getting the most out of OS/2 will often depend on how you use it. A system tuned for best performance on your system may not work well for someone else. For that reason, OS/2 is tuned for "overall" performance, which means it'll work for all of us, but on most systems, there is room for improvement.

Understanding how CONFIG.SYS is used will help you find your way around this file. OS/2 doesn't just process the statements in CONFIG.SYS from start to finish; it is done in several passes. During the first pass of CONFIG.SYS, OS/2 is still in the early stages of initialization. In subsequent passes, OS/2 has loaded basic functions, and can process more advanced functions. In each pass, the statements in CONFIG.SYS are processed in order, so the position of the lines in CONFIG.SYS are important. Moving just one line can make OS/2 unusable, so unless you know what you are doing, leave the statements where they are.

The Base-Device Statements in CONFIG.SYS

The first group of statements processed in CONFIG.SYS is the "base device" statement group. These statements load device drivers that allow OS/2 to communicate with required hardware. A "base device" statement begins with "BASEDEV=," followed by the name (and parameters) of the device driver. BASEDEV drivers will not contain a drive and path name, just a file name. All base device drivers should be in the \OS2\BOOT subdirectory of the boot drive (or the root directory if booting from floppy). Some of the more common BASEDEV drivers are:

10 Advanced Warping

Driver	Description
IBM1FLPY.ADD	Supports diskette drives on non-Micro Channel computers.
IBM2FLPY.ADD	Supports diskette drives on Micro Channel computers.
IBMKBD.SYS	Supports the keyboard hardware.
IBM1S506.ADD	Supports MFM, RLL, and IDE disk controllers.
IBM2ADSK.ADD	Supports ABIOS-based disk devices.
IBM2SCSI.ADD	Supports Small Computer System Interface (SCSI) controllers on Micro Channel computers.
IBMINT13.I13	Uses BIOS to support disk controllers (if no other base device driver can be used).
OS2DASD.DMD	The OS/2 disk device driver manager.
OS2SCSI.DMD	The SCSI device driver manager.
PCMCIA.SYS	Supports Personal Computer Memory Card Interface Association (PCMCIA) peripherals. If your computer does not have PCMCIA expansion slots, your CONFIG.SYS shouldn't include this driver.
PRINT01.SYS	Supports printer ports on non-Micro Channel computers.
PRINT02.SYS	Supports printer ports on Micro Channel computers.
XDFLOPPY.FLT	Allows floppy drivers to access diskettes using XDF format.

There is usually nothing you need to do with the base device driver statements. However, if your system has to use the IBMINT13.I13 driver, your system performance will suffer. From an OS/2 command prompt, type `RMVIEW /IRQ`. If you see one of the IRQ levels being controlled by "IBT13BIOS Int 13 BIOS Support," you are not getting the most from your OS/2 system. If you have an IDE hard drive, make sure the statement `BASEDEV=IBM1S506.ADD` is in your CONFIG.SYS. Hopefully, adding it and rebooting will change the IRQ owner to "ST506/IDE Controller." If not, you may need a third-party device driver to get a performance improvement.

After *base device drivers* are loaded, additional device drivers can be installed. These drivers give OS/2 access to additional hardware. These statements begin with "`DEVICE=`", followed by the driver name and parameters. A `DEVICE=` driver can contain a drive letter and path. DOS device drivers that should be loaded for *all* DOS sessions are loaded via `CONFIG.SYS`. If a DOS device driver is only needed in one session, using the `DOS_DEVICE` property of the DOS object will save memory. To load a DOS device driver into Upper Memory Blocks (UMBs), `DEVICEHIGH` should be used instead of `DEVICE`.

In many cases, a driver consists of two files—the *physical* device driver and a *virtual* device driver. The physical driver actually controls the device, and the virtual driver supports access to the device by DOS sessions. Most virtual device drivers will have the same name as the physical driver, with a "V" added to the beginning—for example, `COM.SYS` and `VCOM.SYS`.

Some of the `DEVICE` statements you're likely to encounter (and find most interesting) include:

- `DEVICE-\OS2\MDOS\ANSI.SYS` — This statement loads ANSI console support for DOS sessions (ANSI support for OS/2 sessions is available without a device driver).

- `DEVICE=\OS2\BOOT\APM.SYS` — This statement supports Advanced Power Management (APM). If your computer does not support APM (a method of reducing power consumption by turning off unused peripherals), you can remove this driver.

- `DEVICE=\OS2\MDOS\VAPM.SYS` — Virtual device driver for `APM.SYS`.

- `DEVICE=\OS2\BOOT\COM.SYS` — This statement loads support for serial ports. For Micro Channel machines, all standard ports are configured. For ISA/EISA, COM1 and COM2 are configured by default. To configure COM3/COM4, use:

10
Advanced Warping

```
DEVICE=\OS2\BOOT\COM.SYS (3,3E8,i,h) (4,2E8,i,h)
```
where:

- *i* is the IRQ used by the COM port (1–15). COM1 uses IRQ4, COM2 uses IRQ3, and on ISA systems, each port must have its own IRQ. Many COM boards don't allow settings other than IRQ3 or IRQ4, so you may need a new adapter to access all 4 COM ports.

- *h* is the way errors should be handled. Specify `D` to disable communications support if 1000 unexpected interrupts occur. Specify `I` to ignore unexpected interrupts (`D` is the default).

- `DEVICE=\OS2\MDOS\VCOM.SYS` — This statement loads the virtual driver for `COM.SYS`.

- `DEVICE=\OS2\BOOT\DOS.SYS` — This statement loads the device driver that supports software reboot of the system.

- `DEVICE=\OS2\MDOS\EGA.SYS` — This statement loads support for DOS applications which use EGA display registers. You will only need this driver if you use DOS graphic programs that expect EGA compatibility.

- `DEVICE=\OS2\BOOT\EXTDISKDD.SYS` — This statement allows you to access external floppy disks using a logical drive letter.

- `DEVICE=\OS2\LOG.SYS` — This statement activates the System Logging Service.

You must add `RUN=\OS2\SYSTEM\LOGDAEM.EXE` to `CONFIG.SYS` when loading `LOG.SYS`.

- `DEVICE=\OS2\BOOT\MOUSE.SYS` — This statement loads a device-independent mouse driver.

- `DEVICE=\OS2\MDOS\VMOUSE.SYS` — This statement loads the virtual driver for `MOUSE.SYS`.

- `DEVICE=\OS2\BOOT\OS2CDROM.DMD` — This statement loads a device manager for CD-ROM drives. By default, the `/Q` parameter is appended to this line, which tells the driver to be "quiet" (don't display any information) when loading.

- `DEVICE=\OS2\MDOS\VCDROM.SYS` — This statement loads the virtual driver for `OS2CDROM.DMD`.
- `DEVICE=\OS2\MDOS\VPCMCIA.SYS` — This statement loads the virtual driver for `PCMCIA.SYS`.
- `DEVICE=\OS2\BOOT\PMDD.SYS` — This statement loads a driver that provides mouse, keyboard and timer interrupt time events.
- `DEVICE=\OS2\BOOT\POINTDD.SYS` — This statement loads a driver that provides mouse support for text-mode OS/2 sessions.
- `DEVICE=\OS2\BOOT\TESTCFG.SYS` — This statement loads a driver that is used by the Install and Selective Install programs to determine your hardware configuration.
- `DEVICE=\OS2\BOOT\TOUCH.SYS` — This statement loads a device driver that provides support for touch-screen displays.
- `DEVICE=\OS2\BOOT\VDISK.SYS` — This statement creates a virtual disk in RAM. The syntax for the `VDISK.SYS` statement is:

  `VDISK.SYS` *dsize ssize dirs*

  where:
  - *dsize* is the size of the virtual disk in kilobytes. The default value is 64KB, and the range is 16 KBytes to 32768 KBytes (32 MBytes).

  - *ssize* is the size of each sector in bytes. Acceptable values are 128, 256, or 512 bytes. The default value is 512 bytes.

  - *dirs* is the maximum number of files that can be put in the root directory of the virtual disk. Acceptable values are 2 to 1024 entries. The default value is 64.

Notes for VDISK: When using the `VDISK` statement, the memory specified in `dsize` is allocated to the virtual disk and is not available to the rest of the system, even if no files are stored on the virtual disk. If enough RAM is *not* available, a default-size disk (64K) is created. The placement of the `VDISK` statement in `CONFIG.SYS` determines the drive letter assigned to the virtual disk.

10 Advanced Warping

Placing the VDISK statement at the end of CONFIG.SYS ensures that all other drives will receive drive letters that come before the virtual disk.

- DEVICE=\OS2\MDOS\VDPMI.SYS — This statement loads a driver that provides DOS Protected Mode Interface (DPMI) support for DOS sessions. DPMI is a method by which DOS programs can run in protected mode, and gain access to memory above 1MB.
- DEVICE=\OS2\MDOS\VDPX.SYS — If you use DPMI, you must add this statement to CONFIG.SYS so that DPMI support will be initialized for DOS sessions.
- DEVICE=\OS2\MDOS\VEMM.SYS — This statement loads a driver that provides Expanded Memory Support (EMS) for DOS sessions.

Suggestion: If you change the statement to: VEMM.SYS 0, OS/2 will not allocate EMM to a DOS session unless you override the setting in that session's DOS Settings. Most programs do not require EMS, so disabling EMS by default can save RAM.

- DEVICE=\OS2\MDOS\VSVGA.SYS — This statement loads a driver that provides Super VGA graphics support for DOS sessions.
- DEVICE=\OS2\MDOS\VVGA.SYS — This statement loads a driver that provides VGA graphics support for DOS sessions.
- DEVICE=\OS2\MDOS\VWIN.SYS — This statement loads a driver that provides Windows support for DOS sessions.
- DEVICE=\OS2\MDOS\VW32S.SYS — This statement loads a driver that provides 32-bit Windows support for DOS sessions.
- DEVICE=\OS2\MDOS\VXMS.SYS — This statement loads a driver that provides Extended Memory Support (XMS) for DOS sessions. This statement must be placed *after* VEMM.SYS.

Suggestion: Add: /XMMLIMIT=4096,0 /UMB to the VXMS statement. This will allocate a maximum of 4MB of XMS for the entire system, but it will *not* give any XMS memory to a DOS session unless you override the setting in an individual session's DOS Settings. DOS sessions won't get XMS by default, which will save memory (since most DOS programs can run without XMS). If you want `DOS=HIGH` to be the default (usually, this is *not* required), use `/XMMLIMIT=4096,64  /UMB` instead. If you replace `/UMB` with `/NOUMB`, no DOS session will be able to use upper memory blocks (`LOADHIGH` and `DEVICEHIGH` will not work).

Performance Statements in CONFIG.SYS

The next group of statements in `CONFIG.SYS` could be considered "performance" items. These statements specify what features of OS/2 you want activated, and how they should operate. Modifying some of the statements in this section will have a significant effect on the performance of your OS/2 system, while others will change the appearance and operation of OS/2. You may not find some of these statements in your CONFIG.SYS, so if you want the performance enhancement they provide, you will have to add them.

- `AUTOFAIL=YES` — This statement suppresses pop-up messages for hard errors. Instead, OS/2 will pass the error code to the application. `AUTOFAIL=NO` will display a pop-up before passing a hard error to the application.
- `BREAK=ON | OFF` — Instructs DOS sessions to check for **Ctrl+Break** key presses. If set to `ON`, Control-Break checking is more frequent, but DOS programs may run slower.
- `BUFFERS=90` — This statement specifies how many 512-byte disk buffers to allocate. These buffers are used to hold disk I/O requests that are less than one sector. Increasing this number may make disk-intensive programs run faster, but they consume extra RAM. The FAT filesystem uses buffers to
- `CODEPAGE=437,850` — This statement specifies which codepages to load. Codepages allow keyboard and screen I/O to change to support a different language or alphabet. Codepage 437 is the United States codepage, and 850 is the multilingual codepage. The `DEVINFO` for keyboard and screen must be changed if you want to load additional codepages.

10 Advanced Warping

- `COUNTRY=001,d:\OS2\SYSTEM\COUNTRY.SYS` — This statement sets country information, which controls how dates, times, decimal points, sorts, and codepages are used. The three-digit number is the country number (in most cases, it's the telephone-prefix for the desired country). The filename is the driver that contains the country information (usually `COUNTRY.SYS`).

- `DEVINFO=KBD,US,d:\OS2\KEYBOARD.DCP` — This statement sets the keyboard for codepage switching. The first parameter is the country to use (in this case, United States), and the second parameter is the file containing the translation tables for that country (usually, `KEYBOARD.DCP`).

- `DEVINFO=SCR,VGA,d:\OS2\VIOTBL.DCP` — This statement sets the display for codepage switching. The first parameter is the display type (CGA, EGA, VGA, etc.), and the second parameter is the file containing display codepages (usually `VIOTBL.DCP`).

- `DISKCACHE=size,LW,threshold,AC:drive(s)` — This statement installs a disk cache for FAT drives. The parameters are:
  - `size` is the size of the disk cache in kilobytes. The minimum size is 64KB. The maximum size is 14400KB.

     Instead of a size, you can put a "D" in this parameter, which sets a default size based on available RAM. The following table lists the default sizes.

System RAM	FAT Cache Size
4MB or less	48 KBytes
5MB or less	64 KBytes
6MB or less	128 KBytes
8MB or less	512 KBytes
Greater than 8MB	10% of RAM, up to 4MB

  - `LW` turns on the *lazy-write* option. When `LW` is specified, disk writes can be held in memory temporarily to increase throughput. Without `LW`, disk writes are done immediately. `LW` does increase disk performance, but an unexpected power outage may cause data loss.

- *threshold* is the size (in sectors) of the largest disk request to be cached. Large I/O requests will use a significant piece of the cache, so you may want to limit cache access to the smaller requests. The minimum threshold is 4 sectors, and the maximum is 128.

- AC: This parameter activates "auto-check." If the system is powered off without shutting down the file system, OS/2 will perform a CHKDSK /F on any drive listed in the AC list (the drives letters following the colon). This will automatically repair any file system damage caused by the loss of power. For example, AC:CDE will check Drives C:, D:, and E:. If you want a drive to be checked on *every* startup (even if it was powered off properly), insert a + before the drive. For example, AC:C+DE will check Drives C: and E: only if they were improperly stopped, but Drive D: will always be checked.

• DOS=LOW,NOUMB — This statement controls the default use of both the High Memory Area (HMA) and Upper Memory Blocks (UMBs) in DOS sessions. This setting only defines the default action for DOS settings. These settings can be overridden by using the DOS Settings for individual DOS sessions. LOW specifies that DOS should not use the HMA, and will load into conventional RAM. Change this to HIGH, and DOS will use the HMA and free more conventional RAM for DOS programs.

If your default is HIGH, each DOS session will need at least 64K of XMS for each DOS session (add /XMMLIMIT=4096,64 to the VXMS statement).

NOUMB prevents DOS from controlling upper memory blocks (unused addresses between 640K and 1M). Change this to UMB, and DOS will fill these areas with RAM, and allow you to use LOADHIGH and DEVICEHIGH to place device drivers in UMBs. LOW,NOUMB is normally the best choice, since most DOS sessions

10   Advanced Warping

do not need the extra memory gained by UMB and HMA use. By not using these areas, DOS sessions will consume less RAM.

- `FCBS=16,8` — This statement allows you to allocate File Control Blocks (FCBs) for DOS sessions. Using FCBs is one way for DOS programs to open files. Older DOS programs may still use FCBs, but most new DOS programs do not. The first number is the total number of FCBs for each DOS session. The second number defines the number of FCBs that can't be closed and re-used if too many FCB open requests are issued. In most cases, these values can be lowered to save RAM (for example, `FCBS=4,4`).

- `FILES=20` — This statement specifies the maximum number of file handles available to each DOS session. File handles are an alternate to the FCB method of opening files in DOS sessions. By default, each DOS session can open 20 files, but if you increase the `FILES` statement, a DOS program can increase the handle count beyond 20.

    For most systems, the `CONFIG.SYS` setting should stay at 20, and if an individual DOS program needs more than 20, you can modify the DOS settings for that particular session.

- `IFS=d:\OS2\CDFS.IFS /Q` — This statement loads the "Installable File System" for CD-ROM drives. An Installable File System (IFS) is a method by which OS/2 programs can access drives with a structure that isn't recognizable by OS/2 itself. If you have a CD-ROM drive, the `CDFS.IFS` is required to access files on your CD-ROM drive. Otherwise, you can remove this `IFS` statement.

- `IFS=d:\OS2\HPFS.IFS /CACHE:nnn /CRECL:nn /AUTOCHECK:C /F:n` — This statement loads support for the High Performance File System (HPFS) file system. If you have formatted any drives to use HPFS, this `IFS` statement is required. If all of your drives are FAT, you can remove this `IFS` statement to save RAM, but you will have to replace it before formatting a drive for HPFS.

    – The `/CACHE:` parameter sets the size of the HPFS cache in kilobytes. The maximum value for this parameter is `2048` (2MB).

    – The `/CRECL:` parameter sets the cache threshold size in kilobytes. Any disk request larger than this size will not be cached.

This can keep large requests from filling the cache quickly. The maximum value for this parameter is 64 (64KB).

- /AUTOCHECK: specifies which HPFS drives should be checked on startup. If an HPFS disk was not closed properly (by using SHUTDOWN or **Ctrl+Alt+Del**), the drive cannot be used until CHKDSK /F is performed. AUTOCHECK will perform the CHKDSK /F for any drive listed that was not closed properly, and it will run CHKDSK unconditionally if the drive letter is preceded by a '+'. For example, /AUTOCHECK:C+EF will check Drives C: and F: if they were not shut down properly, and will always check Drive E:.

- /F:n specifies the level of CHKDSK to be run during the AUTOCHECK. The default is /F:2, but if you want a faster (but less thorough) CHKDSK during startup, specify /F:1.

- IOPL=YES — This statement grants programs the I/O Privilege Level, which allows programs to gain direct access to hardware devices. Without it, some programs may not operate properly. To grant IOPL only to programs that you specify, use the following form of the statement: IOPL=*program1*,*program2*...

- LASTDRIVE=d — This statement specifies the last available logical drive letter for DOS sessions. DOS devices that create a logical drive (networks, virtual disks, etc.) are assigned drive letters after all physical devices are assigned. The LASTDRIVE letter (*d*) must be high enough to make room for all the logical drives. LASTDRIVE=Z allows DOS sessions to create a logical drive with any drive letter.

- LIBPATH=.;*d*:\OS2\DLL;*d*:\OS2\MDOS;*d*:\;*d*:\OS2\APPS\DLL — This statement specifies the path for Dynamic Link Libraries (DLLs). A DLL is a library of utilities that programs can load at runtime. If a program cannot find a required DLL, it will not run. Many programs that install DLLs will add items to the LIBPATH, but since "." (the current directory) is at the beginning of LIBPATH, a program will be able to find any DLL in the directory where you start it from.

Adding directories to LIBPATH may increase the time it takes to find DLLs. Put the most common DLL directories at the start of the LIBPATH.

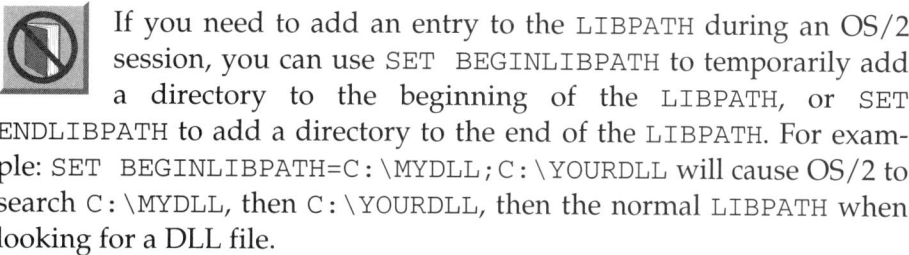
If you need to add an entry to the LIBPATH during an OS/2 session, you can use SET BEGINLIBPATH to temporarily add a directory to the beginning of the LIBPATH, or SET ENDLIBPATH to add a directory to the end of the LIBPATH. For example: SET BEGINLIBPATH=C:\MYDLL;C:\YOURDLL will cause OS/2 to search C:\MYDLL, then C:\YOURDLL, then the normal LIBPATH when looking for a DLL file.

- MAXWAIT=3 — This statement specifies the number of seconds a task must wait before getting an automatic priority boost. If your system is under a heavy load, a program may have to wait for execution time. Receiving a priority boost will put it ahead of other waiting programs. By decreasing this number, you will help programs get execution time faster, but your overall performance my suffer. Increasing this number will allow the OS/2 scheduler to resolve requests for system time based on the true priority of the programs (maximum is 255 seconds).

- MEMMAN=SWAP,PROTECT,NOCOMMIT — This statement configures the OS/2 memory manager. The memory manager controls how OS/2 handles virtual memory. The parameters are:
  - SWAP (or NOSWAP). SWAP tells OS/2 to create and use a swap file (on the disk drive) to handle memory requests that exceed system RAM. NOSWAP causes programs to fail if they attempt to access more RAM than is physically available. NOSWAP should only be used in systems where a known set of programs will fit in RAM, and system response time is critical.
  - PROTECT allows access to protected memory through certain OS/2 function calls.
  - NOCOMMIT (or COMMIT). This option tells OS/2 when to allocate memory. NOCOMMIT (the default) tells OS/2 to allocate memory when it's actually used. COMMIT tells OS/2 to allocate memory as soon as it is requested. This causes the swap file to grow

quickly, but it ensures that programs can run to completion without requiring further growth of the swap file.

You may also see the parameters MOVE or NOMOVE. These are no longer used in OS/2, but are still allowed to maintain compatibility with older versions of OS/2. Another parameter you may see is DELAYSWAP. This parameter is used to boot OS/2 without a SWAPPER.DAT file. The SWAPPER can then be specified at a later time. It is usually used by the OS/2 installation program to format the partition that will eventually contain the SWAPPER.DAT file.

- PAUSEONERROR=YES — This statement determines if OS/2 will pause if it encounters an error during processing of CONFIG.SYS. If set to NO, OS/2 will continue, ignoring any errors.

- PRINTMONBUFSIZE=134,134,134 — The statement sets the buffer size for the print monitor buffers. The sizes are in characters, and are for LPT1, LPT2, and LPT3, respectively. Increasing these values will increase print performance *only* if you have installed a print monitor that can use the extra memory. The maximum size is 134 bytes, and for most systems, that will be enough. Do not set the size to 0; it will actually use more system resources than leaving it at the default.

- PRIORITY=DYNAMIC — This statement specifies how OS/2 determines thread priorities. Default is DYNAMIC, which lets OS/2 determine priority based on system activity. ABSOLUTE prevents OS/2 from modifying priorities based on usage observations.

- PRIORITY_DISK_IO=YES — This statement defines how disk I/O is prioritized. If this option is set to YES, disk requests are given the priority of the task that issues the request (high-priority tasks will get high-priority disk access). If set to NO, all disk I/O is done on a first-come, first-served basis, regardless of the priority of the requesting task. For most systems, this setting should be YES.

- PROTECTONLY=NO — This statement controls access to DOS emulation. If set to NO, DOS sessions are available. If set to YES, only protected-mode access to memory is available, so DOS sessions cannot run.

- PROTSHELL=*d:*\OS2\PMSHELL.EXE — This statement defines the protected-mode shell. Normally, this should be left set to

`PMSHELL.EXE`, but if an optional shell program is available for OS/2, this statement will load it. The shell controls the multitasking capabilities of OS/2. As an example, you can change this setting to `C:\OS2\CMD.EXE`, which will replace the OS/2 Workplace Shell with `CMD.EXE`. Doing so will limit the OS/2 system to a single, full-screen OS/2 command prompt.

- `RMSIZE=640` — This statement controls the default size of DOS sessions in kilobytes. The maximum size is `640`, but since OS/2 uses less of this memory than DOS, nearly all DOS programs can run with a smaller number. If you run many DOS sessions, you can decrease this number to save RAM, and only increase it in the individual DOS sessions that require the RAM.

- `SHELL=d:\OS2\MDOS\COMMAND.COM d:\OS2\MDOS` — This statement defines the "DOS shell." Normally, this will be `COMMAND.COM`, but different command interpreters are available for DOS.

- `SWAPPATH=d:\path minfree_size initial_size` — This statement defines the location and size of the swap file. The swap file is where OS/2 stores any data that can't fit in RAM. When the program requests access to data in the swap file, other data is moved to the swap file, and the requested data is returned to RAM. The parameters for `SWAPPATH` are:

  - `d:\path` is the drive and subdirectory where you want the swap file located. The location of the swap file is important—there must be enough free space on the selected drive to satisfy swap requests (depending on the programs you run, swap requests can be significant). Placing the swap file on the fastest hard drive on your system will improve performance. Placing it in an HPFS partition will reduce disk fragmentation. There is no need to create a separate drive for the swap file. The swap file can co-exist with your data, as long as adequate free space exists.

  - `minfree_size` is the amount of storage (in kilobytes) that cannot be used by the swap file. The swap file will continue to grow until all free space on the disk is used. If you were to set *minfree_size* to `2048` (2MB) a warning message will appear when there is less than 2MB free on the swap drive. At that point, you must close programs or free more space on the drive.

- *initial_size* is the size of the swap file (in kilobytes) when the system starts. Most systems will require swap space, and by defining an initial swap size, you can increase performance by pre-allocating space for the file. The *initial_size* should be set to the expected normal running size of the swap file. To determine the normal running size of the swap file, check the swap file size periodically (use the DIR command, or the details view of the folder containing the swap file).

 If the drive containing your swap file runs out of free space, you may see a warning screen that looks like:

```
┌────────────────────────────────────────────────────┐
│ PROGRAM NAME                                       │
│                                                    │
│ SYS1477: Warning! The partition containing the     │
│ SWAPPER.DAT file is full. You may lose data. Do    │
│ not ignore this message! Select                    │
│ Display help below for an explanation and          │
│ possible recovery actions.                         │
│                                                    │
├────────────────────────────────────────────────────┤
│                                                    │
│ End program/command/operation                      │
│ Ignore the error and continue                      │
│ Display help                                       │
│                                                    │
└────────────────────────────────────────────────────┘
```

If you end the program (listed on the first line of the error screen), you may lose data. You can ignore the message, but then you'll have to act fast. *Immediately* close other programs or delete files on the drive containing the swapper. This will allow the swapper to grow, and avoid an out-of-memory condition.

- THREADS=256 — This statement sets the maximum number of execution threads. A thread is a separate executable task. DOS pro-

10 Advanced Warping

grams only allow one thread for each DOS session, but OS/2 programs can create many threads. Reducing this number will slightly reduce memory requirements, but if you run many programs at the same time, you may run out of threads. The PSTAT command can show you how many threads are allocated at any time. THREADS can be set to any value from 64 to 4096.

Environment Variable Statements in CONFIG.SYS

The last group of statements in CONFIG.SYS pertains to the *environment variables*. These statements are used to activate features in the OS/2 environment. Each command begins with SET=. If you type SET from an OS/2 command prompt, you can see all the current settings in effect, and you can change the settings for an individual OS/2 session by typing in a new value for any environment variable. Adding extra environment variables only consumes enough extra memory to store the variable settings, but *each* OS/2 session creates a new copy of the environment. The settings you are likely to see (if they aren't there, you may want to add them) in your CONFIG.SYS include:

- SET AUTOSTART=
  PROGRAMS,TASKLIST,FOLDERS,CONNECTIONS, LAUNCHPAD

  This statement tells OS/2 what type of objects should be opened at startup. Removing any of the options can cause your system to be unusable. For example, removing FOLDERS will not allow the Desktop to open (it is a folder). CONNECTIONS refers to network connections that were active during the last session.

- SET BOOKSHELF=C:\OS2\BOOK; — This statement sets the "path" for finding .INF files (on-line documentation).

- SET COMSPEC=C:\OS2\CMD.EXE — This statement sets the name of the OS/2 command processor, and can be used by programs that offer an "exit to shell" option.

- SET DELDIR=C:\DELETE,512;*d:*\DELETE,512; — This statement activates the UNDELETE feature for OS/2 sessions. For each drive you want UNDELETE to be activated, specify a subdirectory on that drive (usually \DELETE) and a size (in kilobytes) for the deleted files. With this feature active, if you delete a file, it is stored in the DELETE subdirectory, and can be recovered using the UNDELETE command. If you delete more files, the first ones deleted will be discarded if the total size of the deleted files on that drive is larger than the specified size. DELDIR is not active by default (REM in front of any statement in CONFIG.SYS deactivates it). If you activate DELDIR, you may also want to activate it for DOS sessions, by adding a similar statement to the AUTOEXEC.BAT file.

- SET DESKTOP=path — This statement sets the location of the Workplace Shell "desktop" directory. Normally, this directory is the \DESKTOP directory on the OS/2 boot drive.

- SET DIRCMD=/ON /N /P — This statement controls how the DIR command in OS/2 sessions reacts. This command is not added to CONFIG.SYS by default, but you may add it. In this example, DIRS are sorted by name (/ON), the display is in HPFS style, with the filenames on the right and EA sizes displayed (/N), and the display will pause after each screenful (/P).

- SET DPATH=C:\OS2;C:\OS2\SYSTEM;C:\OS2\MDOS\WINOS2; — This statement sets an optional *data file path*. Programs may use this path to find data files that are not in the current directory.

- SET EPMPATH=C:\OS2\APPS; — This statement sets the directory where the Enhanced Editor (EPM) files are located.

- SET GLOSSARY=C:\OS2\HELP\GLOSS; — This statement sets the path where the Glossary and Master Help files are located.

- SET HELP=C:\OS2\HELP;C:\OS2\HELP\TUTORIAL; — This statement sets the path OS/2 will use to search for Help files.

- SET IPF_KEYS=SBCS — This statement tells the Help Manager how to determine the type of keyboard translation to use.

- SET KEYS=ON — This statement activates command line editing and retrieval in OS/2 command sessions. This is similar to the DOSKEY function in DOS.

- SET MENUSTYLE=SHORT=path — This statement configures the

Workplace Shell context menus to use "short" style. This removes such menu items as: Help, Move, Create Shadow, and Find.

- `SET OS2_SHELL=C:\OS2\CMD.EXE` — This is the name of the OS/2 command processor, which will be started whenever an OS/2 session is opened.

   If you would like all OS/2 full-screen and windowed sessions to automatically run a .CMD file when they start (just like the AUTOEXEC.BAT file in DOS sessions), add: "/K *filename*" to the end of the OS2_SHELL statement (where *filename* is the path and filename of a REXX or batch .CMD file).

- `SET PATH=C:\OS2;C:\OS2\SYSTEM;C:\OS2\MDOS\WINOS2;.` — This statement sets up the list of directories that you want OS/2 to search to find executable programs.

- `SET PROMPT=$i[$p]` — This defines the command prompt in all OS/2 sessions. The `$i` parameter activates a help line at the top of each command screen.

- `SET RESTARTOBJECTS=YES | NO | STARTUPFOLDERSONLY |`
   `REBOOTONLY` — This statement controls what objects are started when the system starts. OS/2 remembers what programs were open when the system was shut down, and will re-open them when you restart OS/2. By using the `RESTARTOBJECTS` setting, you can limit what objects are started. If set to `YES`, all objects are restarted. If set to `NO`, nothing is restarted. `STARTUPFOLDERSONLY` specifies that only objects placed in a startup folder will be started. `REBOOTONLY` can be specified to only process restart objects when the system boots (instead of each time the Workplace Shell starts, which can be more than once per session).

- `SET RUNWORKPLACE=C:\OS2\PMSHELL.EXE` — This statement specifies which program should be used as the Workplace. Normally, `PMSHELL.EXE` will be used, but alternative Workplace programs may be available. For example, if you change `RUNWORKPLACE` to `C:\OS2\CMD.EXE`, the OS/2 command interpreter will be used. The system will start a single OS/2 command window, and you can use `START` commands to start other OS/2, DOS, or PM sessions.

You will not have the features of the Workplace Shell, but your system memory requirements will be greatly reduced.

- `SET SYSTEM_INI=d:\OS2\OS2SYS.INI` and
- `SET USER_INI=d:\OS2\OS2.INI` — These statements name the default *System* and *User*.INI files. There is little need to change these, unless you are experimenting with alternate .INI files.
- `SET VIDEO_DEVICES=VIO_SVGA` — This statement sets the name of the OS/2 environment variable that contains the base video driver names. There must be a `SET` statement that defines the video devices. For example, if you use `SET VIDEO_DEVICES=MYVIDEO`, you must have a `SET MYVIDEO=` to define what the actual video device is.
- `SET VIO_SVGA=DEVICE(BVHVGA,BVHSVGA)` — This statement selects the base video support. The name of this environment variable is set by the `SET VIDEO_DEVICES` variable. In this case, `BVHVGA` (the VGA base video handler) and `BVHSVGA` (the Super VGA base video handler) are defined. For most adapters, `BVHVGA` is used for standard support, and another handler will provide add-on features.

Extended Attributes

Extended attributes (EAs) are used to attach additional information to a file or directory. OS/2 can attach some extended attributes; your OS/2 applications can attach others. For example, if you assign a long file name to a file on a FAT drive, the long name is stored in an extended attribute.

The total size of the extended attributes for any one file or directory cannot exceed 64 KBytes. You can see the size of any extended attributes on files with the DIR /N command. You can use the EAUTIL command to split or rejoin EAs to a file.

Normally, you don't need to be concerned with EAs. OS/2 will preserve EAs when you copy and move files, and will delete the EAs when you delete the file. The only time EAs can be a problem is when you use

10
Advanced Warping

native DOS and manipulate files with EAs. If you use a DOS session under OS/2, the OS/2 file system will make sure the EAs are handled properly. Without OS/2, native DOS will not preserve the EAs. In general, you should avoid deleting, copying, or moving OS/2 system files if you run native DOS. If you use Dual Boot, when you return to OS/2, CHKDSK is run to see if any EA cleanup is needed.

EAs are built into the HPFS system, but FAT was not designed with EAs in mind. Because of this, EAs take up more space, and take longer to process on a FAT drive. Since the OS/2 system includes hundreds of files with EAs that are used often, your OS/2 boot drive should be placed on an HPFS drive.

Using the Print Spooler

OS/2 Warp comes with a sophisticated printer spooling system that can accept print jobs from many applications at the same time, and route the print jobs to printers attached to one of several output ports. Printer drivers can format the print output to match the capabilities of specific printer devices. All of this is carried out by the operating system, while the user is presented with a simple graphical interface for printing.

The heart of the print subsystem is the printer object. These objects connect the various components of the print subsystem to create a path between an application that wants to submit print data, and the printer itself. By configuring a printer object, you can specify the physical port where the printer is connected, the printer driver (which defines the printer commands used to control fonts and graphics), and other options such as queue type, paper selection, and use of separator pages.

Printing a text file is as simple as dropping a text-file object on the printer object. To see what jobs are in the printer queue, open the printer object. Normally, you won't need to modify printer settings, but if you would like to take advantage of some of the advanced printer options, this section will show you the options available.

Printer Object Settings

When you click on a printer object with the right mouse button, you will see the printer object's context menu, as shown in Figure 10.1. The last two items are specific to a printer. The first option allows you to suspend printing. This is useful if you have a portable computer and send jobs to the printer while you are on the road. It is also useful if you install two printer objects on the same port. If you set the status to *Hold*, all jobs will be held in the queue until you change the status to *Release*. The last option on the menu allows you to select the default printer object.

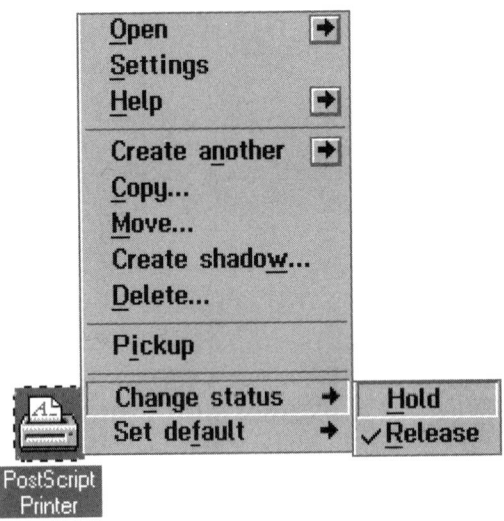

Figure 10.1. The context menu for a printer object allows you to suspend printing and see the default printer.

When you open a printer object's settings notebook, you will see a window similar to the one shown in Figure 10.2.

10

Advanced Warping

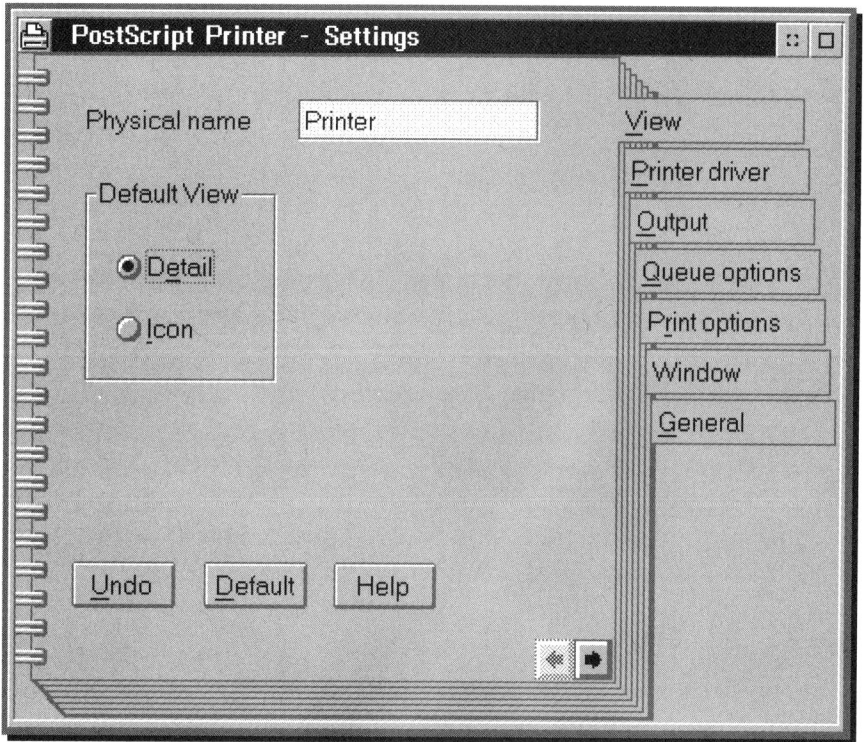

Figure 10.2. *The printer object notebook allows you to set all print options.*

The first page is the View page, which allows you to select what you see when you open the printer object. The default is Icon View, but if you'd like to see more information about your print jobs, select Details View. This page also shows you the physical name of the printer, which corresponds to the directory in the \SPOOL directory where the print jobs are stored. You cannot change this name; it is set when you create a printer object.

The Printer Driver

The next page in the settings notebook controls the printer driver used for this printer.

The OS/2 Warp Survival Guide

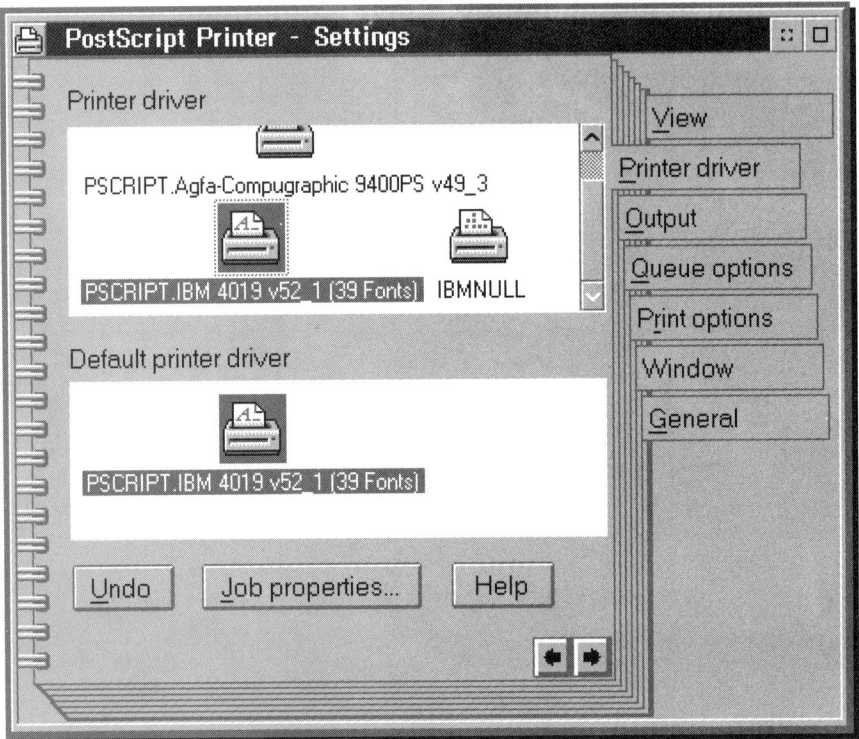

Figure 10.3.   The printer driver page selects the driver for this printer object.

Each type of printer will have its own driver. If you don't see the driver you need in the list of installed drivers in the top box, click on any driver's icon with the right mouse button, and select *Install* from the context menu. Select one of the drivers from the top box, and it will appear in the bottom box, which specifies the currently active driver. Each driver will also have settings that can be accessed by opening the driver object. You can also modify job settings by clicking on the *Job properties* button.

The Printer Port

If you install a new printer, you will connect it to your computer through an I/O port. Normally, you will use a *parallel* port. OS/2 recognizes ports LPT1, LPT2, and LPT3. If you are connected to network printers, you may be able to access logical ports LPT4 through LPT9. Some printers are connected through a *serial* port. Serial ports are slower than parallel ports, but they require less wiring, and the cables can be much longer. OS/2 recognizes serial ports COM1 through COM4. You can also specify that print output should be sent to a file. When you select this option, Warp will prompt you for the file name for each print job. Port and file selections are made from the Output page on the printer object settings notebook.

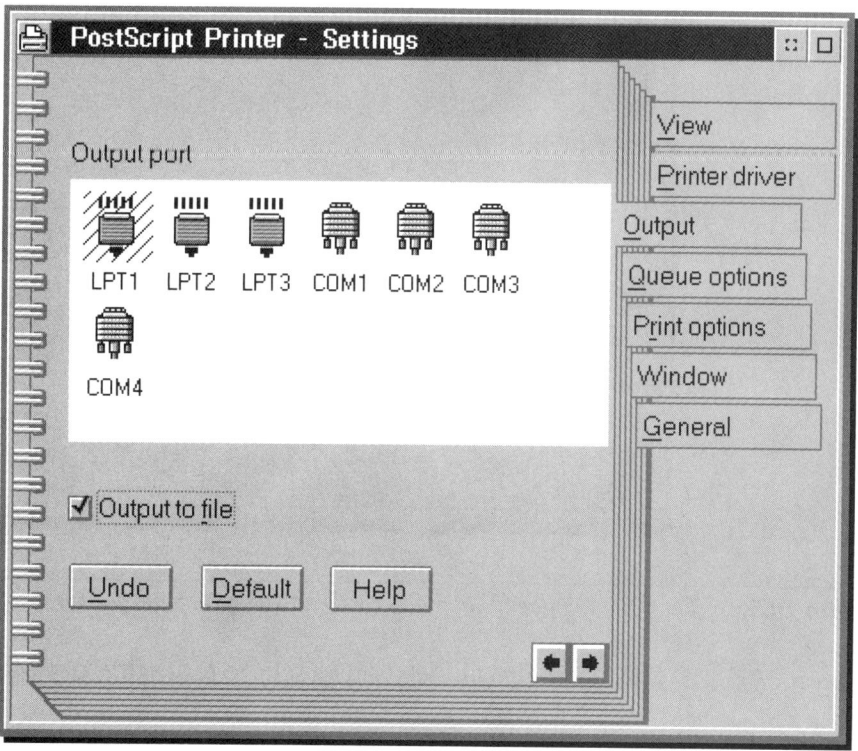

Figure 10.4. *The Output page defines the printer port.*

The next page on the settings notebook is the Queue page. This page allows you to select the queue driver for this printer object. Normally, you will select the PMPRINT queue, but if you connect a plotter, you may need to use the PMPLOT queue, which optimizes output for plotter devices, avoiding making the pens re-draw the same area more than is necessary.

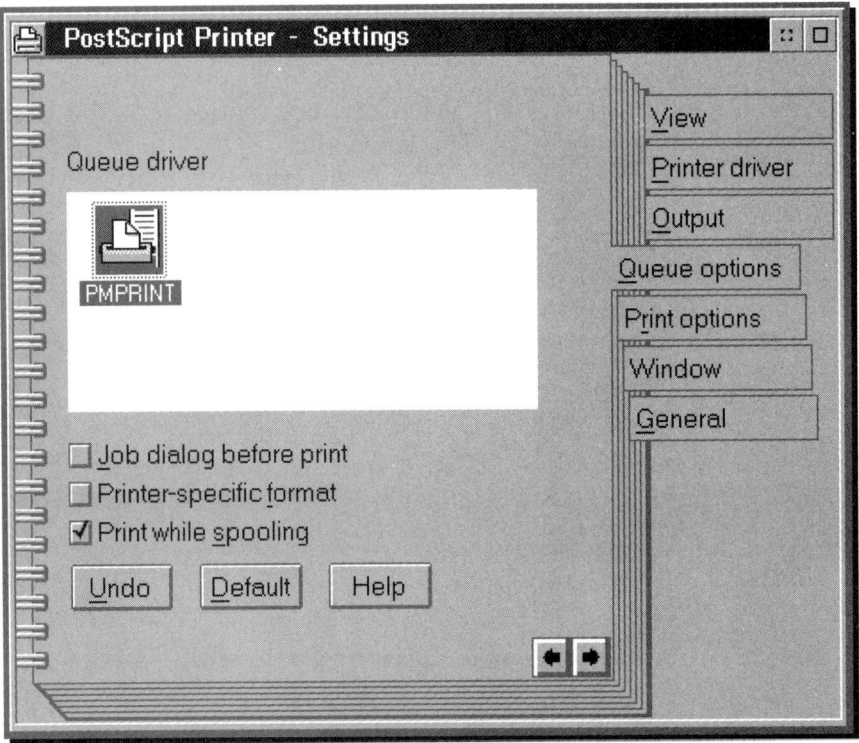

Figure 10.5. *The Queue page allows you to select the queue driver for the printer object.*

This page also allows you to set the following options:

- *Job dialog before print*—If you select this option, a dialog box will pop-up each time you send a job to the printer, allowing you to set print options for each print job.
- *Printer-specific format*—Select this option for remote printers that don't understand OS/2 print drivers. This will cause the printer object to format the print job in the printer's native format. If the computer controlling the remote printer understands OS/2 printer

drivers, you do not need to select this option, and the printer object will send the job in device-independent format.

- *Print while spooling*—If you select this option, the print job will start to print even as the print job continues to spool. If you send a large job to the printer, this will allow it to start sooner, but no other job can print until it is finished.

The last printer-specific page is the Print Options page, which allows you to specify a separator page. This is useful if you have many people printing to the same printer. Sample separator pages included with OS/2 show you how to create a separator page with your user name, print name, and the time the print job was submitted.

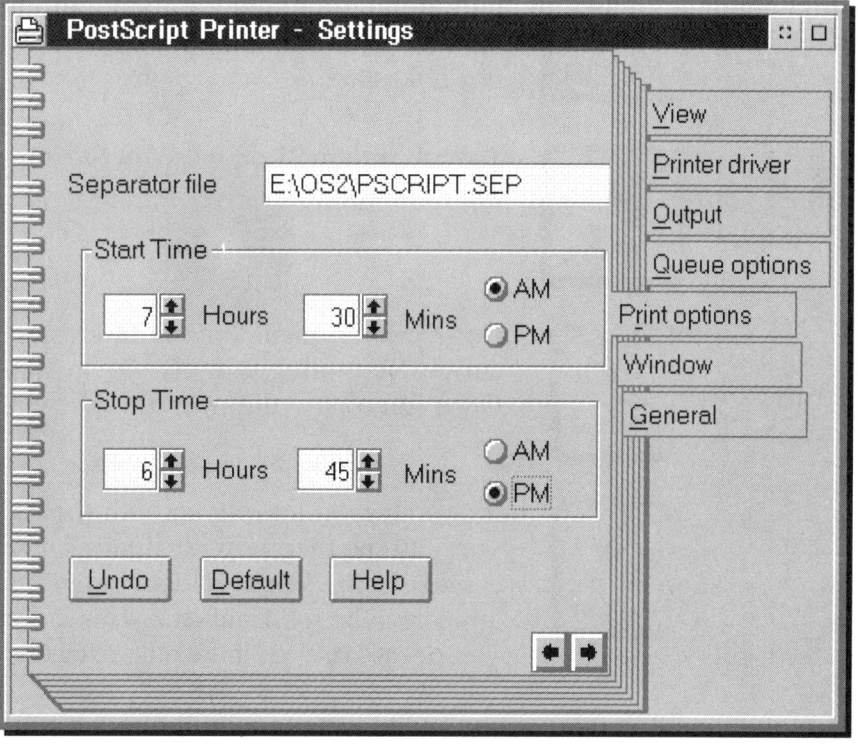

Figure 10.6. *The Print Options page allows you to specify a separator page.*

The Print Queue

When you open the printer object itself, you will see the jobs in the print queue. You can open the printer object in either Icon or Details View. From either view, you can view, delete, hold, or change the order of print jobs. In Icon View, the icon for each print job represents its status:

 The job spooling icon tells you the job is still being sent to the queue. Unless the print object is set to print while spooling, the print job will not begin printing until the entire job is received by the queue.

 The job waiting icon tells you the job has been sent to the queue, but it is waiting to be printed, either because another job is currently printing, or the printer queue is in a hold state.

 The job printing icon tells you the job is currently being sent to the printer.

 If the printer queue detects an error, the icon of the job currently printing will change to the print error icon. Once you correct the error, this job will resume printing.

 If you click on a print job with the right mouse button, you will see that individual jobs can be held from their context menu. If you hold an individual job, its icon will appear as the Job Held icon. This job will not print until you release it, even if the queue itself is released.

If you open the Details View of a print object, you will see a window similar to that shown in Figure 10.7.

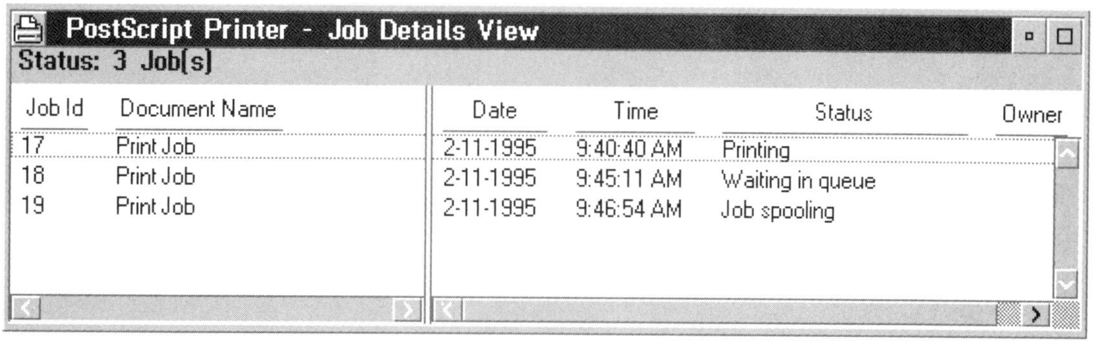

10 *Advanced Warping*

```
PostScript Printer - Job Details View
Status: 3 Job(s)

Job Id  Document Name       Date        Time        Status            Owner
17      Print Job           2-11-1995   9:40:40 AM  Printing
18      Print Job           2-11-1995   9:45:11 AM  Waiting in queue
19      Print Job           2-11-1995   9:46:54 AM  Job spooling
```

Figure 10.7. *The Details View of the printer object displays print job status textually.*

You can delete, view, or re-arrange individual print jobs. To view a job, simply open it. To delete a job, select delete from the job's context menu. To change the order in which the jobs in the queue print, select *Print next* from the print job's context menu.

Chapter

11

Warping with REXX

Very few people who use an operating system such as OS/2 consider themselves "computer programmers," but everyone who uses a computer could probably benefit from a little programming talent. Your goal is to make the computer work for you, and that goal is accomplished by "programming" the computer to perform the tasks you need to accomplish.

Most of the tasks we ask the computer to perform are already programmed for us, in the form of application software. Packages such as a word processor, a spreadsheet calculator, or a database manager are applications that you can use under OS/2 to get a job done. OS/2 also has built-in functions that can help complete a job—functions that can format disks; backup data; and copy, print, and delete files to mention a few. You can use these built-in functions through direct manipulation (such as dragging a data object to the shredder to delete it), or through the command line interface (such as typing DEL C:\DATA.OLD to delete the file). As your use of OS/2 Warp increases, you may find yourself spending more time at the command prompt doing maintenance chores. This is when you'll want to have a computer programmer on call to simplify your job. With a little guidance, *you* can become that programmer!

A Simple Programming Exercise

To illustrate how you can program your computer, we'll spend some time at the OS/2 *command prompt*. Remember, the OS/2 command prompt is similar to the DOS command prompt, but it does have some useful enhancements. We'll want to make use of those enhancements, so make sure you are at an OS/2 prompt when you try these exercises.

Let us assume you often find yourself formatting a floppy disk, copying files from your hard drive to the floppy, and then erasing the files from your hard drive. From the OS/2 command prompt, you would type something like:

```
FORMAT A:              (to format the floppy diskette)
COPY C:\FILES\*.* A:\  (to copy the files to the floppy)
DEL C:\FILES\*.*       (to erase the original files)
```

Typing in these statements once wouldn't be too much of a chore, but if you do the same task every day, it would be nice to have the procedure automated. Besides, it takes time to format the floppy, and you're using OS/2—a multi-tasking operating system. You could be off doing other things while the floppy is being formatted, without having to return to the command prompt to issue the COPY command. The simplest form of programming is to tell the computer all the tasks you want it to perform, in the order you want them performed, from a single command prompt. For example, on the command line you could type:

```
FORMAT A: & COPY C:\FILES\*.* A:\ & DEL C:\FILES\*.*
```

The "&" character (the *and* command) tells OS/2 to perform each command in order. If you translate that command to English, it would read, "format a floppy AND copy files to the floppy AND delete the original files after they've been copied." If you type this *compound command*, you can work on other tasks while the commands are being processed. If you try this command, you may spot a problem or two. If so, consider yourself a true computer programmer! Spotting and fixing "bugs" in your program will be your biggest challenge.

Debugging Our Simple Program

The first problem is fairly easy to solve. The FORMAT command requires input from the keyboard. It asks if the correct floppy is in the drive, and after formatting, it asks for a volume label. It also asks if you want to format another floppy. If we want to start our "program" and then go do something else, it doesn't help to have the program stopping in the middle to ask us questions. If you look at the options on the FORMAT command, you can solve this problem. For example, consider the following:

```
FORMAT A: /ONCE /V:"My Files"
```

By using these options, the FORMAT program won't stop and ask questions. The /ONCE option tells FORMAT that we only want to format one floppy, so it won't ask us if we want to format another. This option also bypasses the prompt to insert a diskette. This could be dangerous, but we'll worry about that later (another bad habit of computer programmers). The /V:"My Files" option tells FORMAT the volume label we want on the floppy, so it won't stop to ask us. We now have a FORMAT command suitable for our programming exercise.

The second problem may not be as easy to spot. What would happen if the files couldn't be copied to the floppy? If the floppy doesn't have enough free space to hold all the files in C:\FILES, OS/2 may blindly obey your command and erase the originals, even if it didn't finish copying them to the floppy. In our example, OS/2 will automatically ask "Are you sure?" before deleting the files, but we want more protection than that. If you were typing individual commands from the command line, you would see that the COPY failed, and could decide what to do before deleting the originals. What we need in our program is a way to say: "Format the floppy *and* copy the files to the floppy *and if that was successful*, delete the original files." Fortunately, OS/2 has just such a command: &&. Our program would look like this:

```
FORMAT A: /ONCE /V:"My Files" & COPY C:\FILES A:\ && DEL
C:\FILES\*.*
```

The "&&" command tells OS/2 to continue only if the previous command was successful. This can be a very useful programming tool. To see the difference between "&" and "&&" type the following:

```
DIR ZZZ & ECHO Hi There!
```

You should see the DIR (which should fail, because there is no file named ZZZ in the current directory), and then you'll see "Hi There!" The ECHO command simply displays on the screen whatever you type after it. Now try:

DIR ZZZ && ECHO Hi There!

This time, you see the results of DIR, but the "Hi There!" is not displayed. The "&&" tells OS/2 to perform the ECHO command only if the DIR command was successful. In our "format/copy/delete" program, using "&&" will prevent the DELETE if the copy was unsuccessful. OS/2 also provides other ways you can test for the success or failure of a command.

Using Return Codes

OS/2 commands typically report their success or failure through a *return code*. A return code of zero (0) means everything completed normally, and a non-zero return code (anything but zero) means there was a problem. You can see return codes by setting up a "programmer's prompt" using the PROMPT command. On an OS/2 command line, type:

PROMPT RC=$R [$P]

This will change your command prompt from something like [C:\] to something like RC=0 [C:\]. The return code from the last command will always be displayed in your command prompt. To see it in action, type the following DIR command:

RC=0 [C:\]DIR ZZZ

Unless you have a file named "ZZZ" on your drive, you should see something like this:

11

Warping with REXX

```
The volume label in drive C is OS2.
The Volume Serial Number is E20B:6414
Directory of C:\

SYS0002: The system cannot find the file specified.

RC=18 [C:\]
```

Notice that the return code is 18, as reported in the command prompt following the results of the DIR command (RC=18). Since it is non-zero, the last command (DIR) was not successful. The number 18 is what DIR returns to say "file not found." The actual number is usually not important; it's enough to know that the last command failed.

Using the FOR Command

Another interesting programming technique is the FOR command. This command is available in DOS and OS/2 command prompts, and is perhaps one of the best-kept secrets of the command prompt. Many of the tasks we do from the command line involve handling a group of files. When you type DIR *.DAT, you tell OS/2 to find any file with a .DAT extension and display the file name. For example:

```
ABC.DAT
NEW.DAT
OLD.DAT
XYZ.DAT
```

However, some programs don't work with more than one file at a time. For example, if you wanted to remove the extended attributes from all files with a .DAT extension, the following command would not work:

```
EAUTIL *.DAT /S
```

473

You must specify one file at a time. A quick "program" can do the work for you. The program would be:

```
FOR %a IN (*.DAT) DO EAUTIL %a /S
```

This may look confusing, but spend a minute with it. In English, the command would be "For every file with a .DAT extension you find, run the command EAUTIL /S." Let's look at each part of this "program."

The middle of the statement is where the actual "program" lives, so we'll start there. The statement, IN (*.DAT) tells OS/2 to build a list of files that end in .DAT to process, one at a time. If you specify wildcard characters (* and ?) in your list, OS/2 will create a list of files that match. You can also explicitly specify items in the list. For example, (*.DAT 1 2 3) will create a list containing any files that end in .DAT as well as the numbers 1, 2, and 3.

The FOR %a portion of the statement defines a *variable*. When OS/2 sees the variable %a in the last part of this program, it will change it to each name in the list. The letter after the percent sign is not important, as long as it matches the letter used in the variable in the *template*.

The last portion of the program is the template. Anything after the DO is the template. For each item in the list, OS/2 builds a command from the template (substituting an item in the list for any variable in the template). The command is executed, and then the next item in the list is processed. So, if we try our example program, OS/2 would execute the commands:

```
EAUTIL ABC.DAT /S
EAUTIL NEW.DAT /S
EAUTIL OLD.DAT /S
EAUTIL XYZ.DAT /S
```

Remember, your list does not have to be built from filenames. For example, try the following command:

```
FOR %x IN (1 2 3) DO ECHO Line %x
```

11

Warping with REXX

Creating Command Files

Once you see how many powerful commands you can create, you'll want to save them so you don't have to re-type them every time. *Command files* are just what you'll need. Under DOS, these were called *batch files*, and were given a .BAT file name extension. DOS .BAT files will work under OS/2, but in order to tell the difference between a DOS .BAT file and an OS/2 command file (remember, OS/2 command prompts have features that DOS lacks), OS/2 uses a .CMD file name extension. If you are used to .BAT files, you can think of .CMD files the same way. The only difference is that a .CMD file will run in an OS/2 session, while .BAT files run in a DOS session.

Any command you can type from the command prompt can be used in a command file. The only noticeable exception is the FOR command. When typing the variables, you must use two percent characters instead of one (for example, %%z). This is because the percent character has special meaning in command files.

You can use any text editor to create command files (there are no less than five programs included in OS/2 Warp that can create a command file). Use an editor to create this sample command file, called MYTEST.CMD:

```
REM This is a comment line
C:
MD \TEST
CD \TEST
ECHO Hi There! > TEST.TXT
ECHO You said: %1 >> TEST.TXT
```

When you run this command file, it switches to Drive C:, makes a subdirectory called C:\TEST, then changes to the C:\TEST subdirectory. The next line may look familiar. ECHO Hi There! will display the message Hi There, but this statement does more. The > TEST.TXT portion of the statement tells OS/2 to put the message in a file, not on the screen. So, this line creates a file called TEST.TXT that contains the words "Hi There!". The last line is even better; the >>

TEST.TXT portion of the statement is similar to the previous line, but the >> specifies that the text should be added to the end of the file. (If we used a single >, the text would overwrite any data in the file.)

The other trick on this line is %1, which is a variable. When you run MYTEST, the variable will be replaced with the first word you type after typing MYTEST on the command line. For example, type the following (after creating the MYTEST command file):

MYTEST HELLO

The last line of the command file would put the text "You said: HELLO" into the file named TEST.TXT. You can use variables %1 through %9 on the command line (even more if you use the SHIFT instruction). The %0 variable will display the name of your command file itself.

When you run MYTEST.CMD from a command prompt, you will see it execute each instruction in sequence. Now that you've come this far, you may be ready to explore the advanced programming functions available to you. You may want to look for a book dedicated to batch-file programming, or you can use the on-line OS/2 Command Reference to learn about advanced features.

REXX Programming

Using a command file to automate commands at the command prompt is useful, but if you are familiar with computer programming, you will want quite a bit more power. Command files are very limited in areas such as looping, decision-making, and error-handling. DOS-based batch programming requires add-on utilities to provide these functions, but OS/2 provides these functions through a language called Procedures Language 2/REXX (widely referred to as REXX). When you use REXX, your command files can become powerful programs, without investing in a complete software development system. Everything you need to create REXX programs, including a GUI-based debugger, are included with OS/2 Warp.

11
Warping with REXX

Teaching REXX programming isn't something that can be covered in a single chapter. Others have filled entire books on the subject. If you look for a REXX book, you may find some that don't even mention OS/2. REXX is available on many operating systems,  from mainframes to PCs. Even PC-DOS version 7 includes REXX support. The OS/2 Information object contains an on-line REXX reference manual, so you could teach yourself with a little time and patience. Rather than attempting to teach you REXX, we'll give you enough of a taste here, and if your interest warrants, you can look into a REXX programming book to take you further.

Testing REXX Features

If you want to try REXX syntax, you may want to use the REXXTRY program. This program interprets REXX statements one at a time, so you can see the results. From an OS/2 command session, type REXXTRY and then try some REXX statements. This method can be helpful when you are first learning REXX, as you can read the REXX reference, type in a statement in REXXTRY, and see the results before you use it in a REXX program.

Testing Your REXX Programs

Once you have created some REXX programs, you may want to use PMREXX to test them. PMREXX allows you to step through a REXX program one statement at a time, and check the progress as you go. To run PMREXX, from an OS/2 command session, type: PMREXX /T (program name). The /T tells PMREXX to start in *trace* mode, which stops execution before each statement, so you can watch the program's progress.

REXX and Extended Attributes

REXX makes use of OS/2's extended attributes in a unique way. In order to improve performance, REXX programs are "tokenized," which means they are converted to a form that is easier for the computer to read (but nearly impossible for humans to read). The first time you run a REXX program, the tokenized version is stored as an extended attribute. When you run the program again, the tokenized version is used. This will make REXX programs run faster. If you modify a REXX program, the next time you run it REXX will re-tokenize and store the tokenized changes. You don't need to concern yourself with tokenized REXX, but just realize that REXX is working hard to make your programs run faster.

REXX Basics

A REXX program is a text file, just like a .CMD file. In fact, REXX programs share .CMD file extension. OS/2 identifies a REXX program by the two characters of the file. All REXX files must start with a comment, enclosed in the characters /* */. What's in the comment doesn't matter, as long as the characters /* are the first two in the file.

Although REXX has a completely different syntax than a batch command file, you can use statements from a command file in your REXX programs. To do so, just enclose the statement in quotes. For example, a line from a .CMD file can be put in a REXX file as follows:

```
/* Following is a batch command in a REXX program */
'ECHO Hi There!'
```

To do the same thing in native REXX, the command would look like:

```
/* Following is a REXX statement */
SAY 'Hi There!'
```

11

Warping with REXX

The SAY command in REXX allows you to display information on the screen. As you'd expect, it has many more functions than the ECHO command in batch files.

One great improvement where REXX differs over batch programs is in its handling of variables. In REXX, you can assign and manipulate variables in countless ways. For example, type the following REXX statements (use REXXTRY):

```
TEST=5
TRY=10
ANSWER=TEST * TRY
SAY "The answer is" ANSWER
```

The output of this program would be: The answer is 50.

Variables can store and manipulate numeric data as well as text. To assign text to a variable, enclose it in quotes—either single or double quotes (which allows you to use quotes in your text). For example:

```
TEST="What's up"
NAME='Doc?'
SAY TEST NAME
```

The output of this program would be: What's up Doc?

REXX also includes sophisticated looping and program control functions. This allows you to repeat a series of REXX instructions until a certain condition is met. For example:

```
DO 5
   SAY "Looping"
END
```

This displays the word "Looping" five times. More complex loops can be created with a DO WHILE or DO UNTIL loop, as in:

```
TEST=1
DO WHILE TEST < 5
   TEST = TEST + 1
END
```

```
DO UNTIL TEST = 1
   TEST = TEST - 1
END
```

The first loop adds 1 to TEST as long as TEST is less than 5, and the second loop subtracts 1 from TEST until TEST equals 1.

The IF/THEN/ELSE loop can be used to selectively repeat a series of REXX statements. For example:

```
TEST = RANDOM()
IF TEST < 500 THEN
   SAY 'Heads'
ELSE
   SAY 'Tails'
```

The first line of this program introduces a new concept: REXX functions. The RANDOM function is a built-in REXX function that returns a random number. You can write your own functions in either REXX or another language, or add function libraries written by others. In addition to the built-in functions, OS/2 Warp comes with the REXXUTIL function library. After using the RANDOM function (which will return a number between 0 and 999), the IF statement determines if the number is less than 500. If it is, the next line is executed, which displays the word "Heads." If TEST is 500 or greater, the line following ELSE is executed, which displays the word "Tails." You might find this program handy in settling disputes where a coin toss is useful.

Putting REXX to Work

This is just the beginning. The power of REXX can only be discovered by using it. In order to convince you of this power, we will provide you with a couple of sample REXX programs.

- Workplace Shell Open Command (WPSOPEN.CMD)
- Go Wild Command (GOWILD.CMD)

11

Warping with REXX

Workplace Shell Open Command

WPSOPEN demonstrates how REXX can interact with the Workplace Shell. If you create a program object for WPSOPEN.CMD, and put either ICON, TREE, DETAILS, or SETTINGS in the parameters field for the program object (also select *Start minimized* on the Session page of the object settings), you can drop any folder on it, and WPSOPEN will open the specified view of the folder. You might find drag-and-drop opening easier than using the open selection from the folder's context menu.

```
/* WPSOPEN.CMD - Opens Workplace Shell objects
   Copyright (C) 1995, Doug Azzarito - all rights reserved.

   This program opens Workplace Shell objects in the specified view.
   It's useful as a drag-n-drop object for opening folder objects
   in a non-default view.

      Syntax:   WPSOPEN (view) (filename)
                view is one of: ICON, TREE, DETAILS, SETTINGS or DEFAULT
                filename is the fully-qualified filename of the object
*/
   parse arg type filename
   Call RxFuncAdd "SysSetObjectData","RexxUtil","SysSetObjectData"

   type = TRANSLATE(type)
   if WORDPOS(type, "TREE ICON DETAILS SETTINGS") = 0 then type="DEFAULT"
   rc = SysSetObjectData(filename, "OPEN="||type)
```

Go Wild Command

GOWILD is a fancy version of the FOR...DO example provided earlier in this chapter. You can use GOWILD to execute a command on a group of files, but it will do so one file at a time. GOWILD also allows you to process files anywhere on your hard drive, to process files in random order, and to process them continuously.

Why would you want such a thing? Consider a slide-show program. You have a program that will display a graphic image as a "slide." You would like to find every graphic image on your hard drive, and display them one-by-one. When the last one is shown, you want to start all over again (a never-ending slide-show). For fun, you want them to show up in a different order each time. To do this, you might spend some time writing a batch file, or use the power of REXX and run GOWILD.CMD.

We won't explain all of the concepts used in GOWILD.CMD, but you can use the REXX command reference to learn about each REXX function being used. After a study of GOWILD, you will be able to understand some of the concepts of REXX, and will probably come up with improvements to this sample for your own use.

```
/*
 *   GOWILD.CMD - A REXX SAMPLE Program
 *   Copyright (C) 1995, Doug Azzarito
 *
 *   Syntax:  GOWILD "template" filespec [/S] [/L] [/R] [/D]
 *
 *   The "template" is any valid OS/2 command, enclosed in quotes.  Somewhere
 *   inside the template, the characters '%1' should appear.  GOWILD will
 *   replace '%1' with each file specified via the 'filespec'
 *
 *   filespec    Specifies the files to look for.  Wildcards are acceptable.
 *   /S          Will search subdirs for matches
 *   /L          Will continuously loop through the matches
 *   /R          Processes matches in random order on each loop
 *   /D          Displays debug messages on console, does not execute command.
 *
 */
address cmd                        /* Send commands to OS/2 command processor. */
signal on error                    /* When commands fail, call "error" routine. */
signal on syntax name error        /* let me know about syntax errors */

trace off                          /* Disable tracing */

/* Tell the user what we are */

SAY 'OS/2 WildCard Command Processor   -   Copyright (c) 1995, Doug Azzarito'

/* initialize variables */

PARSE VALUE 1 0 WITH TRUE FALSE .   /* TRUE=1, FALSE=0 */

FILESPEC=''                        /* The name of the file to process */
SUBDIR=FALSE                       /* search subdirs for files? */
LOOP=FALSE                         /* loop through the files forever? */
RANDOM=FALSE                       /* Process in random order? */
DEBUG=FALSE                        /* turn off debug mode */
NOERROR=0                          /* Exit code for NO ERROR */
NOTFOUND=2                         /* Exit code for NOT FOUND (same as CMD.EXE) */
BADCOMMAND=22                      /* Exit code for BAD CMD (same as CMD.EXE) */

/*
 * This section of code parses the command line.  The command line is
 * broken into three sections.  The template, the filespec, and the options.
```

11

Warping with REXX

```
 * The template is required, and must be enclosed in quotes.  To be flexible,
 * we'll allow either single (') or double (") quotes for the template.
 * The filespec is also required, and can contain * and ? wildcard characters.
 * The options are handled by the KEYWORD function - options can be specified
 * in any order.
 */

parse arg CMDLINE                 /* get the entire commandline */
CMDLINE=strip(CMDLINE)            /* remove leading/trailing blanks */
                                  /* now separate the template from the options */
parse var CMDLINE Delim +1 =1 (Delim)TEMPLATE(Delim) FILESPEC CMDOPTS
if DEBUG then say 'Template="''TEMPLATE'" Filespec="''FILESPEC'" Op-
    tions="''CMDOPTS'"'

/*
 * We now have TEMPLATE, FILESPEC and CMDOPTS.  For strict checking,
 * we could see if DELIM is a ' or ".  We'll leave that as an excersise
 * for the reader.
 */

if FILESPEC = '' then do
    call Help                             /* no filespec?  Show the help & exit*/
    exit BADCOMMAND
end
say '  Filespec='FILESPEC

if \(CMDOPTS = '') then call keyword CMDOPTS    /* Parse the options, if any */

/*
 * The subdirectory search is provided by SysFileTree, which is in
 * REXXUTIL.DLL.  The following statements load the DLL and initialize
 * the options used by SysFileTree.  Then we let SysFileTree find our files.
 */

/* Load the Utility DLL */
call RxFuncAdd 'SysFileTree','RexxUtil', 'SysFileTree'

if SUBDIR then SEARCHOPTS = 'FSO'
else SEARCHOPTS = 'FO'

say '  Searching for files...'
call SysFileTree FILESPEC, 'FILELIST', SEARCHOPTS
if FILELIST.0 = 0 then do
    say 'No files found'
    Exit NOTFOUND
end
say '  'FILELIST.0 'files found.'

/*
 * Here's the main loop - we call the function WildWorker once for each
 * file found by SysFileTree.  If LOOP is true, we will keep going
 * forever (until the user presses CTRL-BREAK).  If RANDOM is true,
 * we'll jumble the list of files each time through the loop.
 */

do until \LOOP
```

```
      if RANDOM then call Jumble
      do i=1 to FILELIST.0
         if DEBUG then say 'Processing 'FILELIST.i
         FILE=FILELIST.i
            call WildWorker
      end
end                         /* end until \LOOP */

exit NOERROR                /* normal end of program */


/*
 *   WildWorker:
 *
 *      This function builds the OS/2 command line and executes the command.
 *
 *   INPUT: FILE      The complete filename to use in the command
 *          TEMPLATE  The command template to use
 *   OUTPUT: NONE     The command is executed
 *
 *   To build the command, we place the template in a temp variable (TmpCmd).
 *   If there is a '%1' in TmpCmd, we break the string into what is BEFORE
 *   the token, and what is AFTER the token.  We append what is BEFORE
 *   the token, plus the current FILE name to a built command, and then
 *   repeat the process on what was left AFTER the token until there is
 *   nothing left.
 */
WildWorker:
   BuildCmd = ''
   TmpCmd = template
   do while TmpCmd <> ""
      if POS('%1',TmpCmd)>0 then do
         parse var TmpCmd NextPiece'%1'TmpCmd
         BuildCmd = BuildCmd||NextPiece||FILE
      end
      else do
         BuildCmd = BuildCmd||TmpCmd
         TmpCmd=''
      end
      if DEBUG then say "CMD SO FAR="BuildCmd"      STILL TO PROCESS="TmpCmd
   end

   if DEBUG then say 'Command to execute: 'BuildCmd
   else BuildCmd
return

/*
 *   KeyWord:
 *
 *      Parses the command line, looking for keywords.  When found, the
 *      value for each keyword is set.  Any unrecognized words on the
 *      command line will be flagged as an error, but processing continues.
 *
 *   INPUT: Command line
 *   OUTPUT: Any recognized keywords will be set
```

11

Warping with REXX

```
 *
 */

keyword:
   arg param
   do until param = ''
/*
 * All of the options are in the form, /X, where X is the key value.
 */
      parse var param junk'/'key param
      if DEBUG then say 'Parsing key=/'key
      if \(junk='') then say '  extra characters "'junk'" ignored.'
/*
 * we use a SELECT clause to handle each keyword.
 */
      select
         when key = 'S' then do
            SUBDIR=TRUE
            say '  Subdirectory search enabled'
         end
         when key = 'L' then do
            LOOP=TRUE
            say '  Continuous loop enabled'
         end
         when key = 'R' then do
            RANDOM=TRUE
            say '  Random order enabled'
         end
         when key = 'D' then do
            DEBUG=TRUE
            say '  DEBUG mode enabled'
         end
         otherwise say "  Unrecognized option: /"key
      end
   end
return

/*
 *   Jumble:
 *
 *      Randomly sorts the elements of the FILELIST array.
 *
 *    INPUT: None - we're using FILELIST - Element 0 must be the count
 *           of items in the array (not counting element 0 itself)
 *   OUTPUT: None - the elements are sorted.
 *
 * To randomly sort the array, we first copy the array to the "orig"
 * array.  Then we pick a random number (x).  Element X in the original
 * array becomes element 1 in the sorted array.  We close up the empty
 * space in the original array, then repeat until we've filled in all
 * the slots in the sorted array.
 */
```

```
Jumble:
say '  Randomizing file order...'

   do i=0 to FILELIST.0                  /* Make a copy of the FILELIST array */
      orig.i=FILELIST.i
   end
   size=FILELIST.0
   do i=1 to FILELIST.0                  /* For every slot in FILELIST */
      pick=RANDOM(1,size)                /* generate a random number */
      FILELIST.i=orig.pick               /* and put that element into FILELIST*/
      if pick < orig.0 then orig.pick=orig.size   /* then fill in the hole */
      size=size-1                        /* and adjust the size of the array */
   end /* do */
return

/*
 *  Help:
 *
 *      Display command syntax help
 *
 *    INPUT: none
 *    OUTPUT: none
 *
 */
Help:
   say
   say 'This command file searches a drive for files matching a wildcard file'
   say 'specification, and then executes an OS/2 command for each match. Syntax:'
   say
   say '  GOWILD "command" filespec [options]'
   say
   say 'The "command" is the command to be executed (enclosed in quotes).'
   say 'Somewhere in the command, GOWILD expects to find "%1", and it will'
   say 'replace all occurances of "%1" with the name of each match to the'
   say 'filespec.  The filespec can contain path info and "*" and "?" wildcards.'
   say
   say 'The following options may be specified after the filespec:'
   say '  /S   search subdirectories for matching files'
   say '  /L   Process matched files in a continuous loop.'
   say '  /R   Process files in random order.'
   say '  /D   Debug mode - displays debug info, does not execute command.'
return
/*
 *  Error:
 *
 *      Trap handler for external errors.  Cleans up and exits
 *
 *    INPUT: Return code from failing operation
 *    OUTPUT: error return code
 *
 */

error:
   ErrRC = rc
```

11

Warping with REXX

```
    say errortext(ErrRC) '('ErrRC') at line' sigl ', sourceline:' sourceline(sigl)
    exit ErrRC                  /* exit, tell caller things went poorly */
/*
 * END OF PROGRAM
 */
```

Chapter

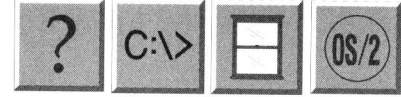

12 *When Things Go Wrong*

OS/2 Warp is a large, complex system. That means there's lots of places where things can go wrong. Fortunately, there are lots of procedures you can use to find and fix problems. Unfortunately, using these procedures can be a complex, confusing proposition. Fortunately, we'll describe them in this chapter so you'll know what to do when OS/2 Warp needs your help.

 Read through this chapter *before* problems arise. Many problems can be avoided by using preventative maintenance measures.

Let's start with the first thing that can go wrong while using or installing OS/2 Warp: The system hangs before it even gets up and running. This problem may seem insurmountable, but if you stay calm, you may be able to get through the problem without a call to the technical support hotline.

When OS/2 Warp hangs during installation, or early during the boot process, the first step in repairing the problem is to identify the part of OS/2 Warp that is hanging. Remember, OS/2 Warp is a multitasking operating system. There's always dozens of things going on at the same time, and during the boot process just one device driver can halt everything. So, how do you find the problem? It's time for a "magic keystroke."

The Magic Keystrokes

When you start OS/2 Warp, whether from the installation disks or from the hard drive, the first thing you should notice is the message, "■ OS/2" in the top-left corner of the screen. This message has two purposes: to let you know OS/2 Warp is on the boot disk, and to tell you it's ready for a "magic key press." These special key sequences signal OS/2 Warp to activate special features during the boot process. The two "magic keystrokes" available while the OS/2 message is displayed are **Alt+F1** and **Alt+F2**. If you don't see the "■ OS/2" message, something very fundamental is wrong. If you see a message similar to "OS/2 !! SYS1475," you probably have the wrong diskette in Drive A:. If you see a non-numeric message, it is probably coming from your computer's BIOS. Check your hardware, and double check the diskette in Drive A:. Once you see "■ OS/2," you're ready to try the "magic keystrokes. We'll discuss **Alt+F2** first.

Alt+F2: Device Driver Display

As soon as you see the OS/2 message in the top-left corner of the screen, press **Alt+F2**. This tells OS/2 Warp to display the name of each device driver as it installs. When OS/2 hangs during the boot process, knowing what device driver was loading at that time can usually help narrow the search for the problem. The OS/2 message only lasts for a second or two after you turn on your computer, so be ready for it. Once it disappears, the screen will display the OS/2 logo. This lets you know the OS/2 boot loader is running.

The boot loader's job is to load the OS/2 Kernel, the "heart" of OS/2. Once the kernel is loaded, the device drivers start to load. The kernel reads the CONFIG.SYS file (which must be in the root directory of the boot drive) for the list of device drivers that should be loaded. The first group is called "base" device drivers. They provide basic function for OS/2 Warp (disk, keyboard, printer). If you pressed **Alt+F2**, you'll see the name of each device driver at the bottom of the screen as it loads. Once all the base device drivers are loaded, the screen will clear and the other device drivers load. These device drivers provide higher-level function for OS/2 Warp (graphics, mouse, communications). If OS/2 Warp halts, the name of the last device loaded should be where you start to determine the problem. The connection between the device driver name and the device it controls may not be immediately obvious, but most of them aren't too hard to figure out. Here are some examples:

IBM1FLPY.ADD — floppy drive support

12
When Things Go Wrong

XDFLOPPY.FLT — support for XDF™ floppy disks
OS2DASD.DMD — the disk device manager
IBM1S506.ADD — the IDE/MFM/RLL disk device driver.
IBMINT13.I13 — the BIOS-compatible disk device driver
SBCD2.ADD — CD-ROM support for SoundBlaster™ cards
CHINCDS1.FLT — CD-ROM support for Chinon™ drives
PRINT01.SYS — Printer support for non-Microchannel computers.
PRINT02.SYS — Printer support for Microchannel computers.

What you do with this new-found information depends on the nature of the problem. Here are some scenarios that may point you to an answer:

- If the driver that causes the hang-up controls a device that has configuration switches and options, check with the owner's manual for that device and see if your settings are not the default. Most drivers can detect non-default settings, but sometimes the hardware cannot be queried, so you'll have to provide the information to the driver. For example, the SBCD2.ADD file needs to know the I/O port of the CD-ROM. The default is 220, but if you re-configured your card to 240, you can edit the CONFIG.SYS file and add /P:240 to the SBCD2.ADD device line.

- If the driver that causes the problem seems to be used for a device you don't have in your computer, try removing the driver from CONFIG.SYS. Device drivers have to "find" the devices they want to control. They do so by sending low-level messages to the devices, hoping for an answer. With all the possible combinations of devices and drivers, there are bound to be "deadly" combinations. A driver that you don't need is almost always harmless, but sometimes it can upset another device in your system. Besides, if you know exactly what drivers you need and remove all the others, OS/2 Warp will take less time to boot. Once OS/2 Warp installs, the CONFIG.SYS file should have only those drivers you actually need, but the installation disks must load all device drivers to weed out the unnecessary ones.

If those ideas don't help, and you can't come up with anything else to try (remember, you *can* experiment—it's hard to "break" software. Just make a backup copy of any file you modify), you'll have to surrender and call technical support. At least you'll be able to give them the information from the **Alt+F2** list of device drivers, which will give the support personnel a head start in finding an answer for you.

Alt+F1: The "Recovery Choices" Display

If you press **Alt+F1** when you see the OS/2 message, OS/2 Warp will display a screen similar to the following:

```
                            RECOVERY CHOICES
   Select the system configuration file to be used, or enter the option
   corresponding to the archive desired.

   ESC - Continue the boot process using \CONFIG.SYS without changes
   C   - Go to command line, (no files replaced, use original CONFIG.SYS)
   V   - Reset primary video display to VGA and reboot
   M   - Restart the system from the Maintenance Desktop (Selective Install)

   Choosing an archive from the list below replaces your current CONFIG.SYS,
   Desktop directory, and INI files with older versions.  These older versions
   might be different from your current files.  Your current files are saved in
   \OS2\ARCHIVES\CURRENT.

   1) Archive created 12-23-94   8:04:45PM
   2) Archive created 12-02-94   6:15:07PM
   3) Archive created 11-18-94   7:46:20PM
   X) Original archive from INSTALL created 10-03-94   1:07:14PM
```

Figure 12.1.   *The Recovery Choices screen is displayed when you press **Alt+F1** during bootup.*

The Recovery Choices screen is not of much use during the installation of OS/2 Warp, so there's no reason to press **Alt+F1** when you start OS/2 Warp from diskette. Once OS/2 Warp is on your hard drive, this screen has many uses, which we'll discuss now. If you ever get to this screen accidentally (by pressing **Alt+F1** instead of **Alt+F2**), you can press **ESC** to continue the boot process as normal.

Option C: Command Line

The first option on this menu is activated by pressing **C**. When you do this, OS/2 Warp starts a full-screen command prompt instead of the Workplace Shell. This has several uses. If something happens to your system that prevents the Workplace Shell from starting, you can start this text-mode prompt and either attempt to repair the system or restore files from backup. You may also find this option handy if you just need to start OS/2 Warp to copy a file or perform some other simple operation. It takes less time to start the text-mode session, so you can save some time if you don't need all of OS/2 Warp's graphical features.

The text-mode session is also convenient when you're doing backup and restore operations, or other maintenance tasks that don't require the Workplace Shell. Just because you select this option, don't think you can't use a graphical OS/2 application. If you start a graphical application from the full-screen session, OS/2 Warp will start enough services to allow the program to run. You won't have full access to the Workplace Shell, but if you want to run a single application, go ahead. When you are finished with that application, press **Ctrl+Alt+Del** to shut down and reboot. Don't just flip the power switch when you're done. **Ctrl+Alt+Del** will make sure the OS/2 disk cache shuts down before you cut the power. If you return to the full-screen session, you can type `EXIT` and OS/2 Warp will reboot.

Option V: Standard VGA

The next option is activated by pressing **V**. When you do this, OS/2 Warp will reset the video configuration to standard VGA. This option has several uses. When you install OS/2 Warp, it automatically detects the video hardware in your system, but you can override this selection. If you make a choice that results in a totally "garbled" video display, it would be difficult to reconfigure (since you can't see what you are doing). If this happens, use the *V* option to reset to standard VGA, and then you can use Selective Install to reconfigure your video.

Another time this option is useful is when you upgrade your video hardware. If you replace your video card or monitor, OS/2 Warp may need to be reconfigured. The easiest way to do this is to use the *V* option to reset the video to standard VGA, upgrade your hardware, and then use Selective Install to reconfigure OS/2 Warp.

Option M: The Maintenance Desktop

The next option is activated by pressing the **M** key. When you do this, OS/2 Warp will start using the "Maintenance" desktop. This desktop is the one that was used while OS/2 Warp was installing itself. You may not have noticed a desktop during install, but there was one behind the scenes. It doesn't have all the objects as the standard desktop, but it does have enough function to be useful. You can use the maintenance desktop if you would like to run a graphical program that manipulates the desktop or configuration files. The maintenance desktop allows you to run graphical programs, but it does not use the standard desktop files.

Option X: Original Desktop Archive

The next option is activated by pressing the **X** key. When you do this, OS/2 Warp will restore the desktop and configuration files (including CONFIG.SYS) to the way they were just after OS/2 Warp was installed. Your current configuration files are saved, but you'll have to manually restore them if you use the X option (we'll explain how later in this chapter). The main reason to use this function is if you do something to your configuration that makes you want to reinstall OS/2 Warp (dropping every desktop object on the shredder, for example). If you use this option, *all* changes to your desktop are erased, which means some programs that you have installed may lose configuration information.

Options 1, 2, and 3: Numbered Desktop Archives

The next set of options is the most important on this screen. OS/2 Warp will, if you select, make a backup of the desktop and configuration files each time you start OS/2 Warp. You can restore one of the previous three backups by its assigned number on this screen. The date and time of the backup is listed so you can choose the backup you want to restore. As with the X option, if you choose to restore one of these backups, your current desktop and configuration files are saved, but you will have to manually restore it if you want to go back to the current desktop. In order to use this function, you have to tell OS/2 Warp to back up your desktop. This is probably *the most important thing you can do* to keep your system running smoothly.

The OS/2 Warp desktop configuration files contain everything OS/2 Warp knows about the desktop—all the information in any object on the desktop: program settings, all your desktop folders, templates, shadows, and printer objects are all stored in these files. Other OS/2 applications you install may also store configuration information in these files. These files are constantly being updated as you use OS/2 Warp. Not only does the Workplace Shell access these files, but other OS/2 applications can be reading and writing them at the same time. One errant write can cause big problems. You wouldn't forget to back up your most critical data files, so don't forget these files either.

The only problem is the way OS/2 Warp saves these files. If you look at the settings notebook for the desktop, you'll see a page labeled "Archive." This page has an option that allows you to create an archive at each system reset. This isn't the best idea. For one thing, it takes time to save all these files (they can be several megabytes in size). This adds quite a bit of time to each system boot.

Another problem with creating an archive on each system reset is that you might reboot your system several times before you realize the system configuration files have a problem. Since only the last three backups are saved, you may lose the last good backup before you realize that you should restore your files.

Don't worry, it isn't hard to use this option properly. Every time you make significant changes to your desktop, and you are comfortable with these changes, open the desktop settings notebook, activate the "create archive at each system restart" option, then shut down and restart your system. This will make a backup of the system files. Once the system has restarted, turn the "create archive" option off. Set a periodic alarm in your IBM Works calendar to remind you to make a backup every week or so as well.

The OS/2 Desktop Archive

It might be helpful to understand how the archives work. In the desktop notebook, you can set the archive location. By default, this is

\OS2\ARCHIVES. In this subdirectory, you'll find the files ARCHIVES.$$$ and OS2.KEY. ARCHIVES.$$$ is a data file that records the date and time each backup was made, and where the backup is stored. It is not a text file, so it can't be edited with a text editor. The OS2.KEY file is a text file, and it lists all the files that should be saved when the desktop is archived. The only reason you'd need to edit this file is if you want some of your own files backed up along with the desktop archive.

Some OS/2 programs create their own .INI files instead of saving them in the OS2.INI file. If so, you can add this file to the OS2.KEY file. It is a read-only file, so before editing, either use the command: `ATTRIB -R OS2.KEY`, or use the Drives object to change the read-only attribute on the file. When you edit the file, add any lines to the *end* of the file. Do not add a line in the middle, as this may cause confusion with other backups. If you decide you want to save the file C:\DATA\VITAL.DAT, add a line that reads:

```
FILE:C:\DATA\VITAL.DAT
```

and save the file. Turn the read-only attribute back on, and you're ready to archive your desktop. Set the *Create archive* setting in the desktop notebook, shut down, and reboot. OS/2 Warp will save the desktop and all files listed in the `OS2.KEY` file. When it does this, it creates a subdirectory in the ARCHIVES directory. The name of this subdirectory matches the "backup number," either 01, 02, or 03. There is also a subdirectory named 0X, which is the configuration saved after OS/2 Warp installed. If you look in any of these subdirectories, you'll find a complete "Desktop" subdirectory; several files with names such as 0, 1, 2, and so forth; and a file named `KEYS.$$$`. The numbered files are the files that were specified in the `OS2.KEY` file. They don't maintain their original name because you might specify two files with the same name (but a different drive or directory) in the `OS2.KEY` file. The number corresponds to the line number in the `OS2.KEY` file. That's why it's important to add lines only at the end of the `OS2.KEY` file.

The `KEYS.$$$` file is a data file that records the full path and filename of all the numbered files in this archive. This is used if you ever restore the archive. See, even if you ignore our advice and add a file to the middle of the `OS2.KEY` file, then restore an archive that was created

12 — When Things Go Wrong

before this change, OS/2 Warp will be able to use the `KEYS.$$$` file to properly restore the archive.

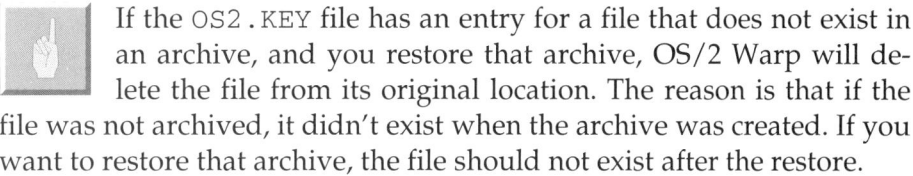

If the `OS2.KEY` file has an entry for a file that does not exist in an archive, and you restore that archive, OS/2 Warp will delete the file from its original location. The reason is that if the file was not archived, it didn't exist when the archive was created. If you want to restore that archive, the file should not exist after the restore.

Restoring Your Current Configuration

If you select one of the backup configurations, and then decide to return to the "current" configuration, OS/2 Warp does not offer this as an automatic choice. It's not hard to do—restart your system, and press **Alt+F1** to get to the "Recovery Choices" screen. Press **C** to start the OS/2 Full Screen session. If you type:

```
CD \OS2\ARCHICES\CURRENT
```

you'll find the configuration files OS/2 Warp saved when you switched to the archived desktop. There will be a Desktop subdirectory, and a subdirectory for each drive specified in the OS2.KEY file. The XCOPY command can put these files back in place. For example:

```
XCOPY DESKTOP C:\DESKTOP /S/E
XCOPY C$ C:\ /S/E
```

There are other things you can do from the "Recovery Choices" screen that aren't apparent from the information on the screen. You can create custom "CONFIG.SYS" files, and activate them from this screen. Why would you want a replacement CONFIG.SYS file? Let's say you have a laptop connected to a docking station. You access a hard drive, CD-ROM, Network, and sound card through the docking station. When you pull the laptop out of the docking station, none of these devices are available, so you want a "lean-and-mean" `CONFIG.SYS` that doesn't try to load all those device drivers. To do this, edit your `CONFIG.SYS` and remove all the unwanted device drivers. Save this file as `CONFIG.?`

The OS/2 Warp Survival Guide

(where ? is any letter of the alphabet except C, M, X, or V). When you activate the Recovery Choices screen, you can press the letter of the alphabet matching your `CONFIG.?`, and OS/2 Warp will start using your replacement for CONFIG.SYS (the original `CONFIG.SYS` file will not be touched). The next time you start your system, the original `CONFIG.SYS` will be used, unless you return to the Recovery Choices screen and press the proper key again.

If that's not fancy enough for your custom boot needs, you can create a `.CMD` file that performs whatever function you need (copying files, backing up configurations, testing for attached devices). Name this file `\OS2\BOOT\ALTF1?.CMD` (where ? is any letter of the alphabet except C, M, X, or V). Now, when you activate the Recovery Choices screen and press the letter matching your `ALTF1?.CMD` file, OS/2 Warp will start that command file *before* processing `CONFIG.SYS`. Your `.CMD` file can even copy over a new `CONFIG.SYS` file. If you have both an `ALTF1?.CMD` and a `CONFIG.?` file, the `.CMD` will run, and then the `CONFIG.?` file will be used instead of `CONFIG.SYS`.

If you want the Recovery Choices screen to appear each time you boot (without having to press **Alt+F1**), you can activate the *Display Recovery Choices at each restart* option, which is on the Archive page of the Desktop settings notebook. You can also specify how long the screen is displayed before OS/2 Warp will stop waiting for you to make a choice and boot normally.

If you like the display of device driver names at boot time, but don't want to bother pressing **Alt+F2** every time, there's a solution. As you have just read, OS/2 Warp allows you to activate **Alt+F1** on every boot, but in order to activate **Alt+F2** every time, you'll need to apply a "patch" to the OS/2 Kernel. Unofficial patches are *never* supported by IBM, so proceed with caution. Also, this patch will only work with the *original* kernel file, not beta or subsequent releases. To apply the patch, create a file named `ALTF2.PAT` containing the following lines:

```
FILE OS2KRNL.
VER BFFD 80FC697505
CHA BFFD 80FC699090
```

12 When Things Go Wrong

This file contains instructions to change the OS/2 Kernel file so it will think you've pressed **Alt+F2** every time. Once you've created the file, open an OS/2 command prompt and type:

```
ATTRIB -r -h -s OS2KRNL
COPY OS2KRNL OS2KRNL.SAV
PATCH ALTF2.PAT /A
```

The first command "unhides" the OS/2 Kernel so that the PATCH utility can find it. The second command saves the original kernel in case you want to reverse the effects of the patch. The third command applies the patch to the kernel. If you've done everything right, the next time you start OS/2 Warp (and every time after that) you'll see the device driver names without pressing **Alt+F2**.

If you see the message "The verification failed for OS2KRNL," either you made a mistake entering the lines in ALTF2.PAT, or you don't have the *original* Warp kernel. If you're a real computer pro, you can use the DEBUG command to search the kernel for the proper offset and apply the patch manually. Here's how. At an OS/2 or DOS prompt, type the following:

```
debug
n os2krnl
l ds:0
s ds:0 FFFF 80 FC 69 75 05
```

At this point, debug should display something like:

```
12A0:BFFF
```

Record the four characters to the right of the colon. To exit debug, type **Q**. Edit the ALTF2.PAT file to replace the two instances of BFFD with the characters you recorded. This new ALTF2.PAT file should allow the PATCH program to find and patch the OS2KRNL file.

Resolving Resource Conflicts

Anyone who has spent time with a personal computer has probably agonized over the task of adding a device to the system. There are drivers to install, configuration switches to set, and cables to connect. The toughest part of this job is usually resolving resource conflicts. It's common for the new device you want to install to require access to a hardware resource that is already being used by another device—and these devices don't like to be shared. OS/2 Warp is the first operating system for personal computers that gives the user a fighting chance in this battle, using something called the *resource manager*.

What Are Hardware Resources?

Your computer has a complex collection of circuits that allows you to add options to the system. The IRQ (Interrupt ReQuest) lines allow hardware devices to tell software they need attention. DMA (Direct Memory Access) channels allow memory to be transferred directly to and from devices. I/O (Input/Output) ports allow software to communicate with the hardware devices. When you add a new device to your system, it may need one or more types of resources, and you won't usually find any help when it comes to selecting which ones. Let's use an example:

You just purchased a new Media Vision Pro AudioSpectrum 16 sound card. After reading the manual, you learn you must assign the following resources:

DMA Channel: 0, 1, or 3 (8-bit) or 5, 6, or 7 (16-bit)
IRQ Channel: 3, 5, or 7 (8-bit) or 10, 11, 12, or 15 (16-bit)
I/O Port for SoundBlaster emulation: 210, 220, 230, 240, 250, or 260
DMA Channel for SoundBlaster emulation: 1
IRQ Channel for SoundBlaster emulation: 2, 3, 5, or 7
I/O Port for MPU-401 mode: 330
IRQ Channel for MPU-401 mode: 2

12

When Things Go Wrong

The only help you'll get from the manual is the recommendation for SoundBlaster I/O port (220). You'll have to choose the rest, making sure you don't choose anything that another device is already using. You probably have no idea what resources are already in use. What do you do? Before OS/2 Warp, you'd probably pick settings at random until things seemed to work, or you gave up and did without the new device. Now that you have OS/2 Warp, you can ask the operating system what to do.

OS/2 Warp includes a *resource manager*, which keeps track of all hardware resources and what devices are using them. Device drivers that know about the resource manager can ask for an unused resource, or ask to share a resource with another device. In any case, you can use the Resource Manager Utility to find out what resources are being used.

The Resource Manager Utility (RMVIEW)

In the Command Reference, you'll find the options for the RMVIEW utility. This utility let's you see what resources are currently being tracked by the Resource Manager. If you are trying to select an IRQ channel for your ProAudio Spectrum, go to the OS/2 command prompt and type: RMVIEW /IRQ and you might see something like:

```
RMVIEW: Physical view
   IRQ Level =  1   PCI Pin = NONE   Flg = EXCLUSIVE     KBD_0 Keyboard Controller
   IRQ Level =  4   PCI Pin = NONE   Flg = MULTIPLEXED   SIO - Serial Port(s)
   IRQ Level =  7   PCI Pin = NONE   Flg = SHARED        PARALLEL_0 Parallel Port
Adapter
   IRQ Level = 11   PCI Pin = NONE   Flg = SHARED        PCMCIA_0 Socket Controller
   IRQ Level = 12   PCI Pin = NONE   Flg = SHARED        AUX_0 PS/2 Auxiliary Device
Controller
```

Figure 12.2. *The RMVIEW utility displays hardware resource assignments.*

It looks like IRQ10 is available for the ProAudio Spectrum, IRQ5 is available for the SoundBlaster emulation, and IRQ2 is available for the MPU-401 mode. The commands RMVIEW /DMA and RMVIEW /IO will help you make the DMA and I/O port choices as well. When you installed OS/2 Warp, it might have found a resource conflict in your system that you never knew about. If your computer was running DOS, there was no protection against resource conflicts, so you would only find them when your system crashed. Hopefully, all your devices will have "Resource Manager-aware" device drivers, so they can make all these resource decisions for you, and change on-the-fly if you add a new device to your system.

Disk Failure: Not IF, but WHEN!

Your disk drive is an important piece of hardware in your system. Without it, your computer can't function. If you lose everything else, but your disk drive is intact, you can reconstruct your system without losing a bit of data. If you are shopping for a new disk drive, you'll see lots of facts and figures: size, speed, transfer rate, and something called MTBF, or "Mean Time Between Failures." This rating tells you how many hours the manufacturer expects the drive to run before it fails.

A good drive might be rated at 100,000 hours, MTBF, which means the drive is expected to operate for eleven years without stopping. However, this figure is an average, and it doesn't take into consideration the forces that threaten your data: power surges, lightning strikes, floods, computer viruses, the cup of coffee spilled on your computer, and theft. Any one of these can cause premature death to your system, and when the drive dies, your data will go with it. With all of these enemies, you *must* have a disaster recovery plan. Have we scared you enough? If not, consider this next fact: The maintenance tools that come with OS/2 Warp do *nothing* to protect your data. True, there is a BACKUP/RESTORE utility, but it isn't adequate for today's disk capacities. The CHKDSK utility is designed to repair OS/2's own file structures, not your data. It's simple: *If you don't buy, test, and use a data backup utility, you will suffer data loss!*

Hopefully, our scare tactics prompted you to put this book down, visit your local computer store, buy a tape backup device with an OS/2 backup program, and do a complete system backup—which will take some time, so you can read on while your system backup is in progress.

12

When Things Go Wrong

If you aren't making backups yet, read on, as we discuss other causes and possible remedies for disk failure. OS/2 Warp uses very sophisticated tactics to improve disk performance. Data is read and written through a software cache, so there is sometimes a delay between the time an application requests that data be written to disk and the time the data actually is written. If the cache is not shut down properly, disk writes can be lost, which could mean scrambled data. When you use the Shutdown option or press **Ctrl+Alt+Del**, the cache will have time to clear any pending I/O commands, but if you flip the power switch, data loss is possible. Another way you can lose data is when software causes corruption. The corruption could be accidental (a bug in the software) or intentional (a computer virus). OS/2 Warp does not provide complete data protection, so any program on your computer can read and write any data on your disk. Programs can also access the disk directly, which can put the disk structure itself in jeopardy. Often, OS/2 Warp can't even tell when your data has been corrupted. Hopefully, your application can. What OS/2 Warp *can* do is tell when its own data has been corrupted. The main remedy is the CHKDSK utility.

CHKDSK: What and Why?

CHKDSK is a utility that checks, and attempts to repair, the file system structures on your disk. When you format a disk drive, the FORMAT utility creates these structures. If these structures are corrupted, you may lose access to your files. Any time an OS/2 Warp system loses power unexpectedly, CHKDSK is used on the next system restart to make sure these structures weren't damaged.

You can also run CHKDSK at other times to make sure things are running properly. Remember, CHKDSK is making sure the disk structure is intact, not your data (however, the only way you're going to get to your data is if the disk structure stays intact). Fortunately, a corruption that would cause data loss doesn't happen often (unless you frequently flip the power switch off while OS/2 Warp is running). If it does, and you have a recent backup, there's nothing to worry about. If you don't have a backup, you'll want to proceed with caution.

Once CHKDSK runs, if any of your important data seems to be missing or corrupted, *stop using your system immediately!* There are several disk utilities that can recover lost data from a disk drive, and the less you do after the corruption, the better the chance of a complete recovery. It would also be a good idea for you to practice using a disk recovery tool, or find someone else who has *before* you need these skills. That knowledge could make the difference, but the fact remains: When your disk fails, the best medicine is preventative medicine. A good backup plan will save you from any problem.

Errors, Traps, and IPEs

When something goes wrong with a program running under Warp, you'll probably encounter either an error, a Trap, or an IPE. Knowing the difference between these results will make it much easier for you to decide how to diagnose and correct the problem so you can get back to work.

Errors

This is the least-dangerous class of OS/2 error messages. You will get an error message if you type an incorrect command, or try to access a device that isn't ready. If you have been using DOS for a while, you are probably used to cryptic error messages whenever you do something wrong. OS/2 Warp is also full of error messages, but they're not quite as cryptic. How the error message appears depends on where you are when you cause the error, and the nature of the error itself. For example, if you type XYZZY from DOS (expecting to run the program named XYZZY, which doesn't exist), you would see the message:

```
Bad command or filename
```

12

When Things Go Wrong

If you do the same from an OS/2 command session, you'll see the message:

```
SYS1041: The name specified is not recognized as an
internal or external command, operable program or batch file.
```

Other than the wordiness of the OS/2 message, there are differences. First, you should notice the OS/2 error message number. In this case, it's SYS1041. This can help you further diagnose the problem (although in this case, you probably don't need any further help). From an OS/2 command session, type: HELP 1041 to get more information about the specific error. In this case, you'll see:

```
SYS1041: The name specified is not recognized as an
internal or external command, operable program or batch file.

EXPLANATION: The name specified should be one of the following:
o   The name of a batch file whose file extension is .CMD.
o   The name of an executable program whose file extension
    is .EXE or .COM.
o   The name of an OS/2 external command.
o   The name of an OS/2 internal command.

For the first 3 cases (if a path for the command was not specified at
the command prompt), the file must reside in the current directory or
in one of the directories specified by the PATH environment variable.

ACTION: Retry the command using a correct name or path.
```

Figure 12.3. *OS/2 Warp's errors are numbered to help identify the exact error condition.*

For most errors, you will see the error message, an explanation, and a suggested action. Remember HELP when you get an error message you can't figure out.

Sometimes, OS/2 Warp will display the error message in a "pop-up" box, along with radio buttons that allow you to select an action. For example, if you type: DIR A: from an OS/2 command session, but there is no diskette in Drive A:, you'll see a pop-up message similar to the following:

The OS/2 Warp Survival Guide

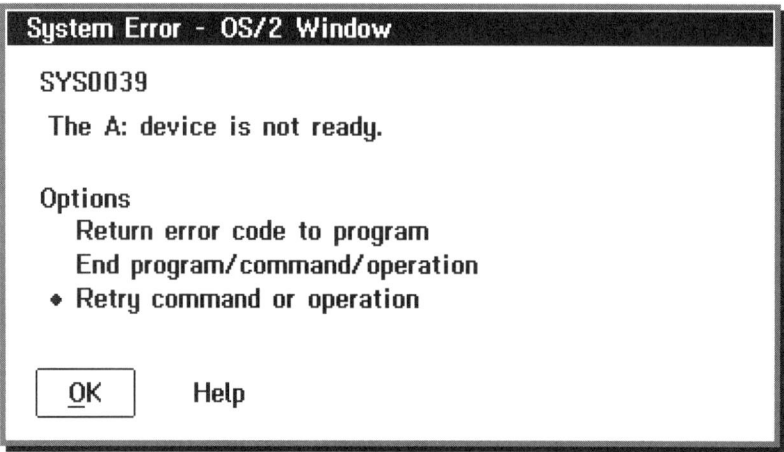

Figure 12.4.   *System Errors are presented in dialog boxes with radio button options and a Help button.*

You can select one of the actions and press *OK* to dismiss the dialog box. As long as the dialog box is displayed, you cannot switch to any other program. You must select an action first. Notice, the error popup also includes an error number, so you can use HELP to get more information. In this case, HELP 39 would display:

```
SYS0039: The *** device is not ready.

EXPLANATION: One of the following has occurred:
1. The device is not ready or is empty.
2. The device driver for COMn is not installed or COMn was
   shut down and further use of it is disabled.

ACTION: Do one of the following and retry the command:
1. Insert a diskette in the drive and close the drive door or
   wait until the drive is available.
2. a. Check the CONFIG.SYS file for the DEVICE=COM.SYS statement.
   b. Shut down the system.  During restart, note and refer to
      any messages regarding COMn.
   c. Issue MODE COMn from a command prompt to see if COMn exists.
3. Be sure there is hardware for COMn.
```

Figure 12.5.   *The Help for an error condition is context sensitive. Help provides an explanation and recommended actions.*

12
When Things Go Wrong

OS/2 Warp takes error recovery seriously; you won't find this type of help for error conditions on many operating systems, not even on "big iron" mainframes.

Traps

A *trap* message is more serious than the error messages we just discussed. Traps are provided by the computer hardware to allow operating systems to detect and correct errors. Normally, a trap is a sign of a "bug" in the software. If you weren't the person who wrote the software, you may not be able to do anything about the trap (other than report it to the author), but sometimes traps can be caused by configuration problems, faulty hardware, or even a bad interaction between two programs.

The Intel 80386 architecture defines the following standard traps. This list may not mean anything to you, but if you see one of these specific trap messages, the explanation in this list may give you just enough information to solve the problem (or know when to give up and call for help). The OS/2 HELP system will also give you information on traps. Add 1930 to the trap number to get the HELP number. For example, type HELP 1932 at the OS/2 command prompt to get a description of trap 02.

TRAP No.	Explanation
TRAP 00	Divide by Zero. Usually a software bug that causes an illegal mathematical operation.
TRAP 01	Single Step. The processor is capable of executing one instruction at a time, for debugging purposes. You should never encounter this trap.

TRAP No.	Explanation
TRAP 02	NMI (Non-Maskable Interrupt). This is usually caused by bad RAM, which triggers a PARITY error (parity is a simple method of detecting RAM corruption). Devices that access hardware directly can also cause a TRAP 02, but not as often as bad RAM. Just because your computer has run without complaint under DOS, don't assume OS/2 Warp should have no problems. DOS makes little use of the RAM above 1 Megabyte, while OS/2 makes full use of every byte.
TRAP 03	BreakPoint. A Breakpoint is a debugging instruction in the program that stops the computer so that the programmer can see exactly what is going on. Only the "debugging" version of OS/2 allows breakpoints. The standard OS/2 Kernel considers this an error, and will terminate any application that executes a breakpoint. If you see a TRAP 03, it usually means the programmer has left in "debugging" code, either by accident, or because he or she never expected that code to execute.
TRAP 04	Overflow check. Used to determine if a results of a mathematical operation on signed numbers is too large to be represented.
TRAP 05	Bounds Check. The processor BOUND command checks to be sure an index is within a specified range, and will generate a TRAP 05 if not.
TRAP 06	Illegal Instruction. This error will sometimes occur with DOS or Windows programs that try to execute protected mode instructions that OS/2 does not allow (because it would jeopardize system integrity).
TRAP 07	Device not Available. This trap is used for floating-point instructions on systems without a Floating Point Unit.

When Things Go Wrong

TRAP No.	Explanation
TRAP 08	Double Fault. This occurs when a trap is generated by a trap handler. It is usually caused by a program that consumes all the "stack" space (an area of RAM used to store temporary data). If the program traps because it overruns the stack area, OS/2's trap handler will take over, but it requires a small amount of stack space itself, so the result is a "double" fault.
TRAP 09	Reserved.
TRAP 0A	Invalid TSS. This is caused by a task switch to a segment with an invalid Task State Segment.
TRAP 0B	Segment not Present. This is the 16-bit version of TRAP 0E.
TRAP 0C	Stack Exception. This is caused by either putting too much information on the stack, or taking too much information off the stack.
TRAP 0D	General Protection. This is the most common trap a user will see. A program tried to access memory that was beyond its boundaries. Under DOS, this program would continue without an error message, but it would probably be corrupting memory. Under OS/2, these problems are caught before the corruption can take place.
TRAP 0E	Page Fault. An attempt was made to access a page of virtual memory that was not in RAM. This trap occurs constantly with OS/2, but the OS/2 page manager intercepts this trap, and retrieves the page from the SWAPPER.DAT file and loads it into RAM. The TRAP E is the basis for OS/2's virtual memory support, and the only time a TRAP 0E message appears is when the pager can't complete its task.
TRAP 0F	Reserved.
TRAP 10	Floating Point Error. This trap occurs when an error is detected in a floating-point instruction.

The OS/2 Warp Survival Guide

TRAP No.	Explanation
TRAP 11	Alignment Check. This error occurs when data is not properly aligned in RAM. Some instructions require that an operand be stored in an address that is evenly divisible by 2 or 4.
TRAP 12	Machine Check. Not used.

When traps are detected in an application, OS/2 Warp issues an error message in a dialog box. A trap dialog box looks something like the following:

Figure 12.6. Traps are more serious than system errors. You have fewer options in the Trap Dialog Box.

The trap dialog box contains an error message (including an error number), and an options menu. If you would like more information, you can click on the *Help* button, or use the error message number with the HELP command. If you select *Display register information*, you will see a screen similar to the following:

12

When Things Go Wrong

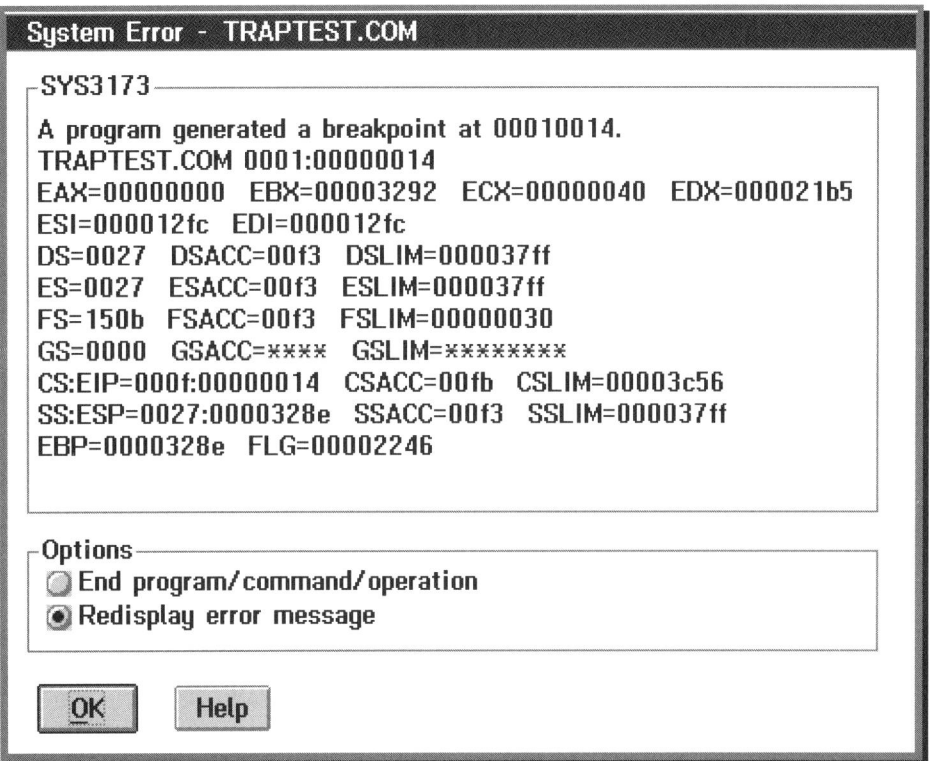

Figure 12.7. For Trap conditions, you can display the contents of the microprocessor's registers. This information can help support personnel diagnose the problem.

This information is useful only to the author of the program that caused the trap, but if you are going to contact a technical support representative about a problem, make sure you have the information from this screen before you call. This will probably be the first thing the representative will ask you.

When you select *End program/command/operation*, the program that caused the trap will be terminated. OS/2 Warp makes sure other running applications are protected from the offending application, so they should continue to run without a problem.

Internal Processing Errors (IPEs)

Hopefully, you will never need the information in this section. An IPE is the most serious error message displayed by OS/2. Basically, an IPE is a trap that was generated by a "trusted" component of the operating system. Some parts of OS/2 run in a privileged state, exempt from the protection mechanisms that keep OS/2 programs safe from one another. If a trusted OS/2 component traps, there is no guarantee that another application's data was corrupted before the trap. The trap could be caused by a violation detected by the hardware, or a "software initiated" IPE. There are fatal error routines in OS/2 that periodically check the status of certain data structures. If a problem is detected, OS/2 will generate the IPE itself. In either case, OS/2 Warp will immediately halt, and display a message similar to the following:

```
TRAP 0003        ERRCD=0000  ERRACC=****  ERLIM=********
EAX=29340009  EBX=fc854001  ECX=00000060  EDX=fff202f9
ESI=fc8504e6  EDI=ffffffff  EBP=00005254  FLG=00002017
CS:EIP=07d0:00000714  CSACC=009b  CSLIM=00002933
SS:ESP=0030:00005254  SSACC=1097  SSLIM=00004633
DS:07c8  DSACC=0093  DSLIM=0000c97f  CR0=8001001b
ES:07c8  ESACC=0093  ESLIM=0000c97f  CR2=fc8c1000
FS=0000  FSACC=****  FSLIM=********
GS=0000  GSACC=****  GSLIM=********

The system detected an internal processing error at
location ##0160:fff5c34c - 000d:a34c.
6000, 9084

048600b4
Internal revision 8.162, 94/09/19

The system is stopped.  Record all of the above information and
contact your service representative.
```

Figure 12.8.   OS/2 handles IPEs by displaying the contents of the registers and halting the system to protect any further data corruption.

This screen is meant to help OS/2 support personnel diagnose the reason for the IPE. With some guidance, you can decipher some of the information on the screen, but only the overly curious user will find anything interesting. Notice the TRAP 0003 at the top of the screen. That corresponds to the trap numbers discussed in the previous section. If this IPE was initiated by software, a message describing the nature of the failure may appear here. The next section gives details about the state of the computer at the time of the IPE. Just below this is the IPE message, and location. The location (in this case, `##160:fff5c34c`) is not always the most important information on this screen. Often, it just reports the location of OS/2's internal trap handler. Below this you'll see two numbers, separated by a comma. If this is a software-initiated IPE, this is the file and line number where the trap occurred, so with just these two numbers, an OS/2 support representative can look right at the instruction that generated the error. In the case of a hardware-detected trap, it is the location of the trap handler. Next is a number that describes your computer's CPU (in this case, an 80486, level B4), and the date and internal version number of the OS/2 Kernel. Finally, there's a message that reminds you to record this information, and call your service representative. The only way to record the information is to write it down. The system is halted (stopped), so you can't write it to disk or printer.

Once you've recorded any information from this screen, you can press **Ctrl**+**Alt**+**Del** to restart OS/2 Warp. Some IPEs are very intermittent, so OS/2 Warp may restart and run without another problem, but if you have an IPE that you can repeat, your best remedy is to contact OS/2 support personnel. Often they will already have a fix (if the same problem was reported by another user), so you'll be up and running in no time. Other times, the problem will require in-depth debugging by the highly-skilled OS/2 support technicians. With your help, they'll find and fix the problem, but you should remember that software development is still more of an art than a science.

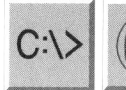

Appendix

OS/2 Warp File Listing

T his appendix lists the files that are typically installed to your hard drive by OS/2 Warp. Only the base OS/2 files are listed; BonusPak files are not included. The files installed on your system may be slightly different, based on your hardware configuration. You may want to use this list to "clean up" those files that are not needed on your system. Many of the files copied to your disk are only needed by certain hardware options, which you may not have on your system.

Why does OS/2 leave these extra files around? Doing so makes it easier to add options after the initial installation. Other files are installed in more than one place on the hard drive. Why?—to make options such as creating utility boot diskettes easier. If you clean up these extra files, you can reduce the disk space OS/2 Warp uses by several megabytes. However, if you delete a file that is required by your system, you may prevent certain features of OS/2 from working. You could even make OS/2 fail to boot. Use caution when deleting any OS/2 system file. If you are in doubt, MOVE the files to a temporary location, and then delete them when you're sure OS/2 Warp doesn't need the file.

You may notice that many files (usually device drivers) have two similar versions: one with a "1" in the name, and the other with a "2" (for example, IBM1FLPY.ADD and IBM2FLPY.ADD). The "1" version is for ISA/EISA systems, and the "2" is for Micro Channel systems. You will only need one of each, but sometimes the Warp leaves both on your system. You can save some space if you delete the version you don't need.

Root Directory (C:\)

The root directory is where OS/2 stores some of the most important "base" files. Many of these files are hidden (to keep you from deleting them), so if you want to see them, you should use the command `DIR C:\ /A`. If you didn't install OS/2 Warp on Drive C:, substitute the correct drive letter.

AUTOEXEC.BAT	This is the file used by DOS sessions to initialize the DOS environment.
CONFIG.SYS	This file defines the device drivers and other configuration options during the boot of OS/2. It is quite different from the DOS CONFIG.SYS.
EA DATA.SF	This is where the Extended Attributes are stored on FAT drives. If you install OS/2 on an HPFS drive, you will not see this file. Never delete this file!
OS2BOOT	This is the "mini-loader." When OS/2 boots, this file is responsible for starting the process of loading the OS/2 base operating system.
OS2DUMP	This program allows you to take a "snapshot" of system RAM in the event of a system failure. The "dump" file can then be inspected by OS/2 support personnel.
OS2KRNL	This is the heart of OS/2. The "kernel" provides all the basic functions of OS/2, such as memory management, file I/O services, multitask scheduling, and device driver interfaces.
OS2LDR	This is the "boot loader" for OS/2. The "mini-loader" loads this file, which in turn loads the kernel.
OS2LDR.MSG	The text messages used by OS2LDR.
OS2LOGO	A compressed graphic image that is displayed while OS/2 boots.

OS/2 Warp File Listing

OS2VER	A file listing the programs that only work if they think they are running under OS/2 version 2.0. OS/2 will "lie" to these programs when they ask for the OS/2 version number.
README	A text file with last-minute documentation changes and information.
TEDIT.EXE	A text-mode editor, useful for modifying CONFIG.SYS.
TEDIT.HLP	The help file for TEDIT.EXE.
WP ROOT.SF	The root directory's Extended Attributes used by the Workplace Shell.

The Desktop Directory (C:\Desktop\)

The Desktop directory is where the Workplace Shell stores all the objects you place on the desktop. Many of the directories inside the desktop will appear to be empty, but that's because most objects on the desktop are "virtual" (shadows, program objects, devices). While they look empty, the directories have Extended Attributes attached to them.

If you are using the Workplace Shell properly, and keeping your "real" and "virtual" objects separate, the only directory in your desktop with real files in it should be the templates folder. Some of the typical folders in the desktop are:

- DOS Programs
- GAMES
- Information
- Multimedia
- Network
- OS!2 Programs
- OS!2 System
- OS!2 System\Command Prompts
- OS!2 System\Drives
- OS!2 System\Games
- OS!2 System\Games\Mahjongg Solitaire

- OS!2 System\Minimized^Window Viewer
- OS!2 System\Productivity
- OS!2 System\Startup
- OS!2 System\System Setup
- WIN-OS!2 Groups
- Windows Programs

The Templates Directory (C:\Desktop\Templates)

This desktop folder contains the templates you can use to create new objects. Some are "virtual," and others are real. The real objects in the templates folder are:

`Bitmap.BMP`	A graphics bitmap template.
`Data File`	A generic data file template.
`Digital Video.AVI`	A software-motion video template
`Digital Video.FLC`	A new-style Autodesk Flic file template.
`Digital Video.FLI`	An old-style Autodesk Flic file template.
`Digital Video.MPG`	An MPEG video file template.
`Folder`	A folder template.
`Icon.ICO`	An icon file template.
`Metafile.MET`	A metafile (graphic image) template.
`MIDI.MID`	A MIDI audio file template.
`PIF file.PIF`	A Windows PIF file template.
`Pointer.PTR`	A pointer file (cursor) template.

The IBMVESA Directory (C:\IBMVESA)

This directory contains a program that provides DOS-mode VESA compatibility on IBM ThinkPad computers with a Western Digital video chipset.

`FRATE.DAT`	A data file that describes your monitor's capabilities.

A

OS/2 Warp File Listing

TPADVESA.DOC	Instructions on how to modify FRATE.DAT for your monitor.
TPADVESA.EXE	The VESA BIOS program for ThinkPads.

The LANLK Directory (C:\LANLK)

This directory is usually empty, and is created during the installation of OS/2 multimedia support.

The Maintenance Desktop (C:\Maintenance Desktop)

This directory holds the objects in the "maintenance" desktop, which was used during the installation of OS/2. You can boot to the maintenance desktop by using the **Alt**+**F1** "Recovery Choices" keystroke (described in Chapter 12, "When Things Go Wrong").

The Multimedia Directory (C:\MMOS2)

The following list represents a typical OS/2 Multimedia support installation. Files are stored in the MMOS2 subdirectory. Your installation may differ, based on your multimedia hardware.

ADSHDD.SYS	Obsolete audio stream handler device driver (replaced by R0STUB.SYS).
AMPM.EXE	The Master Volume control program.
AUDIODD.MSG	Text messages used by the audio device driver.
AUDIOVDD.SYS	The audio virtual device driver (for DOS session audio support).
CDPM.EXE	The music CD player program.
FFC.EXE	The multimedia data converter program.
MCIREXX.INF	A hypertext help file describing how to use

	multimedia functions in REXX programs.
`MIDITYPE.INI`	A data file that describes the MIDI capabilities of your system.
`MINSTALL.EXE`	The multimedia feature installation program.
`MME.MSG`	Text messages used in multimedia support.
`MMPM.INI`	A data file containing multimedia configuration information (system sounds)
`MMPM2.INI`	A text file containing hardware & software configuration settings.
`MMPMCD.INI`	A data file containing settings for all supported CD-ROM drives.
`MMPMMMIO.INI`	A data file containing information about all supported multimedia I/O types.
`MPMCDIMG.CMD`	Obsolete REXX program that copies multimedia installation disks to a hard drive.
`MPPM.EXE`	Player program for digital audio, video, CD/XA, music CDs, and Laser Discs.
`PLAY.CMD`	Command-line audio/video file player program.
`R0STUB.SYS`	The audio stream handler device driver.
`RECORD.CMD`	Command line .WAV file audio recorder program.
`RGBTOYUV.LUT`	Color conversion lookup table.
`SB16D2.SYS`	Specific sound card device driver (this one is for the SoundBlaster 16).
`SPI.INI`	A data file containing configuration information for stream control functions.
`SSMDD.SYS`	The sync/stream manager device driver.
`STPM.EXE`	The multimedia setup program.
`VAUDIO.SYS`	Audio virtual device driver for IBM ACPA card (for DOS mode access).
`VCSHDD.SYS`	Video capture stream handler (for Video IN).
`WEPM.EXE`	The digital audio player/recorder program.

A

OS/2 Warp File Listing

The Multimedia DLL Directory (C:\MMOS2\DLL)

The files in \MMOS2\DLL are the dynamic link libraries for OS/2 multimedia support. Dynamic link libraries contain functions that can be loaded on demand by a multimedia program.

AMPMMRI.DLL	Help and control text for the master volume control.
AMPMXMCD.DLL	Amp/Mixer media control driver functions.
AUDIOIF.DLL	Audio interface functions. Known as the "Audio Vendor-Specific Driver (VSD)."
AUDIOMCD.DLL	Audio functions for Media Control Interface commands.
AUDIOSH.DLL	Audio stream handler functions.
AUTOPROC.DLL	Video file I/O functions.
AVCAPROC.DLL	Video file audio converter functions.
AVCIIOPR.DLL	MMIO functions for AVI files.
AVIO.DLL	AVI file I/O functions.
CARDINFO.DLL	Text messages for multimedia card setup.
CDAUDIO.DLL	CD audio functions.
CDDASH.DLL	CD digital audio stream handler functions.
CDPMMRI.DLL	Help and control text for the CD player program.
CDTBL.DLL	Functions that list the capabilities of installed CDs.
CODECSH.DLL	Compression/Decompression stream handler functions.
DIVE.DLL	Direct Interface Video Extensions functions.
FFCMRI.DLL	Help and control text for multimedia data converter.
FSSH.DLL	File system stream handler functions.
GENCDVSD.DLL	CD vendor-specific drivers.
GENIN.DLL	Generic install functions.
GENINMRI.DLL MMMRI.DLL	Install message text.
HHP.DLL	Multimedia I/O manager functions.

IBMCDXA.DLL	CD/XA functions.
IMAADPCM.DLL	Audio compressor/decompressor functions.
IMGCLASS.DLL IOBASE.DLL	C++ class functions.
INDDEC32.DLL INDEO.DLL INDEOR31.DLL INDFSR31.DLL INDRTR31.DLL	Intel Indeo support functions.
IOPRNLS.DLL	Multi-language translation functions.
ITERM.DLL	Installation functions.
LVDP8000.DLL	Videodisc support functions.
MCIAPI.DLL MCIERR.DLL MCIMRI.DLL	Media Control Interface functions.
MDM.DLL	Media Control Interface device manager functions.
MEMSH.DLL	Memory stream handler functions.
MIDIIO.DLL MIDIMCD.DLL MIPM.DLL MISH.DLL	MIDI functions.
MMIO.DLL WAVEPROC.DLL	Multimedia I/O functions.
MMOTPROC.DLL	I/O functions for M-Motion video.
MMPM.DLL	General multimedia functions.
MMPMCRTS.DLL	Standard runtime functions.
MMSND.DLL SND.DLL	SOUND object functions.
MMSNDMRI.DLL	SOUND object text.
MONDO.DLL	Monitor/display code.
MPGIO.DLL	MPEG I/O functions.
MPPM.DLL	CD and Laser Disc player functions.
MPPMMRI.DLL	CD and Laser Disc text.
MTSH.DLL NULLSH.DLL SSSH.DLL	Stream handler functions.
OS13PROC.DLL	OS/2 1.3 bitmap functions.

A

OS/2 Warp File Listing

OS20PROC.DLL	OS/2 2.0 bitmap functions.
PCDIO.DLL	PhotoCD I/O functions.
QRYCD.DLL	CD-ROM identification functions.
QRYCDMRI.DLL	CD-ROM identification text.
RDIBPROC.DLL	RIFF Device-independent bitmap functions.
SMVSMRI.DLL SMVSPAGE.DLL	Video adjustment setup text.
SNDBLAST.DLL	SoundBlaster functions.
SSM.DLL SSMINI.DLL SSMRES.DLL	Sync/Stream manager functions.
STDL.DLL	Multimedia setup functions.
STDLMRI.DLL STPMMRI.DLL	Multimedia setup text.
SVMC.DLL	Software motion video functions.
SVMCMRI.DLL	Software motion video text.
SVSH.DLL	Software motion video stream handler functions.
SW.DLL	Secondary window functions.
ULCOASYM.DLL ULCORT.DLL ULDC.DLL ULDC16.DLL ULDC8.DLL	Ultimotion compression functions.
VIDVCI.DLL	Video capture functions.
WEPMMRI.DLL	Digital audio player/recorder text.
WEPMPINT.DLL WEPMPLUS.DLL	Digital audio player/recorder functions.
WI30PROC.DLL	Windows bitmap functions.

The Multimedia Help Directory (C:\MMOS2\HELP)

The files in this directory are the help files for the multimedia programs.

AMPMH.HLP	Master volume control help.

CDPMH.HLP	Music CD player help.
FFC.HLP	Multimedia data converter help.
MCIREC.HLP	Sound recorder help.
MMEINDEX.HLP	Multimedia master index help.
MMINSTH.HLP	Multimedia install help.
MMSNDH.HLP	SOUND object help.
MPPMH.HLP	Media player help.
SBLASTER.HLP	SoundBlaster driver help.
SMVSH.HLP	Video setup help.
STDLH.HLP STPMH.HLP	Multimedia setup help.
SVMCH.HLP	Software motion video help.
WEPMH.HLP WEPMPLUS.HLP	Digital audio player/recorder help.

The Multimedia Install Directory (C:\MMOS2\INSTALL)

This directory contains various files used during the installation of multimedia support.

AUDFILE.ICO AUDPLAY.ICO AUDREC.ICO AVSFILM.ICO CDPLAYER.ICO DATACONV.ICO FILMFLDR.ICO MIDIFILE.ICO MIDIPLAY.ICO MMPMDATA.ICO MMPMFLD2.ICO MMPMFLDR.ICO MMPMINST.ICO MMSETUP.ICO MOVIE.ICO SOUNDS.ICO	Workplace Shell icon files.

A

OS/2 Warp File Listing

VDSCPLAY.ICO VIDPLAY.ICO VOLCTRL.ICO	
BASECONF.CH SMVCONF.CH	Files used to control changes to CONFIG.SYS.
CDPM.EAS MIDIICO.EAS MINSTALL.EAS MOVIES.EAS MPPM.EAS SOUNDS.EAS VIDICON.EAS WAVEFILE.EAS WEPM.EAS WAVEICO.EAS	
COMPLIST.INI	Data file describing the installed multimedia components.
DINSTSND.CMD	REXX command that uninstalls multimedia system sounds support.
FOURMEG.SCR SMVINI.SCR VAPM.SCR	Scripts that define all the operations to be performed during multimedia install.
IBMLANLK.EXE	Program to allow installation of locked files on network systems.
IBMLANLK.SYS	Device driver used by IBMLANLK.EXE during installation.
INSTSND.CMD	REXX command that installs multimedia system sounds support.
LSI.MSG	Text messages used when installing on LAN workstations.
LSIH.MSG	Error messages used when installing on LAN workstations.
MINSTALL.LOG	Log of all multimedia files/options installed
RESPONSE.TXT	Setup information for multimedia install.
SYSLEVEL.MPM	Version information for the SYSLEVEL command.

The Multimedia Macro Directory (C:\MMOS2\MACROS)

This directory contains sample multimedia macros for spreadsheet applications.

`AUDIO.WG2` `AUDIO2.WG2`	Sample 1-2-3 macros.
`AUDIO.XLM`	Sample Excel macro.

The Multimedia Movie Directory (C:\MMOS2\MOVIES)

This directory contains sample digital video files. Because they are large, only a small sample is copied to your hard drive. You can find more video files on the OS/2 Warp CD.

`MACAW.AVI`	Short video clip of two birds.

The Multimedia Sounds Directory (C:\MMOS2\SOUNDS)

This directory contains sample sound and music files.

`BACH.MID`
`BALLGAME.MID`
`BLUEJAM.MID`
`HOLIDAY.MID`
`IBMRALLY.MID`
`BBEE.MID`
	MIDI music samples.

`BEEOONG.WAV`
`BELLS.WAV`
`BOING.WAV`
`BOO.WAV`
`BWAAANG.WAV`
`BWEEEP.WAV`
`CUCKOO.WAV`
	Digital audio samples.

A

OS/2 Warp File Listing

```
DOINK.WAV
DOORCLS.WAV
DRUMROLL.WAV
DRWCLOSE.WAV
EEEOOOP.WAV
EEERRUPP.WAV
JET.WAV
LASER.WAV
POP.WAV
SHRED.WAV
SHUTDOWN.WAV
STARTUP.WAV
TAKEMY.WAV
TWIP.WAV
WM_TELL.WAV
WOOEEP.WAV
```

The Nowhere Directories (C:\Nowhere and C:\Nowhere1)

The NOWHERE directory is where the Workplace Shell stores temporary objects. The NOWHERE1 directory is where the Workplace Shell LaunchPad stores temporary objects. These directories will always appear empty, but **do not delete** them.

The OS/2 Directory (C:\OS2)

This directory contains most of the OS/2 programs and utilities that are designed for end users to use from an OS/2 prompt. You might think of it as the OS/2 counterpart to the old C:\DOS directory.

8514.RC 8514M.RC CGA.RC EGA.RC PLASMA.RC VGA.RC VGAM.RC XGA.RC	Files describing the color tables of various video modes.
ANSI.EXE	Program to enable/disable ANSI screen/keyboard functions in OS/2 sessions.
ARCINST.EXE	Program to create the original Workplace Shell archive.
ARCRECOV.EXE	Program to restore a Workplace Shell archive.
ATTRIB.EXE	Program to change file attributes.
AUTODRV2.INI	Text file describing PCMCIA cards in your system.
BACKUP.EXE	Program to back up files to diskette.
BLDLEVEL.EXE	Program to display specific build version of an .EXE or .DLL.
BOOT.COM	The "Dual Boot" program.
CACHE.EXE	Program to display or set parameters of the HPFS cache.
CHKDSK.COM	Program to check your hard disk structure.
CLIPOS2.EXE	The Clipboard Viewer program.
CMD.EXE	The OS/2 command prompt program.
COMETRUN.EXE	The "Comet Cursor" feature of the mouse cursor.
COMP.COM	A file compare program.
DISKCOMP.COM	A disk compare program.
DISKCOPY.COM	A disk image copy program.
E.EXE	The OS/2 System editor.
EAUTIL.EXE	A program to split/join Extended Attributes and files.
FDISK.COM	A disk partition manager program.

A

OS/2 Warp File Listing

`FDISKPM.EXE`	A PM version of FDISK.COM.
`FIND.EXE`	A text search utility.
`FORMAT.COM`	A disk format utility.
`HELP.CMD`	A batch file turns on/off the HELP line in OS/2 command sessions, or calls HELPMSG.EXE to display help on other OS/2 functions.
`HELPMSG.EXE`	A program that displays help screens for OS/2 functions.
`HPFS.IFS`	The HPFS file system program.
`IBM1SS01.SYS` `IBM1SS02.SYS`	PCMCIA socket services drivers.
`ICMEMFMT.EXE`	PCMCIA RAM drive format program.
`ICONEDIT.EXE`	OS/2 Icon file editor.
`INI.RC` `INISYS.RC`	Text versions of the OS/2 .INI files (for use with MAKEINI.EXE)
`KEYB.COM`	Utility to select a keyboard codepage to be used by all OS/2 and DOS sessions.
`KEYBOARD.DCP` `VIOTBL.DCP`	Keyboard and video translation tables.
`LABEL.COM`	Sets the volume label on disks.
`LD2FIX.EXE`	Obsolete program for patching Lotus 1-2-3 for use with OS/2.

`LINK.EXE`
`LINK386.EXE`
`RC.EXE`
`RCPP.ERR`
`RCPP.EXE`
	Programmers' utilities to create OS/2-compatible .EXE files.

`LOCK.RC`	MAKEINI source file that will reset the Workplace Shell lockup password.
`LOG.SYS`	System error log device driver.
`MAKEINI.EXE`	Program to make .INI files from .RC files.
`MODE.COM`	Program to set video, serial port, parallel port, and diskette operating modes.
`MONITOR.DIF`	Text file describing capabilities of various video monitors.
`MORE.COM`	Filter for pausing display of output in OS/2 and DOS command sessions.

`OS2.!!!` `OS2SYS.!!!`	Temporary files where the next changes to the .INI files are written.
`OS2.INI` `OS2SYS.INI`	Data files that contain system and application configuration. Do not delete these files!

`OS2_13.RC`
`OS2_20.RC`
`WIN_30.RC`
	Source files for MAKEINI.EXE that will configure your desktop to look like OS/2 1.3, OS/2 2.0, or Windows 3.0.

`PATCH.EXE`	Program that applies patches to data and executable files.
`PATCHWP.CMD`	Batch file that uses PATCH.EXE to patch WordPerfect 5.2 for OS/2.
`PCM2ATA.ADD`	PCMCIA disk card device driver.
`PCMCIA.SYS`	PCMCIA device driver.
`PMCHKDSK.EXE`	Graphical version of CHKDSK.EXE.
`PMCONTRL.INF`	Text file that list the printer drivers that can be installed.
`PMFORMAT.EXE`	Graphical version of FORMAT.EXE.
`PMREXX.EXE`	Graphical REXX debugging tool.
`PMSHELL.EXE`	Program that starts the Workplace Shell.
`PMSPOOL.EXE`	The OS/2 print spooler program.
`PRINT.COM`	Program to print files from OS/2 and DOS command sessions.
`PSCRIPT.SEP` `SAMPLE.SEP`	Sample printer separator pages.
`PSTAT.EXE`	Program to display the status of running processes.
`PWRMGMT.SYS`	Advanced Power Management device driver.
`RECOVER.COM`	Utility to recover damaged hard drives (use extreme caution on FAT drives).
`REPLACE.EXE`	Program that selectively copies files from one drive to another.
`RESTORE.EXE`	Program that restores files saved with BACKUP.EXE.
`REXXTRY.CMD`	Program that allows you to try individual REXX statements.
`RMVIEW.EXE`	Resource Manager status viewer program.
`RXQUEUE.EXE` `RXSUBCOM.EXE`	REXX language support programs.

A

OS/2 Warp File Listing

SCREEN01.SYS SCREEN02.SYS	Base video screen device drivers.
SETBOOT.EXE	Program to select a bootable partition and reboot the computer.
SETVGA.CMD	Command file to install VGA support from the OS/2 installation diskettes.
SOMDD.EXE SOMDSVR.EXE	
SORT.EXE	Filter used to sort data files.
SPOOL.EXE	Program to redirect printer output from one device to another.
SRD2FIX.CMD	REXX command that turns off LaunchPad to make desktop look like OS/2 2.x.
SVGA.EXE	DOS-mode program that determines the capabilities of a Super VGA adapter.
SVGATMP.BAT	DOS batch file that runs SVGA.EXE.
SYSLEVEL.EXE	Program that displays exact version levels of all installed components.
SYSLOG.EXE SYSLOGPM.EXE	OS/2 System error log formatter.
TEDIT.EXE	Text-mode editor.
TEDIT.HLP	Help for TEDIT.EXE.
TRACE.EXE	System event trace facility.
TRACEFMT.EXE	System trace format utility.
TREE.COM	Program to display directory lists as a tree.
TUTORIAL.EXE	The OS/2 Tutorial.
UNDELETE.COM	Program to recover deleted files (if support is enabled in CONFIG.SYS).
UNPACK.EXE UNPACK2.EXE	Programs to unpack compressed OS/2 installation files.
UPINI.RC	
VIEW.EXE VIEWDOC.EXE	Hypertext viewer program (for viewing .INF files).
VIOTBL.CDP VIOTBL.ISO	Screen translation tables.
WPDSACTV.EXE WPDSINIT.EXE	Workplace Shell DSOM server.

XCOPY.EXE	Utility to copy multiple files and directories.
XDFCOPY.EXE	Utility to create XDF diskettes from image files.

The OS/2 Applications Directory (C:\OS2\APPS)

This directory contains the "productivity and games" applications that come with OS/2 Warp.

BOX.EX DRAW.EX E3EMUL.EX EPM.EX EPMLEX.EX EXTRA.EX GET.EX HELP.EX MATHLIB.EX PUT.EX	EPM function extensions.
CARDSYM.FON	Klondike Solitaire card file.
CASTLE.MAH DEFAULT.MAH GIZEH.MAH TAJMAHAL.MAH TOWERBRI.MAH	Mahjongg tile setup files.
DEFAULT.BMP	Mahjongg background image.
DRAGON.WAV NOMOVES.WAV REMOVE.WAV REMOVEC.WAV SELECT.WAV SUCCESS.MID SUCCESSC.WAV WARNING.WAV	Mahjongg sound files.
EPM.EXE	The Enhanced Editor program.
EPMHELP.QHL	Help for EPM.EXE.
KLONDIKE.EXE	Klondike solitaire program.
MAHJONGG.EXE	Mahjongg tile game.

OS/2 Warp File Listing

MAHJONGG.ICO	Mahjongg icon.
MJFOLDER.ICO	Mahjongg folder icon.
OS2CHESS.BIN OS2CHESS.EXE	The Chess game.
PICVIEW.EXE	Picture/metafile viewer program.
PMSEEK.EXE	File search program.
PULSE.EXE	CPU monitor program.
TILEDEF.DLL TILEHK.DLL	Mahjongg support files.

The OS/2 Application DLL Directory (C:\OS2\APPS\DLL)

This directory contains Dynamic Link Libraries for the productivity and game programs.

CHESSAI.DLL	The Chess "brain."
ETKE551.DLL ETKR551.DLL ETKTHNK.DLL	Function libraries for EPM.
KLONBGA.DLL	Functions for Klondike solitaire.
PICVIEW.DLL	Functions for PICVIEW.EXE.
PMSEEK.DLL	Functions for PMSKEEK.EXE.

The OS/2 Archive Directory (C:\OS2\ARCHIVES)

This directory is where OS/2 Warp stores archives of the Desktop and system files. You can change where the archives go, and enable archiving in the settings notebook for the Desktop.

ARCHIVES.$$$	Data file that describes what archives have been saved.
OS2.KEY	Text file that lists the files that should be saved with each archive.

The OS/2 Installation Archive Directory (C:\OS2\ARCHIVES\0X)

This directory is the archive that is automatically saved after you install OS/2 Warp. If you restore it, your desktop and system configuration will look just as they did after installation. If you have enabled archiving, you will see other directories similar to 0X, which will contain the latest archives.

0, 1, 2, 3	These are the saved system files in the archive (usually, `OS2.INI` `OS2SYS.INI` `CONFIG.SYS` and `AUTOEXEC.BAT`).
`KEYS.$$$`	Data file that contains the original path and filename of the system files backed up in this archive.

The OS/2 Installation Desktop Archive Directory (C:\OS2\ARCHIVES\0X\DESKTOP)

This is where the Workplace Shell desktop is saved in the archive. Most of the directories will appear empty, but don't delete them.

The OS/2 Current Archive Directory (C:\OS2\ARCHIVES\CURRENT)

If you ever restore an archive (using the Recovery Choices magic keystroke), your current desktop and configuration will be saved here. There is no automatic way to restore this archive, but a manual method is explained in Chapter 12, "When Things Go Wrong."

A

OS/2 Warp File Listing

The OS/2 Bitmap Directory (C:\OS2\BITMAP)

This directory contains graphic files that can be used as folder backgrounds and lockup pictures.

AAAAA.EXE	This is the program that displays a list of the OS/2 Warp developers. To see the list, click on the OS/2 desktop, then press **Ctrl**+**Alt**+**Shift**+**O**.
AAAAA.MET	This is the picture file that is displayed when AAAAA.EXE is running.
BLOCKS.BMP BLUES.BMP BLUJEAN.BMP BOX.BMP BRICK.BMP BUTTERFL.BMP COLUMNS.BMP DELFT.BMP FERNS.BMP FLAMINGO.BMP FLEUR.BMP GMARBLE.BMP LEAVES.BMP LINES.BMP LINKS.BMP MAZE.BMP MERCADO.BMP ORCHIDS.BMP OS2TILE.BMP PINES.BMP POOL.BMP RAINFOR.BMP ROOF.BMP SCALES1.BMP SCALES2.BMP SHELLS.BMP SPIRAL.BMP STARS.BMP STUCCO.BMP	Small bitmaps suitable for "tiling" to create a background.

SUNFLOW.BMP SWIRLS.BMP TIEDYE.BMP TILE.BMP TOOTH.BMP WAVE.BMP WEBB.BMP WMARBLE.BMP WOOD.BMP ZIGZAG.BMP	
OS2LOGO.BMP	The OS/2 Warp logo.

The OS/2 Electronic Book Directory (C:\OS2\BOOK)

This directory contains the HELP files for OS/2 Warp. Objects that reference these books can be found in the Information folder on your desktop.

APPLBK.INF	The "Application Considerations" book.
CMDREF.INF	The OS/2 "Command Reference" book.
MULTIMBK.INF	The "Multimedia" book.
PERFBK.INF	The "Performance Considerations" book.
PRINTBK.INF	The "Printing in OS/2" book.
REXX.INF	The "REXX Information" book.
TRADEMBK.INF	The "Trademarks" book.
WINOS2BK.INF	The "Windows Programs in OS/2" book.

A

OS/2 Warp File Listing

The OS/2 Boot Directory (C:\OS2\BOOT)

This directory contains device drives and other files that are needed to start OS/2. This directory should not be in your PATH or LIBPATH, as these files are only accessed during startup. That's why this directory is separate, so Warp doesn't have to search through them when looking for programs in your PATH.

ABIOS.SYS	The Advanced BIOS device driver.
AHA152X.ADD AHA154X.ADD AHA164X.ADD AHA174X.ADD AIC7770.ADD AIC7870.ADD	Device drivers for Adaptec™ SCSI controllers.
ALTF1.CMD	Batch program to process the **Alt+F1** magic keystroke.
ALTF1BOT.SCR ALTF1MID.SCR ALTF1TOP.SCR	Text for the **Alt+F1** screen.
APM.SYS	Advanced Power Management device driver.
ARCHBASE.$$$	File that is used to locate the archive directory.
AUTODRV2.SYS	PCMCIA auto-configurator device driver.
CDFS.IFS	CD-ROM file system.
CHINCDS1.FLT	Chinon CD-ROM device filter.
CLOCK01.SYS CLOCK02.SYS	Real-time clock device driver.
COM.SYS	Serial port device driver.
CONFIG.M	The CONFIG.SYS for the "maintenance desktop" restore.
CONFIG.X	The CONFIG.SYS for the "original archive" restore.
DOS.SYS	Software reboot device driver.
DPT20XX.ADD	Device driver for DPT SCSI controllers.
EXTDSKDD.SYS	External floppy disk device driver.
FD16-700.ADD FD7000EX.ADD	Device drivers for Future Domain SCSI controllers.

The OS/2 Warp Survival Guide

`FD8XX.ADD`	
`HITCDS1.FLT`	Hitachi CD-ROM device filter.
`IBM1FLPY.ADD` `IBM2FLPY.ADD`	Floppy device driver.
`IBM1S506.ADD`	IDE and MFM disk device driver.
`IBM2ADSK.ADD`	ABIOS disk device driver.
`IBM2SCSI.ADD`	IBM SCSI device driver.
`IBMIDECD.FLT`	IDE CD-ROM device filter.
`IBMINT13.I13`	BIOS disk device driver.
`IBMKBD.SYS`	Keyboard device driver.
`ICMEMCDD.SYS` `ICMEMMTD.SYS`	PCMCIA memory card device driver.
`KBDBASE.SYS`	Base keyboard device driver.
`LMS205.ADD` `LMS206.ADD`	Phillips LMS CD-ROM device drivers.
`MITFX001.ADD`	Mitsumi CD-ROM device driver.
`MOUSE.SYS`	Mouse device driver.
`NECCDS1.FLT`	NEC CD-ROM device driver.
`OS2ASPI.DMD`	Advanced SCSI Programming Interface driver.
`OS2CDROM.DMD`	CD-ROM device driver manager.
`OS2DASD.DMD`	Disk device driver manager.
`OS2SCSI.DMD`	SCSI device driver manager.
`PCLOGIC.SYS`	Logitech mouse device driver.
`PMDD.SYS`	Presentation Manager mouse, keyboard and timer interrpt device driver.
`POINTDD.SYS`	Device driver that draws the mouse cursor.
`PRINT01.SYS` `PRINT02.SYS`	Printer device driver.
`RESERVE.SYS` `RESOURCE.SYS`	Resource Manager device drivers.
`SBCD2.ADD`	SoundBlaster CD device driver.
`SCREEN01.SYS` `SCREEN02.SYS`	Video screen device driver.
`SONY31A.ADD` `SONY535.ADD` `SONYCDS1.FLT`	Device support for Sony CD-ROM drives.
`TESTCFG.SYS`	Device driver that allows other device drivers

A

OS/2 Warp File Listing

	to determine hardware configurations.
`TMV1SCSI.ADD`	Device driver for Trantor SCSI controllers.
`TOSHCDS1.FLT`	Device filter for Toshiba CD-ROM drives.
`VDISK.SYS`	RAM-disk device driver.
`VIOTBL.DCP`	Screen translation table.
`XDFLOPPY.FLT`	Filter to add support for XDF floppy disks.

The OS/2 DLL Directory (C:\OS2\DLL)

This directory contains the Dynamic Link Libraries used by the base functions of OS/2.

`ANMT.DLL`
`TUT.DLL`
`TUTDLL.DLL`
`TUTMRI.DLL`
`TUTORMRI.DLL`
`SELECT.DLL`
	OS/2 Tutorial functions.

`ANSICALL.DLL`	ANSI screen/keyboard support.
`BDCALLS.DLL`	Bi-directional text support.
`BKSCALLS.DLL`	Base keyboard support.
`BMSCALLS.DLL`	Base mouse support.
`BUTTON.DLL`	PM Button controls.

`BVHINIT.DLL`
`BVHMPA.DLL`
`BVHSVGA.DLL`
`BVHVGA.DLL`
`BVHWNDW.DLL`
`BVSCALLS.DLL`
	Base video support.

`CDTBL.DLL`	CD-ROM support.
`COMETDLL.DLL` `WPCOMET.DLL`	Mouse "comet cursor" support.

`COURIER.FON`
`HELV.FON`
`MISC.FON`
	Screen fonts.

SYSMONO.FON TIMES.FON	
CPISPFPC.DLL DTM.DLL STXTDMPC.DLL	Text-mode entry panel support.
DISPLAY.DLL	OS/2 Display support.
DOSCALL1.DLL	OS/2 system API support.
DOSRFICO.DLL	System install Icon refresh support.
DSPRES.DLL SYSFONT.DLL	OS/2 resident display fonts.
EHXDLMRI.DLL	OS/2 System Editor functions.
FDISKPM.DLL	Functions for FDISKPM.EXE.
FKA.DLL	Function key support functions.
HELPMGR.DLL HPMGRMRI.DLL	Help Manager functions.
IBMDEV32.DLL IBMGPMI.DLL SVGA.DLL SVGAINST.DLL VIDEOPMI.DLL	SuperVGA support.
IBMVGA32.DLL	PM VGA support.
IMP.DLL	Input Method profiler.
INACALL.DLL	Installation aid functions.
INSCFG32.DLL	CONFIG.SYS update functions.
INSPGM32.DLL	"Add Programs" support.
KBDCALLS.DLL	Keyboard support.
MDMI.DLL MIPMINI.DLL MMPMCRTS.DLL MMPMINI.DLL MMSNIFF.DLL	Multimedia support.
MINXMRI.DLL MINXOBJ.DLL MMIOI.DLL	Master Index support.
MIRRORS.DLL	Windows-to-PM conversion support.
MONCALLS.DLL	Device monitor functions.
MOUCALLS.DLL	Mouse support.
MSG.DLL	OS/2 messaging support.

A

OS/2 Warp File Listing

NAMPIPES.DLL	Named pipe support.
NLS.DLL	National language support.
NPXEMLTR.DLL	Floating point emulator support.
NWIAPI.DLL	Network API support.
OASIS.DLL	OS/2-to-Windows device driver support.
OS2CHAR.DLL	VIO initialization support.
OS2MM.DLL	Multimedia installation support.
PARALLEL.PDR	Parallel port support.
PICV.DLL	Picture viewer support.
PMATM.DLL	Adobe Type Manager support.
PMBIND.DLL	Language binding support.
PMCHKDSK.DLL	Functions for PMCHKDSK.EXE.
PMCLIP.DLL	Functions for PMCLIP.EXE.
PMCTLS.DLL PMDCTLS.DLL	PM controls.
PMDDE.DLL	Dynamic Data Exchange support.
PMDRAG.DLL	Drag-and-Drop support.
PMFORMAT.DLL	Functions for PMFORMAT.EXE.
PMGPI.DLL	Graphics primitives support.
PMGRE.DLL	PM Graphics Engine functions.
PMMERGE.DLL	The "combined" DLL. Many functions from other DLLs are copied here to optimize the system.
PMMLE.DLL	Functions for multiline edit controls.
PMPIC.DLL	Functions for the Picture Interchange program.
PMPRE.DLL	Printer graphics engine.
PMPRINT.QPR	PM Print queue processor.
PMREXX.DLL	Functions for PM REXX.
PMSDMRI.DLL	Dialog box messages.
PMSHAPI.DLL SHPIINST.DLL	PM Shell API functions.
PMSHELL.DLL	Task list functions.
PMSHLTKT.DLL	Private Shell toolkit functions.
PMSPL.DLL SPL1B.DLL SPOOLCP.DLL	Spooler functions.
PMTKT.DLL	PM Application support library.

`PMVDMH.DLL` `PMVDMP.DLL`	Virtual DOS Machine support.
`PMVIOP.DLL` `VIOCALLS.DLL`	Text-mode window support.
`PMWIN.DLL`	PM Window manager functions.
`PMWP.DLL` `PMWPMRI.DLL`	Workplace Shell functions.
`QUECALLS.DLL`	Queue functions.

`REXX.DLL`
`REXXAPI.DLL`
`REXXINIT.DLL`
`REXXUTIL.DLL`
	REXX functions.

`SEAMLESS.DLL`	Seamless window support.
`SERIAL.PDR`	Serial port support.
`SESMGR.DLL`	Session Manager functions.

`SOM.DLL  SOMD.DLL`
`SOMEM.DLL`
`SOMIR.DLL`
`SOMS.DLL`
`SOMTC.DLL`
`SOMU.DLL`
`WPDSERV.DLL`
`WPDSRVP.DLL`
	System Object Model support.

`STARTLW.DLL`	HPFS Lazy-write cache functions.
`SYSLOG.DLL`	System error log formatter support.
`TRACEFMT.DLL`	Trace formatter support.
`UCDFS.DLL`	Utility functions for the CD-ROM file system.
`UHPFS.DLL`	Utility functions for the HPFS file system.
`VCFGMRI.DLL` `VIDEOCFG.DLL`	Video configuration support.
`WCFGMRI.DLL` `WINCFG.DLL`	Win-OS/2 object support.
`WINPRF.DLL`	Windows profile library.
`WPCMPNP.DLL`	Plug and Play class library.
`WPCONFIG.DLL` `WPCONMRI.DLL`	System setup folder functions.

`WPPRINT.DLL`
`WPPRTMRI.DLL`
`WPPWNDRV.DLL`
	Workplace Shell print functions.

A

OS/2 Warp File Listing

The OS/2 Null Printer Directory (C:\OS2\DLL\IBMNULL)

The IBMNULL directory is where the "generic" text-mode printer driver is stored. This printer driver can be used to print to devices (or files) where no printer-specific commands are required.

IBMNULL.DRV	The generic printer driver.

The OS/2 LaserJet Directory (C:\OS2\DLL\LASERJET)

If you install a LaserJet-compatible printer, OS/2 Warp will install the driver in this subdirectory. In addition to the driver, many cartridge font files will be installed (most of which you don't own).

LASERJET.DRV	The LaserJet device driver.
LASERJET.HLP	Help file for LaserJet driver.
ACARTCO0.FNTBARCODE0.FNT BCARTTM0.FNT BRILLIA0.FNT BROKER.DLL CCARTIN0.FNT DCARTPR0.FNT DISTINC0.FNT ECARTLE0.FNT FCARTTM0.FNT FORMSET0.FNT GCARTLE0.FNT GLOBALT0.FNT GREATST0.FNT HCARTLE0.FNT INTERNA0.FNT JCARTMA0.FNT KCARTMA0.FNT LCARTCO0.FNT MCARTPR0.FNT	Cartridge fonts.

543

```
NCARTLE0.FNT
PCARTTM0.FNT
PERSUAS0.FNT
POLISHE0.FNT
PRETTYF0.FNT
PROCOLL0.FNT
QCARTME0.FNT
RCARTPR0.FNT
S1COURI0.FNT
S2TMSRM0.FNT
TCARTTA0.FNT
TEXTEQU0.FNT
UCARTFO0.FNT
VCARTFO0.FNT
WCARTBA0.FNT
WORDPER0.FNT
WORDPER1.FNT
XCARTBA0.FNT
YCARTPC0.FNT
Z1ACART0.FNT
ZMICROS0.FNT
```

The OS/2 PostScript Directory (C:\OS2\DLL\PSCRIPT)

If you install a PostScript driver, it will be installed in this directory.

`pscript.drv`	PostScript printer driver.
`pscript.hlp`	Help for PostScript driver.

The OS/2 Drivers Directory (C:\OS2\DRIVERS)

Additional device drivers and driver utility functions are stored in this directory. Many of the programs in this directory are used to detect devices so a device driver can be installed.

OS/2 Warp File Listing

`152XPRES.EXE`
`154XPRES.EXE`
`164XPRES.EXE`
`174XPRES.EXE`
`7770PRES.EXE`
`7870PRES.EXE`
	Programs that check for the presence of various Adaptec SCSI controllers.

`BTKPRES.EXE`	Program that checks for the presence of a Buslogic SCSI controller.
`CSPMAN.DLL`	SoundBlaster Creative Sound Processor manager.
`DELIVPRC.EXE`	DELIVERY.SYS presence check.
`DPTPRES.EXE`	Program that checks for the presence of a DPT SCSI controller.

`FD16-700.EXE`
`FD7000EX.EXE`
`FD8XX.EXE`
	Programs that check for the presence of various Future Domain SCSI disk controllers.

`IBM16AFS.EXE`	IBM 16-bit AT Fast SCSI controller presence check.
`IBM2SCPR.EXE`	IBM2SCSI presence check.
`MIDIMAP.CFG`	MIDI configuration file.

`SB16AUX.DRV`
`SB16FM.DRV`
`SB16SND.DRV`
	SoundBlaster 16 Windows drivers.

`TMV1PRES.EXE`	Trantor SCSI presence check.

The OS/2 SOM Directory (C:\OS2\ETC)

The files in this directory are for support of the System Object Model (SOM) object management functions.

`SOM.IR`
`WPDSERV.IR`
`WPSH.IR`
	SOM Objects Interface Repository functions.

The OS/2 C:\OS2\ETC\DSOM

The files in this directory are for support of Distributed SOM (DSOM). The addition of DSOM allows programmers to write SOM programs that can access objects in other processes, or even on other computers.

SOMDCLS.DAT SOMDCLS.TOC SOMDIMPL.DAT SOMDIMPL.TOC	DSOM object functions.

The OS/2 Help Directory (C:\OS2\HELP)

This directory contains help data files for various OS/2 components. In most PM programs, a HELP menu item is available, which uses these files to provide help.

BOOTDISK.HLP	Help for the "create utility disks" function.
CASTLE.HLP DEFAULT.HLP GIZEH.HLP MAHJONGG.HLP TAJMAHAL.HLP TOWERBRI.HLP	Help for Mahjongg Solitaire.
CLIPVIEW.HLP	Clipboard Viewer help.
DDINSTAL.HLP	Device driver install help.
DSPINSTL.HLP	Display driver install help.
EHXHP.HLP	System editor help.
EPM.HLP	Help functions for the Enhanced Editor.
FDISKPMH.HLP	Help files for FDISKPM.EXE.
HMHELP.HLP	Help for Help.
ICONEDIT.HLP	Help for the Icon editor.
INSTALL.HLP	Help for Selective Install.
KLONDIKE.HLP	Help for Klondike Solitaire.
MIGRATE.HLP	Help for "Add Programs."

OS2CHESS.HLP	Help for the Chess game.
OS2MHELP.HLP	Help for multimedia device installation.
PICVIEW.HLP	Help for the picture viewer.
PMREXX.HLP	Help for PMREXX.
PMSEEK.HLP	Help for PMSEEK.EXE.
PULSE.HLP	Help for pulse.
README.INS	Installation notes and tips.
SYSLOGH.HLP	Help for the system log function.
TRACEFMT.HLP	Help for the trace formatter.
UNINSTAL.HLP	Help for Selective Uninstall.
VIEWH.HLP	Help for the INF viewer.
WPHELP.HLP WPMSG.HLP	Help for Workplace Shell functions.

The OS/2 Glossary Help Directory (C:\OS2\HELP\GLOSS)

This directory holds the help data file for the "glossary" object (found in the information folder).

WPGLOSS.HLP	The OS/2 Glossary help file.

The OS/2 Tutorial Help Directory (C:\OS2\HELP\TUTORIAL)

This directory holds the help file for the OS/2 Tutorial (found in the information folder).

TUTORIAL.HLP	The OS/2 Tutorial help file.

The OS/2 Install Directory (C:\OS2\INSTALL)

This directory holds files used by the OS/2 installation program.

4029OW21.EXE	Win-OS/2 printer setup program.
ATIM32.DSC ATIM64.DSC PSATI.DSC	Device description files for ATI video cards.
BLISTLAY.OUT	Text file listing installation file locations.
BOOTDISK.EXE	Program to create "utility" diskettes.
CARDINFO.DAT	Text file describing settings for video/multimedia adapters.
CDROM.TBL	Text file describing supported CD-ROM drives.
CL54X.DSC PSCL.DSC	Device description file for Cirrus Logic video cards.
CLEANUP.EXE	Program that deletes temporary files after installation.
CONFIG.SAV	File containing non-standard CONFIG.SYS statements during install.
CONFIG.SYS	The initial CONFIG.SYS used by installation.
DATABASE.DAT	The database used by "add programs" to recognize installed programs.
DATABASE.TXT	Text version of the "add programs" database.
DBTAGS.DAT	Text file describing the settings changes in DATABASE.TXT.
DDINSTAL.EXE	Device driver installation program.

A

OS/2 Warp File Listing

DMPC.EXE ISPD.MSG ISPM.MSG	Text-mode entry panel program.
DSP$REP	Response file used during display installation.
DSPINSTL.EXE	Display driver installation program.
DSPINSTL.LOG	Progress log of the display installation.
ESSTART.BAK	Batch file that cleans up old OS/2 files.
HPFS.IFS	The High Performance File System driver.
INSTAID.CNF INSTAID.EXE INSTAID.LIB INSTAID.PRO INSTAIDE.EXE	Installation aid program files.
INSTALL.EXE INSTALL.INI	OS/2 Install and Selective Install program files.
INSTALL.LOG	Progress log of all files installed during installation.
INSTALL.RC PHASE2.RC	Text files used by MAKEINI.RC to create installation .INI file.
MIGRATE.EXE	The "Add programs" support program.
MMUNINST.EXE	Multimedia uninstall program.
MOS2DET.LUT MOS2OS2.LUT MOS2SUP.LUT MOS2WIN.LUT	Multimedia setup data files.
OS2.INI OS2SYS.INI	OS/2 configuration files used during installation.
OS2MM.LOG	OS/2 multimedia installation progress log.
PARSEDB.EXE	Program that creates DATABASE.DAT from DATABASE.TXT.
PCMCIA.TBL	Text file describing PCMCIA-compatible systems.
PRDESC.LST	Text file listing the supported printers in Warp.
PRDRV.LST	Text file listing available printer drivers, and on what diskette they reside.
PSBGA32.DSC	Text file describing the 8514 display installation disks.

`PSCGA16.DSC`	Text file describing the CGA display installation disks.
`PSEGA16.DSC`	Text file describing the EGA display installation disks.
`PSHEAD.DSC`	Text file describing the Headland Technology display installation disks.
`PSMONO.DSC`	Text file describing the monochrome display installation disks.
`PSS3.DSC` `S3864.DSC`	Text file describing the S3 display installation disks.
`PSSPDW.DSC`	Text file describing the IBM VGA 256c display installation disks.
`PSSVGA32.DSC`	Text file describing the Super VGA display installation disks.
`PSTRID.DSC`	Text file describing the Trident display installation disks.
`PSTSENG.DSC` `TLIW32.DSC`	Text file describing the Tseng display installation disks.
`PSVGA32.DSC`	Text file describing the VGA display installation disks.

`PSWD.DSC`
`PSWDC24.DSC`
`PSWDC31.DSC`
`WDC33.DSC`
	Text file describing the Western Digital display installation disks.

`PSXGA32.DSC`	Text file describing the XGA display installation disks.
`REINSTAL.INI`	Data file describing the installation choices you selected.
`RSPDDI.EXE` `RSPDSPI.EXE`	Programs that install device drivers via response files.
`RSPINST.EXE`	Response-file installation program.
`RSPMIG.EXE`	Response-file migration program.
`SAMPLE.RSP`	Sample response file for installing Warp with pre-selected options.
`SCSI.TBL`	Text file listing the SCSI adapters supported by Warp.
`SHUTDOWN.EXE`	Workplace Shell shutdown command.
`SYSLEVEL.GRE`	Data file containing the version information

A

OS/2 Warp File Listing

	for the Graphics Engine.
SYSLEVEL.OS2	Data file containing the version information for the base OS/2 components.
SYSLEVEL.SDS	Data file containing the version information for the DSOM server.
SYSLEVEL.SEM	Data file containing the version information for the SOM event manager.
SYSLEVEL.SIR	Data file containing the version information for the SOM Objects Interface Repository.
SYSLEVEL.SRK	Data file containing the version information for the SOM runtime kernel.
SYSLEVEL.SUT	Data file containing the version information for the SOM Objects utility classes.
UNINSTAL.EXE UNINSTAL.RSP	OS/2 Uninstall utility.
USER.RSP	Text file describing the choices you made during Warp installation.
WINSUP.IAM	Text file containing the location of installed Windows support.
WP9000.DSC WP9100.DSC	Text file describing the Weitek display installation disks.

The OS/2 Installation Boot Disk Directory (C:\OS2\INSTALL\BOOTDISK)

This directory contains the files used by the "Create utility disks" function to create bootable diskettes that can be used to perform system maintenance.

CLOCK01.SYS CLOCK02.SYS	Real-time clock device drivers.
CONFIG.SYS	List of device drivers and bootup commands for the utility disk.
HPFS.IFS	High Performance File System support.
IBM1FLPY.ADD	Floppy device driver.

551

IBM2FLPY.ADD	
IBM1S506.ADD	IDE/MFM disk device driver.
IBM2ADSK.ADD	ABIOS disk device driver.
IBM2SCSI.ADD	IBM SCSI device driver.
IBMINT13.I13	BIOS device driver.
ODPANS.DLL OSDELETE.EXE ODPRTDRV.EXE	Program to uninstall OS/2 Warp.
OS2LDR.MSG	Text messages used by OS2LDR.
PRINT01.SYS PRINT02.SYS	Base print device driver.
README	Text file describing the utility diskettes.
SCREEN01.SYS SCREEN02.SYS	Base screen device driver.
SYSINST1.EXE	Shell program for the utility disk.
SYSINSTX.COM	Program to make an OS/2 drive "bootable."
UHPFS.DLL	HPFS utility functions.
VTBL850.DCP	Screen code page data file.

The OS/2 Installation VGA Directory (C:\OS2\INSTALL\VGA)

The files in this directory are used by the "Recovery Choices" screen to restore your desktop to VGA resolution.

VGA VGA.DSP VGABUN	VGA support data files.

A

OS/2 Warp File Listing

The OS/2 MDOS Directory (C:\OS2\MDOS)

This directory contains the DOS support files used by OS/2. Some of the files are for Specific DOS sessions (real DOS boot disks used under OS/2). Others are for OS/2 DOS sessions, and others are virtual device drivers. A virtual device driver is loaded by OS/2 (via CONFIG.SYS), but it provides support so that DOS sessions can access hardware devices in a protected manner.

ANSI.SYS	ANSI screen/keyboard support device driver.
APPEND.EXE	Utility to attach directories to the current directory.
ASPISTUB.SYS	SCSI ASPI device driver.
ASSIGN.COM	Utility to switch drive letters.
BASIC.COM BASICA.COM	BASIC language interpreters (for IBM PCs with BASIC in ROM).
COMDD.SYS	
COMMAND.COM	DOS command interpreter.
DEBUG.EXE	DOS program debugger.
DOSKEY.COM	Keyboard command key retrieval utility.
DOSKRNL	DOS-to-OS/2 system support.
EDLIN.COM	Simple line-mode editor.
EGA.SYS	EGA graphics device driver.
EMM386.SYS	Expanded memory support driver (for Specific DOS sessions only).
EXIT_VDM.COM	Program that closes DOS sessions.
FFIX.EXE	Fix for DOS search problems (should only be used when directed by OS/2 support).
FSACCESS.EXE	Program that allows Specific DOS sessions to access physical drives.
FSFILTER.SYS	Device driver that allows Specific DOS sessions to access OS/2-controlled drives.
GRAFTABL.COM	Graphics mode support for extended ASCII characters.
HELP.BAT	Program that allows DOS sessions to access OS/2 help.

`HIMEM.SYS`	Extended memory support driver (for Specific DOS sessions only).
`ISWINDOW.COM`	Utility that allows BAT files to see if the DOS session is in a window or full-screen.
`JOIN.EXE`	Utility that allows a drive to be accessed as a subdirectory on another drive.
`LPTDD.SYS`	Device driver that sends direct printer I/O to the OS/2 spooler.
`MEM.EXE`	Program that displays DOS session memory usage.
`MORTGAGE.BAS`	Sample BASIC program (a mortgage calculator).
`MOUSE.COM`	Mouse driver (for Specific DOS sessions only).
`QBASIC.EXE` `QBASIC.HLP`	BASIC language interpreter/editor.
`SETCOM40.EXE`	Program that sets DOS session BIOS COM port settings.
`SQ4FIX.COM`	Patch file for Space Quest IV.
`SUBST.EXE`	Utility that allows you to substitute a directory for a drive.
`V8514A.SYS`	8514 display-mode virtual device driver.
`VAPM.SYS`	Advanced power management virtual device driver.
`VASPI.SYS`	SCSI ASPI virtual device driver.
`VBIOS.SYS`	BIOS virtual device driver.
`VCDROM.SYS`	CD ROM virtual device driver.
`VCGA.SYS`	CGA display mode virtual device driver.
`VCMOS.SYS`	CMOS memory virtual device driver.
`VCOM.SYS`	COM port virtual device driver.
`VDMA.SYS` `VDMAAT.SYS`	Direct Memory Access virtual device driver.
`VDPMI.SYS` `VDPX.SYS`	DOS-Protected Mode Memory virtual device driver.
`VDSK.SYS`	Hard disk virtual device driver.
`VEGA.SYS`	EGA display mode virtual device driver.
`VEMM.SYS`	Expanded memory virtual device driver.
`VESA.EXE`	VESA video mode support program.

A

OS/2 Warp File Listing

VFLPY.SYS	Floppy disk virtual device driver.
VKBD.SYS	Keyboard virtual device driver.
VLPT.SYS	Printer virtual device driver.
VMDISK.EXE	Program that turns a Specific DOS diskette into an "image" file.
VMONO.SYS	Monochrome video virtual device driver.
VMOUSE.SYS	Mouse virtual device driver.
VNPX.SYS	Numeric co-processor virtual device driver.
VPCMCIA.SYS	PCMCIA virtual device driver.
VPIC.SYS	Peripheral Interface Controller (IRQ) virtual device driver.
VSVGA.SYS	Super VGA virtual device driver.
VTIMER.SYS	Timer virtual device driver.
VTOUCH.COM	Touch-screen virtual device driver.
VVGA.SYS	VGA virtual device driver.
VW32S.SYS	WIN32s virtual device driver.
VWIN.SYS	Windows virtual device driver.
VXGA.SYS	XGA display virtual device driver.
VXMS.SYS	Extended memory virtual device driver.

The OS/2 WIN-OS/2 Directory (C:\OS2\MDOS\WINOS2)

If you install Warp with WIN-OS/2, the windows support files are installed here. If you install Warp without WIN-OS/2, Warp will use a previously installed copy of Windows 3.1x to support Windows programs.

The OS/2 Pointers Directory (C:\OS2\POINTERS)

This directory contains pointer images that can be used to change the look of the mouse pointer in OS/2. You can use these pre-defined pointer sets, or draw your own (with the ICONEDIT program). To change the pointer, open the Mouse object (in the System Setup folder). The pre-defined pointer sets are:

- C:\OS2\POINTERS\BIG_BLAC   Big, black pointers.
- C:\OS2\POINTERS\BIG_WHIT   Big, white pointers.
- C:\OS2\POINTERS\BLACK   Normal, black pointers.
- C:\OS2\POINTERS\WHITE   Normal, while pointers.

Each directory contains a version of each of the following pointers:

ARROW.PTR	The normal pointer icon.
ILLEGAL.PTR	The "don't drop here" pointer.
MOVE.PTR	The window-move pointer.
SIZENESW.PTR	The resize (left-to-right diagonal) pointer.
SIZENS.PTR	The resize (top-to-bottom) pointer.
SIZENWSE.PTR	The resize (right-to-left diagonal) pointer.
SIZEWE.PTR	The resize (left-to-right) pointer.
TEXT.PTR	The text "ibeam" pointer.
WAIT.PTR	The wait "clock" pointer.

The OS/2 System Directory (C:\OS2\SYSTEM)

This directory contains files used by the OS/2 Kernel. Typically, this directory contains:

COUNTRY.SYS	The codepage device driver.
DEV002.MSG	Text messages used by device drivers.
HARDERR.EXE	Program that displays OS/2 error pop-up screens.
LOGDAEM.EXE	System error log gathering program.
OSO001.MSG	Text for all OS/2 system messages.
OSO001H.MSG	Help text for all OS/2 system messages.
REPAIRWP.FIL	Patch file for WordPerfect 5.2 for OS/2 (used by \OS2\PATCHWP.CMD).
REX.MSG REXH.MSG	Text messages used by REXX.

A

OS/2 Warp File Listing

SOMD.MSG SOME_OS2.MSG SOMK.MSG	Messages used by DSOM server.
SPL.MSG, SPLH.MSG	Messages used by the spooler.
SWAPPER.DAT	OS/2 virtual memory SWAP file.
UCDFS.MSG	Messages used by CD-ROM file system.
XDF.MSG	Messages used by XDF floppy support.

The OS/2 System Trace Directory (C:\OS2\SYSTEM\TRACE)

This subdirectory contains files used by the system trace facility to record system events. These files are used when diagnosing problems or performing performance tuning on an OS/2 system.

SYSTEM.TDF SYSTEM.TFF	System trace support files.

The Adobe Fonts Directory (C:\PSFONTS)

This directory contains the ATM fonts available to OS/2. You can install more fonts using the Font Palette object. Each font will have an OFM file and a PFB file. The default fonts available are:

COUR.OFM COUR.PFB	Courier
COURB.OFM COURB.PFB	Courier Bold
COURBI.OFM COURBI.PFB	Courier Bold Italic
COURI.OFM COURI.PFB	Courier Italic
HELV.OFM HELV.PFB	Helvetica

HELVB.OFM HELVB.PFB	Helvetica Bold
HELVBI.OFM HELVBI.PFB	Helvetica Bold Italic
HELVI.OFM HELVI.PFB	Helvetica Italic
MARKSYM.OFM MARKSYM.PFB SYMB.OFM SYMB.PFB	Symbol
TNR.OFM TNR.PFB	Times New Roman
TNRB.OFM TNRB.PFB	Times New Roman Bold
TNRBI.OFM TNRBI.PFB	Times New Roman Bold Italic
TNRI.OFM TNRI.PFB	Times New Roman Italic

The OS/2 Printer Font Matrix Directory (C:\PSFONTS\PFM)

This directory contains the printer "font metrics" files. There will be one PFM file for each font installed in the \PSFONTS directory.

COUR.PFM COURB.PFM COURBI.PFM COURI.PFM HELV.PFM HELVB.PFM HELVBI.PFM HELVI.PFM SYMB.PFM TNR.PFM TNRB.PFM TNRBI.PFM TNRI.PFM	Printer Font metrics for ATM fonts.

A

OS/2 Warp File Listing

The OS/2 Spool File Directory (C:\SPOOL)

This directory is where the OS/2 spooler stores print files while waiting for the printer. For each printer object you install, OS/2 will make a subdirectory in this directory for the print output. These directories will be empty, unless you have pending print jobs.

Index

Symbols

.AVI files
    Indeo video compression, 390
    Ultimotion video compression, 390
.CMD files
    differences from .BAT files, 475
.INI files
    MAKEINI utility, 423
.WAV files, 395
3270 Telnet, 157
3270 terminals, 157
80386 DX, 3
80386 SX, 2
80486 DX, 3
80486 SX, 3

A

abstract objects, 324
ActionMedia II adapter, 208
active partition, 16
active window, 91
Add Programs, 70, 265
Add Programs utility, 361
Adding and Editing Fonts, 273
Address/Phone Book, 176
Advanced Installation, 26
Advanced Power Management, 28
Advantis, 160
Alarm Tab, 310
Alarm..., 167
Alt key, 94, 272, 288
Alt+Esc key combination, 92, 400
Alt+F1 key combination, 253, 492
Alt+F2, 490
Alt+F2: Device Driver Display, 490
Alt+Home, 354, 363, 400
animated icon, 248
ANSI, 403
Application Considerations, 127
Appointments, 164
Archive attribute, 241
archive location, 252
Archive Tab, 252
ARCHIVES.$$$, 496
ARCRECOV, 403
ASSIGN, 403
associating data files with programs, 261
associating sounds with system events, 293
Association Tab, 261
AUDIO_ADAPTER_SHARING, 367

AUTOEXEC.BAT
  in DOS sessions, 353
Automatic lockup, 249

B

Background Images, 234
Background Tab, 233
BACKUP, 403
BIOS, 490
bitmap editor, 115
Bitmap.BMP, 123
BonusPak, 6, 79, 141
BOOT, 404
Boot Manager, 14, 37, 38, 41, 42, 43, 74
  partition, 16
  SETBOOT utility, 430
Boot Options, 14
Borders, 102
Break, 69
Buffers, 67

C

CACHE, 405
CALL, 406
cascade menu, 96
Cascade Menus, 96
CD, 406
CD-ROM Device Support, 29
CD-ROM Drives, 8
  recommendation, 9
changing
  colors, 216
  default folder view, 303
  fonts, 216
  how objects appear, 216
  how objects disappear, 216
  mouse button assignments, 284
  number formats, 270
  resolution of your screen, 217
  the behavior of things, 217
  the order of things, 217
  the pointer, 285
  titles and icons, 216
  your desktop, 216
Changing Colors, 279
Changing Fonts, 272
Changing Schemes, 288
Chart, 191
CHDIR, 406
Check Box, 98
check boxes, 58
CHKDSK, 407, 503
chord, 84
CIM for OS/2, 145
click, 84
clipboard, 113, 338
Clipboard Viewer, 112
CMD, 407
cold start, 74
Color Backgrounds, 235
Colors, 102
COM_DIRECT_ACCESS, 367
COM_HOLD, 367
COM_RECEIVE_BUFFER_FLUSH, 368
COM_SELECT, 368
Comet Cursor Tab, 286
COMMAND, 408

Index

Command Prompts Folder, 105
Command Reference, 128
commands, 34, 65, 105, 128
    ANSI, 403
    ASSIGN, 403
    BACKUP, 403
    BOOT, 404
    CACHE, 405
    CALL, 406
    CHDIR, 406
    CHKDSK, 407
    CMD, 407
    COMMAND, 408
    COMP, 408
    COPY, 408
    DATE, 408
    DEL, 409
    DETACH, 409
    DIR, 409
    DISKCOMP, 412
    DISKCOPY, 414
    DOSKEY, 412
    EAUTIL, 413
    EDIT, 414
    EDLIN, 415
    ENDLOCAL, 415
    EXIT, 415
    EXTPROC, 416
    FDISK, 416
    FOR, 418
    FORMAT, 419
    FSACCESS, 420
    HELP, 421
    KEYB, 422
    KEYS, 423
    MAKEINI, 423
    MODE, 424
    MOVE, 425
    PATCH, 426
    PMREXX, 427
    PROMPT, 427
    PSTAT, 428
    READLINE, 428
    REN, 429
    RMVIEW, 429
    SET, 430
    SETBOOT, 430
    SETLOCAL, 431
    SHUTDOWN, 432
    SPOOL, 432
    START, 432
    SYSINSTX, 434
    SYSLEVEL, 434
    TEDIT, 435
    TIME, 435
    TRUENAME, 435
    UNDELETE, 139, 435
    UNPACK, 436
    VER, 437
    VIEW, 437
    VMDISK, 438
Common User Access (CUA), xxx
COMP, 408
Compact Disc (CD), 394
CompuServe, 144
conditional cascade, 96
Conditional Menus, 96
CONFIG.SYS, 33, 66, 439–58, 490
    Base device drivers, 440
    base-device statements, 440
    environment variables, 455
    in DOS sessions, 353
    performance statements, 446
    Physical device drivers, 442

563

Virtual device drivers, 442
What is it?, 439
Confirmations Tab, 300
Contact List, 183
context menu, 80, 93, 99, 107, 109, 152, 218
Context Menus, 80, 99
COPY, 408
Copying an Object, 87
Country, 267
Country Setting, 27
Create new window, 244
Create Utility Diskettes, 271
Creating a Shadow Object, 87
Creating Command Files, 475
Ctrl+Alt+Del, 493, 503
Ctrl+Esc, 363, 400
Ctrl+Esc key combination, 101
Ctrl+Insert key combination, 113
cursor, 103
cursor blink rate, 275
Cursor Shapes, 103
Custom DOS Objects, 355
customizing OS/2 Warp, 215

D

Data Exchange Tab, 314
Data File, 123
Data File objects, 82, 123, 322, 323
Data Filer, 193
database, 164, 193
DATE, 408
Date Tab, 269
Date/Time Tab, 308
DEL, 409
Deleting an Object, 88
desktop, 73, 77, 80, 104
Desktop Tab, 253
DETACH, 409
Details View, 107, 227
Device Driver Install, 271
device drivers, 55, 271, 298, 299, 354, 370
Device objects, 82, 324
Device Support Diskettes, 271
Dial Other Internet Providers, 157
Dialog Boxes, 97
Digital Audio, 123, 395
Digital Video, 392
DIR, 409
directories, 19
Disk Failure, 502
disk fragmentation, 19
Diskcache, 67
DISKCOMP, 412
DISKCOPY, 412
Display Adapter Utility Program, 72
Display existing window, 244
dithering, 236
dithering pattern, 292
DMA, 500
DOS
    existing software, 11
DOS from Drive A:, 354, 361, 399
DOS Full Screen, 354, 365, 399
DOS Images, 363
DOS objects, 217
DOS Sessions, 354
DOS settings, 259, 358, 366

DOS Software, 11
DOS under OS/2, 353
DOS Window, 354, 399
DOS_AUTOEXEC, 369
DOS_BACKGROUND_EXECUTION, 369
DOS_BREAK, 369
DOS_DEVICE, 370
DOS_FCBS, 371
DOS_FCBS_KEEP, 371
DOS_FILES, 371
DOS_HIGH, 372
DOS_LASTDRIVE, 372
DOS_RMSIZE, 372
DOS_SHELL, 373
DOS_STARTUP_DRIVE, 373
DOS_UMB, 374
DOS_VERSION, 374
DOSKEY, 412
double-click, 84
DPMI_DOS_API, 375
DPMI_MEMORY_LIMIT, 375
DPMI_NETWORK_BUFF_SIZE, 375
drag, 84
Drag-and-Drop, 88
   support for starting program objects, 258
Drives Folder, 106
Drop option, 88
Drop-Down Lists, 98
DSC (description) file, 55
Dual Boot, 14, 31, 45, 106, 402, 404
Dynamic Data Exchange, 314
Dynamic Data Exchange (DDE), 113

E

Easy Installation, 34
EAUTIL, 413
EDIT, 414
Editing a Color, 280
Editing a Scheme, 289
editor, 114, 115, 116
EDLIN, 415
Electronic Books, 126
Electronic Indexes, 126
e-mail, 145
emergency system-recovery, 271
EMM386.SYS, 362
EMS_FRAME_LOCATION, 376
EMS_HIGH_OS_MAP_REGION, 376
EMS_LOW_OS_MAP_REGION, 376
EMS_MEMORY_LIMIT, 377
ENDLOCAL, 415
Enhanced Editor, 114
ERASE, 409
Errors, 504
Event Monitor, 170
Exercise 1
   Copying a Program File Object, 328
Exercise 2
   Creating a Program Object, 330
Exercise 3
   Creating a Work Area, 332
Exercise 4
   Using the Virtual Clipboard, 338

Exercise 5
  Creating a Desktop Window, 342
Exercise 6
  Building a File Manager, 343
Exercise 7
  Virtual vs. Real, 345
Exercise 8
  Using Find, 346
EXIT, 415
EXIT_VDM.COM, 363, 415
Exiting OS/2 Warp, 89
Extended Attributes, 20, 241, 242, 413, 458
Extended Partitions, 16
EXTPROC, 416

F

fast format, 46
FAT, 67
  Cache parameters, 447
FAT (File Allocation Table), 15, 19
  drawbacks to, 19
FAT file system, 46
FaxWorks for OS/2, 199
FDISK, 36, 416
  Command-line options, 416
file management, 343
File names
  wildcard characters, 411
file names under HPFS, 19
File Objects, 320
File System Objects, 319
file systems, 18
  FAT, 15
  HPFS, 15
File Tab, 238
File Transfer Protocol, 158
Find, 346
finding files, 118
first boot, 74
flag attributes, 241
FLC, 389
FLI, 389
Flowed icons, 223
Folder, 123
Folder Object Settings, 221
Folder objects, 82, 320
Font Palette, 124, 271
FOR, 418
form designer, 193
FORMAT, 419
Frame, 94
FSACCESS, 420
FSACCESS.EXE, 364
FSFILTER.SYS, 362, 421
FTP-PM, 158
full pack, 1

G

Games Folder, 109
General Tab, 246, 277, 287
Glossary, 129
Go Wild, 481
Gopher, 151
GOWILD.CMD, 482
Graphical User Interface (GUI), xxx, 78, 153

Index

H

Hard Disk Drives, 6
    access limitations, 6
    partitions, 15
    recommendation, 7
hardware
    CD-ROM drives, 8
    hard disk drives, 6
    math coprocessor, 2, 3
    memory, 5
    microprocessor, 2
    minimum requirements, 2
    miscellaneous, 10
    multimedia, 10
    pointing device, 8
    video adapters, 7
    video displays, 7
Hardware Requirements, 2
Hardware Resources, 500
Hatch Lines, 102
HELP, 421, 505
    OS/2 and DOS commands, 421
    OS/2 System messages, 422
Hidden attribute, 241
Hide button, 244
Hide window, 244
Hide/Minimize Button, 94
High Memory Area (HMA), 448
HIMEM.SYS, 362
HPFS
    Cache parameters, 449
    Cache settings, 405
    CHKDSK options, 407
HPFS (High Performance File System), 15, 19
    benefits of, 19
HPFS file system, 46, 67
HSB color values, 281
HW_NOSOUND, 377
HW_ROM_TO_RAM, 377
HW_TIMER, 378
HyperACCESS Lite, 146

I

IBM Works, 163
ICO files, 115
Icon Editor, 115
Icon View, 107, 223
Icon.ICO, 124
IDLE_SECONDS, 378
IDLE_SENSITIVITY, 378
Include Tab, 229
Incoming Calls, 181
Information Area, 95
Information Folder, 104, 126
Information Superhighway, 143
InfoZIP, 350
input fields, 97
Input Tab, 304
installation
    BonusPak CD-ROM, 142
    BonusPak Diskettes, 142
    decisions, 13
    from diskette images, 32
    hardware requirements, 2
    making a partition installable, 36

multiple operating systems, 37
partitioning examples, 37
Quick versus Advanced, 25
reducing required disk space, 64
special video adapter, 72
the easy way, 34
installing
    additional OS/2 programs, 267
    DOS programs, 267
    Windows programs, 267
installing DOS programs, 267
Installing Multimedia Support, 389
installing multiple operating systems, 37
installing OS/2 programs, 267
installing Windows programs, 267
INT_DURING_IO, 379
Internal Processing Errors (IPEs), 512
Internet Access Kit (IAK), 143
Internet Connection for OS/2, 147
Internet Customer Service, 160
Internet Dialer, 148
Internet Utilities, 156
IPE. *See* Internal Processing Error
IRQ, 500

K

KBD_ALTHOME_BYPASS, 379
KBD_BUFFER_EXTEND, 380
KBD_CTRL_BYPASS, 380
KBD_RATE_LOCK, 380
KEYB, 422
Keyboard, 274
Keyboard Setting, 27
KEYS, 423
KEYS.$$$., 496

L

Launch..., 168
LaunchPad, 78, 136
Light Table, 211
list box, 51
Lockup Tab, 249
logical drives, 37
Logical Drives (Partitions), 16
Logo Tab, 306

M

Magic Keystrokes, 489
maintenance desktop, 74, 494
MAKEINI, 423
Mappings Tab, 275, 283
Master Help Index, 130
math coprocessor, 2, 3
Maximize/Restore Button, 94
maximized window, 93

Maxwait, 67
MEM_EXCLUDE_REGIONS, 381
MEM_INCLUDE_REGIONS, 381
Memman Protect, 68
Memman Swap, 68
memory, 5
   recommendation, 5
Menu Bar, 94
Menu settings, 236
Menu Tab, 236
Menus, 96
Metafile.MET, 124
metafiles (MET), 117
Microprocessor
   recommendation, 4
Microprocessors, 2
MIDI, 395
Minimize button, 244
Minimize window to desktop, 244
Minimize window to viewer, 244
Minimized Window Viewer, 110
Mixed Color Palette, 123, 277
MMPM/2, 389
MODE, 424
mouse, 52, 78, 84, 281
mouse buttons, 84
Mouse Setting, 27
MOUSE_EXCLUSIVE_ACCESS, 381
MOVE, 425
Moving an Object, 86
MPEG, 389
Multimedia, 131

Multimedia Data Converter, 397
Multimedia Device Support, 29
Multimedia Extensions, 209
Multimedia Folder, 104
Multimedia Hardware, 10
Multimedia Install, 396
Multimedia Objects, 391
Multimedia Presentation
   Manager/2 (MMPM/2), 389
Multimedia Setup, 396
Multimedia with REXX, 396
Multiple Operating Systems, 14
Musical Instrument Digital
   Interface (MIDI) files, 395

N

NewsReader/2, 153
Normal size icons, 224
Notepad, 184
Numbered Desktop Archives, 494
Numbers Tab, 270

O

Object Icon, 93
Object Linking and Embedding, 314
Object open behavior, 244
object-oriented interface, 81, 317
objects
   copying, 87
   creating shadow, 87

Data File, 82
deleting, 88
Device, 82
Folder, 82
moving, 86
opening, 83
opening a folder, 86
picking up, 87
Program, 82
selecting, 85
starting a program, 86
open an object, 83
Open FCBs, 69
Opening a Folder Object, 86
Option Controls, 96
Options Menu, 65
Original Desktop Archive, 494
OS/2
32-bit software, 12
advantages of, xxxi
Configuration, 26
existing software, 12
history of, xxix
installing from CD-ROM, 31
with multiple operating systems, 14
OS/2 2.1 applets, 111
OS/2 command line
FOR command, 473
return codes, 472
OS/2 Desktop Archive, 496
OS/2 Full Screen, 365, 399
OS/2 settings, 259
OS/2 Software, 12
OS/2 System Editor, 116
OS/2 Tutorial, 75
OS/2 Window, 365, 399
OS2.KEY, 496

OS2KRNL, 499
Outgoing Calls, 179

P

P2P, 201
Parameters, 257
partitions, 15, 31, 36, 65, 67
examples of, 21
Primary, Extended, Logical, 15
recommendation, 18
with multiple drives, 24
passing program parameters, 257
password protection, 251
PATCH, 426
PCMCIA Support, 29
Pentium, 3
Performance Considerations, 132
Person to Person/2, 201
Personal Information Manager, 163
Phone Dialer, 181
Phone Log, 182
Picking Up an Object, 87
pickup, 87
Pickup Feature, 80
Picture Interchange Files (PIF), 117
Picture Viewer, 117
PIF File.PIF, 124
PKZIP 2.x, 350
Planner, 171
PMREXX, 427, 477

Index

point, 84
pointer, 84
Pointer.PTR, 124
Pointers Tab, 285
Pointing Device recommendation, 8
Pop-Up Controls, 99
pop-up menus, 284
Primary and Secondary Displays, 28
Primary Partitions, 16
Print Monitor Buffer Size, 66
Print Priority Tab, 296
print queue, 137, 466
Print Screen Tab, 305
Print Spooler, 459
PRINT_SEPARATE_OUTPUT, 382
PRINT_TIMEOUT, 382
printer, 59, 125, 137
Printer Driver, 461
Printer Object, 137, 460
Printer Port, 462
Printer Setting, 29
Printing in OS/2, 133
Priority, 68
Productivity Folder, 111
profile control files, 271
Program, 125
Program (Reference) Objects, 321
program file object, 255
Program File Objects, 321
program object, 125, 255
Program Object Settings, 254
Program objects, 82
Program Settings, 264
Program Tab, 256

PROMPT, 427
Protected FCBs, 69
PSTAT, 428
public, 315
Pull-Down Menus, 96
Pulse, 118
Push Buttons, 98

Q

QBASIC.EXE, 355
queue, 137
Quick Installation, 26

R

Radio Buttons, 98
RAM, 5
READ.ME, 133
READLINE, 428
Read-Only attribute, 241
Real DOS, 362
real objects, 326
reassigning keystrokes, 275
reassigning mouse buttons, 284
recovery, 252, 271
Recovery Choices, 253, 403
Recurring..., 169
REN, 429
RENAME, 429
repeat rate, 275
Report Writer, 197
Resolving Resource Conflicts, 500

Resource Manager, 501
Resource Manager., 501
REXX, 134, 476
    Debugging, 470
    difference from batch .CMD files, 478
    DO WHILE/UNTIL loop, 479
    Extended Attributes, 478
    Go Wild Command, 481
    IF/THEN/ELSE loop, 480
    PM interface, 427
    Programming Exercise, 469
    Return Codes, 472
    SAY command, 479
    use of extended attributes, 478
    use of variables, 479
REXX Programming, 476
REXXUTIL function library, 480
RGB color values, 281
RMSIZE, 69
RMVIEW, 429. *See Resource Manager*

S

sample files, 390
Scheme Palette, 125, 287
screen resolution, 298
Screen Tab, 298
Scroll Bars, 95
SCSI Adapter Support, 30
search for and install programs, 266
searching disks and files, 118
Seek and Scan Files, 118
Selecting an Object, 85
Selective Install, 289, 389
Selective Installation, 63
Selective Uninstall, 291
Serial Device Support, 28
service providers, 160
Session Tab, 259
SESSION_PRIORITY, 382
SET, 430
SETBOOT, 430
SETLOCAL, 431
settings, 66, 69, 99, 122
    DOS, 259
    OS/2, 259
    Windows, 259
settings notebooks, 215, 217
Setup Tab, 282
Shading, 102
shadow objects, 83, 240, 323, 325
Shift key, 95
Shift+Ctrl key combination, 325
Shift+Delete key combination, 113
Shift+Insert key combination, 113
Shredder Object, 120, 139
Shutdown, 89, 432
    from an OS/2 command prompt, 432
Small size icons, 224
Software Configuration Menu, 66
software motion video, 392
Software Requirements, 11
Software Updates, 150
Solid Color Palette, 123, 292
Sort Tab, 232

Sound, 293, 397
Sound Tab, 293
Special Needs Tab, 276
Specific DOS, 354, 361
Specific DOS sessions
    Boot diskette images, 438
    direct disk access, 420
    disk access through OS/2, 421
Spin Buttons, 99
SPOOL, 432
Spool File Support (SPL), 117
Spool Path Tab, 295
Spooler, 295
Spreadsheet, 189
START, 432
Starting a Program Object, 86
Startup Folder, 120
surfing the net, 143
swap file, 20, 68
Swap Minfree, 67
Swappath, 68
SWAPPER.DAT
    Initial file size, 453
SYS1475, 490
SYSINSTX, 434
SYSLEVEL, 434
System Architecture, 4
    recommendation, 5
System attribute, 241
System Clock, 307
System Configuration, 26, 48
    Advanced Power Management, 56
    CD-ROM Device, 58
    Country, 50
    Keyboard, 51
    Mouse, 52
    Multimedia Device, 60
    PCMCIA Support, 57
    Primary Display, 54
    Printer, 59
    SCSI Adapter, 61
    Secondary Display, 56
    Serial Device Support, 53
System folder, 104, 219
System Information Tool, 311
System Memory, 5
System object, 297
system recovery, 252
System Set up Folder, 121
System Setup, 215
System Setup folder, 264
System Setup Objects, 264

T

TEDIT, 435
Telnet, 159
Templates, 104, 122, 162
Templates Folder, 104, 122
The Maintenance Desktop, 494
Threads, 67
TIME, 435
Time Tab, 268
Timing Tab, 274, 281
Title Bar, 93
Title Tab, 301
To-Do List, 173
trap message, 507
Traps, 507
Tree View, 107, 225
TRUENAME, 435
Tutorial, 75, 126, 135, 284

type ahead, 304
Type Tab, 263

Ultimedia Mail/2 "Lite", 154
Ultimedia Video IN, 210
Ultimedia Viewer, 211
UNDELETE, 139, 435, 455
Uninstall, 291
UNPACK, 436
Upper Memory Blocks (UMB), 448

VDM, 353
VER, 437
VGA, 298
video adapters, 7
video device drivers, 7
Video Displays, 7
    device drivers, 7, 28
    recommendation, 8
VIDEO_8514A_XGA_IOTRAP, 383
VIDEO_FASTPASTE, 383
VIDEO_MODE_RESTRICTION, 383
VIDEO_ONDEMAND_MEMORY, 384
VIDEO_RETRACE_EMULATION, 384
VIDEO_ROM_EMULATION, 385

VIDEO_SWITCH_NOTIFICATION, 385
VIDEO_WINDOW_REFRESH, 385
VIEW, 437
View Tab, 221, 308
Views, 80
virtual devices, 82
Virtual DOS Machine, 353
Virtual DOS Machines, 353
Virtual Floppy, 363
virtual reality, 318
VMDISK, 438
VMDISK.EXE, 364
Volume Control, 398

warm start, 74
Warning Beep Tab, 295
Warp Drive, 343
WebExplorer, 150, 152
WIN_ATM, 386
WIN_CLIPBOARD, 386
WIN_DDE, 386
WIN_RUN_MODE, 387
Window Controls, 90
window disappears, 110
Window List, 84, 94, 99, 101, 284
Window Tab, 243, 302
Windows
    existing software, 12
    OS/2 with and without, 1
Windows 3.1 Session Tab, 313
Windows objects, 217
Windows Sessions, 365

Index

Windows settings, 259
Windows Software, 12
Windows under OS/2, 353
WIN-OS/2 Settings, 366
WIN-OS/2 Setup, 313
Word Processor, 188
Work Area Folders, 238
Work Areas, 332
Workplace Shell, 77
Workplace Shell Objects, 82
WPSOPEN.CMD, 481

X, Y, Z

XMS_HANDLES, 387
XMS_MEMORY_LIMIT, 387
XMS_MINIMUM_HMA, 388
Year Calendar, 172
ZIP utility, 350